Power to Dissolve

Frontispiece. THE MAKING OF THE CODE RECOUNTED

Cardinal Pietro Gasparri describes his principal part in the creation of the Code of Canon Law to the International Juridical Congress, at the old Apollinaris, Rome, November 14, 1934.

The maker of the Code, aged eighty-two, speaking three days before his death, is out of sight; his empty chair is front row right.

Among the audience are many members of the Roman Curia, including Eugenio Pacelli, front row left, and Angelo Roncalli, third row right.

(photograph courtesy of Stephan G. Kuttner, pictured to the rear right)

Power to Dissolve

Lawyers and Marriages in the Courts
of the Roman Curia

John T. Noonan, Jr.

The Belknap Press of Harvard University Press

Cambridge, Massachusetts   1972

Acknowledgments

Chronologically to enumerate the many acts of assistance of which I am aware, I began work on this book with a fellowship from the John Simon Guggenheim Memorial Foundation, which supported my initial investigations in Rome. These inquiries continued with the encouragement of Joseph O'Meara, Jr., then Dean of the Notre Dame Law School, and the financial aid of the University of Notre Dame.

Stephen Kelleher, then *officialis* of the tribunal of the archdiocese of New York, and John Quinn, then *officialis* of the tribunal of the archdiocese of Chicago, opened to me the workings of modern diocesan chanceries and, in addition, did much to make easier my research in Rome. The late Francis Cardinal Spellman, Archbishop of New York, introduced me to the Sacred Congregation of the Council, the Sacred Congregation for the Propagation of the Faith, and the Secret Archives of the Vatican. The late Francis Cardinal Brennan, then Dean of the Sacred Roman Rota, gave me complete access to the records of his tribunal. Other auditors, staff, and advocates of the Rota, Secretaries of Congregations, and other officeholders still on active curial service provided information and perspectives on the functioning of the modern Curia.

Moving from Notre Dame to Berkeley in 1967, I was then assisted by the resources of the University of California — first by the International Legal Studies Committee of the School of Law (Boalt Hall), then by the Robbins Canon Law Fund. Thomas Reynolds, Foreign Law Librarian, was indefatigable and extraordinarily effective in obtaining needed references. Richard Helmholz, then a graduate student in history, aided me on my third expedition into the archives of the Congregations. Kathleen Casey and Ruth

Acknowledgments

Kittel, graduate students in history, critically checked citations. Steven Finell, a law student, edited the first chapter for its publication in the *California Law Review* (May 1970).

Individual chapters of the book were read by my present colleagues, Stephan G. Kuttner and Albert Ehrenzweig of the Law School and William Slottman of the Department of History; by my old colleagues at the University of Notre Dame, Robert E. Rodes, Jr., and John Dunne, C.S.C.; by John Tracy Ellis of the University of San Francisco; by Antony Honoré of Oxford University; by my sister, Marie Sabin, and by my father. Vera Nielsen, Gay Campbell, Sandra du Fossé, and Deborah Watson typed the manuscript. Throughout the writing of the book, my wife, Mary Lee, has been a source of ideas, inspirations, and encouragement; and she provided critical assistance in the reading of the proofs.

To these institutions and to these individuals whose interest, help, and generosity have contributed so much, I extend my warmest thanks.

John T. Noonan, Jr.

Berkeley, May 30, 1971

Contents

Hostiensis fatetur tamen quod quamdiu papa vivit, dominus dicitur, et potest mutare quadrata rotundis et omnia disponere tamquam dominus, salva violatione fidei. Tamen vere loquendo nec ipse nec alius praelatus est dominus.

Joannes Andreas, *In libros decretalium commentaria novella*, 2.1.12

Hostiensis, however, acknowledges that as long as the Pope lives, he is called Lord, and he can change squares into circles and dispose of all things as Lord, saving violation of the faith. Yet, truly speaking, neither he nor any other prelate is Lord.

Joannes Andreas, New Commentary on the Books of the Decretals, 2.1.12

Preface

This book centers on the functioning of the courts and committees of the Roman Curia in the dissolution of marriage. It looks to the role of law within a religion founded on commandments of love; it looks to the place of love in an institution molded by law. Jurisprudentially, it is the examination of a legal system, arguably the oldest and certainly the most universal in the world. Theologically, it is an investigation of the content of Christian marriage. The method used to conduct these inquiries is historical, an effort to understand the impact of the canonical system on individual persons.

By the system, I mean the application of rules by those in charge, a series of interactions of persons mediated by a set of doctrines and shaped by the positions held by the interacting persons within the organization. Classic canon law has consisted of rules, and the study of these rules has constituted the study of canon law. The rules, however, have affected individual human beings and in this process have become incorporated in the acts of persons. The significance of the law cannot be grasped apart from this process carried out by persons. The process, as it necessitates choice by the decision-makers, is the focus of this book.

Six principal cases have been selected to present the system. They are surrounded by citation, summary, and comparison of several hundred other cases which indicate their place within the spectrum of the law. They themselves are not statistical averages. Each has its quirks, flukes, anomalies, and flavor. They have been chosen to show persons in the system making critical choices about the structure of marriage. They are intended to illuminate the decisional process and the theory of marriage. Viewing each case in its uniqueness one may touch the individuals in whose lives the system lived.

The process is presented over a broad span of time and place. The suit of Charles of Lorraine against his duchess Nicole comes from the system in its prime in the seventeenth century, when, if ever, doctrine meshed with European social expectations. The matter of Luis Quifel Barberini and Joanna Carnide y Almeida and that of José Perez de Guzman and Ana Ponce de León arise in the eighteenth century, when the courts were being brought to a fine point of perfection just before collapse. The cases of Filippo Folchi and Pauline Bailly, Boni de Castellane and Anna Gould, Frederick Parkhurst and Marie Reid, all occur in the restored system, expanded and transformed in the twentieth century when the Church of the seventeenth century, almost identified with those who ruled civil society, had become a dispossessed Church largely composed of peasants and the petite bourgeoisie. Geographically, one case is from independent Lorraine, one from Portugal, one from Spain, one from Italy, two from the United States. They were participated in by ecclesiastical judges in Córdoba, Lisbon, New York, Paris, Portland, and Toul, and they were heard in Rome by the Apostolic Signature, the Sacred Congregation of the Council, the Sacred Congregation for the Propagation of the Faith, the Sacred Roman Rota, the tribunal of the Vicariate, and various special committees of cardinals. In four, dissolution of marriage was ultimately denied; in two it was granted. In the final chapter, the shape being given the marriage law of the future is described; its development is intimately related to the problems, values, and ways of acting found in the six principal cases.

Cases which come before a court may be analogized to the cases which come before a physician. They are specimens of pathology. Marriages so imperfectly made or so unsuccessfully continued as to be candidates for nullification cannot stand for all the healthy marriages nurtured by the system. Yet from the pathological one may draw useful lessons about the healthful and the conditions necessary for health. More fundamentally, the cases are the basic material by which to measure the impact of the legal process upon its participants; in the cases there may be observed those whose acts constituted the system. My aim has been to obtain evidence of the education it provided these participants, to explore the needs of theirs it met, to assess the principles it realized in their persons.

Chiefly educated by the process were those any legal system educates most richly — the active participants in making the system work, the judges, professors, advocates, and counselors. In the foreground stand two: the great systematizer, Prospero Lambertini; and the modern molder of the canon law, Pietro Gasparri. The formation of the system has not been dependent solely on the will of any single man; yet without Lambertini, Secretary of the Congregation of the Council and Pope, and without Gasparri, never Pope but the lord of the papal law of marriage through four pontificates, the balance of the system would have been different. Lambertini and Gasparri got from the system the best education it could give. From it they drew their own purposes, in it they found their own equilibrium.

Less thoroughly educated by the system, but its patient scholars, were the advocates, such as Celio Piccolomini, Francesco Pitoni, and Filippo Pacelli. Well-connected and persuasive spokesmen for their suppliant clients, they were formed in their professional character by the system's actual operation. Their techniques were learned from it, their values shared with it. Almost equally well-instructed by the system were those who played the role of counselor or spiritual adviser, that obsolete kind of specialist who once flourished as the visible embodiment of the books of casuistry, of whom Fathers Cheminot and Marochim are representative. Finally, beneficiaries of the education offered were curial committeemen such as Agostino Sili and diocesan bishops such as William O'Connell, who, playing subordinate parts in the system, were afforded lessons in its methods.

For the passive recipients of instruction, the spouses whose marriages were litigated, their families and lovers, the educational benefits were not so large, although sometimes unforgettable. The education imparted to these miscellaneous figures who entered the system's labyrinthine ways tended to be haphazard. They were not assured instruction of the same quality as that received by those who had acquired established roles and were designated by their office or activity as steady and assiduous pupils.

Petitioners were, in all events, less related to the system by their aptitude for instruction than by their needs. Undeniably, anyone who was a petitioner was in want. Consciously, he sought clearance and restoration. He wanted the past wiped clean. He wanted to be made again a member of the community. He wanted his freedom from the past and his acceptance for the future to be public, certified by the guardians of the community. Latently, he may have had other wants, such as the need to pay for guilt or the need to be restricted in freedom or the need to stand in some relation to his former spouse. If a petitioner failed to satisfy his overt desires, any latent need to be penalized and inhibited was, at any rate, amply satisfied.

Apart from serving in some fashion its petitioners, the system met other needs of the active participants beyond their education. For the most acute professors of canon law it was indispensable. Without the courts, the theorists would have lacked material for analysis, arrangement, and speculation. They would have lacked a focus for their own efforts at instruction. They would have been without an audience. For the advocates the system of marriage law provided a moderate part of their income and a larger opportunity for their ingenuity and the exercise of professional skill. For the counselors the system was as essential as the treatises of moral theology themselves. Above all, for the managers of the Curia the system satisfied multiple wants — a didactic need to assert principle; a corporate need to respect precedent; an administrative need for suppleness; a paternal need to show mercy. From Francesco Barberini to Alfredo Ottaviani, the leaders of the Curia felt these needs and, feeling them, met them in the process which they shaped.

In almost any contemporary system, the compatibility of law with love is an issue; in a Christian system, it is crucial. According to evangelical authority, to love God with heart, mind, and soul, and to love one's neighbor as oneself are fundamental; the disciples of Jesus will be recognized by loving each other as He loved them. These principles, difficult of realization in any event, are particularly difficult for a legal system to incorporate. They are not realized if a system leads its responsible officials to think of the human beings in the process only in abstract aspects of their persons; or if concentration of attention on the machinery of procedure leads to forgetfulness of the system's subordination to these principles. If such effects appear to be inevitable in any system of law, so that men whose business it is to apply law to other men can never love them or be loved by them, no legal system is compatible with Christian principles. If, however, men are able to accept law as necessary for the creation of a community, pursuit of the communal purposes may bridge the unbridgeable gap between the general norm and the individual person. Realization of the principles of love will then depend on how consciously the common purposes are held, how effectively they are communicated, how faithfully they guide action. The difficulties and degree of success of the canon law in terms of these criteria will be apparent in the course of this book.

Of a medieval petitioner for an annulment it was written:

> He to the court of Rome, in subtil wyse
> Enformed of his wyl, sente his message
> Comaundynge hem swich bulles to devyse
> As to his crueel purpos my suffyse,
> How that the Pope, as for his peples' reste,
> Bad hym to wedde another, if hym leste.
>
> I seye, he bad they sholde countrefete
> The popes bulles, makynge mencion
> That he hath leve his first wyf to lete
> As by the popes dispensacion
> To stynte rancour and dissencioun
> Betwixte his peple and hym; thus seyde the bulle
> The which they han publiced atte the fulle.

(The Clerk's Tale, lines 737–749)

Such is the first reference in the mainstream of English literature to the papal dissolution of marriage. The story, it may be recalled, is the effort of Walter to test his patient wife Griselda by obtaining a fictitious dissolution of their marriage from the Roman Curia. Walter is rich, noble, and knowledgeable; Griselda is poor, common, and ignorant. Walter's intent is cruel; his subtlety succeeds at Rome. The stated purpose of the Pope's bull is benevolent, but no reason is given for it except public policy. The annulment is a fiction, obtained as an adjunct to a hoax. The unspoken implications of the story are that annulments are the magical product of an incomprehensible process in which legal reasons play no part and curial discretion is absolute. A papal dissolution appears as an appropriate device for the fictitious termination of a real union.

Among contemporary authors the image of the tribunals of marriage has not improved since Chaucer. Not to mention Morris West's full-scale plea for reform in *Scandal in the Assembly*, caustic references to the curial process are made through dialogue or plot in John Updike's *Couples*, Louis Auchincloss' *The Rector of Justin*, and Muriel Spark's *The Mandlebaum Gate*. In the last two novels, true annulments are given on facts believed to be genuine by the Rota but actually concocted. The petitioners themselves believe the facts are true, but they are uninterested in the facts; for them the great event is the declaration of nullity by the Rota. Implicitly each story asks: If what counts is the Rota's pronouncement, does it make any difference to any human being that the facts are not what they appear to be? Auchincloss and Spark join Chaucer in suggesting the artificial, arbitrary, magical character of dissolving a marriage by the decree of a court of the Court of Rome.

This book will afford material to measure these images of fiction and to determine the accuracy of these unfavorable impressions. I will not anticipate the verdict. Three preliminary observations may, however, be appropriate as to the artificial, the arbitrary, and the magical. Annulment appears to be artificial in contrast to the reality of a marriage or the reality of the breakdown of a marriage. Yet, marriage itself appears in history as an institution whose constituent elements depend upon law. If the law did not designate particular words and actions as betokening the public commitment of a man and a woman to each other, how would marriage be distinguished from other forms of sexual association? In the mass of human gestures, the law has isolated the phrases and deeds which constitute a marriage. Legal dissolution of a marriage may be no more artificial than its creation. The importance of the rules which marriage must follow at its beginning has also been celebrated by literature. All of Manzoni's *I promessi sposi* hangs on Lorenzo and Lucia's efforts to exchange their marital vows in the form prescribed by the Council of Trent; his book is not an indictment of the system which created these artificial requirements.

For centuries it was argued whether a corporation was something real or something fictional; it is now apparent that the term designates neither a metaphysical reality nor an imaginary entity, but relations in a legal system. *A pari*, marriage is a term which designates relations in a legal system; only by reference to the system's rules does it have intelligibility and existence. Outside of a system the term appears to be metaphor or nonsense. Yet does not human instinct suggest that marriage is more than the legal form? This paradox troubles much of the legal analysis of the subject. If "true" marriage — marriage as it might be in the eye of God — is different from its definition by the rules, can its constituents be measured by a legal system?

"Paternity" provides a parallel. In any culture the meaning of paternity depends on rights and duties the system attaches to fatherhood, its recognition depends on law. But paternity is founded on an event which occurs in a discrete moment of time, and the meeting of spermatazoon and ovum has its own dynamism which interlocks with the cultural consequence of being a father. Analogously, in the volitional rather than biological order, an event with its own dynamism of personal interaction marks a marriage. The stubborn reality of this event prevents the neat reduction of marriage to form and consequences within the legal system which gives it significance.

More, perhaps, than any secular law, the canon law has been preoccupied with the relation between the form of marriage and the personal acts constituting the events to which the legal consequences attach. From the flux of individual actions, the canon law has sought to isolate a commitment which, given legal form, will stand secure above the flow. Consequently, it has given extraordinary attention to the event it has chosen as the real, extralegal event, the initial exchange of consent to be man and wife. The thrust of the law, as it has developed, has been to mold marriage as an inner commitment to long-range goals, consciously apprehended and consciously accepted in the instant of consent. This preoccupation has not saved the system from a large measure of artificiality — partly because the moment of consent investigated is artificially identified, partly because securing any form above the flux is a precarious enterprise, partly because concern for public order and concern for interior dispositions are difficult if not impossible to combine coherently.

The arbitrariness which has been observed in the canonical process of terminating marriage may be conveniently distinguished from the artificiality. The arbitrariness is rooted in the relation of petitioner and priest. Although the system styles some terminations "annulments" and others "dissolutions," the result for the marriage is the same, and the kind of power exercised is functionally difficult to distinguish. To terminate a marriage within the system a priest must be asked; and to ask puts one as a petitioner.

Among religious acts, prayers of petition have an ancient lineage as appropriate ways of addressing God. Religious practice has made them seem not inappropriate to address to men in a hierarchical religious institution; and one kind of religious man may find nothing demeaning in his dependence on another man for bestowal of a grace. Curial style has designated the Pope as "the Most Holy" and called the governing committees of administration either "holy" or "sacred." Vocabulary of this kind and the pattern of petitions to God have made it seem not unnatural to make the dissolution of marriage dependent on asking the Pope for his good will and pleasure.

No modern system of law, however, could operate with a single chief determining the disposition of every individual case. Volume of business alone prevents the exercise of such discretion. Organizational pressures rule out personal decisions. The papal system has not been exempt from these limitations. Just as *Sanctissimus* became Ss. and the Sacred Congregation of the Council became the S.C.C., so that to a modern curialist the English translations seem awkwardly grandiloquent, rhetoric about papal supremacy over marriage has been reduced by routine. Sovereign freedom has been translated into bureaucratic licensing.

What of the curious independence of facts which writers since Chaucer have implied that the system possesses? Is there an element of magic in the Curia's transformation of twenty-year-old marriages into nullities, in its turning once indissoluble bonds into unions terminable in favor of the faith? When it comes to marriage can the Pope change squares into circles?

Claims advanced for papal power by curialists have sometimes stretched credulity. Apologists have attributed to the Pope a power to terminate the marriages of almost all the world, including the marriages of persons who have never heard of the Catholic Church, never known of the Pope, never been informed of the vast legal domain within which their unions are said to fall. Much of the magical view of papal actions has been the Curia's own doing. As long as magniloquence is engaged in at Rome, the ironic response of literature will be unavoidable.

Magic, the whisking away of difficulties by a nod, the replacement of reality by illusion, is, however, but one step away from creativity, the transformation of a situation by energetic innovation. Like magic, creativity connotes spontaneity and freedom from iron law, but it also implies labor and increase by organic development. Obfuscatory satire and apology set aside, the curial system at its best has been creative. Too bound to traditional categories to acknowledge its role, the Curia has not had credit for its creations.

For over eight centuries the canon law has asked the questions necessary to develop marriage as an institution and a symbol: what are the conditions for free marital consent? what public registration of marital consent is necessary? can classes of marriage be constructed? If the need for these questions was not at once grasped as indispensable, if experience was necessary to develop even provisional answers, if the costs imposed on individuals in developing the answers were large, no questions without experience and no answers without pain were available. To an extent unmatched by other organs of the Church, the Curia asked the questions and provided answers which, if neither final nor infallible, were often shrewd, imaginative, instructive, and, if sometimes harsh, unrealistic, or oversubtle, were sometimes soberly convincing.

Many cultures use the lives of their gods to state their ideal of sexual relations. The symbolism of marriage derived from Saint Paul takes the relation of Christ to the Church as the pattern of human marriage and reciprocally invests human marriage with symbolic value as the exemplification of the ecclesial union. To endow fragile human relations with this significance, to maintain that the pattern once laid stands imperishably above the flood, has been a bold enterprise. Preservation of the ideal of indissolubility, whatever the pain to individuals, has been the great conscious enterprise of the Curia. Coupled with a universal vision which in aspiration rises above race and class to reach all men, this undertaking has not lacked grandness.

The most substantial theological and legal accomplishment of the curial system has occurred in the effort to fit this grand design to the multitude of human desires. The result has been the creation of a variety of types of marriage distinguished by their degree of dissolubility, manner of dissolubility, sacramental character, symbolic role, and procreative possibilities. Without setting out to do so from the start, the Curia has designed classes of marriage and provided the basis for the further formation of classes more deliberately fitted to the needs of the community.

Creating these classes, the Pope and Curia have had to choose among options ultimately limited by the nature of the Church and the character of its charge and mission. Their choices have never been free, made in the air without resistance and without cost, although sometimes the resistance has been impalpable and the cost disguised or uncalculated. The choices have been constricted by the several contexts of secular European and non-European society, theological tradition, organizational structure, and scriptural admonitions. Each context has molded the shape of the choice made, while the free creative energy which made the choices cannot be totally accounted for by any context. Individual authors outside the Curia have made notable contributions — for example, Alfonso de la Veracruz, the Spanish theologian of the Indians; Isaac, the fourth-century Roman lawyer; Paolo Zacchia, the seventeenth-century Roman physician. But the main decisions, especially in modern times, have been made at the Curia. Exercising their freedom to shape a central human institution, the makers of the system have been co-makers with the Lord of institutions. Focusing upon them, this book shows the participants in the process of choice, both those who acted and those who suffered.

To pierce the curial style, to look at what happened, is a species of demythologizing. But to have a judicial system at all is to start on the road from myth. A judicial system is not omniscient, it needs to know the facts, it has to listen to argument, it delivers split opinions, it makes mistakes and reverses itself, it does not exist in a sacred sphere above time. The canon law has been the forerunner of secular law, both in the use of written briefs by lawyers and in the delivery of written opinions by the Rota. It has also been incurably historical. Every decision has been identified by the system itself in terms of the place where the case arose and the time the opinion was issued, as here: *Toul, January 15, 1653; West Lisbon, July 8, 1724; Córdoba, March 26, 1763; Baltimore, June 30, 1910; New York, February 8, 1915; Rome, November 23, 1923.*

Thinking first in terms of places and of dates, the system has always been embedded in human history and its movement on earth.

Plus ça change, one may be tempted to observe as one looks at these cases from 1653 to 1923 and at the development which has followed from Pius XII to Paul VI. Features of the system do repeat themselves. Yet the society in which the system lives is not the same, nor is much of the doctrine which it teaches. Transformation has occurred. That the transformation has been at least half conscious seems undeniable. That the changes have had a direction, that the creative innovations have been organic, that the evolution has not ended, seem hypotheses worth defending.

Power to Dissolve

I

The Steady Man

Emblems, epigrams, and epithalamiums; horoscopes and riddles; acrostics cut in the shape of crowns, diagonals, and hearts; replications of the alerions and the crosses of Lorraine proclaimed at Pont-à-Mousson the wedding of that university's most prominent alumnus, Prince Charles, to his cousin Nicole in the spring of 1621. Magnificence and gallantry never appeared in Lorraine with such éclat as in his reign. His passion for Béatrice of Cusance, Princess of Cantecroix, was to be unabated until it had taxed the benevolence of two Popes, the subtlety of the subtlest casuists, and the resources of the Sacred Roma Rota. That interconnection of persons, however, was not among the prognostications proffered by the students whose artful compositions celebrated the promise of the cousins' union in May 1621.

THE SPOUSE OF TWO

Charles was the grandson of "le grand Henri," the Duke of Lorraine. His father, François, Prince of Vaudémont, was Henri's second son. His mother, Christine of Salm, was the daughter of neighboring nobility. One of nine children, Charles was his parents' oldest surviving son. He was originally destined by them to hold the place of the House of Lorraine in ecclesiastical life. At five he was tonsured, made a canon of Strasbourg, and appointed coadjutor bishop of Toul. When his older brother died, his parents changed his destiny. He was now to succeed his father and to produce an heir.

At ten Charles was sent to Paris for schooling at the French court. At fourteen he was sent to study under the Jesuits at Pont-à-Mousson, a university of two thousand students, now no more, then at its apogee, founded by Charles' grandfather, the Duke, and his great-uncles, the Cardinal of Lorraine and the Cardinal of Guise, and agreeably situated on the Moselle, equidistant from Metz to the north, Toul to the south, and Nancy to the southwest, in the duchy of Bar. Pont-à-Mousson, the locus for the dissemination of Tridentine Catholicism to the educated Catholics of Lorraine, was to make not insignificant contributions to Charles' life beyond his two years of schooling.[1]

At sixteen Charles was sent to accompany his father, commanding general of the Catholic League, in the war against the Protestants. He had a year of service in Germany, but was kept out of the League's glorious victory, the Battle of Prague. In 1621, when the story proper begins, he was seventeen, with the forces of the League in Germany.

Charles was fair-headed and handsome and charming to women. He was to be a bold and resourceful military commander. He was sometimes generous, and he was always nonchalant. He was also unchaste, imprudent, and quarrelsome.

In 1621 Charles did not know Béatrice but he could not help knowing his young cousin Nicole. Nicole was the oldest daughter of the reigning Duke of Lorraine, Henri II, the older brother of Charles' father. On her mother's side she was the grand-niece of a queen of France, Marie de Médicis; the granddaughter of the Duke of Mantua; the daughter of Marguerite of Gonzague.*

When Nicole was very young, Henri IV of France had thought of her as the mate for his son, her cousin, Charles' classmate at Paris, the future Louis XIII. When politics made a Spanish match desirable for a French monarch, Nicole was dropped. Her father chose for her then a good connection and a stalwart soldier, Louis

* The immediate family tree of Charles and Nicole:

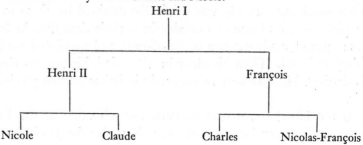

2

de Guise, Baron d'Ancerville, a son born out of wedlock to the Cardinal of Guise assassinated at Blois in 1588, illegitimate but still a member of the great family of Lorraine. Louis and Nicole were betrothed, though, as the betrothal was made when she was below the canonical age for marriage, it was not binding until Nicole reached the age of consent, twelve, and ratified the contract. Born October 3, 1608, in the spring of 1621 she had recently become old enough to marry.[2]

Nicole was well-formed but not beautiful. She was pious, good-hearted, and stubborn. If, at the age of twelve, she had affection for any man, it was directed at the mature soldier her parents had chosen for her.

Charles knew Nicole as he might be expected to know a cousin five years his junior. When she was a woman in her thirties, he could declare graciously that she had the most beautiful arms he had ever seen, but there is no record that he was drawn by any part of her anatomy when she was twelve, and her attainments at this age could not have attracted a young soldier and courtier. At the time it was settled that he should marry her he was still with the army in Germany. He had no other girl on his mind as a prospect for matrimony, but he had not expected to have this one.

Charles and Nicole were matched to be married because their fathers had quarreled. François, petulant younger brother, claimed that the Salic law of France, by which a woman could not inherit the throne, applied to Lorraine, then a country independent of France. By 1618 it was probable that Henri would not have any boys by his present wife; so that on this theory, François stood to inherit the dukedom if his brother died leaving Nicole as his heir. Henri rejected the theory and even more vigorously rejected its implications for his family. Nicole, he supposed, would succeed him and be protected in her succession by the strong arm of Louis de Guise. While the feelings between the brothers were running high, a trusted aide of Guise was murdered. Henri inferred that François had helped to arrange the killing. François inferred that he was in jeopardy. Hence, in 1618, he departed for Germany and there rendered his signal military services to the Catholic League.

The relations between the two brothers distressed the Emperor and the Pope. Their quarrel jeopardized the security of a small but strategic state arrayed on the Catholic side in the Thirty Years'

War. The Emperor and the Pope worked to reconcile the brothers. The Pope, Paul V, sent an emissary to Lorraine with this design. He was Dominic de Calatayud, a charismatic Discalced Carmelite, who had been a hero of the Battle of Prague, carrying the cross before the troops of the Catholic League in their assault. The emissary was well-chosen to reunite two proud and pious families. He proposed that the brothers be reconciled by their children's marriage.[3] Many noble girls were married at Nicole's age; her youth was not an obstacle; she was half a year past the age of consent. Henri hesitated, however, thinking what he had thought of his brother. He was finally convinced by Father Dominic's eloquence and prophecies. François considered half a loaf better than none, particularly when half was the way to the whole. His son would rule the dukedom. Nicole would be controlled by her husband. He agreed to be reconciled.[4]

Consanguinity in the fourth degree was an impediment to the union, but it was certain that the Pope would grant the dispensation. While waiting for it to arrive from Rome, Father Dominic officiated on May 22, 1621, as Charles and Nicole took each other as man and wife. The point of this anticipation of the Pope was to seal the agreement of the fathers as firmly as possible. Yet ecclesiastical propriety was also respected. Consummation was postponed until the dispensation arrived, as it did within three weeks of its request. Trinity Sunday, June 6, 1621, the marriage of Charles and Nicole was again celebrated. Jean des Porcelets de Maillane, the Bishop of Toul, presided in the palace chapel of Saint George. The families and a huge crowd of notables of the realm attended, the people of the town celebrated, Nicole and Charles appeared to be elated, and their joy was echoed by the student celebrations at the University of Pont-à-Mousson.[5]

After they were married they lived together. Charles found life with his twelve-year-old cousin not very agreeable. He murmured about the fate of princes forced to marry for reasons of state. Nicole fell in love with Charles.[6]

Three years later, in 1624, Duke Henri died. The Estates-General of Lorraine, called into session, acknowledged François as his successor. After having enjoyed the title for a week in order to establish that the succession passed through him to his heir, François resigned. Thereafter Charles and Nicole reigned as joint sovereigns.

Their domestic life, meager as it was, might have gone on indefinitely if it had not been interrupted by great political events. Charles exercised his martial temper by actions which provoked his neighbor France, then under the government of Cardinal Richelieu. Richelieu saw the advantage of dominating Lorraine, and he was not sorry to be provoked. In September 1633 a French army invaded Lorraine and captured the capital, Nancy.[7]

Charles fled. Accompanied by some of his troops, he was permitted to enter the neighboring state to the south, Franche Comté, and he took up residence there in Besançon. Nicole stayed behind in Nancy. When Charles left in the midst of war she did not expect the separation to be long. She never expected it to be for twenty-three years. After the French took Nancy, her freedom of movement was restricted, although she was not imprisoned. Her sister Claude escaped in disguise; so did her sister-in-law Henrietta.[8] Nicole hesitated, fatally. In May 1634, the French moved her to Paris. As De Brassac, Louis XIII's commander in Lorraine, observed, she went at the King's order, against her will. She had no way to resist. At the French court she was not physically a prisoner, but she could not leave. She lived on a small pension from Louis XIII and was in the postion of a pawn for Richelieu.[9]

Charles seemed to miss Nicole. At least he worried about her and about the use which could be made of her by his enemies. He wrote her while she was still at Nancy, "I die not hearing news of you." He wrote her on April 6, 1634, before her removal to Paris, assuring her that, whatever his fate, "all which will remain to me in this world will be absolutely in your hands." He wrote her on June 16, 1634, referring to matters which "I desire no person in the world to see or know of except you." [10] These letters might be attributed to a desire to placate Nicole in order to keep her from becoming a tool of Richelieu; or they could be taken at face value as testimonies of affection. They reflected no doubt that Nicole was his wife. Suspicion on this score assailed Charles only after he became better acquainted with Béatrice of Cusance.

Béatrice was the daughter of the Marquis of Bergues, now dead. She lived in Besançon with her wealthly widowed mother, the Marchioness of Bergues. She was a great beauty — painted by Van Dyck as one of the great beauties of the European world — and she had a vivacious and indomitable spirit. In 1634 she was twenty.[11]

Charles, bored, lonely husband, thirteen years married, gallant military hero down on his luck, ex-duke in exile, met Béatrice, a star in any circle and beyond challenge the belle of Besançon. After the acquaintance had ripened, Nicole worried about him. Charles wrote upbraiding her for her suspicions. He denounced "the traitors" who had made "these wicked reports." "I will be," he declared, "with passion all yours." Again he wrote, "I pray you always to love me and to believe that my greatest care is to know how you may be happy." [12]

These letters — available to posterity through the later exertions of Nicole's lawyers — were not necessarily insincere. Charles liked to please the person he addressed, and he knew what Nicole wanted to hear. Yet the letters, too, could have been cries for help, good resolutions, self-addressed exhortations. They were written as Charles found himself ever more drawn to Béatrice.

Eventually Charles asked Béatrice to be his wife. Her mother objected that he was married already.[13] At this rebuff Charles went north to be with the imperial troops at Brussels. His decisive sister Henrietta, in a sisterly desire to keep him out of trouble, arranged a match for Béatrice. For some years the mother of Eugène Léopold d'Oiselit, Prince of Cantecroix, a Besançon resident of importance, had wanted Béatrice as a bride for her son. With Henrietta's aid the match was made. Béatrice became the Princess of Cantecroix.[14]

The marriage was not the end of the story of Charles and Béatrice. The Prince of Cantecroix died on February 6, 1637. Charles, who had offered "3000 masses" for this result, was on hand to press his suit with the widow. Charles and Béatrice were betrothed, within a week of the funeral, on February 15, 1637. They moved quickly because Béatrice was pregnant, and perhaps she was pregnant by Charles. Charles was to claim the child as his after he was born in September. Under the circumstances Béatrice's mother agreed to the marriage. She signed the marriage contract assuring that the couple would have from her an ample dowry.[15]

Charles' alma mater, the University of Pont-à-Mousson, whose students' horoscopes and riddles had celebrated his union with Nicole, now made a new contribution to his life. His most pressing riddle — how he could seem to be married to Nicole, but actually be free to marry Béatrice — was answered by an ex-professor of moral theology at the University, Didier Cheminot. In May 1635,

Cheminot, a forty-five-year-old Jesuit and a patriotic Lorrainer, was expelled by the French from Pont-à-Mousson. He gravitated to the Duke-in-exile, and in 1637 he became the confessor of both Béatrice and Charles. Without his help they could have had an affair. Without his help they could not have been married. Anxious to have two souls in his charge in the state of grace, anxious to show his skill, sympathy, and mastery of moral theology, anxious to serve his country, Cheminot was a resourceful casuist and an indispensable adviser.[16]

Cheminot found good reasons why Charles' marriage to Nicole was null: Charles had lacked free consent, having been coerced by his father; the marriage in the chapel of Saint George had not been performed before the parish priest or his delegate as the law required; the parties were consanguineous; Nicole was not even a Christian, for she had been baptized by a priest later condemned as a notorious sorcerer. Hence, the marriage was null because of coercion, lack of form, consanguinity, and disparity of cult. Cheminot's formal conclusions were joined in by Le Moleur, Charles' chancellor; Sonnet, a canon of Besançon; Periquet, a priest of Besançon; and Catulle, vicar-general of Tournai. Theirs were not big names, but one could say that "five theologians" had held the marriage null.[17]

As the nullity of first marriage was clear, Cheminot reasoned, Charles had a duty to marry quickly. It was a duty owed to his country. He must provide an heir for Lorraine. In time of war delay could not be tolerated. Any day he might be killed by his enemies and his dukedom deprived of his descendants. He must act, and he need not wait for a formal ruling of nullity by a court of the Church.[18]

The last conclusion — the most vital if Charles and Béatrice were to marry at once — was the most daring. It meant ignoring, at least for the moment, the mighty judicial structure of the Church. Sanchez, the most famous of Jesuit authorities on marriage, could be read to support this conclusion but only by forcefully resolving ambiguities Sanchez had left unresolved. To reach Cheminot's desired result took ingenuity and chutzpah.*

* See Tomás Sanchez, *De sancto matrimonii sacramento* (Venice, 1737). Sanchez taught that a spouse conscious of the invalidity of his marriage could not be compelled by the Church to have intercourse, because to do so, unmarried, would be sin and the Church could not compel him to sin or to consent to the marriage

Sincere and strong religious sentiment opposed Cheminot's plan for his penitents. Béatrice's younger sister, Delia, the foundress of a convent of Visitation nuns at Gray, pleaded with her sister and with Charles not to take the step. Pierre Fourier, a septuagenarian canon regular of the abbey of Pont-à-Mousson, was consulted on the case in late 1636, when Cantecroix was still alive, by two religious favorable to Charles. Fourier told them, "His Highness has a lawful spouse." Later, as the Duke proceeded with his purpose of marriage, Fourier composed a memorial on the case and sent an emissary to Besançon to dissuade him. The venerable voice of this religious reformer of Lorraine, a spiritual man who was beatified in 1730, was not enough to shake Charles. The counsels of the devout were heard, but not heeded.[19]

Still, the attitude of Charles and Béatrice was not that of persons flouting the Church and defying it to do its worst, nor was it that of Aucassin who would rather have gone to hell than have given up Nicolette, his "trèsdouce amie." When they came to marry, they scrupulously observed the form for the ceremony required by the Council of Trent for the validity of any Catholic marriage. They attended to this law to assure that Béatrice became a legal wife and that Charles got good title to the dowry; and yet their motivations cannot be reduced to the purely cynical or mercenary. They had their confessor's opinion that they were not defying the Church, that they were indeed acting virtuously. They made sure that their adviser had the approval of high authority. On March 25, 1637, Charles formally appointed Cheminot "his confessor and

(2.39.8). Unless there were scandal in separation, there was no obligation to live with the spouse in the invalid marriage, although invalidity could not be proved (2.39.11). Suppose a man whose wife told him that she had not given true consent to their marriage. What kind of certitude must the husband have to act on his wife's admission? Sanchez answered, "that certitude is required — and is sufficient so that he can believe the woman and enter another marriage — which would make a prudent man morally certain of the fictitious consent of the other." He added that "hence" the man should submit "to the discretion of a judge" the evidence of fictitious consent for the judge to determine its sufficiency (2.45.4). By judge, he may have meant an ecclesiastical judge who had heard the evidence of nullity in a formal trial. In this sense he was cited by counsel for the Inquisition, Cesare Carena, who held that any man presuming to marry without a decision of an ecclesiastical court was to be punished by the bishop even if he subsequently proved to the Inquisition itself that the marriage was null (Cesare Carena, *De officio Sanctissimi Inquisitionis* [Cremona, 1655], part 2, title 5, 5.30). But Sanchez could have meant to refer to the opinion of a prudent man acting as a judge ad hoc. If the second reading were made, Sanchez could be used as authority for the right, in at least some circumstances, to circumvent the ecclesiastical machinery.

counsellor in matters which concern our conscience;" and Mutio Vitteleschi, General of the Jesuits, formally ratified the appointment.[20] They had the theologians' opinion concurring in their confessor's counsel. The Béatrice, who at the end of her life asked to be buried in the habit of the Poor Clares, the Béatrice who is painted in this habit, kneeling before the Mother and Child in the church of Daubs, Saône, is the Béatrice who asked her confessor how to handle Charles. The Charles, who much later wrote his daughter, "Ask God that He give you the grace of dying rather than of offending Him," is the Charles who had masses offered for the death of Cantecroix. However conventional Béatrice's pose, however conventional Charles' piety, it was in these religious categories that they spoke and thought. For them justification in terms of the canonical system of marriage was vital.[21] Legalistic but not necessarily cynical, rationalizing but not nakedly hypocritical, Charles and Béatrice and Béatrice's mother resembled the characters in the hypothetical cases in the books of moral casuistry then in their heyday, or a certain kind of modern businessman who will try any scheme to avoid a tax if he has the advice of counsel. Charles and Béatrice wanted to achieve their will, they wanted to do what the law on its face forbade, but they wanted to do it legally and with a blessing. They had the blessing.

Authority to marry them was sought from the pastor of St. Pierre's parish church in Besançon by the Duke's physician, Foget. The pastor authorized a priest of the parish, Antoine Guyot, to administer the sacrament in the house of a citizen named Daniel Beatrix within the parish limits. On the evening of April 2, 1637, Foget summoned Guyot to this house and introduced him to the waiting couple. Guyot, so he swore later, did not know that Charles was already married. What he thought of the secrecy, the use of an intermediary, the unusual setting is not recorded.

Shutters were drawn. Foget and the Duke's major-domo appeared as witnesses. Guyot was told that he would be the officiating priest required by Trent and was sworn to absolute secrecy. Charles and Béatrice consented to each other as man and wife. They kissed, drank wine from the same cup, and ate bread from the same loaf, according to the ancient wedding customs of Besançon.[22]

Despite a façade of caution, the marriage was an ill-kept secret. Charles and Béatrice lived in the same house. Their servants addressed her as "Your Highness," if strangers were not around.[23] In August, in what was meant to be great secrecy, Béatrice went to the chateau of Scey to await the birth of her child. He was born in late September, and in November, Charles recognized him as his heir. The baby very soon contracted a fever, was put out with a nurse, and died in the village of Belle-Herbe. Tragic as the event was, their religious advisers no doubt could point to the appropriate scriptural parallel: God had taken from David and Bethsheba the son conceived by them in adultery — the son whose disputable parentage would always have haunted the line of succession; the next child born to the royal couple, now legally married, had been Solomon.[24] David was no more publicly committed to Bethsheba than Charles now to Béatrice.

Three other marriages are relevant to the story: two for the light they throw on the attitudes of participants in Charles' case; one because it provided vital motivation for the man who in strategic ways was the most important person in the story of Charles' annulment. The first occurred in May 1621: when Charles took Nicole as wife, Louis de Guise wed Charles' sister Henrietta. In this way Nicole's old betrothed was disposed of and brought into the family reconciliation. Henrietta — she who later arranged Béatrice's marriage to Cantecroix — was then sixteen and had other desires. She ran away and hid in a convent, so that her marriage to Louis, supposed to coincide with that of Charles and Nicole, was delayed four days. The marriage underlined the views of Charles' parents on the obedience owed to parents in the choice of a spouse.[25]

In January 1632, Gaston, Duke of Orléans and brother of Louis XIII, married Marguerite, another younger sister of Charles. The marriage, which took place in Lorraine without Louis' permission, was one cause of the French wrath toward Charles. Three years later, in July 1635, the bishops of Montpellier, Sées, Chartres, Saint-Malo, and Nîmes reported to the Assembly of the French Clergy that French custom required the consent of the king to the marriage of a prince of the blood; Gaston thereupon announced that he would treat his union with Marguerite as null. Marguerite appealed to Rome. In this way, before Charles' turn came, Urban VIII had had occasion to hear the appeal of a Lorraine princess against a spouse repudiating her on the advice of his spiritual counselors. The Pope found the marriage to be unaffected by such an 'incanonical repudiation.[26]

The third relevant marriage involved siblings of the principals. Nicolas-François, five years Charles' junior, had been brought up in his shadow. Destined to replace his brother in an ecclesiastical career, he had been given more time for studies at Pont-à-Mousson. His panegyric in honor of Saints Ignatius and Francis Xavier — delivered at the age of fourteen — was found worthy of commemoration in the University's annals. Equally remembered was his defense at age seventeen of his thesis on "Universal Philosophy," sustained before a public which included his father and his brother. That same year he was made Bishop of Toul — that is, though unconsecrated and not in holy orders, he was given the juridical and administrative powers of the bishop. Urban VIII, noting that the House of Lorraine had been "always regarded as the rampart of the Catholic Church," made him a cardinal when he was eighteen. He was then studying theology at Pont-à-Mousson; and when he continued to attend classes, it was suggested from Rome that a cardinal should be educated in private. Quiet, studious, well-educated, he waited for his hour.[27]

On January 18, 1634, Charles abdicated the dukedom in his brother's favor, hoping thereby to placate Richelieu. But as long as Claude, Nicole's twenty-two-year-old sister, remained unmarried, there was the danger that the French might somehow use her as a claimant to the throne. Nicolas-François had never taken holy orders. The family had already anticipated one contingency in which they would have been in the way: the marriage contract of Charles and Nicole, to which he was a party, had expressly provided that in the event of Charles dying without issue, Nicolas-François should marry Nicole. Nicolas-François clearly believed that a bishop could divorce himself from his see: here at least, prior tradition to the contrary, marriage was dissoluble.* Now in the

---

* Tradition as old as Saint Gregory Nazanien and Saint Gregory of Nyssa taught that a bishop was indissolubly wedded to his see (Raoul Naz, "Translation," *Dictionnaire de droit canonique*, VII, 1321). Innocent III developed this doctrine in decisions which became decretal law. According to the Pope, "the spiritual bond of the marriage" was begun by election, ratified by confirmation, and consummated in consecration. Man could not dissolve this bond, for, as the Lord had said, "What God has joined together, let no man put asunder." Only the Vicar of Jesus Christ, the Pope, could release the bond, X.1.7.4, "Licet in tantum." Not by human, "but rather by divine power the spiritual marriage is dissolved when a

year of crisis he was free to meet another family need and was not slow to meet it. He consulted Fourier's canons-regular as to whether he could dispense himself from any ecclesiastical impediments to marrying. They consulted their copy of Tomás Sanchez and assured him that he could.[28] Acting as bishop, he dispensed himself to marry, and, with the French army at the gates of his chateau of Useville, on February 11, 1634, he resigned the cardinalate and episcopate and married Claude.[29]

Immediately thereafter Nicolas-François became the prisoner of the French. The "conscience of the King of France" would not permit the newlyweds to remain alone, as only the Pope could validly dispense cousins to marry each other. No doubt the French commander knew that an unconsummated marriage could always be dissolved. Virtually by return mail, however, Urban VIII granted the dispensation, which arrived March 19, and the couple escaped surveillance to marry again on March 20, 1634.[30] The dispensation for Nicolas-François had come as quickly for him as for his brother thirteen years before. Papal chagrin at his casual treatment of the cardinalate easily yielded to the desire to frustrate a France allied with the Protestants. Nicolas-François still stood high in Rome. He now had business of a domestic and political character which would make his standing in Rome to be of the greatest consequence.

In April of 1637 Nicolas-François undertook to give his sister-in-law Nicole advice. If Charles was validly married to the sterile Nicole, Nicolas-François or his son would inherit Lorraine; if Béatrice's marriage with Charles could be made good, any son of theirs would be at least arguably the heir. Nicolas-François may have genuinely liked his sister-in-law; he may have had a strong religious conviction about the sanctity of marriage; he may have had

---

bishop is removed from his church by translation or deposition or even by resignation, by the authority of the Roman Pontiff, who is established to be the Vicar of Jesus Christ," X.1.7.2, *Inter corporalia*. Nicolas-François was the bishop-elect of Toul (*Hierarchia catholica*, IV, 349) when he resigned his see.

In contrast, a contemporary prelate who was later canonized, François de Sales, Bishop-in-exile of Geneva, held the classic Christian notion that a bishop was married to his see. When it was proposed that he become coadjutor archbishop of Paris with right of succession, he declared to Cardinal de Retz that he "would wish to be made unmarried only to be no longer married." (François de Sales to Mother Jeanne de Chantal, February 26, 1620, *Oeuvres*, ed. by the Religious of the Visitation of the First Monastery of Annecy [Paris, 1919], XIX, 152; Francis Trocher, *Saint François de Sales* [Paris, 1940], IX, 647.)

an intelligent younger brother's disdain for an older brother who so carelessly wasted his advantages. These motives alone cannot account for the determination with which he was to pursue Nicole's cause. The studious student of theology at Pont-à-Mousson, the young cardinal who knew the Barberini and the Roman congregations, the man of decision who could change his status in a crisis from a cardinal to a husband, Nicolas-François did for Nicole what she could not do for herself. Assuming that Charles would want the dukedom back if Richelieu would let him have it, Nicholas-François looked to the succession. Whenever he appeared there were signs of a decisive intelligence at work, and this directing genius made the struggle between the Duke of Lorraine and his castoff Duchess at least an equal contest.

Perhaps the news of Charles' action of April 2 had already reached Nicolas-François in Lorraine, perhaps he knew only that it was likely. In any event, he did not allude to Béatrice, but he did speak generally of the difficulties Nicole might face, and he offered to send her sister Claude to accompany her or even to come with her himself. His advice was: leave Paris, seek Charles where he is. Only by being on the spot could Nicole win Charles back.[31]

The advice may have been sound, but the French would not let Nicole leave Paris. At this point Richelieu saw no advantage in her retrieving Charles. Over a year later, when the fact of Charles' life with Béatrice was notorious — she rode with him when he went on campaigns for the Emperor — did Nicole appeal for help to the Pope.

MAGNUM IN CHRISTO

Urban VIII had both conciliar and papal legislation — his own in fact — to guide him in responding to Nicole's cry. By the provisions of the Council of Trent a married man living with a concubine was to be admonished by the bishop three times, then excommunicated; a woman "living publicly" with an adulterer was to be admonished thrice and then to be punished by the bishop, with the help of the secular arm, if necessary.[32] These provisions presumably came into play if Charles had merely taken Béatrice as his mistress.

More serious yet was Charles' position if he were found to have married Béatrice when he already had a wife. Bigamists were customarily claimed by the Inquisition. A bigamist, or polygamist as the inquisitors would describe him, was gravely suspect of heresy. A contemporary case from Cremona showed the limits of the mercy of the Inquisition: a woman convicted of remarrying without adequate proof of her husband's death — he was in fact alive — was sentenced to abjure her heresy *de vehementi* and to work at the Hospital for Mendicants for six months. Ordinarily the penalty set by law was harsher.[33]

On this subject Urban VIII had himself pronounced as recently as June 20, 1637. *Magnum in Christo* ran his bull:

Great in Christ and in the Church is the sacrament of matrimony, as a lawful, indissoluble partnership for life between man and woman, in which by reciprocal consent one must give himself to the other. Therefore, by grave and fitting penalties those are to be corrected, who, unmindful of the commandments of the Lord and putting second their own salvation, do not hesitate to violate the holy laws of this sacrament.

The Pope went on to say that reports had reached him of "sons of iniquity" who passed to second marriages in the lifetime of their first wives. He had consulted with the cardinals of the Inquisition, and he had determined on condign punishment to repress this practice. He decreed that such men were to be "condemned to the galleys in perpetuity." [34]

This constitution may have been drafted before the Pope heard of the second marriage of Charles, yet its timing — three months after the event, two months after Duke Nicolas-François could have brought it to the attention of Rome — is coincidental enough to make one suppose that Charles may have been one of those so anonymously classified as sons of perdition. As events developed, no such crude and general legislation was to be applied to him. The bull stood as testimony to the official Roman view of the man who challenged the doctrine on marriage by taking a second wife. Nicole had set in motion a formidable machine.

To the attention now given his affairs by Rome, Charles had but one answer: the adviser who had told him that he was within the law should be given the opportunity to persuade the central authorities of the soundness of his casuistry. Father Cheminot was to be sent to Rome. There was additional urgency for regularizing

Charles' position: Béatrice was again pregnant. Cheminot carried with him a memorial to the Pope which he had prepared and Charles had signed. In it Charles explained why the marriage with Nicole was null, and how his duty to his country had required him to marry Béatrice. Béatrice, he was made to say, was his "wife of conscience." [35]

In a separate memorandum to Cardinal Barberini, Cheminot set out the technical way in which the Pope could handle the case and offend no one. The requirements of the internal forum and the external forum were to be kept distinct. The implied suggestion was that, although Charles might not have a provable case in the ecclesiastical courts ("the external forum"), he could be told that morally, in his conscience ("the internal forum") his actions were justified. In any event the Pope was requested to communicate his desires to Charles privately before they were published: Cheminot wanted a chance to review the decision. He added, as a respectful advocate will add, that Charles was ready to obey whatever the Pope should ask. [36]

Cheminot in Rome took the initiative in getting support from his Jesuit colleagues. He wrote up a hypothetical case involving one Titus and one Bertha, described as having "contracted marriage through the kind of fear which would affect a steady man." The hypothetical gave no hint of the real parties. This textbook example was then circulated in the Jesuits' Roman College, and Cheminot got thirteen theologians, including the famous Juan de Lugo, to pronounce the hypothetical marriage invalid. Apparently he found other theologians, but no Jesuits in Rome, to agree that in the circumstances described the parties did not have to wait for a decision from a church court. [37] He had achieved the equivalent of a staff ruling of the Federal Trade Commission that an accomplished merger was legal. The scrutiny of more powerful agencies and more important persons had still to be survived.

Coercion as a ground for annulling an arranged royal marriage was not an unfamiliar ploy. In the annulment proceedings in 1498 of Louis XII against Jeanne of France and in the annulment proceedings of Henri IV against Marguerite of Valois, coercion of the bride had been alleged. As precedents in a strict legal sense neither case was very useful because other grounds — consanguinity and spiritual relationship — had been present, and the judgments of nullity did not make plain the basis of decision. As precedents in how a marriage might quickly be annulled if the Pope was willing to cooperate, they were highly instructive. In both the trick had been turned by persuading the Pope (Alexander VI and Clement VIII respectively) to name judges-delegate who would act in his name without the case coming to Rome for decision. In both the process had taken less than a year once the Pope had agreed to the procedure.[38]

Through Cheminot, Charles asked that the bishops of Toul, Metz, and Verdun be appointed by the Pope to hear his case against the validity of the marriage with Nicole. The Bishop of Toul was Charles Christian Gourray, who had been Nicolas-François' suffragan since 1624 and had become Bishop of Toul in 1636 under him; Charles gambled on his loyalty. Who the bishops of Metz and Verdun would have been is not clear, since in the confusion of ecclesiastical affairs in the area there were no bishops recognized by the Pope in these cities.[39]

Nicole, well-counseled, responded to the legal petition by recusing all three nominees as prejudiced. She asked Urban VIII to judge in person. She also wrote Charles directly. Doubtless she was counseled here too, but the accent appeared to be her own: "You are going to expose us in the theatre of the world . . . to make those who once pitied our condition now laugh at our misfortune." She expressed her incredulity that anyone had forced him to marry her. But her incredulity was not directed only at the ground of Charles' case: "I have been so long incredulous about my disaster." She would not give him up: "I loved you passionately." "You will one day return to yourself, and you will regret having so mistreated one who loves you more than life." "All your outrages have not uprooted from my heart the affection I have for you." [40]

In Rome the decision, not as to the validity of the marriage but as how to handle the case in its preliminary phase, rested largely with one man — Francesco Barberini. Barberini was "the cardinal-nephew," the institutional embodiment of that nepotism which many Popes had thought necessary to employ in government. He was also, as the inner organization usually called him in memoranda, the *cardinale-padrone*, the "cardinal boss," or the "director of affairs." In 1639 he was a veteran of sixteen years of high office, having been created a cardinal by Urban VIII at the age of twenty-six. In those sixteen years of service he had reaped a great fortune, and he had been the intelligent instrument of the will of his imperious uncle.* Now at forty-two, he was in charge. His uncle was far from senile, but he was seventy-one and accustomed to trusting his nephew. The Secretary of State, nominally the Pope's prime minister, was Cardinal Ceva, but Barberini, holding the office of Prefect of the Holy Office of the Inquisition, was in fact above him; in an affair of this kind, involving high political interests and yet presenting questions of special interest to the Inquisition, Barberini might be expected to take personal control.[41]

Barberini gave Cheminot's memo to two theologians, Giustiniani and Hilarion. Both reported back that it was very unlikely that Charles' marriage with Nicole was null.[42] Upon receiving their preliminary report the *cardinale padrone* proceeded with dispatch to isolate Charles from his erring counselor, whose advice had been sufficiently individualistic already to have caused brother Jesuits in Besançon to complain to the Jesuit General about him and the Jesuits of Brussels to refuse to receive him at their college. Barberini now made a note to tell the General that Cheminot should be rebuked for the partisanship with which he had defended his advice. In the face of this pressure and with their own men in the field at least divided, the Jesuits at headquarters were not prepared to back up Cheminot, however many theologians subscribed to his hypothetical. Nothing stood in the way of action against him at the direction of the Holy See. By brief of June 18, 1639, Urban VIII ordered Jacques Boonen, Archbishop of Malines, to conduct an inquiry into Cheminot's conduct. If he was found to have counseled Charles' marriage to Béatrice, he was to be imprisoned or suspended from the exercise of his priestly functions.[43]

In the same month the first response of the Holy See to the marriage was broadcast to the diplomatic service. Barberini advised the nuncios to the Emperor, France, Venice, Poland, Savoy, Florence, Naples, Cologne, and the Swiss of Urban VIII's initial impression of the case. The Pope, they were told, had heard that Charles had

---

* On Francesco Barberini's power and fortune, see J. Grisar, *Päpstliche Finanzen, Nepotismus and Kirchenrechte unter Urban VIII, Miscellanea historiae pontificiae* (Rome: Universitas Gregoriana, 1943), VII, 244, 261. Grisar estimates that the total annual papal income from all sources ecclesiastical and civil, was over 2,000,000 scudi; the three Barberini nephews enjoyed a legal income of at least 400,000 scudi, not counting presents and other sources of income.

fallen into the error of "by his own authority repudiating the duchess of Lorraine" and of "temerariously contracting a new marriage with the princess of Cantecroix." [44]

To Claude d'Achey, Archbishop of Besançon, went a third directive. The Pope commissioned him to determine if Charles and Béatrice had in fact gone through a marriage ceremony. Charles was close to being tried for polygamy. Secret hearings were conducted early in September 1639 by the Archbishop. Charles and Béatrice were not heard, but indisputable evidence of the wedding was furnished by Father Guyot, who had celebrated it. Barberini now had in hand all he needed to make life for Charles unbearable. [45]

On October 14, 1639, Urban VIII upheld Nicole's complaint against the judges nominated by Charles. He wrote Charles that the matter had been assigned for hearing to Jacques Boonen, the Archbishop of Malines, within whose jurisdiction Charles fell as long as he resided at the imperial court at Brussels. At the same time he assured Charles that the case would be heard by a special commission of prelates if "really, truly, and canonically" he would separate from Béatrice. Boonen was simultaneously directed to press for this real separation and to require Béatrice to enter a convent until the case was decided. [46]

Nicole did not remain entirely passive. On January 7, 1640, she permitted a public manifesto to appear in her name, addressed to Charles. She spoke because "in our name the sacraments are besmeared and especially that sacrament which represents the indissoluble bond of Jesus Christ with his Church." [47] The nub of the interest of the case for Catholic Europe lay in that theological symbolism requiring indissolubility.

Charles treated Nicole's memorial as propaganda from Richelieu. In his capacity of a successful general for the Emperor, he remained at the imperial court in Brussels, insisting that Béatrice be treated as his wife. Archbishop Boonen was in no position to shake him. [48] This sorry state of affairs, as it seemed to Georg Stravius, the secretary of the nunciature in Brussels, was reported to Rome in March 1640. Cardinal Barberini replied at once, instructing Stravius to try a "sweeter and suaver" approach; if that did not work, harsher measures would be necessary. [49]

Father Cheminot was still at the root of the problem in the minds of some authorities. Nicolas-François had written the General of the Jesuits on July 2, 1639, warning him about his dangerous subordinate. Urban VIII, despite his own suspicions, still referred to him as "our beloved son" in his note of October 14, 1639, to Charles. Nicolas-François then caught him on his way back from Rome and had him detained in Nancy in the fall of 1639. When he was searched, the answer of the Roman theologians to his hypothetical was found on his person, and Nicolas-François wrote angrily to the General demanding an explanation of this extraordinary opinion of Jesuit theologians. Vitteleschi replied that the theologians had not known who the actual persons were that the hypothetical referred to, nor had they been given any concrete circumstances; they had answered an abstract inquiry. Cheminot, however, had been allowed to rejoin Charles in Brussels, and Boonen had not been able to shake him from Charles, any more than he had been able to separate Charles from Béatrice.

After Charles' public display of Béatrice in Lorraine, the Pope was heard to describe Cheminot as a "bad man." Thereafter the General of the Jesuits did his best to detach him from the Duke. On July 14, 1640, Vitteleschi ordered Cheminot, "by the virtue of holy obedience," not to speak to anyone of Charles' marriage. A series of letters from Jesuit headquarters pressed home the message; the fifth and last, December 15, 1640, warned him that he would be *ipso facto* excommunicated if he persisted in his disobedience. Cheminot, however, persisted.[50]

Galileo Galilei, one-time friend of Urban VIII, who had published his *Dialogue on the Great World Systems* in February 1632, was summoned before the Inquisition in October 1632, put on trial in April 1633, and sentenced June 22, 1633.[51] Monarchs, ex-monarchs, and successful generals differed from scientists. They were also harder to catch. The Pope continued to choose a milder course than the full rigor of the law on polygamy permitted. Sweeter and suaver methods continued to be the order of the day, although the Barberini will to bring Charles to book did not waver. On October 5, 1640, Urban VIII wrote him once more urging him to separate, at least temporarily, from Béatrice. The Pope, as an old friend of his House, still wanted "to act paternally." Béatrice, he added, need not enter a convent. She could go to Lucerne, although she must not see Charles while the nullity of his marriage to Nicole was being tried.[52] This tone, this concession, the model of reasonable compromise in Roman eyes, did not strike a response in Charles.

In March 1641 Charles came to Paris to talk to Richelieu. He would not stay with Nicole at the family house in Paris, the Hôtel de Lorraine, but it was arranged for him to see her. He made the gallant remark, related above, on the beauty of her arms, but he addressed her as "my cousin." She asked, "Am I no longer your wife?" [53]

On March 29, 1641, Charles signed a humiliating peace treaty with Richelieu in return for which his dukedom was restored. Nicolas-François, the nominal duke, protested the treaty, but he was in Vienna, and no one was in a position to prevent Charles from resuming his old role.[54] He returned to Lorraine, taking with him Béatrice as his duchess. For the country the return of the old duke was a triumphant occasion. For Pont-à-Mousson, whose students had been dispersed by war and whose faculty had been so harassed by the French, the return marked the resurrection of the University. Patriotism as much as theology accounted for the warm reception Charles and Béatrice received from the largely Jesuit faculty when they visited his alma mater on June 2, 1641.[55]

That Charles should be re-established in Lorraine in a posture which the Holy See regarded as polygamous was galling to the Barberini. The preservation of respect for a ruler could not outweigh the harm done by such a public display of defiance. A German Jesuit, Toccius Gerard, was ordered to travel to Lorraine and personally inform Father Cheminot of his excommunication. The mission was at the risk of the messenger's life, given the sensitivity of Charles and Béatrice to interference within their state. Father Gerard was "stupefied" to receive the charge, but he executed it to the letter, without immediate effect. On June 1, 1641, another warning letter to Charles from his paternal pastor in Rome arrived. The Duke did not comply.[56]

As a last check on precipitate action by the Holy See, Barberini arranged for a commission of cardinals to give advice to the Pope. In all probability, Juan de Lugo — Cheminot's chief catch in the signatures on the hypothetical, now the most prominent theologian in the College of Cardinals — joined in the opinion given Urban VIII. As in the Galileo affair the Pope had taken particularly to heart what he regarded as an attempt to acquire an intellectual ascendancy over him. The ruling obtained by Cheminot on his hypothetical had been "fraudulently and treacherously extorted from certain theologians." The theologians, informed of the true facts, had revoked their *responsum*.[57]

After hearing from his cardinals, the Pope took the ultimate step within his power. On February 13, 1642, he signed a bull describing Charles' affair as "a scandal" and "a detestable offense known to all the Christian Commonwealth." Charles and Béatrice were excommunicated and were to be avoided by all Christians. On April 9, 1642, the bull was published with the direction that it be posted in Lorraine and announced in the churches on three successive Sundays.[58] In its own sweet time and way, taking about three years from the date on which official urging had begun, and five years from the date of Charles and Béatrice's wedding, the administrative machinery of the Curia had moved to protect the institution of marriage, its own jurisdiction, and the rights of Nicole.

Predictably, Charles' initial response to the bull was defiance. It was, he declared, founded on erroneous facts and therefore null. He appealed "from the Pope badly informed to the Pope better informed." The Attorney General of Lorraine issued a brochure bitterly attacking the nepotism of the Barberini, the espionage of the Nuncio, the tyrannical behavior of Archbishop Boonen.[59] No doubt Henry VIII of England's was the case everyone had in mind when such ducal wrath was shown; and a ruler less devoted by ancestry and conviction to the Catholic Church might have been tempted to suggest that he always had the option of a different ecclesiastical regime. But all Charles' bravado did not frighten the Barberini nor improve his own position ecclesiastically. A year and a half after the bull, two years and a half after his own excommunication, Cheminot capitulated and sought pardon. The Jesuits sent him to do penance at Genoa; though he died in good standing some twenty-one years later back at Pont-à-Mousson, Charles was deprived of the counselor who had always sustained him.[60]

Urban VIII died July 29, 1644, and was succeeded by Innocent X. The hostility of the new administration to the Barberini may have helped persuade Charles that now was the time to try to get his case heard in Rome. After "eight whole years without being separated" he arranged to live apart from Béatrice long enough to get his excommunication lifted.[61] Then, in 1646, Innocent X issued a special papal rescript. The big favor of a cardinalitial commission to hear the case was not granted, but the substantial grace was conceded that the matter be tried in Rome by the ordinary hearing officers of the Pope, the Sacred Roman Rota. Charles also obtained what he had probably asked for: appeal from the Rota "was removed," so that it could function as a court of first and last resort.[62]

Proceedings at law then stayed in abeyance while the family of the principals tried to work out a settlement. Gathered in conclave in Paris, the princes and princesses of the House of Lorraine determined that husband and wife should make up their differences. As a result of this resolution, negotiations were opened between the parties with the Nuncio to Paris, Nicolas de Guise, another member of the family, acting as a kind of referee. On May 26, 1647, in the Nuncio's presence, a formal emissary from Charles met a formal emissary from Nicole. Charles' offer was "to reunite souls and bodies and to supply the consent which may have been lacking on his part in the first marriage." Nicole's response was that she could not accept a clause which would "prejudice her marriage which was valid from the beginning." [63] Negotiations collapsed. Only a judicial decision could determine a status which the wife asserted was a marriage and which the husband asserted was a nullity.

Proceedings in the Rota now became more serious.* In March and June of 1648 the tribunal gave its first view of the case. The time elapsed since the issuance of the papal rescript was two years, but the decision in March was less than a year after the failure of negotiations, and the lawyers had had to do much preliminary work before they asked the court for rulings on the "remissorial letters" to be issued. These letters were commissions to local representatives of the Church outside of Rome, empowering them to hear testimony and indicating the areas of dispute. In this case they were directed to officials in France, Lorraine, and the Low Countries. They necessarily gave some evidence of how the court viewed the

---

* It was possible for a wife to obtain from the court an order directing her husband to pay her living expenses during the suit (*alimenta*, the original alimony) and the expenses of litigation. So, for example, in *Toledo, Of Marriage, June 15, 1624*, the wife, Maria, had an order for 600 scudi per year for *alimenta* and 200 scudi for the expenses of litigation; *Decisiones Sacrae Romanae Rotae coram R.P.D. Clemente Merlino*, ed. Marcello Merlino (Venice, 1652). There is no indication that Nicole sought such support from Charles.

law.* The Rota noted that Nicole would attempt to prove that the marriage was contracted by new expressions of consent emitted after the arrival of the papal dispensation from consanguinity. It observed further that a marriage might be proved by witnesses as well as by the parish record book required by Trent; that the palace chapel of Saint George was exempt from the bishop's administrative, but not from his pastoral jurisdiction; and that long cohabitation might be a defense against a claim of coercion.[64]

During the next several years the witnesses were examined. The lawyers' briefs were prepared. The parties waited, but not wholly passively. Shortly after they learned of the unfavorable Rota rulings of June 26, 1648, Charles and Béatrice must have come together, for Béatrice, aged thirty-five, again became pregnant. Their first child, born in 1637, had died. The second, born in late 1639, was a girl, Anne. On April 17, 1649, a male heir, Charles-Henri, was born.[65]

Thereafter Charles and Béatrice appear to have lived apart for twenty-eight months, practically from the date of the birth. Was it because Charles had developed doubts about the child's paternity? Béatrice on her own had lived a gay life, courted by Prince Charles of England and Prince Radziwill of Poland. Was it because Charles had achieved his objective and no longer needed Béatrice? Was it because he was once more told such a real "canonical separation" was essential if his case was to go ahead in the Rota? At all events, the separation occurred and embittered relations between the couple. Reports of Béatrice's flirtations reached Charles in Brussels and were enlarged on by his relatives, who were anxious to discredit her. Charles was heard to say that if the marriage case was

---

* Remissorial letters, or letters rogatory, set out "articles" or major questions on which the petitioner wanted his witnesses examined. The respondent had the opportunity to have the Rota approve "interrogatories," a kind of cross-examination, made up in advance, of the petitioner's witnesses. The interrogatories typically began by reminding the witness of the importance of an oath and his moral obligation to make restitution for any loss caused by his lying; see *Tullen matrimonii: Processus remissorialis executa a R.D. Officiali Tullenisi* (June 1651–January 1652), S.R. Rota: *Processus Actorum* 116, Secret Archives of the Vatican. The grant of remissorial letters was an opportunity for the Rota to pronounce on the law of the case, as an Anglo-American court would rule on a demurrer. For example, in *Venice, of Marriage, November 29, 1604*, Auditor Francisco Peña refused to give remissorial letters; though the petitioner, Michaele Syrum, alleged fear of his father had led him to marry, he had alleged "conditional," not "absolute" fear. The distinction made by Peña ended Syrum's case. See the report of the decision printed in Paolo Zacchia, *Quaestiones medico-legales* (Lyon, 1661), II, Decision 58.

ever resolved in his favor, Béatrice might expect "to be chastised with light irons." On November 19, 1652, he went to see her in Antwerp, upbraided her coldly, and removed from her possession all the jewels he could claim as his; he returned to Brussels the next day, demonstrating that his visit had no hidden motive of enjoying her companionship for any length of time.[66]

In the fall of 1652 the coolness between them made Charles' family believe that now was the time to have judgment pronounced on the marriage. Nicolas-François took the initiative in urging the Pope to act. He was now a widower, Claude having died after giving birth to her fourth child in 1648. Two sons, Ferdinand born in 1639 and Charles born in 1643, stood, after him, as claimants to Lorraine if his brother died without lawful issue.[67] Nicolas-François was at the court in Vienna in good standing with the Emperor. The empress, his aunt Eleanor, joined him in his appeal to the Pope, working through the Archbishop of Rhodes, one of the Gonzague family, to the same end. Another Gonzague relative, the Queen of Poland, used Cardinal des Ursins to recommend papal action. Still the Pope hesitated, fearing that Charles would not return to Nicole and that a decision would provoke him to scandalous disobedience. Marguerite, Duchess of Orléans, another of Charles' younger sisters who liked to manage her brother's business, tried to persuade him to send a written promise to the Pope that he would accept and obey the Rota's decision. She was so successful that Charles accepted her draft of the promise, merely changing the "pretended wife" of her text to "Madame Béatrice" when referring to his former love. Nicolas-François, the Emperor, and the princes of the House of Lorraine then jointly asked the Pope to have the case decided.[68]

THE WRITTEN LAW

The Sources

If law is conceived of as what is written down in official law-books, the law was what was contained in the *Concordance of Discordant Canons* of Gratian, the decrees of the Popes, and the canons of the Council of Trent. Gratian was a law teacher's collection of conflicting authorities with his own resolution of the conflicts. By common acclaim, then by papal action, this extraordinary manual composed in 1142 had been accepted as law itself.[69] Wrenched from use as a teaching instrument, it had become a source of familiar texts, decrees, and principles. To it had been added in 1232 the *Decretals* of Gregory IX, an excellent terse summary of the case law of the past century. Divided into five major books — Book 4 being devoted to marriage — these excerpts from pontifical letters began to function as legislation in which the *ratio decidendi* of each case was treated as a universal rule, modified as it might be by its companions in the collection. Innovative papal lawmaking on a large scale ended with this massive effort, but the Sext, Clementines, and Extravagants completed the collection — the Sext, or sixth, book added by Boniface VIII in 1300; the Clementines, or constitutions of Clement V, attached in 1317; the Extravagants, or still further additions of John XXII in 1330, supplementing the existing legislation. The canons emanating in broad statutory form from the Council of Trent between 1548 and 1564 were the last word, building on the earlier decisions and sometimes overriding them. Together, these several documents of the past five centuries answered to the description "law" if one sought to know what official texts governed Charles' case.

Written law could also be understood to include the civil law, the law determined by the state. When a canonist in Rome entered upon this topic, he turned primarily to the Digest, Code, and Institutes of Justinian — the responses of Roman jurisconsults and the decrees of Roman emperors as collected, digested, and codified in Byzantium over a millennium ago. Whenever this law did not expressly conflict with canon law, a court of the Church in Rome would regard it as good authority or as apposite precedent; and sometimes where it did conflict with the canon law, it was glossed to harmonize. It was regularly regarded as good current law. Its antiquity, its varied and sometimes obscure origin, its provenance from Constantinople were ignored.

Canonical and civil texts did not stand alone. They had been interpreted by glosses, by treatises on specialized subjects, by comprehensive summations, by collections of answers to real or hypothetical cases. Like the responses of the old Roman jurisconsults, these applications of the texts by learned legal writers had become difficult to distinguish from the written law itself. No emperor gave the commentators the *ius respondendi*. Yet, as the right of judges or jurisconsults to declare the law was the power to make law, so the authority attributed by practice to the commentators conferred upon them an analogous power, though the fictions employed by courts and lawyers concealed their creative task.

Marked difference did not exist between the authority accorded a canon and the authority accorded a commentator who had gained recognition among legal men by the solidity of his work. Three distinctions between commentaries and official texts could, however, be observed. First, the texts were the normal starting point for explaining a new decision or writing a new commentary; a writer did not so easily jump off from an existing commentary as from the official law. Second, flat contradiction of official texts was likely to be eccentric and unpersuasive; they were undermined by fictions, while flat rejection of a commentator could occur. Third, no permanence was guaranteed the commentators, although writers like Hostiensis had been cited since the thirteenth century. In distinction, the official texts were assured of being regarded as relevant by a new generation of lawyers as long as no official action was taken to repeal or amend them.

Of at least equal standing with the commentaries were the applications of law made by the courts of the Church. Case law — in particular that decided within the preceding seventy-five years — formed part of the corpus of written law. Decisions of the Congregation of the Council here held a special place. This committee of cardinals of the Roman Curia was authorized by the Pope to interpret the disciplinary decrees of Trent; its rulings had the force of legislation. Decisions of the Congregation, however, were neither collected nor published, and therefore could only be cited when some commentator incorporated an account of one of its rulings in his text.[70]

Far more numerous and almost as authoritative were the opinions of the Roman Rota, which was remarkable among curial courts and committees in providing reasoned judgments. By papal direction the judge-reporter had to provide the parties with copies of the Rota's decision together with "the laws and the reasons."[71] Two large, albeit unofficial, printed collections of these reports existed: *Diverse Decisions*, collecting a number of cases from 1530 to 1612, and *More Recent Decisions,* covering, with greater comprehensiveness, the years after 1612. In 1650 the most recent volume available was for the year 1641. In addition, many rotal cases could be found in separate collections of opinions by individual auditors published and sold by the auditor himself or by his heirs. These collections were well prepared for practical use by the members of the bar who edited them. Cases were not identified by the names of the parties — from time immemorial the Rota had affected a certain indifference to the parties' names — but by city of origin, date of decision, and subject matter. Each case was preceded by a one sentence summary of its main holding and by a numbered series of propositions of law extracted from the opinion. The opinion itself was correspondingly numbered. A good editor would also annotate with references to the *Decretals,* the Roman law, the commentators, and related cases. The arrangement was not unlike the syllabus and headnote system of modern American law reports.

The Rota had no strict rule of *stare decisis.* Individual decisions sometimes conflicted with each other, and the conflicts occasioned criticism. A handbook on the Rota by one of its members found the criticism rash; the conflicts arose, he said, from "the love of truth" and "the necessities of the human condition." What was important as precedent was not so much the individual result as the settled line of decisions, the *stylus* or practice of the Rota, which could take precedence over the *Decretals* or all the official law denoted by the word *ius.* The new auditor was advised by another member's handbook that "often more depends on the practice than on the law." [72] By two papal constitutions decisions were to be made "neither against the law nor against the practice and the old decisions of the Rota which have been printed"; doing "equity" was not an excuse for abandoning precedent. Yet a new path might be taken with "the greatest reason and discussion and by a two-third vote." [73]

The Controlling Legislation

The main issue in the case, parental coercion, was dealt with by Gratian in terms of the more common case, coercion of a girl. "Can a daughter," he asked hypothetically, "be given to a man against her will?" After a review of authorities — meager and conflicting in 1142 — he answered with an explicit negative: "By these authorities it is evidently shown that no woman is to be coupled to anyone except by her free will." [74]

The broad principle enunciated by Gratian was embodied in several decretals where enforcement gave it concreteness. In *Veniens*, Alexander III (1159–1181) disposed of the case of a man in bed with a girl surprised by her father and compelled to marry her. If the fear inflicted on the bridegroom had been one "which could fall upon a steady man," his consent was null.[75] In *Consultationi tuae*, X.4.1.28, Honorius III (1216–1227) applied the same standard to women who complained that, compelled by fear, they had publicly consented to marriage while dissenting in their minds. As a consequence of these decretals, a "steady man" became the standard for measuring fear. He was a fictional man of average fortitude, who functioned in fear cases as in modern tort law a "prudent man" functions to measure negligence.

Betrothals — easier to dissolve because unconsummated by sexual intercourse — provided occasion for expansion of the rules on coerced consent. In *De illis qui*, X.4.2.9, the Archbishop of Genoa was instructed by Alexander III that the consent of children to a betrothal was invalid if it resulted from "violence." Urban III (1185–1187) told the Archbishop of Pisa that a betrothal was unenforceable if a girl had been "impelled by the threats of her parents," *Ex literis*, X.4.2.11. In the analogous case of religious profession, a vow at "the command of parents" was said to be not binding, *Quum virum*, X.3.31.12. In *Gemma*, X.4.1.29, the concept of coercion was extended to include the threat of a penalty: a betrothal by the parents of children under seven had provided that a sum was to be paid by whomever broke the agreement; Gregory IX, observing that marriages "ought to be free," held that collection of the penalty could be enjoined by ecclesiastical censure. *Gemma* provided a basis for arguing that coercion could be shown in many ways beyond actual violence.

If these canons tended to support the case of one claiming coercion, a procedural canon posed a bar. *Ad id*, X.4.1.21, a decretal of Clement III (1187–1191), taught that after a girl had lived with a man a year and a half, she could not be heard to say that she had married him without consent: "delay of such a great time excludes proof of this kind." Applied to Charles' case, *Ad id* barred him without inquiry.

All of these canons from the *Decretals* were cast in a new light by the comparatively recent legislation of the Council of Trent in 1563. The form of celebration of a valid Catholic marriage was prescribed by the Council in its twenty-fourth session, November 11, 1563. Asserting the accepted power of the Church to determine competence to marry, the Council legislated the form in terms of capacity: one was incapable of contracting validly except before one's parish priest, or his licensed delegate, and at least two witnesses.* Banns read in church three times on feast days were to precede the marriage; and the priest was to record the marriage in a book. The purpose of this legislation, according to the Council, was to remedy the evils of clandestine marriages, especially the sins committed when a secret first wife was abandoned for a second wife publicly taken. The legislation's effect on marriages invalid in their inception, but ratified in time, was not spelled out.

A series of decisions of the Congregation of the Council determined that the banns were not necessary for validity, but that validity was absolutely dependent on the presence of the proper priest. Far from applying the law only where necessary to carry out its proclaimed purpose, the Rota, too, tended to treat any technical breach of this rule as fatal to validity. It proclaimed as a principle, "The more a matter is one of will [i.e., the more a matter is one of positive legislation and not natural reason], the more it is to be fulfilled in specific terms." †

---

* The casting of the rule on form in terms of "capacity" to marry reflected a division of opinion as to whether the Church had power either to change the form of the sacrament of marriage — i.e., the exchange of consent — or to invalidate the marriage of two persons capable of marriage (Council of Trent, General Congregation, July 24, 1563, *Acta*, IX, 643–645). No one could deny, however, that the Church had already ruled that some persons—e.g., priests—were incapable of marrying. Hence, no one was able to challenge a new incapacitating rule. Substantively, the result was the same as if the Church had declared null in advance all marriages not contracted in the Tridentine form. Either rule would have done the job; a formula incapacitating persons was easier to accept than a formula affecting the substance of the sacrament. The arguments in the debate between 1547 and 1563 are collected and reviewed in Reinhard Lettmann, *Die Diskussion über Die Klandestinen Ehen und Die Einführung Einer zur Gültigkeit Verpflichtenden Eheschliessungsform auf Dem Konzil Von Trient* (Münster: Aschendorffsche Verlag, 1966).

† *Florence, June 16, 1579, October 23, 1579*, and *Florence, February, 1580*, before Visconti *Sacra Romana Rota, Decisiones novissimorum Sacri Palatii Apostolici*

Taking the canons on their face, Charles could win if he could show coercion. He would be blocked, however, by *Ad id*, unless this procedural barrier was interpreted to rest on a presumption that long cohabitation equaled consent and a rebuttal of this presumption were permitted, or unless the requirement of form set down by Trent had to be met when delayed consent to a coerced marriage was eventually given — in that event, no matter how long one stayed in an apparent marriage, no valid consent would be given unless the ceremony was repeated to record the consent in Tridentine style.

The Civil Analogies

The most apposite civilian text, *Si patre cogente*, came from the Digest. It read: "If at the compulsion of one's father, one takes a wife one would not take of one's own will, one has still contracted marriage; for marriage is not contracted between the unwilling, and so one seems to prefer the marriage." [76] The reasoning was paradoxical or backward. It implied that the son preferred marriage to disobeying his father and by obeying must be taken to have consented to getting married; it was so expounded by the great glossator Accursius.

Other texts, good by analogy, were to be found in the Code dealing with property. The general rule was that "transactions undertaken because of fear are not to be treated as ratified." [77] But the standard set for fear restricted the breadth of this rule. In a title headed "Of those matters done because of force and fear," it was specified that invalidating fear had to be fear of death or bodily harm. Mere threats or arguments did not suffice, but "cruelty of act" had to be proved.[78] Fear caused by someone holding at least intermediate jurisdictional authority in a province would suffice to

---

auditorum (Venice, 1590). Two citizens of Florence got married outside the city in a rural area where they lived for three months of the year for recreation. They had a priest and two witnesses, but not the parish priest of either party. The Rota held that the "equivalent" of a parish priest was not good enough to uphold validity. The reason for Trent's requirement of a parish priest, it said, was not to prevent clandestinity, for this could be avoided by publication of the banns. Nor was the parish priest required in order that the marriage be proved, for there could be other witnesses. The reason for the requirement was "to restrict one to one's own parish."

invalidate, but not merely the fear caused by one's adversary being a senator. Fear of being compelled to assume an onerous civic office was not enough. Payment without protest made it improbable that fear was operative as did the presence of friends at the transaction.[79]

Taken together, these laws did not recognize the fear of one in authority unless the person feared was one whose authority permitted him to inflict bodily harm. A father was such a person; but read with *Si patre cogente* these provisions probably did not invalidate the consent of a boy who married under mere moral pressure from his father. Their thrust was in conflict with canons like *Gemma*, which treated the fear of losing property as invalidating, and canons like *Quum virum*, which treated a parent's command as preventing free consent. Measured by the civil law alone, Charles did not have a case. In theory, this conclusion did not reduce his rights in canon law; in practice, the harmonization of canon law with civil law could affect the meaning of his rights when his judges considered the canons on coercion.

The Law of the Commentators

The commentators presented a law more favorable to Charles than either canons or civil law in two principal respects: in the standard set for the fear which invalidated consent, and in the standard for consent necessary to convert a marriage from invalid to valid. Both differences were strikingly illustrated in the writing of Tomás Sanchez, the Spanish Jesuit who taught and wrote at Córdoba at the end of the sixteenth century. His *De sancto matrimonii sacramento*, The Holy Sacrament of Marriage, was among the first investigations by a specialist into the requirements of Christian marriage. Not merely a pioneering effort, his book was to stand as the fullest, most learned, and most acute of scholastic treatises on marriage. Sometimes he was betrayed by lawyer's vices of which he was not free — a fondness for distinctions, a formalism which attempted to win substantive points by the rearrangement of abstract concepts — but beneath the surface of formulas and distinctions, shifts and turns, a grave and just and subtle spirit was at play. Sanchez succeeded in dominating the massive matter of a millennium of marriage law with the suppleness and firmness of a supreme craftsman or a true artist. In his own day, his authority was great; and his fame swelled even higher after his death in 1610. By 1650 the treatise had gone through fourteen editions and had been published in Venice, Lyon, Antwerp, Brescia, and Genoa.[80] Its use by the advisers of Nicolas-François before he married Claude in 1635 was indicative of its serviceability to the most practical of men in the most crucial of hours. In the instant case Sanchez was cited in the briefs and rotal opinion a total of sixty-five times, far more than any other commentator or the *Decretals* themselves. Through Sanchez a master's estimate of existing precedent and a master's shaping of this precedent were provided: what he put forward as the law in 1600 was the law which served litigants and court in 1650.

The Holy Sacrament of Matrimony explored the essence of canonical marriage — the consent to marry — in three areas highly relevant to Charles' case: it examined the relation of coercion to consent; the knowledge required for consent; and the content of consent. It related all these topics to the procedural barrier of *Ad id* and to the rule imposed by Trent that consent must be given before one's parish priest and two witnesses. The domain surveyed and charted by Sanchez was the broad field from which Charles' lawyers could draw all they needed for their case, and in which Nicole's lawyers might find all they required to rebut it.

That consent of both spouses was absolutely necessary; that consent must be more or less free; that consent had to be knowing; that consent was related to affection — with these simple, almost irrefutable propositions Sanchez set out to map the complicated cross-patterns the propositions implied, among which the judge must thread his way. Consent must be free, but consent was compatible with coercion. The *Decretals'* standard of the steady man required a certain level of fear before consent became ineffective. "Reverential fear" — a subject's fear of his superior, a boy's fear of his father — did not invalidate: it did not "seem to have such strength to compel the will that a steady man should be terrified of it." [81] The Roman law plainly reflected this view; the classical canonists, Pope Innocent IV and Cardinal Hostiensis, made the same estimation; it was concurred in by modern sixteenth-century theologians such as Silvestro da' Prieras and Domingo de Soto. The canons that appeared to be contrary could be explained away; they dealt with compulsion greater than that created by the relation of a subordinate to the one with lawful authority over him. By Sanchez' standard, if Charles wanted to show he was coerced because he responded to his father's command, he was out of court.

If other circumstances were conjoined with the parental relationship, the case stood differently: "what steady or prudent man would not repute it a grave evil always to be faced with an angry father?" If a father were ferocious, or long-enduring in his anger, or prompt to execute his threats, his order to his offspring could be coercive enough to invalidate consent. Menaces could be found in what purported to be requests when they were "most pressing, often repeated, and uncivilized"; when such importunities came from a parent, they coerced. The son's own attitude to his parent was also to be considered; his readiness to obey must be considered in determining the effect of a father's words. If reverential fear alone did not invalidate, its presence was an index to a situation requiring close scrutiny of the facts. Sanchez instructed the judge to look to the context, to weigh a variety of related variables, to find consent ineffective if the combination of elements would have invoked fear in a steady man.[82]

All of this analysis, in its ultimate conclusions so favorable to Charles' case, was counterbalanced by another concept: "just fear" or justified fear, felt where a person's actions warranted him apprehending punishment if he did not marry. It arose "from the law and the nature of the crime; and hence it comes from within rather than from without, in this sense that the just cause of the fear, its start and root, is within the man." For Sanchez, the internal origin of the fear created a vital distinction, or at least he used the distinction to rationalize current social and ecclesiastical practice. An example was a seducer's fear of imprisonment if he did not marry the girl seduced. His "just fear" did not invalidate consent to marry which he gave in order to avoid jail. Analogously, a man might be lawfully forced under pain of excommunication to carry out his promise to enter marriage, for one "is not said to be unwilling when compelled to stand by one's promises." Still, one reason for invalidating coerced marriages was that an unhappy outcome might be expected: was not this reason equally good where the fear was just? "Not so unhappy an outcome," Sanchez replied, was to be anticipated if the fear were justified: the bridegroom's "soul" would be "somewhat quieted" by the sense of justice being done. Was not the fear inflicted by the outrage father in *Veniens*, X.4.1.15, justified, and had not Alexander III still invalidated the marriage? The threat of death, Sanchez answered, was so excessive as to be unjust; the Pope had not had the occasion to speak of the moderate fear which would have been appropriate.[83]

With the category of just fear established despite its neglect in the *Decretals*, Sanchez turned to a question which would be critical in the case of Charles and Nicole: "Do sons commit a fault in not obeying parents who command them to enter a marriage?" If disobedience to such a command was sinful, then the coercion used to obtain obedience might be analyzed as the infliction of just fear. "Regularly" a son had no duty to obey a parental order to marry: so taught the great majority of canonists, led by Hostiensis, and so taught the great majority of theologians, led by Scotus. Sanchez concurred: "As to contracting marriage, a son is free and *sui iuris*." [84] Yet there was the inevitable exception: "If it is of much importance to the parents that the son enter such a marriage, the son is bound under mortal fault to obey his parent commanding it," because, "by the virtue of piety, sons are bound to help their parents in need." [85] The exception came close to swallowing the rule. As long as the standard of parental need was not spelled out, the interested parties could argue whether or not a son was bound to obey; and the judge was left to make, case by case, an intuitive estimation of "need" and "importance." If the analysis of just fear were combined with the theory of filial duty, a son refusing to obey his father's wishes regarding a marriage "of much importance" to the father could be compelled to enter the marriage. Recalcitrant, he would be in mortal sin; the cause of the fear would be within; the fear he experienced would be just. Sanchez did not combine these principles into a single statement. If the combination were made, and the importance of the marriage to Charles' father proved, Nicole had won her case.

To have a right to coerce, however, was not to have a right to use all coercion possible. The analysis of just fear had established that the coercion must be appropriate to the situation — as in American common law you have a limited privilege to defend your property: you may use force but not all possible force to achieve this end. Fathers of seduced daughters could coerce their seducers, but not threaten them with death. The punishment threatened must be proportionate to the interest preserved. Even the ecclesiastical judge acting for the Church in forcing a man to carry out his betrothal pledge did not have unlimited power to achieve this end. A degree of freedom must be left to the delinquent fiancé, so that in the end his consent to marriage would not be wrung from him wholly against his will. The judge could compel "moderately, but not conclusively." [86] When it came to fathers coercing sons to obey their commands to marry, what threat exceeded the measure was left to the judgment of the wise.

Concrete contingent facts to be weighed in every case — this was what emerged as decisive in this extended analysis. Formulas such as "reverential fear" or "just fear" could have dispensed the judge from thinking and evaluating. In this presentation they became directions to him to weigh certain factors with special care; the formulas were not to be automatically invoked. Sanchez left open for decision in each case whether reverential fear had been combined with such circumstances of the parent-child relation that freedom had been denied; and, if it had been denied, whether the interest of the parent had been such that piety required the son's sacrifice; and, if piety had called for his obedience, whether the parent's measures still had been disproportionate to the parental stake in the issue. One can say that such conclusions decided nothing or that they were sheer common sense. But they decided much in providing guidelines, even though the guidelines did not relieve the judge of the duty of evaluation. They were common sense vindicated by reflection. The average abstraction of the *Decretals*, "the steady man," melted away and was replaced by a particular person acting in a situation where the intensity and proportionateness of the pressures applied to him where to be individually gauged.

Knowledge was the second element of consent which Sanchez analyzed at length, in the particularly relevant context of the knowledge required for consent subsequent to the ceremony. Suppose consent had been coerced and was therefore ineffective; if the putative spouses continued to live together, the person who had suffered coercion might eventually consent to the other freely. Was his consent effective if he was under the erroneous impression that the marriage was already valid? "Nothing willed, unless first known," ran a general principle of scholastic psychology. If one did not know his marriage was invalid, he did not know that he was still free to marry or not marry; he could at most "intend to ratify the first marriage," when what was required — the first marriage being null — was the simple intent to marry. His consent would be given in ignorance and so would be no consent at all.[87]

Did both spouses have to know of the invalidity to make the later consent good? If one spouse had freely consented in the original ceremony, while the other had been coerced, a marriage could be made if the coerced person alone knowingly consented later without great delay. Simultaneity of consent was not essential. Analogy was made with other contracts: if there was long delay in acceptance, consent was revoked; otherwise it remained in force. A prudent man must judge in the circumstances how quickly the true consent of the coerced party must be given for the uncoerced consent of the first spouse to have lasted: "several months" was a suggested period.[88] But if the uncoerced consent had lapsed, there came into play the same reasoning that required knowledge of invalidity on the part of the spouse giving free consent for the first time. Consent had to be knowing, and if the free consent had lapsed, it could be given effectively again only by a person who knew he was in fact unmarried.

Illogically, some fifteenth- and sixteenth-century writers held that knowledge of invalidity was unnecessary for effective subsequent consent by a spouse in this position. They argued that a mere "error of law" did not prevent consent to a contract, and to believe mistakenly that one was already married was an error of law. They argued further that the classic canon law did not admit mistake of fact as a general ground for invalidating consent to marriage. One could think one's spouse was rich, beautiful, and virtuous; she could turn out to be a poor, ugly whore. The marriage was good. Mistakes as to "quality" were not permitted to affect consent to marriage.[89]

To meet this reasoning, Sanchez turned to two exceptions Gratian had recognized to the general rule, mistakes "of person" and "of condition." If a man married A, thinking she was B, he failed to consent to her person; if a free man married a slave girl in ignorance of her servile condition, his consent was not binding. Artificial as Gratian's distinctions were in logic, they were grounded in social realities and had survived in the canon law. Sanchez pressed them and insisted that if the original marriage was null, and consent had lapsed, both parties had to give knowing consent afresh for there to be a marriage. If a man was ignorant of the fact that the woman with whom he was living was not his wife, he was in error as to her person and her condition; if he renewed his consent to their marriage in this ignorance, he intended "to consent to his own, when in fact she is not his own." [90] His consent was therefore ineffective.

If this abstract scheme were applied to Charles' case, he could argue, perhaps plausibly, that he had not realized until 1637 that his original consent was invalid under the law of the *Decretals*. With even greater plausibility he might argue that Nicole had never known of the invalidity of his consent, and so could never have given the fresh consent necessary to make a marriage even if it were admitted *arguendo* that sometime after his father's death Charles, free of undue coercion, had knowingly consented to her as his wife. By what Sanchez characterized as the "much more probable" opinion, there had been no subsequent consent capable of constituting the marriage.

Consent must not be improperly coerced, and it must be informed. What was the content of consent? The answer of Sanchez which had potential relevance to Charles' case began with analysis of the acts which constituted consent subsequent to the ceremony. In this irregular situation, where nominal but ineffective marriage promises had been exchanged and the couple, unmarried in reality, were living together, consent could be evidenced by coitus; by continued living together when there was opportunity to leave; by accepting wedding presents; or even by calling one another "husband" and "wife." [91] These guidelines, if applied to Charles' conduct, seemed to preclude him utterly: he had consented. But Sanchez added a proviso of the first importance — all of these simple acts established marital consent, provided they were done with marital affection. Without this specific extra factor the behavior of the putative spouses proved nothing.[92] Marital affection was the essential ingredient of marital consent.

What did Sanchez mean by marital affection? Both civil and canon law used the term, defining it not by an express equivalent but by pointing. In a lover's attitude to his concubine that transformed the relation from concubinage to matrimony, or in a master's attitude to an *alumna* (a freed slave girl) which made her a wife, the civil law marked the presence of marital affection. In the undivided fidelity of Mary and Joseph, or in the treatment owed a true wife, or in the ministering to a leprous spouse to the point of living with him, the classic canon law found "marital affection." * Although colored by emotion, marital affection was not lust, infatuation, desire for intercourse, or momentary delight. It was a will to regard the other in a special way, in the special status of "husband" or "wife." If love is understood as more than sentiment, it was love of the other as spouse.[93]

If marital affection was so crucial in the civil and canonical analysis of consent, it may seem that this conclusion was obvious: whenever consent was at issue, marital affection must be proved. What was dangerous, even revolutionary, in Sanchez was that he insisted on this point, even if he did so only in the limited context of acts establishing delayed consent. Classical canonical practice, despite its use of marital affection as a concept, did not attempt to ascertain the existence of such affection in the ordinary, undelayed consent to marry. It seemed to be tacitly assumed that, when one publicly took a spouse, marital affection should be presumed from the language used in the ceremony. But the concept referred to a state of mind and heart, not language. If marital affection was essential to consent, why could not the presumption of its presence always be challenged, its absence always shown? If Sanchez was right in requiring that marital affection be proved to have characterized the acts constituting later consent, rigorous logic led to the same requirement being imposed wherever the validity of consent was questioned.

To use marital affection as a criterion for measuring the validity of any consent to marriage was to look to internal states of mind,

---

* Civil law usage: *Digest*, 5.4.26 (affection for one's *alumna* makes her a wife); *Digest*, 5.27.11 (affection for a concubine makes her a wife). Canon law usage: Gratian, *dictum post*, c. 16, C. 32. q. 5 (a man and a woman are married, once "they have adhered to each other with conjugal affection"); Gratian, *dictum post*, c. 29, C. 27, q. 4 (Mary and Joseph were united by conjugal affection); Alexander III in *Ex parte*, X.4.19. (a husband must return to his wife and treat her with marital affection); Alexander III in *Veniens*, X.4.1.13 (a husband must "receive the said Marietta and strive to love her as his wife and to treat her with marital affection"); Alexander III in *Pervenit*, X.4.8.1 (spouses are to be exhorted to follow their consorts who had been stricken with leprosy and "to minister to them with conjugal affection").

to explore the kind of love required toward a spouse, to challenge the existing social order's system of arranged marriages. The canonists never entirely identified the canon law with the existing social order, but they were inevitably influenced by its practices. Sanchez, the boldest and brightest of them, did no more than open up the possibility of challenge to these practices by a new standard for valid consent; he did not develop and supply the standard. Marital affection remained a concept with an ancient lineage, a range of meaning, and a potentiality for unsettling development. Whether it would be invoked and developed in a case like Charles' depended on the ability of his lawyers to take an established concept beyond its established range and upon the willingness of the court to be more daring than the commentators.[94]

In his entire analysis of consent Sanchez was respectful to decretal law and yet proceeded with enough independence of the texts to give the impression of charting the natural constitution of consent — what God would say was true marriage if the canons never existed. Two procedural laws, however, were of such a precise and positive character that no one could have believed they were part of the nature of things. One was the statute of limitations, *Ad id*; the other the requirements of "capacity" set by Trent. Taken literally, the one-and-one-half-year limit set by *Ad id* shut out completely someone like Charles who been married more than twenty years when he first sought to attack the validity of his marriage. But curial commentators long ago had eroded the line *Ad id* had drawn: Innocent IV and Hostiensis had interpreted the decretal's reference to a specific time as "narration of a contingent fact" in the particular case the decretal decided; it was not to be taken as a general statute of limitations after whose expiry no action could be brought. As Sanchez now explained its teaching, cohabitation was only evidence of consent, and the length of cohabitation which conclusively betokened consent was left to "the judgment of a prudent man." Consent might be shown in a month's cohabitation, or it might be absent in a dozen years of life together. *Ad id* was absorbed in the general analysis of consent and became no more significant than a suggestion to the judge to take prolonged cohabitation into account as partial evidence.[95]

The canons of Trent did not seem to yield so easily to the comprehensive vision of a Sanchez. Their specific dictate that capacity to consent required the parish priest and two witnesses seemed proof against evasion; in particular, they seemed to constitute an insurmountable barrier to effective consent being given after the ceremony. How many invalidly married persons would acquire capacity to consent by reappearing before parish priests and witnesses? Would not insistence on capacity, as defined by Trent, make validation by coitus or cohabitation impossible? The obvious answers to these questions suggested that Trent could not be taken too rigidly. Scandal would be caused if a large number of apparently valid marriages remained invalid for lack of later consent being given in the proper form. Moreover, the rationale of the Tridentine decree — the prevention of clandestine marriages — did not extend to marriages already contracted in the face of the Church. A distinction must be introduced — had indeed already been approved by the Sacred Congregation of the Council and the Sacred Penitentiary under Pius V. If the impediment causing the initial consent to be invalid was secret, the Tridentine ceremony need not be repeated for the later consent which made the marriage.[96] Only where the impediment was public must Trent be applied literally and a second ceremony required to create the capacity to give consent.

In this analysis, everything depended on what was a "public impediment." Sanchez gave a definition weighted in favor of a petitioner for annulment: a public impediment was one which could be proved by two witnesses other than the spouses themselves. Lack of internal consent resulting from fear was not such an impediment: fear not perceived by the priest or formal witnesses to the original ceremony must have been hidden.[97] But there was no logical necessity that the formal witnesses to the ceremony also witness the alleged coercion. If coercion could in fact be proven, then by Sanchez' own reasoning subsequent consent would have to be accompanied by a new ceremony that complied with the prescriptions of the Council of Trent. Under this theory, if Charles could produce two witnesses to coercion, he simultaneously established the right to prove that he had not consented later in the public form required by Trent.

On each topic — reverential fear, justified fear, filial obedience, moderate coercion, knowledgeable consent, marital affection, compliance with the Council of Trent — Sanchez made distinctions, sketched alternatives, balanced values. In his hands the law became supple. Applied by judges inclined to challenge the social order, his views could have been revolutionary. Judges are not apt to be unconventional, however, and perceived from the typical judicial perspective, Sanchez was not subversive; he merely left room for a wide discretion, still hedged by rules. The flexibility he made possible would come to nothing if the judge were unintelligent; it could be abused if the judge were corrupt; but the wise judge was given scope to weigh comparative values in each case. Sanchez invited a litigant with good facts to try his case.

Case Law

Four leading cases of the early seventeenth century were "fear cases," providing possible precedents, analogies, and contrasts. The first, from Seville, had been decided between 1607 and 1609 in a series of opinions by Alessandro Ludovisi, a learned Bolognese auditor who later became Pope Gregory XV; it provided counsel for Charles with a model of successful litigation. Antonia, Marchioness of Alcalá, was married to Don Felipe de Aragón y Guzman. She claimed to have been coerced by her father, the Marquis Pedro Lopez Portocarrero, now deceased. The evidence for Antonia showed she had writen a letter promising to marry another man, Don Francisco de Zuñiga, so that marrying Don Felipe went directly against her declared will. She had wept, protested, and pleaded not to marry Don Felipe. The Marquis was severe, bitter, and "very terrible" when crossed. Threats to kill her or disinherit her unless she obeyed her father's command to marry had been conveyed to her by her stepmother and a priest. These allies of her father, joined by the Apostolic Nuncio, Rodrigo de Castro, had importuned her to obey. She had no freedom to leave her home, except to attend one nearby church. Her own mother was dead, and she was in fear of her stepmother. After her marriage she was "deformed" by sadness. In his first opinion on these facts, *Seville, June 18, 1607*, Ludovisi sketched the law much as outlined by Sanchez, holding that reverential fear of a father, coupled with other circumstances, could be coercive; that importunities by a father were coercive; and that the threat of loss of an inheritance was coercive when the inheritance was "as if owed to a daughter." [98] This statement of the law Ludovisi would apply became the later text of Charles' counsel.*

On January 28, 1608, seven months later, Ludovisi ruled on objections to the Marchioness' eighteen witnesses. Sustaining their competency, he modified the rule that two witnesses "above exception" — that is, not open to any of the recognized exceptions to competence — must prove lack of consent; the requirement did not apply in this kind of case. Relatives and domestics of the petitioner — normally persons who were not "above exception" — became admissible witnesses. "In household matters," Ludovisi reasoned, "those of the household are more to be believed than outsiders." The number of witnesses could make up for their lack of quality, and this compensatory law held, "especially where the matter is hard to prove, as it is hard in our case to prove paternal threats." [99] Almost six months later, on June 23, 1608, Ludovisi applied the rulings of the first two opinions to the case at hand and held that not only had coercion been proved by competent witnesses, but it was coercion sufficient to invalidate the consent of the Marchioness of Alcalá. The "steady man" rule did not entail the absurd proposition that only if she had been coerced by the fear that would have coerced a steady male was her consent invalid. Instead, the standard to be used was the fear which would have affected "a steady woman" of her quality — the fear which would have affected a motherless girl of the nobility. Applying this standard, Ludovisi held that Antonia had been coerced. [100]

Don Felipe's counsel now argued that Antonia had given consent after her fear had been "purged." Six months later, on December 15, 1608, Ludovisi ruled that as long as her father was alive fear of him was presumed to have continued. [101] He put over for further consideration whether the fear had been purged after her father's death. On January 26, 1609, Ludovisi held that the Lord Auditors

---

* Disinheritance as a device to coerce marriage was a familiar tactic. For an English instance, where it was held to invalidate, see *Haryngton v. Sayvell* (York, July 31, 1443), set out in Richard Helmholz, "Marriage Litigation in Medieval England" (unpublished doctoral thesis, University of California at Berkeley, 1970), pp. 352–358. Use of this kind of tactic was also attacked in another way by the theologians and canonists: it was taught that a father at the point of death could not be absolved unless he first revoked his will disinheriting a child who had disobeyed him in marrying, Juan Valero, *Differentiae inter utrumque forum, iudiciale videlicet et conscientiae* (Majorca, 1624), fol. 187r.

would not have to consider evidence of consent after her father's death, because no evidence of later consent would be effective without compliance with the requirement of Trent of a parish priest and two witnesses. Was this requirement binding where consent was later given to a marriage invalid for fear? The older authorities said that it was, and so the Lords judged despite the contrary opinion of "moderns from Córdoba." The Sacred Congregation of the Council had already ruled that if something essential had been lacking in the first ceremony the Tridentine requirements had to be met again. Nothing could be more essential than consent, and if consent was impaired by coercion, the ceremony had to be repeated. Then, with a final bow to the leading "modern of Córdoba," already an authority in his own lifetime, Ludovisi said that "all scruple" was removed in this case because the fear had been public, so public that it was observed by the officiating priest. Certainly the new consent must have the form prescribed by Trent; "and so there is followed Tomás Sanchez, *De matrimonio*, 2.37.11." [102]

These five opinions of an auditor of great prestige — the auditor who as Gregory XV had authorized Charles' marriage — were a treasury of citations for Charles. Every major point he would have to make was covered in them in a way favorable to him. True, the facts could be distinguished; but in outline the law of the case was the law he wanted to rule his own.

An opinion by Ludovisi's successor in the prestigious Bolognese seat on the Rota, Matteo Buratto, could be cited as contrary authority. Buratto never became Pope, but his opinions stood as high as Ludovisi's in legal estimation. He not only had the erudition appropriate for the Bolognese auditor, he had the independence of temper to be twice-married; and, although he ultimately took orders, he was one of the few laymen and few married men to have played a part in the development of the canon law on marriage.[103] In *Venice, May 25, 1622* he ruled on the claim of a maternal aunt that her niece Cecilia had been coerced into marriage by her father. Buratto, upholding the validity of the marriage, followed another path marked by Sanchez. Reverential fear of a parent by itself did not invalidate. As Sanchez himself taught: "No love or counsel is superior to parental love or counsel." If such counsel was to be treated as coercive, then the fear caused by the parent must be proved "not in general but with qualities and circumstances." Sweepingly, he departed from Sanchez to fortify his conclusion by a general principle: "Any force or suspicion of fear is excluded by the subsequent coupling and consummation." [104]

That the suit was by the aunt, not the wife; that Cecilia's view of the facts was not given; that no evidence on marital affection or its absence was stated in relation to "the subsequent coupling" — all of these factors made the case distinguishable from Charles'. Taken abstractly, Buratto's unqualified statement on the effect of subsequent intercourse meant Charles' case was hopeless. His basic view, found in Sanchez and the society at large, that a parent brought love and prudence to his choice of a child's spouse, embodied the kind of presumption which Charles' lawyers would have to overcome with facts.

Coimbra, December 19, 1614, also decided by Buratto, provided almost the converse of coercion of parents — the coercion of a mother's suitor by her sons.[105] Its relevance to Charles' case was that it gave the seventeenth-century Rota the paradigm of a fear case, one which involved no grave challenge to social convention or parental authority, and was close to the situation of extreme physical peril dealt with by Alexander III in the decretal *Veniens.* Brutally, the paradigm underlined the difference between the case the law easily admitted and the kind of case Charles presented.[106] A nobleman, Emanuele, had been courting Bianca, a rich noblewoman, twice-widowed, older than her lover, and the mother of grown children. Bianca expected the affair to turn into marriage and was disappointed when Emanuele procrastinated. Her two sons and her son-in-law shared her disappointment. By prearrangement Bianca called Emanuele one night to her country villa, his servant was put up at an unused house, and Emanuele was surprised naked in bed with Bianca by the boys and their attendants, armed with guns and swords. Bianca's parish priest was summoned in the middle of the night, on the pretext that his parishioner was sick and wanted to confess; in his presence Emanuele was forthwith married to Bianca. In the morning Emanuele escaped and with a sick heart immediately protested to the Bishop of Coimbra and the authorities; he never returned to his new spouse. Armed force, surprise at night, immediate withdrawal by the coerced spouse offered a model of coerced marriage strikingly different from the situation of Charles and Nicole. Buratto invalidated the marriage.

Bianca's counsel then successfully argued that Emanuele and Bianca had been validly betrothed several months before the raid. He pressed for enforcement of the betrothal in accordance with the prevailing interpretation of the decretal *Ex litteris*, X.4.2.11.[107] The court recognized that Emanuele had a moral duty to carry out his promise so that fear inflicted to this end would be "just" if inflicted by a court and not by armed men at night. It also recognized that these were circumstances which excused performance of a promise to marry. Such circumstances existed here: the forced marriage itself; the prolonged litigation. Fulfillment of the betrothal was not ordered.[108]

Emanuele's plight seemed to contrast with Charles'. Yet the final judicial result could be a precedent in Charles' favor. In agreement with Sanchez, Buratto refused to identify a right to have a duty enforced with a right to use all possible coercion to enforce it. If Charles had had a duty to obey his father, as Emanuele had had a duty to marry his betrothed, circumstance, too, might be shown which made performance of the duty a submission to unjustified force.*

Toul, November 7, 1616, still another opinion by Buratto, provided a valuable precedent for Charles in the analogous area of parental coecion to enter religion; it involved a boy from Lorraine not much younger than Charles himself had been in 1621. René, fourteen years old, was sent by his father from his home in Toul to the island of Malta, to make profession as a Knight of St. John. He spent his time in Italy, wasted his father's money, and returned to his father's home without ever having been to Malta. His father

---

* Considerable discretion was exercised by judges in ordering the enforcement of a betrothal. Compare *Toul, April 17, 1617* before Cavalerio (*Decisiones recentiores S.R. Rotae*, IV¹, decision 451) and *Seville, February 8, 1616*, before Manzanedo (*Decisiones*, III, decision 742) both cases where enforcement was ordered, with *Calahorra, March 13, 1643* and *February 11, 1647* before Melzi (*Decisiones* IX¹, decision 163 and X, decision 19), where the girl's subsequent reputation for unchastity, the indignation of the boy's relatives, and the "very great" aversion of the boy for the girl were treated together as reason for not enforcing. In *Córdoba, May 21, 1664*, before Verospio (*Decisiones*, XIV, decision 185), the coercion exercised on Ferdinand to enter the betrothal (civil judge's sentence to marry or pay the girl 2,000 scudos and leave town) was considered reason for the "grave enmity" between the pair, and this enmity was sufficient not to order enforcement.

expelled him from the house, threatened him with total disinheritance, and requested the family's friends not to take him in. René lived in a hut on the castle grounds, fed by pitying servants. After a few days of this treatment he capitulated and consented to do his father's will by becoming a knight.

In an analysis which captured the spirit of Sanchez, Buratto weighed the facts. Less fear was needed to be coercive when it was linked with the reverence owed a father and when the emotion was experienced by a boy, as the standard phrase even then had it, "of tender years." The threat of the loss of his inheritance was itself coercive. Such a threat, as Sanchez had already observed, could induce fear in a steady man. René's profession of religious vows had been "fearful and violent," it was therefore null.[109]

Such a decision in the field of religious profession was of the greatest relevance because of the recognized parallelism between profession and marriage. In solemnity, in absolute commitment, in free dedication, the utterance of vows to God was like consenting to take a person as spouse, and the ceremony of profession invoked the symbolism of marriage. Profession consisted in promises made under oath to God rather than in a promise made to another human being; but marriage — its indissoluble bond a symbol of Christ and the Church — was also a type of faithful commitment to God. Profession was easier to renounce than marriage, as power was recognized in the Pope to commute the vow, while no power to dissolve a consummated Christian marriage was recognized to exist; yet the parallel held because annulment of the vows for lack of valid consent was the preferred route for a religious seeking to leave religious life. The Council of Trent had seen the danger of coercion in religious profession and set up procedures to prevent abuses in the admission of girls.[110] No similar steps had been taken to safeguard marriage. Yet, if coercion invalidated one, it must invalidate the other. Buratto specifically drew the parallel: "as marriage made in fear is not valid, so neither is profession, which is equated to it as a certain spiritual marriage." Decisions on coercion in religious profession and in marriage reciprocally influenced each other. *Toul, November 7, 1616* was to be cited thirty times by Charles' counsel.*

* Over fifty religious profession cases were cited in the briefs in Charles' case. One, a very recent decision, *Trier, December 14, 1648*, was even printed as an appendix to a brief on Nicole's side: Anna, to escape punishment from her parents, had entered a convent and made profession. She now sought to annul her vows.

If case law of the past half-century were used as a guide for pre-diction, the precedents (apart from *Venice*) indicated that Charles might overcome the presumption that a parent's love and counsel were for the best. At least Charles' most likely witnesses, rel-atives and servants, could be heard as witnesses. The last opinion in *Coimbra*, all of the opinions in *Seville*, the decision in *Toul* offered good analogy and hope. If the case law was read in the wider perspective afforded by Sanchez, there was enough in the facts to make litigating worthwhile. If the Rota could be persuaded to accept *Seville* as a model, Charles' case was almost made.

THE THRONE OF JUSTICE

The Court

Charles' case was before the Sacred Roman Rota. In the course of four hundred years' evolution the Rota had acquired some aspects of an independent court, but literally its members were "the hearing-officers of causes of the Sacred Apostolic Palace." As recently as 1561, the reform bull of Pius IV, *In throno iustitiae*, had described it both as a "tribunal" and as "the hearing-place of Our Palace." [111] Rotal auditors were judges, but they did not enjoy that sovereign freedom which the supreme bench of a modern state might possess. The Pope decided where a case would be judged, by whom it would be judged, when it would be judged. By his powers of patronage and preferment, by his legislative and execu-tive authority, by his position as religious teacher and head of the Church, the Pope controlled the Rota.

Throughout the period Charles' case was before the Rota, the Pope was Gianbattista Pamphili, Innocent X, the rotal auditor par excellence become Pope. From early manhood to maturity, for

---

The court held that parents could justly punish delinquent children, and that it was not fear of her parents but something attributable "to her own fault" that had led Anna to profess. Moreover, her witnesses testified only to what they had heard from Anna herself or what they had heard from others who had heard from Anna. Their testimony constituted "no degree of proof," especially as "a presumption of law" must be overcome. In this one-page opinion, issued by Auditor Cerri the same year Charles obtained his remissorial letters, analogy was provided for hold-ing that just fear of one's parents did not invalidate a marriage, and an evidentiary standard was set down which it was hard for Charles to meet.

nearly thirty years, he had labored in the Rota. He had begun as an assistant in the *studio* of his uncle, Auditor Geronimo Pamphili. He had become an advocate and then a Consistorial Advocate. When his uncle was promoted to the cardinalate, he succeeded him as Auditor and held the post from 1604 to 1628. His highest lawmaking office was Prefect of the Congregation of the Council from 1639 to 1644; but the Rota had made him. As he himself observed as Pope, "We owe Our exaltation to God and to the Rota." [112]

In ordinary affairs of state the Pope's sister-in-law, Olimpia Maidalchini, often played a dominating role; she was known to entertain rotal auditors.[113] But in Charles' litigation there was no sign of her influence. Anxious for the honor of his old house, Innocent X would want the treatment of ducal litigation be a credit to the institution which had nurtured him. He took office in reaction to the Barberini, but in legal matters of this kind there was continuity; rotal auditor Panziroli, Francesco Barberini's legal adviser, had become Secretary of State. If the Pope had any preconceptions of the case, his experience with the marriage litigation of Charles' cousin, Henri II, Duke of Guise, might have engendered expectations unflattering to the House of Lorraine.[114] But he had no reason to favor either side. Assigning the case to be treated in his old home, the Pope acted to assure reasoned argument of the merits.

The Sacred Roman Rota was, in the words of *In throno iustitiae*, the tribunal where "the more serious cases of all the Christian faithful may be known and decided." [115] Its jurisdiction was worldwide, although the bulk of its business came from Italy. It handled a large variety of ecclesiastical conflicts and a quantity of property disputes, both ecclesiastical and secular. Marriage cases were less than 5 percent of its load.[116]

Twelve men made up the Rota. The senior man was the Dean, who enjoyed particular perquisites and responsibilities; otherwise the auditors were equal. The Rota was a collegial body, whose judgments were announced as those of "the Lords." Each case was, however, assigned to a panel of five, of which one member was the *ponens* or judge-reporter. He issued all opinions in the case under his own name, but *In throno iustitiae* prescribed that without the vote of his coauditors he was not to give definitive judgment or other "prejudicial rulings," even if his decision seemed to be "clear law," unless the parties "expressly consented on the record." Despite this restriction, the *ponens* had a dominant role in shaping any decision. The Rota reached its decisions by the entire body of twelve, seated at a round table, hearing the case presented by the judge-reporter. The presentation of the *ponens* was usually determinative, although only the four auditors seated to the reporter's left — *co-responsales* or coresponsibles — were entitled to vote; the reporter himself was disqualified from voting. The decision had to be by a majority. If there were a tie, the reporter could not break it, but the case was put over another session and, if the tie persisted, two more auditors were added.[117]

Each auditor had one or two "auditors of the *studio*" drawn from the junior bar and "distinguished for birth, talent, and learning." Like law clerks in higher courts in the United States today, these men were on the first rung of a career. They would move on to become advocates in the Rota or auditors in a nunciature abroad. Ultimately they might be raised to the Rota itself. At this junior stage they provided the research assistance indispensable to a learned court. They helped "compile decisions," and did "other things which the auditors, occupied with heavier matters," could not. Forty-eight notaries — four per auditor — carried out the clerical and administrative tasks of the tribunal.[118]

Auditors of the Rota were appointed by the Pope. They were not charged for the appointment. In this respect the Rota was distinguished from many other curial offices which were used to raise public revenue. Places in the Signature of Grace and Justice were sold, although this body had judicial functions. Even the cardinalate had a price attached, although appointments to it were supposed to be made on merit and the Pope might waive the fee. The Rota stood with the principal congregations of the Curia as exempt from an undignified commerce which ran the risk of restricting merit by ability to pay a purchase price.[119]

Papal discretion in choosing auditors was limited by the Rota's international character. Beginning with concessions made to the kings of Aragon and Castile, the practice of conceding rotal nominations to particular states had developed. In 1640 there were two Spanish seats (Aragon and Castile each had one), a seat for the Holy Roman Empire, one for France, one for Milan, one for

Venice, one for Tuscany (Florence, Siena, or Perugia), one for Ferrara, and one for Bologna (papal territory, but entitled to special consideration as the seat of the ancient university center of canon law).[120] Three seats were left completely open to papal choice. The prevailing custom gave the Rota the weakness and the strength of a modern international court. Although the appointees thought of themselves, to a considerable extent, as representing their areas, the cosmopolitan nature of the body was much to its benefit.

Class as well as country restricted eligibility. Auditors were customarily chosen from the richer and the nobler families; a person not of noble birth was either ennobled by the Pope or formally dispensed from the requirement; and there was a requirement that an appointee have an income outside his salary.[121] These considerations, in theory at any rate, were not designed to perpetuate upper-class control of the judiciary, but to assure honesty in the judicial office.

Apart from these limitations and the usual pressures of politics, friends, and favorites, selection to the Rota was on merit; at least competence was sought and often the Popes found first-rate lawyers. The meritocratic aspect of selection was symbolized by a rite: a nominee to the Rota had to conduct an argument before the assembled incumbents of the tribunal. This public trial was followed by a second private session before the body. The candidate was interrogated in turn by each of the auditors from the most recent to the most senior up to the Dean, who gave the correct answers to the questions the candidate had been asked. This ritual was designed to deter the presumptuous rather than to detect the incompetent, for it occurred after the Pope had made the nomination. Like other initiations, this "novitiate" — the term from religious life was used—functioned principally to create an *esprit de corps* among those who had undergone it.[122]

Once an auditor was seated he had both a respected office and a good income. Fifty scudi per month was paid each auditor as a salary by the papal treasury, the Apostolic Chamber.* In lieu

* In comparison, the best paid professor of canon law at the Sapienza, the Roman training-ground for canonists, received 400 scudi per year, and the pay scale of lesser professors ran from 250 down to 75 scudi per annum. Filippo Maria Renazzi, *Storia dell'Università degli studi di Roma detta communemente La Sapienza* (Rome, 1805), III, 259.

of an ancient tax exemption, each received fifty scudi annually from the papal tax collector. Every year the Pope gave each member an additional hundred scudi and the Dean two hundred. If a Pope died, the auditors received two hundred more scudi apiece, a not negligible windfall. They also had the privilege of holding multiple, nonresident benefices, and, "since their salaries were not commensurate with their many labors," the Pope assigned them a number of such sinecures.[123]

Compensation did not exhaust the rewards of rotal appointment. An auditorship was an excellent way to acquire experience in the Church as a system. By custom, all auditors became chaplains to the Pope; the Dean and next two senior men were voting participants in the Congregation of Rites on the canonization of saints; one auditor was named consultor to the Inquisition; the Dean was canonical examiner for the Congregation for the Examination of Bishops; one auditor was lieutenant to the Chancellor of the University of the Sapienza; and all the auditors collectively were administrators of a poor boys' school, the Nazareth.[124] Auditors were also drawn on for work by the Secretariat of State. They lived, on the whole, in neither monastic nor judicial isolation; they were enmeshed in the administrative business of the Curia.

Experience like this was preparation for even higher position in the Church, and to experience was joined the indispensable requirement for promotion — visibility to those with power to promote. As a consequence, the prestige of the Rota rested not only on the dignity of its role and the quality of its performance but on the careers of its members. From the beginning of the pontificate of Julius III in 1550 to the end of the regime of Innocent X in 1654, ninety-one men became auditors. Of these four became Pope, twenty-four more became cardinals, and twenty-five became bishops. In all, over half advanced in rank and almost one-third entered the highest circle of the Curia.[125] The two main tribunals, the Signature and the Rota, were, in the critical metaphor of Cardinal De Luca, "so many Trojan horses from which issue Sovereign Pontiffs."[126] Nothing could better demonstrate the extent to which the Curia viewed the Church as a legal system than the success of these men of law. Nothing could better emphasize the crucial effects of rotal litigation upon the government of the

Church. The lessons learned in such litigation were the education of the ruling elite.

Du Nozet, Ghislieri, Roxas, Peutinger, Cerri, Bichi, Melzi, Verospi, Ottoboni, Corradi, Arguelles y Valdes, Celso — these were the Dean and Auditors in 1646 — the Dean, Edmund Du Nozet, of Auxerre, appointed in 1626; Francesco Maria Ghislieri, of Bologna, appointed in 1627; Francisco de Roxas, of Valencia, appointed in 1635; Christophe Peutinger, of Amiens, appointed in 1639; Carlo Cerri, of Rome, appointed in 1639; Celio Bichi, of Siena, appointed in 1639; Geronimo Melzi, of Milan, appointed in 1641; Leo Verospi, of Rome, appointed in 1642; Pietro Ottoboni, of Venice, appointed in 1643; Giacomo Corradi, of Ferrara, appointed in 1643; Guttierez de Arguelles y Valdes, of Lerida, appointed in 1644; Angelo Celso, of Rome, appointed in 1645.[127] From this body came the judges of Charles and Nicole.

To start with, the *ponens* was Ghislieri. The senior member after the Dean, he had been assigned to the litigation by the Pope, and his selection reflected his reputation: he was a Bolognese who had succeeded to the prestigious seat held before him by Matteo Buratto and Alessandro Ludovisi; from a family with a long tradition of distinguished canonists, he arrived in Rome with law degrees from Bologna and a personal income, and in twenty years as an auditor he had become known as an outstanding scholar.[128] He made the initial rulings on the remissorial letters in the spring of 1648, and he had every expectation of remaining in charge. Unlike judges-delegate outside of Rome, auditors of the Rota could not be recused for partiality to a party, an immunity justified by their collegial exercise of responsibility and by their "outstanding integrity." [129]

In the summer of 1648 rumors circulated in Rome that the Rota could be bought. Touched at a very sensitive point, Innocent X asked the Dean to investigate. On August 3, 1648, the Dean assembled all the members at the Nazareth on the pretext of discharging their administration over it and, once assembled, he proposed that they determine for themselves where the guilt lay. One by one the auditors left the room and were discussed by their colleagues. Hearsay pointed to a single man, Francesco Maria Ghislieri. While serving as *ponens* he was reported to have been paid 500 scudi by Cardinal Montalto in one case, 1500 scudi by Prince

Borghese in another, 400 scudi by the Princess Verula in yet a third, and 2000 scudi in the Robigni partnership litigation. His alleged receipts totaled about six times his annual legitimate income as an auditor.[130]

Rules on gifts to the Rota had been emphatically laid down by the reform bulls, *In throno iustitiae* of Pius IV and *Universi agri Dominici* of Paul V. Litigants might make small payments, *sportulae*, to an auditor. These payments were a species of court fee, public, recognized by law, and regulated in the reform bulls. By a decision of the Rota in 1641 they were pooled, so that they could not be considered as given to an individual. They worked out to about 50 scudi apiece per year. Beyond such payments, any gift to an auditor, his servants, or his blood relatives, with the exception of food or drink that could be consumed in three days, was forbidden.[131] Ghislieri had no chance of maintaining that he was within the rules, and he apparently could not deny the allegations. He pleaded instead with his colleagues to spare his reputation, the reputation of his family, and the reputation of Bologna. His plea was, in measure, heeded. No public trial, no public denunciation followed the scene at the Nazareth. He was removed from office and made Bishop of Terracina, a small seacoast diocese with an income somewhat greater than his Rota salary.[132]

Students of courts and public administration may deduce from the fate of Ghislieri something of the character and status of the Rota. A member of the highest court is not tried like a common criminal, even if documentary evidence exists to suggest his guilt. The contempt of his colleagues was expressed to him. The distress of the Pope was evident. But it was more important to save the face of the Rota than to punish a bribe-taker. The kind of treatment accorded Ghislieri was that given the member of an established governmental elite — say a high civil servant in the British Foreign Office — who has bungled badly. High office that might have been his was forever denied him. Ghislieri could not be Dean of the Sacred Roman Rota, Archbishop of Bologna, cardinal — all rewards within his grasp after twenty years of service. He was sent off to a minor post, to exile from the center of power. He was not tried like a common criminal, for the scandal would have hurt the institution, and, besides, the victims of his bad behavior were those outside the center.[133] Litigants, like Charles and Nicole, were left to draw what lesson they liked as to why Ghislieri was no longer responsible for their affairs.*

No breath of bribe-taking had occurred in Charles' case, but when Ghislieri abruptly left in the middle of the summer of 1648, it had to be assigned to someone else. Innocent X gave it to the man brought from Bologna to the Rota on March 17, 1649, as Ghislieri's successor, Antonio Albergati.[134] As the inheritor of the Bologna seat, Albergati was the logical choice for the case. He was also the Pope's nephew.[135] Waiting for his appointment from August to March may have caused delay for the litigants, but such delays counted little against the papal interest in a nephew taking charge of such an important case. After the talk of corruption Innocent X wanted someone he could trust to do what he was told and to be loyal, discreet, and honest. Albergati was an archpriest in Bologna; he was already "very rich"; he had a degree in civil and canon law from Padua; and he was a good man. He lived long enough to become Dean of the Rota in 1669 and to die in office in 1686. His

---

* Ghislieri was later able to manage a partial comeback. In 1664, under Alexander VII, he was transferred from Terracina to Imola, a substantial town near Bologna, with an episcopal income of 7,000 scudi (*Hierarchia catholica*, IV, 209). This income, combined with a papal pension of 1,000 scudi, was ten times his Rota salary. Ghislieri's unostentatious removal and re-emergence may be profitably contrasted with what happened to Francesco Canonici, called Mascambruno, Under-Datary under Innocent X and much esteemed by the Pope. In the performance of his office of supervising appointments to benefices within the Pope's gift, he was accused of forging official documents, obtaining the Pope's signature to them by fraud, and selling them for personal profit. He was tried, convicted on April 15, 1652, and executed; Pastor, XXX, 43–44. Why should there have been this difference in the treatment of two corrupt curial officials? Mascambruno had indeed betrayed the confidence and friendship of the Pope and imposed upon him personally. But the Pope felt that the honor of the Rota, too, was peculiarly associated with his own, and he had no apparent ties with Ghislieri to mitigate his anger at his activity. Was it more of a crime to cheat the Pope in person than to cheat those who sought the Pope's justice, or was preservation of the Rota's reputation the most important objective to Innocent X?

The seventeenth-century Rota's reputation was, in fact, not above challenge. During the next pontificate, a Rota official of twenty-eight years' service presented Alexander VII a list of abuses in the court which included bribetaking by some auditors ("Disordini che occorrono nel suprema tribunale della Rota," summarized in Pastor, XXXI, 28–29). In 1663, Cardinal Spado drew the same Pope's attention to the improper intervention of cardinals and other curialists on behalf of litigants in the Rota (*ibid.*, 29). Perhaps if Innocent X had made an example of Ghislieri a purer atmosphere would have been fostered. In the eighteenth-century history of the Rota, the removal of Ghislieri is noted without mention of his crime or that his punishment involved being made a bishop, Bernini, *Il Tribunale*, pp. 153–154.

success was owed to longevity, not erudition. In 1649, he was still learning the ropes, and his intellectual abilities were not outstanding. His uncle, the Pope, advised him to be diligent imitating the other auditors, "and for some space of time to pretend nothing else but to learn." [136] In handling Charles' case at this stage of his career he must have relied on his assistants and the parties' lawyers to marshall the facts and law for him. Uncle and nephew, Pope and *ponens*, worked together to channel the litigation to its termination in decision.

The Bar

Like the modern English bar, whose ancestral relative it was, the Rota bar was divided into "advocates" and "proctors." Advocates, like English barristers, presented the case to the court and were valued for their knowledge of the law and their ability to persuade the court of their client's case. Proctors, like English solicitors, arranged conferences between the parties and the advocates and briefed the advocates in advance by written analyses of the matter. At the conference with the client they decided how the case "should be instructed and prosecuted." They also prepared "the articles" or topics on which witnesses would be interrogated and performed the critical task of selecting the parts of the record that would go into the *summarium* for their side. If their client won, they drafted the judgment for the court. Less honored than the advocates, as managers of the case they carried out tasks requiring at least equal legal skill.[137]

Since the time of Paul III, it had been agreed by the bar and approved by Pope and Curia, that argument be in writing. The reason for this rule is hard to see.[138] Perhaps it was a combination of practical motivation, for compensation was based on written documents, an academic sense of the dignity of the written word, and an experience of oral argument as too often noisy shouting. The spread of printing favored the practice, although not all rotal briefs were printed. Advocates were admitted to the Rota bar not to speak, but "to write." * Theory, however, was softened by

---

* Fees were customarily determined in terms of the papers filed. Advocates were paid 24 *juliani* per writing submitted to the court, and 1 *julianus* for every

practice, for advocates were not without an opportunity to address auditors orally and to present in person the considerations they knew would be most striking. The day after the submission of the *restrictus* or briefs to the *ponens*, it was customary for advocates, proctors, and the litigants themselves or their gentlemen to appear at the *ponens'* residence and argue the case. Consistorial advocates had a place of precedence at these presentations which was envied by those not so favored.[139] The process of oral argument was repeated the following day at the residence of the *ponens'* principal assistant. The procedure was praised in Emerix's seventeenth-century handbook because "the proctors so clearly and distinctly set out the facts, and the advocates so learnedly and wisely conclude with laws and reasons, that the auditors who attentively hear them and effectively suggest the difficulties they feel, reach a resolution when the written submissions are made with much less — and sometimes very little — labor." [140]

Practitioners were usually in minor orders, sometimes priests, occasionally laymen. Decretal law limited priests and religious to practicing law only on behalf of themselves, the Church, or the poor.[141] Papal dispensations were routinely given the secular clergy to authorize them to engage more generally in practice in the ecclesiastical courts, and a cleric who knew the civil law could usually be dispensed also to obtain a "decent livelihood" in civil litigation.[142] While laymen were not unwelcome — as Buratto's career illustrated — orders were necessary if a lawyer was to pursue his career to the highest ranks.

Within the two main divisions of the bar there was a hierarchy that did not depend on clerical status. At the top was the College of Consistorial Advocates, a body of twelve, "fully proved in birth, morals, and doctrine," and distinguished on public occasions by clothes they alone could wear. Consistorial advocates were appointed by the Pope and were subjected to examination by the

---

folio of every copy of the original writing. A six-folio brief with ten copies would then be worth 84 *juliani*. Such a sum was a minimum. Men of wealth would be more liberal when the labor or gravity of the case required it. A happy by-product of this emphasis on written word for historians of canon law is that the files of the Rota as far back as the seventeenth century are jammed with legal briefs. In contrast, in England, where reliance was placed on the lawyer speaking to the court and the court usually ruled upon his speech, legal history must be constructed from the end result, the judge's opinion, or from a court reporter's notes of the oral contentions. Finished specimens of the lawyer's craft are missing.

Rota before they could assume their title. Collegially the twelve constituted the governing board of the Sapienza and so had supervision of the school of most Roman canonists. From the ranks of the College were drawn auditors of the Rota and bishops, and some consistorial advocates became, in season, cardinals and Popes. Membership in the body was the highest recognition a practicing canon lawyer could receive.*

Undoubtedly there was an advantage in having counsel who had associations with the Pope, with auditors of the Rota, with other high ecclesiastics. The reform bulls had attempted to eliminate crude and blatant influence. An auditor was supposed not to hear a case in which a lawyer appeared who was related to him by blood or marriage within the second degree.[143] The standard set was roughly that prevailing in modern American statutes — and indeed somewhat higher, since the not uncommon American evasion of the rule by a relative's partner appearing would not have been possible in the Curia where lawyers did not practice as partners. Still, with deference to the formal standard, it was desirable to have lawyers who stood well in the Curia on one's side — to get attention for interlocutory requests, to counteract pressures, to have prestige — the sorts of reasons which often prompt the hiring of prominent counsel in any age. There was also the psychological value to the client of such an array. Charles and Nicole each had the comforting assurance that a small army of talent was deployed on their respective behalfs.

For Charles, counsel were Carlo Emanuele Vizzani, V. de Vermiglioli, Celio Piccolomini, Hercule Ronconi, Prospero Bottini, and Armindo Ricci. Vizzani and Vermiglioli were both consistorial advocates, but they were at different states of life. Vizzani was at the peak of his powers, recently elevated to the consistorial rank by Innocent X. He was well regarded by his colleagues, who in 1658 elected him rector of the Sapienza. Bolognese, he could be expected

---

* "Advocate" itself, as well as "consistorial advocate," was a title which could not be assumed at will. Aspirants had to label their writings "briefs of fact" rather than "briefs of law." The two types of briefs were similar but the "brief of fact" was longer on a narrative statement of the case and shorter on citation of authority. After some years of trial, an aspirant was awarded the designation "Advocate of the Holy Roman Rota" by action of the Dean after examination. Proctors also might be admitted "to write" in the Rota and so advance to the rank of advocate, but often they did not desire this promotion. They had their own hierarchy, in which precedence and privilege was held by the twenty-four members of the College of Proctors.

to have rapport with Albergati. Vermiglioli, in contrast, seems to
have been added to the petitioner's team chiefly for his name. A
Perugian, who had served in Rome as auditor of the prelate Serlupo
and then had had a sinecure as "conservator of the Capitol," he
was the author of *Consilia criminalia ad defensionem in Romana
Curia*, published in Rome in 1651.[144] Eighty years old when he appeared as Charles' counsel, he filed only a meager two-page brief
on his behalf.

Of central importance to Charles was Piccolomini, who was not
a consistorial advocate but who was in his prime as a lawyer. A
member of the great Piccolomini family of Siena which had produced Pius II, he was a graduate of the *studio* or law course at
Siena. He had been *locum tenens* of an auditorship in the Apostolic
Chamber, and he was now nicely beneficed as a canon of Saint
Peter's. When he undertook Charles' case he was midway in his
career. In 1656 Alexander VII was to name him Nuncio to France.
A cardinal in 1664, he came home to Siena in 1671 to rule for
twelve years as archbishop, a not unpleasant role in old age for an
experienced diplomat and curialist. As his history suggests, he was
a man of talent, energy, and luck: a man to have as one's advocate;
his brief, with over two hundred authorities cited, was the most
learned contribution to the case.[145]

Rounding out the team were an advocate and two younger lawyers. The advocate, Hercule Ronconi, was in sufficiently good
standing in the Curia to act as a censor of books for the Master of
the Apostolic Palace in 1646.[146] Of the younger men, Prospero
Bottini, only twenty-nine in 1650, was at the beginning of professional life, and he was to have a very respectable career in the
Curia — not as distinguished as Piccolomini's, but as good as a reasonable man would have wished. By 1675 he was a consistorial advocate and so at the summit of his profession. He was also by then
a referee in the Signature of Justice, a canon of Saint Peter's, and
abbot of Saint Jerome in his home town of Lucca. In that year
the Consistorial College chose him as Rector of the Sapienza, a
post where "he carried out many public improvements with great
éclat." That same happy year he became titular Archbishop of
Myra. For over forty years he held the honorable office of Promotor of the Faith, or "devil's advocate," in canonization cases.
He continued a vigorous practice, filling the role of chief coun-

sel for the Apostolic Chamber in a famous case in the Rota in 1680, and living to the age of ninety-one.[147]

Armindo Ricci, not yet admitted as an advocate, was a lawyer from the Marches, from the village of Monte San Martino near Fermo. He had reached the ladder of preferment but had not yet begun its ascent. Under Alexander VII he became Under-Datary, and in 1669, because of the incumbent's age, he became acting Datary. He died a rich man, leaving his fortune to support scholars and to establish a charitable foundation for children in his home village.[148]

In short, Charles had working for him a future cardinal-arch-bishop, a future papal datary, two future rectors of the Sapienza, and two veterans of curial practice — a balanced team, strong in youthful energies and not lacking in connections and reputation.

For Nicole, counsel were Paulo Buoncampagni, Eusebio de Eusebii, Tommaso Balbani, Carlo Saraceni, Alessandro Caprara, and Alessandro Saracinelli. The structure of this group paralleled that of Charles, but it was slightly less prestigious. Buoncompagni was distinguished chiefly by belonging to a family which in one branch or another produced three canonists who became Pope; in prominence of name he came closest to matching Piccolomini.[149] Eusebii, a lawyer of about the same experience as Charles' Vizzani, sought to become a consistorial advocate only in 1653.[150] Balbani and Saraceni never held a prominent office in the Curia. The two youngest men were, in the long run, to be most celebrated. Measured by their subsequent careers at least, they slightly outpointed Charles' young lawyers, Bottini and Ricci. Alessandro Caprara graduated from Bologna with degrees in canon and civil law in 1647 and was ordained in 1650. He became a consistorial advocate in 1662, auditor of the Apostolic Chamber in 1675, and finally auditor of the Rota in 1686, taking the Bolognese seat left vacant by Albergati's death. He lived to a ripe age, becoming acting Dean of the Rota and Regent of the Sacred Penitentiary in 1696 and leaving the Rota only to become a cardinal in 1706.[151] The son of Bolognese nobles, he supplied the essential Bolognese element to the staff, and he made up for his inexperience by his energy. Alessandro Saracinelli was the junior man, about Ricci's age, and, like him, not yet admitted to the bar as an advocate. From a hill town close to Rome, Orvieto, his career paralleled Ricci's, but he preceded him as Under-Datary in the regime of Alexander VII.[152] On balance, the two sides were as fairly matched in counsel as ever happens in legal contests.

THE ASCERTAINMENT OF THE TRUTH

Summaria

Describe the nature and function of *summaria*.

By means of the articles the proctors sketched out the case. The court approved these topics for interrogation in approving remissorial letters or in ordering examinations in Rome. Answers by the witnesses on the topics were then taken down, not verbatim but in substance. The proctor then culled the record for testimony favorable to his side. The *summarium* was made up of this testimony and documents selected by the proctor to establish his case. Its composition was frankly partisan, although the material itself was faithfully taken from the hearings, and normally each side would submit a *summarium*, so designed that "the auditors in a short time may examine the most voluminous records and be freed from an inspection of the original proceedings."

What was the aim of Charles' *summarium?*

To present the testimony establishing the presence of initial coercion and the absence of subsequent consent.

What did the *summarium* show as to motives for coercion?

That François stood to lose all chance of the dukedom for himself or his heirs unless he somehow achieved reconciliation with his brother Duke Henri; that François wanted the marriage "because of the persecution by Duke Henri and to keep the dukedom of Lorraine" (Testimony of Charles' chamberlain, Gabriel de Bruuijers, Baron de Chalabré).[153]

What did the *summarium* show as to coercion?

Hearsay that François would put Charles out of the house, deprive him of all his goods, and reduce him to a state of misery if he did not agree to the marriage. That Charles, in fact, left his father's bedroom weeping and "complaining of the aforesaid threats" (Chalabré, supported as to circumstances by François' former valet, Walter Platel, and as to the hearsay's content by a courtier, Nicolas Mareschal).

Was there no eyewitness to the coercion?
Only Charles himself, a spouse, whose testimony could not invalidate his own marriage.[154]

What evidence was there that François would have carried out a threat?
He "maintained the greatest authority over his sons" (Father George Gérard of the Franciscans of the Strict Observance). He was "somewhat choleric," "greatly venerated," and "strongly feared" by his children (Lady Marie de Thomesson, a friend of Charles' mother). He had "the best morals," but was "strict and particularly austere toward his children"; he was "accustomed to carry out his threats"; people believed that Lutzbourgh, Louis de Guise's agent, had been killed at his command (Marie de Haurecourt, now a nun).

What was shown as to Charles' parents' consciousness of their own behavior?
François admitted "forcing" Charles to marry Nicole (Chalabré reporting hearsay). Christine, his wife, opposed the marriage because Charles was forced; at the same time she objected to marrying his sister to Louis de Guise but was "compelled to sacrifice her daughter to Louis as Jephthah dedicated his daughter" (Father Dominic Gillet, another Observative Franciscan).

Was there any evidence of coercion of Charles by Duke Henri?
If Charles refused to sign the betrothal contract, Duke Henri said, he would give Nicole to Louis de Guise and the dukedom with it (Chalabré, and one Jean Regnault, reporting what they had heard).

What evidence was there as to the feelings between the parties?
As to Charles' attitude toward Nicole, prenuptially: when Charles was summoned home from Germany to be matched with Nicole, he left instead for Italy at once (Chalabré and Gabriel de Cherisy, another noble of Lorraine). Charles' first gentleman had said that Charles told his father he did not love Nicole (Regnault's hearsay testimony of what the first gentleman had said). Lady

Marie de Haurecourt was told by Charles that he could not marry
Nicole because she did not love him; his frigid behavior toward her
drew the comment of the court (Marie de Haurecourt). Charles
would become upset at the sight of Nicole; he would often refuse
his mother's requests to visit her; when the dispensation from Rome
arrived, he threw to the ground the cards he was playing with and
showed his anger and his grief (Marie de Thomesson). Charles also
told her more than once, "Princes are of the worst condition because they are forced to marry at the will of others in order to
help their state" (Marie de Thomesson).

As to Charles' feeling for Nicole after one night of marriage:
Lady Hélène Pelitia, Countess of Tornielles, and Nicole's mother
visited the couple's bedroom the morning after the wedding night.
Charles and Nicole were in the same bed, but they were "sad and
morose, with their faces turned from each other." There were no
signs that they "had treated each other with pledged love" (Lady
Hélène Pelitia).

As to Charles' feeling for Nicole after further postnuptial experience: according to Charles' first gentleman, consummation was
delayed four months (Claude Durant's hearsay testimony of what
the first gentleman had said). For extended periods of time Charles
would take up residence outside the palace in order to avoid Nicole; her mother vainly protested this behavior (Jacques Bernier
d'Hagecourt, a Lorraine noble). When Charles was in residence at
the palace he would go hunting and, on return, keep his study door
shut so as not to see Nicole (Charles de Mitry). After Duke
Henri's death, Charles withdrew from Nicole's bed, board, and
dwelling and lived apart "for several years" (Chalabré).

As to Nicole's attitude toward Charles, premaritally: Nicole and
Louis de Guise were in love. Louis joked with Nicole often. Once
he had held her out a window so that she could see a ball game
below. These intimacies were signs of love to the witness (Marie
de Thomesson). By written contract Duke Henri had promised
her to Louis (Chalabré's eyewitness account of the document; Father Gillet's testimony of the common report of it).

As to Nicole's feeling for Charles in the first few months of marriage: Nicole "refused to love Charles" after the wedding, so that
her father struck her and threatened to substitute her sister Claude
as Charles' wife if she would not consummate the marriage (Cha-

labré, reporting common rumor of the court). Nicole would lie abed chatting with her chambermaid Martha until Charles morosely withdrew (Marie Raison, reporting what she had learned from other of Nicole's chambermaids). Charles' father made gifts to Martha to persuade Nicole to consent to consummation (Claude Durant, repeating a story heard from Charles' first gentleman).

As to Nicole's continued disposition: she would refuse to gratify Charles by playing on the *testudo* for him (Caroline Bailly, her former lady-in-waiting). She cried when she talked to Louis de Guise and was forbidden by her father to talk to him again (Marie de Haurecourt). Louis said that he had wanted to marry her and still "possessed her good-will" (a Jesuit, Jean Fagot, relating a conversation he had with Louis, sometime after Nicole's marriage).

Was there any documentary evidence?

First, an excerpt — not authenticated — purporting to be from the will of René II of Lorraine, decreeing that males alone should rule Lorraine.[155] Second, a marriage contract, executed by Duke Henri and his wife Margaret and Nicole and François and Charles, dated the day of the first wedding ceremony, May 22, 1621, by whose terms Nicole's parents promised to give her in marriage to Charles; she consented; he agreed to accept her; if Nicole died without children from Charles, her sister Claude would then be married either to Charles or to his brother, Nicolas-François; if Charles died without children, Nicole was to be married to Nicolas-François; in any event Claude was to marry no one but Charles or Nicolas-François, "in order to keep the said states, lands, and signories in the proximate stirps." [156] Third, a "protest," executed five days before the wedding by François and Charles, in private, with Jean des Porcelets de Maillane, Bishop of Toul, as witness, whereby father and son asserted that the marriage contract was prejudical to their rights as male heirs of Lorraine; rejected in advance the clause in the wedding contract declaring Nicole universal heir; and declared that whatever they did "in this part" they did "by force and coercion arising from the fear which can fall upon the steadiest man." [157] Fourth, two of the letters written by Charles to Nicole in Paris, apparently intended to show that Nicole had abandoned Charles, although containing the declaration "I shall be with passion all yours." [158]

Was there anything else in the *summarium?*

A brief genealogy of Charles. A list of the witnesses, giving the total, thirty-one; their clerical status if any, seven priests and one nun; their rank, if any, twelve nobles; and their names.[159]

On the basis of his witnesses' testimony, could Charles win his case?

If the hearsay were accepted, Charles had proved that he had been subjected to fear sufficient to coerce a steady man. If the hearsay as to François' threats were rejected, it had at least been shown that Charles had entered a marriage arranged for him by his parents with a girl whom he did not love and who had not loved him. Whether such a marriage was invalid depended on what the court would say of a parental command to marry and how it would regard the absence of initial marital affection. Coercion by Duke Henri had not been proved except by hearsay. The claim that Charles later consented to the marriage had been anticipated with only partial effectiveness by Chalabré's testimony of his withdrawal from Nicole for some years after Duke Henri's death.

What was the plan of Nicole's *summarium?*

To show the elements of a valid marriage and the continuation of the marriage and of Charles' affection for twelve years; to demonstrate the unreliability of Charles' witnesses.

How did it begin?

With the marriage contract of May 22, 1621, including the names of seven witnesses to this agreement on the first wedding day.[160]

What other relevant document was produced?

Gregory XV's bull of dispensation from consanguinity wherein the Pope pronounced the marriage, made at "the exhortations and persuasions" of Father Dominic, to be "greatly useful to the public good." [161]

How was the marriage itself proved?

Not by the parish record book required by the Council of Trent, for it had not been kept, but by both Nicole's first witness, her father's old grand chamberlain, and by the witnesses called by Charles.[162]

How was the absence of coercion shown?

By the festivity, gaiety, joy admitted by all as accompanying the ceremony; by the presence of relatives, friends, and high ecclesiastics who had not objected to the ceremony; by the testimony of thirty witnesses for Nicole that François was mild, humane, just, good, and benign.

What motives were given for the marriage?

As Charles' witnesses were quoted, "to conserve the dukedom in the house" and "to avoid wars and quarrels which could break out on Duke Henri's death."

How was consummation proved?

By hearsay and common report, and by Charles' former first chamberlain, who had seen Charles and Nicole in bed, "showing by their words and acts that they were very happy." [163]

What later acts of Charles were used to show that he considered Nicole his wife long after he might have ceased to fear his father?

The minting of coins with the images of Charles and Nicole upon them; the publication of edicts in their joint names as duke and duchess; a letter from Charles dated April 22, 1629, giving a grant to the Franciscans with the obligation that in perpetuity they say a mass a day for his father, himself, and "Madame his wife"; the act of cession of Lorraine to Nicolas-François executed by Charles, February 24, 1634, with the confirmation of "our most beloved and dearest consort, Madame the Duchess"; a letter from Charles to his aunt, the Empress Eleanor, on December 2, 1626, referring to the prerogatives of "Madame my dear Spouse." Climactically, five letters from Charles to Nicole, including the two from Besançon also printed in Charles' *summarium* and here boldly captioned, "Letters of the Duke to the Duchess after his Departure from Lorraine about his Marital Affection," and three other letters, all evidently sent after Nicole had learned of his dalliance with Béatrice. On June 6, 1634, Charles had written Nicole: "If some love remains in you for me, I say nothing of what I have for you since I want you to experience it." In another letter, undated, he had denounced the traitors who spoke "horrible things" about him to her. He had asked her if she had the least doubt "that I love you as in the past." He had closed with "Meanwhile I shall with passion be all yours." [164]

What objections were made to the Duke's witnesses?

Chalabré was a chamberlain of Charles, doubly biased by owing his present appointment to Béatrice. Walter Platel was the guardian of Charles' wardrobe. Jean Regnault worked for an appointee of Charles. Baron Hagecourt was Charles' captain of the guards, had received many gifts from Béatrice, and in earlier days had been beaten several times at Nicole's order. Father Gérard had been arrested for "certain letters" when he came to Toul to testify, and he had been freed from jail at Charles' command. Gabriel de Cherisy was Béatrice's head groom. Father Fagot, consulted at Besançon in 1639 on Cheminot's hypothetical "Titus" and "Bertha," had declared this hypothetical union invalid. Antoinette de Malabarbé had spent "almost her whole life" with Charles' mother. Marie de Thomesson had been maid of honor to his mother for seven years. Martin de Remon was Charles' wine steward. Marie Raisin had failed to get a favor for her son from Nicole.[165]

Procedural irregularities, both slight and substantial, invalidated much of the testimony. Chalabré and Platel had both been examined by an official of Luxembourg who had no commission from the Rota. Most of the witnesses had testified in areas dominated by Charles' armed troops. Acute danger awaited the witness who gave away anything to Nicole's case; one Lafontaine had been crucified at Béatrice's command when he had publicly doubted that she was married to Charles. Finally, the testimony was the product of coaching by counsel. In the language of this bar, Chalabré had been "instructed"; Charles' proctor had furnished him with a paper "to help his memory"; other witnesses of Charles, according to their own admissions, had been shown in advance the articles on which they were to be examined.[166]

Substantive contradictions in the testimony of key witnesses completed their discrediting. Chalabré had first testified that Charles and Nicole continued to live together after Duke Henri's death. Only on re-examination did he change his story and provide the helpful evidence about Charles' leaving once his father-in-law was dead. Platel had undermined his own story of having seen François threatening Charles by giving a flat negative to the question, Did François use force to compel Charles to marry Nicole? Other witnesses produced by Charles had answered "No" or "I don't know" to the articles on fear: their unawareness of any coercion refuted his principal contention.[167]

On the basis of her *summarium* could Nicole win her case?

She had proved the celebration of a wedding with a dispensation from the Pope. She had offered circumstantial evidence and character evidence tending to disprove the hearsay reports of the coercion exercised by the two brothers on Charles. The court had been given reason for doubting or disqualifying the chief witness to the hearsay, Chalabré. Nicole had also provided substantial evidence that Charles had spoken of her as his wife. If the court found initial coercion, it would have to decide if this evidence established marital affection and delayed consent. Charles' counter-evidence of withdrawal from Nicole had been seriously undermined.

Briefs of Fact, Briefs of Law

What facts were emphasized in the briefs of fact?

In Ricci's brief for Charles: the motives François had for forcing the marriage, these being described as "the crown" of Charles' case; the secretiveness of princes, making the coercion exercised hard to prove; François' austere and harsh character coupled with the story of Lutzbourgh's death; Nicole's love for Louis de Guise, and the mutual aversion of Nicole and Charles, said to continue after the marriage; the continuing coercion constituted by the mere existence of François until his death in 1632; the failure to clothe any later consent in the Tridentine form.[168]

In Saracinelli's brief for Nicole: the public circumstances of the celebration of the wedding and the notables present at it; the duty Charles had to obey his father in order to reconcile the families; "the very humane" character of François; the long duration of the conjugal union as shown by Charles' own witnesses; the affection shown by Charles' letters from Besançon; the unlawful night marriage of Charles and Béatrice; the objections to the credibility of Charles' witnesses and the irregularities in their examination.

What were the principal points of the law briefs?

As argued for Charles by Consistorial Advocate Vizzani: where, as here, a father had "the maximum interest in the contracting of the marriage," where the father had a tenacious memory for injuries to be avenged, where the son could consequently expect his father's anger to remain unabated if he refused to obey, the son's reverential fear of his father invalidated his consent. Fear of the loss of the duchy, his by right, was itself coercive; Duke Henri's alternative plan to marry Nicole to Louis de Guise forced Charles to save his title by agreeing to take Nicole himself. No subsequent consent by Charles could turn this marriage into a good one unless it were expressed in the Tridentine form before a priest and witnesses.

As argued further by Piccolomini: Nicole's consent was coerced as well, for she had wanted to marry Louis de Guise. As argued further by Ronconi, resistance to threats made by one with paternal authority was not the action of a steady man but a rash man: Charles in acceding to his father's importunities yielded to pressure which would coerce a steady man. As argued piecemeal in individual briefs by Vermiglioli, Piccolomini, Ronconi, and Bottini, and then jointly in an eight-page brief filed by all Charles' advocates: standards of proof were relaxed where a matter was so hard to prove as fear inflicted by a father on a son. Signs and circumstances sufficed to prove what had been done in private. From necessity, members of the household must be heard as witnesses. If supported by hearsay witnesses, one eyewitness was enough. Less fear sufficed to invalidate consent to a marriage than consent to other contracts or to a religious profession. In doubt as to whether consent was given, the presumption was for no consent. Finally, as to subsequent consent, documents such as Charles' letters from Besançon to Nicole proved nothing as to his marital affection; they were written with the political intent of assuring her loyalty to Lorraine.

As argued for Nicole by Saraceni: the marriage of June 6, 1621, met all the requirements of the Council of Trent. The banns were dispensed. The bishop as the parish priest of parish priests officiated. The ducal chapel of Saint George was exempt from his jurisdiction as to his property, but not as to his care of souls. The parish priest himself was also present; his failure to record the marriage in the parish register was a sin but did not invalidate the marriage. Regular in form, the marriage had not been invalidated by coercion. François and Henri were mild of temperament and Charles bold and martial; the son could not have felt fear which would affect a steady man. In obeying his father he properly sought to end family strife and assure possession of the dukedom. No good contrary evidence to the voluntariness of his acts had been presented: witnesses had to be above exception if their testimony was to be heard against a marriage.

As argued further by Balbani: reverential fear alone did not invalidate. Fear easily removed by negotiation, such as Charles' alleged fear of Duke Henri, did not invalidate. As argued further by Buoncompagni: if fear ever existed, it was purged and the marriage validated by the long cohabitation of the couple. Renewal of the Tridentine form was unnecessary for such later consent when the fear, if any, was secret and not provable in court by witnesses above exception. As argued further by Caprara: the protest of Charles and François touched on the dowry not on coercion to marry. In doubt, the marriage must be upheld. As argued in all the briefs: Charles' witnesses were subject to legal objection, related mostly hearsay, and were often contradictory. Chalabré's story of Charles' total separation from Nicole in 1624 ran counter to all credible evidence. Charles treated Nicole as a wife for twelve years. He believed that he was married to her, and in any event his later consent was given to her as a spouse.

Did the arguments examine first principles, reason abstractly, innovate creatively, afford fresh insight into the law?

They did not proceed in these ways.

How did the arguments seek to persuade?

By authoritative analogy. First, in the sense that every application of an old case or old text to a new set of facts assumes a fundamental likeness in the factual configurations, the advocates relied on analogy to urge the appositeness of the Venice or Seville decisions or the observations of Sanchez. Second, dissimilar areas of law were drawn on for precedent; evidentiary standards, for example, were drawn from cases such as *Lerida, March 1, 1641* (on tithes); *Majorca, June 13, 1643* (on the rights of parish priests); *Perugia, May 22, 1643* (on pensions); and *Reggio, March 18, 1639* (on rights of patronage). The force of the analogies, if the likeness was accepted, lay in their authority.

How was authority related to the facts of the case?

Authority was employed to emphasize, to explain, to garland

the facts. It functioned to make constellations of fact legally significant.

How was authority related to the law of the case?

Authority constituted the law of the case. The legal significance of every major assertion and of many minor assertions was established by citation.

Were Scripture, the Fathers and the Councils of the Church of major importance as authority?

They were not of major importance. Only Balbani quoted, "What God has joined together, let no man put asunder" (Matthew 19.6), ending his brief for Nicole with a triumphant appeal to it. Leviticus, Numbers, and Proverbs were cited by the patriarchal Vermiglioli to provide epigrammatic wisdom and a literary flourish to his short brief. Otherwise no writer quoted Scripture. Little more attention was paid the Fathers of the Church. Saint Augustine and Saint Ambrose were invoked, without specific citations, by Vermiglioli, again for flourish; no other patristic names appeared in any brief. Most of the Councils of the Church were not employed. Trent was an exception, but even it was cited no more than ten times and only by Charles' advocates.

What role was played by Justinian, Gratian, and the *Decretals*?

Roman law was used some thirty times to show the effect of fear on promises and obligations or to settle minor points not controlled by the canons. Gratian was cited only twice. The *Decretals* were a major source, invoked almost sixty times. Together, decretal and Roman law often gave direction to the argument, without playing a decisive role.

What were the most used authorities?

Cases and commentators. Cases came from the Sacred Congregation of the Council, from the archepiscopal court of Naples, from other provincial courts, but above all from the Rota. Approximately two hundred rotal opinions were cited. Taken chiefly from the last fifty years, they were the most modern, most persuasive, most vital authority invoked.[169] When Charles' matter was in turn decided by the Rota, the court showed a marked preference for its own precedents over other forms of authority. Nicole's superior legal position was perhaps reflected by a two-to-one ratio in the citation of rotal precedent in the briefs on her behalf.[170]

Only two books which were not canon law or moral theology were cited: Aristole's *Ethics*, in a thirteenth-century translation, was referred to twice on the nature of voluntary acts. *Opera politica et historica* of Jean Jacques Chifflet, a physician and historian of Besançon, was presented by Charles' counsel to Albergati just after its publication in 1650 to show that the Salic law governed Lorraine.[171] Otherwise no use was made of works of philosophy, psychology, political theory, or history; and no use at all was made of scriptural exegesis, dogmatic theology, or spiritual, ascetic, or mystical writing. The postulates of the judicial universe did not require exploration or justification; the theological and social bases of the case were taken for granted; the legal world was self-contained.

Moral theologians as they touched on marriage were employed, but usually in a judicial context and usually when they were, like Sanchez, as much canonists as moralists. Civilians, expounding the texts of Justinian, were frequently cited. Above all, the canonists themselves dominated. All of the treatises were in Latin, so that no partiality for a contemporary or a national tongue affected the choices made, but legal writers tended to come from Bologna, Rome, Venice, Naples, and Florence, so that authorities from these cities predominated. Modern authors were not supposed to be used, "unless serious and approved," so that on principle very recent commentaries, not yet approved by custom, were excluded.[172] A respectable number of books written in the last fifty years were used. At the other end of the spectrum, no canonical treatise written before the thirteenth century had been printed, so that available canonical writing began with the Gloss, Hostiensis, and Innocent IV. The curve of usage swelled and reached its climax with the authorities of the sixteenth century.

Put to use in the briefs all the commentaries were on an equal footing. A Spanish writer was as good as a Paduan, a fourteenth-century text as helpful as a seventeenth-century one. In the democratic world of jurisprudential reason, both national origin and age were effaced, and each authority was as good as any other. The Council of Trent overrode earlier decisions. The canon law controlled civil law, but, apart from this preference given later legislation, there was no sense of evolution in the law, although more recent works such as Sanchez had fuller analyses and were therefore more often on point. To a greater extent than would be conceivable in any modern legal system, books written from one hundred to four hundred years before the argument were relevant. To an extraordinary degree, books written twenty-five to one hundred years before the decision were influential. In all its written manifestations — canons, Digest, decisions, and treatises — the law was treated as a single, timeless whole, universal in its force.

Were the authorities cited accurately, fairly, comprehensively and effectively?

Accurately, except for occasional misprints: texts were not misquoted. Fairly, to a degree: passages were not twisted out of context, but contrary, difficult, and embarrassing passages were unmentioned. Comprehensively, in giving a wide range of decisions and commentators, but not in being explored in depth. Effectively, in conveying to the court the major decisions and texts on coercion; ineffectively, in leaving wide latitude for the court to choose among competing and conflicting authorities.

JUDGMENT

Albergati announced the decision in *Toul, Of Marriage* on Tuesday, January 15, 1653. "At the admonition of the Supreme Pontiffs and at the suasion of other Princes," Duke Henri II of Lorraine had promised to give his daughter Nicole, "the betrothed of Louis de Guise," to his nephew Charles in marriage. His purpose was "to remove dissension" over the inheritance of the duchy. Charles and Nicole had given their consent. Lack of a record by the parish priest did not prevent proof of observance of the Tridentine form. The fortuitous presence of the parish priest at the wedding had been sufficient to comply with Trent. Moreover, the bishop, who presided, was the parish priest of parish priests; the exemption of the chapel from his jurisdiction did not prevent his performance of a pastoral office. A lawful exchange of mutual consent in the form required by Trent was proved.

Coercion had been alleged, but proof of coercion failed. "Almost all" of Charles' witnesses were his servants or from his household or camp, and so were open to objection as biased. Several of his witnesses had not testified in a court or place prescribed by law; others had testified to hearsay or public rumor without identifying its source. Most of them had failed to specify circumstances but had testified generally that François forced Charles to obey; such "general evidence" was insufficient. Chalabré, Charles' first witness, had given details, but he had not spoken "out of certain knowledge"; what he had repeated of Charles' statements was wholly inadmissible, because if a spouse could not testify against his marriage he could not accomplish the same result through having his assertions repeated at secondhand. Chalabré, moreover, had been invalidly examined out of court.

Even if all Charles' witnesses were accepted, he had failed to show coercion that would have moved a steady man. Suasion by parents was lawful. Reverential fear of them did not prevent consent. Given François' mildness and Charles' greatheartedness, the threats of François were "of no importance." Moreover, not a single witness testified to coercion at the time of the second exchange of vows on Trinity Sunday, June 6, 1621, before the Bishop of Toul. The circumstances of this occasion proved positively that consent had been freely exchanged. There was the mutual gaiety of the spouses; the presence of blood relatives and other nobles; the active participation of the bishop and Father Dominic; the very fact that the consent was being given a second time. Finally, there was the subsequent consummation; the "fifteen years" of cohabitation; the edicts, coinage, and letters referring to Nicole as Charles' duchess and wife; "the letters and other acts showing marital affection." "Hence," Albergati declared, "the Lords have judged that validity is established." [173]

Hard issues were not faced in this opinion. The authority of *Seville* and *Coimbra* permitting servants to testify in marriage cases was unmentioned: Albergati was basically skeptical of Charles' witnesses. Qualifications on the duty to obey a father were unanalyzed: François' acts constituted "licit and permitted persuasion." The relation of Trent to delayed consent was unexplored: the marriage was valid in inception. *Toul, November 7, 1616,* Buratto's opinion on the profession of the Knight of Malta, was not distinguished; it was not even cited. *Venice, May 25, 1622,* Buratto's opinion on Cecilia's arranged marriage, was treated as controlling.

That Charles' marriage, too, had been arranged was emphasized. No difficulty in reconciling arrangement with freedom was acknowledged. The line between persuasion and coercion seemed patent to Albergati; it was a line drawn to permit royalty and nobility to arrange their children's marriages; it was not a line which the Rota was prepared to challenge.

The relation of marital affection to an arranged match was not explored by Albergati, except obliquely in referring to the later evidence of Charles' attitude. After all, Charles' counsel had not argued that marital affection had been absent at the start; why should Albergati have examined an issue which the advocates had ignored? Yet, compliance with the Council of Trent had not been challenged by the briefs for Charles, and Albergati had devoted almost half his opinion to showing that compliance was established. The difference was that not only did Nicole's briefs aid him on this issue, but the Tridentine form was a clear, technical, controllable requirement. Marital affection was an essential element of marriage which it seemed dangerous to explore. If marital affection was measured at the inception of a marriage, how many marriages could survive the test? A balance between the free choice of children of their mates and gross pressure coercing a steady man had been struck. Marital affection at inception could not be required without a different balance being sought; Albergati was not the man to attempt such innovation. The broad, the easy, the conventional path led to affirmation of the arranged marriage.

An opinion of the Rota was not a final judgment but "a compilation of the advice of the auditors, set out before judgment to both litigants by the judge-reporter for this purpose: that, before that limit is reached, the litigants may bring out anything they have to bring out in fact or in law for confirmation or revocation of those statements; and thus it is that many times, when the matter is better elucidated, the Rota withdraws from what it had said." [174] Nonetheless, Albergati's thorough rejection of Charles' contentions and complete acceptance of Nicole's must have seemed formidable to overcome. Especially was this true when Albergati received Innocent X's permission to derogate from a constitution of Urban VIII that the vote in all cases was to be kept secret. The vote, he announced, had been unanimous.[175]

Charles' counsel made one last effort by asking for remissorial letters to reexamine the witnesses whose testimony had been invalidly taken; Chalabré, no doubt, was the man they wanted most to rehabilitate. The request was turned down on January 12, 1654, as contrary to rotal practice after the record had been published and put in the hands of the parties. "Strong danger existed of subornation." Moreover, no witness had given specific circumstances as to the infliction of fear; such deficiency in firsthand knowledge could not be made up by new examination. Matrimonial cases, Albergati added, without apparent irony, "needed swift determination." [176]

Briefs were then presented on a petition for rehearing, Charles now being represented only by his most junior counsel, Ricci. On February 6, 1654, the auditors met to decide this issue. Albergati told them with little subtlety what his uncle had in mind: "The Most Holy did not intend to favor one side more than the other, but he only reminded them that this case had been committed to the Rota fourteen years ago and had been in process there for a long time. For the rest, the Rota should proceed by observing what should be observed. His Holiness did not intend that the practice of the tribunal be changed." [177]

Three days later the petition was denied. Chalabré, besides having been invalidly examined, was "strongly suspect since he deposes with too great partisanship and of his own belief." The other witnesses on coercion were unconvincing. The positive evidence of free consent was great. With this short review of the facts, the Lords "stood unanimously on what has been decided." Along with the citation of canons, Albergati now invoked the commandment of the Lord: "What God has joined together, let no man put asunder." [178]

Judgment itself was issued the following month on March 23, 1654, in accordance with the opinion. The decision became "executive." Silence was imposed on Charles; that is, further judicial recourse was denied him. In the same year, the judgment was published in the vernacular in Nancy.[179]

EPILOGUE

One month before the rotal judgment in 1654, Charles was arrested by the Spanish in Brussels, where he had been a general in the Emperor's employ, and transported to the Alcazar in Toledo, where he was forced to remain.[180] He was arrested because the Spanish had become uncertain of his loyalty. Yet Charles had always been a restless ally, and the Spanish were so far from having a concrete case against him that he was accused of no crime. He was treated with the cold civility used for important political hostages. It seems probable that the arrest was triggered by fear that Charles, angry and frustrated by the final result in the Rota after seventeen years of insisting that Béatrice was his wife, would go over to the Protestants. Detention in Spain afforded him time to reconcile himself to the voice of the Church. That Nicolas-François arranged the arrest has been suspected, is plausible, but has not been proved.

Nicole, still in Paris, worked for his release, and although her efforts were unavailing, her concern was sufficient to touch her depressed and deserted husband. Disillusioned with his brother, Charles, on February 28, 1655, gave Nicole all his authority over Lorraine and the troops of Lorraine.[181] From this point on his relation to her was one of trust, if not of love.

On January 14, 1657, he wrote her from Toledo: "I have so much evidence of the good will you have kept steadily toward me that I forget the memory of what I have been, in wishing for a chance to be able to make you know that nothing could ever be so much yours as I am." [182] This was the last communication between the two spouses, if indeed his letter ever reached her. Nicole died in Paris on February 20, aged forty-eight, married thirty-six years, separated twenty-three of them.[183]

After Nicole's death, Béatrice expected Charles to marry her. Their correspondence since his arrest had not been great, but he still wrote tenderly to their daughter Anne, and as late as 1654 he still had hoped for a "remedy in Rome." [184] On Nicole's death, Béatrice sent an emissary, one Pelletier, to Spain to arrange the marriage, or what she referred to as "ratification of my marriage." [185] Forty-three, she wanted established ecclesiastically what she had always held to be the truth, that she was Charles' wife. "I want to be before the world," she informed Pelletier, "what His Highness knows very well in his conscience we are before God." [186]

Charles, however, had cooled. In part he was chagrined at Béatrice's failure to act energetically in getting him released from Spanish captivity. In part he was irritated by her "extravagance," while he led a confined existence, and by her failure to leave the court at Brussels, where he knew well she was exposed to temptations; the "most innocent things at Brussels," Béatrice observed, "are reported as criminal to H.H." [187] In part, he had known remorse and had developed a new sense of Nicole. Finally, he had not seen Béatrice for three years, and when he had last seen her, their feelings had scarcely been friendly.

Pressed by Béatrice, Charles balked. A marriage with her, he argued, might irritate his brother, alienate France, and jeopardize his release. There was no need to act precipitously. Later he argued, he needed a dispensation from Rome to wed her.[188] The law forbade an adulterer to marry a paramour with whom he had attempted marriage during the life of his lawful spouse.*

Béatrice's response was predictable. She was, she wrote Pelletier, "becoming crazy" with his excuses. She "needed the patience of Job" to endure them. She was "filled with shame" at "His Highness taking no action since p. N's death or at least since he knew of it." She encouraged Pelletier to continue his efforts: "May God do all for His glory and our salvation and assist you in all things in a cause which is as just as the one you undertake for me — the ratification of my marriage that there cannot be better before God." [189]

Charles was finally released from captivity as part of a general European peace settlement made by the Treaty of the Pyrenees in 1659. In eclipse, he spent his time at the court of Louis XIV in what may be imagined as boredom, intrigue, and amorous dalliance.

---

* For the law, see X.4.7.3 and 5. When the Princess of Clèves refuses to marry the Duke of Nemours after her husband's death, she does so because she believes his love for her cannot survive in marriage and because she believes she has a duty to her dead husband. Although she had avoided manifesting any affection for the Duke in her husband's lifetime, she had loved the Duke, her husband had known that the Duke loved her, and her husband's belief that she had committed adultery with the Duke had caused her husband's death. Psychologically, the widowed Princess is incapable of overcoming the barrier which "her duty" to her husband creates (Lafayette, *La Princesse de Clèves*, part IV, pp. 171–177). The legal barrier of the canon law, which reached only to acts of adultery and conjugicide, is replaced by a self-imposed spiritual law which punishes the princess and her lover for defects of will and imagination. Charles did not have the delicacy of a Princess of Clèves, but, with the removal of his legal spouse, the real obstacles to union with Béatrice were no doubt psychological.

Béatrice continued in pursuit. In 1661 she came to Bar in search of Charles. Nicolas-François noted her arrival and did not relax his vigilance. Not now would he let happen what he had tried for over twenty years to stop. He wrote the Pope, Alexander VII, as he had written the General of the Jesuits back in 1641. The Pope, he advised, should not consent to the dispensation Charles would need to marry.[190]

Nicolas-François was probably alarmed without cause. Charles' advocate in the Rota, Celio Piccolomini, was now Nuncio to France. Charles sent a Jesuit to discuss the dispensation with him, and on July 1, 1661, Piccolomini wrote that there would be great difficulties in getting it. Union with Béatrice would be a fresh scandal for the Church. Exercise of the papal prerogative to waive the barrier of adultery could not be expected.[191] This letter from an old advocate had the marks of what an old client might have asked him to provide. What better way to rout Béatrice, now that Charles was in pursuit of another girl, Marie-Anne Pajot?

Louis XIV saved Charles from marriage by popping Mlle. Pajot into a convent.[192] But Charles continued in his search for youth and beauty. In 1664 at Mirecourt in Lorraine he betrothed himself to a new girl, Isabella, Countess of Ludre.

Béatrice felt badly enough about this project to go to Mirecourt to let Isabella's mother know that Charles was already married to her.[193] This trip was the last expedition of her life. Returning to Besançon, she fell ill, and her end was predicted. She wrote Charles, asking as her dying wish that he marry her and legitimate the children. Assured that the tie would not last long, responsive perhaps to the memories of their great passion, pleased to have a lawful male heir, Charles agreed, but without inconveniencing himself. He sent a proxy. The Archbishop of Besançon dispensed the couple from the impediment of adultery. On May 20, 1664, Charles and Béatrice were married.

Béatrice died two weeks later. Her will, executed just after the proxy wedding, spoke of Charles as "my very dear husband." [194] She returned the diamond he had given her on that other wedding day of theirs in 1637 when Charles had become the spouse of two and entered on the course which would risk the punishments of *Magnum in Christo*, lead Nicole to the throne of justice, and provide opportunity for the advocates and auditors of the Sacred Roman Rota to ascertain the truth as to the nature of his marital consent.*

* In 1665 Charles, aged sixty-two, married Marie-Louise d'Apremont, aged thirteen. The ultimate heir to Lorraine was Charles V, the son of Nicolas-François and Claude, "the glorious conqueror of the Turks," fittingly remembered in the annals of Pont-à-Mousson as its most illustrious pupil, Delattre, *Les établissements de Jésuites à France*, IV, col. 118.

II

"If Conditions Are Attached . . ."

Rolando Bandinelli, professor of canon law at the University of Bologna, veteran curialist, Chancellor of the Roman Church, and the first master of canon law to rule as Pope, ended a controversy of centuries by deciding, as Pope Alexander III, that sacramental marriage was not, in all circumstances, indissoluble. Bishop Bartholomew of Exeter, English moralist, Becket's contemporary, laid this case before him: A noble betrothed a girl, swearing an oath to marry her; before the man could carry out his obligation, he experienced a call to enter religious life and make profession as a monk. What should he do, or how should Bartholomew advise him where the choice was between violation of a promise to God and denial of a divine vocation? The Pope had a complete answer. The noble should be instructed that "it would be safer for him to keep the religion of an oath": he should carry out his sworn duty to marry. Yet he could still follow his vocation: "afterward, if he chooses, let him pass to religion, provided, however, that no carnal coupling has intervened." A man could not abandon his wife, even to enter religion; but this, it was implied, was different. The nobleman of Exeter could marry, but he would be able to end his marriage.[1]

SAINT JOHN'S DIVORCE

Alexander III's solution had the appearance of a legal trick, of a lawyer's way of satisfying contradictory purposes by keeping form and sacrificing substance, of nominally honoring the oath to marry while permitting the actual subversion of the oath. But, technically, what was wrong with his answer? "Consent, not coitus, makes a marriage" ran a dictum of Roman law adopted by Gratian and firmly established by Alexander III himself as the foundation of the canon law of marriage.[2] By exchanging vows with his bride the Englishman would enter a true marriage and so fulfill his oath; sexual intercourse need be no part of the undertaking. The most celebrated married couple in Christendom, Mary and Joseph, had entered a virginal marriage, intending from the start to have no intercourse and observing sexual abstinence throughout their married lives.* For the canonists of the twelfth century the reality of this virginal marriage at the beginning of Christian history was as indisputable as its paradigmatic character.[3] If the parents of the Lord were not married, what could marriage mean? Any account of marriage in a canonical context had to be so shaped that the basic institution for couples did not exclude the couple who were Christ's parents. That central requirement — no mere hypothetical speculation but a most pressing religious exigency — forced the canonists to acknowledge that marriage without intercourse had or intended was still lawful and valid. Measured by the criterion Mary and Joseph supplied, the marriage approved by Alexander III was a fulfillment of the vow to marry.

The second part of the solution was more controversial. If the marriage was good, how could the nobleman have the option to abandon his wife to pursue the celibate life of a religious? "A wife does not have power over her body, but the husband; similarly, the husband does not have power over his body, but the wife," Saint Paul taught in 1 Corinthians, and the canons interpreted his text as forbidding unilateral decision of a spouse to withdraw from marital life to enter religion.[4] Alexander III did not deny Saint Paul or the standard interpretations of Paul's dictum; but he held that, although a marriage was lawful and valid upon the exchange of consent, it could be truly dissolved, ending all marital ties and obligations, by the religious profession of one spouse, provided that profession took place before any act of postmarital intercourse had intervened.[5] The Pope made a sharp distinction between a valid

---

* In a dictum *post* c. 2, C. XXVII, q. 2, Gratian declared it was "wicked to think" that Mary ever intended to violate her vow of virginity. No Catholic theologian had challenged Mary's perpetual virginity since Jerome had routed Helvidius who had speculated that she had borne children after the birth of Jesus; see Jerome, *Contra Helvidium de perpetua virginitate Beatae Mariae*, PL 23, col. 198.

union and an indissoluble union. The commandment of the Lord not to put asunder those whom God had joined applied to "a marriage consummated by carnal coupling." Those who had taken each other as man and wife and had then had no intercourse "had not become one flesh." The reason for indissolubility was therefore lacking. As for precedent for dissolution in the circumstances, an excellent example was presented by Saint John the Evangelist, as his life was seen by the English historian Bede: God had called John from his own marriage to remain a virgin in becoming a disciple of Jesus. The miracle at Cana, described in Chapter Two of Saint John's Gospel, was itself a symbol of how "the wine of marriage" yielded to the invitation of the Lord to embrace virginity.[6] In this exegesis Cana was not the prototype of Christian weddings but the prototype of Christian divorces. Nothing prevented the noble, once validly married, from imitating Saint John and validly terminating his union.

Twenty years after Alexander's answer, one of the ablest and best-educated of medieval Popes, a graduate of Paris in theology and of Bologna in canon law, Lotario de' Segni, took office as Innocent III and mused aloud as to whether Alexander's analysis of the dissolubility of unconsummated marriages had been correct. After reflection, "not wishing in this matter to depart abruptly from the path of our predecessors," he stayed with the position Alexander had staked out.[7] But in 1212 he decided a case which suggested a question unraised by Alexander yet essential to his analysis: what was the content of consent to marry? A bishop presented these facts to the Pope for guidance: a man had found that the only way to persuade a girl to have intercourse with him was to marry her; after adopting this expedient under the false name of "John," he sought an annulment, and the bishop found as a fact that "he did not intend to marry or to consent to her." Innocent III accepted this finding; on the basis of it he ruled that the marriage lacked "substance" and "form" and was therefore null.[8] His decision assumed that there was a substance to marital consent beyond the ceremonial words of acceptance. But what was the "substance" lacking here and present in the proposed marriage of the nobleman from Exeter?

In 1232, the compilation of the *Decretals* under Ugolino de' Conti, Gregory IX, further complicated the law. Alexander III's answer to Exeter became the decretal *Commissum*; Innocent III's decision on the man not named John became the decretal *Tua nos*; both were placed in the first title of Book IV under the heading "Betrothals and Marriages." In title five, "Attached Conditions," the compilers considered the variation of marriage by agreement between the spouses. To what degree was the institution susceptible to contractual modification? A response to this question required consensus on the substance of marital consent; and this consensus new legislation, *Si conditiones*, imposed. It ran as follows:

> If conditions are attached against the substance of marriage — for example, if one says to the other, "I contract with you if you will avoid the generation of offspring, or until I find another richer in honor or in resources, or if you will give yourself to commit adultery for money" — the matrimonial contract, albeit favored, lacks effect; although other conditions attached in marriage, if they are shameful or will be impossible, should, because of the favor for marriage, be regarded as not added. (X.4.5.7)

Unlike most decretals, *Si conditiones* was not a judgment on a particular set of circumstances, but a broad rule to cover a subject, to fill a gap. Its principal draftsman was presumably the collection's editor-in-chief, the octogenarian Pope's secretary, the future patron saint of canonists, Raimundo of Peñafort. He incorporated the theory developed by Saint Augustine in the fourth century, and reaffirmed in the twelfth-century revival of Augustine, that there were three "goods" or values justifying marriage: offspring, indissolubility, fidelity.[9] The awkward professorial technique of stringing three hypotheticals together — resulting in a canon reading like an American Law Institute "Illustration" — followed Augustine with academic comprehensiveness. As there were three goods constituting marriage, the contractual denial of any one of them negated the substance of marriage. To this extent, at any rate, private agreement would not be permitted to alter the orthodox structure of marriage. Negatively, the elements which must be present in marital consent were defined.

When *Si conditiones* was compared with Alexander III's answer to Bartholomew, *Commissum*, the difficulty created by Raimundo appeared. If exclusion of procreation nullified a marriage contract, how could the noble of Exeter have entered a true marriage intending to exclude intercourse and enter religion? More fundamentally, how could the Virgin Mary have validly married Joseph if she had vowed to maintain her virginity? The model of marriage set up by *Si conditiones* in obedience to the dominant Augustinian theory of marriage conflicted with the model of marriage derived from a central theme of Marian theology. The canons were symptoms of a basic theological division — on the one hand, the complex Augustinian synthesis of teaching on sin, concupiscence, and sexual intercourse, which justified marriage by positing procreation as its principal end; on the other, the complex synthesis of symbols centered in the exemplary virginity of the mother of God. Both lines of thought were so entrenched in theological tradition, in popular piety, in institutional practice that neither could be sacrificed to the other. Nor was there need to sacrifice either if it were recognized that in Christendom there were two types or classes of marriage, virginal and procreative, neither reducible to the other.

Open recognition of two distinct forms of marriage, however, was not made. Canonists and theologians alike struggled to elaborate a single theory of Christian marriage, and ecclesiastical practice maintained a single model. The reasons for this response may be surmised. Theorists preferred simplicity to multiplicity; practical men preferred clarity to complexity: these preferences converged to support a unitary vision of marriage. Simplicity seemed essential for the structure of an institution designed for the mass of Christians. Variability in design endangered stability which simplicity assured. If one variation of the standard form was permitted, others might occur. The case of the virginal marriage was, moreover, so special, indeed perhaps so hypothetical, that no pressure required its accommodation as a distinct institution; a single form met the needs of virtually everyone, let theologians speculate as they might on the possibility of virginal matings. Considerations such as these, however unarticulated, must account for the general unwillingness to declare bluntly that there were two kinds of consent and consequently two kinds of marriage.

Virginal marriage not only deviated from orthodox Augustinianism by excluding procreation. By virtue of the decretal law established by Alexander III and typified by *Commissum*, the first mutation carried with it a second. Virginal marriage was inherently dissoluble. Its structure gave to either spouse an open option to end the marriage by religious profession. Nonrecognition of virginal marriage as a separate type permitted the ignoring or obscuring of this second characteristic, of this possibility of entering a valid Christian union with the permanent right of disaffirming the union by unilateral decision. The impairment of the ideal of indissolubility that such a definite class of marriages might effect was a further reason for maintaining the fiction that marriage always had the same three essential components.

At the level of the judicial order, conflict between *Si conditiones* and *Commissum* could be avoided. *Si conditiones* had been designed to protect the public form of marriage from public alteration: its thrust was institutional. The elimination of procreation as a goal of marriage by the contemporary Cathar Church was a target within the decretal's range; trial marriage in Croatia was soon found also to fall within its compass.[10] But marriages which were virginal by private intention or by vow constituted no threat to the institutional structure. They did not have to be brought within the decretal's terms; as a matter of technical legal distinction, since such intentions were not agreements, they were not touched at all. Saint Raimundo, at least, saw no incongruity in accepting *Commissum* and adding *Si conditiones* to the law.

Suppose, however, one looked not only at *Si conditiones*, but at Innocent III's contribution to the problem, *Tua nos*. This decision went beyond a consideration of legal contractual variations of marriage to a case where the hidden intention of the bridegroom had negated the substance of consent. If that substance, as *Si conditiones* implied, involved the good of offspring, must not every virginal marriage be fraudulent and null for lack of substance and of form? At a technical level *Si conditiones* might be reconcilable with *Commissum* and the marriage of Mary; it was irreconcilable with them if its teaching were used to define the content of internal consent, and if internal consent were crucial as Innocent III had determined in *Tua nos*.

The canonists moved to suppress one element of the problem — that most dangerous to the upholding of marriage as a judicial institution — the use of internal intention as judicially controlling. As marriage was a religious act and the conferring of a sacrament, the mental state of the participant was important; but, as marriage was a social form, it seemed foolish, even self-contradictory, to let internal intent be decisive. In its general approach to marriage, decretal law took the way of ordinary contract law: the common meaning of what the parties publicly expressed to each other over-rode any private meaning one party might attach to the words in his mind, *Ex literis*, X.4.1.7. Should not this same rule control *Tua nos?* Innocent III himself had suggested this possibility even as he accepted the bishop's finding of lack of intent and consent. "We do not see," he wrote, "how you ascertained this." The Pope's puzzlement suggested to the canonists that in judicial proceedings a claim of fraudulent consent and intent should not be heard. Only in the tribunal of penance, "the internal forum," should what had gone on in the mind be recognized. By the end of the thirteenth century this interpretation of the teaching of *Tua nos* was stand-ard.[11] The bifurcation ignored the actual result in the case; it created the potential problem of a man being unmarried according to his conscience and married according to the courts of the Church; but it saved the public judicial order. Marriages could not be under-mined in court by a spouse contending that he had not meant in his heart what he had said with his mouth.

Tua nos was not permitted to destroy the judicial order; yet to recognize its force in the forum of conscience was to reinstate the conflict between *Si conditiones* and *Commissum*, Augustinian the-ology and Marian theology, which was avoided at the public, ex-ternal level when internal intent was treated as irrelevant. If off-spring were an object of marital consent, was not every marriage begun with the intent of avoiding intercourse null in the tribunal of conscience? When *Tua nos* was combined with *Si conditiones*, was it not evident that Alexander III in *Commissum* had proposed a fraud, even if no judicial remedy for the fraud was recognized? More fundamentally, at the sacred level of conscience, how could the Augustinian notion of marriage coexist with the Marian theory? The conflict was academic, impalpable, impractical; at an institu-tional level nothing seemed affected by it; but it tormented the theorists. The most influential of theologians, Peter Lombard and Thomas Aquinas, and the acutest of canonists, Tomás Sanchez, tried in vain to resolve the dilemma. The proposed solutions tacitly eliminated the procreative purpose of marriage, or the possibility of intending to enter a virginal marriage, or the necessity of effective internal consent. The failure of the efforts of the most capable analysts to combine successfully all the given elements verified by experiment what inspection of the terms of the problem would have led one to predict: no way could be discovered to reconcile in a single unitary account of marriage the discordant notions.

The most plausible and most influential explanation was that attempted by Sanchez.[12] One may marry, he argued, if one accepts the obligation of having children, even though at the same time one intends to avoid execution of this obligation. His distinction made sense if the public language of matrimonial consent was decisive in creating the contract. Then a person could be said to intend to accept the obligation by uttering the appropriate words, and his private intent not to carry out his obligation could be treated as irrelevant and ineffective to impair the contractual undertaking. In an example urged by Sanchez, a man is held to assume the obligation to tell the truth by taking an oath as a witness. He could not escape being charged with perjury for failure to observe the oath by claiming that he had secretly repudiated his public words. His purely private resolution to lie would be regarded as ineffective to relieve him of the obligation he publicly assumed. His intent not to execute the oath would not have negated the substance of the obligation undertaken. This analysis was convincing when the publicly spoken words were decisive in creating the obligation. If internal consent were decisive in creating a marriage, this approach failed. If what counted was internal assent, it was nonsense to suppose the coexistence of assent with a resolution not to carry out what was accepted by assent.*

* The other principal solutions to the dilemma were these:

(1) Mary's consent was a consent not "of carnal coupling" but "of conjugal society"—a cautious genitive eliminating procreative purpose from her marital consent (Peter Lombard, *Libri IV Sententiarum* [ed. The Fathers of the College of St. Bonaventura, Quarrachi, 1916], 4.26.2). The same opinion was stated more clearly in Pierre de la Palu, O.P., *In quartum librum Sententiarum* (Venice, 1493), 30.21: "I contract with you on the condition that you do not seek the debt" does not destroy the essence of marriage. This view was characterized as a minority view but still "probable" in Sanchez, *De sancto matrimonii sacramento*, 5.10.1, and it was followed by Sanchez himself in his analysis of *Commissum* and and in his analysis at 2.29.20 of "the marriage of the Blessed Virgin."

(2) "If a woman says to a man, 'I consent to you in order that you do not know me,' there is no matrimonial consent because there is something there against the substance of the said consent," Thomas Aquinas, *In libros Sententiarum Petri Lombardi*, Vol. II² of *Opera omnia* (Parma, 1852–1873), 4.28.1.4, Reply to the Third Objection. This opinion eliminated the possibility of a virginal marriage if the intention was put in the form of an "express condition." While Thomas

Verbal reconciliations had to content the theorists; the underlying difficulties did not disconcert practical decisionmakers. Virginal marriages must have been rare; their validity was not litigated; there was no need to translate into action the tangle which teased the theorists. Yet powerful theological traditions maintained in existence all the elements of the problem. The possibility remained that an actual case could force a confronting of the conflict, a clear suppression of an essential theological component, or a deliberate recognition that marriage itself had more than one shape and function.

Almost six hundred years after the *Decretals* had been definitively issued as the law of the universal Church, no case had come before the Curia to pose the problem — at least in 1721 no precedents could be found juxtaposing the conflicting laws and deciding between them.* Yet the texts of the *Decretals*, even when ignored for centuries, were not dead. As the Bible was the ultimate Christian book, to whose pages fresh appeal was always possible, so the *Corpus iuris canonici*, in its more limited sphere, was a book always alive to each new generation of canonists; recourse to it was also always open. In the eighteenth century, *Si conditiones*, *Tua nos*, and *Commissum* came to life through the acts of a Portuguese couple, the skill of a Roman advocate, the scholarship of a famous canonist, and the judgment of a central committee of the Curia.

Aquinas denied that Mary had posited such an express condition (*ibid.,* 4.30.2.1, Reply to the Second Objection), he also taught that Mary had vowed to remain a virgin (*ibid.,* 4.28.14). He did not explain the difference between an explicit condition and an explicit vow.

A third solution, avoiding a choice, was given in the mature work of Thomas Aquinas, *Summa theologica* (Leonine ed., Rome, 1950), III, Q. 29, art. 2: Mary and Joseph "each consented to conjugal coupling, but not to carnal coupling save under the condition 'if it should please God.'" The ambiguity of the phrase "if it shall please God" concealed the problem: if it were used as in the expression "I shall go, God willing," as an expression of one's own intent to do an act unless prevented, then there was effective consent to intercourse overriding the postulated vow of virginity; if it were used to suspend intercourse unless a specific contingency occurred, then there was incomplete consent to intercourse. If either choice were made, one element of the problem disappeared; the perfect ambiguity of the language preserved all the elements.

* *Si conditiones* had been applied by the Inquisition in reference to marriages where a condition against indissolubility was found to be part of the marriage ceremony; that is, where the bridegroom promised to keep the bride as long as she remained faithful, *Bosnia, December 2, 1680* (Calvinist marriages in Transylvania), and *Capuchin Missionaries, July 23, 1698* (marriages of pagans or Mohammedans); Pietro Gasparri, ed., *Codicis iuris canonici fontes* (Rome: Vatican Polygot Press, 1955), IV, 35, 40.

In the interaction of these persons the viability of the Marian mutation of marriage was measured.

THE MARRIAGE OF LUIS QUIFEL BARBERINI AND JOANNA AGNETE DE ALMEIDA Y CARNIDE

On May 6, 1718, this document was signed by a young single
woman of Lisbon:

> While Signor Luis Quifel Barberini owes nothing to my honor, yet
> as the reputation of my honor has been harmed by the ease with which
> my parents led him to my house, and by the continuation of the prac-
> tice, I have prayed the said gentleman to cover this discredit of mine
> by receiving me for his wife, and I promise that, if this is done, within
> fifteen days, I will select a convent and at the end of the year forthwith
> profess the state of a religious, either in that convent of the Rosa or in
> any other, and never use the marriage nor consummate it, to which
> end I now immediately renounce all right which I can have to the
> person of the said gentleman. I do this of my own very free will with-
> out any violence. And if I fail any one of these conditions whatsoever,
> I do not doubt that the said marriage is and is judged as if it had never
> been made, to which now I give my free and constant consent.[13]

What necessity had led a young girl to subscribe to this lugubri-
ous legal document carefully drafted by a Lisbon lawyer? Who
were the parents who had permitted such dishonor? Who was the
gentleman who would cover her dishonor on these precise terms?

The girl, Joanna Agnete de Almeida y Carnide, was an orphan;
that is, her father, Bernardo da Costa, was dead; and her mother,
Isabella de Favia Carnide, of an old noble family, had stepped from
the ranks of the nobility by first marrying Bernardo, a fish-dealer's
son who "worked with his hands," then, widowed, by marrying a
second commoner, Vicente Francisco, who was not only ignoble
but poor. Joanna lived with her mother and stepfather, and was not
a promising match for a gentleman.[14]

Luis Quifel Barberini was a gentleman of distinction, the third
son of Bartolomeo Quifel Barberini, whose father had migrated to
Portugal from Antwerp about 1650. Connected by collaterals to
the Barberini who had produced Urban VIII, the family had a name
to which the papal eminence gave luster, and settling in Portugal,

its members prospered financially and were accepted as Lusitanian nobility.[15] Luis, the grandson of the successful immigrants, became a prosperous lawyer in Lisbon, and in time a Judge of the Royal Court of Appeals and a Senator in the Senate of West Lisbon. In 1718 he was over forty and a bachelor when he undertook to cover the discredit of Joanna.[16]

Senator Barberini did not set out on this task in any professional capacity, but whether love or altruism or perversity or sheer bad luck and stupidity brought him to it is not easy to determine. To begin with, he was the creditor of Vicente Francisco, in the amount of 5,500 cruzeiros.[17] How and why he had loaned this sum is not explained by the records, but if the fact of creditorship is taken as the starting point of his relation with his debtor's stepdaughter, one theory of his bizarre role may be developed. As a creditor, he came to visit Vicente Francisco's home. As a visitor, he met Joanna. Her mother saw an opportunity which adroit management could exploit. She encouraged his visits, and they gave him time to know her daughter. In the Lisbon of 1718, an unmarried girl could be compromised by attentive courtship. Joanna's mother and stepfather created a situation in which Senator Barberini appeared as a suitor; then they set in motion a plan whereby to repair the wrong he had done the girl's reputation he would feel obliged to marry her. Their scheme was commercial in design, and Senator Barberini was their unfortunate and passive dupe. This simple, cynical view of what had happened was later taken by Barberini's counsel in Rome.

What made the Senator susceptible to management? Documentary evidence of his feelings is lacking; but circumstances create inferences, which, if not irresistible, have plausibility. Barberini's position, before he agreed to marry, was secure; he could not have been frightened into marriage by his debtor; he could have callously dismissed the talk of damaged honor. He may have been manipulated by the parents, but he must have had a desire of his own which made him malleable. That desire was surely sexual. Of love for Joanna in the sense of responding to her as a person cherished for herself there is no sign. Of marital affection in the sense of wanting her as a spouse for life there is little indication. What is manifest toward her is ambivalent emotion, a pity controlled by calculation and fed from a sexual source. When finally, long after the curious creditor's courtship, long after the marriage, there was intercourse between them in the midst of legal warfare, it was a sudden satisfaction of desires which had been banked but smouldered. The bitter passion which charged their later behavior toward each other had not a commercial but a sexual shape.

Prudence and sexual attraction, mixed in equal parts with pity, determined the agreement to marry and the form which that agreement took. For various reasons Barberini did not want to marry Joanna in the conventional sense. Her mother said she had an ample dowry, but she brought with her the association with Vicente Francisco. She had brothers who served the King at court as befitted those belonging to a great family, but she brought with her the tarnished nobility of her mother. For a judge of senatorial rank and gravity from a family still aware of its alien origins, she was not an attractive catch. Barberini had two older brothers, but one was too old and sick to marry, the other was simply unfit. The family line depended on Luis and he would have to do better than Joanna. If she spoke to him, if she engaged his interest, if he continued to visit, marriage was not the end he could have had in view.

Then he was confronted with a plea: "Rescue me." She was, Joanna wrote, in danger of her life in her stepfather's house (between the lines, because of him). All she wanted was "her salvation" (on earth or in heaven?) and "her honor" (on earth). She implored his aid, "by the most holy Virgin and the wounds of Christ." By these sacred invocations she asked for delivery from "this hell." The rescue could be made without further responsibility. Once rescued, she wrote, "I will immediately become a nun." [18]

Joanna's love letters were five in all. Tender, piteous, demanding, they could never have found their mark if the Senator had not already been in some sense her captive. Caught in a haze of emotion and tenderness, he pondered the alternatives. He accepted the idea that Joanna was compromised. Conscience or convention made him believe that what had conversationally passed between them had created expectations in her and in others. He also accepted as believable her claim to be in danger. Her stepfather he must have come to regard as surly, cruel, untrustworthy. He had no desire to negotiate a settlement with him. What he could do with only the cost of a small dowry was to arrange for Joanna to enter a convent or to marry someone else. His resources were sufficient to provide the money, and his status such that he could prevent her stepfather from interfering. As Joanna had to be rescued, was not the convent or marriage the sensible solution?

Senator Barberini elected to combine the alternatives. The combination may have been suggested to him by a priest who now played a great part in the arrangements, Father Francisco Marochim. Like Didier Cheminot, in the case of Charles and Nicole, Father Marochim was the indispensable intermediary between the parties and their indispensable counselor on morality. A Spaniard, of the order of Our Lady of Ransom, founded to rescue Christian slaves of the Moors, Marochim was Joanna's confessor, and, knowing of her trouble, he worked to effect her delivery from danger. Her ally, he became Senator Barberini's adviser.

The plan agreed to with Marochim was presented by the priest to a lawyer, Francisco Figuiero de Goes, as follows. He had a friend who had had a relationship with a girl, but his friend would not marry her because she was of "an inferior sphere." His friend would marry the girl, however, if she agreed to become a nun. Could Figuiero de Goes draft a contract which would make such an agreement legally binding? Contracts of this kind could not be found in form books, so the lawyer said that he would need time to prepare an appropriate document. Father Marochim pressed, and Figuiero de Goes wrote out a draft.[19]

The solution now had a legal form and clerical approbation, but why did Barberini elect to adopt it? Why was he willing to believe Joanna could become a nun only if she were first properly married? Why was he willing to be the person to carry out the ceremony of marriage with her? Barberini yielded to Joanna's plea and to his feelings for her. She wrote that she would only be happy if she married him before she entered religion. Her touching stubbornness seemed credible. As an honorable, moral, religious man he could not have her outside of marriage, and he wanted to assure her honor. As a royal judge he could not have her in marriage, and, if he could not have her, he wanted to assure that she would belong to no one else. In the solution taking shape he salved his jealousy, he punished her for attracting him, and he punished himself for being attracted. In the history of his older brother was there not something which indicated a malaise he may have shared? Was not this kind of sublimated marriage exactly suited to his needs? Did he not achieve all ends but the suppressed sexual goal, and do so with a minimum of risk? Faced with Joanna's prayers, counseled by Father Marochim, Senator Barberini made a vow to the Virgin Mary: he would rescue Joanna, he would assure her honor, he would marry her as she asked.[20]

A final reason for the arrangement existed. It was given in Barberini's will, executed in Madrid in 1722 when the Senator believed himself on the point of death, and introduced in evidence when the validity of the marriage was tried in Rome. It is possible to suspect that the will was altered to introduce into the case a new, unmentioned, and unmentionable contention which would work upon the judges' minds. If so, the fantasy concocted has a psychological interest in itself. More probably, the will was genuine, and revealed what Barberini could not make public in Lisbon and would have written only in the desperation of dying. He could never marry Joanna validly, his will declared, because he was barred by "the impediment of consanguinity in the first degree." This declaration was not meant literally — he was not confessing that he was Joanna's father — but, as his Roman counsel understood him, he was admitting a relationship in the first degree of affinity to her: he had been, in fact, her mother's lover.[21]

If this testamentary admission is taken as the truth, the motives of many acts may be guessed: why Barberini should have been lending money to Vicente Francisco whom he loathed but who was married to his paramour; why he should have visited the house often; why a current of fascination and repulsion should pass between him and Joanna. That Vicente Francisco, knowing or not knowing of the relation, should try to trap him; that Joanna, unknowing of the relation, should come to appeal to him; that he should convert sexual desire into sado-masochistic repression, all cohere with the fundamental fact that he once had had and lost her mother.

The plan hatched, it was necessary to obtain the cooperation of Joanna's parish priest, so that the requirements of the Council of Trent would be fulfilled. The priest, Antonio Rodriguez, was uncooperative. Marochim first asked him to obtain a dispensation from the Tridentine requirement that the banns be read at three Sunday masses; publicity would have subverted the scheme whereby Joanna's reputation was to be mended in a very private way. Father Rodriguez told Father Marochim to get the dispensation himself.

Two days later the Senator came in person and explained how the marriage must be celebrated in secret and on the condition that the bride enter a convent. Rodriguez asked why, if the object was to restore the girl's reputation, the marriage was to be secret. He also gave his opinion that a marriage on such a condition would be invalid. Barberini assured him that he had consulted two Jesuits, who had advised that the plan was legitimate. The parish priest observed that in such matters he preferred to consult God first, then men of letters.[22]

The hierarchy of values of Father Rodriguez forced Senator Barberini to enlarge and to perfect his plan. He had already enlisted another ecclesiastical adviser besides Marochim: Father Manuel de Oliveira, a Portuguese Jesuit much esteemed for learning and devoutness, who was later the tutor of the King's daughter, Maria Barbara.[23] In securing this priest as an active ally, Barberini seemed to assure himself of a high order of spiritual and political counsel. The convent of Santa Rosa was the site of relics associated with recent miracles, on whose account, three years before, the Senate of Lisbon had memorialized the Pope as to "the great devotion which this court and city of Lisbon have to the glorious virgin Santa Rosa of Viterbo."[24] Saint, relics, and fame made Santa Rosa seem the appropriate place to deposit Joanna. But before approaching the convent, arrangements were made with higher authorities. As emissary of the Senator, Marochim went to Vincenzo Bichi, the papal Nuncio to Portugal, and obtained from him a rescript permitting Joanna to enter Santa Rosa and to remain there without taking the habit.[25] How much Bichi was told of the reason for this request is not clear, but it seems unlikely that Marochim did not let him know as much as he had told the lawyer Figuiero de Goes. The rescript was the first step in moving Joanna out of her home and into marriage and the convent. Armed with the Nuncio's permission, Fathers Marochim and Oliveira approached a civil justice, Antonio de Basta Pereira, and asked for a writ authorizing them to take Joanna from her home and lodge her in Santa Rosa.[26] The writ, of a kind used to prevent parents from interfering with their daughters' freedom to enter religion, was promptly issued. Possessed of documents from Church and State, Marochim persuaded the prioress of Santa Rosa to let Joanna reside at the convent, and to the convent she was moved.

Petition for a dispensation to marry at the monastery was soon made to Tomas de Almeida, the Patriarch of West Lisbon. The troublesome parish priest was thereby circumvented, for the requirements of Trent were satisfied by the presence of the bishop or his delegate; and the most important ecclesiastical figure in the kingdom was brought into the scheme. A request to marry in a monastery was scarcely a routine request, and when the beneficiary of the dispensation was a royal judge, it might be supposed that an energetic ecclesiastic of Almeida's stature would be personally informed of the matter by his chancery. His Vicar-General, João Cardoso Castello, however, handled the matter. A graduate in canon law from Coimbra, a priest of twenty years' standing, and Vicar-General for over a year, Cardoso must have asked for some explanation of the choice of Santa Rosa as the site for a wedding and been satisfied by the answer. He signed the permission to marry at the convent, he dispensed from the banns, and he chose as the official witness of the wedding the pastor of the fashionable church of São Lourenço where Almeida himself had once been pastor.[27]

With Oliveira, Bichi, Almeida, the elite of the Church in Portugal, all in some fashion approving his plan, Senator Barberini seemed proof against misadventure. As a final assurance he now had Joanna sign the document which counsel had prepared and which has been set out in full above. By its terms she renounced the right to intercourse and bound herself to make a religious profession. In effect, she created a virginal marriage which would last a year and then would be dissolved in accordance with the decretal law established by Alexander III; Barberini surrendered his own freedom for the year during which she would be a novice before solemnly professing. In the form of an alternative conditional, Joanna agreed that the marriage was null if the promises were not kept. In effect, she agreed that her virginal marriage could be condemned by Augustinian criteria. The contract had, as it were, two locks, keeping Barberini from lifelong marriage whatever happened. Three further provisions reflected a lawyer's effort to cover all contingencies — a promise to enter some other convent in the event that Santa Rosa rejected her after her novitiate; a denial that coercion had been used upon her; an admission that she had no claim upon the Senator's honor. If legal formulas added to friends in high place could guarantee immunity, Barberini was protected.

Joanna signed the paper on May 6. The evening of that day Barberini enlisted two more priests to act as the witnesses required by Trent in addition to the officiating priest. The recruitment of these men, Fathers Collares and Gomez, drawn from the parish of São Cristovam, caused more difficulty, for at least one of them had doubts about the validity of the marriage. Barberini could have used servants as the witnesses, or he could have used Oliveira and Marochim. Out of a superabundance of caution, he must have wanted two persons who had not been involved with him before, who could testify to the condition on which he married, and he must have wanted these persons to be priests because of the regard for their credibility in ecclesiastical proceedings. Hence, he went to the trouble of finding the men from São Cristovam, explaining the terms of the arrangement to them, and overcoming their scruples. They came to understand the paradox of a marriage on the verge of entry into religion. "The lady is spirited," the pastor of São Lourenço explained to them. "She wants to enter religion with honor." [28]

On May 7, 1718, at ten o'clock in the morning at the grill of the monastery of Santa Rosa, Joanna Agnete de Almeida y Carnide was joined in marriage to Luis Quifel Barberini. The pastor of São Lorenço, the delegate of the Patriarch of West Lisbon, officiated, and Fathers Collares and Gomez were witnesses.[29] No reception followed the ceremony. Senator Barberini left immediately. Joanna remained in the cloister. Father Collares congratulated her on her entrance into religious life. Joanna did not reply.[30]

On May 14, 1718, Joanna Agnete de Almeida filed a petition before the Vicar-General of the Patriarch. She deposed that she was the lawful wife of Luis Quifel Barberini and that he was not living with her. She sought "the restoration of her conjugal rights." She prayed that her husband be compelled, under pain of excommunication, "to come within three days to live with your petitioner." Five days later Senator Barberini was formally notified that he was a defendant.[31]

At that instant Barberini knew that he had been deceived by Joanna, by Father Marochim, by Vicente Francisco, by Isabella, by all of them. They had let him enter a marriage which was a formality, a courtesy, a play, and they were now making it the most serious reality in his life. Barberini himself had entertained the idea of a proceeding before the Patriarch to establish his freedom to wed if Joanna failed to keep her agreement; his feelings for Joanna or her mother could not have been so strong that he was ready to renounce forever the possibility of another match; and he knew that his marriage to Joanna, officially recorded at the office of the Patriarchate, would bar him if Joanna did not make profession of religion. But if he realized that sometime a legal process might be necessary, if he had prepared the ground for that process by document and witnesses, in no conscious and acknowledged thought had he contemplated that twelve days after the wedding he would be in court resisting the claim of Joanna to be treated as his bride.

The process in the court of the Patriarchate moved with amazing dispatch. Under other circumstances, the Senator might have been grateful for this industry. But, when he was not psychologically prepared, when Joanna was prepared both legally and psychologically, all this hurry seemed contrived. Joanna named two proctors to represent her on May 16. On the same day the depositions of the formal witnesses to the wedding were taken. On June 21 the priests were examined by Cardoso, the Vicar-General who had licensed the wedding. On July 18 he gave judgment on its validity.

Coercion to marry, his opinion began, had not been shown — how familiar the claim of coercion must have been in ecclesiastical suits! Cardoso moved on to the heart of the case: the effect of the agreement signed by Joanna. In the language of *Si conditiones* it was an "attached condition" and a condition which was "shameful" and "contrary to the substance of marriage." These conclusions, however, did not move him to apply *Si conditiones* and pronounce the union null. His two-page opinion followed a different track: one ought to make every interpretation excluding sin; therefore, one ought to assume that the will of making this condition did not continue to the moment where consent was given. In fact, the condition had not been repeated at the time of the ceremony at the convent grill; in the face of the Church pure and unconditional consent had been given. The interior intention which Joanna may have had to become a nun could not be recognized in the judicial forum; the canonists' standard commonsensical exclusion of an undeclared state of mind, the commentators' inversion of *Tua nos*, governed the situation; and instead of a recognizable contractual change in the terms of marriage, all Senator Barberini had produced was evidence incompetent to alter the public meaning of the publicly pronounced consent to marry. Refusal to believe that the condition of nonintercourse had lasted to the moment of consent did honor not only to Joanna and the presumption that she had not meant to sin; it did honor to the Senator. He had promised Our Lady to marry Joanna; he should not be supposed "to have paid a real debt and promise to the Virgin Mary with a feigned satisfaction." Cardoso concluded that the condition alleged had not been attached to the consent given. The marriage was valid.[33]

The process used to this point had been the procedure described as "summary," designed to handle simple issues where the facts were not hard to determine. It was now open to the Patriarch to confirm the judgment or to order a full trial of validity in the "ordinary" way. Barberini did not wait for this decision. He appealed at once to the Nuncio in Lisbon. This move was an announcement that he had more to hope for from the papal representative than from his compatriots.

In giving up on Almeida, Barberini could be regarded as giving up on the King. Although he was a canonist trained at Coimbra, Almeida had entered the royal service and had become successively Procurator of the Treasury, President of the Ecclesiastical Department and Pro-Chancellor of the Kingdom; he was now Secretary of State. If ever a bishop were identified with his patron, Almeida was identified with João V. His elevation to the patriarchate had been both a tribute to his service and a testimony to the King's concern for the dignity of his kingdom. Having responded to Clement XI's plea to help the Venetians against the Turks and thereby acquired a claim to conspicuous if not costly reward in Rome, the King had asked the Pope to grant Portugal, like Venice, the extraordinary distinction of a patriarch. Clement XI had raised the royal chapel of São Tomé to patriarchal status, assigned to it some 200,000 souls in the newly created archdiocese of West Lisbon, and appointed Almeida, the King's choice, as Patriarch. Only two years old, the patriarchate still pleased João V by the European sensation it had caused and the splendor of its connotations: next to the Pope himself, who was higher than a Patriarch? And this Patriarch was the King's servant, friend, and selection. When Barberini had obtained his permission for the wedding at the grill of Santa Rosa, he had seemed to secure the approval of both miter and crown. To turn from Almeida after sampling his court was to risk being regarded as disrespectful to both.[34]

What did Barberini gain by going to Bichi? Both Almeida and Bichi were trained lawyers; either might have been expected to appreciate the precautions he had taken and to give due weight to the letter of his contract with Joanna. Both were of noble birth; either would have understood his qualms about marrying Joanna indissolubly. There was no obvious advantage in the Nuncio's court in terms of competence or social rapport. Barberini, however, may have assumed that the Patriarch would stand behind his Vicar-general, and wanted no more of Cardoso's approach to his predicament. Conceivably, he knew of some distant blood tie between Joanna's relatives who were Almeidas, and the Patriarch, even though the latter, second son of the Count of Avintes and Marie Antoinette de Borbón, was far above Joanna's circle. But the family connection he certainly counted on with the Nuncio was his own tie to the Barberini. He drew Bichi's attention forcefully to the prominence of his name, he reminded him of the respect due even the collaterals of a papal family, he insisted on his genealogical privileges.[35]

Vincenzo Bichi embodied the Roman Curia in Lisbon and seemed to be, if anyone in Lisbon could be, independent of the Crown. He was a career man from a Sienese ecclesiastical family — a nephew of Cardinal Carlo Bichi of the Curia and a collateral of Celio Bichi, auditor of the Rota in the time of Duke Charles' case; a graduate in canon law from the Sapienza; a former Deputy Nuncio to the Swiss; the occupant for nine difficult years of the important and demanding nunciature in Portugal.[36] If the title bestowed upon him by Rome in sending him to Portugal — Archbishop of Laodicea — had scriptural associations which could make it seem comic or ironic, the Curia must have come to value his sound moderation. He was now fifty-one years old, an envoy of experience, with a certain weight and position of his own; he could reasonably expect recognition of his services by still higher office in the Curia. If anyone could be counted on to apply impartially the law of the *Decretals* and respect the dignity of a Barberini, he seemed to be the man; and the Senator could turn to him with the consciousness that he at least had no reason to truckle to the King's appointee.

Bichi's auditor, Aloisio Bernabo, another Italian, moved as

swiftly as his counterpart in the patriarchate. Summarily, on October 14, 1718, he handed down a one-page opinion and a ruling. "Many very grave doctors" could be cited to support the invalidity of such a marriage as Senator Barberini had entered. Manifestly its validity could not be determined by the summary process used in the patriarchate. The sentence of the Vicar-General was accordingly revoked. The parties were to be heard in the ordinary way on two questions: Was the marriage valid? If it were valid, could Joanna still be compelled to carry out her agreement to enter religion? Barberini was invited to pursue his case.[37]

By now the affair was notorious in Lisbon, and the King himself became a factor to be reckoned with. João V's own history, psychology, pastimes, and even physiognomy made him regard this marriage of a royal judge gravely.[38] He was the son of Pedro II who had come to power in a palace coup which had ousted Pedro's older brother and given Pedro that brother's wife as his own after a timely annulment on the ground of impotence had dissolved his brother's marriage. With these bold deeds in his recent family past João had assumed kingly responsibility in 1707, at the age of seventeen, with a determination to maintain royal respectability. Half-German, half-Portuguese, he combined compulsiveness with passion. Educated by Jesuit tutors, he was compulsively and passionately devout. Diminutive in stature, he insisted on respect. If to modern eyes his religiousness appears one part superstition and one part hypocrisy, he was unflagging in his orthodoxy and impeccable in his sentiments. For religion, as for royalty, there could only be immense respect; and Senator Barberini's escapade endangered both; annulments were not to be the games of courtiers.

All of João's own zeal for God, for public religion, for form, coexisted, moreover, with a fierce sexual appetite. His loves were legendary, and, even if all the legends are not equally credible, in 1719 he was indubitably engaged in a love affair with Mother Paula Teresa da Silva of the monastery of Odivelas. A child was born from their union in 1721. The guilt of this affair with a real nun, preying on a consciousness trained to think in categories of sin — the sins in which he personally was engaged were sacrilege and adultery — was a factor which might well have exacerbated his feelings toward Senator Barberini. The King was only twenty-nine in 1719. He still felt the heat of youth; he would repent in time;

meanwhile he was not attempting to deny the procreative risks of his relation. The Senator was over forty, an old man who should be setting an example, and instead he was discovered attempting to conceal a disgraceful liaison by turning a real wife into a pseudo-nun. The Senator's marriage, his effort to deny it, his inept invocation of the law of annulment, had made him a laughingstock; far worse, he had stained the image which João V cultivated of his court. The respect due the King and religion had been wanting. João V now deprived Barberini of his judgeship and his senatorial rank: neither were compatible in the royal eyes with his unworthy marriage.[39]

This convincing evidence of royal displeasure made Barberini doubt whether Bichi would hold firm. Rome itself seemed a surer haven. He addressed a petition to the Sacred Congregation of the Council asking for an annulment. Meanwhile he delayed the proceedings in Portugal.[40]

The Senator was right to doubt Bichi if the Nuncio's attitude may be read between the lines in a report from him to the cardinals of the Congregation when they asked for more information on the case. Bichi was skeptical of the alleged relation to the Roman Barberini: "the truth of this will shine more clearly in Rome," he observed sagely. The reputation of the Portuguese Barberini had always been good; but "good reputation," he added drily, "now is related to good property."[41] He said nothing to encourage the Congregation to remove the case from his jurisdiction, and the Congregation did not intervene further.

Formal trial proceeded before two Portuguese judges-delegate, designated by the Nuncio, Luis de Silva da Pedrozo and Aleixo Rodriguez Vilas de Boas. The ecclesiastical pace slowed, but not to the Roman walk. Barely one year after the appeal, on August 11, 1719, their judgment was given. The hope raised by Bernabo's preliminary holding was dashed. The auditors of the Nuncio stood with the auditor of the Patriarch in finding the marriage good. Once again, *Si conditiones*, the decretal which Barberini had assumed would govern any litigation, was found inapposite. The controlling law was that of *Tua nos* — not the decision in *Tua nos* but the commentators' interpretation of it which had put considerations of civil policy above theological intuition. The Nuncio's auditors actually cited as definitive the standard Gloss, composed by

Joannes Andreas, that star of the University of Bologna, which rewrote the canon. Suppose, this university teacher had said, a man protests before others that he is about to do something without the intention of marrying, and then says to a woman, "I consent to you." In that extreme case, even, a marriage had been made — the "common understanding of the words" was decisive. If the man contended that he had persevered in his intent not to marry, even while uttering the language of marital consent, why, he should not be believed: "interpretation ought to be against the one practicing deception." [42] Institutional concern for social stability and justice triumphed over theological concern for personal commitment. The judges-delegate found *Tua nos*, as glossed, admirably suited to Barberini's case. There was no credible evidence that the condition he attached had "entered the act of marriage." Whatever he had said before the ceremony at the grill, at the wedding itself he had publicly consented without conditions to take Joanna as his wife. In two distinct but harmonious opinions the auditors confirmed the decision of the Vicar-General for validity. [43]

Barberini's own feelings after the judgment of the nunciature may be imagined, and probably there was color to the contention laid before a criminal court that he was plotting against Joanna's life. She was back with Vicente Francisco and now sought to protect herself not from her stepfather but from her husband. On September 16, 1719, a month after the second ecclesiastical verdict, the criminal praetor enjoined Barberini from molesting Joanna or her family and informed him that he would be held accountable if any harm came to her. He was also ordered not to speak, as he had spoken, "words unbefitting her reputation." [44]

Within a year and a half Barberini had learned a lesson: no one in power in Portugal — royal or papal, ecclesiastical or lay — was going to help him escape from the trap he had sprung on himself. Almeida and Bichi might have known of his plan when he had embarked upon it, neither was ready to admit that he had connived in a mock marriage. The King and Bichi had once had differences. Now the King's minister and the Nuncio stood together, and Barberini may have felt that he had been passed from Pilate to Herod. The consequences of his grave offense were evident everywhere. The orthodoxy of the scheme itself came into question. The Inquisition, an ecclesiastical adjunct of royal authority, took Father

Marochim into custody and interrogated him on his part in the arrangements. He spent four months as the Inquisition's prisoner, emerged, so the Inquisitors reported, "gravely penitent," and vanished.[45] Barberini may have taken a morose pleasure in his late adviser's plight, but the intimation that his plan had aspects of heresy to it must have had a chilling effect on his weakened spirit. Rome was the only refuge left, and to Rome, Barberini appealed from Bichi's judgment. Seven months after the date of decision in the nunciature, his appeal was on the docket of the Sacred Congregation of the Council for action on March 16, 1720.

The case as it came to the Council, summarized by its Secretary, presented the key question: "Did *Si conditiones* apply?" [46] In favor of its application was "the whole" of Sanchez on "Conditioned Consent." Against application was the example of Mary and Joseph. If this example controlled, the Secretary suggested, *Si conditiones* should be read as applying only to the avoiding of children by illicit means; to avoid offspring by continence would be licit, and Barberini's marriage would be valid. Alternatively, an analysis might be made in terms of ownership and use, concepts borrowed from long service in the arguments on usury. Transfer of one's body to one's spouse was essential to marriage; but to transfer the ownership and reserve the right to use it were not inconsistent. Joanna, therefore, married validly though intending to remain a virgin. On the other hand, in terms of these concepts it could be argued that neither use nor ownership had been transferred, and the marriage was invalid. The Secretary's memorandum was so evenly balanced in terms of law that the Congregation could not help realizing that choice would be difficult. Faced with the classic dilemma of choosing between Augustinian and Marian marriage, the Congregation exhibited the caution for which it was celebrated and gave the interim judgment most characteristic of its processes: "Delay." "Delay," its official decision ran, "and let the parish priest, both spouses, and the witnesses of the wedding be examined formally to the extent that they have not been examined formally." [47]

Months were certain to elapse before the Congregation's order was executed. Yet Barberini could believe that within the year his case would be decided. In a kingdom so devoted to the Holy See as Portugal there could be no difficulty in Bichi carrying out the requirement of further formal interrogations. But a new cause of delay intruded beyond the intent of the Congregation of the Council, beyond the expectations of Barberini — a cause of delay so beyond calculation when Barberini had begun his case, so irregular, and so implausible as to appear monstrous. The Curia was deprived of effective representation in Portugal. In a most Catholic country, with a sovereign distinguished for his devotion to the Holy See, the Curia was denied control of its own extension in the country, the Nuncio. The situation arose from a trivial diplomatic contretemps which ballooned to the proportions of a quasi-schism as João V's ego became involved. The incident, entirely unrelated to the business of Senator Barberini, turned on the recall of Bichi.

Not everyone in Rome apparently appreciated Bichi's skill, and his uncle in the Curia had died.[48] João V did not resist his recall as such, but if Bichi was to go home, the King was determined that he return a cardinal. Proper deference to Portugal and to the King himself required it. Precedent — the recognition given two nuncios in the reign of João's father — made it mandatory. Until the Curia agreed to this reasonable and modest request, Bichi should not leave Portugal nor would his replacement be permitted to act in Portugal. The Curia was unwilling to yield: a principle of administration was at stake; the King of Portugal, who had already chosen two cardinals, could not compel the Curia to reward a recalled career man with the cardinalate, nor, alternatively, could the King determine who the papal representative would be. The issue was bigger than the personality of any Pope. For almost a decade "the Bichi affair" blocked relations between the devout King and the Holy See. When, years later, the incident long past, Benedict XIV bestowed on João V the title *Fidelissimus*, the double irony may not have been intentional, but it was surely evident to those who recalled the King as husband and as friend of the Pope. In the clash of royal and curial wills, Barberini was an accidental, insignificant, wholly unfortunate casualty.

The Sacred Congregation of the Council did not need Bichi to carry out its order of an examination of witnesses in Portugal; an apostolic notary could do this. But it did need the influence of a nuncio if any appeal were made to the secular courts to stop its process. Bichi in early 1719 was still styling himself, in normal curial parlance, as "the most humble, most devoted, most obliged servant of the Most Eminent and Most Reverend Fathers." By the summer of 1720 he was unwilling to do anything for the Fathers which would jeopardize his support by the King. No one else in Portugal was in a position to play his role. The Curia, so deeply at odds with the King over Bichi himself, had no leverage to force the King's hand when his courts entered the case.

Barberini decided to go to Rome in person to press his case; he had nothing to lose in leaving Portugal. But, at this threat of desertion by the man legally established as her husband, Joanna went to the courts of the Crown. On July 9, 1720, she obtained a criminal order forbidding him to leave Lisbon. He uttered new threats against her and the family who had arranged the trap; on September 5, 1720, Joanna obtained a criminal injunction that he "guarantee the life and person of the Lady Joanna, her parents, and her servants." [49]

In the spring of 1721 it appeared that the impasse created by the Bichi affair would be resolved, but in a way which could only be prejudicial to Barberini. Clement XI died, and Michele Angelo Conti was elected Pope as Innocent XIII. Conti, a collateral of Gregory IX, had been Nuncio to Portugal from 1699 to 1707, had known João V when he was an adolescent, and had held the curial designation of "Protector of the Crown of Portugal." Immediately after his election, he set to work to repair the breach and addressed a cordial letter to the King. [50] The Pope's benevolence continued from May 1721 to November of that year, when he granted João V a six-year extension of the Crusade Bull, giving the King formal permission to use for royal purposes certain contributions made to the Church in Portugal. If these propitiary moves, designed to win back the King without giving way on Bichi, had succeeded, the influence of the Portuguese Crown in Rome would have again been great and told against Barberini. They did not succeed because the King was implacable in his demand for the cardinalate for a disobedient nuncio. "Bichi must obey," the Pope declared. [51] As long as this was his position, the Pope could not be the King's friend. The stalemate, although it hurt Barberini in Portugal, was not without its long-run advantage for him in Rome.

In Portugal, Joanna pressed her case before the criminal courts of the Crown and obtained an injunction ordering Barberini "to treat her as his wife," with "that decency with which men of property are accustomed to treat their wives." The judge noted that Barberini had already been commanded to do so "divers times," and warned that if he failed to comply now he would be committed immediately to the Tower.[52] By virtue of this order, Joanna moved into his house. What he had most feared, most fought, most repressed had happened, and Joanna was his. In his testamentary confession, Barberini maintained that even in this extremity he shared neither room nor bed with her, but in Rome his counsel were to argue his case conceding that intercourse had occurred. Joanna became pregnant and then miscarried; her mother attributed the conception to Barberini and the miscarriage to his treatment of her daughter.[53]

Continued compliance with the court's orders was in any event intolerable for Barberini. He could not live yoked in hatred and torment to the woman who had so fatally tricked him, and yet he had not reached the end of his fall. Less than three months after the court's last injunction, he was taken to the Tower of São Vicente de Betelem for its violation. He obtained his release some four months later only by agreeing to place a quantity of money with a court-appointed depositary who would henceforth pay Joanna twenty scudi per month as his wife.[54]

Out of jail, Barberini at last took the road in person to Rome. En route he fell sick in Madrid. For over two years he had been sick with "phlegmish catarrh with excessive pains in the head and dizziness." Now his years of physical and psychological suffering seemed about to bear their final fruit, and he appeared at the verge of death.[55] In October he wrote the will which confessed the canonical incest he was fleeing.

Barberini did die in Spain. He lived and came to Rome and pressed his appeal in the Curia. Stripped of his governmental dignities, a judge become a prisoner, a sick man married to his mistress' daughter, Barberini came in person to Rome to ask the Sacred Congregation of the Council to apply *Si conditiones* and free him of his burden.

BEFORE THE S.C.C.

The Committee

The Sacred Congregation of Cardinals for the Interpretation and Execution of the Council of Trent, to give to the body its official name, or the Congregation of the Council, to use its usual short title, or the S.C.C., to employ the bureaucratic abbreviation for *Sacra Congretatio Concilii* customary in its own records, was set up in the aftermath of Trent and had been in continuous existence for a century and a half.[56] Why did Barberini's counsel select it as their forum rather than the Sacred Roman Rota?

The most important fact about the S.C.C. was that all its voting members were cardinals. That single fact gave it extraordinary standing and authority. Auditors of the Rota were in mid-career. Cardinals were at the apex. However true it might be that an individual cardinal might want to be Pope or even Datary or Secretary of State, however much even a cardinal's influence could rise or fall with shifts of power in the Curia, cardinals had arrived; their careers were made; and if ever disinterested sagacity might be expected from the judgments of man it could be expected from this lofty and secure pinnacle.

The S.C.C. was not a regular court of appeals set above the Rota, but it did have the right to order the Rota to revoke a decision not following its interpretation of the law and in rare instances it exercised the right.[57] To other curial bodies the S.C.C. occasionally deferred in comity or prudence; heresy or a heretic would be referred to the Supreme Congregation of the Inquisition. The Pope, of course, stood apart and above. Except in the most important and controversial cases, however, the S.C.C. judged definitively without papal participation. Within boundaries largely set by themselves, the cardinals of the Congregation of the Council were supreme.

For a case requiring a bold application of ancient and dormant law the S.C.C. was an attractive court, and, its official name to the contrary, the case fell within its jurisdiction. Originally designed to "execute" the laws of Trent — only the Pope could "interpret" them — then specifically authorized to "interpret" Tridentine decrees "pertaining to the reform, discipline, and government of morals and the judgments of the Church" — everything in fact except "dogmatic matters," which were still reserved to the Pope — the S.C.C. had splendidly expanded its scope by simple willingness to take new business.[58] Few issues could not be cast, if the Curia so chose, as questions pertaining to a decree of Trent. As to marriage, the Congregation had begun by ruling on technical questions presented by the banns and witnesses specifically prescribed by Trent. Insensibly its jurisdiction widened to include substantive issues such as coercion affecting consent. Although marriage did not amount to 5 percent of its business — most of the time it dealt with issues of internal ecclesiastical administration — it had a competence and interest in marriage cases. No Pope said that it had overstepped its limits; and in 1720 no one in Rome would have found it incongruous for the body charged with the interpretation of Trent to apply decretals of Innocent III and Gregory IX and judge the validity of a marriage made in Portugal.

Availability and authoritativeness were not the only reasons which attracted Barberini to this forum. Its actual membership was also of importance to his counsel, and not only its membership but its staff and structure. The S.C.C. was a committee — if the latinizing instincts of our forefathers had not foisted "Congregation" as the standard translation of *Congregatio* upon us, "Standing Committee" would be the translation to convey the flavor of the institution. It was a committee with a normal membership of over two dozen cardinals, a regular attendance of six to eighteen, scheduled meetings twice a month, and in 1720 about one thousand questions a year to decide by majority vote of those present.[59] Any committeeman or any student of Parkinson will know that a committee of twenty-four could not decide one hundred issues a year, much less one thousand, if resolution required democratic discussion and deliberation by the full body. The S.C.C. worked as an effective organ of the Roman Curia only because of its structure and its staff.

Two officers were the fulcrum of power: the Prefect and the Secretary, arranged in the familiar tandem of commander and sergeant, chief and executive assistant. The headman, the Prefect, was a cardinal chosen by the Pope in forming his administration. In 1720, when Barberini first came before the Council, the Prefect was Pietro Marcello Corradini, who had the distinction of an almost optimal curial career. From Segge in the little coastal diocese of Terracina, he had come to Rome and acquired the doctorate in both laws, that qualification as mandatory for legal office in the Curia as a Ph.D. for university appointment today. Putting off ordination until he was forty-four, he had been successively auditor to Cardinal Benedetto Pamphili; a practicing advocate in the Curia; deputy Under-Datary; canonist of the Penitentiary; auditor of the Pope; titular Bishop of Athens; cardinal in 1712; Prefect of the S.C.C. at the relatively young age of sixty in 1718. In the center of curial life, he was a serious contender for the papacy itself in the elections of 1721, 1724, and 1730, falling short of success by only three votes in 1730. As a young man he had written a book *The Law of Prelacy*, and his academic interests were marked even as a senior administrator. This strong, experienced man had selected as Secretary of his Congregation the most brilliant person ever to hold that office, Prospero Lambertini.[60]

The competence of the Secretary — a younger man not yet a cardinal but likely to become one — was crucial. He had five critical responsibilities: the reception and handling of all communications from the parties; the determination of the docket, including the decision to schedule some matters for summary disposition, others for full argument; assignment of the case to one cardinal as that cardinal's special responsibility; the written report of the case to the committee, where he set out the facts and law he deemed relevant; and the transmission of the committee's decision to those affected by it. Although these tasks would be done in consultation with the Prefect, the Secretary would have the close mastery of detail which made the process work.

The Secretary in 1720, Prospero Lambertini, was not only the most outstanding Secretary the S.C.C. ever had; he was to be in time the most remarkable lawyer since Alexander III to hold the papacy. Bolognese, a graduate at nineteen from the Sapienza with a doctorate in both laws, he had devoted himself since his graduation to the work of the Curia and the mastery of canon law. His apprenticeship had begun in the Rota — a time happily recalled when he was Pope: "We were a Secretary who wrote and spoke." He was an assistant there for seven years to Auditor Alessandro Caprara, who had been the youngest of the counsel of Nicole of Lorraine. Lambertini had then become an advocate himself; in 1707, by the time he was thirty-two, he was a Consistorial Advocate. In 1708 he also became assistant to the Promoter of the Faith, Prospero Bottini, another member of Nicole's old team of lawyers. He became a canon of Saint Peter's, a consultor of the Congregation on Rites, a consultor of the Inquisition. In 1716 his colleagues in the College of Consistorial Advocates chose him to be Rector of the Sapienza. He was forty-three when in 1718 Corradini made him Secretary of the Council.[61] To this task he brought energy, intelligence, scholarship, and a high sense of order. The affair of Senator Barberini he saw at once as presenting a fresh, difficult, and classic question, which the S.C.C. was in an excellent position to resolve.

If Corradini as Prefect and Lambertini as Secretary made a combination appropriate for the argument of an academic case like Barberini's, the membership of the Congregation also had to be considered. After all, here were the votes which would decide. In 1720, all of the members had been born in Italian cities; the only two with Portuguese connections were Cornaro and Conti, the former nuncios. Barberini could fear that the one Jesuit member, Tolomei, a theologian, would not like the theological implication of his case for virginal unions or hope that he would appreciate the nicety of the theological advice he had received. There was one man whose response could be critical, his namesake and possible relation, Francesco Barberini. Cardinal Barberini's descent from the papal family was beyond dispute. He had entered the College of Cardinals at the age of twenty-seven, when two uncles were already members; in 1720, a cardinal of thirty years' standing, he might be expected to have the experience, the mellow wisdom, and, if convinced of his genealogical claims, the interest to see that Luis Barberini's plea was attentively considered.[62]

Between 1720, when the case was begun, and the date in 1724, when it was actually decided, the membership altered in a way to make it, on balance, slightly less propitious for Barberini. The theological level rose with the addition of two more Jesuits. A conscious effort was made to internationalize the body with seven non-Italians. Of these the Spaniard, Luis Belluga y Moncada, might be unsympathetic to the Portuguese Crown. The two old Nuncios to Portugal, Cornaro and Conti, both died. These changes favored Barberini. On the other hand, Corradini was promoted to Datary and replaced as Prefect by a Roman, Curtio Origo, who did not have his reputation for scholarship and did have a reputation for cunning. Alvaro Cienfuegos, the leader of cardinals responsive to the Emperor in the conclave of 1724, could be expected to be in the Portuguese camp. Above all, a Portuguese cardinal, José Pereira, was added as part of Innocent XIII's effort to placate João V. Still the essentials were unchanged, twenty-four members remained the same as in 1720, Francesco Barberini advanced in seniority, and Prospero Lambertini was still the Secretary.[63]

Preliminary Skirmishes

During the time he was in Rome, Barberini worried about what Joanna might do to prevent his fine legal case from coming to a conclusion. He obtained an opinion from several anonymous theologians that his marriage was null. He addressed a memorial to the Pope alleging bribery of the auditors in Portugal by Joanna. He obtained, as an extra precaution, a papal rescript confirming the S.C.C.'s present jurisdiction. Portuguese cases had a reputation in Rome for chicanery; Barberini's efforts to be sure of his court appear to have occasioned no surprise.[64]

In an effort to get the case moving again after the long delay since 1720, counsel obtained a summary hearing from the S.C.C. on the order to examine witnesses; and on July 21, 1723, the Council ordered that Joanna herself be interrogated further. A lawyer, a notary, and one of Barberini's brothers attempted to discharge this mission. In doing so they fell afoul of the Portuguese injunctions forbidding Barberini or his agents to harass Joanna. She went to the secular courts, and the trio was thrown in jail.[65] In the view of Barberini's counsel in Rome, Joanna by her action automatically incurred the excommunication, from which only the Holy See could absolve, imposed by the bull, *In Coena Domini*. That great catch-all of papal sanctions excommunicated a broad variety of offenders from pirates in the Mediterranean to any civil authority taxing ecclesiastics without papal permission, and, among others, persons using the lay courts to prevent the execution of letters issued by the Pope or his judges. Joanna had already flouted *In Coena Domini* by impeding Barberini's access to Rome in 1720. Doubtless she had advice that the bull had not been specifically promulgated in Portugal, and that, according to one line of authority, it had no force in countries where it had not been promulgated. At worst, her counsel may have told her, another small debit would be added to her record in Rome.[66]

The Roman response was perhaps predictable. If Joanna would interfere with the process, the court would not on that account invalidate her marriage, but it would threaten not to delay further. On November 23, 1723, the S.C.C. ordered the case to be set down for argument. At this juncture, Joanna's proctor—she now had counsel in Rome — told Lambertini that she had revoked his authorization to represent her. This tactic was regarded as dilatory by the Secretary, but the S.C.C. did not yet move to actually decide the case. Innocent XIII still reigned and he still had hesitations about adding another irritation, however small, to the relations between the Holy See and the Crown of Portugal. The case was judicial in form; it was to enter history as a great judicial precedent; but more than judicial considerations entered into its decision. The S.C.C. needed information outside the record; and the S.C.C., after all, did have its man in Lisbon. He was Archbishop Giuseppe Firrao, an experienced diplomatist, later papal Secretary of State. Firrao had been designated as Nuncio by the Pope. Although he was unrecognized by the King, he was in fact in Lisbon. The S.C.C. solicited his views.

Firrao made an unexpected answer, writing directly to the Secretary of State. Anything sent in writing to the Council, he said, would become public. What he had to say could only be upsetting in Portugal. He asked to be excused from reporting and to be given further instructions from the Pope himself.[67] His letter was instructive in more than one aspect. It revealed how extraordinarily sensitive the Barberini matter appeared in Portugal; it implied that Firrao's own views would be unwelcome to the King; it indicated an awareness of Innocent XIII's own interest in the process.

Before Firrao's letter reached Rome, Innocent XIII had died. The new Pope, elected on May 29, 1724, Pietro Francesco Orsini, had been, thirty years ago, Prefect of the S.C.C.; he had retained his membership in the Congregation after becoming Archbishop of Naples; he was an admirer of Lambertini and no special friend of Portugal. No doubt he wanted the Congregation to proceed with its business. On June 22 the case was set down for resolution for the regular Saturday meeting on July 8.

Joanna's friends tried to stave off decision. A memorial on behalf of her mother, Isabella, was presented to Lambertini along with the medical certificate of Joanna's miscarriage in 1719. Isabella could not persuade her daughter to argue in this court a marriage already judged valid by Church and Crown in Portugal, but Isabella prayed the Congregation not to act hastily, to delay at least until the formal examinations of the witnesses ordered in 1720 had been carried out.[68] As Joanna had been blocking such examination in Portugal, this plea was bold to the point of impudence, but it was received with courtesy and kept in the file for the case. Its statements, however, were not treated as part of the record, and Joanna in fact was without legal representation before the court. Yet Barberini could not destroy a marriage merely by his adversary's ineptness or default. He had to persuade the Council that no marriage existed. For that an advocate was indispensable and was obtained.

The Advocate

Recalling the case almost twenty years later, Prospero Lambertini, who had seen the lawyers of the Curia in hundreds of instances, remembered with special warmth the senior lawyer Barberini found to represent him. The marriage, he wrote, "was attacked by Advocate Pitoni, then famous; and he sought to show its invalidity in many ways with all his might." [69] No advocate could have asked for a higher testimonial from a still-famous fellow-craftsman.

Francesco Maria Pitoni, to judge by his other accomplishments, was the kind of workman the Curia produced when it formed a capable but not extraordinary man. He was an ecclesiastic, beneficed as a canon of Santa Maria Maggiore. He was the editor of a collection of papal constitutions. He was, in the later 1720's, an auditor of the Pope, and bishop, in a titular capacity, of Himeria in Mesopotamia.[70] The character he bore, however, was not that of priest or bishop, scholar or hearing officer, but of lawyer — of a counselor who could provide astute advice and a rhetorician who could carry his opinion to victory by written argument to the court. Jurisconsult and advocate, he was a shrewd, learned, determined servant of his client's cause.

Long experience — he was fifty-three in 1720 — had prepared Pitoni for the situation of distress which Barberini presented. Most of his practice was, necessarily, in disputes among ecclesiastics, but matrimonial matters with harsh facts and messy consequences were not unfamiliar to him. Three consultations, which he himself later published, show how splendidly his profession had educated him to handle cases like Barberini's.[71] In a Portuguese affair actually involving betrothal subject to a condition, Pitoni had been consulted by the boy's parents. Their son and heir, a student at Coimbra, had betrothed a girl without their knowledge, but, so his parents understood, on the express condition that they consent. Their consent was not forthcoming. Could the girl enforce the promise to marry? Pitoni assured them that by the express terms of the *Decretals*, 4.5.5, *Super eo vero*, when betrothal was made contingent on a condition which was not immoral, and that condition failed to occur, the promise to marry could not be enforced; and this, of course, was what the parents wanted to be assured. In a second case of advice to parents, a very rich boy betrothed a very poor girl after her father had chased him, naked, from her house and applied further pressure to bring about the engagement. At the request of the boy's parents, Pitoni wrote their bishop that it was his duty to break up the match: the difference in wealth made scandal and family enmity likely, a sufficient reason to disrupt the agreement; at the very least the bishop should postpone the banns until fully informed by the boy's father. In a third case, a youth found himself "most ardently in love" with a girl he had known for a day; at the day's end, after much drinking of wine, the young man pledged his troth and tendered a ring. Pitoni advised this boy's parents that their son could be only "moderately" forced by the ecclesiastical judge to carry out his promise; if he adamantly resisted, he could not be made to marry. None of these opinions, exact solutions to the questions asked, required more than the basic legal competence of knowing where to look in the *Decretals* or Sanchez. As exemplary specimens of the regulation of love by contract, of the subordination of passion to convention, of the importance of social prejudice, they were appropriate legal and psychological preparation for the matter of Senator Barberini.

Pitoni was struck by three aspects of his case. Two judgments of ecclesiastical authority had upheld the marriage; to overturn them would be difficult. The legal issue presented was "new" — no one, so far as he knew, had ever attacked a virginal marriage under *Si conditiones*. The proper result, "the most just" result, would be a judgment of invalidity. So he pronounced when asked his opinion as a jurisconsult; so he argued when retained as an advocate.[72]

Pitoni's brief to the S.C.C. began on an aggressive and rhetorical note: "I address a new case of the cunning of a woman of Portugal, who built snares for a man of higher status and laid plans for deceiving him." Notoriously, women were "more cunning than men," especially in making a marriage: "They tender traps for rich and noble men, whose equals they are not, so that by these damnable arts of theirs — would they were not contrived with the counsel of their relatives! — they seek fortunes for themselves, loss and shame for others." The law, as maxim had it, "does not aid the crafty." [73]

After these generalities, Pitoni developed a picture in black and white — on the one hand, Joanna, a poor, ignoble, scheming, fortune-hunting woman; on the other, rich and noble Senator Barberini, who "proceeded with all sincerity and caution," in sincerity because he sought to help the girl, with caution because he took appropriate steps not to be bound to her in marriage. The Senator had been an honorable man making amends where he had no obligation, a benevolent man performing a generous act, a *finezza*. His compassion had been rewarded by Joanna's treachery.

Rhetorical flights without firm support in the record were not, however, the mainstay of Pitoni's brief. He advanced a three-pronged legal argument against the validity of the marriage: *Si conditiones* applied, and the marriage was null because of the condition against intercourse; *Si conditiones* applied, and the marriage was null for a condition against indissolubility; in view of the parties' agreement, the marriage was a pure fiction. The whole was elaborately interlaced with apposite authority. As a skilled pianist can supply the right chords without apparent effort, so Pitoni seemed effortlessly to invoke the appropriate citations at the appropriate times.

The last contention, that the marriage was a fiction, was theoretically inconsistent with the first two which supposed true consent undone by conditions. Like most lawyers Pitoni saw nothing cynical in giving a court alternative routes to the desired result. The advantage of the third approach was that it got over the difficulty that no conditions were expressed at the moment of consent — the conditions tendered to Joanna could still be used as evidence that Barberini intended to enter a fictitious marriage. The problem with this tack was that it ran directly counter to the common canonical interpretation of *Tua nos:* evidence of intention contrary to the public words of consent would not be heard.

The second contention, that indissolubility had been contracted away, avoided both the thorny areas of internal intention and of virginal marriages by focusing on the terminability of the marriage according to the note signed by Joanna. Either she made solemn religious profession in one year, thereby dissolving the union, or she agreed that the marriage should be judged null for noncompliance; on either contingency the marriage would end. *Si conditiones* itself declared that the clause "until I find a richer woman" invalidated consent to marry; so here marriage terminable on a contingency destroyed indissolubility and fell within the express terms of the decretal. Pitoni invoked "the noteworthy caution" of Gerardo de Petrasancto to young men visiting their lovers at night, if they should be caught *in flagrante* by the relatives: Marry the girl at once on the condition that "you do not do with someone else what you have done with me." [74] Such a condition, the canonist had observed, was unlikely to be refused, and it would nullify the consent to marriage by making indissolubility contingent on the good behavior of the bride. This advice to sophomores, Pitoni suggested, was conclusive analogy for a marriage conditioned on entry into a convent.

The heart of the agreement and the case, however, was the renunciation of sexual intercourse, which, as Pitoni maintained, was the equivalent of the clause "if you will avoid the generation of offspring," expressly condemned by *Si conditiones*. Pitoni eschewed the intellectual luxury of reconciling Marian theology with the law. He stuck to the operative phrases subscribed to in contractual form by Joanna, "never use the marriage nor consummate it" and "renounce all right which I can have to the person of the said gentleman." Each phrase constituted the placing of a condition of the very kind treated as invalidating by Saint Thomas Aquinas, by

Sanchez, by a dozen other cited canonists and theologians. The very "substance of marriage," Pitoni argued in the wake of Sanchez, "consists in the right of using and the obligation of offering the body of the spouse; and hence, when this mutual obligation of bodies is taken away, the contract cannot be called carnal marriage."

The most crucial point for Pitoni, that the condition once placed should be presumed to continue to the moment of consent, was argued in terms of both facts and precedent. Joanna had signed the note on the eve of the wedding; there was no sign that she had changed her mind so recently expressed. But, even if she had, Barberini clearly had married on these terms when he had gone to such pains to have them drafted, when he had explained them to the official witnesses, when he had no reason to repeat them at the monastery grill. Authority superior to the decisions of the Patriarch and Nuncio supported Pitoni's analysis. The Salamancan theologian, Basilio Ponce de León reported this of his knowledge in early seventeenth-century Spain: A woman declared before the marriage, but not at the ceremony itself, that she "would rather suffer death" than marry her fiancé if he were of Jewish blood. Later, her husband was discovered to have Jewish ancestors. Almost all the jurisprudents of the royal court and the most learned theologians of Salamanca, Valladolid, Toledo, Compluto, and Madrid advised that the marriage was null, and a Spanish diocesan court so ruled.[75] Giacomo Pignatelli, a Neapolitan canonist, reported similarly from his experience. Approximately an hour before the wedding, in the presence of the bride and others, Caius declared, "I will accept Bertha as a wife if she has 10,000 gold pieces." After the ceremony Bertha was discovered "to have nothing." The condition placed by Caius, Pignatelli advised, was possible, completely decent, and effective; the marriage was null.[76] The third and best authority was a decision by the S.C.C. itself in which Pitoni himself had written for the successful petitioner. Marcello de Rege, an older son disfavored by his father, solemnly professed as a Carthusian monk at Asti but not before he had registered with the Senate at Turin a declaration that he would enter religious life with the intention of not accepting the vows he pronounced. Later, when Rege attempted to invalidate his profession, the S.C.C. held that he was bound; on reargument, Pitoni successfully urged that his earlier declaration controlled and nullified his public vows. A copy of this decision of 1710, certified as authentic by Lambertini, was part of Pitoni's presentation. His old victory established that contradictory conditions need not be uttered in the same breath with formal consent in order to invalidate it; *Asti, September 20, 1710* presaged victory now.[77]

The Vote

In late June 1724 Lambertini circulated his report of the case to the cardinal members for decision.[78] He opened with the full text of the note signed by Joanna on May 6, 1718. He stressed that its contents had been mutually agreed to by the parties and communicated to the officiating priest and the official witnesses. In a page and a half he set out these essential facts. In a page he sketched the proceedings to date, summarizing the judgments below as resting on a finding that the condition had not been expressed in the act of consent. A page more gave the canon law and theology favorable to Barberini. The foundation of the case was *Si conditiones*. Panormitanus, Petrus de Ancharano, Joannes Andreas, Henricus Boich, Alessando de Nevo, and Prospero Fagnani were cited to show that the canonists agreed that the decretal applied to any condition against the substance of marriage. The theologians showed that an agreement of the kind entered into here "contained many things against fidelity, offspring, and the sacrament." Saint Thomas on the *Sentences* was quoted and buttressed by Domingo de Soto's enlargement of this text in his *Commentary on Book Four of the Sentences of Peter Lombard* (Salamanca, 1557–58). To Soto were added references to "the more recent authors" — "Sanchez, Laiman, Gonzal., Barbos., Pirhing." * In addition, the marriage could be

---

* In other words, Lambertini referred to Sanchez, The Holy Sacrament of Matrimony (Madrid, 1602); Paul Laymann, S.J., Moral Theology (Munich, 1625); Agostinho Barbosa, Three Books of the Whole of Ecclesiastical Law (Lyon, 1645); Manuel Gonzalez, Lasting Commentaries on Individual Texts of the Five Books of the Decretals of Gregory IX (1673); and Heinrich Pirhing, S.J., The Whole of Canon Law Distributed According to the Titles of the Decretals and Explained in a New Way (Dillengen, 1674-1677). To these citations provided by the briefs Lambertini added two very modern works: Franz X. Schmalzgreuber, S.J., All of Ecclesiastical Law Explained by a Short Method for the Utility of Learners, or Canonical Studies on the Five Books of the Decretals (Ingolstadt, 1719); and The Salamancans' College of the Shoeless Brothers of the Primitive Observance of St. Mary of Mount Carmel, Course of Moral Theology (Madrid, 1717-1724).

seen as a fiction entered in order to restore the girl's honor; as a fiction it was invalid under *Tua nos*, X.4.1.26. In four pages Lambertini summed up facts, law, theology, and authority favorable to Barberini.

In opposition, it was evident that the condition had not been attached "in the act of marriage," and simultaneity was required by the Gloss on *Tua nos*, which refused to pay attention to a nullifying condition attached by one party without the knowledge of the other. In such a case fraud was established, and the Gloss insisted that fraud should not be rewarded. It was otherwise, however, if the condition was composed by a lawyer on the woman's initiative, if she wrote asking the man "to hear her in this affliction, in this struggle, to draw her from this hell and she would become a nun," if the man consulted theologians on the validity of the condition, if the parish priest refused to be present because of the condition, if the condition was explained to the priest and witnesses a little before the marriage — "all of these things joined together show that it is doubtful that he desired to withdraw from these conditions in the act of marriage." If these facts were proved, "it seems that there should be no doubt as to nullity."

Yet was not the condition revoked by intercourse? The decretal *Per tuas literas*, X.4.5.6, held that there was a definite "presumption" that a condition to marry "only if father and uncle approved" was revoked by marital coitus; the decretal *Insuper*, X.4.18.4, provided that if someone contracted marriage with a girl below the age of marriage she could withdraw on reaching twelve, but if she had intercourse with the man after this age, she ratified the marriage. Raising the objection, Lambertini said there were three answers: the man here denied the fact of intercourse; the judgment of the Lisbon court did not mention it; after the Council of Trent, such unwitnessed consent to marriage would be ineffective, as Sanchez, 2.45.21, taught.

Omitted in Lambertini's account was all of Pitoni's coloring, his aspersions on Joanna's motives, his emphasis on the difference in rank and wealth between the spouses, his misogynous maxims. Omitted also was a suspicion Lambertini had voiced in his 1720 report as to Barberini's premarital defloration of Joanna. Omitted too was any reference to the principal figures in Portuguese ecclesiastical life, Patriarch Almeida and Nuncio Bichi; the lower court judges mentioned were "the Vicar-General of the Patriarch" and "the auditor of the Nuncio." Nor did Lambertini say anything of the battles waged in the Portuguese civil courts or of Joanna's liability to the pains of *In Coena Domini*. The cardinals, he noted, could read an account of the civil litigation, if they cared to, in a separate memorandum which would be hand-carried to anyone wanting it.

Clean of irrelevant detail, stripped of complexity, the report of Lambertini to the S.C.C. focused on the issues as Pitoni had put them: Was a condition against the goods of marriage attached to the consent given? Alternatively, was the marriage a fiction? Lambertini did not say that the facts alleged were true. The cardinals were to make their own judgment. But if they accepted the facts as established, they were left little choice. The Secretary had reached the conclusion that a marriage of this kind could not stand. He put the issue to the cardinals incisively, inviting them to apply *Si conditiones*.

Eleven cardinals voted. As a body composed of cardinals, accountable only to God and the Pope, the S.C.C. gave no reasons for its decisions, and the arguments which moved the cardinals can only be inferred from the Secretary's report. Decision was by a majority of those present, and was then announced impersonally in the form "The S.C.C. has judged." An interoffice memo addressed to Lambertini gave the tally. No one voted to uphold the marriage; the choice was between a Yes for nullity and Delay; although as Parkinson has more generally shown, a judgment of delay could have been the most deadly denial of the appellant's claim.[79] Barberini had, in fact, been denied in this deadly way for six years.

In the S.C.C., Pereira, the Portuguese cardinal, voted for delay, along with one Jesuit, Salerno; a Sienese, Zondadari; and Pico della Mirandola. Voting "Yes" were another Jesuit, Tolomei; a Spaniard, Belluga; a Neapolitan, Ruffo; a Roman, Colonna; the Secretary of the Inquisition, Giudice; the Prefect, Origo; and, at the head of the list, Francesco Barberini. By a vote of seven to four, invalidity was ruled to be established.[80]

That the judgment ended all Senator Barberini's difficulties; that he returned to Lisbon a well, free, and unmarried man; that at least after the Bichi affair was resolved several years later, the King forgave him and restored his judgeship would be to the credit of the

S.C.C. to report; but the records are silent, and imagination must supply how much vindication in the Curia meant to the petitioner and how responsive the respondent was to the curial termination of her union. For canonists the fame of *West Lisbon, July 8, 1724* rested not on what it did to rule the lives of its protagonists, but on its contribution to canonical jurisprudence. Like those long-suffering Jehovah's Witnesses, whose difficulties with local American ordinances have given rise to litigation with such unlikely factual bases and such large constitutional implications that it has been suggested that the cases were designed and promoted by professors of constitutional law, so Senator Barberini seemed to have been propelled into a proceeding designed by an academic mind to test the paradoxes and limits of the canon law of marriage.

Prospero Lambertini, who from the start had grasped the academic significance of the case, was able to bring it to the attention of the legal world fifteen years later, when, Cardinal Archbishop of Bologna, he began to publish the reports he had made as Secretary of the S.C.C.* With this move the tradition of secrecy a century and one half old was broken, and the professional bar throughout the Catholic world was enabled to know how each formal case decided by the S.C.C. had appeared to its Secretary at the time of decision. Prominent in the first volumes of the *Treasury*, as it was called, were the 1720 and 1724 reports of the Secretary in *West Lisbon*. For Lambertini, the fascination of the case lay in

---

* Early seventeenth-century practice discouraged even unofficial reporting. Agostinho Barbosa, the most eminent of Portuguese canonists, had his *Remissiones doctorum* condemned by the Congregation of the Index of Prohibited Books in 1621, and his *Collectanea bullarii et decisionum* similarly condemned in 1642, because their combination of commentary and collection of rulings by the S.C.C. constituted interpretations of Trent and required a special papal license; Americo do Conto Oliveira, "Agostinho Barbosa, canonista portugues," in *Aufsätze zur Portugiesischen Kulturgeschicte*, ed. Hans Flasch, II, 29, 37. Theologians and lawyers were still interested in the S.C.C.'s rulings, but with these restrictions, and with no effort at publication by the S.C.C. itself, the rulings and the reasons for them were hard to get. As Prospero Lambertini sadly observed in 1739, "The decrees and responses of the Congregation are either entirely unknown or incorrectly understood" (*De synodo diocesana*, preface, p. 1). It was to fill this gap that Lambertini began the publication of his reports as Secretary, covering the years 1718 to 1726 in the first three volumes which appeared in 1739. By 1742, when he became Pope, reporting of the S.C.C. was on a current annual basis and remained so, with a few interruptions, until 1868. Prior to Lambertini's edition, the Secretary's Reports were printed as *Folia Sacrae Congregationis Concilii* in Rome at the press of Geronimo Maynard; this printing, made as early as 1732, was without any indication of authorship or editorship.

the clash between Marian and Augustinian theology as he indicated in his Report in 1720, and in the clash between *Tua nos* and a broad interpretation of *Si conditiones*, as his Report in 1724 revealed. Public order and the sure administration of the law called for a single unitary model of marriage established in court like other contracts. Paradoxically, however, as Pitoni's precedents demonstrated, the more marriage was treated like any other contract, subject to modification by agreement, the easier it became for individuals to write their own terms. The limit on that reworking of marriage had to be those private agreements which destroyed the substance of the institution. As long as fraud was not rewarded, Lambertini believed, the courts could only invalidate the marriage whose public mutation broke the boundaries.

Alexander III's *Commissum* taught that a dissoluble, virginal marriage satisfied an oath to marry. *West Lisbon, July 8, 1724*, as reported by Lambertini, taught that intent to enter a dissoluble virginal marriage, contractually expressed, nullified the marriage. Between these poles, set up by its brightest and strongest minds, the curial system was held in tension; it did not break; the balance it maintained was, as yet, secure.

III

Captive in Mind

Prospero Lambertini was elected Pope on August 17, 1740, after a six-month conclave in which the divisions between Austria and Spain and between the cardinals of Clement XI and the cardinals of Clement XII had produced the longest deadlock since the Great Schism, broken only by unanimous agreement to settle on the best. His election brought to the papacy as Benedict XIV the most knowledgeable, the most energetic, and the most humane canonist ever to be chosen as the supreme ruler of the Church. The author of the definitive treatise on the canonization of saints and the negotiator of the settlement of papal claims in Sicily, equally esteemed by the envoy of the Emperor and by Voltaire, celebrated even in Protestant, deistic England, he was, as Horace Walpole wrote, "A Man whom neither Wit nor Power could corrupt." Apprenticed in the Rota, Consistorial Advocate, Secretary of the Congregation of the Council, he came to the summit not only after a long career in the Curia, but after twelve more pastoral years as archbishop of his birthplace, Bologna. If intelligence seasoned by experience and joined to goodness could make just law, no man was better fitted for his work.[1]

HOW THE POPE REFORMED THE LICENSE OF THE POLES

Elected when he was a vigorous sixty-five, Lambertini had eighteen years as Pope to bring his ideas to execution. Within a year he described himself as "meditating on salutary laws" for matrimonial litigation.[2] Little over six months later he announced his plan. He left on the treatment of marriage cases an indelible imprint — yet not so much his personal mark, but the stamp, energized and made effective through him, of centuries of accumulated curial experience in the juridical handling of marriage.

Reason was to rule the process — not the doubting, restless intellect of eighteenth-century skepticism, but the related faculty, which, although it asks questions and sifts evidence, delights above all else in systematization. Out of the speculations of canonists and the practical knowledge of curialists, a superior system was to be constructed. No knight of La Mancha ever set out with greater confidence in the written word, in the power to make unmalleable matter conform to his vision of order, than did the former Secretary of the S.C.C. in his work of reform.

The order for which the Pope spoke was not only the abstract domain ruled by the canon law; it was the concrete curial world he had known as Caprara's secretary in the Rota and as Corradini's executive in the S.C.C. In 1720, when Lambertini was Secretary of the Council, that world had been expressed in a yearbook, the first in a series which continues to the present day to announce names, rank, function, and origin in the Curia.[3] Almanac, organization chart, and directory, *Notizie per l'anno 1720* contained, in this sequence: the time from the creation of the world, 6,919 years; the time from the universal deluge, 4,677 years; the time from the founding of Rome, 2,472 years; the time from the Incarnation, 1,720 years; a dedication to Monsignor Pietro de Cardis, governor and apostolic visitor of the Mark, whose virtues made him "shine in the exercise of his career"; Perpetual Tables enabling one to tell the hour of the occurrence in Rome of dawn, midday, and midnight on every day of the year; the feasts of obligation, the feasts of devotion, the feasts observed by the Tribunals of the Auditor of the Camera, the feasts observed by the Capitoline Curia or City Hall, the feasts observed by the Bank of the Holy Spirit and by other banks paying returns on shares in the public debt; the religious orders in Rome and their Roman addresses; the parishes of Rome and the number of their parishioners; the number of bishops (49), priests (2,479), brothers and religious (3,866), monks (1,946), prisoners (260), communions (108,439), and persons (137,129) in Rome; the parish churches possessing baptismal fonts; the heads and procurators-general of the religious orders; the birthdates of the sovereigns and princes of Europe; the principal deaths of the last year, all those commemorated being monarchs; the names, birth-places, birthdates, creation dates, and curial congregations of the cardinals, arranged in order of creation; an analysis of the creations of each Pope by national origin; recently deceased cardinals; the governors of municipalities within the States of the Church; the bishops with residential sees within the States of the Church; the patriarchs; the nuncios with their birthplaces and birthdates; the vice-legates in the States of the Church; the birthplaces, birthdates, and dates of being "made" of the auditors of the Rota; the secretaries of the curial congregations with their birthdates; miscellaneous officeholders in Rome, including the President of Prisons; the day of the week on which the auditors of several of these officers held office; the prelates of the Apostolic Palace; the order of precedence for those marching in the Pope's procession on the feast of Corpus Domini; the archconfraternities of Rome; the schedule by hour and day throughout the year on which the Inquisition met with the Pope (Thursdays), the cardinal members (Wednesdays), and the consultors (Mondays). This hieratic structure on the horarium of Italy, which opened with the date of the creation of the world, continued with the dates of the creation of the cardinals, and closed with the schedule of committee meetings of the Inquisition, was the universe of Prospero Lambertini, in which he lived, for which, perforce, he spoke as Pope.

As Benedict XIV saw the scene at the start of his reign, there existed dioceses which were "well set-up." In these, through careful observance of the rules of Trent, "almost never or rarely" was there litigation about marriage. In other areas, above all in Poland, the ready dissolutions of marriages were a scandal. The fault lay, to begin with, in the failure to comply wholeheartedly with Trent. In Poland, banns were frequently and unnecessarily dispensed with, and the lack of public notice facilitated the later claim that the marriages were coerced. Led by an "easy humanity," pastors frequently let marriages be performed by other priests, and the informality of these permissions made it easier to claim later that the Tridentine requirement of the presence of the pastor or his duly authorized delegate had not been met. Sloppiness of this sort became dangerous because of the practice of the courts. The ecclesiastical judges, so the Pope thought, improperly recognized claims to nullity fostered or made possible by the slackness in the formation of marriages.* The Polish courts were characterized by "excessive freedom," and Polish marriages were dissolved "with great ease." [4]

The quantity of dissolutions which provoked the Pope was not clear. He spoke of men and women married "three or four times" in the lifetime of their first spouse—that is, of men and women who had gone through two or three annulments. Probably these were the extreme cases. If the Pope took "almost never" as the proper norm for matrimonial litigation, fifty annulments a year would have looked enormous, particularly if they were concentrated in the nobility. He spoke of Poland, but this distant realm, reeling from recent war and menaced by mighty neighbors, was easier to single out than places nearer home which the Pope referred to vaguely as "some other regions" where there was also the "wicked practice of this kind in the dissolving of marriages." The problem, in short, was general enough for papal prescriptions to be necessary for its solution. In a good diocese, the Pope said, the pastor would take seriously his obligation of celebrating marriage; he would delegate only if prevented by "the most serious lawful cause." Before he even announced the banns he would interrogate fiancés as to their freedom; he would inform himself about the existence of impediments. In doubt he would refer the matter to the bishop. Only after such interrogation and inquiry would he have the banns read on three successive Sundays or feast days, as Trent prescribed. If all this were done, Benedict XIV believed, there would be few claims of invalid marriage.

But there would be cases. To regulate them the Pope issued on November 3, 1741, a bull of reform, *Dei miseratione*.[5] "By the mercy of God," he began, he had been made Pope and charged to root out abuses arising from the wiles of the devil and the malice of man which were pernicious to the salvation of souls and brought injury to the sacraments of the Church. No longer should it be possible for a spouse to seek and obtain dissolution of a marriage because the other spouse did not appear. No longer should it be

---

* In the latter nineteenth century Johann Döllinger referred to a custom "among the Polish aristocracy in earlier days" of a father boxing his daughter on the ear at the marriage ceremony so as to provide ocular proof that her marriage was coerced and to give a basis for annulment if later desired, *Conversations with Dr. Döllinger recorded by Louise von Kobell*, trans. Katherine Gould (London, 1892), pp. 32–33.

possible for a judgment of nullity to go unappealed because the parties were content. No longer should it profit the spouses to simulate conflict while collusively cooperating to secure an annulment. No longer should one spouse win a judgment over his mate's objections because the latter ran out of money for litigation. In each diocese there was to be a "Defender of Marriages," chosen for legal skill and moral probity, who was "to be cited in every judicial act" of a matrimonial process. He was to attend the examination of witnesses, to defend the validity of the marriage "orally and in writing," and to bring out everything he judged necessary to sustain the union. The Defender was to be a necessary party to the validity of a judgment; any judicial act done without citing him would be null. He was to be appointed by the Bishop in a diocese, by the Dean in the Rota, by the Prefect in the S.C.C. His fee, if there was no spouse arguing for the marriage to pay him, was to come from the tribunal he served. In each situation he would be a man bound to the judge as his appointee, as the judge would be bound to him by having appointed him.

The establishment of the Defender as a necessary and quasi-official party was the first plank of *Dei miseratione*. The second was the requirement that, for spouses to achieve freedom to marry, one judgment of nullity was not enough: there must be two "similar and conforming judgments," from the second of which no one elected to appeal. No room was left in this legislation for casuistry, equivocation, or claim in conscience. Once a person appeared to be married he could not marry again without these two concurring judgments unless he cared to incur the pains and penalties of polygamy.

The office of the Defender meshed with the requirement of the two judgments. Whenever a diocesan court held for nullity, the Defender had the duty to appeal—from a suffragan diocese to the metropolitan diocese, from either suffragan or metropolitan diocese to Rome. In the Roman tribunals such as the Rota, the S.C.C., or special commissions of the Curia the same duty of appeal existed. In the Rota a new panel of auditors had then to consider the case. In the S.C.C., it was unavoidable that the same body as a whole be asked to reconsider its judgment. Even after two conforming judgments of invalidity, the Defender's office was not necessarily discharged. If he thought the result still "manifestly unjust or invalid," he must appeal; and if later he discovered something new, a marriage decision was never *res judicata:* in the Defender's discretion he could reopen the case.

The requirement of two judgments worked only one way. The petitioner lost by one unappealed judgment that the mariage was valid; he won only by two judgments for invalidity. If there was a split of decisions — say, invalid, valid, invalid; or valid, invalid, invalid — the Defender had a right and apparently a duty to appeal; if this sequence occurred, the petitioner seemed condemned to see the case go to a total of at least four decisions. The Pope contemplated that a party defending a valid marriage might run out of money and instituted the office of the Defender against this contingency. No special provision was made for the party attacking an invalid marriage who was impoverished by litigation.

Mature experience came to fruition in the provisions and sanctions of *Dei miseratione.* They were the work of a lawyer interested in mechanisms for preventing the evasion of law; the work of a religious man grieved "beyond words or tears," as he expressed it, by improper dissolutions of the marital bond; above all, the work of a man who had been for a decade the Secretary of the S.C.C. and who in his first years as Pope, as in his last, drew upon the knowledge he had gained and the decisions he had made in that central post. To anticipate evasion, to forestall corruption, collusion, and connivance, to discourage negligence, Benedict XIV recollected what he had learned as Prospero Lambertini and constructed a set of rules to rationalize, channel, and control the process. *Dei miseratione* was a supreme act of systematization.*

Paradox nonetheless abounded when so regular, so careful, so calculated a process was designed to measure unions brought about by passion, prudence, chance, or love and to uphold in the flux of time a symbolic value with such high theological content and such

---

* When Prospero Lambertini had been a member of the Curia, he had exercised for fifteen years the office of Promoter of the Faith, charged with raising both substantive and procedural objections to candidacies for beatification and canonization. In that capacity he had argued that, before the Pope declared a martyr for the faith to be a saint, four miracles should be certified as having occurred at the intercession of the candidate. The incumbent Pope, Clement XI, rejected his plea, keeping the old rule of two miracles. In the first year of his own pontificate, Benedict XIV changed the requirement to four. Doubling the number of miracles seemed to him to increase the security of the former procedure; see Benedict XIV, *De Dei servorum beatificatione et beatificorum canonizatione* (Prato, 1839) 1.37.5.

deeply idiosyncratic embodiments as the bond of marriage. Nothing was new in preserving marriage by the law. *Dei miseratione* only doubled the defenses. To have been protecting the symbol of love by lances and to have brought in artillery did not seem to strain comprehension too severely. Yet the perfection of plan risked making the ironies of the enterprise palpable. If the system rationalized by *Dei miseratione* were faced by irrationality itself, the tax on understanding might even be excessive.

HOW THE POPE CAME TO DISSOLVE CHRISTIAN MARRIAGES

The theologians, confronted with the canons of Alexander III set out in Chapter II, had had to explain how an unconsummated but valid, confirmed, sacramental marriage of Christians could be dissolved by religious profession. Henry of Ghent hazarded the thought that the marriage was not dissolved at all; if the spouse remaining in the world remarried he enjoyed a licensed bigamy, having one spiritual spouse in religion and a second, carnal spouse in his new marriage. This solution measured the difficulty of the problem, the embarrassment of the exegetes. Ultimately, recourse to another metaphor prevailed. Everyone knew that death ended the marital bond. In professing religion, one "died to the world." Whether it was "a certain spiritual death" or a form of "civil death," profession was indisputably "death" in contemporary parlance. The theologians, led by Thomas Aquinas, employed the enlarged sense of the term to explain how religious profession terminated unconsummated unions. Entering religion — dying — one ended one's incompleted marriage. The canons did not create a form of dissolution; they recognized a subdivision of death.[6]

The canonists, led by Hostiensis, chose to emphasize the active role of the Church in establishing this result. They were led to ponder the ecclesiology implicit in the canons. Was not "the Church confirmed by marriage, rather than marriage by the Church, since by marriage there is signified that by which the Church is confirmed?" Even if the common distinction between consummated and unconsummated unions was accepted, so that only a sexually completed marriage symbolized the indissoluble union of Christ and the Church, how could the Church make and unmake marriages so easily? For Hostiensis at the center of the Curia, these questions had to be answered by invoking the special powers of the Pope. As Innocent III had already established in *Inter corporalia*, X.1.7.2, the Pope could dissolve the marriage between a bishop and his see; he could do so by virtue of his extraordinary power as the Vicar of Christ. So here, "we" — Hostiensis seemed to include the Curia with the Pope — "can legislate whatever pleases." True, it was inexpedient and unsafe "to relax the reins very much." But the canons on religious profession were only an example of a wider papal power over marriage.[7]

Until the fifteenth century no one knew of Popes acting on Hostiensis' hint. Then Antonino, Archbishop of Florence, formerly an auditor in the Curia of Eugene IV, reported that he had seen "bulls of Martin V and Eugene IV containing a dispensation or dissolution of unconsummated marriage for those who had later contracted marriages to others" — that is, he had seen bulls permitting the rectification of an existing marriage by removing the obstacle of a previous unconsummated union. Antonino was not prepared to denounce the practice of pontiffs he had served and bulls he had seen "with my own eyes"; neither was he ready to accept as definitive such unprecedented, theologically unexplained action. He ended by announcing that such dispensations were "not to be condemned, neither were they to be counselled to anyone." *

Recent exploration of the archives of Odo Colonna, Martin V, suggests that the practice was established and had a history predating his pontificate. In 1417, the first year of his reign, the Pope was asked by Stephan Puetrich to dissolve his marriage to Ursula Paet on the grounds that after the marriage Ursula had given birth to someone else's son, leading Stephan to refuse to consummate the marriage and creating great danger of the relatives of the two spouses committing mayhem. The Pope instructed the bishop of Augsburg to ask both Stephan and Ursula to enter religious life, but

---

* Antonino took the same position — neither to condemn nor counsel — on the lawfulness, under the rules on usury, of selling the bonds of Florence at a discount (*Summa theologiae moralis*, 2.1.11). In that case, too, the conflict of practice and theory helped to make him hesitate. Yet sometimes even curial practice was not enough to make Antonino set aside his theory. He condemned as usurious the profits made by the exchange-bankers, and when it was objected that "the Roman Church favors the exchange-bankers," he observed that members of the Roman Curia had concubines, but that no one concluded from the curial practice that concubinage was lawful (*ibid.*, 3.8.3).

if either or both refused the bishop was given power to dissolve their marriage and dispense them to marry others, provided Ursula did not object. In a second case, arising in 1425, Conrad von Martpurg asked the Pope to delegate authority to divorce him from Elizabeth Knelinges on similar grounds: she had borne another's child; he had refused to consummate the marriage; the relatives were at the point of bloodshed. The Pope delegated authority to dissolve to the deacon of the church of St. Severus in Erfurt, if both parties agreed. Apparently Elizabeth objected, for two years later Conrad sought an annulment on the ground that he had consented to marry her only on the condition that she was a virgin. On his allegations alone, the Pope granted this prayer. In 1427, Andrea of Perugia and Caterina, a German girl, jointly petitioned the Pope to dissolve their marriage on the grounds that Caterina had married at her mother's command, not consenting in her heart; that Caterina had returned Andrea's ring; and that no consummation had occurred. The Pope delegated authority to Hermann Dwerg, an apostolic notary, to dissolve the marriage if he found these facts to be true.

The Pope's answer in Stephan Puetrich's case combined the old rule of dissolution by religious profession and the new dissolution by papal authority. Martin V, himself an experienced canonist, may have been acting on Hostiensis' text, or he may well have been following an established custom. The routine way these petitions were handled and the easy delegations of power scarcely indicated an awareness that an extraordinary power was being exercised. But these documents were not available to theologians until five centuries later. All they knew was the undetailed account of Antonino. With his doubtful endorsement, the curial practice was disclosed to the larger theological world.[8]

For over a century, the papal power to dissolve remained in the limbo in which Antonino placed it in 1450. Two leading sixteenth-century theologians, Cajetan and Navarrus, claimed the Pope had the power without further theological elaboration; they pressed the fact that at least two Popes had exercised it. Another leading sixteenth-century theologian, Domingo de Soto, dismissed the power as a "dream," put forward "without a shadow of probability"; he doubted that Antonino had read the bulls of Eugene IV and Martin V aright. The controversy was warm; no theological consensus existed. When, on November 11, 1563, the Council of Trent enacted its canons on marriage, it asserted, against the denial of Luther, that religious profession dissolved an unconsummated marriage; the rule of Alexander III was put forward as a solemn truth to deny which was to incur anathema. But nothing at all was taught about papal power to dissolve. The silence of the Council, like the opinion of Antonino, neither condemned nor counseled.[9]

Actual cases continued to be reported in an unofficial, haphazard, incomplete fashion. Between Antonino and Cajetan, a span of fifty years, none was mentioned. Cajetan, a curial cardinal in a position to be informed, knew of several "in our day"; but only one, an action by Clement VII, did he report with such precision as to establish clearly what had happened. Soto knew of Spanish applicants who, relying on Cajetan's opinion, had sought dissolutions in Rome and been denied. Navarrus knew of Spanish applicants whom he had sent to Rome without being certain of how they had succeeded. Throughout this period, stretching from Antonino's accidental revelation up to the end of the Council of Trent, the absence of any public papal pronouncement left the field open to hearsay, conjecture, and debate.[10]

Two papal decrees issued in 1571 and 1583 as limited private rulings reflected increased confidence at the Curia in the papal power. These documents, *Romani Pontificis* of Pius V and *Populis et nationibus* of Gregory XIII, will be discussed in Chapter VI. Suffice it to say here, that, on a liberal reading, they assumed the existence of a power to dissolve unconsummated marriages; but the actual language used, oblique and cautious to the point of ambiguity, reflected hesitation to claim the power openly.[11]

In 1599 a special committee of the Curia assumed that the Pope had the power. Composed of rotal auditors; cardinals who had been rotal auditors; a famous Jesuit theologian, Roberto Bellarmino; officials of the Sacred Penitentiary; and diplomats, this group met to consider the request of Sigismund Báthory, Prince of Transylvania, for a dissolution of his marriage to Maria Christina of Austria, niece of the Emperor Maximilian VI. Impotence on the Prince's part had not been proved; the fact of nonconsummation (the marriage had lasted four years) was unclear to some members of the commission; but they united in affirming the Pope's right to dispense if nonconsummation were proved to the satisfaction of his delegates. The case became a celebrated precedent not because the advice was officially published, but because of the indiscretion of a member, the French cardinal, D'Ossat, who included an account of the decision in his correspondence. In his view the Pope's elaborate consultation was not so much for the benefit of the Transylvanians as for that of Henri IV of France, who was known to be seeking an annulment of his own marriage: the Pope had "wanted to show us in the case of another how he would proceed in our own." * In D'Ossat's understanding of what was done, papal annulment of a consummated marriage as invalid was no different in substance from papal dissolution of an unconsummated union: either could be accomplished if the Pope were willing.[12]

Such a failure to discriminate between invalidation and dissolution — such a hard-headed, functional analysis — would have seemed careless and even cynical to the theologians who attempted to explain the basis of the papal power to dissolve unconsummated marriages. Of these, the chief was Tomás Sanchez, who asked forthrightly: "Can the Pontiff dispense from a confirmed marriage so that its bond is dissolved and the spouses can lawfully enter another marriage?" The answer he found in doubt, but a maxim was of aid — "in doubt, the opinion of superiors is to be observed" — and Popes had in fact used the power. It was a power inherent in the Pope as Vicar of Christ, necessary for the administration of the Church and, therefore, implicit in the papal office: "It must be believed that Christ, Who does not fail in necessities, has conferred on His Vicar full power as to those things which are necessary for the good administration of the Church."[13] Like American doctrine on the inherent powers of the President, the rationale of vicarial power stretched far — it covered almost any action by any Pope undertaken for the welfare of the Church.

Yet, how was marriage indissoluble if lawful, valid, sacramental marriage could be dissolved by the Pope? Marriage was indissoluble, said Sanchez, only in the sense that it could not be rescinded by mutual agreement "in the manner of other contracts." It was not

* D'Ossat may have understimated Clement VIII's interest in the affairs of Transylvania. Sigismund Báthory, a prince educated by Jesuits, had appeared as a champion of Catholicism in this region threatened by Turks and divided among the Orthodox, the Calvinists, and the Catholics. Although in 1599 Sigismund was in retreat, he was still an important client of the Holy See, see N. Iorga, *Histoire de Roumains* (Bucharest, 1938), V, 327-328, 363, 409; *Enciclopedia României* (Bucharest, 1938), I, 762.

indissoluble in the sense of remaining unbroken if the higher authority of the Pope dissolved it. Did not divine law forbid divorce and remarriage, and was not divine law above alteration by the Pope? Such divine laws as "Thou shalt not commit adultery, Thou shalt not lie" were, Sanchez conceded, beyond papal dispensation. But the Pope could affect the human contract on which the divine law operated: he did not change the divine law, "he removed the foundation of the obligation." Divine law imposed the duty of keeping a vow once made; the Pope could not change the duty, but he could, in the name of God, release a religious from his vows; and, once the religious was released, the obligation disappeared. Analogously, he could dispense from marriage by dissolving the contract which gave rise to the obligation not to remarry. Was this to say that the Pope could undo a sacrament? It was only to say that he could "dissolve the contract" on which the sacrament depended. The Pope could not make consecrated bread cease to be the Eucharist; for there the body of Christ had "a necessary connection" with the consecrated species of the bread; but he could "indirectly" disjoin the sacrament of marriage from two persons because the sacrament was not necessarily connected to the two married persons. If the Pope could remove the contract underlying an unconsummated marriage, why could he not also remove the contractual foundation of a sacramental marriage? The latter had a final perfection: it signified "the union of Christ with the Church through the flesh in which is founded in every way the indissolubility of consummated marriage." That signification could not be denied by dissolution.

Sanchez' reasoning assumed the result that he had to reach. No theologian in 1600 could have maintained that all Christian marriages were dissoluble by the Pope. To stop short of this conclusion, yet to justify the dispensations granted by the modern pontiffs, required determination. If the most skilled of writers on marriage had difficulty in making his distinctions persuasive, small wonder that the Curia itself did nothing to advertise or defend a power whose existence was a novelty, whose exercise was useful, and whose justification appeared to be so purely pragmatic.

Regularization of the power occurred in the seventeenth century. The S.C.C. became the agency before which the advocates would show facts and reason justifying dispensation from an existing union. If the Congregation determined that nonconsummation was established and that sufficient reason existed to grant the grace of a dispensation, it so advised the Pope, who routinely followed its advice. The process was well-known to the curial bar, which specialized in the presentation of petitions. No "reasonable controversy" existed over the papal power to dispense, Prospero Lambertini told the S.C.C. in 1719: "the received opinion of the canonists" and the judgments of "many theologians" supported it; and the precedent of the Prince of Transylvania in 1599 was well-known.[14] The Secretary found it unnecessary to cite canons, papal pronouncement, or even theological opinion. By this date the exception to the indissolubility of marriage was taken for granted in the Curia.*

Reduced to bureaucratic familiarity, no longer doubted as a fact, the power to dissolve Christian marriages still had not been formally claimed by the Popes or broadcast to the public. In 1741, in *Dei miseratione*, Benedict XIV did not justify or explain, but he exposed the marvellous power to the world at large. He kept the curial language which avoided shock: the Pope "dispensed," he did not "dissolve." Not for the Pope to use Sanchez' blunter term, "dissolve"; not for him to provide a rationale for a power which was "often" exercised. If his own knowledge of historic precedents seemed to go back no further than the case of the Prince of Transylvania, he was untroubled. The cases which came to the Curia were "frequent." He had handled them himself more than once in the S.C.C. His own aim now was to correct deficiencies he had observed in the procedure. That in passing he gave full publicity to

---

* Other petitions presented by Lambertini for consideration by the S.C.C. were *Rimini, May 16, 1720*, Benedict XIV, *Quaestiones canonicae*, q. 145; *Urbano, January 12, 1726*, *Thesaurus S.C.C.*, III, 254; *Florence, March 29, 1727*, *Quaestiones canonicae*, q. 546. In the Urbano case, the only issue Lambertini thought it necessary to report at length was the availability of the papal dispensation to humble folk: Pasquale Cristino, an inhabitant of the Italian village of San Angelo, married by proxy Isabella Britti, a Portuguese girl selected for him by his brother in Lisbon. Escorted by the brother, Isabella sailed for Italy on an English ship and was kidnaped by its captain who took her off to Gibraltar and married her. Pasquale, validly married for life to a girl he had never seen, petitioned for a dispensation from the bond. Lambertini cited precedents to show that papal grace could be accorded "the small man as well as the great"; and the favor was granted.

a practice over a century old probably did not seem to him the most significant aspect of his action. Yet Benedict XIV's interest in rationalized public process was plainly being served.

By the terms of *Dei miseratione*, a "full and accurate" account of the facts in nonconsummation cases was to be supplied the Pope in the libel of petition, so that by merely reading the petition he could determine whether to deny or commit it to a Congregation (normally the S.C.C.) for an advisory vote. If the petition was assigned to a Congregation its Secretary was to give the Pope an exact relation "of the whole business," so he could decide whether to approve the Congregation's vote or recommit the matter to another court or committee.[15] When the Pope was Prospero Lambertini, no arrangement could have better assured thoughtful supervision. But how many other Popes could be expected to review in detail the petitions of advocates and the actions of curial committees in an unending stream of individual instances? Seeking to centralize responsibility in the Pope, *Dei miseratione* in effect confirmed the treatment of nonconsummation cases in the Curia. Incidentally, almost accidently, nonetheless deliberately, it acknowledged at the highest level that a discretion existed and was employed to terminate one class of Christian marriage.

THE ADVENTURES OF A KNIGHT OF CÓRDOBA AND A LADY OF JAÉN AND BAEZA

The Ponce de León, familiar to readers of American history from the seeker of the Fountain of Youth and explorer of Florida, and to canonists from the celebrated professor of Salamanca, were not lacking in other distinguished members of the family; and if the branch which settled in central southern Spain in the province of Jaén in the small town of Baeza was not in a position to discover Florida, still in a municipality of the size of Baeza, the bearers of the name were persons of dignity and importance. Luis Ponce de León lived in Baeza and enjoyed the title of Lord of the Tower of Don Rodrigo and became the king's governor of the city of Jaén, thirty miles to the north. He married, with the appropriate papal dispensation, his first cousin, Leonor de Quesada, daughter of the second Count of Garzies, and from the union had three daughters, Maria Isabella, Teresa, and Ana, and one son, Miguel Jerónimo.

Maria Isabella married Francisco Canaveral, eighth lord of Benaluá. Teresa married Fernando Carvajal, Count of Humanes. Miguel Jerónimo married Angela Dionisia de Baeza Vicentelo, daughter of the third marquis of Castromonte y Robledo.[16] But Ana, until she was twenty-two, married no one, and whether she married then was to be a question that the procedures devised by Prospero Lambertini would have to decide.

As a third daughter, Doña Ana had less chance of a good marriage than her older sisters, and the amount of her dowry must have been a matter of calculation for the Lord of the Tower of Don Rodrigo. He died before his daughter's future could be secured, and responsibility for her fate fell to her brother, who succeeded to the titles of his father and grandfather and was both Lord of the Tower of Don Rodrigo and the third Count of Garzies. As was natural under the circumstances, Doña Ana was sent to the monastery of Santa Clara, which existed under the eye of the family at Baeza, to try her aptitude for religious life.[17] After some months she was returned to her home, and it was clear to her brother, as in 1728 she reached the age of twenty-two (twenty-one was "over age," a canonical reason for granting a dispensation from a variety of canonical impediments to marriage), that he had an obligation which must be met if the honor and dignity of his sister were to be preserved.

In Córdoba, sixty miles to the west, another obligation troubled the family of Don José Perez de Guzman. The Guzman of Castile had, according to Cervantes, a more ancient lineage than Dulcinea del Tobosa, and the beginnings of the family, of which both Saint Dominic and João V of Portugal were descendants, were lost in the times of the Visigoths. The Perez, who had become Perez de Guzman, numbered among them Gaspar Alonso, the rebel Duke of Medina Sidonia, punished for his part in a separatist movement in Andalusia and deceased in 1660, and Alonso, Viceroy and Captain-General of the King in Valencia, deceased in 1708. The branch of the family which lived in Córdoba at the beginning of the eighteenth century had no such illustrious persons in its immediate ranks, but it had pride in its ancestry, its relations, and its name, and a sense of its great worth and durability and the desirability of continuing to endure.[18]

The father of José de Guzman had died when Don José was still an infant, and he had been raised in Córdoba by his widowed mother, Juana, herself of the noble family of Aguilera de los Rios. At sixteen Don José was in love, and this state proved painful to his mother, for the girl was "of humble condition," and unsuitable to his lineage. His mother feared "the slippery season of youth," and she dreaded not the lubricous allurements of sexual sin but the more serious and permanent entanglement of "an unworthy marriage." In these straits she recalled or discovered the predicament of the Count of Garzies and sent a monk of Córdoba to investigate the Count's willingness to match Doña Ana with her son.[19]

A match was made. Don José Perez de Guzman had an older name and came from a more famous city. Doña Ana Ponce de León had more powerful relations. To be connected with the Perez de Guzman seemed to the Count of Garzies an honor for his family and a satisfactory arrangement for his sister. To have her son win a dowry and become the brother-in-law of the Count of Garzies seemed to Doña Juana the best a widowed mother might arrange for an impressionable orphan. Neither family weighed the disparity in age as serious. Doña Juana's emissary reported the enthusiasm of the Count of Garzies for the proposal. Only one disturbing rumor burdened the negotiations. A noble of Jaén wrote Luis Herrera, Inquisitor of Córdoba, that Doña Ana "was crazy, had always been crazy, and at the present was without improvement." Herrera informed Doña Juana, and another priest, Tavira del Zerro, gave her the same report.[20]

Doña Juana would not have chosen a demented girl to produce heirs or to provide for the sexual needs of her son. In her desperation she was not anxious to investigate, and she refrained from sending Don José to see for himself. She brushed off the information she had received with the supposition that Doña Ana was melancholy after her enclosure in a convent; a change of location and status would cure her. Nonetheless, she took two precautions in arranging for the marriage, which, to satisfy the mutual desire for speed, was to be made by proxy. She wrote to Doña Eleonora of Córdoba, a friend then in Baeza; and she sent a new representative, Don Juan de Salazar, to Jaén. Salazar carried a document, signed by Don José on January 19, 1728, constituting the Count of Garzies his proxy; it was so drafted as to take effect only if cosigned by Salazar; and Salazar was to sign only if he were first satisfied that Doña Ana was sane.[21]

Bribed by the Count, as Doña Juana came to believe, or incompetent, or merely unperceptive, Salazar signed the proxy and delivered it. Doña Eleonora de Córdoba wrote that Doña Ana was an angel and anything said to the contrary was the work of evil tongues. Doña Juana asked no more questions. Contreras, the Pro-Vicar-General of Jaén, dispensed from the banns and gave permission for the marriage to be held "at home or wherever the contracting party is." The dispensation avoided publicity and permitted the Count to have the wedding take place when he wished. The marriage was celebrated at his castle on February 27, 1728, before a parish priest of Baeza, two servants, and a relative of the bride, with the Count acting as his brother-in-law's proxy. Don José himself met Doña Ana outside of Baeza in the village of Menxibar. There, with both principals present, the marriage was "revalidated" before Juan Santos, the Count's own chaplain.[22]

Don José and Doña Ana had been docile pawns throughout this process. If coercion implies the overcoming of resistance, it would be hard to say that either had been coerced. No word or sign has been recorded that they wanted to marry each other, yet no word or sign of resistance to their marriage has survived. Waxenly and woodenly, with a sense of destiny or of duty or of despair, they did what those in whose power they were expected of them; and what they expected of each other they perhaps never put in words.

Man and wife, on the evening of their wedding day in Menxibar, Doña Ana told Don José that she had taken a vow of virginity which she did not expect to violate. Don José, who had had no intimations of this intention, and whose knowledge of scriptural and hagiographic precedent was perhaps limited, was shocked by her declaration. His first thought was to abandon her in Jaén, but in the morning his apprehensions about her brother and his mother, and his view of himself as a Spanish gentleman and potent male, predominated over his initial resolution; and moved by "fear, honor, and shame," he left Menxibar at once, but took Doña Ana with him.[23]

In Córdoba, Doña Ana was presented to Doña Juana and other relatives-in-law. What happened after that was disputed in the later litigation and will be described in that context. Doña Ana's behavior was bizarre and intolerable to her husband, who in 1730 left her and, as Spain entered the War of the Polish Succession, went to Naples as a soldier.[24] Whether the marriage was ever consummated was disputed in the courts of the Curia thirty years after the wedding day.

Excerpts from the record of a provincial criminal court suggest the feelings which developed between the two yoked together, sometime after Don José's return from the wars in Italy. For the purchase of a drug from a Cordovan pharmacist, Juan Ramirez, Don José was prosecuted criminally. Introduced as evidence of the transaction was a letter from Ramirez saying, "I presume the medicine is for your mother or your wife." Doña Ana's relatives regarded the acquisition of the drug as preparation to poison her. That Ramirez thought Doña Juana might have been the recipient of the medication struck them as irrelevant. They had their own view of how Perez de Guzman felt. Yet the prosecution was not for attempted murder, but for buying a drug: Ramirez had made an unlawful sale and was banished to Africa for six years; Don José had made an unlawful purchase and was exiled from Córdoba for four years.[25] Prosecution and punishment were for a technical offense. In severity they seemed to reflect a suspicion, true or false, that the more serious crime had been contemplated.

By 1758, when Don José had returned from exile to his native city, he was determined to end the marriage. In thirty years of being Doña Ana's husband, he may have become reconciled to his life, but now he was stirred by a new hope. His cousin, Pedro Alcántara de Guzman, Duke of Medina Sidonia, was entering old age without a child.[26] More than ever before Don José desired to have offspring to continue the line. Doña Ana was fifty-two. If he were to serve his house, he would have to free himself from her. Whatever allurement poison may once have presented in his own fantasy or in that of his relatives, the course he now chose was the orderly process of the dissolution of an unconsummated marriage provided by the Pope.

IN WHAT WAY THE POPE'S GRACE WAS SOUGHT AND LOST

In 1758 Benedict XIV was eighty-three; it was thirty-four years since he had presented Senator Barberini's plea for deliverance to the Sacred Congregation of the Council; and it was the last year of his life. Meticulous to the end in discharging his legal duties, he read the supplication addressed to him from Spain on behalf of Don José Perez de Guzman to dispense him from a marriage valid and confirmed but unconsummated. The petition was meritorious on its face, the Pope committed it to the S.C.C. for examination, and in the spring of 1758 the Secretary of the S.C.C. wrote the Bishop of Córdoba to hear the case and return his recommendation to the Congregation of the Council.[27]

According to thirteenth-century papal legislation preserved in the *Decretals, Causam matrimonii*, X.2.19.14, and *Literae vestrae nobis*, X.4.15.7, virginity was to be proved, where nonconsummation was an issue, by a physical examination of the woman in question. Although exceptions were not unknown for ladies of great dignity, in a contested case the examination was standard; and the procedural reforms of *Dei miseratione* had done nothing to relax its rigor. Doña Ana, committed by the Bishop to a monastery to await the outcome of the litigation, was ordered to undergo the test. She was inspected by three skilled midwives, who probed her fifty-two-year-old genital tract with the aid of violet oil and a tube. She appeared to be intact. She herself contributed no information verbally, for she was incoherent on oral interrogation.[28]

The bishop, Martino de Barcia, had before him the midwives' report, the oath of Perez de Guzman that intercourse had never occurred, the absence of contradiction from Doña Ana, and her obvious present mental irregularity. He was a new man and a northerner, born in Zamora in 1702 and transferred to Córdoba from Ceuta, Morocco, in 1756. His predecessor, Folch de Cardona, had been promoted to be cardinal-archbishop of Seville; and perhaps the new bishop was more willing to treat Perez de Guzman's old marriage as a new matter. He voted that the favor of dispensation be granted.[29]

Over two years passed before this recommendation reached Rome. Counsel for Perez de Guzman pressed simultaneously the other branch of their case, the alleged incompetence of Doña Ana at the time of the wedding; and the presentation of testimony and procedural conflicts attendant to this course delayed action on the plea for grace. But when the case came to Rome, counsel were put to an election: they must choose the way of grace or of justice. They opted to ask for grace, and buttressed their Spanish evidence with an analysis by two "medico-surgical" professors of Rome, who gave their expert opinion that the midwives had taken appropriate measures and found suitable evidence of virginity.

Perez de Guzman had surmounted two hurdles — the Pope's initial scrutiny and his own bishop's trial — and had proved the negative fact of nonconsummation so far as expert testimony could. The next step was to win the recommendation of the Congregation of the Council which had to precede the final action of the Pope. This body was in all substantial respects the same kind of committee it had been in 1720 when Lambertini was its Secretary. The cardinals were younger, for Benedict XIV had promoted younger men, but none was under forty and there were several septuagenarians. The Jesuits were gone; on the brink of extinction by papal fiat, they no longer gave a special theological cachet to the committee; but men with high reputation as legal scholars, such as Giuseppe Furetti of Bergamo, and former auditors of the Rota, such as its ex-Dean Pietro Bussi, gave the Council a reputation for learning. There were no non-Italians among the resident members — the death, shortly before the case was scheduled, of Cardinal Joaquin Portocarrero, himself a Guzman and the minister plenipotentiary to the Holy See from Spain, removed the person most likely to take a close interest in the families involved. One member, Domenico Orsini, Duke of Gravina, had been a married man; for almost twenty years he had been a widower and a cardinal; if marriage, bereavement, and loneliness constituted a basis for empathy, he stood closest to the petitioner.[30]

Carlo Rezzonico, a Venetian, now reigned as Pope Clement XIII. He was no less a lawyer than his predecessor, though not so great a one, and from 1729 to 1737 he had held the Venetian seat upon the Rota. The three printed volumes of his decisions as an auditor did not contain a single marriage case, but in the midst of judicial business mostly confined to Italy he had handled three ecclesiastical disputes from southern Spain: an accounting of a common fund sought by an archdeacon and a canon from the cathedral chapter of Jaén and Baeza; a suit by the same cathedral chapter against the nuns of Santa Clara who had once tested the vocation of Doña Ana; a quarrel between two claimants to the benefice of San Andreas, Córdoba, the parish church of Perez de Guzman. If the papers of the new case even crossed his desk, they may have evoked recollections of his prime when he had dealt justice with discerning firmness to the stubborn Andalusians.[31]

The Prefect of the S.C.C., Ferdinando Maria Rossi, was the Pope's appointment and his creation as a cardinal, a man like himself trained in the law outside of Rome — at the University of Camerino in Macerata — who had risen through a series of curial appointments until at the end of Benedict XIV's reign he ruled as vice-regent of Rome. Lawyer and administrator, Rossi had brought to the Council as its Secretary Giuseppe Simonetti. Simonetti came from the village of Castelnuovo di Farfa, had acquired the usual credentials at the Sapienza, and, nine years Rossi's junior, had held a variety of curial posts in association with him. Rossi's industrious, circumspect, and knowledgeable executive, he was made a cardinal in 1766, an appointment greeted with what Pastor calls "universal praise," and died almost immediately after receiving this recognition. In Perez de Guzman's case he was the fulcrum.[32]

Simonetti reported the case for the meeting of the S.C.C. scheduled for September 20, 1760. In favor of granting the plea were the bishop's endorsement, the midwives' report, the sugeons' opinion, the petitioner's oath. Doña Ana, now insane, could not be suspected of collusion. Dispensations must be for just cause, and more than one just cause was alleged here: doubt as to Doña Ana's original capacity to consent; her frustration of the purpose of marriage by refusing intercourse; the deception practiced by the Count of Garzies in procuring the original agreement to marry; the objective of keeping the line of Perez de Guzman from expiring; and the recommendation of the bishop. Against granting the dispensation was the rule that cohabitation gave rise to a presumption of intercourse, especially applicable when Perez de Guzman had acquiesced in the marriage for thirty years. The midwives could be wrong; if so, there was no proof of nonconsummation; Perez de Guzman's oath was not evidence; in doubt, a dispensation was to be denied. Evidence apart, just cause for dispensation was lacking. It was not enough to say "a noble house will perish." Indeed, there was a weighty counterreason for denying the grace: Ana would be prejudiced; if denied this marriage, she could never expect to marry again.[33]

Report of argument and counterargument distributed to the cardinals for their meeting of Saturday, September 20, Simonetti was disturbed on the evening of September 19 by a visit from the Defender of Marriages. On the very eve of decision there had reached him from Spain, through the efforts of the Count of Garzies, a deposition taken of Blasia Montalbo, who for the first three years of Doña Ana's marriage had been her lady-in-waiting. The girl deposed that she had seen Don José and Doña Ana together in the act of intercourse — "lying together coupling." Everyone knew that Doña Ana had suffered a miscarriage; she herself had been present when it happened. Still trying to assess the credibility of this report, and no doubt having consulted Rossi, Simonetti on Saturday had the matter passed over by the cardinals.[34]

On November 22 the case was back on the docket. Simonetti added the surprising information which had been communicated to him on September 19. In the intervening two months, counsel for Perez de Guzman had not been able to offset or undermine the story, and the Secretary must have found Montalbo's testimony plausible to make it part of the briefing for November 22. Compared with his summary for the meeting of September 20, his report had a ring unmistakably hostile to the petitioner. The cardinals' action was also unambiguous. To the question "Has a ratified, unconsummated marriage been established so that the Most Holy is to be advised in favor of dispensing?," the S.C.C. responded, "No, and not again."

"Not again" was the moral equivalent of "double costs" imposed by modern courts to express disapproval of a frivolous appeal. It was not an absolute bar to reopening the case, for, after a suitable interval, the S.C.C. as a whole might vote to permit rehearing; but "not again" said that the court considered the case hopeless. The Secretary was commissioned to determine Doña Ana's costs of litigation and her living expenses (*alimenta*) during it; Perez de Guzman was ordered to pay the total.[35] His effort to save his line through the path of grace had come to an expensive and ignominious end.

HOW THE KNIGHT OF CÓRDOBA PROVED
HIS WIFE TO BE MAD

Simultaneously with the hearing on nonconsummation in Córdoba, thirty-two witnesses, eleven of them priests, had appeared before the Vicar-General of Bishop Barcia to testify as to Doña Ana's competence to marry. These appearances occurred between May 9, 1758, and October 25 of the same year, a pace later described by her Roman counsel as "incredible precipitation." The speed was at least so great that no one cited Doña Ana formally as the respondent, and no one seemed to have heard of the Defender of Marriages instituted by *Dei miseratione*. The process could at best be regarded as preliminary.[36]

In 1759, a fresh start was made with the Fiscal, a legal officer of the diocese, appearing as guardian *ad litem* for Ana. The Vicar-General of Jaén, presumably incited to act by the Count of Garzies, enjoined the Córdoba court from proceeding, but this maneuver was without effect. Then, on May 19, the Count presented to the court a mandate signed by his sister authorizing him to represent her. The Vicar-General of Córdoba ruled that Doña Ana, at this point, was indisputably insane, and her mandate void. The Count, bitterly protesting, was excluded from the trial. His chaplain, Juan Santos — the official witness of the marriage at Menxibar — and the Count's steward, Leonardo Carbanell, were commanded to attend as witnesses, refused, and were compelled by threat of excommunication. Other witnesses from Jaén and Baeza avoided testifying out of fear of the Count. Still, on the evidence presented, the Vicar-General ruled that Doña Ana's "perpetual" insanity had been proved; and the Bishop pronounced the marriage null.[37]

Dei miseratione, of course, had not been complied with: no appeal had been taken by a "Defender of Marriages," and two concurrent decisions of different tribunals had not been given. Under the new law, Doña Ana could have done nothing, and Perez de Guzman would have been guilty of polygamy if he married again. But the Count of Garzies was not satisfied with a situation where the Bishop of Córdoba had determined that his sister was unmarried. He could have gone to Toledo, the metropolitan see, where Cardinal Luis Fernandez de Córdoba, a Guzman connection, was the archbishop.[38] He preferred to go where he had won before. An appeal signed in Doña Ana's name was filed with the S.C.C.

In 1760, when the petition for a dispensation had been heard, Don José had given up his right to defend against this appeal. Once the chance for a dispensation disappeared, Don José regretted the renunciation of his claim to justice. He obtained new counsel, of whom the chief was Filippo Durani, a recent Consistorial Advocate and Co-Adjutor of the Advocate of the People in the Campidoglio or administration of the city of Rome. Durani set about remedying his predecessors' mistake. No renunciation of rights, he argued, could make an invalid marriage valid. The S.C.C. should not force a litigant to live in sin because of a mistaken waiver by his proctor. This line of persuasion was effective; Don José was not barred from argument.[39] What did the evidence establish as to his wife's competence?

Two physicians of Córdoba had examined Doña Ana in 1759, pronounced her beyond doubt "a mad, crazy woman, who did not know right from wrong," and declared her madness to be "without intervals." The parish books of San Andreas, Córdoba, showed her incapable of receiving the Eucharist in 1760 and 1761. She had not been capable of rational speech throughout all the proceedings before the Vicar-General. When she first came to Córdoba with her husband, she had screamed obscenities and run naked in the sight of the household; and she had walked nude in the garden making piles of snow. In 1731, sick and on the point of dying, she had been refused the Viaticum because she was judged incapable of receiving a sacrament.[40]

Doña Ana's resistance to intercourse was positive proof of her madness on the very day she met Don José and went through the second ceremony of marriage. At the ceremony itself she spoke the words of consent "with some delay and hesitation," according to Juan Santos, the Count's chaplain, a witness favorable to validity; and she barely extended her hand in sign of consent, according to a witness for Perez de Guzman. Sebastiano de Espexo, his steward, had found her stupefied and speechless when he had come to Jaén with a gift before the wedding. Even her brother had recognized her condition, according to Don José's witnesses. His mother, Juana, related how the Count had visited the newlyweds in Córdoba and told her that his sister would have to be locked in the house.

When Doña Juana asked why he had arranged for Doña Ana to be married if she were mad, he had answered that the madness came from a tightness of the uterus which marriage would cure.[41]

Before the marriage Doña Ana's state had been no different. What but mental incapacity could have led the poor nuns of Santa Clara to reject their patron's sister? Bartolomé Hidalgo, a casual visitor to Santa Clara in 1727, had stumbled on her near the choir of the monastery church, and with shrill cries and laughs she had told him the devil would carry him off. Another caller at Santa Clara in 1726, Francisco Delgado, had seen her in the visitors' parlor behaving oddly, and had been told by other nuns that she was the crazy sister of the Count of Garzies. The Count's chaplain, Santos, admitted that Doña Ana had been sick while at the convent and suffered "a period of foolishness," although it lasted no longer than her sickness. Sebastiano de Morente, an order priest from Baeza, had heard from a nun of Baeza that, at Santa Clara, Ana had "to be bound sometimes as one in a frenzy." Gaspar de los Cobos, formerly an ecclesiastical judge in Baeza, wrote Juana in 1737 that the Bishop of Jaén had actually ordered the nuns to refuse Doña Ana because her madness impeded the divine office; this letter, accepted in evidence, was the best approximation to an official explanation of why she had not been allowed to remain at Santa Clara. The evidence went back to Doña Ana's childhood. Don José's old steward, Espexo, had visited Jaén when her father was governor and had seen boys throwing rocks at a window where they said "the governor's daughter was." Counsel argued that such contempt for the governor's daughter would not have been displayed unless Doña Ana's accepted madness gave the boys immunity or she had started the fight by throwing rocks herself. From the age of four to the age of fifty-four her behavior had been mad.[42]

Counterevidence began with the depositions of the present abbess and prioress of Baeza that Doña Ana was sane while at the monastery. Parish records from Jaén showed that Doña Ana had fulfilled her Easter duty in every year she had lived in the town except 1722 and 1725; the record from San Andreas showed she had received Easter communion in Córdoba in 1729 and, intermittently, in succeeding years thereafter. Three witnesses from Jaén — Santos, the chaplain; Leonardo Carbanell, the Count's steward; and a physician—all admitted that Doña Ana had sometimes not been herself, but all attributed these periods to illness from which she had recovered. Contradicting ten witnesses for Perez de Guzman, Doña Ana's uncle swore that Don José had formally visited her several times at Baeza before the wedding. Chaplain Santos attributed her hesitation in pronouncing the words of consent to the modesty usual in strictly reared girls. The former lady-in-waiting, Blasia Montalbo, testified that the marriage was consummated without irrational hesitation by Doña Ana on the second day of marriage, on the way from Menxibar to Córdoba, in the town of Del Rio.[43]

Contradiction ran through much of the testimony—on Doña Ana's health at Santa Clara; on Don José's acquaintance with her before the wedding; on the fact and time of marital intercourse; on the length and character of Doña Ana's illness. No hearsay rule excluded a large amount of secondhand reporting and inference. Yet, if all doubtful or challenged evidence were put aside, it remained undisputed that, as early as 1726, she had suffered bouts of illness which had affected her behavior; that she had on occasion been excluded from the sacraments as incompetent; and that at the time of trial she was unable to respond rationally to interrogation. On this evidence had she been incompetent to marry?

OF THE MANIC, THE NOODLES, THE LUCID, AND THE MARRIED

The texts of the *Corpus juris canonici* which recognized insanity as a bar to marriage were of no help in deciding a case like Doña Ana's. *Neque furiosus*, a scrap of Roman law — "Neither a madman nor a madwoman can contract marriage, but if it has been contracted let them not be separated"—constituted Gratian's contribution.[44] Later, in 1205, Innocent III had ruled on a case where a soldier from Alexandria alleged that his daughter Rufina had married one Opizo Lancavecla, who "suffered from a continuing madness," and "because of the alienation of the madness, consent could not occur." The Pope ordered the separation of the couple; his decision, the canon *Dilectus*, X.4.1.24, stood as papal recognition of insanity as an impediment to marriage. Nothing in the short papal decree explained what constituted this incapacity.

What insanity consisted in, what the signs of it were, when it affected legal relations — these were questions answered by the familiar sources of canonical jurisprudence from Justinian to the Roman Rota. The usual authorities were buttressed by purely medical writers such as Galen and Avicenna and enriched by a new seventeenth-century genre combining medical data with legal conclusions, of which the pioneering specimen and prime example was the *Quaestiones medico-legales* of a Roman physician, Paolo Zacchia. Designated by Innocent X "General Proto-Physician of the Whole Ecclesiastical State," Zacchia was in fact the General Proto-Author of All Writers on Law and Medicine. He was saluted as a new Columbus, who had sailed a new ocean, who ruled a new land.[45] In exemplary jargon, in unabashed self-confidence in a superiority resulting from knowledge of "medical science," in the proprietary view of patients assumed by an authoritative analyst, Zacchia's work was the father of a mighty progeny.* Published in 1621, his treatise was still in 1760 the best authority on what constituted insanity within the canonical system. Supplemented by the insights of that old Cordovan, Tomás Sanchez, Medico-Legal Questions provided all the approved answers.

Insanity was recognizable by an "infinite" variety of signs, which varied with the variety of human temperament. Disordered words and manner of speech, unconventional acts like deliberately walking through mud or giving away property to inappropriate recipients were among the symptoms. To neglect the unneglectable, to fear without cause, to be angry at what caused no anger — these were unfailing signs. In a given case, to decide authoritatively, physicians were "the sole witnesses to be believed." [46] By Zacchia's standards, Bishop Barcia's court in Córdoba had proceeded without flaw in finding Doña Ana presently insane.

Had she been insane, however, when she gave her consent to marry some thirty years before? To answer this question there came into play the concept of the lucid interval: that insanity was intermittent; that intervals of time were "lucid"; that beneficent

---

* As to style: "I have now and have had before, hypochondriacs" (Zacchia, *Quaestionum*, 2.1.23.4)—the possessory "have" is perfect for the proprietary stance. "I am able to follow the nature of the matter more closely," he wrote, apropos of lucid intervals, "because of my knowledge of medical science" (2.1.21.12) — the direct appeal to superior expertise was, at times, made. As to jargon, the book's title is itself the best evidence.

acts done in those intervals would be recognized — these were propositions rooted in Roman law and confirmed by the canons. A man could make a will or resign a benefice in a lucid interval, and his act would be valid and its consequences honored. Indeed, the very fact that an act was appropriate, like a dying man making a will, created the presumption that it was lucidly done: the sanity of the act appeared from its quality.[47]

Not all diseases of the mind, however, were relieved by intermissions. If madness or melancholia, two subdivisions of mania, continued for, say, a month and arose not from fever but from "the brain itself," then the presumption must be that the mania lasted, whatever the outward evidence of its presence. In such varieties of melancholia as coma and catalepsy no lucid intervals occurred, and any acts of the comatose or cataleptic were without legal significance. If the disease were "by its nature, perpetual, incurable, and hopeless," the legal presumption that at every point in time the person was insane could only be rebutted by proof that the act occurred at a moment of actual lucidity.[48]

Half the battle in Ana's case turned on the burden of proof. Was her mania "drawn out from the very nature and organization of her body," as was maintained on behalf of Perez de Guzman — then the Defender of Marriages must show she was sane at the moment of consent. Was her dementia characterized by cyclical returns to sanity, as her counsel argued — then Perez de Guzman had to show she was insane when she married. She could be a melancholic — "captive in mind" in legal parlance — and be either incurably or intermittently demented.[49] Zacchia, providing the appropriate categories, did not determine their application.

The notion of temporary lucidity was paralleled and reinforced by the concept of partial insanity. Both focused on symptoms rather than the affected person as a whole. Both were supported by the most eminent medical authorities, Avicenna and Galen. Both appealed to the observation of persons who were irrational at particular times or in peculiar ways, and otherwise apparently sound. After all, asked Zacchia, "who does not have his heresies?" If peculiar opinions did not demonstrate general incapacity, neither did odd obsessional acts. As Avicenna taught, the imagination could be affected in one particular way without the reason being disturbed.[50]

Sanchez and Zacchia accepted this conventional view; but they were uneasy with it. To Sanchez, Cervantes' contemporary, an "outstanding doubt" was presented by the question, Can a man be rational in almost all matters, and insane on one? Contrary to Avicenna stood Aristotle. In Aristotelian analysis the reason of man depended on his imagination. In any kind of insanity, it seemed to Sanchez, the imagination had been injured; the effect of the injury upon the operations of the reason must be indivisible. If Aristotle were accepted instead of Avicenna, insanity on a single subject made a person incapable of contracting marriage because his reason as a whole must be affected.[51] Zacchia himself told the old joke about the visitor impressed by his knowledgeable hospital guide until they reached a man who said, "I am Napoleon," at which the guide declared, "He is madder than all the others, since I am here who really am Napoleon." In 1621, it was "the Holy Spirit" instead of "Napoleon," and perhaps the joke was not old. It underlined the point that a single delusion might manifest an underlying disease. In this state a man suffered from "a perturbed spirit" and was open to "false imagination"; he should be barred from all acts with legal consequences. If Zacchia were followed to this point, contrary to his own acceptance of Avicenna, a marriage made by one partially insane appeared open to challenge.

Love itself for Zacchia was a subspecies of the larger class of manic melancholia. By love he meant not affection of "medium force," but the kind of passion that arose from the beauty of a woman and banished prudence, made her lover blind to her faults, led him to frequent unaccustomed ways because she dwelt therein, incited him to dress more elegantly, use perfume, and apply ointment, perverted his judgment, and, in short, made him crazy with desire.[52] Tristan's yearning for Iseult, Don Quixote's for Dulcinea, was the sort of emotion which seemed to fall within the manic, and if madness on one subject destroyed capacity to marry, at one stroke those apparently most anxious to enter the state of union were disqualified; a marriage might be overthrown because made in a passion which manifested an unsettled reason. Doña Ana's marriage to Perez de Guzman had no danger of invalidation on this ground, but if imagination and reason were treated as all of a piece, if symptoms of madness were used to establish a general incapacity, then lucid intervals themselves might be discarded and the evidence of Ana's intermittent madness would establish her continuing infirmity.

Alternatively, Ana might have fallen into another recognized branch of dementia, fatuity, to be among those described by Zacchia as the simple, the stupid, the slow, the innocent, the moronic, the thick-grained, to stand with the noodles of whom Sanchez wrote, "we say ironically in Spanish they are not as wise as Solomon." [53] By native constitution, Zacchia observed, such persons were unfit for "even childish elements of learning" and were often inordinately bashful. Such a one might, for example, be afraid to touch his own wife for fear she would complain to his mother of his boldness. Could not Doña Ana's timorousness in marriage, her dull and wooden behavior, establish her as fatuous if not manic?

In Zacchia's simple dichotomy the physicians diagnosed the disease, the lawyers attached the consequence, even if in the process of adjudication the legal consequence thought proper must have played back on the medical classification of the act. Whatever the possible categories in which Ana might be fitted — the organically manic, the intermittently manic, the simple — the consequences attached were determined by the law. Was this kind of mixed medico-legal judgment even inescapable? Are not the demented always incapable in terms of capacity to perform some social act, whether it is speaking or marrying? If insanity always involves some failure to perceive reality, or relate to it, one always reaches the question of how reality is defined, and who defines it. By imperial decree of the Roman Emperor in A.D. 380 all who presumed to reject the Catholic faith were insane.[54] The Soviet Union today has been known to classify dissenters from doctrine as mentally ill. Czelaw Milocz has effectively used "The Captive Mind" as the title of his brilliant description of the response of Polish intellectuals to postwar Russian Communism. The extreme cases of religious or political definition of the real illuminate the character of a judgment which must be social even in a society such as eighteenth-century Spain which distinguished heresy from madness. Was Prospero Lambertini of captive mind if he supposed that regulations issued at Rome could safeguard all Catholic marriages as symbols of a supernatural truth? Was Ana Ponce de León of captive mind when she walked in the snow at Córdoba?

A social system structured the reality which made one question appropriate and the other impertinent.

When the issue was capacity to marry, in the eighteenth century, a strong social reason existed to set capacity in terms of minimal mental requirements. Marriage was the sole lawful channel for sexual intercourse. Celibacy was a gift not given to all. Unless a large class of Christians were to be given no legitimate outlet for their sexual impulses, marriage had to be an institution democratically accessible to all. What Sanchez wrote of the cyclically insane was generally felt to be true: "It would be harsh to constrain them to a life of continence." [55] This consideration, not often articulated, appeared to lie behind the assumption that little should be asked of those seeking to marry.

The low standard was confirmed by two analogies. Little was demanded in religious profession: the simplest soul could not be denied the opportunity to accept a divine invitation; to become a monk or a nun was open to almost anyone; and if one were capable of professing, one was capable of the lower vocation of Christian marriage. Almost everyone, too, was capable of sin. Only the infant, the sleepwalker, and the madman were not accountable to God for their acts. When seven, the age of reason, was attained, a child could offend God; he was capable of rational action. The standard Gloss on Gratian expressly taught that the insanity which made one incapable of sin was the insanity which incapacitated from marriage. Conversely, the Gloss's implication ran, capacity to sin was capacity to marry.[56] If this were true, the seven-year-old seemed to be mentally capable of marriage — it was the need for physical capacity which pushed the marriage age to fourteen for boys and twelve for girls.

Against this whole analysis stood the Augustinian account of the purposes of marriage consisting in the procreation and education of children, the preservation of fidelity, and the maintenance of indissolubility. How could a person of small mental capacity be capable of educating children? How could the recurrently insane be capable? Both Sanchez and Zacchia responded to these questions by teaching that the cyclically insane should be prohibited from marriage. Specifically as to melancholic mania, the category apparently most apt for Ana Ponce de León, Zacchia taught that there was "a peril of reincidence — one can easily recede — and therefore marriage should be entirely prohibited." [57] But prohibition was the least of canonical sanctions; to violate a prohibition was to act illicitly but not invalidly. Even the best authors were unwilling to draw the radical conclusion that incompetence to educate children was as fatal to capacity to marry as incapacity to copulate. Both Zacchia and Sanche affirmed the ability of the fatuous to marry. They were not fit for what required "perfection and integrity of intellect," such as public office, feudal lordship, or the priesthood. Yet they could take religious vows as brothers or sisters; and "they could more easily be admitted to marriage than to enter religion," for, in marriage, "nature itself cooperates and teaches the ignorant." [58] With "nature teaches the ignorant," Zacchia appeared to reduce the ends of marriage to the instinctual; the central Augustinian purposes were neglected; capacity was set at its lowest.

Expressly as to those insane on a single topic, Zacchia affirmed their general capacity to act with legal consequences. They should be prevented from acting; but if they performed some legal deed, it was "manifest" that they had had "sufficient prudence" to perform what they had done; their deeds were not invalid. Marriage might "even be fostered" for the partially insane; some persons by marriage became "of a better mind"; some were totally healed. Therapeutic possibilities outweighed the risk of failure. [59] Expressly as to those sane only in intermittent periods of lucidity, Sanchez taught that they sinned in marrying unless others could educate their children; but they married validly: "it is harsh to confine them to a life of continence, especially if, when they are of sound mind, they are impelled by severe stimuli of the flesh." [60] In this analysis, competence was capacity to consent at a given moment in time; capacity to carry out the obligations of marriage was ignored. The established authors' focus on the moment of consent, their refusal to incapacitate the intermittently lucid, their insistence on the accessibility of the institution, made any effort to invalidate a marriage for insanity difficult and Don José's case perilous.

Proof of the difficulty and peril, if further proof were needed, lay in the paucity of precedents. Apart from Innocent III's decision incorporated in the decretal *Dilectus*, neither the advocates of the parties nor the Secretary of the S.C.C. were able to refer to any instance of a marriage attacked for insanity before any court of the Curia. It would be rash to say that no marriage sanity case had gone to Rome since *Dilectus* had been issued in 1205, but where precedent is unknown it is as good as nonexistent.

In the appendix of a posthumous edition of Zacchia one hundred decisions illustrating medical issues before the Roman Rota were listed. Eleven turned on questions of mental competence, but were no precedent for a marriage case if, as Zacchia explicitly recognized, the standard set for capacity varied with the issue: one involved the appointment of a curator for an incompetent; four the validity of gifts; six the validity of wills. Where marriage was litigated in these selected cases from the years 1569 to 1657, the medical question was always physical; in nine of the hundred, the issue was the capacity to copulate. Only one, *Camerino, Of Marriage, February 9, 1624,* partially raised the issue of sanity. The Bishop of Camerino had annulled a marriage on the ground that the wife was "obsessed by an unclean spirit." Reversing in the Rota, Buratto noted that the Bishop had proceeded as though the woman were "mad or captive in mind," whereas signs of diabolical possession had appeared only when she had entered a convent long after the wedding; the presumption of sanity that "arose from nature, which produces men of sane mind," should have been respected in measuring her state at the time of consent. The case did not explore the mental requirements of marriage and offered no guidance where not supernatural intervention, but continuing or recurrent disease was in dispute.[61]

One well-known case, however, did exist as analogy. Almost a century old, coming from Portugal for decision by the Rota in 1579, its age did not impair its force. It offered a model for Don José's counsel; and on his behalf its teaching was pressed hard upon the S.C.C. Luis Alvarez had arranged for his sister Margareta to profess as a nun. Rejected as incompetent to take the vows by the monastery of Speranza, she had been admitted, through influence, to profession at the abbey of São Denis at Odivelas. She had been reputed to be insane both before and after her profession; her bizarre behavior in the convent was reported at length; two Jesuits had found her incapable of receiving sacramental absolution; during the trial two physicians pronounced her to be mad. Yet she had been capable of going through the long and taxing ceremony of profession. In the suit to invalidate her vows, the defense was that at the moment of profession she had been lucid. The Rota split on the point, but the majority held that with dementia proved before and after profession, dementia must be presumed to have affected Margareta when she uttered her vows, and they were void. The case was citable, useful, controlling in the presentation of Perez de Guzman.[62]

HOW THE MOST REVEREND SECRETARY SUMMED UP THE CASE AND WHAT THE COUNCIL VOTED

Five printed pages, principally devoted to Perez de Guzman's witnesses, condensed some hundred pages of briefs in Simonetti's summary for the S.C.C. The evidence for Doña Ana's bizarre behavior was related, from her childhood to the point of trial in Córdoba, where almost all the witnesses deposed her madness had reached an extreme degree. The Secretary did not attempt to classify it — counsel had not tried to specify the class of dementia within which it fell. From what he did report, a reasonable reader of Zacchia would have been able to conclude that she was "captive in mind." The Secretary concluded his presentation of the petitioner's case with the argument that her dementia, arising from a defect of nature, did not permit lucid intervals; "for those who are demented by a defect of nature never heal, as Zacchia holds, Medico-Legal Questions, 2.1.20." *Lisbon, June 22, 1579* was good precedent. From the evidence establishing insanity at times before and after the exchange of marital consent, she "must be presumed to have been equally insane at the time the marriage was celebrated." [63]

Against these contentions were two procedural points. No Defender of Marriage had been appointed in Córdoba; according to the terms of *Dei miseratione* the entire process in Spain had been a nullity. By practice of the S.C.C. the examination of witnesses had to be on "interrogatories," that is, on specific questions, not on "articles" or broad topics as they had actually been examined; only two years before the S.C.C. had remanded a case of religious profession to Córdoba for this very failure. There was an answer to the first point, urged in the petitioner's brief: the Fiscal, Doña Ana's guardian *ad litem*, had been no mere "material presence," but an active defender of her rights; in accordance with immemorial Spanish custom he had fulfilled the functions of a Defender of Marriages. Yet if the cardinals of the S.C.C. desired to avoid substantive issues and give Perez de Guzman's plea the cruelest denial, there was enough, perhaps, in either point for them to return the case to Córdoba to start again.

The substantive evidence for Doña Ana was set out by Simonetti in a paragraph. Eyewitnesses testified to periods of rationality. She had on occasion been admitted to the sacraments. Perez de Guzman's own witnesses spoke of relapses, which presupposed intervals of sanity. The nuns of Baeza deposed that she had been rational before the marriage. The "proofs alleged to persuade that consummation occurred," presented to the Council on November 22, 1760, supported the conviction that she had been sane at the time the marriage was begun. By the combination of these facts, lucid intervals were established. Superficially, the Secretary's summation was weighted in favor of Perez de Guzman. On closer inspection it was the work of one who thought the petitioner would lose and who was meticulous in reporting what might be counted in his favor before stating the propositions which defeated him.

The Secretary's summary was prepared for consideration by the cardinals at their meeting of February 26, 1763. He asked, "Is nullity of marriage established?" The matter was put over to March 12 and again to March 26. On noon that Saturday, at the Quirinal, the cardinals began with a case from Gubbio, ruling on the election rights, hereditary property, and assessments for wax and other supplies of two newly established canonries. In a case from Ascoli they held that the bishop should appoint the visitor to the prison of Ascoli. In a case from Bagnoregio they referred a separation suit back to the bishop.[64] In *Córdoba, Of Nullity of Marriage*, the S.C.C. answered, "No, and not again." The expenses of the litigation were awarded to Doña Ana, to be paid by her husband. She might sue before the Bishop of Córdoba for authorization to live permanently apart from Don José.[65]

The system devised by Benedict XIV had worked. Despite the irregularities of Spanish procedure, despite the error of local ecclesiastics in Córdoba, despite the personal helplessness of the respondent spouse, the indissolubility of a marriage had been preserved. The combination of appeal to Rome and the institution of the Defender at the S.C.C. had safeguarded the sacrament. The impious attempt of José Perez de Guzman to destroy a bond of thirty years' standing had been defeated. The grim efforts of the Count of Garzies to preserve his sister's honor had been crowned with victory. The cardinals had rejected the aberrant authority of *Lisbon, June 22, 1579* and remained obedient to the commentators who taught that the fatuous, the partially insane, the recurrently manic had the capacity to marry validly. Doña Ana was now at the extremity of madness, her behavior had been bizarre at Santa Clara, she had on occasion been refused the Eucharist, but she had been competent to consent to marriage by the criteria which Sanchez and Zacchia had approved. If they were the law, the result had been foreordained. Marriage had to be accessible to all. Society demanded it, and theory had granted it. Once it was entered, the union was indestructible. The rules drawn from Prospero Lambertini's experience assured that indestructibility would be preserved in law. The spouses could be alienated, hostile, mad; their marriage would serve as the symbol of the unbreakable union of Christ and the Church. The Pope, the cardinals of the S.C.C. and the Secretary, the advocates and proctors, the parties and their relatives, perceived reality within the walls which the system constituted. Captive within it, the Sacred Congregation of the Council appeared untroubled by doubts as it gave its second and final double no.

IV

The Good of Children

1.

That tributary of the Tiber which, turning south, runs with mountain freshness to enter the central stream not long before it plunges to the urban plain, takes its course and form from the rains and melting snows of the thick Apennine backbone of the Italian peninsula, and the turbid city flow, carrying an accumulated sludge between gray banks, recalls only in its unterminated current the country springs, sudden torrents, and translucent rivulets which, in the marches of Umbria, fed the Nera at its source. More than once in these marches the Apennine chain breaks out in one of those sharply austere configurations of rock sufficiently isolated from the rough running ridge of mountain and drawn to such a point of domination over the valley at its feet that the inhabitants of the region, if not disinterested cartographers, recognize in it a force and character which compel attention and require the bestowal of an individual name. Such in the northwest quadrant of Umbria, in the northeast corner of the diocese of Norcia, is Monte Bove, whose rigid form stands, in the language of a native observer, "like a terrible lord, day and night," above the village of Ussita which has come into existence in its shadow.[1]

In the village of Ussita on May 5, 1852, was born to Bernardino Gasparri and Giovanna Sili their ninth and last child, Pietro Gasparri. That he was responsive to his early instruction in religion; that he showed himself, as a boy, to be of a studious disposition; that he was the ninth; that his parents, though not rich were not destitute; that his mother's brother, Monsignor Sili, was the Vicar-

General of Nepi; that opportunity, youthful piety, parental persuasion worked together, all of these observable facts joined in that unobservable realm where human choice, prompted by opportunities and pricked by obstacles, nonetheless operates and led Pietro, still a boy, to elect the ecclesiastical state. At fifteen he left his village and the tutelary surveillance of Monte Bove and entered the provincial seminary at Nepi, not many miles to the west, presided over by his uncle. In 1870, the year of the proclamation of the infallibility of the Roman Pontiff speaking *ex cathedra* on matters of faith or morals, he was eighteen; and he experienced a painful shaking and stirring in the ordered universe he had accepted, as the army of Italy entered the Papal States, and the seminary itself closed its doors as the invader's forces neared Rome. Turning his adversity to good advantage, and with no doubt the continuing benevolence of Monsignor Sili, he enrolled in the Roman Seminary, that central ecclesiastical institution whose candidates could without presumption hope to share in the course of their careers in the exercise of the Petrine power itself.[2]

That a man with only a country curate's training could rise high in the democratic ranks of the clergy of nineteenth-century Italy is not only a pious supposition, but a truth splendidly exemplified by the life of Giuseppe Sarto, Pius X; and it would be temerarious to suppose that a man of Pietro Gasparri's solid determination, sober strength, and quick intelligence would have wasted unnoticed in an Umbrian parsonage if he had not had the fortune of a Roman education. Undeniably, however, without those five preparatory years in scholastic philosophy and theology and canon law, at the core of the system, in the last years of Pius IX, under the supervision of the most reliable of teachers, and in the company of the most favored of students, Pietro Gasparri would never have been able, in his maturity, to have become himself the master of the complex and delicate ecclesial mechanism.

Gasparri graduated, a doctor of philosophy, a doctor of theology, and a doctor of canon law; and, aged twenty-five, he was ordained a priest. He moved at once into the legal orbit and became the secretary of the Prefect of the Signature of Justice, Cardinal Mertel, one of the last of a species, a cardinal subdeacon, and the last President of the Council of State which governed papal Rome. Apprenticeship in administration could not exhaust his energies or curb his appetite for academic exercises. Trained to treat theology and canon law as cut from the same cloth, he taught canon law at the College of Urban VIII conducted by the Congregation for the Propagation of the Faith, and sacramental theology at the Apollinaris, the school of canonical studies of the Roman Seminary from which he had so recently emerged. Very much a junior, he performed the service, indispensable to the organization he had entered, of imparting the information he had received to the succeeding batch of recruits; and his days were spent in arduous cramming, outlining, and lecturing, in organizing his own learning while he conveyed the received doctrine to docile learners.[3]

When he was twenty-eight, in 1880, his career took an unexpected swerve. Since 1878 there had been a new Pope, Leo XIII, and a new administration. Did Gasparri now want for powerful protectors? Did some incident, contretemps, or rupture make withdrawal from the seat of power mandatory or advisable? Alternatively, was he a trusted young man selected for a mission or a useful young man found handy for a chore or a promising young man endowed with a plum? Or did Paris and a life of purely academic research present an irresistible attraction to him on purely personal grounds? One may safely dismiss the last possibility as alien to the solidity, the pragmatism, and the love of his native land which formed such substantial elements in Gasparri's character; but among the other explanations one may hesitate; most probably he was thought trustworthy, competent, and not indispensable at Rome. At all events he left Rome for Paris.[4]

The *Institut catholique*, where Gasparri now became the ordinary professor of canon law, was an embryonic yet potentially important institution. Founded in 1875 as a center for higher studies, it was the focus of sustained intellectual effort by the French Church after a century of revolutions and expropriations had stripped the French Church bare of universities and the means of theological research. In the largest Catholic nation in the world, in the Catholic nation most inclined to speculative investigation of the truths of theology, the Institute was assured of a role, and the young Italian dispatched to hold the chair of canon law could profit from a spirit of inquiry uncommon in the Roman schools and court, even while he himself functioned to embody the *Corpus iuris canonici* which was the instrument of Roman supervision.[5]

For ten years Gasparri was immersed in the regular business of academic life. He gave lectures, a series of commentaries on the five books of the *Decretals*. He collaborated in the editing of a new law review, *Le canoniste contemporain*. He helped found a discussion group for canonists, "the Academy of Saint Raymond of Peñaforte." [6] In 1891 he published his course on Book IV under the title *De matrimonio*.[7] Gasparri's value, it then became apparent, was not unremembered in Rome. Leo XIII himself wrote to express his admiration of his "learning and judgment," and the papal letter formed an introduction to the second edition immediately brought out in 1892. Gasparri was at once famous within the restricted field of interested specialists. In time the book became the most authoritative canonical treatise on marriage since Sanchez. A professor in the Roman seminaries could tell his student, "In matters of matrimonial law, all other opinions are to be rejected — only he who agrees with Gasparri is right." In the twentieth century, on hundreds of occasions, it was cited to the Sacred Roman Rota and cited by the Rota for statement of the governing law.[8]

De matrimonio was not highly original. From Gratian to Gasparri, few canonists have sought originality. It was clear, succinct, balanced, definite. If it trenchantly eliminated avenues of exploration, it did so by choosing candidly one line of accepted authority. Sanchez had been a discoverer of ambiguities, a master of implications, a theorist. Gasparri had in mind the parish priest, who must know the law and even be capable of expounding it to his flock, yet who labored "under the gravest difficulties because of the confluence of positive ecclesiastical law with positive or natural divine law." [9] In these somber and technical words of preface Gasparri indicated his awareness of the complexity and even confusion created by the seven centuries of ecclesiastical legislation since Gratian. For the literate and sensible administrator perplexed in the morass, for the student who wanted to be that literate and sensible administrator, Gasparri's two volumes provided a compendium of rules and information and ratiocination in apparently definitive form.

De matrimonio drew on the old — Gratian and the *Decretals*, supplemented by the legislation of later Popes, especially Benedict XIV, and classic commentaries on moral theology and canon law, especially Sanchez. It drew on the new — Gasparri's notes on dogmatic sacramental theology as taught by Camillo Santori, later Secretary of the S.C.C., and the writings of his canon law teachers, Francesco Santi and Filippo de Angelis. Above all, it was based on what Gasparri "had turned with unwearied hand night and day," the volumes, now numbering over one hundred fifty, containing the reports of the Secretary of the S.C.C.[10] In *De matrimonio* the reporting system initiated by Prospero Lambertini came to full fruition. Decisions as early and as unique as *West Lisbon, July 8, 1724* stood side by side with current decisions from the Rome of Leo XIII; together they constituted a single, timeless line which Gasparri treated as "the law." These disparate pieces of information from law teachers and papal courts were marshaled into a solid whole, informed by Gasparri's earnest spirit, and given an apparent consistency and purpose. Not a vast speculative synthesis, not smacking in the least of frothy French concern for the apostolate to the intellectuals, his sturdy book was a monument to canonical jurisprudence, as though Monte Bove had been moved to Paris and set down to stand in the Elysian Fields.

Seven more years Gasparri remained a professor in Paris. Then, in 1898, someone in the office of the Secretary of State decided to launch him on the path of unusual advancement. He was made Apostolic Nuncio to Peru, Bolivia, and Ecuador and sent on a grand tour of Latin America. Diplomatic missions are almost certain to enlarge the domestic stature of the envoy if he does not empathize too readily with the natives to whom he is accredited; prudence and fidelity to his superiors will be sure to carry him far, in the eyes of his superiors, and few tasks are better designed for showing prudence and fidelity to advantage. Gasparri returned from his trip in 1900, his reputation as a diplomat established, his prestige as a nuncio crowning his fame as a canonist, his knowledgeableness of France second to none as the Church in France entered a period of grave crisis; and in 1901, in the dying years of Leo XIII, under the energetic eye of Cardinal Rampolla, he assumed the sensitive and critical post of Secretary for Extraordinary Ecclesiastical Affairs.[11]

The surprising election of Giuseppe Sarto as Pope in August 1903 and the even more surprising appointment of Rafaele Merry del Val as Cardinal Secretary of State confronted Gasparri with new challenges and new opportunities. The Pope was a man he scarcely knew, mysteriously translated by vote of the College of

Cardinals from Patriarch of Venice to Bishop of Rome, without experience of any sort in the Roman Curia or the diplomatic service. But Gasparri could guess something of the temper of the man, the second of ten children of the clerk of the Venetian village of Riese, educated at the seminary of Padua, for seventeen years a parish priest in two hamlets in the Venetian marches, now at sixty-eight made Supreme Pontiff. Gasparri could imagine how often Sarto "had touched with his hand the difficulties which ecclesiastical legislation then presented . . . how many times, in the exercise of his pastoral ministry, he would have wished for a canonical code on the model of the civil code!" [12] Like the other administrators for whom he had written, Sarto would view the law as a book of clear answers for administrators. Like Gasparri himself he would value simplicity and brevity and would admire candor. Within a week of the election the following dialogue occurred when Gasparri went to pay homage to the new Pope:

> *Pius X:* What do you want to do here now?
> *Gasparri:* I want to make a code of canon law, Most Blessed Father.
> *Pius X:* Can you do it?
> *Gasparri:* Yes, Most Blessed Father, it can be done. Certainly, it is a long and difficult work, but it will be of immense utility to the Church.
> *Pius X:* Let's do it. If We cannot promulgate it, Our successor will.[13]

So Gasparri recollected the conversation three decades later, and, if his tenacious memory idealized at all, the substance of the dialogue which launched his dearest life work must have been recalled by him in its spontaneity and simplicity. The idea itself was not new — several bishops had asked that the Vatican Council in 1870 authorize a code. Nor did Pius X proceed without getting the approval of Cardinal Gennari, the senior canonist of the Curia. But the idea at that hour and the seizing of that moment were the glory of Gasparri. As he looked back in 1934 he could observe, "Having examined the course of my life, I see clearly what the Lord principally willed of me — He willed my cooperation in the formation of the Code of Canon Law. . . . From infancy, He directed all my steps to the post of Secretary for Extraordinary Ecclesiastical Affairs, where alone the compilation of the Code was possible." [14]

In 1891, the same year in which *De matrimonio* was finished, a marriage took place in Rome whose characterization and whose consequences were to be determined in not insignificant degree by the author of *De matrimonio*, the Code which he constructed, and the judicial system in which he placed the Code that he had made.

2.

Filippo Folchi was the fifth of six sons of the family of Arcangelo Folchi and Anna Cavalletti. The Folchi, or Folchi-Vici, as they became in the nineteenth century, were related to Guy Fulcodi, a widower who had become Pope Clement IV in 1265; to Gugliemo de Folchis, Bishop of Fiesole in 1520; to Folch de Cardona, Cardinal-Archbishop of Seville in 1760; and these relations, distant, collateral, and ancient though they were, formed part of the Folchi tradition of service to the Church and gave a sense of dignity and accomplishment to the present, impoverished bearers of the ancient name. In more recent times the Folchi had been closely tied to papal Rome, having moved from Fiesole to Castel Gandolfo in 1570, and from there to the city itself in the eighteenth century. For a century they had been part of the nobility of the States of the Church. Arcangelo Folchi himself was a gentleman chamberlain of the Pope.[15]

His son, Filippo, attended schools of a religious character until he was twenty-one and then struck out in a way of life adapted to his impressionable and imaginative character if not to his capacity for perseverance and discipline. He became a painter, and, freed from the shackles of academic routine, entered on the new pleasures he associated with the life of artists. At the Carnival of 1886, when he was twenty-four years old, he encountered Pauline Bailly.[16]

Pauline was a French girl from Versailles, twenty-eight, unmarried, earning her living by giving language lessons. Filippo's friend, the Marchese Alfonso Antaldi di Astorre, was regarded by Filippo as her lover, and it was under Antaldi's auspices that he made Pauline's acquaintance. The inhibitions imposed by friendship were no stronger than those instilled by family, religion, education, ancestry, and society once her acquaintance was made. After a month of pursuit, on April 19, 1886, Filippo and Pauline were joined in sexual intercourse. In September 1887 their first son, Mario, was born.[17]

Whatever the view of the lovers before, whatever their own unconcern for consequences, the birth of Mario could not but confirm in Pauline a deep desire to be joined to Filippo in wedlock, while it aroused in Filippo painful sensations of predicament and looming responsibility. In the ensuing crisis it was the view of the family which prevailed. Anna Cavalletti, as her sons were to testify, was "a holy woman," "a saint." [18] She could not abide the connection of her son with a woman who appeared to her little better than a French prostitute. Filippo was pleased to welcome any suggestion which would permit him to terminate the affair without incurring further obligation. He took his family's counsel. He joined the army and sailed to join the colonial troops of the King engaged in the pacification of Eritrea.[19]

This correspondence ensued: Pauline, in French, to Filippo, Rome, December 27, 1887:

I beg you, my beloved Pippo, write me, for I am too sad without news of you. I lack life itself. I fear that your family, which detests me so much, is alienating you from me. Who knows what they don't do so that you will forget me and abandon me? But you love me, don't you, Pippo? And you do not doubt my love. Tell me, repeat it to me without ceasing, for I never tire of hearing it. I want you near me to hide myself in your arms, to lock myself against your heart, and to embrace you as much as I want while you could look into my eyes and read my love for you and my sorrow at being far away. You are my life, you are everything for me, if you fail me or if you cease to love me, I would no longer wish to live, I would no longer live. . . . I embrace you and I love you with all my soul. Your wife, Pauline.[20]

Filippo, in Italian, to Pauline, Otmulo, January 12, 1888:

I know that you are saying that I promised to marry you. I never made such a promise, and I could not in conscience have made such a promise in view of the enormous, quasi-insurmountable difficulty which I have always had before me. Only once I told you that I hoped that all would end with a favorable solution for us, but I didn't say that so you might build on these words and make castles in the air, because I could say nothing precise. . . . Pauline, when will you become more experienced in the things of this world? [21]

Filippo to his older brother Stanislao, Hamassat, January 27, 1888:

I believe that I am ready to do anything so that I may know that mama and papa and all of you are tranquil, above all mama.[22]

Filippo to the parish priest of San Vitale, April 4, 1888:

The life of B. is a life which I know only for a certain period, a period which perhaps you know. And that is that of her stay in Rome, in which various of my acquaintances knew B. very intimately. And that is well-known. . . . After all that, can you tell me that I could in conscience give such displeasure to my family, who can only be opposed? I believe that I cannot have any right to inflict this dishonor (it could not be other) on those who have only done me good.[23]

In the fall of 1888 Filippo returned from the campaign, purged, full of resolutions, eager to satisfy his parents, ready to follow the conscience he invoked. In August 1890 Pauline gave birth to their second son, Gian Galeazzi.[24]

Pauline now had an ally. Anna Folchi had been reproved by her own confessor for her pharisaical scorn of Pauline, and she had been moved. A Jesuit, Father Massaruti, joined in urging her and Stanislao to encourage Filippo to do his duty, to marry Pauline. Anna was convinced. Stanislao pressed upon her the imprudence, the disgrace, the needlessness of such a course. Arcangelo was mute. But Anna saw her own responsibilities clearly. Having failed to separate the lovers permanently, she determined to unite them irrevocably. To this end she turned her planning and her prayers.[25]

Filippo was hemmed in, no longer with a mother to invoke against a mistress, but with a mother and a mistress joined in their objective. Still he resisted, pleading poverty. The Folchi had "lost their money," were indeed "ruined." [26] Filippo's earnings as a painter were paltry, and although Filippo in Africa had politely hoped that Pauline in Rome would find her tutoring "most lucrative," he did not expect to support his family by her lessons in French. But he could not hold out forever against the resourceful women animated by piety or passion who pressed him from two sides. Pauline had a benefactress, Caroline Courbally, rich and pious and an octogenarian, who sought to enroll her in the Pious Society of the Via Milano and who offered to find Filippo commissions.[27] Then, to the prayers of his mother and the pleas of Pauline and the work found by Madame Courbally were added the robust counsels of a priest.

The new hand in the shaping of Filippo's future was that of Monsignor Saverio Bacchi, an officer of the legal division in the secretariat of the Vicariate, the diocesan administration of Rome. Bacchi's business was the regularization and annulment of marriages, and he had served for over fifteen years as Deputy Treasury Proctor for Marriage.[28] Discovered by Arcangelo Folchi, he was a godsend for Anna. "Given the frank character of Canon Bacchi," Archbishop Sili was to testify, "I do not believe it improbable that he could have exaggerated the obligation of Folchi-Vici to marry Bailly." [29] By "frank," Sili meant "determined." "In good faith he [Bacchi] could have used equivocal expressions — for example, 'You have trouble in marrying this lady. But before God you are bound to her, since you treated her maritally and had children from her' — expressions which could have meant either that there was an existing matrimonial bond or that there was an obligation to marry the lady in the future." [30] Filippo's own recollection of his conversations with Bacchi were of a less ambiguous exchange: "Monsignor Bacchi said that in conscience I was the husband of Bailly by the procreation of two children, and he added that I had conjugal affection for her. To this I replied, 'No, carnal.' " [31]

Bacchi was undaunted by the expectable coolness of Filippo's reception of his disinterested advice. In place of disorder and sin he offered order and religious sanction accompanied by a complete cleansing and a total restoration to an unimpaired position. Not only could Filippo's sins be forgiven and his future relations with Pauline made holy, but even the record of the past could be set straight. If Filippo would consent to the ceremony, the Church would hold the two boys legitimate; the marriage itself would be recorded as occurring in 1886 on the date of his first intercourse with Pauline.[32]

With speed — but not, the old notary of the Vicariate observed, with greater speed than usual in "patching up any little contretemps" — the ecclesiastical wheels were moved, and Bacchi as a veteran of the Vicariate made them turn.[33] The Bishop of Rome was of course the Pope, but the Vicariate was the Vicariate because the Vicar of Christ himself had a Vicar to administer his diocese — in this instance Cardinal Lucido Maria Parrochi. Cardinal Parrochi dispensed from publication of the banns. The Holy Office dispensed from proof of freedom to marry. Cardinal Parrochi made Bacchi his delegate to perform the wedding. Trent was to be complied with by marriage before the delegate of the delegate of the Ordinary, without the necessity of troubling the parish priest of either Pauline or Filippo. At the end of April 1891 — even Pauline does not seem to have remembered the exact date — in the private chapel of Canon Bacchi's home at Via Frattina 104, Filippo and Pauline took each other as man and wife; and the records of the

Vicariate reflected the marriage as having taken place the day of their initial intercourse, April 19, 1886.[34]

Filippo was happy with his lot. The night before the wedding Pauline had been melancholy, and to cheer her Filippo fitted the wedding ring on her finger, saying, "Now don't ever take it off." [35] Once married he could live openly with her, abandoning the subterfuges he had used to placate his mother.[36] He became — so Pauline was to recall—"very affectionate and religious." He frequented the sacraments so long inaccessible to him. No longer sinners together, his wife and he heard mass together. At his insistence the servants (his poverty was relative) had to attend and receive the sacraments too. The elder Folchi, Arcangelo and Anna, visited Pauline's house; the children became aware of them as benevolent grandparents.[37]

Yet the five Folchi brothers — Giuseppe, forty years old; Stanislao, thirty-eight; Saverio, thirty-four; Pio, thirty-one; and Giulio, twenty-four — never came to call. Many of Filippo's friends were not introduced to Pauline.[38] Above all, she was not yet his legal wife. Under the current regime of strict separation of Church and State, a church marriage was not a substitute for a civil ceremony. In the eyes of the Italian state, Pauline was still a concubine, and Mario and Gian Galeazzi were still illegitimate.

In the winter of 1892 Pauline withered. Suffering from serious congestion in her lungs, on January 29, 1893, she received the viaticum. For this last solemn communion Filippo asked permission from Cardinal Parrochi that they might share a single host. The permission was given, and the single host broken and devoured by the two.[39] Assured, as he recalled later, that she could not live, Filippo agreed to marry Pauline according to the civil law of Italy. On February 5, before an official of the City of Rome, the marriage was celebrated, and the couple executed a legal acknowledgment of Mario and Gian Galeazzi as their children.[40]

In Puccini's opera of love, poverty, and art, there is a sad-happy ending when Mimi dies, and her lover, after he has declared his fidelity to her on her deathbed, will have no more to do for her. Pauline did not die. She grew strong, recovered her health, resumed her wifely role — Filippo's wife before the Church and before the state. Her mother-in-law, once her foe, then her surest ally, did die. With Anna Folchi's death, the equilibrium struck in 1891 was no longer secure.

The precariousness of Pauline's position was not, however, demonstrated until circumstances moved Filippo from his studio at the Porta Pinciana to a more elegant environment. In 1895 he was offered a commission by Roberto, Duke of Parma, who lived on the Tuscan seacoast at Viareggio. Filippo accepted his offer, he moved to Viareggio with Pauline, he entered the world of European royalty.[41] Duke Roberto, himself a Bourbon, was the brother-in-law of another Bourbon, the exiled Don Carlos, recognized by his followers as the lawful King of Spain. The villa at Viareggio housed a princess of the blood in the person of Elvira de Bourbon.[42]

Unmarried still at twenty-five, Princess Elvira was the third child of the second marriage of King Carlos, who as a widower had married Princess Marie-Berthe of Rohan-Montbazon and sired five children. In literal terms Duke Roberto was not her uncle, but he acted as her uncle and her protector, and she lived as his guest. At Viareggio, in late 1895, Elvira and Filippo, thirty-three, and Pauline, thirty-seven, came together.

In the spring of 1896 Filippo eloped with Elvira.[43] By the fall of the year their position invited the speculation of the press. Misbehavior of a Bourbon, a Bourbon princess, a daughter of Don Carlos, could scarcely escape comment and censure. The strength of the Carlists lay in the rugged purity and rigid orthodoxy of their religious faith. The king in exile could not easily reconcile himself to his daughter living openly as a concubine. The Folchi-Vici, poorer and less royal than the Bourbons but no less conscious of responsibilities, could only regard Filippo's public posture as deplorable. *La Tribuna* of Rome suggested that "to end the scandal the Pope will grant the dissolution of the first religious marriage."[44]

Neither Viareggio nor Rome was a congenial haven that year for the new couple. In America, far from critics of their conduct, there awaited them the hospitality of a man who had shared Filippo's tent in Africa and his society in Rome, Giovanni Del Drago. He assured them of a welcome for Christmas 1896.[45] At more than one turn Del Drago was to be their indispensable ally on the long path of litigation which lay ahead of them.

3.

Despite the guess in *La Tribuna*, no precipitous action was taken to dissolve the Folchi-Bailly marriage, and no formal action was taken at all during the pontificate of Leo XIII. Filippo plausibly explained his inaction as a desire to drop from sight "for fear of having given offense." Pauline said that Filippo waited until both Cardinal Parrochi and Monsignor Bacchi were dead.[46]

Bacchi died in the 1890's, Cardinal Parrochi on January 15, 1903; in February 1903 Filippo discussed his situation with a friend of his father in a position to furnish expert counsel. His adviser was Giovanni De Montel, aged seventy-two, for twenty-five years an auditor of the Sacred Roman Rota and currently its Dean. Even in the decrepitude of a Rota no longer concerned with marriage, the assistance of its Dean had some value in the Curia. In the company of De Montel and Monsignor Angelo Sinibaldi, Filippo went to inspect the record of his marriage in the offices of the Vicariate. There he discovered or recalled that the marriage was falsely recorded as having taken place April 19, 1886. The fact of falsification was noted by his counsel and pondered by them.[47]

The next step was to sound out Pauline. This task was entrusted to a noble friend, Louis Hardouin, a duke with a title unrecognized in the country of the dukedom. Hardouin learned that Pauline wanted a civil divorce and was prepared to return to France, where civil divorce for adultery had been available since 1875, to obtain a decree. In Italy there was no divorce; as recently as 1902 a combination of Catholics and Conservative-Liberals had defeated the government's attempt to permit divorce after a decree of separation for adultery, desertion, or cruelty. In Italy, Pauline had obtained a legal separation, but she wished her adulterous husband to have no claims over their sons, an objective she hoped to secure by asserting her rights in France. She was not interested in annulment of the religious marriage.[48]

Hardouin informed her that the Duke of Parma, Uncle Roberto, was prepared to provide a dowry for Elvira, if Elvira was able to marry Filippo. Pauline observed that if Filippo ever came into money, he would have to give his lawful wife and children no mere monthly pension but a lump sum such as 100,000 lira. The negotiations — dated for Pauline by another Roman Carnival, that of 1904 — terminated at this point.[49]

Two more years went by. Elvira, now his mistress of ten years, had borne Filippo three children, and they lived domestically in Florence where Filippo painted and went under the name of Della

Rocca.[50] He was, his lawyers were to say, bound to Elvira "by ardent and mutual affection." Familial, social, political, and personal reasons made worthwhile every effort for the securing of an annulment which would permit the religious regularization of their union. Foregoing Pauline's cooperation, Filippo initiated a formal suit for a declaration of nullity in the tribunal of the Vicariate.[51]

In his counsel Filippo continued to be fortunate, with a fortune that was not the result of chance. His father, Arcangelo Folchi, was not only of that small class of Roman nobility, the Blacks, identified with the Pope in the upheavals which had removed the Pope from the control of Rome. Not only was he an actual employee of the Vatican; in 1895, he had advanced in rank to become one of the four numbered papal chamberlains of honor with cape and sword.[52] In the household of the Pope such chamberlains were of a nobility inferior to those designated secret chamberlains, but their prestige was not that of doormen or policemen. Serving a ceremonial function at papal audiences and paid a modest monetary compensation for their service, they received their true reward in the status traditionally enjoyed by those in immediate attendance on a royal person.[53] In this office, won through friendship in the Curia, the officeholder had opportunity to make friends in the Curia. Arcangelo Folchi's friends were among the chosen, and his son's counsel were the choicest.

Filippo's first adviser had been an old man, Dean of the Rota when his advice was asked. His counsel now in the Vicariate was a younger man, Giulio Grazioli, who was to be Dean of the Rota from 1936 to 1944. In 1906, aged forty-four, he was Substitute or Acting Secretary of the Consistorial Congregation, on whose staff he had served since the 1890's.[54] The modest title of this committee and the modest title of Substitute concealed the importance of Grazioli's office. The Consistorial Congregation was charged with the appointment of bishops to all of the dioceses of the world which did not fall in mission territory or were not regulated by concordat. The Pope himself was the Prefect of the Congregation, and as Pius X was so new to his office and so dependent on his administrative staff, and as there was no administrative official above the Substitute, Grazioli might be supposed to have a large hand in the determination of those who would compose the episcopate of the Church. The very bright future held out by assignment to this key position never became a reality for Grazioli; he was not to know the great successes, in terms of a curial career, of some of his colleagues. But when in 1906 he became Filippo Folchi's advocate, with the future unknown, he was a lawyer with influential friends, high prospects, and a central and strategic post. His home in Rome, Via Lungo Tevere Prati 17, was used by Folchi, for purposes of the case, as his legal domicile.[55]

Grazioli was not alone as Filippo's counsel. With him was a man in fact his senior and in fact to prove a counsel and an ally even more valuable, Oreste Giorgi.[56] Like Gasparri a villager who had been educated at the Roman Seminary, Giorgi had been ordained a year after Gasparri in 1878. He had been an advocate in the curial courts, then auditor for Cardinal Mertel. After this apprenticeship he had taught in the Roman Seminary. In 1891, at the age of thirty-five, he had become one of two substitute secretaries at the Sacred Penitentiary, and by 1899 he had become first assistant to the Secretary. He had moved on to the Congregation of Bishops and Regulars, and now, at fifty, he was the Under-Secretary of this Congregation whose wide supervisory powers over diocesan administration linked with, and overlapped, those of the Consistorial Congregation. In 1904 he was among the first chosen by Gasparri for work on construction of the Code. For almost twenty years he was to be the most effective of Folchi's counselors.

Filippo's case, as conceived by Grazioli and Giorgi, rested on the failure of his marriage to Pauline to have met the technical requirements for a valid contract. Filippo had given his consent to marriage on a condition. The condition had not been met. The condition had been *sine qua non* — how counsel liked that phrase! As the condition had failed, the consent had not been effective. The outline of this argument was clear. Its pieces were not. What had been the condition *sine qua non*? It had been that Filippo was already married to Pauline. In the libel drafted by counsel to set out the case to the new Cardinal Vicar of Rome, Filippo declared that he had been "stupefied" by the assurances of Monsignor Bacchi that he was "before God bound to her"; yet that he had ended by accepting Bacchi's representation as true, and that he had expressed his consent before the priest and two witnesses in 1891 only as a way of registering what he took to be already a fact. The record of the Vicariate showed that everyone concerned had treated the real marriage as made in 1886. The record reflected what he had been told, the condition on which he gave consent in the ceremony. He had consented to be married only on the condition that he was already married. Now he declared the condition had failed. Fornication with Pauline in 1886 or thereafter could not have created a true marriage. As this condition had not been met, his marriage was invalid.[57]

The opening statement of a case prepared by counsel often has imperfections, which, it is trusted, testimony will amend. The adoption of alternative and inconsistent theories to justify the relief sought is not an unusual practice. This libel, however, put forward a second allegation inconsistent with the first, not at the level of legal theory, but of fact: "I truly never had the intention of marrying Pauline Bailly, but I had the will of keeping her as a lover or kept woman, as she had been held by other men before me."[58] The implication was that the marriage should be treated as a sham, invalid under the decretal of Innocent III, *Tua nos*, X.4.1.26. Buried between the two conflicting allegations of an intent to marry and an intent not to marry was the one claim which eventually loomed large in the litigation: "the petitioner manifested to Pauline his firm intention not to procreate other children from her."

Giuseppe Ceppetelli, judge of the Vicariate, took testimony in 1906 and 1907. Filippo gave a deposition, from which what principally emerged was his rancor toward Pauline. It was she who had promoted his affair with Elvira de Bourbon in 1896, to better, so he supposed, her own financial condition. The reason he had given her, in the beginning, for postponing marriage was his economic situation, but he had had a more profound motive for avoiding marriage with her: "My true reason for my strong aversion to this marriage was based on reflection upon, and consideration of, the past life of Bailly. I knew her at the Carnival of 1886 with a lover of hers, and I am persuaded that she had had others."[59] Pauline, then living in Rome at Via Veneto 26, gave two depositions. She declared, "I believed that he loved me truly."[60]

The parties might depose, and their admissions were binding against themselves. But a party's statement by itself could not prove a marriage invalid, and evidence other than a party's deposition was required. No further evidence of Filippo's *sine qua non* condition, his paradoxical intention, was produced. Benedetto Melata, Defender of the Bond, had a good deal of sport with the "Bacchian crime" — the falsification of the matrimonial register, an accommodation which could not impair the validity of the union — and the case was commonly referred to in circles of the Vatican as "the case of the Bacchian crime."[61] On March 14, 1908, the marriage was held valid by the Vicariate.[62]

4.

Appeal lay to the S.C.C. Appeal was filed on March 16, 1908. Giorgi and Grazioli asked that more testimony be taken. The secretaryship being vacant, the Under-Secretary, Michele Lega, acted as "judge-instructor" in hearing the witnesses.

Two new persons were presented in support of the principal, paradoxical claim of Filippo's libel. One was Filippo's first adviser, Giovanni De Montel. Substituting one role for another, De Montel testified about his visit to the Vicariate with Filippo in 1903 and Filippo's account to him of his conversations with Monsignor Bacchi in 1891.[63] In terms of evidence De Montel added nothing. His testimony, however, told the S.C.C. that the seventy-seven-year-old Dean of the Rota believed in Folchi's case.

Of even greater strategic value to the cause was the second witness, Agostino Sili. The meat of his testimony has already been set out: his observations on the candor of Monsignor Bacchi. Sili spoke hypothetically of what Bacchi had been capable of doing, not of what he had seen Bacchi do. His usefulness did not lie in his testimony but in what his adhesion to Folchi's side signified.

The son of one brother of Pietro Gasparri's mother, and a nephew of that Monsignor Sili who had superintended Gasparri's early ecclesiastical life, Agostino Sili was born in the village of Calcara di Visso, a hamlet adjoining Gasparri's birthplace of Ussita. The cousins knew each other from boyhood; six years Gasparri's senior, Sili set an example by his choice of the priesthood and his studies at the Roman Seminary. His academic brilliance appeared to assure him a chair of theology until his instinct to serve the poor led him to enter the Bigi, a brotherhood devoted to the care of old men. Illness forced his withdrawal from the order; in 1901 he was living in seclusion in his birthplace when Gasparri became a leading figure in the Curia. Intelligent, impulsive, idealistic, neurasthenic,

Sili came to Rome in his cousin's wake. Six months after Gasparri became Secretary for Extraordinary Ecclesiastical Affairs, Sili was appointed a consultor to the Congregation. When the development of the Code of Canon Law began, he became a consultor to the Commission and Gasparri's trusted aide in the making of the Code. At the same time Pius X assigned him a post appropriate to his character — he was made the head of the office of papal charities with the titular dignity of Archbishop of Caesarea del Ponti. In late 1908 he was placed on a special committee of the S.C.C. itself.[64] For Folchi he was an ally as important as Oreste Giorgi. His commitment to his cause was proclaimed in his well-intentioned speculations about Bacchi. That commitment was not to weaken in the many turnings of the case.

Giorgi and Grazioli did more than produce two eminent endorsers as if endorsers were needed in addition to their own advocacy of the cause. They also began to press more strongly the contention, barely mentioned in the libel, that Filippo had intended to have no children when he married Pauline, and to draw the legal implication of that intention. The shift in strategy was occasioned by reflection on the shifting state of the law.

Since July 8, 1724, when the S.C.C. had upheld Senator Barberini's claim that Joanna's agreement to become a nun had invalidated their marriage, few litigants in the S.C.C. had based their case on *Si conditiones*, X.4.5.7, and none had invoked the decretal successfully. Parayre's detailed account of procedure in the S.C.C. in 1897 did not so much as mention a condition or intention against offspring as a ground upon which the Congregation might annul a marriage.[65] At the turn of the century, theorists at the Apollinaris were discussing the solution of a case apparently within the terms of the decretal and still hesitating, for fear of scandal, to advise a wife to leave her husband although the couple had married with a written agreement to avoid children.[66] In 1904, thanks to initiative from France, the ancient decretal again became living law. Anne de Crosmières, a widow with two children, had agreed to marry the Vicomte Edouard de Maricourt only if he would agree that they would have no children. By letters exchanged between the principals before the marriage and by the testimony of their two mothers, the existence of Anne's condition was established. On her petition the archdiocese of Paris held the marriage null. On appeal, the

S.C.C. affirmed the Secretary's report, making plain that *Si condi-tiones* had been treated as decisive.[67]

Paris, July 16, 1904 — unlike *West Lisbon, July 8, 1724* — did not turn on a showing that intercourse had been renounced, but on an explicit contract to avoid children, presumably by practicing contraception. Decided under the incumbent Prefect and Under-Secretary, the case should have been good precedent for Folchi. When his libel was prepared in 1905, the Secretary's report had not been published, but the decision was over six months old. It had already been remarked on: *Analecta ecclesiastica* published a summary in July 1904 with the last names of the parties omitted, and *Le canoniste contemporain* pointed to the case with the startled comment: "It should be noted, because examples of nullity on account of an attached condition to avoid offspring are most rare." [68] Giorgi and Grazioli could not have found it difficult to obtain the briefs. They must not have grasped in 1905 that they had been given a model for victory.

The awkward drafting of Folchi's libel suggested that no model had been consulted: "The petitioner manifested to Pauline his firm intention not to procreate other children from her, to such end avoiding the regular use of the conjugal office, as he then immediately declared that he would never consent to complete the civil contract." [69] Pell-mell the refusal to be civilly married was thrown in on top of the avoidance of the "regular use" of intercourse, with which the connection was not apparent. "Regular use of the conjugal office" was itself ambiguous. Did it mean abstinence from intercourse, or contraception? That a condition against the substance of marriage had been attached to Filippo's consent was not, in so many words, stated.

These inadequacies were, in measure, repaired by Filippo's declarations upon judicial interrogation. In the Vicariate, he testified: "There were no properly conjugal relations because, before the religious ceremony, I said to Bailly, 'As for children, speak no more of them.'" [70] In the S.C.C., asked point-blank if he had made a contract with Pauline not to have children, he replied, "Yes. That is, I said before the marriage, 'As for children, speak no more of them,' and I put this as a condition which was accepted by Bailly, who in her turn imposed it on me — so much so that when on some rare occasion I was not using the protective, she reminded me of it and at the psychological moment simply repulsed me." [71] Contraceptive practice and a condition mutually imposed had finally been added to the "firm intention" set out in the libel and the ambiguous "speak no more" of Filippo's oral declaration in the Vicariate. In her interrogation, Pauline was asked, "For what reason did you not have children?" She replied, "If other children did not come after the first two, it was not for lack of matrimonial and marital union, but because the Lord did not send them to us." [72]

At this juncture a witness was found to support Filippo's contention. He was a witness highly familiar with Filippo's affairs — the godfather of his two sons, his tentmate in Africa, his companion in Rome, his host in New York, Giovanni Del Drago of the noble Roman house of the Princes Del Drago. At forty-eight, he was a man of some experience of the ecclesiastical world and of ecclesiastical termination of marriage. His late collateral who died on March 17, 1908, had been Cardinal Gianbattista Casali Del Drago, a member of both the Consistorial Congregation and the S.C.C. His cousin, Prince Francesco, had obtained the dissolution of his unconsummated marriage of five years' standing by act of Leo XIII, in 1902. His own marriage of fourteen years' duration had been annulled in 1901.[73]

Del Drago appeared on June 22, 1908, before an official of the archdiocese of New York. He testified that Filippo had told him many times that "he did not intend to marry Bailly because he was not her first lover." "In the circles of the society I frequented," Del Drago added, "it was held to be not a marriage, but a foul-up." He said, "I know and remember excellently that the contracting parties intended to avoid children, and they both said it together in my presence before contracting marriage and precisely in the house on Via Sette Scale where Signora Bailly lived." It was not a true marriage because "Folchi did not give true matrimonial consent. Moreover, both contracted with the condition of avoiding children." [74] If Del Drago were believed, there was at last evidence to meet the requirements of *Si conditiones*.

Lega moved with briskness in hearing the new witnesses before the S.C.C. By the end of July 1908 all the new testimony Giorgi and Grazioli could find was in. On August 25 Folchi made a few minor corrections to his most recent declaration, taking the occasion to object to the skepticism of his story expressed by the judge in the Vicariate because he was seeking to remarry. "Who is there," he asked, "who seeks to have a marriage declared null if he is not contracting another?" [75]

Briefs were submitted by counsel, the case was ripe for judgment, when on October 20 the administration of the S.C.C. changed. The Prefect, Vincenzo Vannutelli, seventy-two, *papabile* in 1904, now in partial eclipse, was replaced by Casimiro Gennari, sixty-nine, a native of the hill hamlet of Maratea, the founder of the canonist journal *Il monitore ecclesiastico*, and the most highly placed supporter of the project to codify the canons.[76] Gennari might not have shared Vannutelli's commitment to the Crosmières decision, but he would have been sympathetic with modest advances in the law. Changes of greater interest to Folchi occurred just below the top. Michele Lega moved to a new post. Basilio Pompili, a forty-five-year-old native of the Umbrian hill town of Spoleto, a former official of the Penitentiary who had been four years an auditor of the Rota, became Secretary. Into Lega's former position as Under-Secretary stepped Folchi's own counsel, Giulio Grazioli.[77]

What the Defender of the Bond, Carlo Lombardi, a professor of canon law at the Roman Seminary, thought of this shift has not been recorded. What Giorgi thought is known from his next step. The reorganization of the Curia by Pius X, which took effect October 20, had assigned jurisdiction in marriage cases to the Rota. On October 30 Giorgi obtained from the Pope a rescript keeping Filippo's case before the S.C.C.[78]

Lucky turns in administration, prestigious witnesses, recent precedent, helpful testimony were all in vain. On December 12, 1908, the S.C.C. answered the question put by Secretary Pompili, "Is the judgment of the Vicariate of the City of March 14, 1908, to be confirmed or invalidated in this case?" The answer was: "It is to be confirmed." In the ordinary course of law this judgment, concurring with the Vicariate's, was the end of Folchi's case.[79]

5.

There were men involved in the Folchi case who appear as manipulators, as dissemblers, as suspect of perjury or the fostering of perjury. The interest of the case does not center in their pres-

ence — what judicial system has ever been free from their like?
What is instructive is their interaction with the system — how did
these men make the good men do their work?

To answer this question, to understand the system at this time,
is to know something of the characters and careers of four men
who shaped the system's structure or guided its operations: Pietro
Gasparri, Michele Lega, Giuseppe Sarto, and Achille Ratti. They
were not the only devout men, nor the only men in charge, but
they were the highest motivated, the firmest willed, the most
strategically placed. They subscribed to a set of clear ideals, had a
strong determination to realize them, were animated by a conscious
dedication to God. The Folchi case in its long course was touched
by each. It was both their response to the case and the structure
they provided that decided the outcome.

To the biographers of these men a connection between their
subjects and the Folchi case might seem, perhaps, tenuous, if not
irrelevant and impertinent. In their lives it was a small incident, to
which they devoted a small amount of time and thought. It did
not involve their own interests, emotions, hopes or plans. A frag-
ment of the daily grist of legal business with which they dealt, the
case seems insignificant beside the great legal task of their lives,
the reform of canon law. The historians of canon law, too, might
not report the case in setting out the major changes the canonical
system was then undergoing. The creation of the Code and the
creation of a new judiciary might appear as incommensurably
larger events. The history of the law can easily be written in terms
of the enunciation of doctrine without reference to the fumbling
apprehension of principle and its awkward application to the surd
facts of a special case. Chroniclers of the Church might also suppose that the Folchi case had no place in their tale. While the
great failures may receive attention, while the ancient scandals have
been recounted, discounted, deplored, or rationalized, there would
seem to be no room for the bureaucratic breakdown, the modern
inadequacy of words, the contemporary lapse in judgment of rulers
of the Church. Most chronicles of modern pontificates have incorporated the suggestion once proferred by a cardinal of Pius
X: "Why, in the name of all that is reasonable or sensible, bother
our brains or worry our souls with the little, petty, poisonous
intriguing which everyone knew lay beneath the surface, un-

mindful and, indeed, utterly careless of what constituted great and holy Rome, the center of all Christendom, the See of Christ's Vicar, the majestic, eternal Rome?" [80]

Yet, in the detail of many paintings a critic may discern more of the artist's sense of space and form than in a more remote study of the canvas as a whole. The novelist, psychologist, or biographer may find a character expressed in an incident. In the momentary meeting of men brought about by the requirements of law, the historian may grasp the forces and purposes of a system. The history of the Church is not the celebration of a triumphal procession. The history of the law is not a record of the decrees enacted. The history of men is not a list of their aspirations. If all intentional acts have unforeseeable consequences, if execution never matches aim, the gap between ideal and reality can be ignored only at the peril of reporting dreams; it may be explored with the hope of achieving, next time, a closer approximation of the goal. The imprint of Gasparri, Lega, Pius X, and Pius XI was set upon the Folchi case. The case was not their program, code, judicial model, or system, but it is what happened in the program of Pius X, the code of Gasparri, the judicial model of Lega, the system of Pius XI. Adventitious to them as the case was, if they had not legislated and taught as they had, the case would not have happened as it did.

The canonical system for handling marriage cases, already mature in 1650 under Innocent X and perfected in 1743 by Benedict XIV, culminated in the person of the Pope. Michele Lega's authoritative treatise, *Ecclesiastical Judgments*, declared that if a case had been finally lost by judicial decision, one possibility remained: "Supplication may be made to the Supreme Prince not based on any decree of law but commended only to the grace and humanity of the Prince." [81] The Supreme Prince in the canonical system was the Sovereign Pontiff, substituted, in this system, for the Roman Emperor. The Sovereign Pontiff in 1908 was Giuseppe Sarto, Pius X. To him, on behalf of Filippo Folchi, Oreste Giorgi turned.

The appeal to the Pope came at a time strangely inappropriate or strikingly opportune, depending on the perspective taken. In the summer of 1908, Pius X had issued *Sapienti consilio*, the most significant legal document of his administration. Taking "wise counsel," as the opening words of the *motu proprio* proclaimed, the Pope had reorganized the standing committees of the Roman Curia. His aim was that "the Roman Curia, organized in a suitable and lucid way, may more easily offer its work to the Roman Pontiff and the Church." In those modulated phrases an observer could detect compressed impatience with what the Curia had become. Reorganization, the Pope added, was the first step in the process of codifying the law.[82] The new restructuring was the necessary accompaniment of Gasparri's grand design of bringing order into the canonical world.

The tacit premise of the reorganization was the acceptance of the loss of the Papal States. The explicit purpose of the reorganization was to create a more spiritual kingdom — "to restore all things in Christ," as the Pian motto ran. *Sapienti consilio* was restoration legislation after the Fall and the Exile. Like the post-Exilic revisers of the Pentateuch, the priestly legislators looked back, wistfully and idealistically, to the glory of the Temple. Like those earlier reformers, the priestly lawyers advising Pius X saw the glory of the past centered in the observance of law. The post-Exilic quality of the Reform was especially marked in the recreation of the Roman Rota.*

Since the days of Benedict XIV the Rota had declined. The Congregations, composed of cardinals and equipped with administrative remedies, had taken over most of the ecclesial controversies which might have been submitted to it for judicial examination. Wars and revolts had interrupted its secular tasks and reduced its secular scope. By 1821 it had become no more than a court deciding commercial cases and appeals in the Papal States.[83] National auditors had become unnecessary, and with the loss of an international composition had gone a decline in erudition. The doctorate in canon

---

* After the Babylonian Exile, according to Martin Noth, writing about ancient Israel, "'the law' became an absolute entity valid without respect to precedent, time, or history; based on itself, binding simply because it existed as law, because it was of divine origin and authority. . . . It was not now this community which formed the prerequisite for the being and application of the law, but rather it was the law, as the unprecedented primary entity, which fashioned this community, which was nothing but the union of those people who submitted to the law on all points. . . . It is the fate of human institutions which arise out of definite historical situations to decline in the course of history. But the ordinances and statutes, which had their place in the context of these institutions, obstinately maintain their existence, and, after their real basis has disappeared, take on a worth of their own which they had never possessed and which is not their due." Martin Noth, *The Laws in the Pentateuch and Other Studies*, trans. D. R. ap-Thomas (Edinburgh: Oliver and Boyd, 1966), pp. 86–87, 106.

law, so routinely required in the past, was not possessed by a number of nineteenth-century auditors. In 1849 the Dean of the Rota, Emmanuele Muzzarelli, a Bolognese like Lambertini and Ghislieri, abandoned his post and defected to the invaders attacking the papal domain.[84] His flight revealed the Rota's fallen state and portended a further fall. In 1870 the court's civil business stopped, as the Papal States were incorporated into the Kingdom of Italy. A vestigial function remained for the auditors — to act as judges in causes for beatification or canonization. Cast as advisers to the Congregation on Rites, they were far from the career elite of Urban VIII's day.[85] By 1908 they had shrunk to an aged and undistinguished seven.

Sapienti consilio inaugurated the new order. Pius X observed that the Congregations were "too burdened by forensic business." They would be reformed by being deprived of their litigation, by being restored to what they had been. The Pope quoted the eighteenth-century language of Innocent XIII, which Lega had discovered, ordering the Congregations not to receive "contentious cases which require process and proof." The ordinary judicial forum was to be the Sacred Roman Rota.[86] In the Church, now enjoying the centralization predestined by the decree on papal infallibility of the First Vatican Council, the importance of the Rota would be worldwide. Its development, still dependent on the good will of the Pope, might confidently be expected.

As a heroic re-creation, the new Rota was to be purer than the old. Only ordained priests could be auditors. They had to be possessors of the doctorate in theology as well as the doctorate in canon law. They must be men of mature age, but must retire at seventy-five — a notable restriction at the Roman Curia, where great dignities often came with great age. They would not be appointed on the nomination of nations or cities, but by the free choice of the Pope. Each would be assisted by a learned aide possessing at least the doctorate in canon law and approved by the rotal body and the Pope. All of these provisions were set out in "The Proper Law of the Sacred Roman Rota and Apostolic Signature" attached to *Sapienti consilio*. Like the priestly legislation after the paradigmatic Exile, the plan drew on legend of the past to set up an institution of learned priests as guardians of the law.

To ask the author, or at least the authorizer, of this ideal reconstruction to vary the even-handed ways of the law might have struck a lawyer as audacious. According to the theologians, a mortal sin against justice was committed by a judge guilty of "acceptance of persons" — of giving judgment not on the merits of the litigation but from partiality toward the person of a litigant.[87] In the ringing words of Innocent III in *Qualiter et quando*, X.5.1. 17, a judge should "put aside favor and fear, have God alone before his eyes, and walk the royal road without acceptance of persons." * According to Lega, two conditions sufficed to insulate judges from temptation to the sin: observance of the Clementine prohibition against receiving presents from litigants, and assurance of freedom from coercion by a superior. The safeguarding of the judge's independence was a necessary task of the legislator, for, although the laws to be applied were "most just," the judge was beset by "the imaginings" of the parties and needed impartial freedom to give "just judgment." "Hence," Lega wrote, "the canonical legislator must provide for the judge to be immune from the acceptance of persons." [88]

When the Pope, sovereign legislator and judge, was appealed to, he could, at least in theory, have decided the case himself, he could have refused to entertain the appeal, or he could have remitted the case to judges other than himself. What kept him from deciding the Folchi case in person? The theoretical possibility can scarcely have seemed a real one in a system organized in a structure of courts. For the Pope to have made the decision himself, nakedly to have asserted his sovereign power, would have been to show a contempt for the ordinary structures so subversive of their authority as to be in fact unthinkable. Even if Pius X had not been under the eye of a hostile press in an Italy administered by an unfriendly government, the internal restraints of the ecclesiastical system would probably have kept him, in a matter labeled judicial, from taking

---

* "Acceptance of persons" (*acceptio personarum*) is a term taken from the Vulgate translation of the Bible. The Bible enjoins a judge "to hear the little as well as the great, and do not accept the person of anyone, for the judgment is of God" (Deuteronomy 1.17). The New Testament gives a divine model: "With God there is no acceptance of persons," Romans 2.11. To accept persons in judgment is specifically labeled a sin in the Epistle of James 2.9. The glory of the Rota, Pius XII told its members in 1941, has been that in its judgments there has been "no acceptance of persons," Pius XII, "Allocution to the Auditors and Other Officials of the Sacred Roman Rota," *Acta apostolicae sedis*, XXXIII, 421.

the theorists at their word and, as Supreme Prince, personally, publicly judging the marriage null.

What kept Pius X from refusing the appeal after two courts had examined the case on its merits and found it wanting? The Pope did not hesitate to spurn the appeal because of conscious wickedness, pusillanimity of spirit, or skepticism about principles. A simple, radiant, almost palpable goodness made him what he was; and though the testimony to his spiritual stature comes most vividly from persons close to him in his pontificate, there is no reason to doubt the impression he made on his collaborators; it formed the solid foundation for his canonization by Pius XII.[89] This simple goodness was linked inextricably to firmness of purpose. He was a man of determination, of ideals — of stubborn pigheadedness, his enemies said. His course once set, it was almost impossible to deflect him. To such a man, rooted in the fundamentals of orthodoxy, no one could have proposed connivance in a divorce or the arrangement of an annulment on evidence which had been falsified. Bribery would have been repelled with stern retribution if Folchi had been rich (he was not) and impudent enough to attempt to bribe Pius X. Political influence would have accomplished little with a Pope who had been so recklessly disdainful of political consequences in upholding the doctrine of the Church when he believed orthodoxy was at stake.[90] Adamant in his conceptions of what was right, Pius X would have been proof against all attempts to use *raison d'état* as a rationale for freeing a Folchi to marry a Bourbon princess.

What, then, of friendship, or friendship mixed with compassion, as a motive? Arcangelo Folchi was not merely a Black, not merely one of the small band of loyal nobility toward whom a beleaguered Pope might feel benevolence, not merely an aristocrat a peasant might take pleasure in helping in his need. As senior chamberlain with cape and sword he saw the Pope almost daily. Contact made in service of this sort could breed confidence and affection in the Pope. Pius X's responsiveness to those physically close to him had been demonstrated dramatically on a major scale at the opening of his reign when he had selected as the new Secretary of State a thirty-eight-year-old monsignor, Merry del Val, whom he had met as secretary of the conclave and who had been helpful to him in his first days in office. At a more humble level of service, Arcangelo Folchi had helped the Pope ever since he had been installed for life in the Vatican. The plight of his boy, tied for life to a mercenary Frenchwoman while beloved by a royal princess, must have weighed upon Arcangelo. What more natural than for one old man to confide his heartbreak to another old man who could help? What more natural than for a compassionate man to do his utmost to help? From the very beginning of the case Pius X took a personal interest in its outcome. Grazioli and Giorgi, it has been observed, were counsel with outstanding credentials in the Curia; counsel of this kind could not have been chosen by accident. They must have been selected or at least authorized to act by Pius X himself.

If Pius X wanted to aid Arcangelo and his son, he had to do so in accordance with legal form. Italy was torn by fierce anticlericalism. Liberal opinion and the liberal press put on the same level "the scandals of the Black aristocracy and the disciplinary reforms of the Church." [91] The strenuous battle over the first divorce proposal in the Italian Parliament was still fresh in the public's mind. Near the end of the previous pontificate, summing up twenty years of opposition to the introduction of civil divorce in Europe, Leo XIII had told his cardinals that a divorce law "did open injury to God." No one should hope that the Church would relax its opposition: "It will not connive in any way. It will not acquiesce. It will not bear supinely an injury to God and to itself." [92] For Pius X it would have been unthinkable to repudiate in a general way or in a special case this indomitable affirmation of the exigencies of divine law. If he was to help a friend, it had to be within the law. He could not give new ammunition to the anticlericals by giving license to a Black. He could not provide an easy opportunity for knowledgeable people to remark that the Church furnished its own divorces. But if, in these circumstances, where every political and ecclesiastical consideration called for strict observance of the law, the Pope authorized two top career men to be Folchi's counsel, what feeling other than friendship could have prompted him? All had to be done discreetly and legally. The career men assured the necessary discretion, the essential legality.

Now that the case tried in the courts had ended in a double rebuff, and Giorgi came to the Pope with a new request, the famous determination of Pius X came into play. He had undertaken to help Arcangelo. He would not abandon him because two of his courts had denied Filippo's plea. As long as the law could be observed, the Pope would continue to help. That a procedural advantage — rehearing — constituted an "acceptance of persons" probably did not occur to him. If law is viewed as a book of answers, the nature of law as process is apt to be obscured. If law is regarded as a rigid code, personal grace must temper its demands. According to the explicit teaching of Saint Thomas, the unequal gifts given by God to different men do not constitute an "acceptance of persons," for God owes man nothing. According to the same high authority, rulers of men may reasonably discriminate among men in giving dispensations from the law: the administrator owes them nothing and relaxes the law for his own good reasons.[93] That a papal request for rehearing could be coercive was a thought dismissed by recalling the excellence of the Pope's appointments. That the integrity of a judicial system might be impaired by the influence upon it of a Supreme Prince, acting with grace and humanity, was an idea so foreign to the concept the Pope had always held of the Sovereign Pontiff's powers that it would not have troubled his mind. All that he needed to prompt his benevolence was some indication from Giorgi that not everything had yet been considered by the courts.

Within a month of the negative judgment of the S.C.C. of December 9, 1908, Giorgi obtained what he needed to move the Pope. It was already clear that the key might be held by Del Drago. As luck would have it, Del Drago was now visiting Rome, and with Filippo Folchi's encouragement Giorgi arranged to see him to discuss his testimony.[94] On January 9, 1909, Del Drago wrote Giorgi, "Most honored Monsignor, I remit to you my declaration in the terms which I have told you I can use in conscience, grieving that I have not been called to reconfirm it with an oath — that, eventually, I shall always be willing to do. Receive, Monsignor, my sentiments of sincere devotion and profound respect." [95] Attached to this letter was Del Drago's explicit affirmation that Filippo and Pauline as "a true condition" of their marriage had made "a binding agreement" not to have children. Here was something more positive, more precise, more satisfactory, than anything Del Drago had testified to in New York. Here was a piece of paper which Giorgi could put before the Pope as new evidence. Three days later Pius X granted the petition for rehearing.

The choice of forums made by Folchi's counsel and designated in the papal rescript was instructive. By the terms of *Sapienti consilio* only the Rota could hear a marriage case, and if the S.C.C. had understandably been permitted to decide the Folchi case, pending before it at the time of the reorganization, there was no reason why on rehearing the case should not have been referred to the Rota.[96] But the rescript from Pius X gave the S.C.C. "special faculties to inquire further," and kept the case before it.[97] Apparently, to Giorgi, the S.C.C. with Grazioli as Under-Secretary looked far less formidable than the new Rota.

At this point, however, Folchi's interest in winning his case encountered the momentum of the new judicial system which *Sapienti consilio* had inaugurated. One week after the papal rescript, on January 19, 1909, the S.C.C. sidestepped responsibility by choosing the new Dean of the Rota as the judge-delegate to hear further evidence. The Dean proceeded to hear testimony. The Pope was apprised of the course of the proceedings, and on May 17, 1909, the S.C.C. was informed by its Secretary that the Pope had decided to withdraw the case from it. A week after this courtesy of notification, Pius X signed a rescript ordering the case to be heard by the Rota.[98] The strategy of keeping the case in the S.C.C. had been abandoned as fruitless by Giorgi; or the new Dean of the Rota had succeeded in vindicating the proper jurisdiction of his tribunal.

6.

The new Dean of the Rota, who had been acting as the judge-instructor, was Michele Lega, the former Under-Secretary of the S.C.C.; he had heard the evidence in 1908 and had no doubt prepared the basic draft of the report on which the S.C.C. had acted at that time. In his new capacity, Lega headed the court designed, in the reform of canon law, to be the embodiment of judicial excellence. Folchi's friend De Montel and four other auditors had resigned, leaving the reformers a free hand. The new appointments reflected a serious effort by Gasparri to put on the court some of the best men available; their single common characteristic was their origin in small European villages. They included Serafin Many, a Sulpician, who had succeeded Gasparri in canon law at the *Institut catholique;* Franz Heiner, the author of *Grundriss des Katholisches Eherechts;* and John Prior, Vice-Rector of the Beda, the celebrated English seminary in Rome. The recomposed Rota had among its members five former professors of canon law. It numbered one Frenchman, one German, one Englishman, one Austrian, and five Italians, and ranged from forty-five to sixty-seven in age.[99] By curial standards, it was a youthful body. If the court was not completely internationalized, multi-national representation had been attempted. If not all the judges were scholars, scholarship had been respected. If the tribunal was less than the priestly paradigm envisaged as the restoration after the Exile, no comparable college of priests learned in the law existed anywhere.

Except that he was from the Romagna instead of Umbria and had not lived in Paris, its head came from a background remarkably similar to that of Gasparri. Lega had been born in the village of Brisighella in the diocese of Faenza. He had entered the Roman Seminary. He had taught as a young man at the Apollinaris and then become a full professor of canon law, while practicing in the courts and serving as a hearing-officer for the S.C.C.[100] He had published in 1894 an exhaustive treatise on a special branch of canon law, resembling Gasparri's in its close attention to current curial practice. His subject had been procedure in the ecclesiastical courts and committees of Rome. Drawn from lecture notes to students, it was, with kindly humility, also dedicated to the students as a work stimulated by their demands and as "something I share in a way with you." [101] If his experience of the world outside Rome was narrower than that of Pius X or Gasparri, if his mental framework was equally rigid, he did incarnate the energy, solidity, and devotion to duty of the best Roman canonists. When in August 1908, aged forty-eight, Lega became Dean of the Sacred Rota, Gasparri must have looked across at him as one of the bulwarks of the judicial system. Lega took his assignment to the Folchi case with the seriousness which attended all his work. For sixteen years he was to embody the demands of the law in its regard.

Lega took office with a high sense of the past of the Rota:

Our Tribunal is not newly instituted by the Constitution *Sapienti consilio* and The Proper Law, but it is the very same *Tribunal of the*

Roman Rota, heaped with praises in times past and now again called into operation . . . Hence, today's Auditors hold and revere the old Auditors as if they were their own parents and teachers; and, by this, great dignity is conferred upon Our Order.[102]

The liberal use of italics in this passage accurately conveyed Lega's enthusiasm for the institution which he headed. For him "Our Order" or "Our Sacred Order" referred to a body which was collegial, special, continuous with the past, and uniquely venerable. It was to this institution that the matter returned which he had already dealt with as Under-Secretary of the S.C.C., the petition of Filippo Folchi to establish nullity.

Between January 12, 1909, and the formal assignment to the Rota in May, Lega had already heard the new witnesses produced by Folchi's counsel: a painter, Alessandro Frattini; a lawyer, Luigi Pacieri; a Roman landowner, Ottavio Fabi; and a city official, Marchese Alfonso Antaldi di Astorre.[103] All of these old friends of Filippo testified to knowing that he had attached a condition against offspring, but Frattini thought that it was a condition not to have any intercourse; Pacieri had learned of it only after Folchi "had departed with the daughter of Don Carlos"; and Fabi and Antaldi did not know whether the condition attached had preceded the religious marriage. Perhaps the most unexpected witness was Antaldi, who, resorting to French, described Pauline as his *maîtresse* and Filippo as his friend at the time Filippo had stolen her from him. For "reasons of delicacy" he had been reluctant to testify earlier. Now he asserted that Filippo had eventually confided in him that, to please his mother, he had had "to make some sort of systematization of these relations," but that he had done so "irregularly." Three of Filippo's brothers, Stanislao, Saverio, and Giulio, were recalled as witnesses and for the first time testified that they had heard of an agreement not to have children; none specified when the agreement had been reached.[104]

The star witness continued to be Del Drago, who had recently married a forty-eight-year-old American widow. He was interrogated in Rome before Lega on June 12, 1909. His New York deposition was read to him, and he reconfirmed it "in all respects." He was then asked when the agreement of Filippo and Pauline had been made. He replied: "These conversations were carried on approximately after the return from Africa and after the birth of the second baby, some time before the marriage." Pressed by Lega to specify the time further, he said: "I cannot be precise as to how many times and at what period." [105]

An effort was made to get more testimony from Pauline, who was working in Milan. She refused to come to Rome, not, she said, because she was disrespectful of the court, but because she could not take the time from her employment. The Archbishop of Milan was then directed by Lega to obtain her testimony, and she appeared before the Vicar-General of Milan on June 18. Before this official she made a declaration. She supposed that "it was a matter of another attempt by my husband Filippo Folchi-Vici to obtain the annulment of our marriage against every truth of law and fact." She did not intend to respond to further questioning. She had only Sundays free, and she needed her job. On further prodding by the Rota, however, the Milan archdiocese induced her to appear once more in Milan, on July 7. She said that she would testify in Rome if her husband paid her way. She would not appoint counsel to appear for her in court, and she testified nothing further. [106]

Pauline's rights continued to be defended, as they had been in the past, by the Defender of the Bond. In the first months of the case in the Rota this was Luigi Sincero, but when, in May 1909, Sincero was made a rotal auditor himself, his place was taken by Francesco Parrillo, who was to conduct the case for the validity of the marriage with outstanding pertinacity and vigor. Counsel for Folchi — Grazioli and Giorgi both having ascended to higher office — was a lay member of the ecclesiastical bar, Vincenzo Sacconi. [107]

1909 was the first year of cases for the new Rota. There was no backlog, and Lega could move with his usual briskness to keep the docket current. The judgment in the Folchi case was ready for announcement on December 6. Under the rules of the new Rota, a majority vote decided. The *ponens* or judge-reporter was not disqualified from voting; the judge-instructor, who had heard the testimony, was. Hence, Lega could not participate in the decision, and Sincero, the former defender of the bond, disqualified himself. The rest of the Rota voted. The opinion was given by Gustavo Persiani, the senior member, sixty-eight, a native of Rome, and a hold-over from the old Rota.

Counsel had dropped the claim made in the libel and in earlier declarations of Filippo that he had gone through the religious ceremony on the condition that he was already married. Persiani, nonetheless, reviewed this contention, apparently to cast light on the credibility of Filippo. He observed that Filippo alone had asserted that there was such a condition. He concluded that "it was entirely without verisimilitude" that Monsignor Bacchi could have told Filippo that fornication with Pauline made him a married man, or that Filippo could have believed such a statement if it had been made. In two pages Persiani disposed of the claim now urged upon the Rota that there had also been an agreement to avoid children. Filippo himself could not be counted as a witness for his claim, and all of the witnesses, save Del Drago, testified to hearsay dependent on Filippo. None of the witnesses, including Del Drago, could say that the agreement was made at a time in advance of the consent to marry. It was not established that any condition had been attached to the actual consent.[108]

Persiani's analysis of the facts was not only skeptical, but perfunctory, reflecting a sense that the whole claim was preposterous. His statement of law was even more cursory. Here it became evident that he belonged to the nineteenth-century breed of Rota judges, not to the scholars of the reform. He made no reference to the relevant decisions of the S.C.C., nor did he invoke any treatise save the thirteenth-century Gloss on *Tua nos*, X.4.1.26. As he correctly understood the Gloss's teaching, if an intention against the substance of marriage was entertained by one party and uncommunicated to the other before the marriage, "fraud was established," and a court should not let the fraud benefit the party engaging in it; the marriage would be upheld. The decretal *Si conditiones*, X.4.5.7, applied only if there was "a true and proper condition to which the contracting parties tie their consent, and this condition, attached by one of the contracting parties, must be positively accepted by the other."

"Is nullity of marriage established?" This question, in terms of which the reorganized Rota, unlike the old, invariably decided annulment cases, made plain that the burden of proof fell on the party attacking the marriage. The answer given at the end of Persiani's opinion was "No." There then followed the judgment itself, the new Rota, again in distinction from the old, welding the judgment to the opinion. What remained unchanged was the ancient introductory formula: "Having considered all these matters and sedulously weighed them and having invoked the name of Christ, we, the undersigned Auditors, sitting for the Tribunal and having God alone before our eyes, decree, declare, and judge definitively . . ." After this reminder of the religious character of their action and after this declaration that no earthly consideration swayed them — "God alone" before their eyes — the auditors gave judgment.* In this case it was: "*Non constat*" — "Nullity is not established." In the standard clause following this pronouncement all diocesan bishops and court officials were commanded to enforce the judgment by such "executive and coercive means as are most efficacious and opportune in the circumstances."

Once more Folchi's case appeared to have ended. It was "shipwrecked," as Lega was to say, employing a common metaphor that, when applied by the presiding judge, implied satisfaction with the result. But his case was not wrecked, merely stranded. Counsel for Folchi continued to give evidence of that suppleness, stubbornness, dexterity, and staying power which were to sustain his cause, more than once, at the edge of disaster. Counsel went to the Apostolic Signature.

The Signature in 1910 was a reformed successor to the Signature as that ancient body had functioned since Gregory XVI had reshaped it in 1834. Its relation to the Rota and its present availability for an appeal were the immediate consequences of the fresh reorganization made by *Sapienti consilio*, which had given it a limited supervisory power over the judicial system. Of its membership of six cardinals, five were elderly creations of Leo XIII, including its Prefect, Vincenzo Vannutelli, lately transferred to this post from his more significant position as head of the S.C.C. The group's composition suggested that the Signature was principally a place of honorable retirement for cardinals of another day.[109] In theory there was little work for them to do. In the small number of cases falling

---

* "God alone before one's eyes" is a phrase invented or at least made canonically familiar by Innocent III. His use of it in instructions to papal judges in *Qualitas et quando*, X.5.1.17, has already been noted. Earlier, in the Fourth Lateran Council, he decreed that abuses of cathedral chapters were to be corrected by the bishop, "having God alone before his eyes," X.1.31.13, *Irrefragabili*. The formula became common in papal letters of the thirteenth century and was adopted in rotal judgments as early as 1319 (André Jullien, *Juges et avocats des tribunaux de l'Église* [Rome: Catholic Book Agency, 1970], p. 231). For Cardinal Jullien, a modern Dean of the Rota, "having God alone before one's eyes is the first rule for every judge" (*ibid.*, p. 226).

within their limited jurisdiction they would be asked to vote Yes or No after receiving a report prepared by their Secretary, and a *votum* or recommendation prepared by one of their consultors. A kind of House of Lords in the Curia, the Signature effectively combined venerable age, honorable function, and minimal responsibility.

The role of two men in this body made it plausible that the Signature might look with favor on Filippo Folchi's appeal. Its senior consultor — not necessarily the man who would be assigned the case — was Folchi's former witness, Archbishop Agostino Sili. The sixth cardinal — the cardinal of Pius X's creation, appointed to make sure that the venerable oldsters being honored did not put the new judicial system out of kilter — was Agostino Sili's cousin, Pietro Gasparri.

A court of cassation in a strict sense, the Signature did not have the function of judging the merits of a case. The remedies it could provide were three: it could disqualify a judge; it could quash a judgment for lack of jurisdiction in the court rendering it; and it could order *restitutio in integrum*, "restoration to an unimpaired position." [110] In Folchi's case, only the last was even conceivably relevant. "Restoration to an unimpaired position," an equitable device of Roman law, had been designed to give judicial aid to persons under a disability, such as minors, who had suffered serious loss through their inability to protect their rights and needed to be allowed to begin a case afresh. The device had been adopted for the canon law by the *Decretals*, where an entire title, X.1.41, was consecrated to the subject. Cleansing of the judicial slate of earlier judgments was precisely what Folchi wanted. But had he grounds to ask it?

Existing statutory law provided restoration on very limited grounds. The only decretal remotely relevant to the case at bar was X.1.41.4, *Ex literis abbatis*. In this decision from the year 1200, the petitioner's father had asserted that his daughter's marriage had been terminated by judicial decree because she had been fraudulently misled as to the day set for her case and so had failed to come to court; Innocent III, "in favor of marriage," as he said, quashed the judgment against her and granted her a new day for a hearing. Commentators had then expanded the decretal's original notion. Joannes Andreas had said broadly that restoration to an unimpaired position was available for adults as well as for minors if there was a just cause. The view that the remedy was "extraordinary" continued to confine it, yet a modern authority such as Lega's textbook on procedure was not at all clear what its limits were.[111] Folchi had scarcely been denied a hearing, and he was attacking, not defending, a marriage; but within lines so vaguely drawn, the room for judicial discretion was substantial.

Canon 1905 of Book Four of the new Code of Canon Law being drafted under Gasparri's direction permitted restoration to an unimpaired position only in cases of "manifest injustice." This limitation seemed to accord with the view that the remedy was to be an unusual one. "Manifest injustice," however, was itself defined by the Code as occurring when a judgment rested on documents now shown to be false; or when new documents were discovered containing new facts which "decisively demand a contrary decision"; or when "a prescription of law has evidently been neglected."[112] The last two specifications, especially the very last, were of an elasticity such that almost all appeals could appear to qualify. What lawyer who has lost a case does not believe that the court has evidently neglected a prescription of law? If the draft Code corresponded to current conceptions of the remedy, as no doubt it did, only severe judicial self-restraint or conscious impotence could keep the Signature from turning into a court where the soundness of Rota decisions was regularly reexamined.

In any event, the Signature could grant restoration only when a case had become *res judicata;* and, according to *Dei miseratione,* marriage cases never became *res judicata.* If the rules conferring jurisdiction meant what they said, the Signature was powerless to order restoration in a case like Folchi's. This technicality was not an insignificant one for Michele Lega; but the Dean of the Rota was not a member of the higher court.[113] Recent though the jurisdictional rules were, the Signature brushed them aside — leaped over them, if a more vigorous metaphor is preferred — to take up Folchi's petition. In the fall of 1910, it restored Folchi to an unimpaired position.

The basis for the Signature's action was not stated. Unlike the Rota, which was constrained by The Proper Law to give facts and reasons under pain of its decision being null, the Signature was empowered to render judgments without opinions. The old notion that cardinals did not have to account for their conclusions still prevailed. Even the Secretary of this body felt no obligation to publish his reports. The highest court of the reformed Curia was in a position to behave precisely as the S.C.C. had behaved for over a century, until Prospero Lambertini had introduced it to the idea of making public the Secretary's statement of the case. At the apex of the reformed judicial system a body with an elastic jurisdiction had been established without public accountability.

While the Signature itself preserved the sphinxlike posture of cardinals, the terms of the judgment and a letter from the Secretary, Niccolo Marini, hinted at the basis for its action. The cardinals extended the remedy of restoration to Folchi only as "to that part of the judgment related to the attaching of a condition against offspring." [114] In other words, the Rota would be expected to hear Folchi again only on what had become his principal claim. The Secretary was even more explicit in a note to Folchi's counsel. The Rota, he said, had taken the view that to prove his case Folchi had to establish that a bilateral agreement to exclude children had been made by himself and Pauline. But in modern times a different opinion was to be taken as true, "given the authority of distinguished canonists and the nature of the matter itself." A marriage was null if even only one party attached to his marital consent a condition not to have offspring.[115] Marini did not cite the distinguished canonists he had in mind, but the pre-eminent authority who held this position with the greatest conviction, who was even then in the process of engrafting it on the new Code, was Pietro Gasparri himself. If the Rota was reversed by the Signature for evident neglect of a prescription of law, it was because Persiani's opinion had rested on the old-fashioned view which Gasparri was eradicating. Not necessarily to accommodate the Pope and not necessarily to accommodate his cousin Sili, but to establish rotal marriage law on a modern foundation, Gasparri concurred in the reversal of the Folchi judgment and insisted that the Rota measure Folchi's claim once more by the new standard.

7.

Oreste Giorgi was no longer Filippo Folchi's counsel, but his devotion to his old client's cause had not slackened. His tenacity was to be of vital significance as the case progressed; and to account for it, and the measures to which it led, is not easy. Pius X's interest in the case would not by itself have generated this untiring concern; it survived the Pope's death in 1914. Having done his duty as a lawyer, and having had to move on to other business, Giorgi needed to feel no special tie to Folchi. Payment by Filippo himself was improbable, and, though the Folchi family could have compensated him, it does not appear that his motivation was mercenary. Nor does friendship account for such staunch service. Filippo saw little of him; he had no close connection to Arcangelo. The explanation, it may be, lies in Giorgi's psychology as affected by the organization in which he served.

Not merely the Curia in general, but the Sacred Penitentiary in particular, stamped an impression on Giorgi. The Penitentiary, the ancient curial office in which he had first reached prominence, acted on questions presented by penitents or by confessors on behalf of penitents in a variety of cases where the gravity of the sin or the complexity of the sinner's situation required recourse to the Pope himself. Endowed with a comprehensive delegation of papal power, it granted absolutions or dispensations in the Pope's name.[116] Sin was the raw material of its business; it responded to the sinner seeking mercy; its purpose was to reconcile. It was called a "tribunal," but it was very different from a court where rules of proof govern what the judge may do. Its evidence was the statement of its petitioner, and, unless his insincerity was palpable, he was believed. It was even possible for one result to be reached in the regular courts of the Church, the courts of the "external forum," and another to be reached in the Sacred Penitentiary.[117] In this tribunal of "the internal forum," in a direct line with sacramental confession, the Church sought to deal with individuals on their own terms with a minimum of regard for the consequences of such special justice to the ecclesiastical community as a whole.

Yet the Penitentiary was an organization, even a hierarchy. The Grand Penitentiary was at the top, and he presided over the Regent, the Secretary, the Substitute Secretaries, the consultors. The organization operated through channels, and it applied the canon law. The resulting mixture of a mission of mercy and a structure of law ran the risk of making the mercy impersonally bureaucratic or the law arbitrary and whimsical. The tensions between mercy and law experienced by the Penitentiary paralleled tensions in the Church as a whole, but did so in a hothouse atmosphere where everything was secret — confidentiality was an absolute prerequisite — and where the pleas for mercy were directed to those who could grant them most easily by pressing the levers of power. A Grand Penitentiary could be no more interested in disinterested justice than a Grand Inquisitor could be interested in disinterested science. It was only natural that the Penitentiary should try to facilitate, by the legal techniques available to members of the Curia, the return to grace of those eager and humble enough to seek its special ministry. The iron law of bureaucracy is that regulatory agencies of government turn into the servants of those they regulate. The Penitentiary served the clientele it drew. It afforded its petitioners the legal regularization of their situations by the accommodations which were easiest to arrange on a formal legal level.

Giorgi moved in the early 1900's to the Congregation on Bishops and Regulars, but the Penitentiary remained his love. He received an appointment to the Rota in February 1908,[118] but Lega and Gasparri no doubt recognized that he lacked the judicial temperament so particularly necessary for the judges who were to begin the new era of the Rota, and when the great reorganization went through later in the year, he was asked to resign. On February 8, 1909, he returned in triumph to the Penitentiary as Regent or deputy chief. After two years of service he was to move to a still higher curial post, to be Secretary of the S.C.C. (no longer, as reorganized, a judicial body). But ultimately he was to return to the Penitentiary and end his days as Grand Penitentiary.

Throughout the Folchi case, Giorgi was always the Grand Penitentiary. A suppliant had sought his help, convinced him — perhaps in sacramental confession itself — of the sincerity of his fundamental claim. To save that sinner by regularizing his relation with the Church became the great objective. The means to accomplishing the objective — legal devices as he perhaps saw them to be — were entirely subordinate to the glorious end in view. In the heat of litigation, personal pride, pique at opposition, and peasant stubbornness may have also played a part in strengthening his will, but to himself his motive was high and pure-minded. "I undertook the matter from intimate conviction," he told the Vicariate's Defender of the Bond in 1906.[119] That intimate conviction sustained him through eighteen years of solicitude for Folchi.

No longer his counsel in 1911, the Regent of the Sacred Penitentiary exchanged roles. Like De Montel before him, he became Folchi's witness. He appeared, in the rehearing before the Rota ordered by the Signature, to support crucial new testimony by Giovanni Del Drago. Del Drago now declared that in his earlier deposition he had inadvertently omitted a vital fact: the exchange of words between Filippo and Pauline agreeing to the exclusion of offspring had occurred in front of him, Del Drago, on the very afternoon of the marriage performed by Monsignor Bacchi. He added that the record of his 1908 deposition in New York — the record he had confirmed in his re-examination before Lega in Rome in 1909 — showed signs of "suppressions and alterations." His further testimony in Rome was inadequate because he had been "in a hurry." Only now in 1911 was he giving a full and precise account of the agreement of the spouses to the condition against offspring.[120]

Giorgi testified in support of this addendum to Del Drago's story. On the afternoon of Del Drago's re-examination by Lega in 1909, Del Drago had come to his house, discussed the judicial interrogation he had undergone, and asked if he had failed to bring out an important circumstance in not being precise about the time he had heard Filippo and Pauline speak of their agreement. Giorgi had informed him that his omission was important and advised him to wait until all the testimony was published before deciding what to do. Later Giorgi mentioned his conversation with Del Drago to Folchi's new lawyer, Sacconi, and to John Prior of the Rota.[121]

Giorgi's appearance to give this evidence was arranged with care. Offering his new testimony on May 18, 1911, Del Drago said that he could confirm its truth by "a pious and learned priest." However, as his communication with the priest was of a "strict and secret character," he could not reveal his name. With the stage set, Sacconi revealed that Giorgi was the priest in question and called him as a witness on November 25. Giorgi thereupon declined to appear as a witness for a party, but declared his willingness to appear if called by the court ex officio.[122] The Defender of the Bond, Parrillo, objected strenuously to any testimony from Giorgi on the ground that he "had played the part of an advocate." In the General Council of Lyon, Innocent IV had legislated, "In the appeal of a case the appellant's proctor or advocate in the prior judgment is not received as a witness," and the legislation stood as part of the Sext, 2.10.3. By decree of December 20, the Rota overrode the objections of both Giorgi and Parrillo and the text of the Sext and ordered Giorgi to appear as a witness called by Folchi.[123] The power of the twentieth-century Rota to compel testimony was purely ecclesiastical, but of course a churchman like Giorgi would obey its order. Giorgi then appeared as an unwilling witness.

When he did testify at last on December 30 — this witness whose name was a secret in May, who had to be dragged in by order in December — Giorgi not only confirmed Del Drago's story, but contributed the surmise that Del Drago had come to see him because he was afraid that Folchi would attribute his omission of the date "to a base vendetta against him; for, at that time, there was a disagreement between them." [124] Giorgi thereby did the maximum for Del Drago as a witness: Del Drago was truthful, his omission of the date had been due to misunderstanding, he had actually been on bad terms with Folchi when he testified. There was a final bonus in the delay in Giorgi's testimony. By the time he testified he had been promoted from the Penitentiary to be Secretary of the S.C.C. In the concentric tiers of the Curia, the circle formed by secretaries of Congregations stood just below the circle formed by cardinals. In Giorgi's appearance, a very high administrator of the Curia vouched for Del Drago.

The new hearings also produced more precision from other witnesses on the time the condition against children had been made. Two more Folchi brothers, Giulio and Pio, swore that they had learned from Filippo that the condition was made some time before the religious marriage. The old friends, Pacieri, Frattini, and Antaldi, swore that they had heard that the condition was attached to the religious ceremony. An old teacher of Filippo, Enrique Serra, a Spanish artist, came forward as a new witness to the "reciprocal accord" not to have children. A physician, Francesco Saverio Costantini, swore that in 1891 he met Filippo on the street and that Filippo asked him "what means he could use to avoid children." Dr. Costantini advised him and asked the reason for his question; Filippo replied that he had agreed to have no children.[125]

The testimony of Pauline was once more sought. Appearing once again before the archepiscopal tribunal of Milan, she confirmed the little she had testified to before. Asked if she had anything further to say in the interest of justice, she replied, "I declare that I do not want to appear again in this interminable case. In my judgment it has no serious foundation, for the marriage contracted by me with Signor Folchi-Vici must be always held as valid before God." [126]

The case was once again ripe for judgment by the Rota. A procedural skirmish which had occurred after the Signature had returned it to the Rota affected the composition of the court. The Signature had sent the case back with the direction, "All are to see," that is, all of the auditors were to participate in the judgment. Lega, who could not have been pleased with the Signature's reversal of his court and the Signature's disregard of its jurisdictional limits, raised the technical objection that the Rota's own rules disqualified the judge-instructor from judging, and a former Defender of the Bond should not judge in a case he had argued; hence, how could "all see"? The issue was taken with great dispatch by Cardinal Vannutelli to the Pope for settlement. In his own hand, Pius X wrote, "To the Sacred Rota that all may see, notwithstanding anything else." [127] The Pope who had authorized Folchi's counsel in 1906, who had kept the case in the S.C.C. in October 1908, who had ordered a rehearing in the S.C.C. in January 1909, who had transferred the case to the Rota in May 1909, here intervened for the fifth time with a personal command. He appeared to say, "We want no technical trifling from the Rota." The Pope's direction had been sufficient to quell any resistance to the Signature's decision; the case had gone ahead. Now Lega decided that the Pope was to be obeyed rather than the rules, and he would participate in the judgment; in fact he would write the opinion himself. Sincero, however, the Pope notwithstanding, still disqualified himself.

Lega's opinion was the most serious attention Folchi's case had yet received, as though, exasperated by the matter falling within his sphere for a third time, he had resolved that there should be no ground given for its reappearance. [128] Confronting the new testimony of 1911, he invoked the rules of evidence which decretal law, the old Rota, and the commentators had developed on the basis of long experience. First, witnesses could testify to hearsay, but such witnesses suffered "the greatest exception," as taught "innumerable decisions of This Holy Order," recalled by a row of citations to the *More Recent Decisions* of the seventeenth-century Rota. In any event, the credibility of hearsay witnesses could not rise above their source. In this case all of the new witnesses were repeating what they had learned from Filippo. Second, there was the danger of subornation when witnesses were heard after the testimony had been published and was available to the parties. For that reason a constitution of Clement V, issued at the Council of Vienne in 1317 and added to the canons in Clementines, 2.8.2, forbade the examination of witnesses on the same articles after publication of the testimony. Despite this clear law, such examination had been made here, by specific order of the Signature, through favor — Lega did not say to Folchi — but "to a marriage case." The testimony was to be regarded with suspicion, especially as the questions asked had been suggestive of the answers desired. A single witness, Del Drago, testified to the actual agreement of the condition against offspring. He had been "various and vacillating." There was no apparent reason why his latest testimony, "now laboriously extracted," could not have been given earlier. By the afternoon of June 12, 1909, when he talked to Giorgi, Del Drago knew that his dating of the condition was important. He could have asked to correct his testimony after it had been published, as Folchi himself had corrected his statement. There was a clear conflict between the earlier record of what Del Drago had in fact been asked and his present claim that he had never been asked the dates before. The regular rule of proof in marriage cases required that the ground of nullity be proved by two witnesses who were "above all exception." Against Del Drago, "many and great exceptions could be raised and in fact are raised." The substance of his testimony was itself too perfect. He testified for Folchi in such a way "that nothing better could be desired." Without calling him in so many words a perjurer, Lega left little doubt as to his estimate of his credibility.[129]

Lega said nothing about Giorgi's credibility, but what he thought of the effort to rehabilitate Del Drago through Giorgi may be inferred from the dating of the judgment. It was given less than three weeks after Giorgi's testimony. In terms of rotal time, eighteen days was an impossibly short space in which to prepare a decision, obtain the concurrence of the other auditors, and write a long opinion. The swiftness of the judgment after Giorgi's appearance suggested Lega's valuation of his contribution. The opinion was also an answer to other persons besides Giorgi. The new Rota responded to the critique offered by the Signature and to the pressing interest shown by Pius X. Lega's exhaustive examination and repudiation of Folchi's case appeared to preclude further appeal to these higher quarters.

In 1912, the same year as this judgment was given, Lega supervised the publication of the decisions of 1909, the first year of the reorganized Rota. Unlike the opinions of the old Rota, these were to be published by the tribunal. Unlike the decisions of the S.C.C. between 1740 and 1868, they were not to be published currently, but only after a delay. Unlike even the recent practice of the S.C.C., the real names of the parties were to be omitted in the reporting of decisions on petitions for annulment. Both the delay in publication and the anonymity of the cases were related to the Church's exposure to attack in a hostile Italian press. A price was paid for them: justice was not seen to be done, and the protections that the open administration of justice assures were materially diminished. Accustomed as they were to secrecy in so many aspects of ecclesiastical life and ecclesiastical lawmaking, the reformers did not appear to count this sacrifice as a heavy one.

To achieve the anonymity desired, fictitious names were substituted. Whether they were selected by Lega or by an assistant and whether they had any symbolic significance to the man selecting them cannot be demonstrated. Someone indulged a mordant sense of humor in dubbing Monsignor Bacchi "Don Pantaleone," someone savored the irony of disguising Pauline as "Felicitas," and someone was moved by intuition, premonition, or clairvoyance to name Filippo "Patroclus," the fallen warrior who was avenged by his friend, Achilles.

8.

Arduum sane munus, "surely an arduous office," ran the opening words of Pius X's announcement of approval of the project to construct a Code.[130] The brief had been issued March 19, 1904, six months after Gasparri's historic conversation with the new Pope. The words referred to the papal office, but they evoked the difficulty of the task to be accomplished. All during the years the Folchi case had run its course through the courts of the Curia, Gasparri had labored to make the Code. In 1912, the year of the Rota decision, the first complete draft was ready for distribution to the bishops of the world.

Anyone who has served upon a committee knows that however sagacious its individual members, however impressive its collective experience, the group will be limp and flabby unless one person makes its business his own. Some committee members will be sharp and resourceful critics of what is proposed, others will acquiesce in almost any suggestion, but if the matter is to move forward, one member must shoulder the responsibility. Gasparri was that man in the making of the Code. He was under the supervision of the Pope and curial cardinals; he had the advice of the canonists he had chosen; he received the comments of the episcopate; he had the particular aid of four close collaborators of his choosing — his first assistant, Eugenio Pacelli; the Jesuit Benedetto Ojetti; his young nephew, Filippo Bernardini; and his old cousin, Agostino Sili. But throughout the process, it was Gasparri who analyzed the law into the areas of responsibility and selected the men to whom they were assigned, collated their drafts, collated the criticisms of the cardinals and the suggestions of the bishops, revised the drafts and put the individual pieces into a coherent whole. Not unjustly he could state, "I was the principal actor in the formation of the Code," and, "The Code was principally composed by me." [131]

Dominating the composition of the Code was the Curia's Roman view of law as a set of instructions announced by superiors to docile subjects. The instructions themselves were to be lucid, lapidary summations of the prescriptions of earlier authorities. Yet, voice from Sinai that it was intended to be, the Code could not help but bear the stamp of its guiding genius. Nowhere was this special impress clearer than in the prescriptions which, coincidentally, bore so heavily on the case of Filippo Folchi: the rules on intentions and conditions against the substance of marriage.[132]

The starting points for the extraordinary development effected by Gasparri were the two decretals which have already been set out and analyzed in the context of the Barberini case in the first part of Chapter II of this book: Innocent III's *Tua nos*, X.4.1.26, holding null a marriage where consent was simulated; and Gregory

IX's *Si conditiones*, X.4.5.7, holding null marriages where conditions were attached against the substance of marriage, such as "I contract with you if you will avoid the generation of offspring." *Tua nos* had opened up the possibility that the subjective intent of the parties to a marriage would be examined in determining the validity of their consent. The standard Gloss, however, had restricted the decretal to the internal, penitential forum, denying that it applied in the public courts of the Church. Subjective intent had not, in fact, been considered by the courts of the Curia, save in rare cases such as a woman in prison pretending to marry in order to escape, or a joking man and girl who pretended to marry in order to entertain a crowd of friends.[133] In these cases circumstances so plainly controlled the spoken word that the courts had little difficulty in declaring the apparent marriages void. The large area of intent against the goods of marriage, such as the good of offspring, was never explored except where contract had excluded the good as in the Barberini case. Even the recent application of the decretal by the S.C.C. in the Crosmières case in 1904 dealt with an agreement, not a private intention against offspring. What Gasparri did was to bring *Tua nos* and *Si conditiones* together, take *Tua nos* as authority to examine subjective intent against the goods of marriage, and conclude that, if a subjective intent existed in one party's mind against the substance of marriage, the marriage was null by analogy with *Si conditiones*.[134]

The law embodying this startling development was canon 1086 of the new Code which, promulgated by Benedict XV on Pentecost Sunday, 1917, became the law of the universal Church on May 19, 1918. The canon ran:

Sec. 1. Internal consent is presumed to be in agreement with the words or signs used in the marriage ceremony.

Sec. 2. But if either party or both parties by a positive act of the will exclude marriage itself or all right to the conjugal act or some essential property of marriage, the parties contract invalidly.[135]

In this canon there was no mention of "conditions being attached," no restriction, even by implication, to intentions manifested by public agreement. The internal act of one party alone, not necessarily communicated to the other party, sufficed to annul the marriage. All that was necessary to be established was "a positive act of the will," excluding from the consent to marry one of the essential properties of marriage. The immense area constituted by the mental state of persons getting married was opened to the scrutiny of the courts.

Hinging validity on intention, the canon predictably opened the way to self-deception if not to fraud and perjury. These dangers, so vividly exemplified in the Folchi case, had been anticipated in the 1912 draft of the forerunner to canon 1086. After the words which now form the second section this draft added, "As the presumption of consent remains, the one who fictitiously consents to marriage is bound to expunge the fiction and offer consent." [136] In a case such as Folchi's, the petitioner, even if he established that he had excluded an essential property of marriage from his consent, would have been obliged, by ecclesiastical law and under penalty of sin, to consent to marriage properly. If the other party was still willing to have him, he would have gained nothing by his fraud. There would be no "reward" of nullity for the person who married, concealing from his putative spouse that he was not accepting the purposes of marriage.

Ecclesiastical precedent was not lacking for treating a deceitful person as estopped to deny his marriage. Alexander III's decretal, *Propositum*, X.4.7.1, would not let a bigamist deny his second marriage when, after his first wife's death, he attempted to repudiate his second wife on the ground that he had never been free to marry her because of his secret first marriage. The decretals on betrothals provided for "moderate" compulsion to force the carrying out of a promise to marry.[137] Yet, could the Church force one under penalty of sin to give consent if he absolutely refused? The Code, reflecting Gasparri's own conviction, said that marriage was formed by consent "which can be supplied by no human power." [138] If the Church could not supply consent, perhaps its power to coerce consent even for the purpose of discouraging fraudulent profanation of the sacrament was limited. In the final revision of the Code, the canon compelling the offer of a new valid consent was eliminated.

Fraud remained without a practical sanction against it. The risk of fraud, however, had less impact on the courts than the confusion, already present in theory, which now began to have a substantial impact on actual decisions. That confusion, elaborated in the second chapter of this book, arose from the coexistence of one class of marriages, virginal in intention, and another class of marriages, entered with a view to offspring. As long as these two distinct classes were subsumed under a single comprehensive theory, there was the potentiality of serious practical problems arising. For seven centuries the consequences had not been great. Virginal marriages were not common. No more than one Barberini case was decided by the S.C.C. Difficulties emerged only in the latter part of the nineteenth century.

Contraception as a social habit brought the issue to the fore. Beginning in late eighteenth-century France, birth control had spread through most of Western Europe, so that a new and distinct pattern of deliberately regulating family size became evident.[139] The teaching of the Church was that contraception was a sin; not every sin had such a relation to the institution of marriage. By virtue of the teaching that the good of offspring was an essential property of marriage, by virtue of the decretal *Si conditiones*, the validity of a marriage could be affected by an agreement to exclude offspring by contraception. Faced by the decretal and by the practice of contraception, the canonists had to decide: Was procreative marriage the only acceptable model for the institution of marriage? Could the Church accept as valid a third class of marriages which, like virginal marriages, would involve the intentional exclusion of offspring although the exclusion would be by contraception rather than by continence? The Crosmières case showed the determination of the S.C.C. to follow *Si conditiones* in treating any public agreement to have no children as so contrary to the institution of marriage as to invalidate the marriage at its inception. This result was predictable on the basis of *Si conditiones;* but a multiplicity of questions could be raised which the old decretal did not answer. Suppose the rejection of children was not by agreement, but by intention? Suppose it was by the intention of one party only? Suppose it was only for a period — until children could be afforded, or after enough children had been born? Suppose the contraceptive means to be employed did not affect the act of intercourse itself, but only its consequences? Suppose that contraception was to exclude further children for the good of existing children? Gasparri, living and writing in France where contraception had flourished so vigorously, was not unaware of most of these questions. *De matrimonio* embodied an attempt to meet them. But he was handicapped by the analytical tools at his disposal, and, using them, he imported into the new law on invalidating intention the difficulties already present in Thomas Aquinas and Tomás Sanchez.

In Sanchez, Gasparri found the distinctions the Spanish Jesuit had worked out in his unsuccessful effort to reconcile the Marian theology of virginal marriage and the Augustinian account of procreative marriage.[140] Gasparri adopted these distinctions. A person, he held, could intend to avoid offspring by contraception without intending to reject the obligation to engage in procreative sexual acts. A difference, he insisted, existed between intending to reject an obligation and intending only to reject the fulfillment of the obligation. As Gasparri paraphrased Book II, title 24, section 11, of Sanchez' *De sancto matrimonii sacramento*, "The intention of contracting and obliging oneself can coexist with the firm intention of violating the obligation."[141] Accordingly, a person could marry, sinfully yet validly, if he intended to prevent the procreation of any children by the practice of contraception, but did not intend to reject the obligation of having children.

Fine as the distinction is between rejecting an obligation and rejecting the fulfillment of the obligation, it is intelligible if "obligation" is created by what is said publicly. As Chapter II of this book has already shown, a man can be held to the obligation he assumes by taking an oath, whatever his private intent to violate the oath; the obligation publicly created can be regarded as valid. Marriage vows may be similarly treated, and are similarly treated by civil courts. The intent of the parties to violate their vows does not make the marriage contract civilly null; obligation coexists with a private intent not to fulfill it. But the two orders, public and private, external and internal, are unintelligibly confused if obligation is created only by internal consent and yet is supposed to be capable of coexisting with the intent of not fulfilling the obligation. An internal intent to bind oneself cannot coexist with an intent not to perform the obligation. Gasparri, like Sanchez, transposed to the realm of internal intent an analysis possible only where external obligation is different from internal obligation.

Gasparri's resulting perplexity was proclaimed in his attempts to formulate the rule. A mental condition, he wrote, annulled a marriage if it were an intention contrary to *"the right itself* to the body of the other in relation to offspring." [142] A marriage was invalid if the person marrying "intends to exclude the right itself and the related ordination of the right itself to offspring." By typography such as italics or by the verbal equivalent of italics in such a phrase as "the right itself," Gasparri thought to make a distinction between an intention which accepted "the obligation" while rejecting fulfillment of the obligation. Only if *"the right itself"* was rejected was there nullity. But what was the difference between rejecting *"the right itself"* and intending to exclude offspring by contraception? The difference could not be created by the underlining of words. All the emphasis Gasparri could supply would not show why one mental rejection of procreative intercourse was consistent with a valid marriage and another mental rejection of such intercourse invalidated marital consent. Gasparri encapsulated the consequent uncertainty in this formula: "Absolutely attached, this condition excludes the very right according to *De conditionibus, Si conditiones,* unless it is proved otherwise." [143] Compressed in this sentence was the irresolution created by a dilemma insoluble as long as the basic analysis of intention was not clarified. Given Gasparri's analysis, his conclusion had to be that a condition excluding the good of children invalidated, unless it did not invalidate.

Precisely parallel results were reached by Gasparri in considering the effect of an intent to practice contraception for a specific period. In theory, the obligation to give one's spouse a right to procreative acts of intercourse was absolute and indivisible. An exclusion of the obligation, even for a limited time, ran counter to what theory said was an essential property of marriage. Yet it could seem sensible to say that intention to reject the obligation for a period did not invalidate. Unjustified by theory, a rough practical line could be drawn, with only the perpetual exclusion of offspring being treated as invalidating. Gasparri saw the attraction of drawing the line in this way, but his devotion to his basic concepts was such that he could not accept a clear and definite rule which ignored the theoretical requirement that the obligation of procreative acts be indivisible. Consequently, he concluded that the intent to exclude offspring "until better fortune smiles," indicated that the person so intending "wanted to enter a true marriage, unless it is otherwise established." [144] Similarly, "the corrupt popular custom of marrying on the condition that we avoid children after the first or second child" could have one of two effects. The condition annulled the marriage if by it "the spouse intends to give and accept as temporary the matrimonial right itself." [145] It did not annul the marriage if the spouse wished only "to abuse the right." How could a court tell the difference? Gasparri did not ask the question or give an answer. His treatment of nullifying intention culminated in giving discretionary power to the court. This result was inevitable once it was supposed that an internal intent to accept an obligation could coexist with an internal intent to reject an obligation. The judge was necessarily left to decide which of two inconsistent intentions he preferred to find had characterized a party's state of mind.

The consequences of irresolution in Gasparri were not confined to his own work. Not only was he the principal author of the Code; he was the favorite authority of the re-created Rota. Hundreds of times in the first fifty years of its reorganized existence, the Rota cited Gasparri for the law on marriage. The single most cited passage was that in which he attempted to distinguish between the intent to reject the obligation of procreative intercourse and the intent not to fulfill the obligation. [146] Whenever a party to a marriage had intended by acts of contraception to exclude children forever, or for a period, and the Rota decided to uphold the marriage, this passage of Gasparri was used to say that the obligation or *right itself* had not been excluded. Whenever, on the same sort of evidence, the Rota chose to invalidate a marriage, it cited Gasparri on the invalidating effect of an intent to exclude offspring. Gasparri's texts created a judicial system in which a litigant might be given either answer with equal logic. The choice, cut loose from determination by objective evidence, rested with the will of the court.*

* Illustrative decisions are *Of Nullity of Marriage, May 17, 1947, Decisiones*, XXXIX, 297, before Henrico Caiazzo, Agostino Fidecicchi, and Francis Brennan, holding a marriage valid where the wife wanted no children and her intent was interpreted to be a mere intention to abuse the marital right; and *Of Nullity of Marriage, July 7, 1927, Decisiones*, XXXVI, 300, before Massimo Massimi, Julio Grazioli, and Arthur Wynen, holding a marriage null where the husband wanted no children and his intent was interpreted as exclusion of the good of offspring. The Rota decisions and the controversies they caused are reviewed at length in Schmidt, *Kardinal Pietro Gasparris Einfluss*, pp. 67–77. Almost from the issue of

The essential unpredictability created by the view taken of intention by Gasparri was reinforced by a related, but distinct, uncertainty on his part as to the kind of obligation or right which was an essential property of marriage and the kind of acts which excluded this right. The right and the acts affecting the right were correlative, and uncertainty about one rebounded on the other and created a second area of mystification in the law on intention against the good of offspring. Canon 1081, section 2, of the new Code of Canon Law provided: "Matrimonial consent is the voluntary act by which each party gives and receives a perpetual and exclusive right to the body of the other in relation to acts by themselves fit for the generation of offspring." This definition reflected Gasparri's settled conviction. In the edition of *De matrimonio* following the Code he described a nullifying condition as one which "excludes either the *right itself* to the body of the other in relation to acts fit by themselves for the generation of offspring, or *some essential property of marriage*."[147] The key to the right at issue lay in the phrase chosen by Gasparri and the Code: "acts fit by themselves

___

the Code, Gasparri's distinctions were criticized in Germany by Martin Leitner, *Lehrbuch des katholischen Eherechts* (Paderborn, 1920), p. 95. The first decision in a Roman court challenging them was given in the Vicariate by Gerard Österle, a German Benedictine, Rome, February 9, 1949, excerpted *Ephemerides iuris canonici* (Rome: Catholic Book Agency, 1944), V, 142–146. This decision was strongly criticized by rotal auditor Dino Staffa, who reversed it, *Of Nullity of Marriage*, February 23, 1951, *Decisiones*, XLIII, 131–138, before Dino Staffa, Giuseppe Pasquazi, and Pericle Felici. Ultimately, however, these auditors changed their position: "The distinction between a condition by which the right is excluded and a condition by which only the use is excluded is not based on any foundation. . . . The distinction between *a radical right* and *a useful or usable right*, taken from the law of property, cannot be applied in our matter, for in a marriage contract there is transferred not a right to property, but a right to the body" (*Lausanne, Geneva, and Freiburg, Of Nullity of Marriage, June 24, 1955, Decisiones*, XLVII, 561–562, before Staffa, Pasquazi, and Felici). Staffa's point was emphasized by auditor Arturo De Jorio: "the undersigned Fathers deny that one of the contracting parties can exclude offspring to the very end of life — that is, have the intent or mind of generating no offspring — and simultaneously transfer to the other party a right to the body ordained to the generation of offspring. For an assumption of this kind of obligation or bond is a mere fiction of mind," *Chicago, Of Nullity of Marriage, December 14, 1966*, excerpted in "S.R. Rotae Sententiae Recentiores," *Ephemerides iuris canonici*, XXIII, 280. Other rotal auditors have been unwilling to relinquish the old terminology (so, for example, Giovanni Pinna in *Turin, Of Nullity of Marriage, December 18, 1966*, excerpted in *ibid.*, pp. 289–296). Nonetheless the status in 1971 of leading critics of the distinction — Dino Staffa being now Prefect of the Apostolic Signature, Pericle Felici being President of the Commission for the Revision of the Code — suggested that the new Code would end the conflict of Rota decisions which Gasparri's rules had made possible.

for the generation of offspring." Ambiguity in this phrase made the central definition of matrimonial consent and the definition of a condition contrary to it ambiguous.

The basic notion of an act fit by itself for the generation of offspring was taken from Thomas Aquinas, and it served as a pillar of the usual scholastic argumentation against contraception. Concretely and precisely, it referred to male seminal ejaculation in the female vagina.[148] This act was taken as the norm of sexual intercourse, as the natural sexual act. Of all possible sexual acts, it alone was capable of beginning the process of generating a child. It also was the sole voluntary act necessary for generation in the sense that, once this act was completed, generation could occur without further specific human activity prior to the child's birth. In this special sense, seminal ejaculation into the vagina was "by itself" fit to generate offspring. Difficulty arose with the meaning of the notion if one knew in advance that after such an act of intercourse, generation would not occur, as would be the case if the man or woman were naturally sterile or had been sterilized or were using contraceptives. As the act of a knowledgeable human being, the act of intercourse in such circumstances would not be an act capable of generating offspring.[149] A man who strikes the keys of a piano performs an act "fit in itself" to produce music. If he knows the chords are cut, however, he cannot intend to produce music or even do an act fit in itself to produce music. His act as an intentional human act is to produce the moving of a dead key. When one is certain that an act is impossible, one does not intend to do the act which, if circumstances were different, would take place.

All of this seems evident enough to scarcely bear repetition, and it may be wondered what caused confusion. The dilemma was this: If sexual intercourse with a person known to be sterile was recognized not to fall within the class of acts fit by themselves to generate offspring, marriage with such a person would be invalid if one knew of the sterility. Consent could not be given to acts fit by themselves to generate offspring; therefore, the intention of the person marrying must necessarily not include these impossible acts. Yet, to accept this conclusion would be to unsettle the established custom of the Church.* The Church had never made sterility an

* In upholding (against objection from his son) the right of seventy-seven-year-old Count Giovanni Gasto Prosperi to marry, the Secretary of the S.C.C. noted

obstacle to marriage, had never made the intention to marry a person known to be sterile an intention invalidating marriage.[150] Either the definition of the object of matrimonial consent had to be changed or the established practice revised. Gasparri did neither. He seemed to escape from the dilemma by not looking at what it meant to speak of an act fit to generate offspring when a person was known to be sterile because of age or physical condition. Concerned as he was with the problem of contraception, however, he could not avoid the analogous problem posed by various ways of preventing the birth of offspring. According to his thought in 1891, at least three means might be used which would exclude, in a way invalidating marriage, the right to the body in relation to offspring. These were "abortion, onanism, or taking poisons of sterility, etcetera." [151] In this listing, "onanism," or *coitus interruptus*, involved the prevention of seminal ejaculation in the vagina, the act by itself fit to produce offspring. Abortion had no effect on the act of intercourse or upon conception. "Taking poisons of sterility," that is, using sterilizing drugs, prevented conception, but did not prevent the completion of coitus, the act by itself fit to generate offspring. In recognizing that the intention to use such drugs invalidated consent, Gasparri tacitly admitted that if one knew the normal coital act would be sterile, one intended to exclude offspring. But, if he even tacitly admitted this conclusion, how could he save the validity of the marriages, hitherto regularly allowed by the Church, of those unable to bear children?

The extent of his difficulty did not come home to Gasparri, perhaps because he had no precise idea of how the "poisons of sterility" worked. But in the 1904 edition of his book he dealt with a relatively new means of preventing offspring and immediately found himself taking openly inconsistent positions. To the means whose use excluded the right to acts related to offspring, he added "cutting of the Fallopian tubes or extraction of both ovaries or the uterus." [152] Intent to sterilize in these ways was treated as nullifying; yet sterili-

---

that "age is not among the canonical impediments, but the Church permits marriage to the old without distinction; in habit at least they have the potential of generating, Sanchez, 7.92.19, and several others. And it permits it to the dying, although such potential is almost extinct in them, Zacchia, Medico-Legal Questions, 2.1.19"; Report of the Secretary, *Todi, Of Marriage, September 7, 1793, Thesaurus S.C.C.*, LXII, 224.

zation evidently did not affect the act of seminal ejaculation in the vagina which was classically considered the act by itself fit to generate offspring. In the same section in the same edition of *De matrimonio* Gasparri asked if a woman who had been sterilized to avoid bearing children could then validly contract marriage. To hold that she could not, he declared, would be "absurd, because matrimonial consent is an act which depends upon the will." [153] But if matrimonial consent depended upon the will, it was not clear how consent could be given to acts which were impossible; and for the sterilized woman, like the woman using contraceptives or the woman who was to be sterilized, acts of intercourse must by hypothesis be nonprocreative. In the 1932 edition of his book Gasparri dropped his reference to the cutting of the Fallopian tubes and extraction of the ovaries or uterus — a sign, at least, that he perceived an incongruity between treating these means of preventing offspring as destructive of the right to acts by themselves fit to generate and simultaneously teaching that a sterilized woman could consent to a valid marriage. [154] Dropping the illustration did not eliminate the dilemma. Either marital consent had as its object the right to seminal ejaculation in the vagina — then the sterile, the sterilized, and the person intending to use any contraceptive which did not prevent coitus could marry validly — or marital consent had as its object the right to acts capable of procreation — and then the sterile, the sterilized, and the contraceptive-user married invalidly. By not facing the dilemma, by using the notion "act fit by itself to generate offspring" in a shifting sense, Gasparri left almost as much room to judicial discretion as he had by his attempt to distinguish the internal intent to reject an obligation from the internal intent to fail to carry out an obligation.

An "act by itself fit for generation" had presented difficulties to Catholic moral theology since Thomas Aquinas. [155] But before Gasparri it had not been a major source of confusion for the courts, because intent alone would not be held judicially to invalidate a marriage. When Gasparri treated the intent to exclude offspring as a possible ground for invalidation, and when the spread of contraception made such intent likely to occur, the courts were faced with a problem where Gasparri's writing and the Code he had prepared could lead to no consistent result even as to the kind of acts which an invalidating intention against the good of children must envisage.*

A final inconsistency in Gasparri proved more restrictive than confusing to the courts. Abortion affected the possibility of birth

* The kind of question to which no consistent answer could be given in terms of Gasparri and the Code arose both before and after the Code. Four examples may suffice.

(1) The Holy Office had ruled as early as 1877 that a woman whose ovaries had been removed should not be barred from marrying, Holy Office, Response, February 3, 1887, *Le canoniste contemporain* (1888), XI, 140–141; and it took the same position as to a woman whose ovaries and uterus had been removed, Holy Office, Response, July 30, 1890, *ibid.* (1894), XVII, 235–236. Ten other cases were decided in the same way up to 1904, according to a report made to the Commission on the Code of Canon Law (Gasparri, *De matrimonio* [1932 ed.], sec. 536). In no case, however, did the Holy Office do more than not raise objection: it did not want to resolve the theoretical question whether such a marriage was valid (*ibid.*, sec. 536). Giuseppe Antonelli was a vigorous champion of the position that such incapacity constituted impotence; he insisted that absolute incapacity to procreate should be distinguished from sterility which might be cured. (Giuseppe Antonelli, *Pro conceptu impotentiae et sterilitatis relate ad matrimonium: Animadversiones in opus P. Eschbach, "Disputationes"* [Rome, Ratisbon, New York: Fridericus Pustet, 1901], pp. 44–53.) Franz Wernz, the leading Jesuit canonist of Gasparri's day, appeared to favor Antonelli's view, although his true opinion is itself in doubt; see Wernz, *Ius canonicum*, revised by Pedro Vidal (Rome: Gregorian University Press, 1925), V, 259 n. 56). In this state of controversy a compromise was reached in the Code of Canon Law which provided at sec. 1068.2, "If the impediment of impotence is doubtful, by virtue of a doubt of law or of fact, the marriage is not to be impeded." The impotence doubtful in law was the inability to procreate of a woman without ovaries (Wernz, *ibid.*, sec. 226, p. 260). That this kind of question was in doubt for the makers of the Code underlines the impossibility of its resolution without giving up either the procreative content of consent or the traditional practice of letting the sterile marry. As late as 1925 the theologian of the Penitentiary could argue that, if generation "is manifestly known to be excluded or impossible it cannot be the object of consent," and conclude that what he termed "absolute sterility" was the same as impotence and, therefore, a bar to a valid marriage, Wilhelm Arendt, S.J., "De absoluta habilitate sterilium ad matrimonium (Circa Can. 1068.3)," *Ius pontificum* (1925), IV, 87.

(2) If a woman's vagina is so blocked that semen cannot pass beyond it, is she impotent? Agostino Sili, canonist consultor in a case before the S.C.C. in 1899, answered, Yes, and A. Eschbach, a Sulpician, theologian consultor in the same case, answered, No; Munster, *Of Marriage*, May 19, 1900, *Analecta ecclesiastica* (1900), VIII, 251–259.

(3) If a woman uses a diaphragm so that conception cannot occur, may her husband morally have sexual intercourse with her if he deplores her sin, or does her blocking of the flow of semen so alter the sexual act that intercourse is no longer matrimonial and becomes intrinsically evil for both spouses? The bishops of Germany gave the first answer and Arthur Vermeersch followed Sili to give the second, "Occlusio vaginae estne casus impotentiae an sterilitatis?," *Periodica* (1925), XIV, 65.

(4) If a man is vasectomized, is he impotent? The Holy Office, ruling in the case of a man compulsorily sterilized under German law ruled, No. *Response,*

after the act of intercourse was completed and after conception had
occurred. If intent to commit abortion affected the validity of a
marriage, why did not any or all intentions against what had
traditionally been termed "the good of children"? The good of
children (*bonum prolis*) could mean either the good of having offspring or the good of the children had. The ambiguity seemed to
have been preserved by adopting both meanings: in classical ex-
positions the good embraced not only the conception of the child,
his birth, and his physical rearing, but his intellectual and spiritual
welfare.[156] As Gasparri himself, in expounding the elements of marriage, had summarized the classical view, the good of offspring was
"the power of receiving and educating offspring, and the receiving
and educating of the offspring." [157] Exclusion of the education of
the child appeared to be as destructive of the good of offspring as
the intent to abort the child. Gasparri glimpsed the implication,
but instead of discussing it, contented himself with examples denying that an intent contrary to the education of the child nullified
the marriage.[158] It was not made clear why he restricted the good
of offspring so narrowly in this context to the physical life of the
child. The restriction did not appear to perplex the courts. It did
affect their thinking as to what "the good of offspring" was in the
context of invalidating intentions. When asked to nullify a marriage because of an intention against the good of offspring, the
courts looked only at that intention as it related to the physical
existence of future offspring. They did not consider how it related
to the education of existing offspring. They never asked if the
intent to exclude some offspring might not be consistent with an
intent to further the good of children taken comprehensively to
include the education of the children already alive. The good of
children in judicial usage failed to include the good of children,
such as Mario and Gian Galeazzi Folchi, already in existence.

February 16, 1935, reported, twelve years after the decision by Felipe Aguirre,
"De impotentia viri iuxta iurisprudentiam rotalem," *Periodica* (1947), XXXVI, 14.
The Rota ruling in a marriage case a decade later, said, Yes. *Of Nullity of
Marriage*, October 25, 1945, *Decisiones*, XXXVII, 574–592. The Holy Office,
asked in 1963 to rule in a marriage case from Worcester, Massachusetts, stood by
its 1935 ruling; but it expressly refused to give the reasons for its stand, Report
to *The Canon Law Digest* by Timothy P. O'Connell, *officialis* of Worcester, *The
Canon Law Digest Annual Supplement Through 1966*, at canon 1068. On the basis
of Gasparri and the Code, no reasons could be given for preferring one of these
answers to the other.

Innovation by Gasparri had made intent against the good of children capable of nullifying a marriage judicially. Inherited confusion between intent and obligation in the external, public order and intent and obligation in the mind had led him to formulas of perfect ambiguity and rules which a court could only apply by its own choice. Whether contraception was to be practiced for a month or a lifetime, whether contraception was to be practiced after having had ten children or to prevent having any, the intent to practice contraception might or might not invalidate the marriage.

Gasparri made these results possible not from any articulated desire to make judgments in the courts of the Curia dependent on the feelings of the individual judge or the luck of the individual litigant. His intent, as much as Benedict XIV's, had been to systematize. He had approached his task with a deep respect for order and reverence for his authorities. How could he have come to conclusions so troublesome to the administration of the law?

A metaphysical cast of mind is sometimes blamed for responding to dilemmas with verbal solutions of the sort which Gasparri selected. The great antinomies, such as the omnipotence of God and the freedom of man, are treated in such a way in scholastic reasoning that persons exposed to them but uninterested in metaphysics may become insensitive to the abuse of language. Philosophical methods, transposed by such persons to the practical realm which they themselves inhabit, may lead to verbal trifling. Rigorously metaphysical minds, such as Duns Scotus' or Heidegger's, would see such transpositions as caricature. Members of the Roman Curia, however, who underwent cursory training in speculative theology, and had to be practical men, ran a risk of damage; Gasparri himself did not escape. A certain type of modesty also played a part. Gasparri, like many members of the Curia, lacked the scientific interest of some moral theologians and casuists in the details of contraception. He preferred using phrases as ancient as Augustine's "poisons of sterility" to analyzing the mode of operation of the diaphragm. This chaste repression of curiosity limited his imagination and the range of his inquiry when he had to deal with the effect on marriage of an intent to practice contraception.

More fundamental, however, than either Gasparri's tolerance of verbal confusion or his inhibitions about sexual matters was an intuition. He saw that marriage depended on consent — it had been said for two thousand years. He not only saw but believed and felt it. The Code expressed the intuition when it said that consent to marriage "can be supplied by no human power." The Code did not measure the depth of his feeling. Sanchez had asked if God, in His absolute power, could supply consent to marriage if the human beings themselves did not consent, and had cautiously answered that "the more probable" opinion taught that God could not. For Gasparri there was neither doubt nor argument. "God," he said, "cannot make a thing to exist without its essence." [159] Consent was the essence of marriage. Without it even God could not bring a marriage into existence.

Convinced of this insight, Gasparri blurred the line which had been drawn between the internal forum of the Church, the penitential tribunals where intent was weighed, and the external forum, the courts where decisions were made with due regard to the public order. He imported into the judicial realm the standards of the Penitentiary, and made internal consent to marry a necessity which the courts could not ignore. True, the carrying out of his intuition was marred by his irresolution, by his retention of Sanchez' inappropriate distinctions and Aquinas' unworkable norm, by his inconsistencies on sterility and sterilization and on the physical and intellectual good of children. He could not extricate himself from his academic and ecclesiastical authorities, from the concepts and vocabulary he had inherited, from the problematic which tied so much of sexual morality to the Thomistic natural act. In the difficulties inevitably caused by loyalty to his intuition and loyalty to his authorities, Gasparri's formulations expressed, not unwaveringly but predominantly, his insight. Neither God nor man nor court of the Church could make a marriage if consent to marriage was lacking.

The intensity of Gasparri's intuition does not wholly explain why he stuck to it even when following it led to insoluble problems. The intuition was supported by what was happening to the Church. Interwoven with the medieval fabric of society, the Church in the nineteenth century was in the process of assuming a much more limited social role. In the post-Exilic world of Pius X there was the realization that the Church had lost its direct temporal power. Perception of the loss with its full implications was still clouded by sentiment at the beginning of the century. Yet churchmen could not help noticing even as to marriage that the Church's old role of determining the social order was no longer exactly the same. The kingdom of the Church might have to be internal; if it was to be internal, then intention, even in marriage, had to count more than expression.

Gasparri did not formulate the reasons for his innovation in this way. In the very act of reorganizing the judicial system he did not recognize that a judicial system could not operate on the personal, subjective basis of the confessional, that in pressing the standards of the Penitentiary upon a system of public courts he was crippling them. In a time of transition, half-aware of the magnitude of the transformation of the Church's role, he did not calculate the consequences when he installed intention in the external forum as the criterion of valid consent to marry.

The climax of Gasparri's life as a canonist was the promulgation of the Code in 1917; the crown of his career as Secretary of State was the Concordat which, on behalf of the Holy See, he signed with Benito Mussolini in 1929. The Concordat gave up the temporal kingdom of the Church in Italy. It kept the spiritual realm of marriage. It kept it in such a way that the Curia's decisions on marriage had secular consequences: Catholic marriages had civil effects; ecclesiastical tribunals had jurisdiction over cases of nullity; canon law shouldered the work of Italian domestic law and became yoked to the politics of a nation.[160] If marriage had been seen as an exclusively spiritual realm, such a bargain would not have been attractive. But Gasparri — and not just the man but the Curia he represented so ably — could not visualize a canon law in Italy without social consequences; and those consequences were most clearly secured by enactment into law. That spiritual power was thereby commingled with civic seemed not a compromise but a victory. The unwillingness to sever the spiritual and the social, the identification of the social with the legal — these fateful characteristics of the Concordat were also the characteristics of Gasparri's treatment of marital consent, which required it to be internal and unfeigned, yet accorded it decisive authority in the social domain ruled by law.

Filippo Folchi's case was conceived of as a lawsuit when the idea was unknown to the curial courts that intent to exclude children would nullify a marriage even if not manifested to the other party to the marriage, and when the idea had just been judicially recognized that an express agreement to avoid children by contraception would nullify. Folchi's "condition" against offspring increased in importance as his case progressed through the S.C.C. It became the heart of his case in the Rota. Persiani's opinion in 1909 applied the old pre-Gasparri requirement that a condition must be expressed in a contract. The Signature, taught by Gasparri, reversed for this error of law. The Rota in Lega's opinion in 1912 attempted to combine Gasparri with past authority.

An "intention contrary to the obligation itself," Lega declared in his decision of 1912, was "most difficult to prove" unless it were expressed in a contract. The practice of the Church, indeed, was not to invalidate unless the intention was so expressed. Yet, in theory, intention alone could annul if the intention was "most conclusively demonstrated." [161] In this opinion Lega paid just enough deference to Gasparri's views to admit the theoretical possibility of a nullifying intention and took all practical significance from the admission by setting up practice and presumptions against it. He put to use Sanchez' distinction between rejection of obligation and intent not to fufill the obligation, as this distinction could always be used by a court upholding validity. Like Gasparri, he appeared to believe that differences could be created by emphasis, that there was a difference between "demonstrating" and "most conclusively demonstrating." Convinced by the testimony of the flimsiness of Folchi's case, Lega had no difficulty in stating the law of intention in such a way that, even with credible witnesses, Folchi could not have proved his case.

No doubt, in Lega's mind, to fault Folchi both on the evidence and on the law was the most efficient way to sink a hopeless cause. Yet could such a grudging limitation of Gasparri's insight be proof against assault when Gasparri was the maker of the Code? If Gasparri's own statement of the law of intention was so ambiguous that his distinctions could easily be cited to uphold a marriage, could they not as easily be cited to invalidate? If Gasparri was to import the internal standard of the Penitentiary into the new Code, would not the viewpoint of the Penitentiary ultimately prevail?

In 1918, the new Code became the law of the Church. The Folchi case, dead six years, did not at once stir to life.

9.

On January 21, 1922, as Benedict XV was dying, Pietro Gasparri, Oreste Giorgi, and Agostino Sili stood out among the cardinals who surrounded him. Gasparri, his Secretary of State, whose Code he had made law, wept by his side. Giorgi, Grand Penitentiary of the Church, read to the dying Pope the profession of faith. To Sili the Pope turned urging him to pray for him to the Blessed Virgin Mary.[162] The day before this solemn scene, so unrelated by the participants to a marriage case settled in 1912, the advocate A. Carabini had presented to the Roman Rota on behalf of Filippo Folchi an offer to produce two new witnesses in support of his petition for annulment and a request that the Rota "resume the case." [163]

Of the men at the center of power as an old administration ended and an interregnum and a new administration began, Gasparri was the most powerful. For fourteen years he had been a cardinal; for seven years he had been Secretary of State. He was the architect of the existing law. In foreign affairs he had been virtually deputy Pope under Benedict XV. No one could match his knowledge of the men and mechanisms of the Curia. Sili, his cousin and protégé, a cardinal of only a year's standing, now held the honorable if subordinate post of Prefect of the Apostolic Signature. Giorgi, who had been a cardinal for five years, had been, since 1918, the Grand Penitentiary of the Church.

Of these men, probably Giorgi was the most interested in the case of Filippo Folchi. Gasparri, to be sure, was concerned with the sound working of the system and in the theory of internal consent at issue in Folchi's case, but, with his principle securely established in the Code, he had no special reason to pursue further a doubtful exemplification of it already examined by four courts. Sili, who had been Folchi's witness, may have retained a residual sympathy for his cause, and he was now in a position to be of particular help. For five years Michele Lega had been Prefect of the Signature, effectively blocking any possibility of the case being reconsidered, but on March 20, 1920, he had moved to the Congregation of the Sacraments. His replacement by Sili meant that at least the Signature would not be an obstacle to reconsideration. Giorgi had the most personal and the most priestly reasons to revive the case. In the defeat of Folchi he had been defeated. In Lega's definitive opinion for the Rota in 1912 he had been treated as a meddler and almost characterized as a perjurer, or at least been made to appear as the principal character witness of a perjurer. In an old man, tenacious of purpose and of memory, few memories could have rankled so bitingly. Beyond offended *amour-propre*, there was "the intimate conviction" with which he had undertaken the case in 1905, his assured belief that Filippo Folchi was not validly married. His extraordinary role of reconciler recognized by his title, the Grand Penitentiary hoped still to bring back to Christian life the sinner whose invalid public tie prevented him from marrying the woman with whom he lived. It was Giorgi who moved.

The witnesses now discovered for Folchi were found within the precincts of the Vatican itself. Both were laymen from the small circle of Black nobility. One was Count Pietro Della Porta, the senior official in the Third Section of the Secretariat of State, the office charged with the transmission of papal correspondence. He was four year's Filippo's senior and his distant cousin, had known him since he was a baby, and had spent a great part of his youth with him before his own marriage.[164] The other witness was Domenico Orsini, Prince of Solofra. Unlike Count Della Porta, he was not a civil servant in the papal government, but he was the head of the Orsini family, which since the twelfth century had been celebrated for its services to the papacy, and he held a high place among the honorary functionaries of the Vatican. He had been a friend of Filippo's brother Giulio, his classmate at the Collegio Massimi.[165]

Giorgi, Folchi, and Della Porta discussed the case on December 12, 1921, and immediately thereafter Della Porta wrote out a declaration that "he remembered perfectly" being told by Filippo Folchi, when he was about to marry Signora Bailly, that they had made "a precise agreement not to procreate children." [166] Orsini had discussed his recollections of Folchi's agreement with Giorgi and another unnamed cardinal before the war without anything coming of the conversation.[167] Needed now, he was reached in London and replied on December 10, 1921, that "he remembered perfectly" that Folchi had told him at the time of the marriage that they had agreed not to procreate more children and "that the marriage was carried out with that reciprocal condition." [168]

These declarations, put in the hands of Folchi's counsel, were the necessary first step toward reopening the case on the ground of new evidence. Unless Benedict XV's health was weaker than it was publicly believed to be, Giorgi did not initiate this first step with a view to putting the case to a new Pope.[169] More probably, the substitution of Sili for Lega at the Signature in March 1921 had suggested that the opportunity for a new effort had come. When, a month after the declarations had been gathered, Benedict XV suddenly became very sick, a certain haste to get the case started again in the interregnum does appear. The request for reopening was filed the eve of the Pope's death; six days after it was received the Rota set up a turn to hear the evidence with Francesco Solieri, the designated judge-reporter. Solieri, born in Cotignola in 1859 and appointed to the Rota in 1916, had been Giorgi's *summista* or first assistant in 1889 when Giorgi was auditor of the Congregation of Bishops and Regulars.[170]

Meanwhile, Filippo Folchi, on whose behalf the wheels of justice were again being turned, had abandoned his career as a painter and was working as a technician in a film studio outside of Rome. He was as poor as ever. He had had two more children by Elvira, bringing to five the number of children from this union. But the relationship with Elvira, longer-lasting than that with Pauline, had not endured. He was living in Rome with a new woman, whose name never became part of the legal record, and he was, by her, the father of two more children, or, in all, the father of nine.[171]

Solieri began the task of hearing the new witnesses, but on April 19, 1922, the Rota balked at going further, holding that without a new commission from the Pope it could not take up the case which it had decided twice.[172] Unless the Supreme Judge ordered them to look, the auditors would not act; again Folchi appeared shipwrecked on the unfriendly rock of the Rota. Again, if he were to be saved, help could only come from the head of the system.

The interregnum had been brief. Achille Ratti, Pius XI, had been elected Pope on February 6, 1922. Before his election he had in all likelihood never heard of Filippo Folchi, Pauline Bailly, the circumstances of their marriage, or the history of Folchi's long litigation. He was now to play a decisive part in the controversy. What factors help explain his choices?

Achille Ratti shared the economic and social origins and educational experience of men like Gasparri, Giorgi, and Lega. Born in Desio, a small town not far from Monza, the son of a silk-worker, from a very early age he had been shaped intellectually by the Church. He entered the minor seminary at Seveso at the age of ten, continued at the seminary in Monza at fourteen, and, at seventeen, went to study theology at the Seminary of Saint Charles Borromeo in Milan. At nineteen, a very promising pupil, he was sent to Rome, where he acquired the usual degrees — the doctorate in theology from the Sapienza, the doctorate in philosophy from the Academy of Saint Thomas, the doctorate in canon law from the Gregorian. Equipped with this preparation for a career in the Roman Curia, he entered a very different field; he returned to Milan and soon was associated with its most celebrated monument to culture, the Ambrosian Library. Ratti spent the central portion of his life as its librarian, leaving in 1912, at the age of fifty-six, to become vice-prefect of the Vatican Library. When in 1914 he became Prefect, he seemed to have received the maximum recognition he might expect in his career.[173]

In 1918, when he was sixty-one years old, his life was changed by a decision of the Secretary of State. To this point his isolation from the legal, diplomatic, theological and pastoral activities of the Curia had been nearly absolute. Of its standing committees, he had served on none. He was in 1918 merely a monsignor, administering a subordinate division of the Vatican. Unexpectedly, if not unaccountably, Gasparri drafted him for the diplomatic service, and he was sent to Poland as the Pope's representative to the new nation. He returned home in June 1921 to be made a cardinal and Archbishop of Milan, an extraordinary promotion. Taking possession of his see in September 1921, he had exercised his office a little over four months when the conclave opened to elect a successor to Benedict XV.

Merry del Val, Pius X's old Secretary of State, now Secretary of the Holy Office, stood for doctrinal and political intransigeance in opposition to the flexibility of Gasparri. The conservatives voted for him at the beginning, and, according to Gasparri, he engaged in tactics incurring automatic excommunication under canon 2330 of the new Code prohibiting bargaining for the papacy.[174] By the fifth ballot, Gasparri, his most obvious opponent and the logical choice in terms of experience, had a commanding lead. The most serious objection to his candidacy was his nepotism. "He would be a toy in the hands of his relatives," ran the allegation against him.[175] Not all curial cardinals shared this view, and Gasparri's strength held at twenty-four — twelve below the necessary two-thirds — until the ninth ballot when his suporters began to shift to Achille Ratti. Giorgi, an independent, is said to have played a part in rounding up the other votes still needed after the shift was completed on the eleventh ballot. On the fourteenth ballot, after three days of voting, Ratti was elected. Blocked by the fears of the intransigeants and the rumors of his nepotism, Gasparri had not been made Supreme Pontiff; but the outcome was one which he had made possible and which made possible the fruition of his policies.[176]

The election followed a pattern that, to date, has been rigorously observed in twentieth-century papal elections — a man without strong connections or experience in the Curia has alternated with one of the Curia's own. Election of the "outside" man must appear to some curial insiders as the best way of preserving their stake in the government. The tactic does not assure the selection of a weak man — who would call Giuseppe Sarto, Angelo Roncalli, or Achille Ratti weak? — but of a man who, necessarily, must rely on the experts surrounding him. A diplomat of less than two years' experience may be trusted not to disregard the advice of a Secretary of State of seven years, especially when that Secretary of State has launched him in diplomacy. A bishop with less than four months in office will not be unreceptive to curial instruction on the role of hierarchy. A man of sixty-five, who has been a librarian most of his life, can run a legal system only with the help of lawyers.

That the choice of an archivist as its head could be construed as a symbol of the Curia's reverence for a frozen, archaic past was probably not the foremost consideration for the system's managers. But the virtues by which the archivist was distinguished would have been very much in mind. The labor of Ratti's life had been the assembling, cataloguing, deciphering, editing, and arranging of eccelsiastical documents. He had been among that devoted and indispensable band whose mission is to furnish other scholars with evidence for their critical analysis or their creative synthesis. In carrying out this work he had been distinguished by "his calm, his self-possession, his serenity." [177] His own description of an eighteenth-century Milanese scholar revealed his values: Dom Ermete

Bonomi, he wrote, was "conscientious to the point of scrupulosity," modest, devoted to his vocation, and "open to noble sentiments of friendship and gratitude"; "in a troubled and turbulent time, without any noise or fuss, with unwearied care through many years, with inextinguishable and always fresh vigor, this monk collected and prepared for the easy study of those who followed him inestimable treasures of learning and of doctrine, carrying on, in the most honorable way, the most glorious traditions of monastic life." [178] In the same spirit of devotion Ratti had been trained to preserve the past. Accuracy, a sense of relevance, deep fidelity had been demanded by his work; he had displayed these qualities. As Pope he could be expected to preserve the past at the loftiest level, in the most honorable way.

Nothing in Ratti's life had developed in him a sense of the processes involved in a legal system. His view of the place of the Pope in the law was derived from what the new Code proclaimed. Canon 1569 declared: "On account of the primacy of the Roman Pontiff it is irreproachable for any believer in the whole Catholic world to bring his case to the Holy See for judgment or to introduce his case at the Holy See, whether the case is civil or criminal, whatever the grade of judgment, and whatever the stage of litigation." Canon 1597 added: "The Roman Pontiff is the supreme judge for the whole Catholic world according to the norm of canon 1569, and he declares the law either through himself or through tribunals constituted by him or judges delegated by him." Informed by the law that he was the supreme judge, who declared the law "through himself" if he chose, Achille Ratti was bound only by the tacit constraints of custom and those practical limits placed by the Curia on the kind of matter directed to his attention.

Supposing such a matter as the Folchi case to fall beneath his eye, and supposing that those who ran the legal system assured him that here his supreme judgeship might be exercised, what would move the Pope to act? Advice from the maker of the Code or the Grand Penitentiary may have sufficed. In legal matters the Pope was to be guided. The advice met with a willing listener when it was directed not merely to the acknowledged plenitude of papal power but when it appealed to a personal virtue of the Pope.

Achille Ratti had been formed in the intellectual and emotional ambience of Milanese Catholicism whose character had been imparted by the *arte cattolica Manzoniana*. In that learned Milanese world Alessandro Manzoni, dead in 1873, still lived "as an invisible tutelary deity." [179] In that Manzonian universe the rules afforded by the Church were penetrated with life by the great Christian call to forgiveness. The strictest conception of duty was tempered by the highest valuation of mercy. Manzoni's great law, as Ratti saw it, had been "never to say a word which approved vice or derided virtue." Manzoni's *I promesso sposi* was an apotheosis of canonical form: the entire plot hinged upon the necessity of a couple to comply with the Tridentine requirements for a valid marriage. At the same time the novel was a celebration of the quality of mercy, of the loving imitation of divine forgiveness. Ratti's own empathetic grasp of Manzoni's theme had been disclosed in print in 1912 when in his archival investigations he had discovered Cardinal Federico Borromeo's contemporary account of the repentance of Marianne de Leyva, Manzoni's "nun of Monza," and had supposed that if Manzoni had known all the facts, the novel would not have ended without a scene between the penitent nun and the Cardinal, similar to that where the "scalding tears" of the repentant Unknown One fall on "Federico's spotless robes." In the actual case Cardinal Federico had been "so just and so merciful." Knowing all the facts, Manzoni also, Achille Ratti supposed, would have shown "his paternal modesty and pity toward the wretched creature." [180]

When Achille Ratti encountered the facts of the Folchi case, could Filippo Folchi's twenty-year-old quest for legal dissolution of a union have reminded him, almost in reverse as it were, of the long search of Renzo and Lucia for a legal union? Desiring "never to say a word which approved vice or derided virtue," "open to noble sentiments of friendship and gratitude," admiring his great predecessor in Milan who was "so just and so merciful," Pius XI would not consciously have consented to ignoble subterfuge. Could knowledge of "all the facts" have changed for him the aspect of a case so lacking in merit in appearance? If Giorgi presented the matter to the new Pope as one where repentance after decades of sin was possible, would not such a plea to paternal mercy have moved his heart while the law assured him of his power? If the focus of the Pope's attention was Filippo, if Pauline was presented to him as uninterested in the outcome, would it have been too great a distortion of reality for Pius XI to have supposed that he had the opportunity of being sovereignly merciful?

There is no doubt that on his accession to office the Supreme Judge, the Manzonian father, also held the orthodox views of marriage. In 1922, in the first encyclical of his reign, reviewing the social disorder of the day, Pius XI declared that evil had "penetrated the roots of human society, that is, the cell of the family," as spouses "rejected their sacred duties to God and to civil society" and marriage itself was reduced to a civil contract, while "Christ had made it the holy and sanctifying symbol of that perpetual bond by which He is joined with His Church." No doubt too, Pius XI in 1922 held the views he was to express to the world in 1930 in his encyclical on Christian marriage: the Pope had power to dissolve unconsummated marriages, "but no power of this kind can ever affect for any cause whatsover a Christian marriage which has been ratified and consummated. It shines forth in such a marriage that, as the marriage bond has been fully perfected, so, by the will of God, there is also a firmness and indissolubility which may not be destroyed by any authority of men." [181]

On May 8, 1922, Pius XI, acting on the advice of the Signature headed by Sili, issued this rescript: "The Most Holy benignly receives the libel of petition seeking a new examination of the Folchi-Bailly marriage and orders that it be sent to the Sacred Roman Rota with the necessary faculties to judge the matter." [182]

The case now resumed in the Rota, with the Englishman John Prior replacing Solieri as judge-reporter. Prior was the sole remaining member of the Rota who had participated in the decisions of 1909 and 1912. With seniority he had become the Dean, and as the Dean he took charge of this important case. Four other members of the Rota were not unfamiliar with the matter: Federico Cattani had participated as an Auditor in the decision of 1912; Massimo Massimi had been Promoter of Justice of the reformed Rota of 1908, and in this capacity had been associated with the Rota's legal staff until his appointment as an auditor in 1915; Francesco Parrillo as Defender of the Bond had vigorously upheld the marriage in the first two rounds, and since 1919 had been a rotal judge himself. The best-informed Auditor of all was Folchi's old counsel in the Vicariate and the S.C.C., Giulio Grazioli. Since his service for

Folchi, Grazioli had been from 1910 to 1915 Under-Secretary of the S.C.C. When Giorgi had left the Secretary's post on being made a cardinal in 1916, Grazioli had been moved to the Rota, where by longevity he was to become the Dean himself in 1936. Prior, Cattani, and Massimi had no reason to disqualify themselves merely for familiarity with the case. Parrillo tried to disqualify himself, but was overruled by the Pope acting through Sili and the Signature on June 22, 1922.[183] There is no record that Grazioli made any attempt to withdraw.

Pauline was summoned by Prior to appear before the Rota at the Palazzo della Dataria on August 8, 1922. The official citation was published in the journal of papal activities, the *Acta apostolicae sedis* for July 1922.[184] As Pauline's whereabouts were unknown to the Rota, and as it was unlikely that she was a reader of the *Acta*, the citation performed a purely magical legal function of notification.

Meanwhile, the examination of the new witnesses had gone ahead; and they stood manfully by the depositions they had already given. Prince Orsini, the friend of Filippo's younger brother Giulio and twenty-three years old at the time of the conversation, recalled that Folchi's marriage to Pauline had been spoken of unfavorably at the Circolo del Reno, and that on leaving the club he encountered Filippo who disclosed to him the existence of "reciprocal promises" not to have children. Orsini dated this recollection of thirty-one years ago by his return to Rome from his own wedding trip.[185] Count Della Porta's memory went back thirty-three years. He had met Folchi "one evening toward the Ave Maria in the first fortnight of October, 1889, in the Piazza Barberini." When he told Folchi that in four years of marriage he had sired three children, the other exclaimed that he must make "a strict contract not to have children." Two years later Folchi told him that he had indeed married with such an agreement.[186]

A third new witness was produced, Dr. Guido Smiderle. He testified to frequenting Folchi's studio at the Porta Pinciana in the company of Prince Orsini in 1895, at which time Filppo had told them of "the contract not to procreate children." Dr. Smiderle was now from Milan and was perhaps selected as a witness because of acquaintance in Milan with the new Pope. Other qualifications as a witness were not evident. His date of 1895 was late to be helpful in showing an agreement antedating the marriage, and he had Filippo "confirming to me many times that he never had carnal relations with his wife after the marriage was contracted."[187] Only Frattini in the earlier hearings had thought that Filippo claimed to have had a marriage with Pauline without intercourse.

In late 1922 a new *summarium* was printed for Folchi. It was identical with the one unsuccessfully submitted in 1912, except for the addition of the testimony of the three new witnesses. A brief for Folchi was given to the Rota on February 9, 1923. The case was almost ripe for judgment, and John Prior should have been preparing his opinion.[188] Then a curious break occurred in the course of the case in the Rota. For a reason never disclosed on the record, it was necessary to go to the Pope again. On March 3, 1923, Pius XI issued this rescript:

> The Most Holy benignly receives the libel of supplication seeking a new examination of the nullity of marriage between Filippo Folchi-Vici and Pauline Bailly, and orders it to be sent to the Sacred Rota with the necessary faculties to know the matter and to decide it with all participating, notwithstanding anything to the contrary.

The language is so similar to that of the rescript of May 8, 1922, and it seems so superfluous after the earlier command, that one could suspect that the second was a mere doublet of the first with an inaccurate date. Yet it forms a part of the official record in the case in a printed report edited with some care.[189] It relates to the other procedural mystery of the case, the sudden disappearance from it of the Dean, John Prior.

Inferably what happened was this: Prior, when he saw that the three new witnesses, if believed, added only cumulative detail to the case twice decided by the Rota, was unwilling to decide the case again despite Pius XI's order of May 8, 1922. In his view no ground for rehearing and decision could have been established. Hence, Giorgi must have had recourse to the Pope and produced a second order, incorporating within it the June 1922 ruling that no one should disqualify himself. Despite this new command, in its very teeth indeed, John Prior then withdrew from the case. His place as *ponens* fell to the next senior man, Federico Cattani, who had also voted on the case in 1912 and wanted no more part in the business than Prior. On August 8, 1923, he delegated the case to the next in seniority, Rafaele Chimenti, and on September 27 obtained the Pope's express permission not to participate at all.[190]

The tension between the Grand Penitentiary and the Rota, between the Supreme Judge and his judges, was now at a maximum. Decision of the case had been held up seven months while the Rota's most senior members had tried to halt the proceedings or escape contamination from them. If the process of disqualification had continued, the Pope might have been forced to destroy the formal division between himself and the court, and Pius XI might have ended by deciding the case in person.

Chimenti, to whom the lot fell in August 1923, was a man of sixty-eight, who had been an Auditor since 1914. He had not known the case in the Rota, but his earlier service had been in the matrimonial section of the Vicariate, and he had been Chancellor of this section in 1908 when the Vicariate had sustained the validity of Folchi's marriage. He could not have been unacquainted with the celebrated case at that time. Chimenti was another countryman of Gasparri, coming from the village of Monte Leone di Spoleto, in the hills of Umbria, in the diocese of Norcia.[191]

Folchi's counsel were led by Vincenzo Sacconi, who had represented him in 1911. Count Commander Sacconi had been, since 1912, one of the nine Roman lawyers recognized by the special appellation of "Consistorial Advocate."[192] The Defender of the Bond, Enrico Quattrocolo, was a fifty-one-year-old native of Turin. He had been a student-aide to Auditor Sebastianelli when the case had been in the Rota in 1912. From 1917 to 1919 he had served as Parrillo's assistant before succeeding him as Defender.[193]

Chimenti rendered judgment on November 23, 1923.[194] Giovanni Del Drago, "the principal witness in the case," was rehabilitated. Chimenti accepted his testimony of 1909, 1910, and 1911 as truthful. He was an eyewitness of "the condition made by the spouses of a contract to avoid children." All apparent hesitations, inconsistencies, and conflicts in his account were explained. The negative evaluation made by Lega was criticized and rejected. Del Drago had not only testified with clear veracity, his truthfulness was confirmed by that "most excellent prelate, Giorgi, now a cardinal of the Holy Roman Church."

One eyewitness was, by rotal standards, only "half-proof." But, in lieu of a second witness, circumstances and hearsay could converge to supply the other half. Chimenti took the position that the hearsay witnesses were reliable if they had heard of the condition from Filippo at "a nonsuspect time," defined as any time before Folchi was contemplating the annulment of his marriage. Chimenti did not consider the possibility that, as Filippo declared he had always considered his marriage null, there might be no "nonsuspect time." Rather, he treated the period up to the elopement with Elvira, during which Filippo was "living peaceably" with Pauline, as nonsuspect. By this test the testimony given in 1911 by Pacieri, Serra, Constantini, Antaldi, and Filippo's brothers, Giulio and Pio, was probative. To it Chimenti added that of two of the new hearsay witnesses: Prince Orsini, described as "a most exalted person in the court of the Most Holy Lord," and Count Della Porta, whose testimonial inconsistencies as to date Chimenti explained, while accepting the substance of what he swore he had heard thirty-three years before. Chimenti summed up by saying that all of these witnesses proved that Filippo Folchi had resolved in his own mind not to have children. How could one hold otherwise, he asked, "unless the good faith of the witnesses — and such witnesses! [the exclamation point was his] — were called in doubt?"

Once Filippo's mental state was taken as established, the new Code, canon 1086.2, made it easy: "But if either party or both parties by a positive act of the will excludes marriage itself, or all right to the conjugal act, or any essential property of marriage, the parties contract invalidly." There was to be sure the problem of retroactivity if the 1917 Code was applied to a marriage made in 1891. Without expressly alluding to the difficulty, Chimenti avoided it by treating the Code as a mere clarification of *Si conditiones*. The view was now established that a mere intention, not reduced to an agreement, invalidated a marriage: "Today the doctrine which shines with a clearer light through canon 1086, paragraph 2, is to be judged true."

There remained the problem that an intention such as Folchi's could be interpreted as nothing more than an intention to practice contraception without excluding an essential property of marriage. After all, Lega had considered the possibility that an intention against the good of offspring had been proved and that, according to Gasparri, it might invalidate, but had concluded, also citing

Gasparri, that a mere intent to abuse the marital right had been shown even if Folchi and Del Drago were believed. Chimenti candidly observed that, "in these cases the mind of the judge is held in perplexity" as to whether there is "an intention of excluding the obligation" or "an intention of violating it once accepted." But in Folchi's case, after recounting the circumstances of the marriage, the judge had no doubt: "It was absolutely without any limitation excluded that any children in the future be born from Pauline. . . . And in these circumstances the condition excludes the *right itself* not only the exercise of the right. Gasparri, *De matrimonio*, third edition, section 1006: 'The condition [of avoiding children], *absolutely* attached, excludes the very right, unless it is otherwise proved.' " The italics for *right itself* were provided by Chimenti, trusting like his authority to create a difference in substance by typographical emphasis. He adopted one of the two options available to the court in the analysis of an intention against offspring, one of the two options created by Gasparri's indecisive text. Where Lega had chosen to hold that only intent to practice contraception had been shown, Chimenti chose to find a complete exclusion of intercourse related to childbearing. The academic irresolution of Gasparri made possible the zigzag of the rotal opinions.

Chimenti's statement of the case was argumentative, strained, and extraordinary in several ways. It opened with bitterness toward Filippo, who was described as captured by "an insane love" and living in "shameful commerce" with Pauline,[195] then fleeing with Elvira, then deserting her and adhering to a third, and "receiving a plenitude of children from both." Sullen pleasure was taken in showing how little equity Filippo might invoke. Later, bitterness toward Lega appeared; "open equivocation" was found to exist in part of Lega's conclusions on the evidence in 1912. In his own treatment of the testimony, Chimenti was not distinguished by consistency. He held that the existence of a contract between Pauline and Filippo was not proved, although a contract was all that the declarations of Filippo had set forth, all that Del Drago had testified to, and all that the hearsay witnesses reported. Chimenti found this evidence sufficient to prove Folchi's state of mind. Yet the only evidence of the state of mind was the contract said not to be proved. Chimenti was equally inconsistent on the plausibility of Folchi's decision not to have more children from Pauline, though later willing to procreate seven more children. His agreement to avoid children was "so alien from common morals, indeed from Christian decency" that he would never have mentioned it to his friends unless it had been made; no one would have made up a story so discreditable to himself. At the same time the Auditor observed that Filippo had motives of "a moral character" not to marry Pauline, motives consisting in the "indecent morals of the woman who had already been attached to several others." The court here accepted Filippo's surmises about Pauline's past. "There is no one," Chimenti concluded, "who does not see how moral or social considerations of this character demanded the simple, absolute, and perpetual exclusion of offspring from Pauline."

Bitterness toward Folchi, bitterness toward Lega, breaking through an opinion whose prevailing tone was that of an academic exercise in which the topic had been assigned — "Prove by as many arguments as possible that Filippo Folchi-Vici and Pauline Bailly were not validly married and that the Dean of the Sacred Roman Rota erred in upholding their marriage" — the opinion was altogether extraordinary in rotal annals. Inner tumult, internal strain must account for the inconsistencies in statement, in perspective, in emotion of this tortured document. Chimenti concluded, "The nullity of the marriage is established."

Listed with Chimenti as composing the court giving the decision were Grazioli, Parrillo, Solieri, Massimi, and Joseph Florczak, Ubaldo Mannucci, André Jullien, Rudolph Hindringer, and Francesco Guglielmi. Like the reformers' Rota of 1908, this body was still a group of men whose origins lay in the small villages of Europe; it was still a group with multicountry representation and still composed entirely of priests who also had degrees as canonists.[196] Only in scholarly publications was it slightly inferior to the original body of 1908. If a majority of this body acquiesced in Chimenti's judgment, responsibility could not be attributed to a sharp decline in the standards for appointment. Five votes made a majority. Grazioli's and his own were certain. Solieri and Guglielmi had old ties with Giorgi; it is not unrealistic to suppose that these remained a factor. On the other hand, it is plausible to suppose that Parrillo, the old Defender, and Massimi, the old Promoter of Justice, still believed the bond was valid. One vote had to be picked up by the *ponens* from the group of five appointed to the court in the last three years. Who accepted the inevitability of Folchi's victory cannot now be said.

Appeal was taken to the Signature on May 18, 1924. By canon 1603, paragraph 1, section 2, of the Code the Signature now had ordinary jurisdiction of "an exception of suspicion against any auditor of the Sacred Roman Rota." By section 3 it had ordinary jurisdiction over "a plaint of nullity against a rotal judgment." By section 4 it could consider "a request for restoration to an unimpaired position from a rotal judgment which has become *res judicata*." By section 5 it had jurisdiction of "recourses against rotal judgments in matrimonial cases which the Sacred Rota refuses to admit for a new examination." None of these provisions appeared to contemplate the Signature acting as a court of second instance to provide the second judgment of nullity in a case where the Rota had given the first. The Signature appeared to be designed as a court of cassation, not as a tribunal to decide the merits. Yet, in this case, by a specific papal decision, the Signature acted as the court of second instance, passing on the substance of the case.[197]

Of the reasoning of this body, nothing is known save the result. The new Code kept the cardinals' privilege. By canon 1605, "Judgments of the Supreme Tribunal of the Signature have force, although they contain no reasons in fact or in law." But if the reasons of the body have escaped recording, its composition is known. In addition to Sili, the Prefect, there was Federico Cattani, recently released from his rotal office to become the Secretary, and there were eight cardinal members — in order of seniority, Vincenzo Vannutelli, Basilio Pompili, Pietro Gasparri, Donato Sbaretti, Michele Lega, Oreste Giorgi, Giuseppe Mori, and Evaristo Lucidi.[198] In the proceedings before the S.C.C. in 1908, Vannutelli had been Prefect; Pompili, Secretary; Lega, Under-Secretary; Mori, Lega's first assistant; Lucidi, Assessor; Giorgi, Folchi's counsel; Sili, Folchi's witness. In the Rota between 1909 and 1912, Lega had been Dean; Cattani and Mori, auditors; Giorgi, a witness. In the Signature in 1912, Vannutelli and Gasparri had been members. In the Rota in 1922, Cattani had been an auditor; Giorgi, Folchi's sponsor with the new witnesses.

Cardinals were above recusal. The Defender of the Bond did not ask any to withdraw. If all of the cardinals who had actually participated as principals or assistants in decisions holding the marriage good remained unchanged in their views, there were four votes for validity: Pompili, Mori, Lucidi, and Lega. But of these only Lega had made a large personal investment in upholding the marriage. Of votes for invalidity, two were certain: Sili's and Giorgi's. Of the other voters, Vannutelli was eighty-nine and followed Gasparri's lead. Sbaretti, a former diplomat, had been made a cardinal in 1916 and the Prefect of the S.C.C. in 1919; he was part of the administration established by Gasparri. Pompili, Mori, and Lucidi were also Gasparri's men: Mori having been made a cardinal in 1922; Pompili, an Umbrian who had been made Vicar of Rome in 1921; Lucidi, another Umbrian, who had become a cardinal in 1923. All, in short, had been advanced by Gasparri, including Lega who now stood a little apart from his old colleague. In the end the decisive voice had to be that of the man who had made the administration, made the Pope, and made the law.

In deciding, Gasparri had to consider the work of Lega on the case from 1908 to 1912 and to remember that the judgment which Chimenti's opinion so bitterly derided was the elaborate opinion of the reformed Rota of 1912. He could recall that Lega had been one of his principal assistants in making the new judicial system a reality, even if they stood apart from one another now. On the other hand, Sili, his admired older cousin, his kinsman and his protégé, vouched for Folchi, and the plea of a relative, even where his own interest was not at stake, had a value of its own. Oreste Giorgi, he knew, had moved heaven and earth to have the case reopened. Giorgi spoke with the unction of the Grand Penitentiary and the dignity of a man who had played an important role in the conclave to elect the Pope.

Personalities apart, Gasparri was confronted with an opinion which, in a particularly striking way, revealed the effect upon decretal law of the new Code. In this opinion the judicial order acknowledged the triumph of Gasparri's view of the primacy of internal intention. In this case the legal victory was possible only by the acceptance of Gasparri's remaking of *Si conditiones*. How much these considerations of legal policy, how much the interplay of curial personalities bore upon him as he gave judgment cannot be said. Policy and personalities composed the spectrum of influences upon the mind of the maker of the Code. The record shows only that on June 30, 1924, six weeks after the appeal was filed, the Signature, "in a special meeting of the Eminent Fathers, judged conformably to the rotal judgment." [199]

With the help of Giovanni Del Drago, Prince Orsini, and Count Della Porta, Filippo Folchi had won. His friends, the members of his old circle, had given the evidence which freed him at last from his long mismarriage. He had not been abandoned by his set when he had tried to return, ecclesiastically unimpeded, to its shelter.

With the help of Agostino Sili, Giulio Grazioli, and Oreste Giorgi, Filippo Folchi had won. The counselors provided by his father and Pius X had stood by him through thick and thin, through metamorphosis of role, through ascent to the heights of administration in the Curia. The pious hope of his salvation had led them to be patient and cunning in his behalf, and in the end they had been able to press the levers of control to spring him free.

Filippo Folchi had also won because of the law which had been codified by Pietro Gasparri — the process so constructed that the Sovereign Pontiff was still the Supreme Prince, secrecy clothed the litigants, and the highest judicial body, composed of cardinals, did not need to give reasons in fact or law for its conclusions; while the substantive rules deliberately made internal intent decisive even for the public ceremony of marriage and unintentionally left to a court's choice whether the requirements of invalidity had been established. Giuseppe Sarto, Pius X, had launched Filippo Folchi on his trial of the system and had saved him twice when he faltered. In the same sovereign capacity, Achille Ratti, Pius XI, had let Folchi start again and had seen his case through stormy rotal waters to a happy conclusion. In the final decision the word belonged to the man without whom the case would not have been possible, Pietro Gasparri.

At the age of sixty-three, after a marriage which had been performed by the deputy of the Vicar of the Pope, which had lasted thirty-four years, which had been held valid by four judgments of ecclesiastical courts, Filippo Folchi, the father of nine children, was, because of his intent to exclude children, ecclesiastically free to marry, in Pauline's lifetime, whomever he chose.*

---

* Under Italian civil law Folchi would not have been free to marry civilly. The Concordat in 1929 was prudently ambiguous on the effect of an ecclesiastical annulment on a marriage entered before the Concordat. It became arguable, though not certain, that the ecclesiastical judgment terminated the civil union, Vincenzo

Five sentences with their complement or counterpoint run through this history:

1. "This condition, absolutely attached, excludes the right itself, according to the cited final chapter of *De conditionibus, Si conditiones*, unless it is otherwise proved."

And, "Today the doctrine which shines with a clearer light through canon 1086, paragraph 2, is judged true."

2. "I want to make a code, Most Blessed Father."

And, "I undertook the matter from intimate conviction."

3. "In judgments there is to be no acceptance of persons."

And, "To the Sacred Rota that all may see, anything else notwithstanding."

4. "Pauline, when will you become more experienced in the things of this world?"

And, "There is no one who does not see how moral or social considerations of this kind demanded the simple, absolute, and perpetual exclusion of offspring from Pauline."

5. "As it is plain here that the marriage contract has its full completion, so, by the will of God, there is also the greatest firmness and indissolubility which may not be destroyed by any human authority."

And, "The Most Holy benignly receives the libel of supplication seeking a new examination of the nullity of marriage between Filippo Folchi-Vici and Pauline Bailly."

Del Giudice, "Sul potere giurisdizionale dei tribunali ecclesiastichi nelle cause di nullita dei matrimoni preconcordatari," *Il Foro della Lombardia* (Padua, 1931), I, 1–20.

V

Does Intent to Enter a Marriage One Believes to Be Dissoluble Make the Marriage Dissoluble?

A MATCH AT FANNY READ'S

"Under certain circumstances there are few hours in life more agreeable than the hour dedicated to the ceremony known as afternoon tea. There are circumstances in which, whether you partake of the tea or not — some people of course never do — the situation is in itself delightful." Such a tea, such a situation, presented itself to a twenty-year-old American girl one afternoon in Paris in the spring of 1894.

She was young, an American, a girl, in Paris in the spring, and beyond all these possibly accidental ingredients of happiness, she was rich. Her father, to be completely specific, had left to her, on certain terms and conditions, one sixth of his estate, and that estate, sparingly estimated for the purposes of probate in the State of New York to be $72,000,000, had been barely diminished by legacies, the small inheritance levy of the day, and a special payment of $5,000,000 to the oldest son for services in the paternal business, and not at all diminished by gifts to church or charity, which were nonexistent. The sixth was hers in trust for life, with power to appoint the remainder of her share as she chose, to such issue as she had, if she had issue. It was free of control by her husband, if she were to have one, and it possessed the customary muniments against the incursions of creditors or the intemperance of the donee by the provisions commonly called spendthrift which the ingenuity of American lawyers had added to the English device of a trust as additional assurance that a beneficiary should personally and uninterruptedly enjoy the bounty of a munificent ancestor.[1]

She had, then, at least half a million a year, and, her parents dead, it was in her unrestricted control save for two provisions whose weight would be determined by her temperament. She was, until twenty-one, the ward of her older sister and her oldest brother. If she married without the consent of a majority of her trustees — the same brother and sister and two other brothers — her share was to be reduced by half. For one as resolute as she, these restrictions could not, it might be hypothesized, constitute a crushing limitation.

As for appearance, she was small of stature with tiny hands and feet; she did not qualify as "beautiful" by either American or continental criteria; but she did not lack a vivacity which, added to the vigor and gloss of youth and the assurance conferred by wealth, made her a presence to be noticed. Her deportment, sufficiently refined to indicate a conventional schooling in social situations, was not without a certain timidity, although it was also not without determination, even, a completely candid observer might have added, tenaciousness. Her face was unmarked by frustrations, and its freshness might have been mistaken for naiveté if her large, black-blue eyes had not been animated by what her admirers would have taken as intelligence and those who were not her friends would have experienced as malice.[2]

She was rich, and she had the reputation of being even richer, for her father had been the most celebrated of American financiers of his era. The intricacies and defenses of American trusts were not within the ordinary education of European gentlemen, and on this spring day in Paris, Anna Gould enjoyed the homage of a European swarm, who knew only that she was the only unmarried daughter of the most famous of American masters of Wall Street.

Her hostess, Fanny Read, was an American old and knowledgeable in the ways of the Faubourg St. Germain. To introduce a young compatriot abroad to cultivated natives who could appreciate the potentialities of that compatriot was the kind of pleasure with mutual satisfactions which her experience permitted her to arrange and her sensibilities had prepared her to enjoy. No doubt it was her interest in this kind of pleasure, and not unregulated coincidence, that had brought about this occasion where Anna, in gray crepe de Chine, pursued by the pleasurable swarm, should meet the Marquise Anne Marie Madeleine de Juigné de Castellane and the oldest unmarried son of the marquise.[3]

Christened Paul Boniface, and known as Boni, Castellane was from a family ancient yet new — Provençal in ultimate provenance, Bourbon by blood, renewed by Napoleon who had made the senior branch dukes de Talleyrand. *Mai d'ounor che d'ounors*, "More honor than honors," ran the Provençal devise of the family; and in a republican age, where monarchists were in disarray and the discipline of commerce was too dull to be accepted, the family lineage was the most important family asset. Castellane was brought up at the ancestral residence of Rochecotte in the valley of the Loire. At sixteen he passed from its patriarchal life to the Collège St. Stanislas conducted by the Marists in Paris and then to the Oratorians' College at Juilly. Education at these institutions was perhaps tinctured by worldliness, and more Catholic in form than in fact, but if formal education added to ancestry could determine belief, Boni was incorrigibly Catholic. Among the gracious legends of the past which fed his boyhood fancy was his grandmother's recollection of the repentance of her famous great-uncle, the ex-bishop who had become Napoleon's Foreign Minister, and whose final penitence and submission to the Church had been generously received by Gregory XVI;[*] and Castellane had had implanted in his heart the conviction that the strength of the family was not independent of the ecclesiastical regime.[4]

What did he understand by devotion to the Church? How different were his views from those of a nobleman of three centuries earlier such as Duke Charles of Lorraine? Not very different it would have to be confessed. That is to say, for Castellane the Church appeared as a venerable and surprisingly powerful organization, entwined with his family and constituting a support both for the social order in general and their special status within it.

---

* The story of Talleyrand's repentance is set out at length in the autobiography of Boni's father, Antoine de Castellane, *Men and Things of My Time*, trans. Alexander Teixeira de Mattos (London: Chatto and Windus, 1911), pp. 148–150. Antoine's mother, Talleyrand's grandniece, was at the center of devout, liberal Catholics of the Empire; at seven Antoine himself was sent to Orléans to be educated by their ecclesiastical leader, Bishop Dupanloup, *ibid.*, pp. 2–9.

The ruling authorities of this useful body were austere and some-what peculiar men, whose favor was pleasant to receive — he was to get Leo XIII's blessing not long after his wedding — but who were not to be imitated. The prescriptions enunciated by these authorities, especially as they bore upon sexual behavior, were in-capable of being observed, at any rate by a man under seventy, but they were not to be flouted in an institutional fashion. Castellane was not without affection for what he envisioned as an ancient and aristocratic entity both sustaining his self-image and tolerating his peccadilloes, and it would be wrong to suppose that in his long familiarity with the ministers and adherents of the Church no idea of God or love of neighbor had been apprehended by him. "Ego-tist, frivolous, too young" (his self-characterization), living at a level of perception not far from animal, Castellane had a conscious-ness of persons outside himself which was not entirely unawak-ened, however feeble and intermittent were its flickerings. Primar-ily, he saw the Church as an object, and taking a view of it at once sentimental and legal, he did not see that what it was was what its participants, himself included, were.[5]

The Church, on this spring afternoon in 1894, would in any event not have been in Castellane's mind as he contemplated Anna Gould, found his mother approving, caught the young American's attention by his English, and persuaded himself that this small and animated creature was not only rich but charming. Compact and trim, big-shouldered, very fair, Castellane for a decade had been engaged in amorous affairs in which his physical address and in-souciant courtesy had counted for everything in the accomplish-ment of his objectives. Marvel as he might at the stroke of fortune which had brought her within his Parisian radius, he could not doubt his ability to please this inexperienced foreigner.

If he needed encouragement at all after this tea where the radi-ance of a match with Anna had sensibly come home to him, en-couragement was provided by a dinner at which the host was George Gould, the oldest brother whose "remarkable business ability" had been so generously described and so appropriately recognized in Jay Gould's testamentary dispositions. George Gould struck Boni as a man not so different from himself. As a young man, George had impulsively married a pretty actress, his extra-marital behavior was gossiped of in Paris, and the Frenchman thought his ideas on the subject of sexual propriety broad enough to comprehend with equanimity Castellane's own reputation. Shared instincts, however, were not what drew Castellane to the Goulds. The European nobleman nourished the belief that there was, in the last analysis, something different about the very rich. "For the first time I saw some millionaires at close quarters." He had entered a higher sphere and had found a more elevated species when he consorted with beings so magnificently enabled to satisfy their whims. Quite simply, "I made the mistake of thinking they were all remarkable." [6]

The richest heiress in America encountering a descendant of Talleyrands seems to be the classic Jamesian situation written in capital letters; but if the lettering was larger, the colors were less subtle, and the contrasts more palpable. Yet, on the side of neither family was there placed the kind of obstacle which an abstract enumeration of the disparities between them might have suggested. Anna was a girl of vague Protestant antecedents whose father was a trader from upstate New York turned master scalawag, and Castellane was a Catholic whose family was definitively ancient, aristocratic, French. The differences were of no account to the latter, the sources of the Gould riches or for that matter of Anna herself were subjects of indifference, if the riches were there. Having accepted an American at all as a potential member of the family, their focus had to be on the pecuniary value of the arrangement. The Goulds were equally tolerant of the idea of an impecunious foreigner without steady employment at the age of twenty-seven winning the affection of the youngest Gould girl.

The factor which dominated the imaginations of the Castellane family was beyond doubt, although their calculations as to what Castellane might enjoy were imprecise and erroneous. The behavior of the Goulds was more puzzling. Perhaps Fanny Reid had launched the notion with her friends that there was luster in the Castellane name and excellence in its lineage: Boni was a count and would in time be a marquis. But, to put the case with commercial bluntness, the title was not the best money could buy, and George Gould, who had chosen not to go to college so that he could begin work at nineteen in his father's employ, could not have rated very highly the idle holder of a second-rate title. George, in any event, would not have had the possessory or oedipal feelings that might have fed a father's wrath at seeing his daughter conquered by a person whom almost any American entrepreneur would have judged a dapper but common cheat.

There was, indeed, Helen, the oldest daughter, Anna's coguardian, comfortably married and the only member of the Goulds with much religious conviction. A Presbyterian and active in good works in Protestant circles, she struck Castellane as sober and severe. With this prim philanthropist he was forced to draw on his recollections of his Christian education, to show "a clergyman's soul," to be taken for "a little saint"; and Anna, who knew him at least a little better, must secretly have enjoyed this mocking of her devout guardian.[7]

In the end it was Anna's decision to make. Whatever the provisions of the trust, whatever the misgivings of George, the other brothers, or Helen, they knew Anna too well to challenge her when her course was set. Unlike the other marriages chronicled in this book, family influence was not decisive with either individual; it did not override rebellious affection or compel listless spirits to perform their duty. Castellane of course had been formed to think of family interest, but there was an almost perfect coincidence of family interest and his own in what Anna would bring, and he had no consciousness of sacrificing himself for his family. As for Anna, she may have been pleased to become a countess, but her pleasure was not in pleasing her brothers or her sister. Like any American girl, she married the man she had chosen for herself.

Was it, then, a marriage of love? There was first a courtship. Castellane pursued Anna while she remained at Fanny's Read's. He rode by on horseback under her windows, sent her flowers, and wrote her several times a week. Then, relying on the impression he had created to stir her imagination in his absence, he withdrew and, going by way of England, preceded her to America and awaited her arrival. Three months later she arrived, to weigh her Frenchman on her home ground in New York. She began by inviting him to the Horse Show. She had him to dinner at Helen's. She had him for Christmas at the Gothic chateau built by her father at Irvington-on-Hudson. She persuaded George to invite him to share the Goulds' private railroad car on a voyage to Canada; and on the neutral territory of Montreal, in a warm glow of emotion after Sunday mass, Castellane proposed and was accepted.[8]

That each saw the other in a special light, that each seemed eminently desirable to the other, seems undeniable. Gilbert Osmond, it may be recalled, was "sincere" and very much in love with Isabel Archer when he married her "for her money." [9] To say that Castellane did not quite see Anna as a person and did see her primarily as a source of inexhaustible bounty might be accurate, but would not deny that he wanted to marry her as he saw her. To say that Anna had had insufficient exposure to Castellane's character would not gainsay that, to the extent she had seen him, she wanted him. If Castellane seriously asked himself if he could give up the promiscuous pursuit of other women to confine himself to one so fundamentally unsensuous as Anna, he may have qualified what he meant by wanting her as his wife. If Anna took seriously the rumors that perhaps reached her of Castellane's sexual propensities, she may have stifled her doubts by recalling that by the standards of American law her choice was not in every circumstance irrevocable. Each may have measured the commitment freely made, but, however qualified, their commitment was to each other.

The matching of an American heiress to a European nobleman still could have the quality of a fairy tale or nineteenth-century novel, and the match was described to New Yorkers as a delicious fantasy miraculously made real. The physical magnetism of the gallant Count captured the fancy of the press, and it was approvingly observed that, blond and blue-eyed, he and his brother "looked more like Englishmen of Saxon blood than Frenchmen." Anna, in delicate contrast, appeared as "shy, modest, and retiring," a "gentle maiden whose dream had become flesh." [10]

On March 4, 1895, a month after the engagement, less than a year after the tea at Fanny Read's, they were married in a ceremony which took place in George Gould's mansion at the northeast corner of Fifth Avenue at 67th Street. Victor Herbert conducted a twenty-piece orchestra in the Wedding March from *Lohengrin* and the Wedding March of Mendelssohn, Madam Sucher sang Gounod's *Ave Maria*, and Louis Sherry provided breakfast. A civil marriage service was conducted by Justice Andrews of the New York Court of Appeals, but the wedding itself was the religious ceremony celebrated by Augustine Corrigan, the Catholic Archbishop of New York. [11]

The possibility of Anna becoming a Catholic had been present; she had had more than one long and earnest conversation with Archbishop Corrigan; but in the end the Archbishop gave Castellane the necessary dispensation to marry a Christian of a heretical sect, a dispensation conceded with little difficulty in American dioceses where mixed marriages were common. The canonical witnesses of the wedding were Castellane's brother Jean; and a friend Castellane had acquired among the Europeans in New York, Giovanni Del Drago.[12] The homily was delivered by Archbishop Corrigan himself, who had been informed by the Count, he said, that "in your blood flows the blood that once flowed in the veins of St. Boniface." He was led to recount the familiar story of Pope Gregory the Great and the English slaves (not Angles, but angels) and the less familiar legend of Pope Gregory II and the naming of the monk Winifred as "Bonnyface." Saint Boniface was to be an example and guide to his namesake and relative who shared his blue eyes and his fair countenance. The Archbishop remarked on the mysterious design of Providence in bringing the couple together, so that the Count had seen the New World, and Anna would "learn the manners and customs of the Old."[13]

The marriage ran a course of eleven years. Boni was born within the first year of marriage, Georges in the second, Jay in the seventh.[14] To observers, the couple did not seem unhappy. Castellane spent money on a magnificent scale, constructing a yacht of 1600 tons, celebrating the birth of a child with a fete for 3,000 guests, building a townhouse in Paris and a private theatre with 600 seats, and obligating himself beyond the measure of his wife's trust income. His extravagances were irritating to his brothers-in-law and the cordiality that had once existed with them gradually vanished.[15] But Castellane's taste in art was sometimes excellent, his brothers-in-law had no doubt expected some exuberance from him, the trust capital was unimpaired, and Anna herself enjoyed the bouyancy and fresh wonder with which Castellane sought to relieve the tedium of existence. All that she objected to was that among his entertainments was the continued sexual pursuit of young women.

Castellane expected his wife to accept his infidelities. They were not in his view incompatible with the institution he had entered with her. He treated her response as unreasonable jealousy; he felt that he no longer understood her; he regretted the independent spirit of American women.[16] Her husband's belief that faithfulness to one woman was an unattainable perfection seemed cynical to Anna. With some patience she suffered the first lapses known to her, nothing at all having come to her attention in the first three years of marriage. Eventually she became convinced that his habits were inveterate. She did not act precipitately, but she distilled her discontent in what her husband perceived obscurely to be a danger- ous silence. She had been no more wary than Isabel Archer in confronting her destiny, but aware at last of its dimensions she had the will and the resources to strike for herself. A letter from a girl to Castellane was intercepted. Directed by Anna's lawyer, detec- tives followed him to his rendezvous; the irrefutable facts she sought were hers. On January 26, 1906, Anna strolled in the park with her husband; three hours later she and the children had disap- peared and the house was closed. She had left Boni for good. Pos- sessed of the evidence, she sued for divorce on the ground of adul- tery. A French court granted her plea and gave her custody of the children.[17]

With the swift skill that her father had showed in extricating himself from financial morasses and rebounding with greater strength, Anna completed the expulsion of Castellane from her life; in July 1908 she married his cousin, Marie-Pierre-Elie de Talley- rand Périgord, obtaining as a husband a bachelor of fifty-nine, with the benevolence and respectability of a reformed roué, and a better title than she had first acquired. Her new husband was Marquis de Périgord, Prince of Sagan in Silesia, and, in time, Duke de Talleyrand; until her death in 1961, Anna lived as a duchess, the wounds she had received perceptible only in a certain stoic grim- ness with which she now addressed the affairs of life and the deter- mination and ingenuity she exhibited in preventing Boni from achieving his own freedom.[18]

Castellane was left penniless; no part of his wife's property stuck to him; and he was already heavily in debt. At one stroke he had lost wife, children, fortune: "My disaster occupied everyone's imagination."[19] It fully occupied his own for years to come. His wife, marrying his cousin in a London registry office, sailed on, so it seemed to him, intact and even swelled by success. He had but one great talent, the art of marrying a rich woman, and, bound as a Catholic to Anna for life, his single talent had to be buried. To his problems there seemed but one solution, and that solution was so dependent on his spiritual connections, so related to his family's status and inheritance, so congenial to his sanguine expectations, and so appropriate in the light of the eventual outcome of his marriage, that he could not doubt but that it would be granted.

THE DEAN OF MODERN ADVOCATES

Round One

Marcantonio Pacelli was a practitioner of canon law, an advocate of the old Rota in its senectitude, and, from 1851 to 1870, Undersecretary of the Interior in the papal administration of the States of the Church, a faithful servant of the temporal power in the days of its decline and fall.[20] The second of his ten children, Filippo, also became a canon lawyer. Optimistically getting married at thirty-six, only three years after the invading Italian army had swept away his father's world, Filippo Pacelli found his optimism justified. He flourished in the practice of ecclesiastical law at the Curia. In 1910 he was seventy-three, and he had been, since he was sixty, the dean of the College of Consistorial Advocates. He enjoyed a direct income from the Holy See as Legal Counselor of the Reverenda Fabricca di San Pietro, the building authority of the Vatican.[21] He was the sole lay consultant to the Commission for the Code of Canon Law, where his third oldest child, Eugenio, was the right hand of Cardinal Gasparri. It was to Filippo Pacelli that Boni de Castellane turned when his distress put him in need of an advocate at the Curia.

Who financed the case is not entirely clear. Castellane's parents were concerned enough about his situation and possessed of enough money to launch a lawsuit, and, unlike Charles of Lorraine, a litigant in the modern Rota did not need to employ an army of lawyers. As for Castellane's chances of success, it was known that his cousin, the Prince of Sagan, had explored with Roman canonists the defects which might be discovered in Anna's first marriage.[22] It had seemed in order. The law of Trent, though in fact apparently complied with, had no application in the archdiocese of New York, for the decrees of the Council of Trent had never been promulgated in the former English colonies making up the

United States. There was no evidence of coercion exercised on the principals, who had chosen each other with such deliberate will. There had been no lack of consummation, and no exclusion of the good of procreation. The counselors of the Prince of Sagan had concluded that an attack on the marriage was a lost cause, and he had simply disobeyed the law of the Church when he entered a marriage with Anna which, by canonical criteria, was bigamous for Anna and a nullity for him. But the Prince of Sagan had not had Filippo Pacelli as his advocate.

First, the ground was laid to have the case get off to a good start by beginning in Rome. Venue for a sovereign lay in Rome. For Castellane, who was not a sovereign, the normal place for the case to have been tried was Paris, where he lived, or New York, where the marriage had been celebrated. But Paris could be depicted as hostile territory. Castellane's enemies — earned, counsel suggested, by his championing of the Church against the Freemasons — would surely exploit the case if it were conducted in France, secret though canonical hearings were and distant though these maleficent forces were from the ecclesiastical tribunal of the archdiocese of Paris. New York, it appeared, was too inconvenient. By special rescript of Pope Pius X, Castellane was permitted to bring his case to Rome and not merely to the Vicariate but like any sovereign to the Rota itself.[23]

The theory of Castellane's case was this, as set out in the petitionary libel drafted by Pacelli: a quarter of an hour before the wedding Anna stated in the presence of Jean de Castellane and Giovanni Del Drago: "I intend now to say to you, and indeed so that Boni may know it and so that you will make it known to him, that I am a Protestant and an American, while he is French and a Catholic. Marriage does not have the same meaning for us, and I am determined to abandon him and to divorce him if it pleases me and the occasion seems right to me."[24] An intention against indissolubility was the gist of this allegation. Anna had excluded one of the three values constituting the object of marital consent.* She

---

* Strikingly enough, Pacelli did not attempt to establish an invalidating intention much more within Castellane's power to prove: an intention against fidelity. Although fidelity was one of the three goods of marriage in Augustinian analysis and in the decretal *Si conditiones*, a cultural resistance existed to treating an intent against fidelity as fatal to validity. The modern Rota has held some marriages null for such an intention (e.g., *Of Nullity of Marriage, February 7, 1925,*

had willed to enter a dissoluble and impermanent union. She had thereby consented to what was a nullity before the Church.

In the course of 1910 and 1911 Pacelli presented the evidence in support of his case. Castellane amplified his libel by declaring that four days before the wedding there was an exchange of views between himself and Anna, and that "she told me she was an American Protestant, that she was free, that her marriage could not bind her irrevocably, and that she reserved for herself the faculty of divorce if things fell through." [25] Castellane's brother, Jean, read to a judge-delegate of the archdiocese of Paris a paper in which he described a conversation with Anna the evening before the marriage. She had said: "I am very sad to marry. Boni pushed me and pressed me so that I yielded. What reassures me is that I can get a divorce. Boni believes that he will keep me forever. He will keep me only as long as long as I wish, and if it is no longer agreeable for me I will get a divorce. I am a Protestant, and I know that I can get a divorce when I wish." On being asked by the judge if Anna had actually used these words (now recalled as they had been spoken sixteen years before) Jean answered: "These words struck me so much that I have an exact recollection of them." [26] He could not, however, remember repeating them to his brother, and he contradicted the annulment petition by denying that Anna had ever told him to convey such a message to her fiancé.

Kitty Cameron, one of Anna's bridesmaids, now Castellane's friend, testified: "I am certain that, before the marriage, in front of me and several others, Miss Gould said that she would get a divorce if she was not happy. She said that to me in reply to a question I asked her on the subject of the marriage. I asked her if she was sure of being happy with Monsieur de Castellane. Her reply was, 'If he doesn't make me happy, I shall divorce him.' In

---

Decisiones, XVII, 61, before Massimi, Grazioli, and Parrillo: before the marriage the bride accepted a signed declaration by the bridegroom, "I declare that I intend to have my way in everything without opposition of any kind to my will"; the document was interpreted as a charter of sexual freedom for the husband). More typically, recognition of this ground has been grudging. A recent example is *Reims, June 11, 1965*, unpublished decisions of the Sacred Roman Rota. Here the man continued to see his mistress and have sexual relations with her during his engagement and also during his honeymoon. He testified, "I thought that my wife by the legal and religious union was Claudine, by love Marietta." The court held the marriage with Claudine valid.

America, almost all the girls have this intention of making use of divorce if a marriage doesn't make them happy." Kitty Cameron did not relate this conversation to any specific time except that it had taken place before Anna was married.[27]

Star witness of the proceedings was Giovanni Del Drago, who, by the time he was interrogated on behalf of Boni de Castellane, had already made his substantial contribution to the matrimonial cause of Filippo Folchi. The morning of the wedding, Del Drago's account ran, he was in a room next to the bride's in George Gould's house; he heard weeping; he approached the room; he then "was called by the bride herself. In a state of agitation she told me that she was not sure of the affection of the bridegroom and was afraid that she was doing something wrong in marrying him. In any case she declared that she was marrying on the condition of being free to be able to divorce, particularly if she were betrayed by the bridegroom; and she prayed me then to communicate this information to the bridegroom." Del Drago testified that the communication was duly relayed to Boni, "in a corner of a room without anyone else being present," and that his friend "appeared very sad and moved by religious sentiments but in order to avoid a scandal he did not think of breaking off the marriage." [28]

Antecedent intention was the issue, for only antecedent intention against indissolubility would nullify; but declarations subsequent to marriage might be used to confirm the existence of an antecedent intention. Castellane's most helpful witness on this branch of the case was his mother. The Marquise de Castellane recalled that at Rochecotte, the family home, some months after the marriage, Anna had gone to mass with her in the chapel of the chateau, and on leaving the chapel the Marquise had thanked her for attending: "She said to me immediately, 'I will never become a Catholic because I prize the power of being able to divorce.'" In the course of matrimonial life her daughter-in-law had often said, "I will get a divorce." "She said it to a good many people in the most varied circumstances, sometimes in a joking tone, sometimes in a very serious and grave tone. It was a thought that had matured a long time with her." [29] The Marquis de Castellane confirmed his wife's account.

Boni's old school and sporting friend, Honoré Southène, Duke de Luynes, testified that "the young woman constantly had the word 'divorce' on her lips in the most futile circumstances." An Anglican relative-in-law, the Marquise de Talleyrand, recalled Anna saying more than once, "If Boni does not behave as he should, I will get a divorce and remarry," and when she asked her once on a country walk if she would become a Catholic, she replied, "Never in my life, because, if I became a Catholic, I could no longer get a divorce if Boni misbehaved." Count Jean de Montebello stated that Anna had told him: "In America, it is very convenient: when a husband ceases to please, one begins life with another. And I shall not fail to do this if I am unhappy with Boni." Countess de Montebello, who described herself as a friend of Anna, related how at the Castellane chateau of Marais about 1905, Anna told her: "In my religion and in my country, there are advantages — one leaves one's husband when one is not happy." [30]

The bare repetition of Anna's American views on divorce was filled out a little by other observations on her nature and behavior. To Giovanni Del Drago she was "of strong character, resolute and authoritarian, incapable of going back on her ideas." Castellane's mother saw her as jealous and even violent: "In privacy repeated scenes caused by the acts of Anna Gould broke the quiet of conjugal life. Anna went so far as to bite her husband." Her friend, the Countess de Montebello, remembered that, whenever she had visited the chateau, Anna "was always in bad humor, a figure of wood and disagreeable to her husband." The Marquise de Talleyrand described her as "very demanding" and "vindictive": "She will pursue vengeance to the death of one who has offended her. She will do the impossible to prevent Boni from recovering his freedom." [31]

All of these witnesses disapproved of Anna's divorce, and several of them professed to be puzzled or surprised that she had sought it. Castellane's father was not sure what the grounds for the divorce had been, but he seemed to feel that Anna had obtained it in execution of a plan laid years before: Her purpose "was for her so little an intention in the air and so much the expression of a deliberate and fixed will that, in fact, eleven years after the marriage, she divorced my son." The Countess de Montebello declared, "I believe that at bottom the principal reason was that Anna Gould did not wish to bear any correction and wanted to keep her complete independence." The Countess had deemed it her duty to call on Anna at the Hotel Bristol while the divorce action was pending and "to make vibrate in her soul everything which might remind her of conjugal or maternal sentiments." Anna was seated with her dog at her right, a bridge game at her left, and the countess was astonished and saddened to find Anna less interested in her reproaches than in "seeking, with calm seriousness, the solution of a bridge problem." Giovanni Del Drago knew that the divorce was on account of "her husband's infidelity," a reason that struck him as a cultural peculiarity: "I know very well that American girls, more than any others, claim fidelity from their husbands." [32]

Anna herself was summoned to testify by the ecclesiastical court in Paris and was asked the truth of the declaration attributed to her in Castellane's libel. She replied: "I did not pronounce the phrase attributed to me. I do not even remember having said something like it or having the same meaning. I add that my father was opposed to divorce and that he brought me up in his ideas." Had she ever spoken of divorce? Not, she said, in the first three years of marriage, "but when difficulties arose, several times I threatened my husband by asking for a divorce." Did she think at all of divorce and remarriage at the time she married Boni? "At that time I was still very much a child. The thought of the possibility of a second marriage did not occur to me." With what intention had she married? "I was marrying like one ordinarily marries. I did not think of anything else." [33]

She was asked if she had any further witnesses to suggest to the tribunal and replied that she had none, but when she had had the opportunity to read the testimony of Jean de Castellane and Giovanni Del Drago, she changed her mind. First, she entered a denial of their testimony. She had never used the language attributed to her by Boni's brother. As for Del Drago, "he was a friend of Monsieur de Castellane but not of my family . . . The Prince Del Drago had no connection with me, and I had no confidence to make to him. That is a pure calumny." Second, she now suggested witnesses from her own family, and her brothers and sister came forward before a judge-delegate of the New York archdiocese to testify to her feeling for Castellane. "The very eve of the marriage," Edwin Gould said, "she told me that she loved her fiancé a great deal. It was for this reason that she freely accepted the conditions demanded by the Catholic Church for a mixed marriage and that she accepted as well all the consequences that flowed from that undertaking." In a word, "she hoped that nothing could detach him from her." Helen Gould declared, "She was very affectionate toward Paul." None of her siblings had heard her speak of the possibility of divorce before the wedding, nor had two old friends from New York, Addie Woodward Adams and Edwina Montgomery Crane, who were positive in their testimony: Anna had not "believed" in divorce.[34]

Toward the end of 1911, at the same time that the Folchi case was coming to its second judgment by the Rota, the Castellane case was ripe for decision. The rotal turn was composed of the old auditor, Guglielmo Sebastianelli; the new appointee, Pietro Rosetti; and the stalwart Dean, Michele Lega. On December 9, 1911, Lega gave the opinion and the judgment.[35] The sole witness, he observed, to a "true condition" against indissolubility was the Prince Del Drago. Without referring in the least to Del Drago's parallel position in *Folchi*, Lega pointed to one contradiction between his testimony and that of the Marquise de Castellane. Del Drago had asserted with characteristic assurance that he "knew with certainty" that Anna had declared her mind on divorce to Boni's mother at the time of the wedding, because the Marquise had reported this declaration to him. Yet the Marquise herself testified, "Up until the moment of the wedding, I never heard from Miss Gould of any intention." With a certain dryness, Lega concluded, "Not only is the Prince Del Drago the sole witness; he does not inspire belief in his depositions."

Castellane's brother was also contradicted by his mother's depositions. According to Jean, his mother found Anna's opinions on divorce "so frightful that she wept warm tears the eve and also the day of the wedding." But the Marquise herself testified that she had had no communications from Anna to distress her. Other differences existed between the libel and the oral testimony. According to the libel, Jean sought the cause of Anna's tears a quarter of an hour before the wedding, and Anna then set out her condition to Jean and Del Drago together. Castellane stated orally that an hour and a half before the ceremony Anna made her declaration, first to Del Drago, who had entered her room, then to Jean, then to both together. Jean himself said he heard Anna state the condition the evening before the marriage.

Observing these discrepancies, Lega touched upon the fashion in which the petition for annulment had been coordinated with the accounts which would be orally given. Although, as the Dean coldly remarked, there was "a precise requirement" of law, X.2.1.14, *Pastoralis* — "We decree that the facts should be set out by the principals themselves" — the practice prevailed of the advocate drafting the libel. The libel, the Dean added, "does not always signify the real truth, since it is written by the advocate to win the action he has undertaken."

Against witnesses caught in contradictions with each other stood the firm denial by Anna that, neither in words nor in mind, had she expressed any premarital intention to obtain a divorce. Her denial was given credibility by her prompt objection to the testimony of Del Drago and Jean, by the witnesses to her love for Castellane when she married him, and by her failure to bring up the alleged intention as a basis for nullity when the Prince of Sagan had sought a canonical ground for annulment of her marriage. The suggestion that Anna sought vengeance by blocking Boni was looked at, but discounted. She would not have been so tardy in producing witnesses to support her, Lega supposed, if she had calculated from the beginning on telling lies designed to frustrate Castellane's case.

As a precaution perfunctorily added, Lega gave a further consideration accepted by the court: "The Lords have thought that a reason is not lacking for vindicating the stability of this marriage, even if it were conceded that a condition had been attached. The marriage was celebrated in New York, where the Tridentine regulation was not in force.* Hence, as peaceful cohabitation and coup-

---

* The Tridentine rules had been published in much but not all of the territory once ruled by Spain and France. The result in nineteeth-century America was a crazy quilt. When in 1883 all of the archbishops and many of the bishops of the United States gathered to discuss American problems at Propaganda before its prefect, Cardinal Franzelin, the extent to which Trent was in use was on the agenda; the Archbishops of Baltimore, Boston, New York, and Philadelphia indicated that the Tridentine rule was not observed in their dioceses and that they would not want to see its introduction. As to what dioceses Trent had been published in — as distinct from being observed — this was "a thorny question involved in doubts" (*Relatio collationum* . . . , a report printed in Latin at Baltimore containing the minutes of this meeting of November 13, 1883, now in the Gibbons file for 1883 in the Archives of the Archdiocese of Baltimore). According to Gasparri, writing eight years later and drawing on the official views of Propaganda, Trent had to be observed for the validity of a marriage in the ecclesiastical province of New Orleans; in the ecclesiastical province of San Francisco, except that part east of the Colorado River; in the ecclesiastical province of

ling were spontaneously admitted, not only after the unfaithfulness of the husband was detected but for the rest of the eight years, and, indeed, with the result of generating offspring, the spouses cured the pretended defect of consent." [36] The principle of *Ad id*, the old decretal of Clement III, X.4.1.21, so much discussed in the case of Charles and Nicole and so apparently obsolete, was applied with pristine vigor; if Trent was not in force, there was no need for any later consent to be expressed in Tridentine form before a parish priest and two witnesses; and consent would be implied from circumstance. The commonsense result of denying a delayed attack on a long-established union was achieved; Castellane was barred by a virtual statute of limitations; the new Rota, unlike the old, appeared ready to dismiss a stale claim of defective initial consent. Nullity of marriage, Lega concluded, was not established.

Another Point of View

As was his right, Filippo Pacelli appealed to another turn of the Rota. To give force to this appeal, in June and July of 1912 he called again upon some of his old witnesses. Castellane's mother, now sixty-seven, was able to improve her earlier testimony slightly. She had been shocked and pained by Anna's views on divorce which the Marquise had gathered not directly from her but from her behavior in New York. "It happened very often that in worldly conversations, apropos of the presentation of girls not having their mother's name because the mother was divorced and remarried, that all this Protestant world would approve the divorce, and Miss Anna Gould appeared to find all that entirely natural." Thus, though she had never spoken to Anna on the subject, she did have "a crisis of despair" on the eve of the wedding, as Jean had deposed. Jean himself, recalled to testify, was not asked about his contradiction of his brother's account, but only about the time when Anna

---

Santa Fe, except that part north of the Colorado; in the diocese of Vincennes, Indiana; in the city of St. Louis; in the villages of St. Genevieve, St. Ferdinand, and St. Charles, Missouri, and in Kaskaskia, Cahokia, French Village, and Prairie du Rocher, Illinois, Pietro Gasparri, *De matrimonio* (Paris, 1891), "Allegatum VI," II, 518–519. The archdiocese of New York, beyond dispute, was outside the areas where Trent applied.

first spoke of divorcing Boni after the marriage; Jean replied that she had never said to him, "I will divorce your brother," but only that she "did not wish to deprive herself of the advantages of Protestantism, which gave her, in particular, the power to divorce." The Duke de Luynes was little more helpful. No more than a year after the marriage at the most, Anna said to him that it was "natural and legitimate to use divorce as was currently done in America." But he heard Anna herself threaten to obtain a divorce only in August of 1899, five years after the wedding: a boating accident put Boni and the Duke on an English yacht; Anna suspected that the accident covered a prearranged rendezvous for Castellane with a girl; and she spoke angrily of divorcing him in America. This information, at best hearsay, since Luynes was on the English boat, contributed no new light on Anna's mind when she had married. Mother, brother, friend, all showing some consciousness of an obligation to the truth, strained to help Boni, but none of them added an iota of seriously helpful evidence. Their testimony, however, was worth more to Pacelli than its face value. It was stuffing, feeble and flimsy but pliable, which he could push and pat and point to as evidence which had not been considered by the first turn.[37]

Far from being educated in ideas opposed to the acceptability of divorce, Anna came, so Pacelli now maintained, from a divorce-prone family. In the new *summarium*, he introduced this matter under a headnote proclaiming what he sought to establish: "Proof that the Gould family has always lived with divorces and that one of them, Howard Gould, Anna's brother, married Helen Pearsall, a divorced woman." A document from the Supreme Court of New York showed that one Helen K. Gould had divorced one Francis J. Gould on August 23, 1909. A marriage certificate dated June 13, 1912, showed that one Ralph H. Thomas had married Helen K. Gould. Another document from New York showed that Katherine G. Gould had obtained a decree of separation from Howard Gould on June 25, 1909.[38] The exact relation of these records to the family of Anna Gould remained to be explored by Pacelli's adversary.

The main thrust of the new brief was argumentative, its tone was rhetorical, and its colors vivid. Francesco Parrillo, the Defender of the Bond, had been "subtle"; the first court had "too lightly accepted his opinion." When the Defender, with his usual tenaciousness and brusqueness, tore apart Pacelli's new evidence, he became a man of "savage skill," whom the first court had followed by "an evil destiny." As for Anna, she was guilty of "the most foul falsehood." She had been "most false" in denying that she had spoken of her intention of divorcing at will before the marriage; and her lie was demonstrated by the statements of Jean de Castellane, Giovanni Del Drago, and Kitty Cameron. She had lied again when she had said she was "very young" at the time of her wedding; she was in fact twenty-one. She testified she had been educated in ideas opposed to divorce; her claim was belied by "the authentic documents in the record," the Gould Family Divorces, "a wonderful example of education of a family with ideas completely opposed to divorce!!!" The triple exclamation points served to emphasize the preposterousness of Anna's position before the records Pacelli had produced.[39]

What Pacelli described as Anna's "moral figure" was itself subjected to assault. She had led "a scandalous life" with the Prince de Sagan before she married him. She had then led the Prince "to apostasize" from the Catholic religion. She now opposed Boni in the present suit out of "implacable hatred." The first charge was proved by a quotation from the brief of Castellane's own lawyer in the Paris custody case, which referred to Anna's "incorrect behavior" before her second marriage. The second was substantiated by the simple evidence that Anna and the Prince had married civilly. The third appeared to counsel to be self-evident. All Anna's character was classically summed up in the words of the Sixth Satire of Juvenal: "Nothing more intolerable than a rich woman." [40]

In contrast, Castellane had lost the civil divorce case in Paris because of the enemies of the Church. As a member of the Chamber of Deputies he had voted in 1905 against the law separating Church and State in France; he had forcefully waged battle in 1906 against the President of France's Italian visit which had so provoked the Vatican by the President's slight to the Pope. Because of the ambiguity of Latin, which has no definite article, Pacelli's description of his client as *unus* who had done these things could even have been read as "the one" who had led the fight. Catapulted in this fashion into a position of political prominence he had never enjoyed, Castellane was portrayed as the object of very dark machinations.

He had been hated by "the nefarious Masonic sect." Anna had achieved her civil victory through "the robust aid of Protestants."[41]

This ringing contrast of his client's virtue with his adversary's depravity was further distinguished by a typographical style of which the three exclamation marks after the sarcasm on the Goulds is a small sample. The dramatic *unus* was italicized in the statement on Boni, as was the dramatic "scandalous" applied to Anna and the Prince de Sagan; so was the entire quotation from Juvenal. Key parts of Del Drago's testimony were reproduced in large capitals — for example, "She did it immediately BEFORE the marriage." Kitty Cameron's statement appeared as "I am CERTAIN that BEFORE the wedding, before ME and before SEVERAL other persons, Miss Gould *said* that she *would get a divorce*, if she was not happy."

Pacelli had produced a brief which must have been a pleasure for his client to read or have translated to him. Its version of the situation corresponded remarkably with Castellane's own view of his own nobility and his opponents' malignity. The advocate had also produced a new *summarium*, charged for by the page: fourteen pages were a reprinting of Lega's opinion; one page was taken up by a letter of the Paris archdiocese reporting its summonses of witnesses in this and another, unrelated case; six pages consisted in the additional testimony of mother, brother, and friend; and three and one half pages were composed of the documents from the Supreme Court of New York.

Parrillo treated this effort of the Dean of Consistorial Advocates with the attention it seemed to deserve. He asked how Del Drago could be believed when he testified that everyone in George Gould's house must have heard the scene on the morning of the wedding, and yet no one had heard it, he "tells such great absurdities." If Anna had lied about her age, why didn't Pacelli show what her true age was? "A certificate speaks, my advocate." The "Gould Family Divorces" were not merely a matter of overstatement in the headnote, but "what was in the headnote does not appear in the black type below." Pacelli had produced the divorce record of one man, Francis J. Gould, not apparently related to Anna, the remarriage of that man's wife, Helen, to a stranger, Ralph Thomas, and a judgment of separation from a Howard Gould, who might or might not be Anna's brother, but who was scarcely shown to believe in divorce. Even "the Helen Pearsall" mentioned in Pacelli's headnote was not mentioned in the records which followed.* Pithily Parrillo made apparent his estimation of the kind of legal services Pacelli had rendered.[42]

The new rotal turn was composed of the former Austrian court chaplain, Antonius Perathoner, the more recent Italian appointee, Giuseppe Alberti, and, as senior member and judge-reporter, the former Vicar-General of Modigliana, Federico Cattani. Cattani, who in 1924 appeared in the *Folchi* case as Secretary of the Signature, and who eventually became a cardinal in 1935 at the age of seventy-nine, was at this time, in 1913, aged fifty-six and barely launched on his higher ecclesiastical career. His opinion, delivered March 1, 1913, was in marked contrast to Dean Lega's.[43]

As to the reason for Anna's divorce, Cattani repeated the testimony of Jean de Montebello that "the cause of the divorce was especially the possibility of making a new life for herself. Officially, Anna Gould found a pretext in some frivolous acts of her husband." That the divorce was for adultery was not mentioned, and the court quoted Countess de Montebello's account of Anna's solitary bridge game to show "with what great levity Anna Gould deserted the marital home and how little she made of the duties of a wife and mother." She was seen as now defending her marriage not "from love of the truth" but from "implacable hatred for her husband" — the phrase of a witness quoted with approval by the court. Anna was also guilty of five falsehoods. She had lied about her age at marriage, about being educated in ideas opposed to divorce, in saying that the Marquise de Castellane had chosen her for her son, in denying that she had spoken before the marriage of her intention

---

* Pacelli could have shown that Anna Gould's brother Frank had in fact divorced his wife, Helen Kelly, in 1909, after eight years of marriage; later, in 1918, he married an Edith Kelly (Hoyt, *The Goulds*, pp. 256, 283). Somehow, on the track of these public facts, Pacelli lost the thread of relationships and turned up the unrelated Helen Pearsall and Ralph Thomas. The marital life of two other Gould brothers was rather on the "European" style of a Castellane than on the "American" plan of believers in divorce. Howard Gould was legally separated from Katherine but was never divorced from her (*ibid.*, p. 257). George in 1913 took another actress as a mistress and had two illegitimate children by her (*ibid.*, pp. 268, 279). Brother Edwin Gould married only once and had a stable marriage (*ibid.*, pp. 301–302). Sister Helen Gould was still unmarried in 1912, and on January 22, 1913, aged forty-four, married happily (*ibid.*, p. 262). To draw from the lives of the five brothers and sisters a pattern of divorce required imagination.

to get a divorce, and in denying that she had brought up this intention after the marriage before her first quarrel with Boni. To arrive at these conclusions the court had before it only one piece of evidence which, at the time, was undisputed. Roused by Parrillo's gibe as to the lack of documentary evidence of Anna's age, Pacelli had obtained from Castellane a deed of sale executed by Anna in 1896, and had introduced it before the court at the last moment, arguing that it proved that Anna was over twenty-one since she was able to transfer property; Parrillo had had no opportunity to refute this contention, which was now given credit by Cattani. Anna's education in divorce was established by citing as "uncontested documents" the court records Pacelli had produced. The Marquise's indifference to the wedding was shown by the testimony of the Marquise herself, whom Cattani generously characterized as "a most pious woman." The premarital statements attributed to Anna were classed as authentic because of the words of Del Drago, Jean, and Castellane's libel; the discrepancies between these authorities were said merely to touch accessory circumstances. "Indeed," Cattani quoted Thomas Aquinas explaining discrepancies in the four Gospels, "some discord in such things makes the testimony more credible"; and, as he quoted Benedict XIV on the rules of evidence for use in proceedings to canonize a saint, "Agreement in all matters, both substantial and accidental, merely fails to arouse belief and diminishes the credibility of the witnesses." Castellane's witnesses, conflicting on details, were found to corroborate each other in substance. As to Anna's postmarital statements, the testimony of Boni's pious mother was again preferred to Anna's.

The final point of Lega's opinion was still unscathed: coitus and cohabitation had cured the defect of consent. But the principle of *Ad id* was no more acceptable to Cattani's court than it had been to the advocates and auditors of the seventeenth century: it imposed a rigidity of rule where the Curia wanted flexibility of policy. In legal language, subsequent consent to a null marriage was easily shown to be improbable. Anna had never realized that the marriage was null and, hence, could not have willed to cure the defect; as long as she thought the marriage valid, she was not in a position to consent. Moreover, given her views on divorce, there was no evidence that she would have willed to cure the defect if by some chance she had become aware of it while she lived with Castellane. Lega's commonsense contention that eight years of married life manifested consent to marriage melted in the legal air.*

With Anna in effect tried and found guilty of perjury and Castellane's main witnesses rehabilitated, it was evident what the rotal judgment would be. Pacelli's presentation of evidence, his analysis of the facts, his argumentation appeared to have been decisive. The opinion given by the Dean of the Rota in 1911 was subverted, the verdict of 1911 was overturned, the marriage was held invalid. The Dean of the College of Consistorial Advocates had scored an extraordinary victory, whose only palpable deficiency, perhaps, was that it was but the first of the two judgments required by law.

ERRONEOUS BELIEFS AND INVALIDATING INTENTS

Two rotal judgments, given within two years of each other, were in direct opposition to each other. Granted that what testi-

* Cattani's point on ratification was later made by the Rota in invalidating the marriage of another American Protestant heiress, Consuela Vanderbilt, to Charles Spencer, Duke of Marlborough. Coercion by her mother having been established, the Rota observed that it "was improbable that Consuela was endowed with a knowledge of the impediments invalidating marriage." Although the marriage lasted ten years before the couple definitively separated, twenty years before they were civilly divorced, and thirty years before the nullity action was brought, it was presumed that Consuela could never have given free and knowledgeable consent. Southwark, *Of Nullity of Marriage, August 7, 1926, Acta apostolicae sedis*, XVIII, 505. The storm of criticism which the Vanderbilt annulment evoked was partly directed to the Rota responding to the presumed influence of the principals (the Duchess sought the annulment; the Duke also wanted it); partly to a Roman court annulling a marriage contracted by two Protestants before a bishop of the Protestant Episcopal Church; and partly to the invalidation of a marriage which had lasted so long and in which two children had been born (see, e.g., *New York Times*, November 29, 1926, p. 2; *Time*, December 6, 1926, p. 31). American Episcopalians were particularly strong in their criticism; William Manning, Episcopal Bishop of New York, described the Rota's decision as an "amazing and incredible" attack upon the "sacredness and permanence of marriage," *New York Times*, November 15, 1926, p. 6.

Seven months after the Vanderbilt decision the annulment of another Anglican marriage caused a similar protest and depended on the same principle as to delayed consent. Guglielmo Marconi, the inventor, married Beatrice O'Brien in 1905, separated from her in 1918, and was civilly divorced in 1924. Marconi, baptized as a Catholic, had been brought up as an Anglican; Beatrice was an Anglican. In her words, "We were both convinced of the possibility of divorce." A rotal turn composed of Grazioli, Parrillo, and Solieri held the marriage null, *Westminster, Of Nullity of Marriage, April 11, 1927, Acta apostolicae sedis*, XIX, 227. Even Catholics, Grazioli observed, "almost always" did not know a marriage was null for such a reason; *a fortiori* persons educated as heretics could not suspect the nullity and so could not give valid consent during the course of the apparent marriage (*ibid.*, pp. 225–226).

mony was believed was decisive; granted that the second judgment read as though Anna Gould herself had been on trial; granted that, on any theory, the second panel's strenuous rejection of all the first panel had found was startling — still a vital difference lay in the apprehension of the law by the two panels. Apart from the change in the appraisal of the credibility of the witnesses, apart from the shifting fortunes of litigation, the law itself was in flux; and the Cattani court viewed it differently from the Lega court. At the heart of the conflict between the opinions, if one plumbed the depth of the conflict, were questions of policy broader than the individual fate of Boni de Castellane. Would intention alone be held to invalidate a marriage in the courts of the Church? This question, ultimately answered affirmatively in the 1917 Code and the *Folchi* case, became especially grave when joined to a second: Would the marriages of most of the world be treated as null for an intention against indissolubility? Interrelated, the two questions were tied to general theological theory on the intentionality necessary to confer any sacrament of the Church. *Castellane-Gould* was fully comprehensible only in a wider context of policy conflict and theological speculation reaching back to ancient roots and established paradigms.

The Beliefs of Unbelievers

Almost all of the non-Christian world, and a substantial part of the Christian world, had never viewed marriage as an indissoluble union. As early as the twelfth century it was perceived that unbelievers' beliefs might affect the character of their marriages before the Church. In 1130 the English canonist Robert Pullen, later a cardinal of the Curia, observed that "a marriage cannot be confirmed if it is undertaken outside the Church, for both pagans and Jews dissolve marriages which have been contracted." [44] Pullen's idea, adopted by Gratian, appeared in the basic lawbook of the Church. Marriage, Gratian declared, "is not confirmed among unbelievers, because their marriage is not firm and indissoluble: if they give a libel of repudiation, it is lawful for them to withdraw from each other by the law of the forum, not by the law of the City [of God] which they do not follow." [45] These statements, supporting the dissolubility of the marriages of two unbelievers when one became a convert, did not seem restricted to the case of conversion. If indissolubility was one of the three basic goods of marriage according to Saint Augustine's formula, and if an intention against any one of these goods nullified a marriage, a question necessarily existed as to the validity, by Catholic criteria, of all unions of unbelievers.

With this question still undecided in 1202, Innocent III issued a decision which, as the decretal *Gaudemus*, X.4.19.8, became the fundamental law on the subject. Speaking of Palestinians, either Mohammedans or Jews, who were reported to be polygamists, the Pope taught that on conversion they must be regarded as already validly married to a single wife. He did not specify which of several wives was to be considered the lawful spouse, but later commentators supposed that he meant the first woman in the series, even if she had been divorced before the conversion and had remarried someone else: the convert must ask her back as his lawful wife. *Gaudemus* and its interpreters did not explain how, in a society where polygamy and divorce went hand-in-hand, a man could intend to give individual fidelity to one woman or to enter an indissoluble union with her representing the monogamous union of Christ with the Church. *Gaudemus* did not deal with intention against fidelity or indissolubility at all. But noting that the Apostle Paul had treated the marriages of unbelievers as valid, Innocent III reached the decision not to invalidate, on a wholesale scale, the marriages of Mohammedans or Jews in Palestine. The civic good sense, the polity of this position was not mentioned at all; but it is difficult to believe that the Pope's choice was compelled by a text from Scripture. The fate of the Kingdom of Jerusalem, a strip of Palestinian coast precariously held by the Crusaders, was of deep concern to Innocent III. Legislating for this state with its religiously mixed population, would it not have been almost madness to have declared all non-Christian unions nullities? If the choice had to be between saying all were indissoluble and all were null, was not indissolubility the wiser policy? *Gaudemus*, at all events, went unchallenged.[46] The Pope's broad and vigorous affirmations did not invite attack on the ground that it was impossible or improbable that Mohammedans or Jews intended to enter indissoluble unions.

Not until the burst of missionary activity in the sixteenth century did the question of intent against indissolubility receive renewed attention. From Macao to Mexico, from Lima to Tokyo, a chief obstacle to missionary endeavor consisted in the marriages of prospective converts who, on becoming Christian, had to be told by a missionary to return to a divorced or abandoned first spouse. Usually already remarried, a pagan inquirer would turn from a religion which required him to relinquish an existing union and reinstate a spouse he had put aside. If the invalidity of a pagan's first marriage could be recognized by the Church, a powerful deterrent to conversion would be removed.[47] Gabriel Vasquez, a Spanish Jesuit of some theological standing, pronounced on the question in 1594 on the basis of facts reported by Jesuit missionaries in Japan. Some Japanese marriages were entered with the intent "to test the character" of the chosen wife; she would be retained only if she proved satisfactory. These marriages, Vasquez said, were null, for there was "an express intention against perpetuity." Other marriages were entered with no such express intent, but were formed in the context of Japanese custom, whereby the man was free to dissolve the match and where no disgrace would attach to the woman if she were dismissed. Laying great weight on the ease of divorce and the absence of stigma attached to it, Vasquez concluded that these marriages were null, too. "When Japanese contract in this manner of their country, it is as if they expressed a condition" — a condition that the marriages could be dissolved on the usual terms, so that they excluded the indissolubility essential to a valid marriage. Three Jesuit professors at the Roman College reached the same conclusion as to Chinese marriages in 1614. Law of the land in favor of divorce, rather than custom, formed the basis of their judgment. Marriages made in the Kingdom of China incorporated Chinese law; so doing they carried into their structure an invalidating condition against indissolubility: the marriages "made according to the laws of the Kingdom are null, because it is granted by the laws that marriages may be dissolved; and this is against the substance of marriage." [48]

The analysis applied to Japan and China was generally endorsed by the leading Jesuit theologian on marriage, Tomás Sanchez, whose exposition of intention against the goods of marriage was to become classic. Where the intention was against indissolubility, his discussion was not muddied by the requirements of Marian theology or the need to preserve the validity of virginal marriages.[49] Indissolubility was viewed not only as a good of marriage, but as "the essential" good. No distinction could be made between rejecting indissolubility "in principle" and rejecting it "in execution." To marry at all one must intend "at least implicitly" an indissoluble marriage. If one had an intention to the contrary, though it was "retained in one's heart," one did not intend to marry; and one who intended to enter "a marriage which is dissoluble and only for a time truly does not intend marriage." [50] Intention was determinative and intention was established by custom and religion. "If an unbeliever contracts with the intention of giving a libel of divorce as often as it is lawful to him according to his rite, the marriage is null although he does not reduce the intention to any contract." [51] In the broadest of terms a principle was formulated which could bring into doubt the marriages of most of the world.

The Copts' Case

Sanchez, Vasquez, the Roman College — these were powerful authorities; and behind the fine theories of the theologians stood the practical exigencies of the missionaries and the strength of the Jesuit order itself. *Gaudemus*, it seemed, would have to go. The policy of the Curia would have to change. Wholesale, the unions of infidels would have to be held invalid. Nothing of the kind happened. The curial committee charged with supervision of the missionaries, the Congregation for the Propagation of the Faith, met in 1634 and held that marriages in Japan were presumptively valid. The Holy Office in 1669 refused to go further: it was "not expedient to define the matter." [52] *Gaudemus* remained the law. Curial conservatism of mind and temperament — an unwillingness to abandon decretal law four hundred years old; disinclination to believe that foreign mores could be so different from one's own; intuitive shrinking from the radical conclusion that most of the world were not married; reluctance to face the radical consequences of taking seriously the teaching on intent against indissolubility, lest these consequences have repercussions at home as well as abroad — triumphed over need and logic.

The state of mind which prevailed may be observed in a man who was both a Jesuit theologian and a member of Urban VIII's Curia, both a confidant of the missionaries and a confidant of the Pope, Juan de Lugo, who chose to discuss the issues in terms of Ethiopians — a case so exotic as almost to have the freedom from special pressures enjoyed in a hypothetical proposed by a teacher in the classroom. Coptic Christians had married in Ethiopia with the belief that their marriages could, for given causes, be terminated by divorce. If they became Catholics, were they bound by their old Coptic marriages? Lugo gave it as his judgment that "if they contracted because they knew divorce was lawful and otherwise would not have contracted, they have implicitly willed not to oblige themselves in perpetuity": the marriages were null. The result turned on what is known in American law as "but for" causation — "otherwise they would not have contracted." * Put in other terms, the Ethiopians' marriages were valid if "they did not limit their intention at the time of the contract to this estimation, but had the general will of contracting a valid marriage." Their will to act validly carried with it "implicitly" the will to marry indissolubly, "inasmuch as indissolubility is of the essence of true marriage." Custom, law, and rite permitting divorce were all made subordinate to the doctrine that marriage was indissoluble, and so everyone must want to marry indissolubly if they wanted to marry at all.[53]

Central in this analysis was the term "implicitly." Whenever judges are called on to enforce a contract, they have to decide what the parties "really" meant; and often, for various reasons of social policy, they will wish to limit or to enlarge the actual language before them. In those circumstances to find "implicit" in the agreement a qualification to which the parties themselves never adverted is standard judicial technique. "You can," in Holmes's classic epigram, "always imply a condition in a contract." [54] This kind of operation is not cynical make-believe, but a recognized method of importing social considerations into the enforcement of contracts; the condi-

---

* A question of this kind led not to a historical inquiry into what actually happened, but to a hypothetical reconstruction of what might have happened in conditions contrary to fact. In investigating such a subject as marriage it had to be a matter of conjecture whether any given individual would have intended to enter the matrimonial contract if he had conceived its consequences differently. Inevitably, in deciding what factors to weigh as important in reconstructing the mind of the person marrying, general policy on the validity of marriage would affect the choice of factors and their weighing. For a comparable situation in the use of "but for" causation in American tort law, see Robert H. Cole, "Windfall and Probability: A Study of 'Cause' in Negligence Law," *California Law Review* (1964), LII, 770–772.

tions implied will reflect what a judge considers fair, equitable, proper, reasonable in his society. Policy overrides inarticulate or ineffective individual intent. Lugo carried out this sort of exercise in supposing that an implicit will to marry indissolubly existed in the minds of the Copts. The difficulty of this procedure was not its use of fiction, but its importation into the realm of interior intention of a technique appropriate to the external legal order.

Speaking of what was "implicit," Lugo insisted that the intent of which he spoke was "an actual will," not a hypothetical will. But it was not "an actual will" to marry indissolubly. It was "an actual will to contract a marriage valid in every way." [55] The inference that this actual will included a will to marry indissolubly was made by the theologian. The intent to marry indissolubly was necessary for validity. If the marriage was invalid, it was, objectively viewed, an occasion of sin; such a result was neither to be encouraged nor presumed. Anyone wanting to marry wanted to marry validly: "No one is so insane as not to will to make valid an act which in truth he wills to do." [56] The same preference for validity, stability, and universal accessibility of marriage which led to the upholding of such marriages as Ana Ponce de León's operated here to feed another presumption. Not only were those marrying presumptively sane, their sanity included a knowledge of the natural structure of marriage.

Benevolent in purpose, this procedure assumed that heretics, Jews, and pagans desired to be married validly according to the criteria of the Catholic Church. It identified the Catholic structure of marriage with a natural structure of marriage projected as prevailing throughout the world. In the face of contrary laws, customs, rites, and beliefs, the curial theologians supposed that the Catholic pattern was the norm. In effect, they made a policy decision to attribute a Catholic intent to the rest of the world in order not to have to hold invalid the marriages of most of the world.*

* Benevolent use of "implicit intention" was familiar to the theologians from moral casuistry. For example, the Augustinian tradition on marital intercourse required that a spouse seeking intercourse have an intent to procreate. This teaching put a great many married persons in sin. Sanchez argued that married persons, not intending an evil end, who had entered marriage for the Augustinian goods of marriage and who did not actually seek a present evil end, did no sin if they intended "only to copulate as spouses." The reason was that they intended offspring "not formally, but virtually" (*De sancto matrimonii sacramento*, 9.8.31). Attribution to the married of such intention, especially in intercourse in pregnancy

Intending What the Church Intends

Marriage for Christians was a sacrament; whenever a Christian marriage was formed, not only marital intent was necessary; the ministers of the sacrament — that is, the spouses themselves — had to have the intention required to confer a sacrament.[57] Reciprocally, therefore, theory on marital intent and theory on sacramental intent influenced each other. The post-medieval starting point was Canon XI of "The Canons on the Sacraments in General," enacted by the Council of Trent in 1547: "If anyone says that in ministers, when they effect and confer the sacraments, there is not required an intention at least of doing what the Church does, let him be anathema."[58] One did not confer a sacrament unless one intended to. But what sort of intention was required? What was "intending to do what the Church does?" Answer was left to policy or, better, to the interaction of theological speculation and curial decisionmaking. Summing up the state of the discussion one century after the Tridentine decree, Lugo classed as "externalists" those theologians who said that to intend to do what the Church does was to intend to perform seriously the given ceremonial acts appropriate to the sacrament being conferred, that as long as one's intent was not merely joking or fraudulent, intent to perform the acts sufficed. The opinion of the externalists was close to that condemned by Trent. On the other hand, those theologians asked too much who

---

or other known sterility, was a way of giving up the Augustinian insistence on express procreative purpose. A general will to marry as a Christian was made to serve for the old Augustinian specific purpose, and the general will was made specific and actual by calling it "virtual."

To take an illustration from another field, Lugo agreed with several sixteenth-century predecessors that the usury rule, prohibiting absolutely the seeking of profit on a loan, did not condemn a man lending at a moderate profit to a businessman, because the transaction could be justified if three separate contracts were made: one the lawful contract of partnership where capital and profit ran the risk of the business; the next a contract reducing the profit in exchange for a guaranteed return of capital; and the third a further reduction of profit in exchange for a guaranteed amount of profit. The three contracts should be made separately, "but in fact it suffices if these contracts are understood to be made virtually and implicitly, as in fact they are commonly understood as often as one in good faith gives money to a merchant to do business with at a fixed moderate rate, intending to give it in that way which the doctors say can be done and the prudent and godfearing do." (Lugo, *De justitia et jure, Opera Omnia*, vol. II, 30.4.47.) To keep the lender from being a sinner, Lugo attributed to him the correct intentions—basing his attribution in this case on the actual practice of the community in which the lender lived.

said that the required intent was the intent to produce sanctifying grace. Grace, the gift of God, was the effect of the sacrament; the minister of the sacrament need only intend to produce the cause of grace. The intention required in him was "to speak and act not in his own name but in the name of Christ and as the minister of Christ." If he did this, he intended "to do what the Church does"; he met the requirements of Trent; the sacrament he bestowed was valid. The necessary intention could be expressed simply, in words such as these: "I here and now will that this my act not be reputed as my act but be reputed by everyone as the action of Christ." [59] An intention of this kind was necessary for validity in conferring any of the seven sacraments; its existence became an issue in disputes involving the sacraments of baptism and holy orders.

Taken literally, Lugo's description and formulas substantially restricted the instances where a sacramental intention might have been found — just as, taken literally, the requirement of actually intending to marry indissolubly seriously restricted the instances of valid marriage. Well-instructed Christians might be supposed to have the intent to act "in the name of Christ and as the minister of Christ." Established theological opinion, however, held that the sacrament of baptism could be conferred by anyone — Catholic, heretic, or infidel.[60] If complete nonbelievers in Christianity could be said to intend to act in the name of Christ and to intend their action to be regarded as the action of Christ, Lugo's descriptions and formulas could not be meant literally. Rather, he had to find the requisite intent to exist by invoking what was "implicit." Implicit intent to act as the minister of Christ "could occur," he said, "in many ways." It existed "even in one not thinking of the universal Church, if he wishes to do what this particular church does or what such and such a parish priest does or what is done by some among whom he has heard that these signs are applied as religious ceremonies." The right intention could be found "implicit" in each of these instances because "in all these ways one has apprehended that something is hidden under those signs which, whatever it may be, he confusedly intends." [61] The intention to do what the Church does was thus reduced, if not to the Pickwickian dimensions accorded it by the externalists, at least to a will which required only the vaguest of apprehensions to set in motion. The elasticity of "implicit" gave the theologians and the Curia a wide latitude in determining when they would or would not uphold a sacrament. Everything in the end depended on what state of mind the Curia was willing to attribute to the person whose intention was at issue.

In general, the invocation of implicit intent tended to maximize the number of valid sacramental actions, just as implicit intent when applied to indissolubility tended to maximize the number of valid marriages. But because such latitude existed in finding what was implicit, a policy decision could be made by the Curia, in a given situation, to determine that the requirements had not been met. That sacramental intent was a function of policy was dramatically illustrated in the 1890's in the controversy over the validity of Anglican orders. The High Church Anglicans, who wanted Roman acknowledgment of the validity of ordinations in the Church of England, assumed that their bishops had had, at a minimum, the intention of conferring valid orders as instituted by Christ; in Lugo's parlance they had intended to do what the Church does, and, measured by this criterion, their intention should not be treated as defective. But Pietro Gasparri pointed out that if the bishops' beliefs — which ran counter to the Catholic idea that priesthood meant capacity to offer sacrifice — had passed from abstract speculation to positive intent, then the bishops had intended to consecrate non-sacrificing priests, and their general intent to do what the Church does had been nullified by this contrary specific intention; Anglican orders, by Catholic criteria, were null.[62] The Curia had to decide which intent was to be attributed to the bishops.

High Church Anglicans and French Catholic sympathizers pressed for recognition of the orders. Cardinal Herbert Vaughan, Archbishop of Westminster, thought concessions to Anglicans would be disastrous to the Catholic position in England and conducted a vigorous campaign against recognition. When Leo XIII set up a commission to decide the question, Gasparri, then a canonist at Paris, was assigned responsibility for the issue of intention. In *Apostolicae curae*, issued in 1896, the Pope found the orders null for want of both the requisite form and intent. The formulas of ordination, he declared, were defective in their statement of the sacerdotal function of sacrifice. From the use of the formulas, an intent not to do what the Church does was inferred. The rite conferring the sacrament was used by the Pope not only as an index of speculative belief but as decisive evidence of the actual intent of those purporting to confer it. The benign supposition of an implicit but predominating intent to do what the Church does was supplanted by a hostile supposition of an intent contrary to what the Church does. The choice of evidence, the forming of the supposition, appeared to reflect an option taken, a policy judgment that Anglican orders should not be recognized.[63]

Apostolicae curae might appear to be remote from the problems of Boni de Castellane and Anna Gould, but a close connection existed in the paths of curial thought. At each stage of theological development the mode of thinking about sacramental intention in general had influenced the way of thinking about marriage, and vice versa. At the beginning of the seventeenth century, Sanchez had applied to marriage the kind of reasoning used to uphold the validity of sacraments generally.* Did Christians who did not believe that marriage was a sacrament enter a valid sacramental marriage? he asked; and he answered that the marriage was valid if these Christians "intend to do what the faithful do through marriage." [64] This was the same sort of appeal to implicit intent to do what the Church did which Lugo used as a general theory of sacramental intention. It credited persons, contrary to their own conscious beliefs, with intent to do what was necessary for validity. Conversely, in the nineteenth-century controversy over Anglican orders, reasoning and illustration were taken from the theological analysis of the intent required for matrimony. If a man preached against indissolubility and then married, Gasparri argued, an intent against indissolubility in his own marriage might be attributed to him.[65] The point was made against the Anglican bishops — if they had preached against sacerdotal sacrifice, they could not have intended to consecrate sacrificing priests. But if the analogy had force, it was because Gasparri grasped the relation which usually exists between expressed belief and internal intent. When Anglican orders were in fact in-

* Non-Christians, whose marriages were not regarded as sacraments (Sanchez, *De sancto matrimonii sacramento*, 2.8.1), were supposed only to have the intent of marrying indissolubly. Christians, for whom the contract of marriage was said to be inseparable from the sacrament of marriage (*ibid.*, 2.10.6), were both supposed to intend "to do what the Church does" and to intend to marry indissolubly. Formally, these intentions were distinct. They were, in practice, merged. Indissolubility being identified, in Augustine's phrase, as "the good of the sacrament," intent to marry indissolubly seemed to carry with it the necessary intent to confer the sacrament; in marriage cases, argument focused only on the intent to marry indissolubly.

validated for want of intent as well as for want of form, and the evidence of intent consisted in the formulas used and the doctrines taught by the ministers of the sacrament, a parallel question could be put: Was not an express belief in divorce or reference to laws and customs permitting divorce good evidence of an intent not to enter an indissoluble union? If the question was not pressed, it was because the answer required by policy was not as evident.[66]

The Transylvanian Precedent

Did any precedent exist of an actual annulment for exclusion of indissolubility? The leading case was *Transylvania, 1754*, decided by Benedict XIV as Pope and reported by Benedict XIV himself. Two Calvinists had married according to the Calvinist rite in use in Transylvania; the wife, now a Catholic convert, sought to invalidate the marriage. In the marriage ritual an oath was taken by the bridegroom, "I shall not desert her in any distress, so long as she remains in her decency and purity." For Benedict XIV the nub of the matter was: Did the oath form an integrated part of the marriage contract? He found that "one and the same act was formed by the foregoing responses [the exchange of marital consent] and the subsequent oath." The oath was "a constitutive part of the contract," and so the contract was patently dissoluble if the bride committed adultery. By canonical criteria, the marriage was null because of the express condition against indissolubility. The Pope distinguished by these facts a 1680 ruling of the Holy Office on a case from Bosnia where an intention against indissolubility, "not reduced to an agreement," failed to nullify. The Transylvania case was, rather, analogous to *West Lisbon, July 8, 1724*, which the Pope had handled as a junior member of the Curia — Senator Barberini's case where the marriage had been invalidated because of the contractual undertaking to relinquish all right to intercourse. Unless intent was expressed in a contract, the courts did not act. If the parties merely believed that marriage was dissoluble, "there is still place for the presumption that they willed to enter marriage as instituted by Christ." [67]

Benedict XIV's lawyerlike exposition of the leading precedent meant that it could not serve as the basis for across-the-board invalidations of the marriages of schismatics, heretics, Jews, and pagans who believed in divorce. Recognizing the force of ritual, it was carefully restricted to ritual publicly connected with the ceremony of consent; it refrained from looking broadly at ways in which consent could be affected by customs of divorce. It solidified curial conservatism, the policy against undoing the marriages of those outside the fold. Three pontificates later, the Archbishop of Prague wrote Pius VI about the marriage of a Catholic girl deserted by a non-Catholic husband in Belorussia; some of the Archbishop's advisers deemed the marriage invalid because of the husband's belief that marriage was dissoluble. This, the Pope replied, could not be admitted. The "most powerful" reason for upholding such marriages existed: "Unless marriages of this kind by non-Catholics were true marriages, the whole Church would have erred for centuries — the Church which received as true husbands and wives non-Catholic spouses returning to the fold, even though, imbued with error about marriage, they had contracted marriage within their own sect." Whatever their beliefs, they had "the primary intention of contracting according to the divine law confirmed by Christ." [68] Policy had hardened to the point where intent to marry indissolubly appeared to be a presumption required by the infallibility of the Church.*

Native Custom in the Sandwich Islands, Japan, and North America

Anthropology, done by missionaries, confronted this settled rule of the Roman Curia with new challenges in the second half of the nineteenth century. The Inquisition, highest of curial congregations, was called on to reassess the traditional policy. In a series of decisions beginning in the pontificate of Pius IX, the prudence of the past was reaffirmed; but there was one startling break from precedent. The conflict reflected in these rulings formed the proximate background of the issues the Rota faced in *Castellane-Gould.*

* The distinction between "primary" intent and subordinate intent recalled the distinction used in scholastic discussions of the purposes of sexual intercourse in marriage. After theologians had recognized that nonprocreative purposes in marital intercourse were legitimate, the full consequences of this recognition were avoided by labeling such purposes "secondary." A policy determination to treat them as less important was made in order to protect the rule against contraception, see John T. Noonan, Jr., *Contraception: A History of Its Treatment by the Catholic Theologians and Canonists* (Cambridge, Mass.: The Belknap Press of Harvard University Press, 1965), pp. 371–372.

On December 11, 1850, for the Sandwich Islands, and on March 11, 1868, for Japan, the Inquisition rejected without analysis the contention of missionaries that local law or custom of divorce created a presumption that those marrying intended to enter dissoluble unions.[69] At the very close of Pius IX's rule, with the Inquisition under the secretaryship of Cardinal Prospero Caterini, a foreshadowing of a change of policy could be observed. The occasion was offered by an eloquent letter from Vital-Justin Grandin, the missionary bishop of St. Albert, a diocese of a few thousand Catholics in the wilds of Alberta, Canada. As Grandin saw the mating customs of the Indians with whom he worked, "the barbarian unbelievers enter no marriage, they couple experimentally." A man bought a girl from her parents or kinfolk. They delivered her to him willy-nilly. If she was morose, fat, sick, the union lasted only until he found someone better. If she was lovable and serviceable she was kept, though, if in two or three years she had produced no children, she was dismissed or forced to share the man with another woman. Only at the end of seven or eight years was "perpetuity of cohabitation effected." A catechumen whom he reproached with changing his wives replied, "Do you not change your servants?" The relation seemed at most to be concubinage, though there were some Indians who lived together from youth, loved each other, and could not easily be separated from each other. If an Indian wife wanted to be baptized, was she to be refused the sacrament as one who was living in concubinage?

The Holy Office solved the specific question by prudential casuistry. The woman need not be informed that her union was invalid if in good faith she believed that she was married; the missionary, in the circumstances described, could keep silent; baptism, it was implied, need not be denied. A yes or no judgment on whether such a union was in fact invalid was avoided. But, not confining itself to answering the question asked, as it usually did, the Holy Office argumentatively reviewed the evidence. The Indians viewed their unions as concubinage: at least they recognized that there was present a natural contract. The men fed their women: so the Roman Catechism spoke of marriage, first of all, as a union for mutual aid. Indians coupled to sterile women often kept them when they took another: they had not entirely forgotten the dictate of nature to love their own flesh; as Saint Paul had written of the love of spouses, "No one ever hates his own flesh, but nourishes it and cherishes it" (Ephesians 5:29). The Indians sought offspring in these unions: as Saint Thomas Aquinas taught, offspring were the principal end of marriage. They had an exaggerated and distorted view of the subjection of women to men: Saints Peter and Paul taught that wives should obey their husbands. Missionaries were always asserting that "all the marriages of the barbarians" were null on account of error as to indissolubility. But, as the Holy Office had ruled in 1680, in the case presented from Bosnia, mental error not reduced to a contract did not annul. "It was not certainly and clearly known that among these peoples no marriage is established according to the law of nature."

To this point the answer to Grandin was an essay in defense of curial policy. Another hand, perhaps, had added a hypothetical: Suppose there were "a constant and general practice of exchanging or prostituting one's wife on the occasion of certain celebrations in honor of the false gods?" Then there would be "serious reason for supposing that these barbarians generally agreed to couple in marriage with at least a tacit condition contrary to one of its goods." In other words, "proximate or remote circumstances" — not a contractual agreement — could show that a marriage was made with an invalidating condition. The principle of looking at custom was admitted; the insistence on contractual expression was dropped. Benedict XIV and the Holy Office of 1680 were modified if not abandoned in a document which had begun by relying on their firm judicial rule. Still, the Holy Office concluded, a mere custom of divorce, as concretely described by Bishop Grandin, was not enough. The classic case of the pagan marriages treated as marriages by Saint Paul was, for the hundredth time, invoked. If marriage were really entered only experimentally there would be reason for thinking it invalidly entered, but the practice described by the Bishop of St. Albert was so tempered by considerations which made the unions last that they had to be looked at on a case-by-case basis; there could be no "decretal judgment" that all the unions of these barbarians were invalid.[70]

The policy shift half-accomplished in the letter to Alberta seemed to become a full-blown change three years later, on January 24, 1877. Now the Holy Office spoke not of the hypothetical customs of barbarians but of the actual customs of the inhabitants of the diocese of Seattle, Washington, or at least the actual customs of those in "the mountain regions" of the diocese. Methodist clergymen of the area did not believe that marriage was a sacrament or that it was indissoluble. Catholic missionaries reported that some persons married before these ministers, "for no reason save that they believe that in this way they can avoid the perpetuity of the bond which they contract." Were such marriages valid? The Congregation for the Propagation of the Faith referred the question, asked by the Bishop of Seattle, to the Inquisition, and received this response: The Holy Office had "always steadily" followed the doctrine of Benedict XIV that an invalidating condition must be reduced to an agreement. With this bow to precedent, the reply went on to innovate. Use of certain formulas in the marriage ritual, as Benedict XIV himself had admitted, might be invalidating. Even Matthew 5:31–32, or the parallel passage of Matthew 19:9, "If a man puts away his wife for any cause save fornication and marries another, he commits adultery" — even those words of the Lord if used as part of the marriage rite — were "sometimes rightly judged to contain an invalidating condition." Beyond verbal expressions, other facts could establish the existence of a qualification in the consent given to marriage. The Bishop of Seattle had represented that it was "common" among the Protestants to "rescind marriage on account of adultery or other reasons of lighter importance." The Holy Office now judged that this practice in itself did not prevent a "heretic" in the area from contracting a valid marriage. "But," the answer continued, "it can happen that there be a common and almost universal persuasion such that, by force of it, the matrimonial contract is only temporary and conditional and not contracted except under this condition." These circumstances could be considered in determining whether "explicitly or implicitly" there was a contractual condition, and they could be considered in determining "whether marriage was contracted with the wicked will of not consenting to a perpetual bond." The bishop could look at "indications, arguments and presumptions, and the morals of the region." He could "take account that [persons] contract before the Protestant minister in particular with the will that, if the marriage is dissolved according to Protestant practice, they may pass to other vows." From such facts "a definite will" to contract "only conditionally" might be apprehended.[71]

Since the twelfth century the position taken by this document of 1877 had been an option available to the Curia and always rejected at Rome. Now a custom of divorce was made a basis for finding an invalidating intent against indissolubility. The decretal language "condition" was retained, but "condition" in this interpretation seemed identical with interior will, and the document indeed spoke of "a definite will" as the determining fact. The juridical requirement of an express agreement against indissolubility was dropped. Presumption that everyone naturally sought to marry indissolubly was countered by presumption drawn from the actual practice and beliefs of the people involved. Instead of an "implicit" will to marry indissolubly being attributed to those who married, it was supposed that, even among Christians, there could be an "implicit" intent against indissolubility. Although the Bishop of Seattle was instructed to investigate each case on its own merits, the Holy Office appeared to face with equanimity the prospect of a large class of American marriages being judged to be null.*

The Old Christians of Kitzuki and the New Treatise of Gasparri

A major shift in curial policy could not succeed without response from the bishops in America and without settled commitment to the new approach in the Curia itself. By 1891 it was apparent that neither ingredient of success was present. Once again a hopeful Japanese missionary asked about marriage in Japan. This time the question was raised by the Apostolic Vicar for Southern Japan on behalf of a group deserving of special sympathy, descendants of "old Christians" on the island of Kitzuki, who had kept the faith through two centuries of persecution and abandonment. These

---

* No one apparently ever sought a ruling from Rome on the marriages of American slaves. Yet, according to Francis Kenrick, who was for a long time the only moral theologian of any note in the United States, "The majority of their contracts do not have the force of marriage, since the intention of contracting a perpetual bond is lacking to them and a condition is attached to their consent"; Francis Kenrick, *Theologia moralis* (Philadelphia, 1843), III, 333. Since the slaves surely did not regularly make written contracts of marriage, Kenrick appeared to judge by their internal intention, as evidenced by their customs and their attitudes to marriage. Kenrick, a native of Ireland, who had been educated at the College of the Propaganda and then dispatched to Bardstown, Kentucky, reflected very well the judgment of the experienced missionary in contrast to the judgment of the Curia.

Christians had not been immune to the influence of the culture encompassing them. They married with "a custom of divorce." The Apostolic Vicar believed that their marriages were frequently invalid; and, presumably, by the ruling of 1877 the custom of divorce was the decisive factor in finding invalidity.

Now ruled by Leo XIII and under a new Secretary, Cardinal Monaco LaValletta, the Inquisition returned to Innocent III, Urban VIII, Benedict XIV, and its own rulings under Pius IX. "These marriages," the Vicar Apostolic was told, "are not readily to be judged invalid on the ground that they were begun with the opinion of dissolubility or with the intention of divorce. For an erroneous opinion and intention of this kind only invalidate when reduced to an agreement, and such agreement will be evident from the words in which consent is expressed." [72] Internal intention, definite will, evidence from custom, all disappeared. The Curia reverted to the strict criterion of a contract which expressed a repudiation of indissolubility. The policy of 1877 appeared to be reversed.

"Nothing willed except known" was a maxim of scholastic psychology. Intention and consent "presuppose the act by which reason directs something to an end." [73] How could one will what one did not know? Concretely, how could one consent to an indissoluble union if one did not know that marriage was indissoluble? Commonsense experience pointed to the difference between believing a thing abstractly or speculatively and applying it in one's own case: a follower of Proudhon might believe that property is theft and yet assert that he owned his house. But the social institution of property supplied the knowledge the Proudhonist used in his own case. Where a man himself asserted that marriage was dissoluble, and his society confirmed that belief by its institutions, how could he acquire the knowledge that it was actually indissoluble? [74] The theologians in ignoring this question had been sustained by the conviction that marriage was a natural institution whose proper characteristics were known to everyone. As the answers to St. Albert and Seattle suggested, their confidence was being shaken by anthropological evidence. At the same time, the shift of focus to internal intention, which Chapter IV of this book has already traced, made it harder to give answers appropriate only for external juridical rules. Gasparri, publishing *De matrimonio* in 1891 and unaware of the new decision for Japan that very year, reflected not an almost unbroken curial tradition of seven hundred years but the confusion of a transition.

Faithful to Sanchez and to his own strongest intuition, Gasparri insisted in section 802 of his book that consent was internal, so an internal intent against indissolubility nullified. What was "truly and properly called a mental condition against the substance of marriage" included an intention "not to give and receive the conjugal right as perpetual, exclusive, and sacred." In this passage Gasparri seemed at least as broad in his ideas as the Holy Office had been in 1877; and elsewhere he quoted the ruling of 1877 as though it were still good law.[75] Nothing here suggested that he would not be receptive to all the evidence, beyond the marriage rite and contract, which would establish the true mental state — unless reference to "an explicit and positive intention" served to rule out of court inferences to the mental state which might be drawn from custom and cultural beliefs.

Elsewhere, however, in section 793, Gasparri had dealt with what he described as "a simple error of law," including the opinion he ascribed to unbelievers, schismatic Greeks, and "some perverse and ignorant Catholics," that marriage could be ended by divorce. Despite such error in the mind, consent could be validly given by any member of these ignorant, uninformed, or perverse groups: "A marriage is in itself valid where there is a simple error of law, even when the error gives cause for the contract. It is valid if the one contracting in this error wills to enter *a true marriage as instituted by God*, etc., and does not exclude, by a positive act of the will, an essential property of marriage, although he would exclude it if he thought about it." As usual in Gasparri, italicization indicated the point where emphasis was substituted for analysis. Going further than Luga by excluding "but for" causation as a test of intent, he appeared to maintain that all those affected by mere error of law meant to marry as God wanted them to marry, that is, indissolubly. Intent to exclude indissolubility because of their erroneous belief that marriage was dissoluble was "an interpretative will which might exist, but which does not exist." All this was said, although Gasparri held that matrimonial consent was "the act of the will" assenting to a "perpetual" right; that "mutual consent presupposes knowledge in the intellect"; and that "free will does not exist in one making a mistake." [76] At the end of his analysis, however, he became ambiguous: "On account of the favor for marriage, simple error is presumed so long as a condition, properly so called, is not proved; or, rather, such a contrary positive act of the will is a fact, and facts are to be proved." In this section on simple error of law, Gasparri seemed to stand in the tradition of Innocent III, Lugo, Urban VIII, and Benedict XIV, whom he quoted expressly, until the force of the final clause was considered. The last six words again opened the door to proving as a fact an internal intent not expressed in a contract. In Gasparri the tried and true policy which created a presumption against invalidating intent struggled with a new willingness to permit proof of intent; and the outcome of the struggle was by no means clear in Gasparri's mind or treatise.

In recapitulation and summary, curial policy at least as old as Innocent III, and Catholic teaching arguably as old as Saint Paul, treated the marriages of all the world as valid even though entered into by persons who believed that marriage was not indissoluble. Counter to this policy ran the teaching that indissolubility was essential to marriage, and that intent depended on intellectual apprehension. The policy had been severely tested twice: by the customs of Asia and the New World when encountered by Spanish and Portuguese missionaries in the first great missionary effort outside of Europe; and by the same customs as they struck the second wave of nineteenth-century missionaries. The policy, with only one notable lapse, had been maintained, for reasons to be more fully evaluated in Chapter VII. In Gasparri a transition was apparent, but not accomplished.

The American Scene

If the Rota had actually taken evidence on American attitudes toward divorce, *Castellane-Gould* might not have been as instructive as it is in the dilemma of the law. "Our ideas about marriage and divorce are particularly old-fashioned," Newbold Archer advises his cousin Ellen who is separated from a European count. "Our legislation favors divorce — our social customs don't." Later Archer says to Mrs. Welland, "Countess Olenska thought she would be conforming to American ideas in asking for her freedom," and Mrs. Welland replies: "That is just like the extraordinary things foreigners repeat about us. They think that we dine at two o'clock and countenance divorce! That is why it seems to me so foolish to entertain them when they come to New York. They accept our hospitality, and then they go home and repeat the same stupid stories." These fictional conversations took place in the 1870's in the most refined circle of Old New York. It may be doubted that the pace of evolution was so swift that, twenty years later, in less refined circles, American attitudes were appreciably different than those chronicled by Edith Wharton.[77]

Castellane-Gould, however, proceeded on a different assumption. Lega accepted Kitty Cameron's pronouncement that "in America, almost all the girls who marry have this intention of getting a divorce if the marriage does not make them happy." [78] At least he was willing to take it as a fact that Anna had shared this view, that she had expressed something like it to Jean de Castellane, and that it had later emerged in her conversations with her mother-in-law at Rochecotte and with the Duke de Luynes and the Countess de Montebello. Not only was Anna credited with belief in divorce as an American girl, but she had it put to her account as an Episcopalian. In his brief Pacelli had declared in so many words that Anna "was enrolled in the Episcopalian sect which admits divorce." This oversimplification of Episcopalian doctrine, which was not corrected by the Defender of the Bond, was repeated by Lega in his opinion. Curiously enough in a case where so much turned on mental state, no evidence was ever adduced as to what American Episcopalians might believe.* American and Episcopalian, Anna

---

* Anna's actual religion could be disputed. Cattani, in his opinion asserts that she was baptized an Episcopalian four or five weeks "before the wedding"; Cattani opinion, p. 174. The *New York Times*, March 3, 1895, reported that she was still a Presbyterian, and it could be argued at the very least that her Episcopalianism was not very deep. She was married to the Prince de Sagan in the French Protestant Church in London. Undeniably, she was treated as an Episcopalian for the purposes of the case.

The actual position of the Protestant Episcopal Church of the United States, as revealed by its legislation, was also qualified. In 1808 the House of Bishops and House of Deputies had jointly resolved "That it is the sense of this Church that it is inconsistent with the law of God, and the ministers of this Church, therefore, shall not unite in matrimony any person who is divorced, unless it be on account of the other person being guilty of adultery"; *Constitution and Canons for the Government of the Protestant Episcopal Church in the United States of America, Adopted in General Conventions 1789–1922*, annotated by Edward A. White (New York, 1924), p. 722. This joint resolution was not regarded as "law" in the strict sense (*ibid.*, p. 723), but in 1868 a canon was adopted by the General Convention forbidding a clergyman to marry a divorced person, except an "in-was presented as a believer in the dissolubility of marriage.[79]

For Lega this ascription of belief had no legal effect. All it meant for him was that Anna had "made a mistake of law." Quoting Benedict XIV, he declared, "What we have called the general will of entering marriage according to the institution of Christ prevails over and absorbs that private error." Quoting section 792 of Gasparri, he found "a simple error of law," which might have given rise to the contract of marriage, but which had not become a positive intent against dissolubility. Taking the Castellane witnesses at their strongest, Lega could conclude that they had not spoken "of a true and proper condition attached by Anna to the contract, but of an intention of freely and lawfully using the power of divorce which the tenets of her Protestant sect gave her." All of Pacelli's evidence, even if believed, fell harmlessly against the presumption that in marrying, "as one ordinarily marries," Anna intended to marry indissolubly.

Two years later Cattani set out a different law of the case. "It seems wrong to us," he declared, "to adapt to this case those things taken from His Eminence Cardinal Gasparri, where he explains an error of law." [80] Gasparri, section 792, on error of law, was abandoned only to be replaced by Gasparri, section 802, on invalidating intention. The impalpable difference between "belief" and "intent" permitted Cattani to make the necessary characterization of Anna's mental state. She was now described not as holding a belief in divorce, but as having "the intention of contracting something dissoluble and of reserving to herself the faculty of divorce." Analyzed in those terms, her mind at the time of marriage did not consent to marriage "as instituted by God." Her intention, "although not attached exteriorly to her consent" but only determined "mentally," was sufficient. Any will she might have had to marry according to the institution of the Lord was contradicted by her

---

nocent party in a divorce for the cause of adultery" (*ibid.*, p. 724). In 1877 this canon was amended to include not only the clergy but the parties themselves: "If the persons be joined together otherwise than as God's word doth allow, their marriage is not lawful" (*ibid.*, p. 725). Consequently, no American Episcopalian respecting the canons of the Church had the right to divorce a spouse who did not please, although Anna would have had the right to remarry after divorcing Boni for adultery.

In 1901 and again in 1904 and in 1916 the House of Bishops and the House of the Clergy attempted to prohibit remarriage even for the innocent party, but each time the amendment was defeated by the laymen in the House of Delegates (*ibid.*, pp. 725–728).

will to exclude perpetuity. "At least virtually" her will at the moment of marriage contained an invalidating intention. "Clearly she offered not a true but a simulated consent; and so the marriage was invalid." [81]

In Cattani's opinion and judgment, *New York, March 7, 1913,* curial policy of some seven hundred years' standing was decisively rejected. The speculations of Sanchez were preferred to the legal prudence of Benedict XIV. Not only on the facts but on the law the Rota's opinion of 1913 rejected the old-fashioned views of its first Dean. Ambiguity and ambivalence in Gasparri were resolved in favor of recognizing the invalidating effect of a unilateral, internal intent against indissolubility; and a kind of legal fiction — "virtual will" — was invoked to explain how the intent was known to be present at the instant of publicly expressed consent. If *New York, March 7, 1913* was the criterion, how many American marriages could stand the test?

THE THIRD TURN

The Defender's Offensive

The vicissitudes at the Vatican of such a famous marriage did not escape the attention of the press and the comments of interested observers. According to the Jesuit weekly *America,* the second decision provided an opportunity for enemies of the Church. But they "were not the only ones." There were "others, even Catholics, who in good faith feel upset over the affair." It was openly suggested that if this decision stood against the validity of the Castellane-Gould marriage, it would "upset any number of others." *America*'s commentator could only observe that marriages involving a formal intention of divorce were "as yet extremely rare," and lamely add that "the tribunal is not infallible." On the Continent as well as in the United States influential Catholics were reported to be protesting the annulment. [82]

With the awkward but determined sense of public relations that has characterized the Vatican in the twentieth century, an unidentified curial source made it known that "the case in all its bearings is particularly obnoxious to Pope Pius. In the first place marriage is regarded by him as indissoluble, and he is never inclined to allow nullification on a mere technicality." These statements, remarkable when made about the Pope of the Folchi case, *supra*, and the Parkhurst case, *infra*, were buttressed by an interview granted by John Prior, "the representative of the English-speaking element" as vice-rector of the Beda and judge of the Rota, to whom the case on the third turn had been assigned. Given the gravity and complexity of the issues, he made it known that he did not expect to be able to reach a decision before December.[83]

At this point, however, Anna made herself felt. With adroit timing and economy of effort she now appeared as a party for the first time, employed an advocate, and asked the Signature to nullify the second judgment. Her intervention in June effectively suspended consideration of the case by the Rota.[84]

Anna's choice of counsel for this venture into canonical litigation reflected her conservative temper. Her representative was Monsignor Nazareno Patrizi, a relatively young man of thirty-seven from Pagliano in the diocese of Palestrina, who had been a *minutante* or apprentice in the Congregation of Bishops and Regulars. Although Marquis Patrizi held the hereditary post at court of Standard Bearer of the Holy Roman Church, Monsignor Patrizi had only a routine practice before curial committees as an "ecclesiastical agent" and as a lawyer for religious communities. Compared to the curialists like Giorgi and Grazioli, who served Filippo Folchi, or compared to her husband's counsel, the Dean of the College of Consistorial Advocates, Patrizi was a person of undistinguished attainments. His selection betokened an interest, but also a frugal investment by Anna in the case.[85]

Old Vincenzo Vannutelli, that *papabile* of 1904, "honorary citizen of Dublin and lover of America," as the *New York Times* chose to describe him, was still the presiding officer of the Signature, as he had been when round four of the Folchi case had been decided in 1912; and Pietro Gasparri was still the cardinal member with the greatest knowledge of the law. Gasparri's Code, in draft form since 1912, was indeed but three years away from promulgation as the law itself. He acted as the reporter of the case to the other cardinals.[86] Patrizi's chief point, at least as reported in the press, was that Anna had never been officially notified of the second proceeding; because of her custom of never receiving registered mail, her doorkeeper had returned the registered notice sent her by the Archbishop of Paris.[87] Without her participation, it was argued, the second judgment was itself a nullity. Although Patrizi issued an optimistic bulletin of approaching victory to the press, his insubstantial technicality did not succeed. The Signature rejected Anna's appeal six months after it had been taken, "saving the rights of the appellant to produce other matters, if she has them, in the third instance." [88]

Patrizi then asked the Rota to order the appearance of further witnesses, a request granted on February 14, 1914.[89] But Anna, having made a show for eight months, was tiring of a game she had not entered with much panache. On reflection, she may have realized that her posture invited disbelief in her sincerity as she, now the wife of the Duke de Talleyrand, appeared in the Roman Rota as the defender of her marriage to the Count de Castellane. Perhaps she had come to the conclusion that the court-appointed defender of the bond sufficed. Perhaps she had cynically concluded that she might be exploited if she stayed in the battle. Perhaps she calculated that she had accomplished her objective in delaying Castellane for eight months and that it was time to retire content with this accomplishment. To her counsel from the Curia, poor Monsignor Patrizi, she dispatched an icy letter of dismissal. She had entered the case as a litigant only to refute certain lies about her which could affect her children. She had done enough to achieve this end: "My deference to the indissolubility of marriage should not go further." To the press a different story was given. The Duchess de Talleyrand had withdrawn from the case because she was convinced that "she could not obtain justice from the Rota." She preferred "to let the tribunal of the Church take its own biased view and leave her case to the unbiased tribunal of public opinion in Europe and America." [90]

Meanwhile, the defense of the indissolubility of the union remained with the advocate who had so ardently upheld the marriage in the first two rounds, the official defender of the bond, Francesco Parrillo. He did not hesitate to use his brief to draw the attention of the third turn to the publicity which the second judgment had received: "The whole world seemed to be stirred." The daily papers and weekly journals "had been preoccupied with it for a long time as something of scandal or at least as a deed offensive to pious ears." It had been suggested that the Church was more interested "in the wool than in the sheep," and that its doors were open to "those who gave," closed to "those who did not give." [91] Parrillo observed that he did not need such unkind insinuations to win his case; but he had applied the technical terms, ordinarily employed to condemn discredited propositions of theology — "scandal" and "offensive to pious ears" — to the second judgment itself, at least as it looked to the press. Having at the least called the Rota's attention to the public interest in its probity, Parillo directed all his strength to demolishing the reasons advanced in the second opinion.

"The opinion" — or, occasionally, "the judges," but never anything so personal as "Cattani" nor so definitive as "the Sacred Roman Rota" — had committed a rich variety of blunders. It had relied on Castellane's libel as though it were evidence, while admitting that libels did not always tell "the genuine truth." It had accepted the testimony of the Castellane family as crucial, although the *Decretals* themselves provided that marriages were not to be dissolved merely on the basis of testimony offered by a spouse's relatives. It had not only accepted the testimony of relatives of the petitioner but treated that testimony as sacred. The Paris archdiocese had described the Marquise de Castellane as "conspicuous in decency." How had this modest encomium been transformed into "most pious" in the opinion's description of Boni's mother, and how had this testimonial been extended by the opinion to include Del Drago, for whom no one had vouched?

The judges had explained discrepancies between Boni and the other witnesses by saying he had been "blinded by love." So blinded, how had he been able to perceive, "with one hundred eyes," Anna's will to divorce? Other discrepancies between the witnesses had been treated by the opinion as mere differences in circumstantial detail. But how else had Daniel proved that the elders lied about Susannah than by noting that one said she had committed adultery "under a mastic tree," the other "under an oak"? No two witnesses had testified to the same statement of Anna. But divine law itself required that proof be "by two witnesses, above exception, speaking of their own knowledge."

Credulous toward the Castellane witnesses, the opinion had been severe in its evaluation of Anna. Of the five lies charged against her, one depended on accepting her husband's word against hers and two depended on treating the statements of Boni's mother "as though they came from the Holy Spirit." Two lies said to be established by documentary evidence were, in fact, unproved. The New York court records on the "Gould Family Divorces" were irrelevant and inept to prove anything bearing on this case. Pacelli's clinching proof of mendacity, that Anna had lied about her age, depended on the document showing her conveyance of property in 1896. But the Dean of Consistorial Advocates, and the opinion, had forgotten the civil law. By the terms of that law marriage emancipated a minor. As a married woman, Anna, whatever her age, could have conveyed property. The document of 1896 so triumphantly produced could prove nothing. How could a lawyer distinguished in imperial law, Parrillo could not resist asking, have relied on such proof to undermine the bond of marriage? [92]

Keen in laying bare the factual flimsiness of Pacelli's case and Cattani's opinion, Parrillo was far less effective on the law of invalidating intent. Without even a bow to Gasparri's *De matrimonio* and its innovations, he stuck to Benedict XIV: To invalidate a marriage an intention against indissolubility must be expressed in an agreement. Otherwise the intention was "presumed not to be distinct" from the error that divorce was permissible. So little did the defender do on this key issue that he even repeated Pacelli's assertion that "the Episcopalian sect" gave Anna a right to divorce. In his view this error of the heretics could not subvert her general intent of "doing what God instituted."

Ratification was the only legal issue Parrillo pursued with much spirit. The opinion had relied on the teaching of Sanchez that to ratify an invalid marriage one had to know that it was invalid. But this was not the law of the *Decretals*, established in *Ad id*, X.4.1.21; and the Holy Office in 1883 had issued for the ecclesiastical tribunals an Instruction which followed *Ad id*, not Sanchez: if one was forced to marry and later, free of fear, stayed in the conjugal union, he was judged "to consent to and ratify what he had first done unwillingly and with a contrary mind." The Instruction was directed to cases of force and fear; *mutatis mutandis* it should apply where valid consent had not originally been given. Staying with Boni for eleven years, Anna had ratified the marriage.[93]

In his brief for Castellane, Pacelli showed the easy confidence, if not insolence, of a champion who is assured of victory. The question, he believed, was one of law. Despite the efforts, now tolerantly described as "very spirited," of "the distinguished defender of the bond," the resolution of the case was simple because of "the harmony" of the most recent decisions of the Rota and the judgment of the second turn. "A happy outcome" was in prospect for "our most harassed Client." [94] With this sanguine preamble, he reprinted, virtually verbatim, his winning brief of 1913. For the statement of facts, however, he now relied on Cattani, for what could be more authoritative than the facts recognized by the Rota itself? To his earlier presentation of the law the advocate added only two cases: *Esztergom, January 22, 1914,* and *Portland, July 6, 1914,* both containing dicta on the invalidating effect of a purely mental intention of dissolubility.[95] In this fashion, with the addition of a paragraph of introduction, a page of new argument, and the quotations from the 1914 cases, Pacelli produced for his client a new brief, forty-four pages in length, which stood on the firm ground of a repetition of the facts and the law recently enunciated by a judge of the court.

If Pacelli had been less sanguine in his expectations or more sensitive to the structure of one kind of English ecclesiastical mind, he might have been less ready to find a precedent in *Portland, July 6, 1914,* described by him as "the most recent and the most learned decision of today's *ponens.*" John Prior, the only Englishman on the Rota, had in fact written the opinion in the case and was now *ponens* of the turn hearing *Castellane-Gould.* But, what did this most recent and learned decision — the fourth American case ever to reach the Sacred Roman Rota — suggest about the judge facing Castellane? * The facts he had passed on were as fol-

* Besides the Gould case and the Parkhurst case, which is set out in the following chapter, the only other American case to have come before the Rota involved Emil Honnert, a twenty-year-old coachboy, who got pregnant Anna Schelling, an eighteen-year-old housemaid. She had him arrested on a paternity charge. To escape jail, he married her in a civil ceremony, took her to a street car, and left her. Four years later, in 1908, having divorced and remarried civilly, she sought an annulment on the ground that he had been coerced. The archdiocese of Cincinnati, on May 18, 1909, held the marriage null on the ground of simulated consent; on appeal, the archdiocese of Chicago on June 18, 1909, held the marriage null on the ground of fear. As the grounds of decision were not the same, the petitioner had to seek the judgment of a third court. The case was sent to Rome in April 1910 with a request, concurred in by the defender of the bond, for a papal dispensation from the marriage as unconsummated. The Congregation for the Sacraments referred the case to the Rota, which assigned an advocate to

lows: Dinah Smith, a girl of eighteen, married Abner O'Kieffe in 1895, in Pine Ridge, South Dakota. She was deserted by him five months later. In 1905 she wanted to remarry and, a devout Catholic, sought to marry within the Church. Living now in Oregon, she addressed a plea to the tribunal of Portland: Abner had remarried; he had a wife and two children; "he would not think a minute of taking me back in any way." Dinah knew "a man to love who would die for me. . . . He seems to be the only thing I live for." Her dilemma was tersely put: "If the Church decides against me, I will have to leave the Church or the man I love a thousand times more dearly than anything in the world." Her appeal went beyond legal argument: "Oh Father, have mercy on me. Our Lord knows I intend to do the right thing, but it would kill me or drive me crazy if I had to leave this man. Father, I humbly beg and pray that you grant me my freedom if you can." [96]

Dinah Smith's judges in the diocese of Portland held that she was bound for life to Abner and discouraged further activity on her behalf; but her pastor's persistence brought her case to the Rota, which it reached *in forma pauperis*, with Dinah certified as poor by her bishop and assigned counsel by the Dean from among the advocates of the Roman bar. Her Roman counsel did not have the means to develop new testimony, but he put the undisputed facts before the court: Abner O'Kieffe had testified that he married Dinah because he had been going with her for two years and that she had pestered him and embarrassed him into marrying her. It was his intention to leave her if she didn't please him as a wife. He was not a Catholic and had had no interest or belief in Catholic teaching on marriage. As Prior summed up, the testimony established beyond question that O'Kieffe, "by virtue of a difference in religion and morals, foresaw an unhappy outcome for their marriage and so was prepared to take up at will, by his own private authority, a separate bed and board." In the light of Cattani's opinion in *Castellane-Gould* the case seemed an easy one: O'Kieffe had excluded the idea of an indissoluble union; the marriage must be

---

represent Anna without charge; her case was decided the following year by a panel headed by Prior. The Rota found that the fear inflicted on Emil was just and so did not invalidate his consent; but it held that his consent itself was simulated, as his immediate flight after the ceremony proved; the marriage was null, *Of Nullity of Marriage,* July 9, 1911, *Decisiones seu Sententiae,* III, 237–244. (The diocese is omitted, and the names disguised in the official report.)

null. Prior did not refer to the 1913 *Castellane* opinion, but he cited Sanchez, Gasparri, and others to show that intent against indissolubility would nullify consent. He also referred, however, to the thirteenth-century Gloss on *Tua nos*, X.4.1.26: intent could not be proved if intent had not been expressed in contractual language. Faced with a clear and unacknowledged conflict of authorities, he avoided the issue. He found that O'Kieffe's intention had not been contrary to indissolubility but had been contrary to the obligation of living with his wife. Abner had indeed deceived Dinah — "certainly the man acted unjustly toward the girl" — but, "as Gasparri notes, n. 103, 1904 edition, a condition as to not living together at all is not against the substance of marriage but rather against its integrity." Choosing this thin distinction from among the several distinctions available in Gasparri, Prior was able to conclude that O'Kieffe's intent had not been of an invalidating sort. O'Kieffe's injustice and the girl's swift abandonment were not reasons for the Sacred Rota to destroy the bond of marriage; still less did a reason exist in her desire to marry the man she loved, though her letter expressing her desperation formed part of the Rota's files. Nullity had not been established; the inexorable judgment of Portland was confirmed; and Dinah Smith was left to her hard choices.[97] With this decision behind him, Prior turned to contemplate the contentions advanced by Pacelli; he was, at the beginning of 1915, ready to pronounce upon them.

The Unintended Intention

In the third decision of the Rota on the merits of *Castellane-Gould* the difficulty of a definite formulation of the law was apparent; the difficulty was recognized by Prior himself. As he put it, the common opinion was that, if someone contracted marriage and, "by his positive will simply and absolutely intends a dissoluble bond, the marriage is null." In this simple declaration he swept away the long tradition that invalidating intent had to be expressed in a contract: The Gloss, *Gaudemus*, and Benedict XIV fell before the teaching of Gasparri; the new Code, though not yet enacted law, was waiting in the wings; Prior in effect acknowledged that what became Canon 1086 was not only the law of the

future, but the law of the past.[98] But acceptance of one part of
Gasparri was then severely qualified by another part of Gasparri.
"Abstractly," it was true that intent invalidated; "concretely," invalidating intention had to be distingushed from mere noninvalidat-
ing error. To distinguish between the two mental states was not
easy. Accomplishment of the discrimination required "the art" of
the judge. Prior went as far as a court might go with propriety
in implying that the judge operated in a vacuum: "It is an arduous
task to resolve the doubt, and a sure rule for judging is needed." [99]
When it had fallen to him to decide this case, he had experienced
perplexity if not agony in reaching a decision and rationalizing it.

His task had not been made easier by the responses and instructions which the Holy Office had issued since 1680, for Prior, unlike both counsel and earlier rotal judges in the case, resolved to
face this relevant body of curial rulings. Still less was his burden
lightened by his apparent conviction that the Holy Office could
not have contradicted itself and his consequent determination to
harmonize the inconsistencies. He was driven to create a hybrid:
"From these documents [the Holy Office decisions] it is clear that
there can be some kind of intention of contracting a dissoluble
marriage which cannot, however, be called a positive or absolute
will." [100] His language came very close to saying "From these documents it is clear that there can be intentions which are not intentions or which are not recognized as intentions." If the intent to
enter a dissoluble marriage was perceptible at all, why was it not
a "positive" intent? No answer was provided by psychology. The
hybrid was a verbal solution of the conflict between the theology
requiring an intent to marry indissolubly in order to marry validly,
and the curial policy in favor of the validity of marriage whatever
the customs of those marrying.

Coming to grips with the conflict in the particular case, Prior
could not stop with his verbal creation; he had to decide what the
Holy Office rulings meant in practice. Concretely, he found that
they showed that a positive intention against marriage could
"scarcely or never" be found to exist, "unless this intention were
reduced to a contract, or consent were offered under this condition and not otherwise." Taking Gasparri's doctrine of intent as
the common opinion, Prior reached a result that meant it was
"scarcely or never" to be applied. The doctrine was "abstract."

Concretely, Prior remained true to the long judicial practice of requiring a contractual expression. Operationally, he accepted the curial preference for upholding the validity of marriages; and, operationally, he gave the preference vitality by a presumption in favor of a valid intent. Whatever the laws of the country or the religion of the parties marrying, it was "always to be presumed" that they intended to marry indissolubly." Specifically, as to the United States, the intent to marry indissolubly must be supposed to be general: it was "absurd to say that almost all the women of this vast area positively exclude indissolubility of the bond when they give matrimonial consent." [101]

Why was it "absurd" to suppose that most American women excluded indissolubility? It was not that Prior had taken evidence on the point or that he appealed to general knowledge about the Christian origins of American culture. It was because marriage was indissoluble by "the law of nature"; and what was natural was universal or almost universal. A priori, without examination, Prior knew that Americans must generally seek to marry indissolubly because they must generally obey the law of nature. This conviction not only sustained him in honoring the presumption of intent to marry indissolubly; it also furnished him with an explanation of how persons who believed in the dissolubility of marriage could nonetheless intend to marry indissolubly: "Knowledge of marriage is instituted by the Author of nature, and it is not at all obscured even among the greatest corruptions of the people." In the face of contrary laws, custom, or religion, this natural knowledge could be supposed to form the wills of those who married. Whatever their national, ethnic, or doctrinal misconceptions, they could be trusted, in general, to act on their natural knowledge of the constitution of marriage. Beneath all cultural expressions of the impermanence of marriage, the natural knowledge of its true character, in some subterranean way, survived. All mankind could be presumed to intend to marry indissolubly, "to contract marriage as instituted by the Author of nature or by Christ." [102]

Once Prior had decided what the law was "concretely," once he had determined to maintain the policy favorable to validity, the arduous task of deciding Anna's mental state proved not so difficult. Almost all of Castellane's witnesses could be accepted as testifying truthfully without proving his case. The testimony of

Boni's parents, brother, and friends showed nothing more than the belief of Anna that she could, if she chose, obtain a divorce dissolving the bond. Such a belief was a classic "error of law." Nothing translated it into a concrete positive intent to enter a dissoluble union. Anna, intending to marry as one "ordinarily marries," must be presumed to have intended indissolubility.[103] This straightforward application of a presumption founded in policy was embellished with a paradox which had also engaged Pius VI in writing the Archbishop of Prague. Anna believed she could dissolve the marriage by divorce. Therefore, she would not have willed its indissolubility — indissolubility was "already effectively excluded for her, beyond all operation of her own will, by a certain extraneous cause; that is, by the doctrine of the non-Catholic sect to which she belonged: 'I am a Protestant and I know that I may divorce.'" Because of this belief, she had no need to form a specific intent against entering marriage "as instituted by the Author of nature." As she assumed she did not need to exclude indissolubility, she must have had only the general intent of marrying; and intending to marry meant intending to enter a permanent union. By this reasoning the more firmly a person believed in divorce, the less likely he was to intend to enter a dissoluble marriage.

All the Castellane witnesses were disposed of in this fashion but one. Del Drago remained, with his testimony that Anna had consented only on the explicit condition of entering a dissoluble arrangement. But "one witness, no witness" — canon law required two witnesses to constitute proof. Beyond quantitative deficiency, Prior shared Lega's view of the trustworthiness of Del Drago. There were reasons to doubt "the accuracy" of his memory. He had testified that he had repeated the contractual declaration of Anna to Jean de Castellane and that the Marquis de Castellane had heard him, and Boni's father had also testified that he had learned of Anna's mind from Del Drago. Yet not a single one of these witnesses "reported a word about a condition attached to matrimonial consent." Del Drago was undermined by the testimony of the Castellane family. It was, Prior observed mildly, "at least rather probable that after a lapse of ten years he did not recall as accurately as other witnesses the sense of the declaration of the bride." In a judgment joined in by the auditors Giuseppe Mori and Luigi Sincero, Prior concluded, "Nullity of marriage is not established." [104]

FINAL JUDGMENT IN THE CURIA

Unexpected as reversal of Cattani's judgment was, Filippo Pacelli did not despair for his "harassed Client." Beyond the Rota was the Signature and beyond the Signature was the Pope. Prior's opinion had been printed in the June 21, 1915, issue of the *Acta apostolicae sedis*, thereby giving it more prominence than the ordinary rotal judgment. Yet if marriage cases were never *res judicata*, if avenues of appeal were always open, there was no reason to treat Prior's exhaustive analysis as final. Pacelli appealed to the Signature; and a worried note in the *American Ecclesiastical Review* observed that there was no assurance that the judgment of the third turn had ended the case.[105]

Presiding over the Signature as Prefect was one man who could be expected to appreciate the need for finality in Rota judgments and to appreciate the need with a vengeance in this case, the author of the first opinion in *Castellane-Gould*, the author of the leading canonical treatise on procedure, the first head of the re-created Rota, Michele Lega. The Proper Law of the Rota provided no basis for the Signature to act as a court of ordinary review for the Rota; there was no reason for Lega to ignore the law as the Signature had done in 1912 for Filippo Folchi; he could rule that Boni de Castellane was out of court. On June 28, 1915, the Pope, Benedict XV, changed the law: the Signature received authorization to review marriage cases. On July 17, 1915, it ordered *Castellane-Gould* to be heard again, this time by the entire Rota.[106]

Unlike the Folchi case, *Castellane-Gould* had been at every stage publicly reported and publicly debated.* The impression which would be given by a fourth hearing at Castellane's request could scarcely escape the more sensitive members of the Curia. Two weeks after the Signature's unpublicized order for rehearing, Benedict XV reached a different conclusion. Rehearing would be

---

* There was to be sure greater journalistic interest in annulment than in affirmation of the bond. Anna's defeat in the Signature had been front-page news in January 1914; her vindication in February 1915 rated only a small notice in the *New York Times*, February 11, 1915, p. 18.

granted, but in complete secrecy, and at the highest level. By papal rescript of August 2, 1915, the case was committed to a special commission of cardinals.[107] At its head was Gaetano De Lai, Secretary of the S.C.C. in Pius X's administration. Its other two members were Wilhelm Van Rossum, a Dutch Redemptorist, who in September 1915 became the Grand Penitentiary, and Gaetano Bisleti, former major-domo of the papal household. All three were cardinals of Pius X; only De Lai had made a career as a jurist.[108] The Pope's decision was communicated to the Rota by Cardinal Gasparri as Secretary of State; and no doubt in this case where the good name of the legal system was at issue Gasparri played a part in deciding how review would be granted and who would do the reviewing.

The legal grounds on which the Signature had ordered review, the legal grounds on which the Pope then took the case from the Rota and gave it to the cardinals, the legal grounds on which the cardinals reached a resolution of the case — all are unknown. Neither Signature nor Pope nor Secretary of State chose to give reasons. The report of the cardinals was never made public, never communicated to the Rota. Officially, the last reference by the Vatican to the case was the publication in the *Acta apostolicae sedis* for 1915 of Prior's opinion of February 8.[109] Officially the last entry in the Rota file was Gasparri's letter of August 2, removing the case to the secret deliberations of the chosen cardinals.

Unofficially, from that fragile source the *New York Times*, so often unreliable in its reporting of this case but nonetheless a source of news when the court records cease, more may be learned.* The appointed cardinals first met to consider the matter

---

* An observer following the case's progress through the *New York Times* would have learned the following: the case had first been decided by the Congregation of the Council (July 10, 1913, p. 1); Pope Pius X was opposed to annulments on mere technicalities (June 1, sec. III, p. 3); the second decision was given by Cardinal Lorenzelli (January 4, 1914, sec. III, p. 3); in this case Anna had been prevented from testifying because women could not testify in the courts of the Vatican (*ibid.*); in the second round, Castellane produced two new witnesses, Del Drago and a former governess (February 22, 1913, sec. III, p. 3); the basis for the decision was a letter Anna was alleged to have written (March 16, 1913, p. 1); Anna had been converted to Catholicism to marry but the letter showed this a matter of mere expediency (March 23, 1913, sec. IV, p. 5); Anna had been told she could never win the case (May 11, 1914, p. 5); the case would end with Anna's withdrawal (*ibid.*); Anna herself had sued to annul the marriage but withdrew when it appeared impossible to win (May 5, 1916, p. 8); the Pope's ratification of the cardinals' decision in 1916 definitely barred annulment (May 6, 1916, p. 9);

on October 15, 1915.[110] They gave judgment upholding the validity of the marriage on May 4, 1916. The Pope confirmed the judgment the next day with the result, the newspaper said inaccurately, of "definitely barring annulment of the marriage." On July 23 of the same year, Pacelli had "new evidence" he wanted to offer. Benedict XV was reported to have submitted the case once again to the same committee of cardinals.[111]

Pentecost Sunday 1917 the Pope promulgated the Code with the direction that it become law a year later. Canon 1086 was as relevant to *Castellane-Gould* as it had been to *Folchi-Bailly*.[112] If the cardinals had not decided the case by 1918, or if the cardinals had decided the case adversely to Castellane, was there not reason enough in "the clearer light" provided by the Code to consider the matter once again? The new canon seemed to adopt as the law, which judges as well as theologians should follow, the view of the effect of mere mental intention which had been rejected by Benedict XIV and the bulk of Holy Office decisions and given grudging and ineffective recognition in Prior's opinion. Canon 1086 represented a triumph of theological theory over the demand of courts for clear rules of proof. Could not Boni de Castellane, like Filippo Folchi, benefit from the amendment?

As in *Folchi-Bailly*, counsel for Castellane waited until the new administration of Pius XI and found it favorable to their hopes. A new commission of cardinals was appointed. Donato Sbaretti, the former diplomat who had been appointed prefect of the S.C.C. as part of the Gasparri administration in 1919, and Agostino Sili, Gasparri's cousin, were added to De Lai, Bisleti, and Van Rossum. If the commission had been split before, the two new votes shifted the balance. In July 1924, less than two weeks after Folchi had been definitely released from the bond of marriage, the cardinals reported to Pius XI that Boni de Castellane's marriage was a nullity.[113]

Once again the renown of *Castellane-Gould* had consequences

Anna's marriage was finally annulled (November 30, 1961, p. 37, Anna's obituary). These dozen untrue statements resulted partly from reliance, without checking, on the self-serving statements of interested persons; partly from guessing about procedures of which the reporter was in ignorance; and partly, in the last instance, from failure to consult the *New York Times*' own files. Only in the last example was there a formal correction of the misinformation (December 6, 1961, p. 47).

for the petitioner. In 1914 and 1915, even in the Vatican Library, Achille Ratti must have heard of the case. The public impression that would be created by annulling the marriage now could scarcely have escaped him as Pius XI; and perhaps having been prevailed on to permit the Folchi decision, he looked with a little more skepticism on another case presented to him as having been thrice misjudged. He added four cardinals — Pompili, Lega, Mori, and Sincero — to the commission and returned the case for reconsideration.[114]

The new additions were themselves instructive. Mori and Sincero had been the judges who had joined with Prior in the judgment upholding the marriage in 1915. Lega had not only written the first opinion; as the Folchi case had demonstrated, he held Prior's view of the credibility of Castellane's chief witness, Del Drago.[115] The appointment of these cardinals pointed in only one direction.

At the end of March 1925, the newly constituted group reported in favor of the marriage. Four months later the Pope confirmed their verdict.[116] After three hearings in the Rota, two in the Signature, and four before special commissions of cardinals, the validity of the consent exchanged by Anna Gould and Boni de Castellane before Archbishop Corrigan in 1895 had been definitively established to the satisfaction of the Roman Curia.

New York, Of Nullity of Marriage now entered the world of canonical literature. In 1932, in the final edition of *De matrimonio*, in a section devoted to conditions against the substance of marriage, Cardinal Gasparri quoted at length from the 1877 instruction of the Holy Office to the Bishop of Seattle, so favorable to the theory of Castellane's petition, and appended to it a citation of the three rotal opinions delivered in response to Castellane's claims. No summary was provided of the opinions' holdings, no reference was made to the uncertainty of the law these opinions reflected, no hint was given that the case had had a ten-year history after 1915 among the cardinals of the Curia. Classified by Gasparri as illustrative of intention against indissolubility, *Castellane-Gould* became, in spite of its outcome, a citation showing that intent to enter a dissoluble union would make the union dissoluble.[117] In the last judgment of the Curia, in the imperishable, imprescriptible universe of precedent, in Gasparri's treatise, *Castellane-Gould* stood for the law asked for by Castellane.

Elsewhere, in a footnote in the same final version of *De matri-monio*, Gasparri showed a new awareness of the crucial issue of policy: "If the laws or customs of the region admit divorce as to the bond, or polygamy, there seems to be the presumption that those marrying *will to enter a marriage conformable to the laws or customs of the nation*. Hence it follows that all marriages cele-brated in that region must be held as invalid unless in particular cases it is proved that those marrying had a different will in the act of marriage." The italics reflected the author's intense aware-ness of the critical role which law or custom could play. He went on to a revolutionary inference. "The marriages of almost all lands" were invalid. For seven hundred years — from Innocent III's decision in *Gaudemus* to the answer to St. Albert — the Curia had refused to accept this conclusion. If it had wavered in 1877 and again in the second round of *Castellane-Gould*, was it prepared at last to go all the way? But again faced with the simple option of saying, All are null, or, all are indissoluble, the eighty-three-year-old maker of the Code refused to be a revolutionary. His footnote concluded, "It has been shown that this doctrine cannot be ad-mitted." [118]

Why could the doctrine not be admitted? Gasparri's reasons were two. First, "the favor of the law which marriage enjoys" — a restatement of the conclusion. Second, those getting married "at least generally speaking do not even think of the dissolution of the bond of marriage or of marrying again and much less do they think of these things and will them in such a way as to exclude marriage itself" — that is to say, a marriage was invalid only if there was an express intent against indissolubility, although Gas-parri had just recognized that it was a question of choosing one presumption (that people ordinarily entered marriage as an indis-soluble union) or the contrary presumption (that people ordinarily entered marriage as a union dissoluble in a variety of circum-stances). The choice could not be aided by supposing that people did not explicitly consider what they were doing. From Gasparri's statement of reasons emerged only his ultimate adhesion to the ancient curial policy for validity, even while his judicial adoption of intention, now law in canon 1086, exposed that presumption to easy refutation by the facts of custom.

Cynics might draw from the course of *Castellane-Gould* the lesson that in the end the party with the larger pocketbook got what she wanted: her former husband incapacitated for the rest of her life — and she died only in 1961 — from marrying legally in the religion of his ancestors. Yet Anna Gould's part in achieving this objective seems minuscule on the surface and irrelevant when the case is more deeply proped. Others, perhaps more realistically, might compare *Castellane-Gould* with *Folchi-Bailly* and conclude that a doorkeeper in the household of the Pope had a better chance of getting his son's marriage annulled than a French nobleman of ancient title and more illustrious pedigree lacking the asset of access to the Pope. Still, Castellane's counsel was Pacelli, so if not in person, yet in his deputy, he had entree to the highest circle. If any factor could account for the difference between the results in the two cases it would seem to be publicity: the absence of public scrutiny made it possible for the friends of Arcangelo Folchi to do for Filippo Folchi what Filippo Pacelli could not achieve for his client. But the image of the Curia in the press, which never had the case exactly right, did not provide the dynamism which moved the judges.

Observers focusing on the forensic aspect of the case might note that the advantage of having the Dean of Consistorial Advocates had been counterbalanced by the kind of care he gave to preparing and presenting the case, and that the skills he displayed were not such as to persuade even a moderately critical court of the merits of his cause. The advocate's task had not been made easier by the kind of cooperation he received from witnesses such as Del Drago. Judges like Lega and Prior were not to be mocked in every case by the production of pat testimony. But the incredulity stirred by counsel and witnesses was not the most basic reason for Castellane's failure.

Neither the relative position of the parties nor the credibility of the evidence nor the quality of advocacy displayed was at the heart of the result in the case, reached in secrecy by the cardinals of the Curia after three turns of the Rota had passed on the issues in open judgment. In a time of transition in the law, applying a new principle before the eyes of all the world, the Curia was unwilling to abandon the new principle or follow it unflinchingly. If intention was to be a criterion in the courts, intention was not to be proved by rites and laws, customs and beliefs in conflict with the settled curial conviction that marriage was naturally indissoluble and known to be so by all peoples. Hence Prior's grudging opinion, hence the silent, secret, final affirmation by the cardinals. Whatever people believed when they married, they must ordinarily marry in a way which satisfied the criteria designed by the Author of nature and certified as universal by the courts of the Curia.

VI

The American Unbeliever

If, in the course of the year 1901, an alien in Rome, some pensive observer of the city's medley of antique pomp and contemporary vivacity, had come upon an elderly Roman, a younger American lady, and a middle-aged ecclesiastic posed in the act of investigating a museum or a church or halted in their perambulations to enjoy the light upon the cupola of a great basilica perceived over the rooftops, he might easily have concluded that nothing had changed in the half-century or more that cramped New England consciences had come to dilate in the warmth of Rome. Seen from a distance, in the beneficent light of late afternoon, the trio could readily have symbolized the stable relationship of American innocence and European experience under the benediction of religion. Closer observation of the three, however, would have disclosed that there was a striking lack of harmony among them, and that the ecclesiastic, although patently the lady's compatriot, and, by his authoritative air, evidently her coreligionist, was the adversary of both the lady and her dignified supporter.

The Roman who might have been observed in this reserved but chivalrous posture was Prince Giuseppe Francesco Maria Filippo Rospigliosi-Gioeni, eldest son of Clemente Francesco, the late Grand Duke of Tuscany, and distant collateral of Giulio Rospigliosi, Pope Clement X. On his father's death in 1897, Giuseppe, then aged forty-nine, had succeeded him as prince of the Holy Roman Empire and as Duke of Zagarolo, Prince of Castiglione, Marquis of Giuliana, Count of Chiusa, and Baron of Valcorrente.[1] At his mother's death, when he was fifty-one, Prince Giuseppe Rospigliosi had been still a bachelor, and it had appeared that titles and family estates would pass in due time to his brother, Prince Camillo, commander of the *guardia nobile* of the Pope, or to his brother's numerous offspring; for his brother, married to a daughter of the Giustiniani Bandini — had sired ten children, and Prince Camillo's family had fully occupied the ancestral palace of the Rospigliosi in Rome. At the age of fifty-three, Prince Giuseppe had been free for two years from whatever inhibitions devotion to his mother had imposed, when, through the improbable delay of a ship at Naples, he had met an American girl, who, more improbably still, had within a week captured his affections and won from him a proposal of marriage. It was she whom he could have been observed supporting in conversation with the prelate.

This second gentleman, of an ample stature inclining to portliness, with the jaw and mouth of some Cerberus and the steady gaze of one newly accustomed to authority, was none other than William O'Connell, the bishop-elect of Portland, the northernmost diocese of the United States, comprising the entire state of Maine. As much a New Englander as the older breed which had arrogated the character of New England to itself, he had grown up a Catholic in the midst of the hostility manifested to the Catholic religion by the Yankee bourgeoisie of the mill towns of Massachusetts, and embattled from his youth, he had drawn from his own experience his own sense of the classical description of the Church on earth as the Church militant. In Rome, at the training ground of American bishops, the North American College, he had been four years a student and then, after an apprenticeship in Boston, six years the rector. In the ecclesiastical culture of the center of his ancestral faith he had rejoiced as one who had come home. Now a Roman of the old Romans, a New Englander of the New Englanders, he was being returned by his superiors to embody Rome in New England.[2] That assignment had brought him squarely into the path which Prince Rospigliosi and the lady at his side had to cross.

The third member of this uneasy trio was one whose dark good looks might already have diverted the musing observer's attention from the nobleman and the priest. As her intonation, and indeed her whole manner, captivating even in combat, indicated, she was from the Southern section of the United States, although she was evidently a Southerner who had spent some portion of her life in the North. She was at that most interesting of ages, when the ingenuous beauty of youth has by a more ample exposure to the variety of

life been tempered, without its original lineaments being wholly
obscured by polish or by mask. Born in New Orleans in 1870,
Marie Reid had grown up in the national capital. Her parents had
separated while she was still a girl, and she had been brought up
by her mother. Her father a Protestant, her mother a Catholic, she
had been educated in her mother's faith, but her interest in it had
not been intense. No rich American heiress, but a girl of modest
means, she had sufficient charm, sexual attraction, and self-will to
account for her triumph with Prince Rospigliosi without the
benefit of fortune.[3] But if, still a zestful Southern belle at thirty-
one, Marie Reid had the sparkle which could ignite the heart of
an Italian bachelor in his fifties, what complications could prevent
such a piquant union of opposites? The answer to this question lay
in Marie Reid's Northern experience, the determination of a man
from Maine, and the character and structure of the Catholic Church
in the United States.

ROME AND AMERICA

Under the Pope, the American Church was governed by the Sacred Congregation for the Propagation of the Faith. The S.C.P.F.,
or Propaganda — to use the short form of its title made odious
among generations of English-speaking Protestants — had been
created in 1622 to supervise "all matters pertaining to the propagation of the Faith in the entire world." [4] Its mission had in fact been
missionary, and only those portions of the world falling outside
the domestic or colonial domain of those European countries de-
nominated "Catholic" fell within its ample charge. Geographically,
its jurisdiction extended further than that of any of the regular
administrative committees of the Curia; it had supervised for centuries the Catholic clergy and faithful of England and her colonies,
Holland and her colonies, Scandinavia, Russia, the Turkish Empire,
and all of Africa and Asia which was not Spanish, Portuguese, or
French. Subordinate to the Holy Office in matters labeled "faith or
morals," and less centrally located in the administration than the
Secretariat of State or the S.C.C., Propaganda was, by virtue of its
jurisdiction, finances, and personnel, one of the most powerful
standing committees. By its missionary objectives it was oriented,
more than any other curial organ, to the world outside the Church,

and, though still totally clerical in temper, it was, by the effect of this orientation, more open to innovation than other branches of the Curia. Typically, Propaganda initiated the great change in the usury doctrine which occurred in the theological acceptance of interest-taking based on the risk involved in lending.[5] Typically, Propaganda introduced the vernacular, Italian, into its records and correspondence while other Roman congregations stuck essentially to Latin. Propaganda also had a record of success in administration which other curial committees dealing with strong-willed Catholic monarchs, determined anticlerical Latin governments, or subtle theological theorists, could not match. Propaganda acted upon missionaries and through the missionaries upon native converts, usually simple folk recently instructed in the faith, or upon beleaguered Catholic minorities regularly grateful for any succor or recognition from Rome. In supervising American affairs, Propaganda, judged by crude statistics, appeared extraordinarily successful. As immigration from Catholic lands had occurred, the Church in America had grown prodigiously from a mere 25,000 persons in 1784 to over 12,000,000 in 1900.[6] While this five-hundred-fold increase took place, Propaganda was the benevolent observer and the bestower of hierarchical dignities upon those chosen to structure the flow. Organizer, guardian, and arbiter of the American Church, Propaganda presided over what was still officially "unbelievers' territory." Without its word in such territory, no diocese was created, no bishop appointed, no marriage dissolved.

Prefect of Propaganda in 1901 was Miecislas Halka Ledóchowski. Born in 1822 in Gorki, the son of a Polish nobleman, Ledóchowski had served as a papal diplomat in Portugal, Colombia, and Chile before being made Archbishop of Posen. Imprisoned by Bismarck from 1875 to 1877 during the *Kulturkampf*, he, like O'Connell, knew what it meant to fight for the Church, and he drew from men like O'Connell the reverence due a confessor of the faith.[7] Cardinal Ledóchowski had been prefect since 1892, and at seventy-nine was still actively in charge of his congregation when he selected O'Connell for Portland and opened the hearing on the petition of Marie Reid.

The American arm of Rome was the Apostolic Delegate to the United States. Established by Leo XIII in 1893 against the advice of the bishops of the United States,[8] the Delegation was organizationally a simple extension of the Vatican in America. Its principal personnel came from the Curia; they returned ultimately to the Curia. Service in the Delegation was, like service in the nunciatures, a step in a curial career. Not yet the mouth of the Curia in the United States, the Delegation was, more than the bishops, its eyes and ears. Throughout the period relevant to this story, the Delegate was Diomede Falconio, a native of Pescocostanza near Monte Cassino, another order-man turned diplomat, who had been transferred from Ottawa to Washington at the age of sixty in 1902. Falconio was to perform his duties with credit and return to Rome to become a cardinal in 1911, a promotion simultaneously signifying the status of the Curia's American listening post.[9]

Head of the American Church in America — a chief dependent on the Supreme Pontiff and the Curia, yet with a ballast and a posture of his own — was not Diomede Falconio, but James Gibbons, Cardinal-Archbishop of Baltimore. Born in Baltimore in 1834, Gibbons had been brought up in Ballinrobe, Ireland, and returned to the United States, to New Orleans, only at the age of nineteen. Fifteen years later, in 1868, he became Vicar Apostolic of North Carolina and, as titular Bishop of Adramyttum, the youngest bishop in the world. Since 1877, he had been Archbishop of Baltimore, the oldest of American sees, embracing all of Maryland and the national capital. In this position for over forty years, the sole American cardinal for twenty-four of them, Gibbons had established himself as the spokesman and leader of American Catholics, as the adviser of American presidents on matters Catholic, and as the most influential adviser of the Holy See on matters American. A kindly and spirited person, a devoted priest, a consummate diplomat, Cardinal Gibbons was to the Vatican and to the world the embodiment of the Catholic Church in America. As late as 1916 when Gibbons was eighty-two and Pius X had created other American cardinals, Gasparri declared that no prelate in the United States possessed such influence in Rome. In 1901, Leo XIII's only American cardinal, he was in his prime.[10] It was his office which had given Marie Reid the dispensation which enabled her to marry in 1887.

Another member of the American hierarchy, who had already played a subordinate but vital role in the affairs of Marie Reid, was Placide L. Chapelle, a priest of the archdiocese of Baltimore and protégé of Gibbons. The Vicar-General of the archdiocese thought

Chapelle, "deficient in prudence and learning," and when he was proposed for a see of his own, Cardinal Mazzella observed that Gibbons was easily imposed upon. But Gibbons stood by his man, and Chapelle became coadjutor-archbishop of Santa Fe in 1891 and Archbishop of New Orleans in 1897.[11] In earlier days, from 1882 to 1891, he served as the pastor of St. Matthew's Church, 1415 H Street, in northwest Washington. In this capacity, on September 21, 1887, five days before leaving with Gibbons on a trip designed to present the only American cardinal to the West, he presided at St. Matthew's when Marie Reid took Frederick Parkhurst as her spouse.[12]

Parkhurst, the man from Maine so central to the concerns of Marie Reid and Giuseppe Rospigliosi in Rome in 1901, was born to Jonathan Fuller Parkhurst and Sarah Haskell Parkhurst in the village of Unity on November 5, 1864.[13] The next year his parents moved to the town of Bangor, Maine, where his father set up a trunk, bag, and harness factory. At the age of fourteen Fred entered his father's small establishment, and if it had not been such a prospering enterprise and if he had not within him a Yankee curiosity not content with the rudiments of education, he would never have met Marie Reid or heard of Giuseppe Rospigliosi. But ambitious and modestly affluent, he set off when he was twenty-one to study law and to study it in the nation's capital. In the spring of 1887, he received a bachelor and master's degree in law from Columbian University, the predecessor of George Washington University. He spent the summer reading law with Hamlin and Hutchings in Bangor, but he had already met Marie in Washington; and the union of Southerner and Yankee, self-willed belle and self-supporting student, careless Catholic and righteous Protestant was already planned. In September, very much in love, he returned to marry her.

Love, at least on Marie's part, did not survive transplanting to Bangor, a town likely to seem physically cold and socially austere even to inhabitants of Boston. Parkhurst threw himself into running his father's business, and the business began to thrive. Parkhurst threw himself into Republican politics, and he was elected a member of the Bangor City Council, then its president. He took an active part in military exercises and became a colonel in the National Guard. The outlines of the future governor of Maine could already be perceived in Parkhurst's purposeful and energetic life. The couple's first child was stillborn. But a daughter, Dorothy, was born and, then, in 1893, a son, Reid. Determined and devoted as Parkhurst was, their fertile union could have survived the bitter sadness of the first death, the environment of Bangor, and even Parkhurst's dedication to business and civic welfare, if Marie had not engaged in conduct which in self-respect Parkhurst would not accept or tolerate.

"Divorce should not be a panacea for infelicities of married life; if disappointment, suffering, and sorrow even be incident to that relation, they must be endured. The marriage yoke, by mutual forbearance, must be worn, even though it rides unevenly, and has become burdensome withal. Public policy requires that it should be so. Remove the allurements of divorce at pleasure, and husbands and wives will the more zealously strive to even the burdens and vexations of life, and soften them by mutual accommodation so as to enjoy their marriage relation."[14] So spoke Justice Thomas Haskell of the Supreme Judicial Court of Maine in 1886, interpreting the Maine statute which permitted "divorce from the bonds of matrimony" on the grounds of cruel and abusive treatment.[15] These grounds, the court held, comprehended more than physical violence. "Words and deportment" which threatened to impair the other spouse's physical or mental health met the statutory criterion. Despite its misgivings about divorce, such "wilful disregard of marital duty" would be recognized by the Court.

In 1898, in a proceeding before the Supreme Judicial Court sitting for Penobscot County, Parkhurst divorced his wife for cruel and abusive treatment. She did not contest the sentence and accepted a financial provision of fifty dollars a month to be paid by Parkhurst as long as she remained unmarried.[16] By the terms of Maine law she was forbidden to remarry without the court's permission.[17] Parkhurst kept custody of the children. The ungenerous financial terms and the custody arrangements suggested the position from which Marie had bargained.

Parkhurst continued to expand his business. His political career was unaffected, and in 1900 he served as a delegate to the Republican National Convention.[18] Yet he did not forget Marie, who, rejected by her husband and the world she had inhabited for eleven years, from girlhood to maturity, turned to Europe. The news of her marriage on September 2, 1901, to Giuseppe Rospigliosi, at the Rospigliosi family estate at Lamporrechio near Florence, found him vulnerable.

Baltimore–Portland–Rome

One month before the events at Lamporrechio in September a desperate effort had been made to establish the basis for a religious union between Marie Reid and Prince Rospigliosi. Marie had had the hope — or did some lawyer in Rome implant it? — that something had been wrong with her dispensation to marry Parkhurst. Perhaps — was it too wild a hope? — the dispensation had never been given, or, if given, had disappeared and could not be proved. At the end of July 1901, a cable was dispatched by the American consul in Rome to the chancellor of the archdiocese of Baltimore inquiring if a dispensation was recorded. To the imaginable irritation of the Roman advocate who had instigated the inquiry the cable back read: "Chancellor absent. Archives locked." The advocate instructed the consul to press for action. His second cable stirred Cardinal Gibbons' vice-chancellor to force the lock, consult the files, and report the existence in the register of matrimonial dispensations of a dispensation for Marie Reid, identified as Catholic, to marry Frederick Parkhurst, whose religion was not described.[19] The dispensation was from "disparity of worship," the phrase technically used to describe the diriment impediment to marriage created by one person being baptized and the other unbaptized.

The existence of the record ended the possibility of a swift annulment, administratively handled without trial, on the simple ground that Marie, a Catholic, had married a non-Catholic without ecclesiastical permission.* Marriage with Rospigliosi would not

---

* The Inquisition had ruled on June 9, 1889, that *Dei miseratione* need not be followed as to an appeal, but that one judgment sufficed for nullity in cases of disparity of cult; prior, existing marriage; consanguinity, affinity, and spiritual relationship arising out of lawful intercourse; and defect of form — all on the condition that from "sure documents or evidence it is manifestly proved that these impediments exist and were not dispensed by the Church." The S.C.C., setting out this decree, noted that it was meant to apply worldwide; *Warsaw, Doubt as to Marriage Cases, June 10, 1894, Thesaurus S.C.C*, CLII, 778. The Holy Office later emphasized that the impediments must be "certainly and clearly established," Decree, March 27, 1901, *Analecta ecclesiastica* (1901), IX, 286–287.

now wait for what had canonically to be established. Under Article 94 of the Italian Civil Code persons were married by declaring before a civil official that "they willed respectively to take each other as man and wife." However, one "bound by a preceding marriage" could not marry; and the capacity of a foreigner to marry depended on the laws of his own country.[20] Was Marie Reid bound by a preceding marriage? Was she capable of marriage under the laws of Maine? These questions of a lawyer did not trouble the local magistrate at Lamporrechio. Under the existing separation of Church and State in Italy, civil marriage was possible without the concurrence of the Church. Civilly, Marie and the Prince were united at Lamporrechio. But, once Marie had become Princess Rospigliosi in accordance with Italian law, the religious and social reasons making both Prince and Princess desire the churchly regularization of their union intensified.

In the *Libro D'Oro*, the blue book of the Italian nobility, Rospigliosi was described as married to "the widow Parkhurst." [21] This euphemistic lie was a good index of the difficulty of saying or accepting that the head of the Rospigliosi had married an American divorcee. The arrival of the Prince and his bride at the Rospigliosi palace in Rome and the resulting dispossession of Camillo and his ten children put a severe strain on relations between the two brothers and between the two putative sisters-in-law. If Romans associated with the Quirinal might accept the new union, the Black nobility was adamant in its outrage. Marie, as she later told the *New York Times*, was greeted with "nothing but cold stares and uplifted brows." [22]

Technically, Marie's present status appeared to be governed by canon 124 of the Third Plenary Council of Baltimore, over which Gibbons had presided as Apostolic Delegate in 1884. By the usual principles of canon law, affirmed by Propaganda as recently as 1883, the domicile of a wife unlawfully separated from her husband was determined by her husband's domicile.[23] Marie — separated by no ecclesiastical order from Parkhurst — appeared to be a domicilary of Maine, bound by the legislation of Baltimore. According to canon 124, any Catholic who, after a civil divorce, "dared to attempt matrimony," incurred an excommunication reserved to his Ordinary.[24] The ceremony at Lamporrechio looked like an attempt at marriage. By canon 124, Marie had incurred excommunication and could be absolved only by her new Ordinary, William O'Connell.

Poor boy from Massachusetts, the Bishop of Portland in his six years as a prelate in Rome had cherished his acceptance by the Black nobility, and he had delighted in a special way in those Italians who had married Americans of well-known families. High in his esteem had been Camillo Rospigliosi's eldest son, married to a Bronson from New York.[25] He shared the family's shock and indignation. Marie Reid discovered almost at once that he was not a sympathizer of her cause.[26]

As counsel the Rospigliosi chose a priest, Antonio Lombardi, not the most distinguished member of the curial bar but a seasoned advocate before the courts of the Curia with an appointment in the Holy Office.[27] They may have supposed that at Propaganda, with its pastoral orientation, a priest would be more helpful than a layman. Moving with some dispatch, by the middle of December 1901, Lombardi had enough of a story at his command to file with Propaganda a petition to declare null the marriage of Marie Reid to Frederick Parkhurst.

Gibbons' dispensation authorizing the marriage was attacked on three grounds. First, it had been given without a just reason and without promises by Marie to obtain the conversion of her husband and to educate her children as Catholics; hence, the requisites for a valid dispensation to marry a Protestant did not exist. Second, it had not been given at her request but at that of Monsignor Chapelle; Marie could not have been dispensed without having asked to be dispensed. Third, it had authorized Marie to marry a baptized Protestant; it was ineffective because Frederick was unbaptized. Alternatively, the petition alleged that Marie had married because of an "error of person," believing that she was marrying a Christian; Frederick was an unbaptized person, canonically no Christian, whom she would not have married save for her mistake.[28]

The Rospigliosi made some effort to avoid O'Connell by reciting in the petition that Chapelle had manifested his hostility to their marriage and had influenced O'Connell in a hostile direction. But with Ledóchowski in command at Propaganda, slurs on O'Connell were not well received, and the Roman prominence of the Rospigliosi could not change the rule of canon law that the proper place for a trial of invalidity was the domicile of the parties. Three weeks after the petition was filed, Propaganda ordered O'Connell to conduct the trial in Portland.[29]

In any American diocese a trial of the invalidity of marriage was a rarity, and in most dioceses a "matrimonial tribunal" was unheard of. The large and simple Catholic flock of Maine knew nothing of advocates who might probe the legal satisfactoriness of a marriage made before a priest in church. Marriages, once made, seemed to exist immune from legal attack or inquiry. For the new bishop, it was his first experience. Yet, Propaganda had paternally provided for all new bishops with simple flocks by issuing in 1883 its own version of the rules of Benedict XIV.[30] Following this modern manual, O'Connell named his Vicar-General as moderator or judge of the process, his chancellor as notary, and a local priest as defender of the bond.[31] By this expeditious arrangement of the bishop's chancery officials, a court came into existence. The Vicar-General began the trial in his own living room. No provision was made for counsel for the petitioner: Propaganda's instructions required none, there were no trained advocates in Maine, and the Rospigliosi frugally chose not to send an Italian to act for them in Portland. The American part of the case became an inquiry conducted by the moderator, using the questions drafted by the defender of the bond, into the truth of the petition.

Control of the case from Portland led to Marie Reid's being interrogated at the offices of Propaganda in Rome, her questioner being an Italian judge-delegate using questions prepared in Portland, and her answers being translated for him by the later Dean of the Rota, John Prior.[32] Marie gave her residence as the Palazzo Rospigliosi and said she was the Princess Rospigliosi. She had had no part in conversations before the wedding about a dispensation: "I remember that all the necessary practical things were done by Father Chapelle and by my mother, so that I was not asked to do anything." She had never asked Frederick if he were baptized. She had never discussed religion with Frederick before or after the wedding. Had she, at the moment of her marriage, put in words or in mind the condition, "I marry you Frederick because I believe you are baptized and if you are not baptized I do not take you as my husband"? "No, it never entered my head." Nonetheless, she had "intended to be the wife of a baptized Protestant, which was the religion of my father." Her awkwardness of expression betokened sincerity of mind; but her oral declaration was far less artful than the legal allegations her counsel had incorporated in the libel of petition.

In June, in New Orleans, in his own court, Chapelle answered the questions of Portland.[33] He had been the counselor of Mrs. Reid in her difficulties with her own husband. Mrs. Reid had written him before the wedding that the Parkhursts were Methodists. He, in turn, wrote Parkhurst "along the lines that I understood that he belonged to a Methodist family." His notion of Parkhurst's own religion was "a general guess." He did not remember if Parkhurst had or had not told him that he was unbaptized. He had, however, obtained for the wedding not a simple dispensation to marry a baptized Christian but a dispensation for disparity of worship, the dispensation appropriate for marrying an unbaptized person. He regularly read such dispensations aloud during the service to the couples he was marrying. His competence as a pastor challenged, Chapelle was clear that he had done what was necessary to make the marriage valid.

In July, in Philadelphia, before a specially created three-judge tribunal of the archdiocese, Marie's mother gave her testimony.[34] She had never talked to Parkhurst about religion. She had known that something had to be done about a dispensation and that something had in fact been done. Had she and her daughter spoken to the parish priest about the matter? "I was silent." Had she heard the priest say he would get the dispensation necessary? The priest had said that "he would attend to that."

In August, in Bangor, in Parkhurst's own library, the members of the Portland tribunal heard his story of the dispensation.[35] He was politely quizzical about the present fuss: "The question was not treated as one of much importance, and as far as I can remember was only the subject of a single conversation." He had been and was a Christian, "believing in the principles of Christianity." He was not a baptized Christian. Before the wedding he had so informed his fiancée, her mother, and Father Chapelle.

From December 1901 to August 1902 the case had moved with a briskness which testified to the organization of Propaganda and the competence of ecclesiastics to carry out notorial commissions. The case now languished. Had it become plain to the Rospigliosi that on the evidence they could hope for nothing in America? Or had

313

the opportunity presented itself to escape O'Connell? On July 22, 1902, Ledóchowski had died, and Girolamo Gotti had succeeded him as Prefect. Gotti did not have Ledóchowski's long experience with O'Connell. The Rospigliosi renewed their charge of prejudice: Prince Rospigliosi had written O'Connell about the case and never received an answer. This impoliteness, scarcely unknown among high ecclesiastics, did not amount to very much evidence; and O'Connell's friendship with Camillo was not mentioned. Still O'Connell found it prudent to take the opinion of a Roman advocate who gave him the expected advice.[36] None of the recognized grounds for recusing a judge — blood relationship to a party, bribery, or personal enmity — were present. Nevertheless, Gotti decided that the case should be transferred from Portland to Rome.

For almost two years the case stayed inactive, the result either of a temporizing policy by Propaganda or, more probably, a decision of the Rospigliosi counsel not to press but to wait to see if better evidence or a better opportunity would turn up. A consultor of the congregation, Evaristo Lucidi, the later Secretary of the Signature, was asked to give his opinion on the merits of the claim of nullity and reported to the congregation negatively on Marie Reid's contentions.[37] But the *votum* or recommendation of the consultor — an indispensable step before judgment — was undated and was apparently put aside on Lombardi's plea that more evidence could be found. In May 1904 a regular session of the cardinals of Propaganda made the procedural decision, "Let the record be completed."[38]

On June 13 Gotti wrote O'Connell to obtain more evidence about Parkhurst's baptism or lack of it. Plainly, some members of Propaganda had accepted the Rospigliosi contention that the non-baptism of Parkhurst was the crucial fact to be established. Gotti also brought into play the Holy See's own resource in Washington, Diomede Falconio, the Delegate.[39] Where the records of the most influential prelate in America were in question, Rome would use its own man.

O'Connell replied within the month. Parkhurst, on re-examination by the Portland tribunal, had testified that he knew he was not baptized from what his parents had told him. His sister and his grandmother had also been judicially examined and had stated that they believed him to be unbaptized.[40] What the Parkhursts of Maine thought of all this interest in Fred's baptism was not reported. No Parkhurst was ashamed to state what the Rospigliosi regarded as the crucial fact in Marie's case.

Gotti directed other questions to the Delegate in Washington, and Falconio turned them over to his assistant, Francesco Marchetti-Selvaggiani. This young man, who had arrived in Washington with Falconio, was the classmate of Eugenio Pacelli; and while Pacelli served his apprenticeship to Gasparri, Marchetti-Selvaggiani was initiated into the Curia's technical view of marriage by his assignment to the Parkhurst case. Over forty years later, when Pacelli was Pope, Marchetti-Selvaggiani as Secretary of the Holy Office presided over the inauguration of a new form of papal dissolution of marriage for those in marriages such as Frederick Parkhurst's and Marie Reid's.

Scurrying about the streets of Washington in 1904, sedulously scrutinizing the ecclesiastical registers of the famous cardinal of Baltimore, Marchetti-Selvaggiani performed the apprentice's tasks of a legal bureaucracy which qualified him for advancement within the structure. He took the train to Baltimore, made careful notes on how the archdiocesan records of dispensation were kept, and copied down notations in the register on the Parkhurst-Reid dispensation of 1887. He checked the records of St. Matthew's in Washington and interviewed two priests who had been Chapelle's assistants in the 1880's. He wrote the chancery in Philadelphia, where Mrs. Reid now lived, to get more data on her family. The sum of these inquiries was not enormous.[41] Another Reid daughter was divorced and had married a divorced Protestant; Mrs. Reid lived with this couple, "as if she approved of divorce" — remotely relevant facts perhaps if the case had been of another character. The priests of St. Matthew's denied that Chapelle ever read out dispensations during the course of wedding ceremonies — a point against the credibility of Chapelle's claim that Marie Reid knew of the dispensation. No record at all of the dispensation could be found at St. Matthew's. Still, the notation in Gibbons' register was exactly as the vice-chancellor had reported to the consul in 1901: it recorded a dispensation from disparity of worship.[42] All of this information, grist for the legal mills, was sent on by Falconio to Propaganda.

In Rome, in September 1904, Chapelle was interrogated again, this time not in his own archdiocese but in Propaganda's offices in Rome, with Archbishop Barone of Malta acting as judge-delegate.[43] Chapelle now recalled that he had known that Parkhurst was unbaptized and that both mother and daughter had asked for the dispensation when he explained the need of it to them before the marriage. The next day, the Rospigliosi produced Edmund Stonor, titular Archbishop of Trebizond, as a witness.[44] Stonor testified that Chapelle had discussed the case with him in 1901 and had described the Reid-Parkhurst marriage as one of "mixed religion," a description applicable to the marriage of a Catholic and a baptized Protestant but not technically appropriate to the marriage of an unbaptized person. Stonor, an English aristicrat born in 1831 in Stonor, England, was the patriarch of the English colony in Rome.[45] His testimony was meant of course to shake confidence in Chapelle's story that he had applied for the necessary dispensation, but the larger value of the Archbishop of Trebizond as a witness was to convey to Propaganda that not all English-speaking prelates shared the view of Rospigliosi and Reid taken by O'Connell and Chapelle.

The evidence was now in, and briefs were filed with the Congregation. Lombardi, in thirty-six pages, argued that the testimony supported the contentions made in the libel of petition. He was answered by a defender of the bond, anonymous according to the practice of Propaganda. Lombardi filed a reply to the defender. The briefs were given by the Secretary, Luigi Veccia, to two consultors chosen by him from a roster of twenty-four. The opportunity to use the one American consultant, John Keane, was not availed of, and Veccia selected the titular Archbishop of Damascus, Denis Alphonse Steyaert, a Discalced Carmelite from Ghent, aged seventy-four, and Evaristo Lucidi, the earlier consultor.

Lucidi, already familiar with the case, examined in detail the new material. On March 5, 1905, he submitted his recommendation, entitled "Advice as to the Truth of the Matter in the Case of the Nullity of the Reid-Parkhurst Marriage." His task had been to look at all the facts reported to Propaganda, including not only those judicially established by the Portland tribunal and its worldwide interrogatories, but those more informally ascertained by Marchetti-Selvaggiani's inquiries. In sixteen printed pages he analyzed this matter, the law of marriage dispensations, and the rules governing marriage dispensations in the United States, and concluded negatively to the petition. On April 11, 1905, the other consultor, Steyaert, filed an independent analysis of the case; he, too, was negative.[46]

While this work of analysis went on, a rash of stories inspired by the Rospigliosi appeared in the *New York Times*: It was generally believed in Rome that Princess Rospigliosi's first marriage would be annulled, "it being now established that Colonel Parkhurst was never baptized." Monsignor Chapelle had testified that the marriage was "irregular according to the law of the Church." Cardinal Martinelli, formerly the Apostolic Delegate to the United States, had been assigned to the case and had reported to the Pope in favor of annulment.[47]

Lombardi had to deal with the Congregation, not with the press; and after Steyaert's negative report, he made a last effort to save the case in court. In the name of Princess Rospigliosi, he wrote asking for a new examination of Chapelle, pointing out unpleasantly that it was remarkable that Chapelle could not have remembered Parkhurst's baptismal status in 1901 but could remember it in 1904. He also played a final card: Prince Rospigliosi himself had evidence of relevance to offer and was ready to be heard; the Congregation was requested to examine him judicially.[48]

These frantic efforts in early May were ineffective. The cardinals of the Congregation met in regular session on May 22 and answered the question, "Is nullity of marriage established in the case?" Three abstained, eight voted no.[49] Gotti communicated the result to O'Connell a month later, so that he might inform "the parties." [50] O'Connell's letter to Marie Reid is not preserved, but his reply to Gotti is extant. He would not conceal his "satisfaction that the case has finally terminated and in such a way, with immense jubilation of all good citizens in this country." [51] In the conflict between a Protestant Yankee factory-owner and two lifelong Catholics, O'Connell's heart had not been divided. He had stood with his friends, the junior Rospigliosi, with the sanctity of marriage so flippantly flouted by the petitioner, with the stability of Catholic marriages made in the United States. Triumphant, the New England conscience saw the defeat of Italian deviousness, the repulse of trifling with a great institution by a frivolous couple abetted by legal technicians. That it was improbable that Princess

Marie Rospigliosi would ever return to Bangor as the spouse of
Colonel Parkhurst was not the Bishop's concern. He rejoiced in
the triumph of principle.

Rome–Portland–Baltimore

Maria Rospigliosi, the first child of Prince Rospigliosi and Marie,
was born August 2, 1902, and died August 27, 1907. In the same
year, 1907, Marie gave birth to a boy, Geronimo.[52] Maria's death
and Geronimo's birth both may have rekindled the desire of the
head of the Rospigliosi to be rejoined to the Church and to the
society of Rome. At the beginning of January 1908 Propaganda
received a request signed "Marie Reid, Princess Rospigliosi," asking
for copies of the record in the old case. Renewal of the battle was in
prospect.

Pius X's reorganization of the Curia in 1908 doubtless led counsel
to delay going further that year. The accompanying restructuring
of the judicial system established the Rota as the major court even
for missionary territory. At the same time, the reform decree
Sapienti consilio removed the United States from the jurisdiction
of Propaganda.[53] It was prudent for counsel to study the possibilities presented by the fresh terrain. On March 18, 1909, an effort
was made to reopen the case at the highest level. A petition to Pius
X, humbly signed "Marie Reid," asked that the case "be taken up
again" by the Apostolic Signature.[54] The Pope did not fully grant
this request, but he authorized the Rota to hear the case. One month
after the petition was filed, Parkhurst was cited by the Rota and
called to defend the validity of his marriage to Marie.

A nice ecclesiastical term, *admiratio*, is employed to describe the
sensation caused by behavior which does not technically "give
scandal" — that is, lead another person to believe one is committing a sin — but does cause astonishment, wonder, marvel.
Admiratio was what was felt in Maine when the Rota's citation
arrived. Parkhurst responded directly by a letter couched in Latin
and addressed to the new tribunal itself. The case had been "ma-
turely considered" for several years, it had been decided by a
Sacred Congregation, the judgment of the Congregation had been
confirmed by the Supreme Pontiff himself. The renewed allega-

tions of his wife questioning the existence of the marriage were false, and they were harmful to the couple's offspring. He could only "hope and pray that the case is now *res judicata*." [55]

Parkhurst's motive in entering the new contest in person can only be conjectured. What did it matter to him that a wife he had divorced a decade ago should be given a favor by the Pope? No doubt the shock of having the proceedings reopened four years after their apparent close affected his attitude. Who would not resent the unexpected opening of an old wound? Moreover, to any tidy mind there was incongruity bordering on ridiculousness in this interminable process. No doubt, too, his political career was not helped by the kind of rumors that this sort of questioning of his marriage might generate. Finally, the disingenuousness of his wife's position, the sheer frivolity of her case, must have incensed him. But, underlying all his reasons for irritation at the reopening was there not an emotion toward Marie, a compound of love, hurt, and pride? If for no very large reasons Parkhurst tried to frustrate his wife's desires now, was there not a spark of the old relation, pricked to life? Something had once existed between them. Somehow the very term "nullify" seemed to deny this truth, and, the truth recalled, he had to touch her. On January 9, 1910, he wrote directly to her, addressing her as "the Princess Rospigliosi." He had at first thought to let the marriage be defended in the Rota by the official defender of the bond; but now, he told her, he himself had decided to contest her suit "to protect Reid" and "in memory of Dorothy." Her case, he informed her, "is based on something not true." If she persisted in seeking to win on false grounds, he might be forced to reveal "all the truth" about her conduct which led to his action for divorce.[56] Solemn, self-important, blackmailing, the letter seemed also to reveal toward its recipient an emotion which was anguished, inverted, buried, and not dead.

His wife, attempting marriage while still married to him, was, by the criteria of some Catholic authorities, a public sinner. Such was Parkhurst's own bittersweet observation in a brief filed by him in the Rota. Principled Maine man and divorcing spouse, Parkhurst did not hesitate to make his own the teaching of the Church to whose court he argued. He "had heard from everyone" that at stake was not merely the validity of his own marriage. On the Rota's decision in his case hung "the cause of religion, the cause of the law, and the procedures and the tribunals and the doctrine of the Catholic Church itself." [57]

Doubtless, the elements of canon law had not been among the subjects of study at Columbian University in 1887; and the mass of authorities cited by Parkhurst in his twenty-page brief revealed the hand of some clerical scholar, perhaps a Sulpician or a Jesuit, in its preparation. An impressive array of canonists were marshaled to support the marriage, and, beyond canonists, decisions of the Rota itself — not the infant modern Rota, but the glorious Rota of the seventeenth century. The international tribunal of Albergati and Innocent X's day lived once more in this composition issuing from Maine. Whether the Latin was Parkhurst's own is more debatable. A strong classical education and a strong determination could have produced the prose submitted, but more probably the helpful anonymous scholar of the citations provided the words as well as the cases. What was felt beneath the Latin words and canonical citations, however, was a spirit, simple, forthright, and determined. Properly, no advocate signed the brief, for Parkhurst himself *in propia persona* spoke.

Witnesses — witnesses who could conclusively refute his wife's contentions — Parkhurst was now anxious to supply. There were those who would testify that the marriage was contracted only after his lack of baptism had been discussed with the Reids; those who would testify that he had in fact made an oral guarantee to raise the offspring of the marriage as Catholics; those who would testify as to his reputation for veracity and his wife's reputation for lack of it. If the case was to be redone, Parkhurst stood ready to supply the defender of the bond with all the evidence needed to crush Marie Reid's fanciful claim of nullity. [58]

Only a little less excited by the new proceeding than Parkhurst himself was the venerable head of the American Church, Cardinal Gibbons. Who made it a point to inform him of its progress is not clear. O'Connell had moved on to a grander realm than Portland to become Archbishop of Boston. Chapelle was sunk in an increasingly unsatisfactory state in New Orleans. Perhaps mere newspaper gossip, perhaps Parkhurst himself, roused Gibbons' vigilant interest. The case already was familiar to him as a challenge to a marriage made in his archdiocese by virtue of a dispensation granted by him; but it was not merely his jurisdictional connection with the case which stirred him to act. He perceived in its reopening a threat to that balanced image of the Catholic Church, gracious but principled, supple but unyielding, which he personified in the United States.

In the same month in which Parkhurst made direct contact with Princess Rospigliosi, Gibbons wrote to Rome. His antennae had detected some shift in the handling of the case which seemed to call for bold, vigorous, and personal intervention. He addressed himself to the Dean of the Roman Rota, Michele Lega. He wrote:

> Even although no reason why I should speak can be found written in the law, religion and truth prohibit that, as to something which in the judgment of all good men is a matter of the public good of religion and of the Church, I should be silent.
>
> If a decision is given against the validity of this marriage, there will be a clamor about the authority of the Church and its ministers as regards the sanctity and indissolubility of the bond of marriage among the American people. Up to now our place in this matter has been secure, our words endowed with authority. . . .
>
> If invalidity is decreed, it will be a joy and aid for the enemies of the Church, a wound and anguish for her friends.[59]

Some Protestant sects, he continued, said that the Catholic Church admitted divorce under another name. The case was now famous. It had been heard of "ad nauseum," and "now again our newspapers are full of it." Every eye in the United States was watching. The Cardinal ended on a note of history. He invoked a story familiar to good Baltimoreans, Napoleon's attempt to obtain the annulment of Jérome Bonaparte's marriage to Betsy Patterson of Baltimore. As Gibbons recalled it, the case was instituted by one who "dominated France and terrified all of Europe." Pius VII would not give in to the threats and influence of the Emperor. His firmness "served to show that the Church did not make distinctions among persons." The principles of marriage applied to all. The Pope's stand in the end "brought inestimable benefits to the Church." Gibbons trusted that the present case would end the same way.*

---

* The American points of view which Gibbons had in mind had been expressed fifty years earlier by Nathaniel Hawthorne in *The Marble Faun*. For his heroine Hilda, drawn to the Church of Rome, "the exuberance with which it adapts itself to all the demands of human infirmity" was virtually a sign of divinity: "If its ministers were but a little more than human, above all error, pure from all iniquity,

The cardinal's example from history was, perhaps, not as free from ambiguity as he would have wished. Jérome Bonaparte did secure an annulment from the Church in France and did go on to marry Catherine of Württemberg, even though neither the state of Maryland nor the Pope recognized the grounds of the annulment.[60] But, however muddied the actual course of events, Gibbons' point was clear. On occasion, under the gravest pressure, Popes had held out for principle in marriage cases. The injustice, the sin, of deciding cases not by distinguishing principles but by distinguishing persons, had been gloriously avoided. Gibbons' view of the seriousness of the issue and the severity of the pressures now applied was suggested by his example: the senior Rospigliosi cast in the role of the Bonapartes, Pius X likened to the captive Pius VII. The nature of the issue and the nature of the pressures no doubt justified in the Cardinal's own mind his extraordinary demarche outside the normal legal channels and his candid appeal to the Dean of the Rota to decide the case on the basis of public policy.

Longuinqua oceani spatia, "across the long leagues of ocean," Leo XIII had leaped, in spirit, in 1895 to review the prosperity of the Church in America and to congratulate it on its stand on divorce. "Scarcely a greater ill can be thought of," he had declared, "than to wish to be able to break the bond which is perpetual and undivided by divine law." This truth, he had observed, had been perceived by not a few American non-Catholics, who "admired and approved" the Catholic doctrine. Their judgment was "not less the result of the love of country than it was the counsel of wisdom." [61] These words from Rome had echoed Gibbons' own convictions, appealed to his patriotism, flattered his wisdom, heartened his courage. Surely sixteen years later the Roman Curia would not lack Leo's perception of the Church's interests in America, or fail his cardinal.

Splendid rhetoric, shining historical exemplar, and justified reliance were not Gibbons' only resources when he wrote to Rome. In his seventy-sixth year on earth, his thirty-third as Archbishop of Baltimore, he spoke with the weight of his acquired reputation. Later in the same year in which he addressed the Rota he wrote,

what a religion it would be!" For her companion Kenyon, "the exceeding ingenuity of the system stamps it as the contrivance of man or some worse author." *The Marble Faun or The Romance of Monte Beni* (Boston, 1900), II, 271.

for example, to the papal Secretary of State Merry del Val, on another matter, the "mission entrusted to me by the Holy Father through His Excellency the Most Reverend Apostolic Delegate Monsignor Falconio, in regard to a threatened persecution of the Church in Cuba." Gibbons reported that he had executed the mission by calling on President Taft. Taft had responded by sending an American fleet on a courtesy call to Havana, a fleet carrying with it General Leonard Wood who delivered to President Gomez in the name of the United States an "informal protest" about the threatened measures; and President Gomez had responded by assuring General Wood that no legislation would be directed at the Church. As Gibbons wrote Merry del Val, "it was a pleasure as well as a duty for me to be of assistance in a matter of such supreme importance." [62] Gibbons' service of this sort, past and future, in such matters of supreme importance was what gave his exhortation to Dean Lega more than eloquence could bestow.

Scorning subtlety, Gibbons had chosen to make a head-on attempt to influence the court. With equal directness Dean Lega did not keep the letter to himself but made it available to Francesco Parrillo, the defender of the bond; and Parrillo printed it as part of his brief. The Princess had new counsel, Consistorial Advocate Carlo Santucci, a friend from early youth of Cardinal Gasparri.[63] With Gibbons' letter in front of everyone, Santucci responded to it vigorously. Gibbons' missive, he declared, was itself a cause for *admiratio*. The libelous rumors which agitated the cardinal had nothing to do with the case. It was not the Rota's business "to seek the applause and praise of the crowd in administering justice." The function of the marriage courts was other than that so crudely ascribed to it by Gibbons:

The tribunals were not established to break or to preserve the bond of marriage, as the Most Eminent Gibbons says in the cited letter, but, with the help of God and according to the dictates of conscience, to discover the truth without distinction as to person.[64]

The true favoritism, the advocate implied, was what Gibbons sought. On the merits, decision should be for the Rospigliosi.

The Rota spent some months weighing Parkhurst's offer of new witnesses. Santucci counterattacked by producing the bulletin of St. George's School in Newport, Rhode Island. According to the rules stated here, all students of the school were required to attend Episcopalian services; and Reid Parkhurst was listed as a student. This evidence, Santucci maintained, showed Parkhurst's "lack of good faith" in carrying out his prenuptial promise and somehow disabled him from offering more evidence. Parrillo, staunch and tenacious defender of the bond, took a middle ground, arguing that the new testimony could be taken if the Rota thought it necessary, but suggesting that even without it Propaganda's decision of 1905 could be upheld. On June 23, 1910, the Rota ruled that more evidence would be superfluous.[65]

DISPENSATIONMANSHIP

To the dispassionate observer Marie Reid's attempt to escape from the unwelcome bonds of matrimony on the ground of a defective dispensation is likely to seem foolish. Married in church, a wife for eleven years, mother of three children fathered by the man she had wed, what difference to her state could be made by the exact terms under which she had been permitted to marry? The dispassionate observer may share the impatience of Bishop O'Connell and Cardinal Gibbons, their sense that an annulment would have been a travesty of the teaching that marriage was indissoluble.

This sensible viewpoint arguably gives insufficient weight to the highly legal character of the entire ecclesiastical institution of marriage. Indisputably, it ignores the basic intuition underlying Marie Reid's case: there was something special, something different, about marriage with a non-Christian. Obscured by the way the lawyers tried the case, this fundamental fact never became so intelligible as to fully reveal the strength of the Reid-Rospigliosi position. But even in the fashion the case was presented to the court, the special character of marriage with an unbeliever was its premise.

No general canon existed saying that a Catholic could not marry an unbeliever. Such marriages were simply perceived as forbidden by custom, and this perception was enunciated by the masters of the medieval schools. Such marriages were, said Gratian, "contrary to the ordinance of God and the Church"; and a couple who entered into such a union was to be separated.[66] "Difference of cult" between believer and unbeliever, opined Peter Lombard, meant that

324

they "could not contract marriage." [67] These teachers also vigorously disapproved of marriage to a heretic, but it was in a different category from marriage to an unbeliever. Divine natural law, the teachers said, prohibited both kinds of marriage outside the fold — no canon then was strictly necessary — but marriages with unbelievers were not only sinful and illicit but null.[68] On this critical difference in consequence between marriage to another Christian, albeit a heretic, and marriage to an unbeliever, Marie Reid premised her case.

Such a case to be sure meant treating unbelief as equivalent to nonbaptism. Traditional theory supported this approach. The *infidelis* of tradition, the infidel, the faithless one, the unbeliever, was the one who had not received the sacrament of entry into the community of believers.[69] Baptism was the great dividing line between the company of the faithful and the infidel. To twentieth-century minds this division might seem rough indeed. Was a man who had been baptized in infancy and never again been to church a believer? Was an unbaptized person instructed in the Bible with a strong commitment to "Christian principles" an infidel? A distinction with these consequences seemed to work with a logic which gave too little room for the human relation with God involved in faith. Rude as it was, however, the division made by baptism formed the foundation for distinguishing marriages made with simple heretics from those made with unadulterated unbelievers. By this crude criterion, Marie Reid Rospigliosi was a believer, Frederick Parkhurst an unbeliever.

The method employed in classifying Christians accounts for part of the impression of artifice given by the case. But more central to the creation of this impression were the rules which had developed for litigation involving dispensations. Regardless of the impediment dispensed, these were likely to give such litigation the character of an especially artificial game. Although a specifically canonical institution, dispensation was no anomaly in a legal system. Like the civil licensing of marriages, dispensation furnished a record of a distinctive class. Like the licensing of dogs or automobiles, it had the effect of producing a modest revenue. Like the licensing of taverns, it provided a restricted outlet for actions thought undesirable as a general rule in the community. Like all such licensing schemes it set at least a minimal standard of personal competence for the one obtaining the license: he must at least have had the intelligence, knowledge, and good will to apply. Licensing of this kind created flexibility within an ordered structure. The world created by it was not a world of pure individual options. However routinely the clearance was granted if asked, the person who wanted to do the licensed act had to ask permission of the community before he acted. The asking fed authority in the community's representatives, and the granting, when not too stingy or too arbitrary, fostered solidarity in the community.*

Dispensations, it might be argued, were themselves likely to cause trouble. It could be said of each of the principal cases in this book that a broken marriage would have been avoided if the common law had been observed. Refusal to dispense Charles of Lorraine to marry his first cousin Nicole, refusal to dispense Boni de Castellane to marry a heretic, and refusal to dispense Marie Reid to marry an unbeliever would have prevented three misunions. Insistence on the Tridentine procedural requirement on banns might have deterred Barberini and Folchi from their secret marriages and led to José Perez de Guzman being better informed on the mental fitness of his fiancée. Such speculation, however, is unfair argument against the utility of dispensations, when one does not also look at the many unions, made possible by dispensation, which flourished. Dispensation involved a risk, but a risk which only slightly increased the risks of marriage itself.

The unavoidable effect of dispensation was that it lessened the seriousness of the law dispensed from. Save for procedural formalities such as the banns, the marriage law of the Church was supposed to be based on requirements of the moral order. Licensing a departure from one of its provisions emphasized the legal rather than the moral character of the rule and conflicted with the rhetoric often employed to justify the rule itself. When the Church dispensed so that an uncle could marry a niece, it licensed incest as

---

* To the objection that dispensation constitutes the sin of "acceptance of persons," Thomas Aquinas replied that, "when the condition of some person requires that as to him something be specially observed, there is no acceptance of persons if some special grace is done to him," *Summa theologica*, 1–2, q. 90, art. 4, reply to obj. 2. Sanchez taught that it was not the sin of acceptance of persons to dispense the rich and powerful more easily than the poor, because marriage dispensations were given to strengthen peace, and this purpose "was more necessary for the common good as regards the rich and powerful than the poor and plebians," *De sancto matrimonii sacramento*, 8.19.5.

defined by the canons. When the Church dispensed to let a Catholic marry a Protestant, it permitted what Popes had described as a "sacrilegious union." [70] Acts permitted by dispensations could scarcely be evil in themselves. This inference was reinforced by the axiom that what was forbidden by natural law could not be licensed by any ecclesiastical authority. The dispensable rules, in contrast to indispensable natural laws, appeared to be prudential, paternalistic, even legalistic. As the rules suffered a loss of moral flavor, legalism was encouraged in their treatment, and legalism was redoubled in the treatment of the dispensations by which exceptions to the rules were authorized.

The canonical effort to maintain the gravity of the marriage rules, while permitting the exceptions, compounded the legalism still further. First, conditions were laid down for the validity of a dispensation. Then, validity of marriage was made to turn on validity of dispensation. The first teaching was an obvious attempt to justify and to control departures from the general rule; the second employed the extreme sanction of nullity to make the first effective. It was a device which was not an unavoidable dictate of logic. If the conditions for a valid dispensation had not been met, the dispenser could have been held accountable without visiting invalidity upon the marriage itself. Whatever was wanting to make the dispensation valid could have been said to be "supplied" by the Church as a whole. Such a legal fiction was employed where a priest lacked jurisdiction to confer absolution, but through a common error penitents believed he was competent to act; the Church did not treat the absolutions given as invalid, although the requirements for legal validity had not been satisfied. That such a solution was not adopted for marriage dispensations, that the overkill solution of nullity was adopted instead, needs explanation. One not implausible explanation is that this approach gave the Curia discretion not only in the granting of exceptions to the rules for making marriages but in the granting of annulments.

That some significant organizational desire of this kind was being served becomes more apparent in view of the failure to apply ordinary principles of estoppel to those dispensed to marry. One who has benefited from a legal grace and induced reliance upon it by another should not be heard to challenge its validity — the rule seems elementary. Its adoption here would have been equitable and fostered certainty. But canonical practice knew no such limitation on attacks on dispensations. Anyone questioning the validity of a marriage could question the validity of the dispensation he had enjoyed. The most famous of all annulment cases, Henry VIII's attempt to repudiate Catherine of Aragon, took the form of such an assault on the papal license by whose grace Henry had wed.[71] Despite the large, unhappy consequences of this proceeding, the Curia did not change the rule. Its utilitarian justification was that it gave the courts of the Curia broad latitude. *Reid-Parkhurst* was no sport in matrimonial litigation. The advocates followed a beaten track; and at the end of their pedantic labor they stood dependent on the discretionary justice of the court.

Validity of dispensation depended in part on the reason for the dispensation. Any official subject to a superior's law could not exempt from the law without reason — without what was technically termed "a just reason." The Pope could dispense from his own law at will, but he could not dispense from God's positive law without justification. Analogously, a bishop could dispense from his own law, but just reason alone would permit him to dispense from papal law. A bishop, moreover, could dispense from such law only to the extent the Pope had permitted him to dispense. As a dispenser, he was compared to an agent distributing the principal's property: the distribution would not confer title unless made within the scope of the agent's authority. That the bishop, like an agent, might have apparent authority on which others could rely, was denied. Only actual authority sufficed to make his act of dispensation valid.[72]

The Council of Trent itself had provided that dispensations were to be given "with maximum deliberation," and that the reason for the dispensation must be known to the person dispensing if the dispensation was to be valid. Otherwise, the Council had said in a decree of reform aimed at past abuse, "the most sacred canons are to be exactly observed by everyone." That a just reason existed but was not known to the dispenser did not, according to Sanchez, satisfy the terms of this law.[73]

Specific authority for American bishops to dispense from the impediments of mixed religion and disparity of worship was of comparatively recent origin. While certain types of delegation to dispense had been standardized since 1637, only during the American

Civil War had the Pope approved a standard formula for the delegation of his powers to dispense from these impediments.[74] Standardization of the formula had been a tacit recognition of the impracticality of trying to prevent Catholics from marrying non-Catholics in the United States. "If you can't beat them, regularize them" was a curial instinct. Even so, marriages with Jews still required specific exemption from Rome; and the powers which were granted had to be renewed every ten years. American bishops were required to apply for the delegation to Propaganda; its Secretary routinely submitted the request for approval by the Pope and then forwarded the papal authorization to the suppliant bishop in the terms of the approved formula for the United States, Formula D.[75]

Formula D made specific the ordinary rule requiring cause for the dispensing power to be exercised: "His Holiness wills and commands that the said bishop use the faculties referred to *supra* only to the extent that there are just and serious reasons." An Instruction for the treatment of mixed marriages issued in 1858 by Cardinal Antonelli, Pius IX's Secretary of State, was incorporated by reference in Formula D; it reiterated that the Holy See permitted such "pernicious" and "detestable" unions only for serious reasons.[76] In 1868, an encyclical letter put out by Propaganda was equally severe. It lamented that some bishops had misunderstood Antonelli's Instruction as representing a change in papal policy to favor the acceptance of marriages with non-Catholics. Propaganda fiercely reminded the bishops that they would have to account to God if they permitted such marriages, even for "the gravest reasons," and they were reminded once more that no exercise was valid save for "just and serious reason."[77] When the bishops of the American Church assembled at the Third Council of Baltimore, presided over by Gibbons in 1884, three years before the Parkhurst marriage, they repeated on their own account the received teaching: "A just and serious canonical cause is fully required; and without it believers cannot be permitted to place themselves in serious danger as to faith and morals even when guarantees are given."[78]

Formula D would have been a straitjacket if a broad view of what constituted just and serious reasons had not existed. As early as 1822 the Vicar Apostolic of Bosnia had asked the Holy Office if a dispensation to marry a heretic could be given those Catholics "who assert no other motive save insane love," when "it is foreseen that if the dispensation is denied they will enter marriage before an unbelieving magistrate." The Holy Office replied, "Use your faculties as you judge expedient in the Lord." [79] The answer appeared to echo Paul on the freedom of widows to remarry: "Let her marry whom she will, only in the Lord" (1 Cor. 7). It recognized the bishop's freedom to take the force of sexual love into account. A circular from Propaganda itself in 1877 was equally benign, repeating the answer of 1822 and listing sixteen reasons recognized as just and serious in the practice of that paradigmatic canonical body, the Roman Curia.[80] Among the reasons explicitly endorsed for use by those under Propaganda's tutelage were some which were personal to a given couple (for example, the pregnancy of the girl and the danger of scandal therefrom); others depended on age (any girl over twenty-four was officially *super adulta*, and her "over-age" was reason alone to facilitate her marriage to anyone who was willing to marry her); some were geographical (the locality in which the petitioner lived might be so small that there was almost no one to choose except the heretic or unbeliever). Two reasons which would seem to have been particularly applicable in the United States were "predominance of heretics or unbelievers in a given region" and "the probable danger of civil marriage" if the requested dispensation was denied. In short, despite numerous gruff warnings and much paternal headshaking, Propaganda was reconciled to accepting unions of believers and unbelievers if application was made for dispensation in the most usual kind of circumstances.

Propaganda's Instruction was appended to the Decrees of the Council of American Bishops in 1884, and a specific canon of the Council required its sedulous observance. The Council also noted that attention was to be given to "the circumstances of place, matter, and person, especially where there is a danger of a more serious evil, lest in dispensations being denied, a secret mixed marriage be contracted anyhow without the guaranties." [81] Left open was whether the dispensing bishop had to judge the circumstances of each case — the Council's emphasis on circumstances suggested this approach — or whether the bishop could have a standard rule, in the circumstances of his diocese, authorizing dispensations if they were sought. The validity of the dispensation given Marie

Reid turned in part on determining whether Formula D had permitted Cardinal Gibbons to adopt the latter, standardized approach. A related question was whether Cardinal Gibbons personally had to give the dispensation. Formula D permitted a bishop to redelegate his dispensing authority to his Vicar-General, if he were absent from his residence or lawfully impeded.[82] Taken on their face, the restrictions of Formula D and the Council of Baltimore seemed to mean that the bishop should act in person if he was engaged in the regular conduct of his diocese and that he should act with the maximum deliberation and personal knowledge of the just reason required for dispensation by the Council of Trent.

A further relevant condition for validity was that the guarantees, devised by way of compromise when Catholic princes were first permitted to marry Protestants, had been given by Parkhurst. From the Reformation to the nineteenth century the policy of the Inquisition had been constant that Catholics would not be permitted to marry a heretic. Two exceptions existed to this policy, one unofficial, one official. The unofficial exception was broad, that established by contrary custom in Germany, the Netherlands, England, and other countries with large Protestant populations, where Catholics entered mixed marriages without asking any ecclesiastical permission. The official exception was initiated by Clement VIII in 1604 when he permitted the Catholic Prince of Transylvania to marry a Protestant princess. It was thenceforth held that "a very grave public cause, affecting the good of the whole Church," might justify a dispensation, so that princes and even high nobles become eligible.* To guard against what appeared to be the obvious dangers of this innovation, the guarantees were insisted on, and in their subsequent expanded usage they continued to retain something of the flavor of a negotiated marriage. When eventually in the nineteenth century the Popes determined to eliminate the north European custom of undispensed Catholic-Protestant marriages and did so by making dispensation easier, insistence on the guarantees accompanied the liberalization.[83]

The guarantees were three: the non-Catholic spouse must under-

---

* Schenk, citing Cardinal Albizzi, Secretary of the Inquisition, states that the first dispensation to marry a heretic was for the marriage of Heinrich of Bavaria, a Catholic, to Catherine of Navarre, the Calvinist sister of Henri IV of France. Catherine died before the dispensation could be acted on, but policy had been established with regard to rules. Schenk, *Matrimonial Impediments*, pp. 50–52.

take not "to pervert" the faith of the Catholic. The Catholic must promise to take care, to the extent of his ability, to convert the non-Catholic. Both must agree to educate the offspring of both sexes "in the holiness of the Catholic religion." So ran the classical statement of the guarantees in Formula D. The premise was that the Catholic faith was the true faith. No equality of marital rights could override this central proposition. From this premise it followed that a Catholic committed a sin against faith by running any substantial risk of impairing his belief; that the Catholic had a duty in charity to bring the non-Catholic to the light; and that the education of the children, undertaken by both parents as part of the primary purpose of marriage, meant education in the true religion. Not to make these undertakings was to sin against divine natural law. Beyond the sin, Propaganda had attached a judicial sanction. Since the guarantees were "founded in that divine natural law which the Church and the Holy See struggle with all their zeal to preserve in its integrity," the giving of the guarantees was "an express condition" for the grant of a dispensation to marry a heretic or unbeliever.[84]

When the Rota met to decide the petition of Marie Reid it had to decide these questions. Had Cardinal Gibbons, knowing a just and serious reason existed, given the dispensation for this reason? Had Marie Reid promised to raise the children as Catholics and to take care for the conversion of her spouse? Had Frederick Parkhurst promised to raise the children as Catholics and not to subvert the faith of his wife? Literal reading of the rules seemed to make an affirmative answer to all the questions necessary to sustain the marriage. Dispensationmanship made all the answers open to management.

AMERICA AND ROME

The Rota's answer was given June 30, 1910, one week after it had decided that further evidence would be superfluous.[85] Dean Lega delivered a sober, careful, and exhaustive opinion for a court composed of all the auditors, Persiani, Sebastianelli, Many, Heiner, Prior, Sincero, and Mori. One subordinate issue was easily disposed of: Marie's original contention that she had made a mistake of person in marrying an unbaptized person. The modern Rota was not totally unsympathetic to this ground for annulment authorized by Gratian, as the *Wang-Sang* case was to illustrate in 1913.* But Marie had effectively undone her first advocate's claim of a vital error by her testimony that it "had never entered her head" to think about Parkhurst's baptismal state at the time of the wedding. Her advocates before the Rota abandoned the point altogether.

A subordinate claim affecting the dispensation was also disposed of, though with slightly greater difficulty: Marie's contention that she did not know she was being dispensed. According to Sanchez, a person must ask for a dispensation or at least know he has received it, for it to be valid.[86] Lega held that, wanting to be married, she had wanted a valid dispensation; turning everything over to her mother and Chapelle she had authorized them to do everything necessary for the wedding. The familiar legal technique of implying an intention was employed, and an intention to seek the dispensation was found implicit in Marie Reid's behavior.

The court's willingness to attribute the appropriate intention to Marie was matched by its attribution of reasons to Gibbons when it came to consider a more central issue, the just and serious ground for his granting the dispensation. No evidence at all had been proffered as to what his reason had been. Nothing appeared in the records of the chancery beyond the bare fact that the dispensation had been given. Chapelle testified only that he had asked for it. The records of Baltimore did show, as Marchetti-Selvaggiani had reported, that 642 dispensations for mixed religion and 120 dispensations for disparity of worship had been given by Baltimore in a thirty-month period from January 1885 to September 1887. Plainly, dispensations were routinely granted at the chancery. Anyone at all familiar with the operations of a large ecclesiastical see could infer that dispensations were not the personal act of the bishop himself weighing the circumstances of each case, but licenses routinely issued by the designated chancery official upon application by the parish priest performing the marriage. American bishops were no-

---

* A widower, John Wang, sent his son to another village to arrange a marriage with beautiful young Lu Cecilia. When she refused, his son substituted ugly old Anastasia Sang; his father, meeting her for the first time at the altar, accepted her under the impression she was the girl he had heard so much about. The marriage was annulled for mistake of person — the mistake, the Rota said, was not merely of quality: Wang had intended to marry only the person described by Lu Cecilia's characteristics, *Southwestern Ce-Li, April 17, 1913, Decisiones seu sententiae*, V, 242, before Heiner, Prior, and Sincero.

torious for the ease with which they granted dispensations. The very summer of 1901 in which Prince Rospigliosi's lawyers had begun to test the dispensation given Marie Reid, Prefect of Propaganda Ledóchowski had had occasion to address an admonition to Gibbons on American "abuses": in some dioceses, the canonical cause for granting the dispensation and the relevant circumstances were not set out as required by the Instructions of 1877.[87] Ledóchowski was tactfully vague as to where these abuses had occurred. But he could scarcely have supposed that the only American cardinal occupied himself with weighing the reasons in the hundreds of marriages in his archdiocese. Faced with marriages which were canonically invalid for failure to observe the law, the American instinct had been to regularize rather than invalidate. In 1866 the Second Council of Baltimore had observed that marriages were frequently invalid for disparity of cult in dioceses where there were few Catholics; often, when a priest pointed out the invalidity and suggested a dispensation, the non-Catholic spouse would refuse to renew his consent. To meet these situations the Council had asked the Holy See for the delegation of authority to missionaries to cure these marriages by dispensations retroactive to the time of the original exchange of consent.[88] The impulse had been to uphold as many unions as possible. Analogously, to avoid the need for retroactive curing, the American bishops had not been grudging in giving dispensations to marry. Would Rome back them when the letter of the law threatened to undermine their routine? *

* O'Connell gives as a story *ben trovato* that Pius IX on being asked for a certain dispensation, smiled and said, "The Pope cannot grant that dispensation. You must go to an American bishop for it." The American bishops, O'Connell adds, were "so far from Rome" and "so unaccustomed to the minute regulations of the Curia," that they would often regard exact fidelity to the law as unjust and "so take matters into their own hands" (O'Connell, *Recollections of Seventy Years*, p. 154). The Third Council of Baltimore instructed the parish priest to dissuade Catholics from marrying non-Catholics, "with all his strength, with exhortations, persuasions, and upbraiding"; and if the party persisted, he was to make "a careful examination of the grave canonical causes which are required for the dispensation." (Decree 134, *Acta et Decreta*, p. 67). However, it is inferable that a parish priest accepted the case as presented to him by the interested parties. The practice of accepting non-Catholics' statements that they are baptized is described as an abuse leading to "a number" of invalid marriages in Ledóchowski's warning to Gibbons. Four years before the Reid-Parkhurst marriage, Chapelle had asked a dispensation for Senator Tabor, a Protestant, to marry a parishioner of St. Matthew's. Chapelle had received his promises orally, interviewed the father, mother, brothers, and sisters of the bride, "all professing to be good Catholics," and officiated at the wedding after the dispensation had been granted. The Washington correspondent of the *New York Times* then informed Chapelle that Senator Tabor was a divorced man whose first wife was alive. Chapelle wrote to

If the Rota upheld the express terms of Formula D, if it followed Trent's provision that the reason for the dispensation be known to the dispenser, if it took seriously the requirement of the Third Council of Baltimore that the circumstances be considered, if it insisted that the just and serious reason for the dispensation be established in each instance, it would have taught that a standard operation of Cardinal Gibbons' archdiocese was such as to produce hundreds of invalid American marriages. The Rota assumed that common sense required a different result. Accordingly, it reviewed Marie Reid's circumstances in 1887 — her youth, her poverty, her quarreling parents, her suitor's prospects and his great love for her — and concluded: "Surely there was present the danger that the fiancés, if denied dispensation, would enter marriage before a civil magistrate or heretical minister." Knowledge of these circumstances by Chapelle was tacitly supposed by the Rota to have somehow been shared by Gibbons. Without a scrap of evidence before the court the danger of a civil marriage was taken to be the just and serious reason upon which the dispensing authority had acted.

Determined, as it now appeared, to uphold the marriage, Lega faced his most demanding task in explaining the satisfactoriness of the guarantees. Chapelle had testified that Parkhurst had orally promised to respect his wife's religion and to bring the children up as Catholics. Gibbons and the American hierarchy in 1883 had expressed the hope that a standard set of written guarantees be composed for all the dioceses.[89] Nothing had come of this desire by 1887. Under existing practice an oral promise sufficed; and Chapelle's testimony was taken to be adequate proof when coupled with Parkhurst's own testimony that he had raised the children to attend the Catholic Church. But no evidence was given by anyone that Marie Reid had undertaken either to educate the children as Catholics or to care for her husband's conversion; and she herself testified that she had not given the guarantees. A fatal weakness seemed to exist in the conditions necessary for a valid dispensation.

At this point in the case the Rota had to make a choice: to uphold the terms of the papal delegation of power to dispense and, so doing, nullify the Parkhurst marriage on a technicality, or to invoke

---

tell Gibbons that he had been "shamefully imposed upon" and would announce to the press that he had been deceived. (Chapelle to Gibbons, 1883, Archives of the Archdiocese of Baltimore, Gibbons file.) In fact Chapelle had been doubly deceived. Tabor's bride was a divorced Catholic, Elizabeth Doe, the later heroine of "The Ballad of Baby Doe."

a counter principle. In reaching its decision it had to weigh the express requirements of Formula D for a valid dispensation — all the guarantees must be given — against the effect upon the Church in the United States of requiring this kind of compliance with the rules.

Speaking generally, the Curia had no special qualms about invalidating a marriage for failure to meet a requirement that someone unsympathetic with the system would denominate as "technical." After all, the rule-makers could believe, there is not some metaphysical substance known as "true marriage" floating in isolation from the law. A true marriage is a valid marriage, and a valid marriage is one which has met the conditions specified by law. This spirit — legalistic to its critics, lawyerlike to its admirers — was even compatible with a desire to make marriage a better, holier institution. Part of the program of Pius X "to restore all things to Christ" had been the reform decree *Ne temere* issued by the S.C.C. in 1908 which extended Trent far beyond its old limits of parishes where Trent had been published and made it applicable throughout the entire Catholic world — the result being to require all those baptized as Catholics to marry before their parish priest and two witnesses, and to produce a mass of invalid marriages among those who out of sheer ignorance would marry without regard to the new law.[90] Lega had been Secretary of the S.C.C. when this measure entailing wholesale invalidations had been enacted. He could not have hesitated now, merely because a technical flaw was present, to hold defective a marriage which had failed to meet the standards set for exercise of the papal prerogative of dispensation.*

* In composing *Ne temere* it was debated whether the decree should apply even to those who had been baptized as Catholics but who had been born of non-Catholics and educated as non-Catholics, Folchi's friend, Agostino Sili, arguing that it should not, and Carlo Lombardi, the defender of the bond in the first round of Folchi, arguing that it should. "Relatio actorum quae praecesserant decretum 'Ne temere,'" *Analecta ecclesiastica* (1908), XVIII. Lombardi's advice was taken in the decree; Sili's advice was followed by Gasparri in the Code (see Gasparri, *De matrimonio* [1932 ed.] sec. 1024. In the long run — thirty years — Lombardi's position was reinstated by Pius XII in 1948. *Motu proprio*, "Abrogatur alterum comma paragraphi secundae can. 1099," published in *Periodica de re morali canonica liturgica* (1948) XXXVIII, 333-334. The final position returned to that of the S.C.C. in 1907. It adopted as deliberate policy a law which those educated as non-Catholics could scarcely be expected to comply with — how would they know who were their parish priests? — with the intention of facilitating or speeding up the dissolution of marriages probably invalid for intention against indissolubility; see Joseph Creusen, S.J., "Notes" appended to the *Motu proprio, ibid.*, pp. 334-344.

Three considerations to the contrary, however, could not have escaped the court. The American bishops were remarkably free in their failure to follow the requirements for valid dispensations; so that strict enforcement of the rules would make American marriages open to challenge on a massive scale. The American bishops preferred preservation of apparently valid marriages to discovery of what marriages were valid in terms of the letter of the law; the attitude of O'Connell, the testimony of Chapelle, the extraordinary letter of Gibbons proclaimed that preference so that no auditor of the Rota could doubt how deeply it was felt. The American church was now a powerful constituent of the universal Church; its emergence from the control of Propaganda in 1908 marked with some exactness the point at which it was no longer experienced as a missionary enterprise of Europeans but as a vigorous younger partner capable of material contribution to the old organization.* If policy said, "Papal authority should be upheld; papal directives should not be ignored at will," policy also said, "Do not defy the established leader of so fair a flock."

In the end the option favorable to the Americans was made easy by finding at hand an old and settled maxim: dispensations were presumed to be validly given unless the contrary were established. This principle, so commensensical in appearance, took much of the snap out of the game of "Dispensation:" the court could end the game at any point by assuming what was necessary to make the dispensation turn out validly. Selective use of this presumption meant that the Rota retained enormous discretion in determining

---

* One crude measure for the changing place of the American Church is financial. Statistics on contributions do not in general exist, but a good, if rough, index of American development is furnished by one set of published data: the contributions made to the Society for the Propagation of the Faith, a charity founded to finance Catholic missions. When the Society was founded in Lyon in 1822, France was still the most important Catholic country in the world and the United States was pure mission territory. Between 1822 and 1861, the American Church was a recipient of European bounty, receiving over $7,000,000 (Fulton J. Sheen, "Propagation of the Faith, Society for the," *New Catholic Encyclopedia* [New York: McGraw-Hill, 1967], XI, 844–845). By 1875 the United States ranked fifth among contributors to the Society, although the 100,000 francs from America scarcely compared with the 3,900,000 francs from France (*Annales de la propagation de la foi* [Lyon, 1876], XLVIII, 159–181). By 1901 the United States was only behind France and Germany with its contribution of $145,000 still substantially behind France's $1,345,000 (*Annals of the Propagation of the Faith* [Baltimore and New York, 1902], LXV, 111). But, by 1912 the American share had risen to $281,000, more than one-third of the French contribution of $605,000; and the American was the second largest contribution (*ibid.*, LXXV, 40–99).

whether a marriage failed because of a technically defective dispensation or still held because the dispensation was presumed to be effective. Faced with a choice between preserving the celebrated technical traps of the law of dispensation and the public policy favoring the reliability of official acts and the stability of marriage, the Rota now chose reliability and stability. Because the Rota's decision did not abolish the celebrated traps, the Curia would be faced with the same options in other cases. In *Baltimore, June 30, 1910* the demand for stability in the United States was heard: Cardinal Gibbons' dispensation was valid; Marie Reid's marriage to Parkhurst was good. The day after the Rota's decision was announced, letters went from Lega to Gibbons in Baltimore and to O'Connell in Boston informing them of the outcome.[91]

The End of the Affair

Vindicated in Rome, Frederick Parkhurst was able to appraise his situation at home more judicially. Dean Lega had remarked in his opinion upon his great initial love for Marie, "who still, after so many divisive things, cannot be entirely forgotten by him." But perhaps the very struggle with Marie and his crushing victory freed him to turn his mind from her. In his view, the fact that he had once been married was no reason not to marry again. The point he had made against Marie was that their marriage had been a reality not a nullity; his appearance in the case did not commit him to Catholic notions of indissolubility. Within a year of the determination by the Rota that he had been validly married the first time he married again, this time a girl from Boston, Dorothy Woodman. The couple had two daughters, born in 1913 and 1919. Parkhurst's business and political careers continued to flourish, and in 1920 he became governor of Maine. He died from an unexpected illness twenty days after taking office.[92]

Rospigliosi was too old a Roman to be discouraged by even two such rebuffs as the vote of Propaganda in 1905 and the vote of the Rota in 1910. Parkhurst's remarriage provided an opportunity for reopening the battle. On November 29, 1911, the Rota, *en banc*, turned down the request of counsel for Marie that new evidence be taken in the case;[93] but if new evidence would not be taken, the

Signature could still be asked to order reconsideration of the old evidence. Perhaps, too, Rospigliosi took heart from a decision of the Holy Office announced on June 21, 1912. A marriage between a Catholic and an unbaptized person was null, the Holy Office decreed, if "the prescribed guarantees were not given." [94] Proof of the giving of the guarantees was the weakest point in Parkhurst's case. After a fourth year of waiting, the Signature complied with Marie's request. Under date of November 26, 1912, a new citation was on its way to America — unaccountably misdirected to the Archbishop of Baltimore — to be served on Frederick Parkhurst, directing him once more to defend his marriage to Marie Reid before the Roman courts. [95]

Cardinal Gibbons, no doubt wearily, forwarded the citation to the new Bishop of Portland, Louis Walsh, with some intimation of his own views of the matter. Walsh agreed in regretting the reopening very much, but he told the cardinal he was not surprised, "after what I heard in Rome before the decision of the Rota and what I have heard since from Rome." He could not think of "any possible loophole for a reversal"; yet "whispering winds from Rome do create some uncertainty." He proposed to follow Gibbons' example and write the court a letter strongly deploring "any reversal of the Rota decision." [96]

The contest between the senior Rospigliosi and the American hierarchy might have continued indefinitely. Marie resented her ostracism in Rome and the ostracism of her six-year-old son by "playmates of his class." Prince Rospigliosi was "only half-alive" away from Rome. To live in Rome and to be accepted they needed the annulment, although in June 1913 Marie told the press that she had gotten along for a dozen years without the approval of the Church and would continue to do so. [97] The issue was finally resolved in Rome on September 22, 1913, by the death of Rospigliosi himself. His brother Camillo was on hand to deny reports that on his deathbed he had married Marie before the Church. That, Prince Camillo explained, was impossible because the marriage of Mrs. Parkhurst had never been annulled. [98]

Lega's opinion had been excerpted in the August–September 1910 issue of *Analecta ecclesiastica* and printed in the August 1910 issue of *Acta apostolicae sedis*, in both instances with the principals identified by name. [99] The case entered the published records of

Rota judgments, however, in 1913 with the anonymity of the parties restored. "Chalcedon" was substituted as a name for both Baltimore and Washington; Rome became "Vienna." Marie Reid appeared as "Aurelia"; Rospigliosi as "a certain prince." Frederick Parkhurst was entitled "Virgil." His name was a tribute, albeit humorous, to the unbelieving author of the Latin brief, whose cause had served for a dozen years to embody the principle of indissolubility in the United States.

VII

The Seventh Class

Pietro Gasparri, master of the modern Curia — Secretary of State of Benedict XV and Pius XI, patron and teacher of Pius XII, author of the Code of Canon Law, chief architect of contemporary Catholic marriage law — was in 1891 a professor in Paris completing his *De matrimonio*. He focused upon two extraordinary papal documents of the sixteenth century, *Romani pontificis* and *Populis et nationibus*, and presented them under the heading "Full Divorce — That is as to the Bond." The juxtaposition posed a question. Half a century ahead of the Curia, Gasparri was asking if the Pope had power to dissolve valid marriages.

Full divorce by papal will had existed for five hundred or more years in instances where consensual union was not followed by physical union. The circumstances were too special to accommodate easy enlargement of the power exercised. Incomplete matings met a psychologically distinct response among the canonists, as if it were agreed that anyone entering matrimony should be entitled to the experience of marital intercourse; where it was wanting, the marriage should not count. Rough equity seemed to excuse the papal authority assumed and to make comprehensible and restricted a power which neither precedent nor logic explained. Gasparri in 1891 asked about a larger class of unions, a class coterminous, perhaps, with the majority of marriages in the world.

THE CONVERT'S SECOND LIFE

Scripture was at the root of the development which led to Gasparri's inquiry. Questions by converts, speculation by theologians, pressures from missionaries had led to the development which had already occurred from the scriptural starting point. In the century after Gasparri's book the rate and direction of the evolution of marriage doctrine was to be to a striking degree within the control of the courts and committees of the Curia.

The Contemptuous Unbeliever

The biblical text whose cryptic message stood at the beginning of all discussion occurred in Saint Paul's First Letter to the Corinthians. He wrote:

To the married I charge — and not I but the Lord — let not a wife separate from her husband. If she does separate, let her remain unmarried or be reconciled with her husband. And a husband must not send away his wife. To the others, I — not the Lord — say, if a brother has an unbelieving wife, and she is agreeable to living with him, do not send her away. And if a woman has an unbelieving husband, and he is agreeable to living with her, do not send away the husband. For the unbelieving husband is sanctified in his wife, and the unbelieving wife is sanctified in the brother — otherwise your children would be unclean, but now they are holy. But if the unbeliever will leave, let him leave. Neither a brother nor a sister is a slave in these matters; but God has called you in peace. How do you know, wife, if you will save your husband? How do you know, husband, if you will save your wife? (I Corinthians 7:10–16)

This passage was part of a response by Paul to a series of questions on sexual ethics from the community consisting of his recent converts at Corinth. The questions, now lost, provided a specific context that doubtless made his answers intelligible. His reply, as it was to stand for the Christians of all later generations, had a universality and an ambiguity which made it a fertile source of doctrinal development.[1]

When specifically canonical analysis of these words began, there were outstanding two distinct lines of authority. Canonists and Curia had to choose between them. One had as its fount the most influential of all Christian writers on sexual ethics, Saint Augustine. He interpreted Paul as sanctioning separation for the abandoned convert. He denied categorically that Paul permitted the abandoned convert to remarry.[2] The opposing view was found in the first Latin commentary on Paul's epistle by a writer believed in the Middle Ages to have been Saint Ambrose or Saint Gregory and now surmised to have been Isaac, a fourth-century Roman lawyer and convert from Judaism.[3] The predominance of Augustine in the West seemed to assure that his view would prevail. But the canonists did not so much choose by predilection for a favorite author as by the appeal of a doctrine. They opted for Isaac, whose lawyerlike exposition of the passage became as important as the words of Paul himself. Isaac had written:

If the unbeliever withdraws in hatred of God, the believer will not be guilty of the dissolved marriage; for the cause of God is greater than the cause of the marriage — that is, the reverence of marriage is not owed to him who hates the Author of marriage. For a marriage which is without devotion to God is not confirmed, and because of this it is not a sin in him who is dismissed on account of God if he will join himself to another. Contempt of the Creator, therefore, dissolves the law of marriage as to the one who is abandoned, so that he may not be accused when coupled to another.[4]

Paul's text became translucent. "God's cause" outweighed "man's cause" — the value of faith was preferred to the value of marital stability. If these values clashed, the marriage with the unbeliever was not confirmed (*ratum*); it could be dissolved. The convert who remarried could not be accused if he remarried. The unbeliever's contempt of God "dissolved the law of marriage" (*solvit ius matrimonii*). The phrase of Roman law described with exactness the ending of the marital bond.

Ambiguities nonetheless were apparent even in Isaac when his explication became the cornerstone of a canonical structure. Did the believer who left an unbeliever have the same remarriage right as the believer who was abandoned? How long did the right to remarry last? Specifically, what act dissolved the union of believer and unbeliever? What acts constituted contempt of the Creator? Would falling into heresy have the same effect upon a marriage as persisting in unbelief? These questions were all open. All were the subject of exploration and lively argument in the creative period of theology and canon law from the beginning of the twelfth century to the middle of the thirteenth.

Hugo of St. Victoire, pioneer theologian of Paris in the 1130's, taught that the injury done the Creator by the unbeliever's unbelief "also excuses the believer: the believer himself may prefer partnership in faith and with Christian devotion abominate an unbeliever who is willing to cohabit but who refuses to receive the faith." [5] The majority view, with less logic, was more obedient to the texts of Paul and Isaac: only the believer who was deserted could remarry. So taught Gratian in a dictum summing up his views of the matter; so taught the definitive decretal *Quanto te*, X.4.19.7, issued in 1199 by Innocent III.[6]

The convert's right to remarry lasted until he had coitus, post-conversion, with his unbelieving spouse. Then "the law of marriage contracted by the unbelievers and till then inchoate is consummated in Christian faith, and the marriage begun in the manner of the pagans becomes according to Christ." [7] Such was the opinion in 1130 of Robert Pullen, also of the school of St. Victoire, later one of the rare English cardinals of the Curia. On the other hand, the later establishment of the rule by Innocent III in *Quanto te* made no reference to the remarriage right being lost through post-baptismal intercourse. The implication at least of the decretal was that the Christian could remarry if at any point he should be abandoned by the unbeliever. The implication of course was significant: a valid, consummated marriage between Christian and unbeliever was dissoluble.

What actually broke the first union? In the early thirteenth century Guillaume of Auxerre, theologian and representative of the University of Paris at Pope Honorius III's court, took Isaac literally — the unbeliever's contempt dissolved. If possible, the unbeliever's contempt should be proved by witnesses before the Church; but if it could not be proved, the believer should still leave: "No marriage is there." [8] In the next generation, Cardinal Hostiensis, the foremost canonist of Urban IV's Curia, held that only a decree of divorce by the convert's bishop, entered after a finding that the unbeliever had withdrawn, dissolved the marriage.[9] The prevailing view, however, was implied early in the twelfth century by Hugo of St. Victoire and taught explicitly by Thomas Aquinas in the thirteenth century: the first marriage was dissolved by the second marriage. The union of unbelievers was "not wholly firm and confirmed." When one of the spouses in such a marriage became a Christian, was deserted by his spouse, and remarried, the marriage "contracted in the faith of

Christ" dissolved the first union. As Thomas put it, "the more firm" dissolved "the less firm." [10]

The kind of contempt of the Creator which ruptured the marriage, Hugo illustrated by a wife who said: "You have become a Christian, I shall not follow you. Since you do not worship idols, since you have cast aside the rite and the customs of your parents, I am going to another; or, if I am not going to another, I am not now going with you." [11] Unbelief plus refusal to cohabit equaled contempt of God. Innocent III, accepting this rule in 1199, expanded it by supposing the case of an unbeliever willing to cohabit with his converted spouse if he, the unbeliever, might still blaspheme or draw the convert to mortal sin. Here, too, there was contempt of the Creator, according to *Quanto te*, X.4.19.7.

If contempt of the Creator dissolved and if contempt consisted in leaving a spouse in rejection of the faith, could not a marriage originally contracted by two believers be dissolved when one of them became an unbeliever and left his spouse? In the strenuous pontificate of Hiacinto Bobo, Celestine III, this case had been put to the Curia. "In hatred of his wife," a husband "had denied Christ," left her, and married a pagan. With the assent of her archdeacon, the abandoned Christian had remarried and had had children. If her first husband now returned to the fold, was she bound to return to him? To Celestine III, "it seemed not," "especially since she was seen to have withdrawn by the judgment of the Church, and, as Gregory is witness, contempt of the Creator dissolves the law of marriage as to him who is abandoned in hatred of the Christian faith." [12] The Pope's interpretation of Isaac (Gregory in his usage) had created a principle permitting the dissolution of valid consummated Christian marriage. This expansion of dissolubility caused a stir. When the nonagenerian Celestine died in 1198 and was succeeded by Lotari de' Segni as Innocent III, clarification was sought by the day's foremost teacher of canon law, Uguccio. His inquiry provoked a comprehensive answer from his former star pupil, now the Pope. Opening with a graceful tribute to the master's prowess — "So much are you known to us as skilled in canon law" — Innocent III replied with the letter which became *Quanto te*, X.4.19.7. "A greater contempt for the Creator" appeared in a believer becoming an unbeliever or a heretic than in an unbeliever remaining an unbeliever. Nonetheless, "although one of our predecessors seems to have judged otherwise," the marriage of two believers was not dissolved by such a lapse. For believers "the sacrament of marriage" was so confirmed (*ratum*) that "it lasts in a spouse while he lives." To this sacramental reason was added the pragmatic argument of a lawyer: his answer forestalled "the malice of some who, in hatred of their spouses, or when they displeased each other, would simulate heresy to rebound through this to other marriages." Astute to prevent fraud, the Pope would not leave open such a tempting door. When, a quarter of a century later, the official collection of papal decretals was prepared by Raimundo of Peñaforte, Celestine III's decision was edited out of the collection, and *Quanto te* was inserted under the title "Divorces." The Curia had determined to follow Innocent III in limiting the remarriage right to the convert.*

No theorist succeeded in showing why marriages contracted in unbelief were in a different category from marriages made by believers. To say that they were not confirmed was of course conclusory: it restated their dissolubility, it did not explain it. Pullen had suggested that the marriages of unbelievers were dissoluble because unbelievers treated them as dissoluble. Gratian had accepted the suggestion: the marriages of unbelievers were not "firm and

* The Gloss on X.4.19.7 observed that Celestine was a Pope who had said that the bond of marriage was dissolved by heresy and "that you formerly had his saying in the decretal *De conversione*, c. *Laudabilem*. And badly spoke Celestine." The Gloss was referring to the original text of the decretal, before the part referring to dissolution by heresy was edited out by Raimundo as editor. The original was not restored until the Friedberg edition of the *Decretals*, which appeared in 1881. When Gasparri wrote *De matrimonio*, he quoted the Gloss's statement and remarked, "But the glossator was asleep when he wrote these things, for in this chapter there is neither hide nor hair of this matter" (1892 ed., sec. 1083). This remark demonstrated that Gasparri at the *Institut catholique* in Paris in the 1890's did not possess a copy of the Friedberg edition and so in all innocence had consulted a standard earlier text where the original decretal of Celestine would not have been found; hence neither hide nor hair. What is more remarkable is that forty years later, when *De matrimonio* was revised by Cardinal Gasparri as Secretary of State and reissued in 1932, Gasparri did not correct his mistake. Instead he made it worse. His text, *De matrimonio*, sec. 1134, remained unchanged, and he buttressed it with a footnote, "Esmein, *Le mariage*, II, 80." The apparent meaning of the citation was that Esmein agreed with him, but if one looked at A. Esmein, *Le mariage en droit canonique*, published in Paris in 1891, a year before Gasparri's book, Esmein set out plainly — at II, 80, and also at I, 231 — that Celestine had taught that heresy dissolved. In addition, Esmein in these passages interpreted the original text of the decretal *De illa*, X.4.19.6, of Urban III as also holding this view. Was Gasparri incapable of admitting that the Pope could make a mistake of this kind? Did someone give him the reference to Esmein as pertinent and did he or some slovenly secretary fail to check what Esmein said or to look at Friedberg? Or, most probably, did the press of other business lead Gasparri to overlook the correction?

inviolable" because, for unbelieving spouses, "when a libel of repudiation is given, it is lawful to withdraw from each other and be
joined to another by the law of the forum." The difficulty of this
explanation was felt in the thirteenth century when it was taught
by the theologians that marriage was indissoluble by reason of
natural law, and when Gregory IX issued the decretal *Si conditiones*, X.4.5.7, declaring that a condition against indissolubility
nullified a marriage. If the marriages of unbelievers were intended
by them to be dissoluble, by these criteria they were not marriages
at all.[13]

Such a radical conclusion was unacceptable. As early as A.D. 414,
Pope Innocent I had observed that Christ spoke of Jews as married.
In the light of the Lord's language, marriage could not appear to be
a unique Christian institution. Gratian made the similar observation
that Saint Paul had spoken in First Corinthians of an unbeliever
"having a wife." [14] In *Gaudemus*, X.4.19.8, issued in 1201 by Innocent III, the Pope drew the same inference from Corinthians in
asserting that "the sacrament of marriage exists among believers and
unbelievers." If this line of thought were followed, the dissolubility
of the convert's marriage could appear only as a mysterious exception created by one reading of Paul. The two decretals of Innocent
III, *Quanto te* and *Gaudemus*, recognized the convert's right to
remarriage and its limits. They gave sufficient if not complete
guidance for practice. They left unanalyzed and unrationalized the
right which they established; its anomalous character created, within
the firm defense of indissolubility, an opening where development
might, in season, occur.

Unbelievers from the Americas

Stimulus to development was provided three centuries after Innocent III by the discovery of America, the Spanish and Portuguese
colonization, the expansion of the slave trade, and the enormous
increase in missionary endeavor. Many of the potential Indian converts, especially perhaps the chiefs, had several wives in the course
of their lives. Many of the potential black converts had been physically separated from their original spouses in Africa and had taken
new spouses in America. To require Indian chiefs or black slaves,

if converted, to return to their first spouse or remain unmarried was a substantial deterrent to conversion or to reception of the sacraments if conversion had already occurred. Missionaries pressed upon the Holy See the need for change in the law. Theorists produced justification for change. The Curia responded ambiguously and conservatively, preferring stability of doctrine to newfangled theory even if the theory exalted the power of the Pope. The steps not taken, half taken, taken back — the interaction between missionaries, theorists, and the Curia — offer instructive analogies and contrasts with the Curia's response to American unbelievers four centuries later.

To begin with, the response was conventional. In 1532, only a dozen years after the Conquest, the Dominicans in Mexico consulted their most distinguished confrere in Rome, Cardinal Cajetan, about the position of Indians who had been married more than once. Cajetan, a notorious liberal on the dissolubility of marriage, gave the unimaginative response that "it was clear according to *Gaudemus*" that an unbeliever, upon conversion, must treat his first wife in a series of wives as his true wife.* Nothing explicitly said in Innocent III's decretal held that it was the first spouse who must be counted as the real spouse, but the apparent simplicity of the common interpretation, which Cajetan repeated, had carried the day.[15] According to the standard rules, then, an Indian convert would have to leave the spouse with whom he was living and return to whomever had been his first spouse, unless he could show that she now rejected him in hatred of his new faith.

Five years after Cajetan had failed to help, Alessandro Farnese, Pope Paul III, took the first halting step toward a different rule. The Pope who excommunicated Henry VIII for his contumacious sec-

---

* Against what he called "a torrent of doctors" Cajetan defended the proposition that the Gospel permitted consummated Christian marriages to be dissolved by a husband for his wife's adultery. The papal decisions to the contrary he dismissed with the observation, "The pontifical decretals about this matter are not definitive for faith, but are judicial facts. The Popes themselves declare that the Roman Pontiffs have sometimes erred in these judgments on marriages, as is established in X.4.19, 'Divorces,' 7, *Quanto te*, and in X.4.4. 'The Spouse of Two,' 4, *Tua fraternitas nos*," Cajetan, *In quattuor Evangelica et Acta Apostolorum ad grecorum codicum veritatem castigata ad sensum quem vocant litteralem commentarii* (Venice, 1530), f. 44. The text is reproduced in F. von Gunter, O.P., "La doctrine de Cajetan sur l'indissolubilité du mariage," *Angelicum* (1966) vol. 43, p. 66.

ond marriage, Paul III had had acquaintance not only with the problem of multiple marriages, but with the necessities of colonized Indians. On May 29, 1537, he wrote the Archbishop of Toledo to prohibit enslavement of Indians within the Spanish Empire; on June 1, 1537, doubtless as part of the same program, he issued the decree *Altitudo* for "South and West India," that is, for all parts of the New World assigned by Alexander VI to Spain. Rejoicing in the conversion of the inhabitants of these regions who had formerly been "ignorant of the divine law," the Pope addressed the situation brought about when converts, "according to their way of life," had had several wives. If the convert remembered which wife he had taken first, *Gaudemus* applied and he must dismiss the others. But if the convert did not remember whom he had taken first, he was free to choose among his wives and contract marriage now with whichever one he chose.[16]

Altitudo suffered from internal inconsistency. It confined the convert to a choice among the wives he had — as though he must be already married to one of them — while it made him get married again to the one he chose. It apparently assumed that the chosen wife would convert, for it made no mention of the impediment of unbelief. Worst of all, in the hands of scrupulous missionaries, it only helped Indians with a bad memory. *Altitudo* was a boy sent to do a man's job, and it did not do it.

America then returned to Europe a theologian who could argue the cause of the Indians in Rome — Alfonso de la Veracruz. Born Alfonso Gutierrez in Caspueñas, in the diocese of Toledo, the recipient of the best contemporary education in scholasticism at Salamanca, the pupil and friend of Vitoria, Alfonso became a missionary and an Augustinian friar and confronted the academic learning he had absorbed in Spain with the patterns of life in Mexico. Published in 1556, his *Speculum coniugiorum*, Mirror of the Married, was not only among the initial generation of books printed in the New World; in the ancient European discipline of canon law it was a pioneering work — the first major treatise on the canon law and theology of marriage, the American pathfinder which would lead to the great works of Ledesma and Sanchez. His contemporaries hailed him as "the oracle of Mexico." His book would "extirpate scruple and ambiguity." With it as a companion, one might "enter the labyrinth of Dedalus more safely and certainly than Theseus." *

Matrimonial cases were "very frequent" in Mexico; Veracruz had been depressed by their frequency. "Jesus Christ, whose affair it is," had, however, so strengthened him that he "moved the hand with the pen." It was his hope that by his work "the new men, newly discovered, of the New World, may be maximally aided." [17] The difficulties present in the application of the approved rules may be gauged from the success of his attempt.

Veracruz first determined that the men of the New World married. Conversing in their own tongue with "the priests of the idols," listening to the reports of other missionaries, observing for himself among the Michoacans, Veracruz concluded that man and woman in the New World chose each other as man and wife, although only the nobles exchanged consent with much ceremony and humbler folk often established marriage by a man and woman living together on the implicit understanding that he would farm for her and she would make his clothes. Grave Spaniards doubted if these unions were valid marriages because the customary polygamy seemed contrary to marital fidelity and the common practice of divorce by mutual consent seemed contrary to indissolubility. Veracruz argued that, despite intentions hostile to fidelity and indissolubility, the men of the New World entered valid marriages if they followed their customary forms, provided only that they "accept a wife with marital affection." If the marriages, however, were valid, and the Indians had several wives, what happened on their conversion? "Because of their easy conversion and their innate gentleness, no spouse finds the other to withdraw from him because of his conversion to

---

* Alfonso left a promising academic career at Salamanca for Mexico, starting a new life when he became an Augustinian novice at Veracruz. Bringing his books with him, he founded four libraries in Mexico; he has been described as "the cornerstone of the University of Mexico," where he held the first chair in theology. He wrote treatises on Aristotle's logic and physics as well as a moderate but firm defense of the rights of the Indians, see Arthur Ennis, *Fray Alfonso de la Vera Cruz, O.S.A. (1507–1584)* (Louvain: E. Warny, 1957), pp. 14, 18, 20, 47. For the contemporary tributes to his book, Juan Nigret, Rector of the University of Mexico, to Alfonso, Alfonso de la Vera Cruz, *Speculum coniugiorum* (Mexico City, 1556), pp. 4–5; Francisco Cervantes Salazar, Professor of Rhetoric at the University of Mexico, to the Candid Reader, *ibid.*, p. 7. For a bibliography, see Amancio Bolaño e Isla, *Contribución al Estudio Biobibliográphico de Fray Alfonso de la Vera Cruz* (Mexico City: Antigera Libreria Robredo, 1947). For his sympathy to the Indians see his *Defense of the Indians: Their Rights*, ed. and trans. Ernest J. Burrus, S.J. (Rome: Jesuit Historical Institute, 1968).

the faith." Hence there was no immediate occasion to find an existing marriage dissolved by contempt of the Creator. Usually the spouse with whom a male convert was living was baptized with him. If the convert had been married before, he was not conscious of an obligation to be reconciled to the wife he had left. The converts did "not fully understand what is defined by the Church." Only after instruction received postbaptismally did they perceive what the Church taught. Then they would acknowledge the existence of an earlier spouse; but they would not know if she were alive or dead or whether she had had an earlier husband or whether that earlier husband had had an earlier wife. Since in this series, which Veracruz described as "in a way infinite," the validity of an existing marriage depended on whether both parties to it had been free to contract at the time of marriage, it was in fact impossible to be sure whether the most recent union had been impeded by some previous valid union or not.[18]

Veracruz assisted Indians in this situation by invoking a response of Lucius III to Christian prisoners of the Saracens, *Dominus ac redemptor*, X.4.21.2, and another letter of Innocent III to Uguccio, *Inquisitioni tuae*, X.5.39.44. Remarried Christian captives had been told by Lucius III that if they were not sure whether their first wives were alive or not, they could not initiate intercourse in their second marriage, but they could have intercourse if their second wives took the initiative. Innocent III had added to this instruction that it applied only if one had a "probable" doubt about being validly married. If the doubt was "light and rash," and "exploded by the counsel of one's pastor," one need not follow Lucius III's rule. How Veracruz expected the line between a responsive and an initiating role in intercourse to be drawn by male Indians or explained to them by Spanish missionaries was not made clear. A Theseus furnished with this thread might never have emerged from the labyrinth. Teaching was not expected by Veracruz. He cited the two decretals so that missionaries would not feel too uncomfortable in acquiescing in situations where the unraveling of a marital snarl looked hopeless. Like Paul III's *Altitudo*, his solution was intended to authorize dissimulation and forbearance where strict enforcement of the rules gave no answer.[19]

In the pontificate of Michele Ghislieri, Pius V — thirty years after *Altitudo*, a dozen years after Veracruz's book — a fresh effort was made at the Curia to cope with the problems in the field. Vera-cruz had returned to Spain. He did not go to Rome, but his ideas were not unnoticed at the Curia; he helped achieve a significant confirmation of the privileges of the missionaries by a *motu proprio* of Pius V in 1567; his presentation of the situation of Indian converts now had a Roman audience. The Pope himself, a former Dominican inquisitor with a conscientiousness approaching scrupulosity, could scarcely have been content with solutions which involved complaisance in situations of dubious regularity. His instinct, in general, was to demand compliance with the hard requirements of the law, while as a reformer he had an exalted vision of the duties and power of the papacy. In this case, as in others, he set up a high-level commission to advise him. The result was his issuance, on August 2, 1571, of *Romani pontificis*, a decree so balanced in its phraseology and so impenetrable in its theology that it reflected a perfect compromise within the Curia, a document patient of multiple interpretations and enormous development.

The Roman Pontiff, the decree began, had always shown solicitude for the Indians. Pius V had learned that unbelieving Indians were allowed by their customs to have several wives whom they divorced for the slightest reason. The practice had "hence" arisen of allowing those who received baptism to remain with the wife with whom they were baptized. It often happened that she was not the first wife. Priests and bishops were then "tormented with the gravest scruples as they think this not to be a true marriage." The Pope's concern for these tormented souls was evident. The document then came to the crucial language setting out the Pope's response to the practice:

Because it would be very harsh to separate these Indians from the wives with whom they received baptism, especially because it would be very difficult to find the first spouse, We, therefore, of our own motion, from sure knowledge and out of the plenitude of Apostolic power, desire to provide benevolently for the state of the said Indians with paternal affection and to relieve these bishops and ministers of scruples of this kind. So that the baptized Indians as previously set out, and Indians to be baptized in the future, can remain with the wife who is baptized with them, or who will be baptized with them, as with a lawful wife with the others dismissed, We, by apostolic authority, by the tenor of these presents, declare that marriage lawfully exists between those of this kind.[20]

Taken at its face, *Romani pontificis* went far beyond the words of Paul to the Corinthians, Isaac's interpretation of those words, and Innocent III's establishment of Isaac's interpretation. No reference was made to the unbeliever abandoning the convert or showing contempt for the Creator. The state of mind of the unbelieving spouse was ignored. Operating retroactively as well as prospectively, the decree seemed to assume a papal power to set right all existing marriages of converted Indians. Whatever their previous unions, Indian spouses who were converted together were to be treated as validly married to each other. Read in this way, *Romani pontificis* represented a major expansion of papal authority over marriage.

Alternatively, a conservative reading was possible and seems more probable. *Romani pontificis*, it could be said, dealt only with the cases where it was "morally impossible" to find the convert's first wife; in those cases the Pope confirmed the convert's existing union. Where the first wife could be found, *Romani pontificis* had no application. Veracruz gave this interpretation in a new edition of Mirror of the Married published at Salamanca the same year as the *motu proprio*; he pointedly drew attention to the ruling in a new preface to the book. In 1556 he had spoken of dissolution of marriage "in favor of the faith" as in accord "with the intention of Christ speaking through the Apostle"; he had meant the Pauline exception as interpreted by *Gaudemus*. He did not understand "favor of the faith" in a broader sense in 1571; he was clear that Cajetan was mistaken in believing that the Pope could dissolve unconsummated marriages, and he did not suppose that a broader papal prerogative was exercised here.* Given Veracruz's role in posing the question, his clear delight in the Pope's answer, and his access to the document itself — only by his publication of it was the text available in Europe — his interpretation seems to give the authentic sense of the ruling. Any broader interpretation, he said, would run "against the natural and divine law, as is clear in the canon *Gaudemus*." The missionary theologian who knew the Mexican situation

---

* Veracruz appears theologically timorous in clinging to *Gaudemus*. Yet he did not hesitate to criticize the reasoning of this decretal and in so doing to declare that the Pope's plenary power "is not for this, to know the truth, but for this, that after it has been proven by study of Sacred Scripture and by the Doctors whom God has given the Church, the Supreme Pontiff may define that such truth be held," Veracruz, *Speculum coniugorum*, 2.21, "Whether the Pope's Opinion is to be Preferred to the Doctors'."

best, he was content with this modest extension of *Altitudo* and a continued deference to Innocent III's old decretal.[21]

At the Curia itself the same position was taken by the very aged, very acute, very trusted adviser of the Pope, Martino Azplicueta, known as Navarrus. Asked specifically if a converted Indian had to inquire of his first wife if she wished to be baptized with him, Navarrus held that "the Apostolic declaration and decree" (*Romani pontificis*) had not changed the requirement of inquiry, even though that requirement made the decree "rather harsh." By implication, he agreed with Veracruz that, only where it was morally impossible or, as the decree said, "very difficult" to find the first wife, did *Romani pontificis* apply. Indians who could remember their first wives and would readily find them were not helped at all.[22]

At the same time, Navarrus cherished a broader view of what the Pope could do, and this broader view may account for the ambiguity in the *motu proprio*. As shown in Chapter III of this book, he accepted fully the proposition that the Pope could dissolve the unconsummated marriage of Christians. From this premise, he later moved to consider another case put to him for counsel: Lazarus, a Jew, married a Jewish woman according to Jewish law. She then became a Catholic. He divorced her according to Jewish law and married a second Jew. His first wife remained single. Lazarus became a Catholic. Was he obliged to return to his first wife?

The question, Navarrus said, was "new," that is, it was not answered by his sources — Gratian, the *Decretals*, Peter Lombard, Saint Thomas, and the commentators on Saint Thomas. In favor of the dissolution of the first marriage stood the general rule of law set out in the *Decretals*, "Everything is dissolved by the same cause by which it is brought into being," X.5.41.1. The Ordinary Gloss took pain to point out that this rule did not apply to marriage. Marriages were made by consent, but they could not be undone by withdrawal of consent. But the Gloss's comment did not govern here: this marriage could have been dissolved by the abandoned wife if she had married before Lazarus' conversion. Hence, it was implied, the marriage had continued after the conversion only by virtue of her consent, and her consent to dissolution could now dissolve it. Against dissolution, it was argued that marriage was indissoluble "by the law of nature as St. Thomas proves"; by the Roman law definition of marriage as "an undivided way of life"; and by the command "What God has joined together, let no man put asunder." Conversion should not destroy nature, but perfect it. What was naturally indissoluble should be all the stronger when it became Christian. Between these two lines of thought Navarrus chose the second. By the common law of the Church, *Gaudemus*, Lazarus' first marriage remained, and he must return to his first wife.

But there was a further question: Could the Pope go beyond the common law and dispense from the first marriage? To answer, Navarrus divided marriage into its natural and its sacramental elements. He saw no obstacle to the Pope destroying the "inseparability induced only by the law of nature," provided papal dissolution did no injury to any person. Here the only persons affected by dissolution, Lazarus and his first wife, agreed to it, and no injury was done to one knowing and consenting. The sacramental element depended on the spouses being Christian. The first marriage when it had been made was necessarily "naked of sacramental significance." Was not this marriage converted into a sacramental marriage when both partners to it became Christians? Navarraus would not challenge the logic of answering this question affirmatively. He observed, however, that the union had not been consummated as a Christian marriage. After their independent conversions, Lazarus and his divorced first wife had not had intercourse. They were Christians; their marriage was Christian; but, their marriage, in Navarrus' words, "was not consummated by the sacrament," that is, intercourse signifying the union of Christ and the Church had not occurred. As the Pope had power to dissolve other unconsummated Christian marriages, so he could dissolve this one; and Lazarus, if papally dispensed, need not return to his first wife.[23]

The case of Lazarus was individual, to be resolved by a specific dispensation; his first wife did consent. These features distinguished the situation from Pius V's rule-making for the Americas. In advising Lazarus, Navarrus did not cite *Romani pontificis*, but his analysis of a consummated marriage of unbelievers as an unconsummated Christian marriage after the unbelievers' conversion, and his large view of the Pope's power over unconsummated Christian marriage, suggest that before *Romani pontificis* was issued the Curia must have engaged in much introspection on the extent of papal power over the marital status of the convert.

A dozen years after Pius V's ambiguous action, this kind of speculation bore fruit. The ruling Pope was Ugo Buoncompagni, Gregory XIII, an experienced canon lawyer, and he responded in particular to the request of Claudio Aquaviva, General of the Jesuits, voicing the concern of Jesuit missionaries. The resulting document, *Populis et nationibus*, issued January 25, 1585, was a palpable advance over Paul III's *Altitudo*, and it was explicit on issues which compromise apparently had led Pius V's *Romani pontificis* to omit. The specific situation addressed was the lot of slaves captured in Angola, Ethiopia, Brazil, and "other parts of the Indies" and removed without their lawful spouses to "most remote regions." If any such slave wanted to convert, there was no way of telling if the distant spouse from whom he had been separated would show contempt of the Creator so as to give him the right to remarry recognized by *Gaudemus*. Similarly, the spouse whose husband had been enslaved and deported could not convert and know whether her husband's attitude to the faith would give her the right to remarry. Yet it was appropriate that recently converted "peoples and nations" enjoy freedom to contract marriage after conversion, "lest they not persist in the faith." The black and Indian slaves presented the same occasion for expansion of *Gaudemus* which the free Indians had presented in 1536 and 1571. Gregory XIII responded with a general proposition, a procedure, and a blanket dispensation.[24]

Marriages among unbelievers, the Pope observed, "are indeed true marriages, but yet they are not to be judged so confirmed that they cannot be dissolved, if necessity urges." The proposition was extraordinarily broad if any necessity whatsoever justified dissolution of these marriages, and if the Pope were to be the judge of the necessity. For the purposes of the document, necessity seemed limited to the situation of the slaves; and the Pope implied that he was the ultimate judge of the necessity by delegating his power to dispense such slaves and spouses to Jesuit confessors and the ordinaries and parish priests in the affected areas. In this procedural step the Pope authorized his delegates to dispense Christian converts of these regions, "so that each one of them can contract marriage with any believer during the lifetime of an unbelieving spouse without that spouse's consent being sought or response awaited." A proviso was added to the delegation: summarily and extrajudicially, the dispensing priest was to determine that the absent spouse could not be interrogated or had not replied within a fixed time. With this nod to Isaac's idea that it was the unbeliever's contempt for God which dissolved, the Pope's procedure effectively permitted dissolution where no "contempt of the Creator" in the old canonical sense was shown. At the same time, the inconsistency present in both *Altitudo* and *Romani pontificis* was eliminated: the convert was not required to take one of his existing wives as though he were already married; he was freed to marry whom he would. Underlining the breadth of the decree was the rule stated at its close: marriages contracted by virtue of the authorized dispensations were valid even though it was discovered later that the absent spouse had herself already converted. This rule was in effect a blanket dispensation in advance of particular cases, applying to the slaves the theory Navarrus had developed for Lazarus. Relying squarely on the newly established papal authority over unconsummated marriages, the Pope treated the existing marriages of converted slaves with separated, converted wives as unconsummated Christian marriages and provided for their dissolution where their existence would restrict the right to a second marriage.

Papal power to dissolve the marriage of an unbeliever and a believer had been exercised. What was the basis of the power? Writing in the next generation, the great theorist of canonical marriage, Tomás Sanchez, addressed this question. In the early days of Christianity, he said, there were many converts from unbelief, and unbelievers were not as obstinate as they are today. Hence, Saint Paul, when he wrote to the Corinthians, advised his converts to stay with their unbelieving spouses. Experience now showed that unbelievers were rarely converted, so the Church had laid down a different rule: converts should not stay with their unbelieving spouses. When the convert left his spouse in obedience to the law of the Church, he did so because the unbeliever had sinned against God and against the law of marriage in not accepting the faith. By causing the believer to leave, the unbelieving spouse could be said to be the one who left. True, this case was not explicitly in Paul's text, but then neither were the other cases which dissolved the marriage according to *Gaudemus* — the unbeliever's contempt of the Creator or his inducing the believer to mortal sin. Innocent III had rightly provided for these two cases by considering the purpose of the original Pauline permission of remarriage to converts. Generalizing from these several cases, Sanchez concluded that the dissolution of an existing marriage of a convert to an unbeliever was possible "by virtue of the privilege of Christ, who granted it in favor of the faith."

In this bold hypothesis there was one general rule for exceptions to the indissolubility of marriage. It comprehended Saint Paul and Innocent III and Pius V. It was a rule legislated by Christ Himself. Christ's legislative enactment reflected a weighing of values: "Since the good of the faith is greater than the good of marriage, it was consonant with reason that Christ, the Author of faith and of marriages, legislate that, in these circumstances, favor for the faith could dissolve a marriage." The purpose of the Lord's legislation was to provide for the weakness of the neophyte. Unless he could remarry, the married convert had the alternative of leading a celibate life he was unprepared for; committing adultery; or remaining with an unbeliever who created dangers for his faith. To avoid these alternatives, Christ had made his grant of privilege; "and this privilege St. Paul set out in 1 Cor. 7." In today's circumstances, it was within the purpose of the privilege to permit the convert to remarry when his spouse refused conversion. "Hence it is not to be said that the privilege of Christ has now been changed, but from the beginning it was granted for all those circumstances in which it would be unlawful for the believing spouse to cohabit with the unbeliever in unbelief." [25]

Appealing to experience, the power of the Church, and the purpose of the law, Sanchez showed how development could occur within the Church by literal reversal of the letter of a biblical text; Paul's advice to converts was turned on its head. But Sanchez' analysis of the values at stake was not different from Isaac's. "God's cause" was still the value outweighing the indissolubility of marriage. The formula "in favor of the faith" put this valuation precisely. Restating the values of Isaac and Innocent III, Sanchez perceived that the privilege set out by Paul might be only illustrative of the kind of case where the faith could be supposed to count for more than indissolubility. By contending that the basic legislation was Christ's, Sanchez hypothesized the existence of a general rule which could be applied as appropriate. When this hypothesis was coupled with Sanchez's view of the Pope's power as Vicar of Christ — the Pope, he taught, enjoyed as Christ's deputy whatever power over marriage was necessary for the good of the Church — the elements were present for a far bolder papal expansion of dissolubility than *Populis et nationibus* had attempted. Sanchez himself did not attempt to tie these elements together in a concrete expansion; they lay inactive, to be employed in the twentieth century.

Six From Florence

From *Altitudo* in 1537 to *Populis et nationibus* in 1583, from Cajetan in 1532 to Sanchez in 1600, apparently an orderly, organic development had occurred in less than a century under the impulsion of missionary experience with American unbelievers. Most theorists, however, were not as bold as Sanchez. The Curia itself apparently considered the effect which innovation in America would have in Europe. The result was a reconsideration parallel to what happened in the treatment of marriages not intended to be indissoluble, as set out in Chapter V; and of course the two matters overlapped, for, to the extent that the marriages of unbelievers did not qualify as true canonical marriages, they were dissoluble. As caution prevailed in judging the validity of Japanese, Chinese, and Indian marriages, so it also prevailed in the use of papal power to dissolve them.

Urban VIII convened a commission in 1631 with Cardinal Pamphili, later Innocent X, as reporter, to consider a request from a missionary in South America for faculties to dispense Indian converts with several wives so they could choose the wife they wished to be married with. The request asked no more than *Populis et nationibus* had granted missionaries for the slaves and spouses of slaves. But several established theologians — Basilio Ponce de León, the Augustinian moralist at Salamanca; Giles Connick, the Jesuit moralist at Louvain; Gabriel Vasquez, the Spanish Jesuit — had denied that the Pope had power to dissolve the marriages of unbelievers which had been consummated before their conversion. If their reasoning was accepted, the kind of blanket dispensation given by Gregory XIII was impossible. The theologians and canonists of Pamphili's commission — they included Abbate Hilarione, who was later to advise on Charles of Lorraine's case — accepted the conservative position. They reported that the requested facilities should be refused, "because according to the truer opinion of the doctors the Pope cannot dispense." This phraseology did not deny that the opposite opinion might be true, but even those who granted the Pope the power — Navarrus and Sanchez — said he could only dispense for a just cause. Now, the commission concluded, the Pope could not make a general dispensation in advance as though there would be a just cause in each case. Missionaries must apply to Rome in writing where the circumstances were compelling.

Propaganda, with Urban VIII presiding in person, reviewed the committee report, softened "cannot be granted" to "is not to be granted," and made the report less official by issuing it as "the opinion of the theologians and canonists" rather than as a decree of the Congregation.* The Curia would not flatly repudiate the action of Gregory XIII; but the new policy was substantially more cautious.[26]

The decision taken in 1631 was controlling six years later when the standard formulas to delegate papal dispensing authority were composed by a joint committee of cardinals of the Inquisition and Propaganda. The missionaries received authority to allow a convert with several unbelieving spouses to marry the wife of his choice only if the first wife refused to be converted. *Gaudemus* was back in favor. In equating nonconversion with contempt of the Creator, the committee followed Sanchez, but only this very limited distance. No authority to dissolve all marriages contracted in unbelief

---

* Greco, *Le pouvoir*, p. 94, identifies the disappointed petitioner as an Augustinian friar, Pedro Hieta. He distinguishes his petition from one presented by Juan De Lugo on behalf of Jesuit missionaries in Paraguay, although it may be that both petitions provided the stimulus for Propaganda's negative action. Urban VIII had issued briefs on October 20, 1626, and September 20, 1627, employing the broad language of *Populis et nationibus*, and Lugo had cited these in his petition (excerpted in Greco, *ibid.*, pp. 92–93, and in Antonio Ballerini, *Opus theologicum morale*, ed. Domenico Palmieri [Prato, 1900], VI, 356–357). Ballerini indicates that Jesuit practice in Paraguay was not affected by the decision because the pagans' unions were treated as invalid marriages. In the initial presentation Lugo had pointed to the fact that polygamy was usual; that abandonment of a wife was common; and that often it was hard for an Indian to determine what woman he had first chosen as a wife.

was claimed by the Curia or granted to the missionaries. The free style of Gregory XIII was ignored, the missionaries were left with their scruples, and the papal power to dissolve was kept, unmentioned, in Rome.[27]

Altitudo, Romani pontificis, and *Populis et nationibus* were not easily available to interested theologians; they were not published as official documents. They were limited, special concessions for particular groups, dispatched to the parts of the world affected by them. They received no general circulation. Their confined, almost confidential character was both a signal of the doubts the Curia had experienced in issuing them and a reason why the evolution accomplished in them could be ignored without much public fuss. Sanchez himself knew *Romani pontificis* only as "a certain *motu proprio* reported by Veracruz." A century later Prospero Lambertini, when Secretary of the S.C.C., knew the decree only through Veracruz; and, even as Pope, Lambertini had only Veracruz at hand. In 1750 Alfonso de' Ligouri did not even know the names of the edicts, although he had obtained their content through the book of Benedict XIV. With this kind of distribution it was not surprising that their existence could drop from view.[28]

The depth of curial doubt about the extraordinary power apparently manifested in *Populis et nationibus* became clear in two celebrated cases centered on Jewish converts and their marriages. Israel Pinto and Stella Enriquez, Jews of Florence, were man and wife. Stella became a Catholic, with the baptismal name Maria Rosa. Israel divorced her according to Mosaic law and married his niece Esther. He and Esther then became Catholics themselves, with Israel being baptized as Ferrantes Maria. In a court of the Church, Maria Rosa sued Ferrantes Maria to compel him to return to her as her lawful husband. The case came to the S.C.C. for disposition. Its theologians, following Thomas Aquinas, held that only a marriage by a convert subsequent to conversion dissolved a marriage contracted in unbelief; the Mosaic divorce was treated as ineffective against the rights of a Catholic. As Maria Rosa had never remarried, her marriage to Israel was still in force. The canonists of the S.C.C. disagreed — on what basis was not recorded. The S.C.C. upheld the theologians, and in 1680 advised Pope Innocent XI that Ferrantes must be ordered to return to Maria Rosa. In the brief report of the S.C.C.'s official action, no mention at all was made of the possible papal power to dispense or the possible precedent in *Populis et nationibus*.[29]

Forty years later these possibilities were explicitly explored by Florentines who proceeded more cautiously than Israel Pinto. Abramo and Ricca Esther, Jews of Florence, were man and wife. Ricca Esther became a Catholic; Abramo divorced her and in 1721 married the couple's former servant Bianca. In 1726 Abramo and Bianca desired to become Catholics but first wanted to know if Abramo would have to take Esther back.[30]

Giuseppe Maria Martelli, Archbishop of Florence, raised the question before the S.C.C. His inquiry gave the proceeding the shape of an administrative process rather than a trial and put prime responsibility for management of the case upon that exceptionally able secretary of the S.C.C., Prospero Lambertini. After diligent research, Lambertini thought the Pinto case controlling and the Congregation followed him, holding that the marriage of Abramo and Esther still bound them. Esther had no desire that Abramo return to her, and Lambertini pointed out there was still the question of papal dispensation. Before tackling this question, the S.C.C. tried to see if there was a less controversial solution. Was Esther planning to marry or to make religious profession? How hard would it be to get Abramo back to Esther? To these expedients Archbishop Martelli replied that Esther, "at the advanced age of forty," had no plans to marry and had not much desire to become a religious. Abramo and Bianca said only death would separate them. Abramo, the Archbishop added, was bound to Bianca by more than "marital affection"; their tie was "deep-rooted and in their natures" and went back to the time Bianca was Esther's servant, "and this, in my opinion, will make their separation much more difficult."

Faced squarely with the issue of papal power over a marriage made by unbelievers, the S.C.C. asked for opinions from consultors chosen by Lambertini. They divided. Domenico Ponsi, a Dominican, and Francesco Zavaroni, a Franciscan, doubted the existence of the Pope's power or at least the wisdom of exercising it. In *Gaudemus*, Innocent III had described the marriage of unbelievers as "a sacrament." Evidently he had not meant "sacrament" in the strict sense, for only the baptized could receive sacraments of the

Christian faith. He must have used the term in a broad sense as "a mystery and so a signification of the union of Christ and the Church." On the showing of *Gaudemus*, then, even "natural" marriages, contracted by non-Christians, could have this symbolic significance. Marriages signifying the union of Christ and Church could not be broken by the Pope. Moreover, it was "absurd" to call a marriage unconsummated where multiple acts of intercourse had occurred. The legal fiction proposed by Navarrus — "the unconsummated Christian marriage" — was rejected. The awkward papal precedents were boldly rationalized and explained away: *Romani pontificis* assumed that the absent spouse had not been actually converted; *Populis et nationibus* assumed that the absent spouse had not actually been found.

To the contrary were the other two consultors: Ludovico Sparieri, a Jesuit and the theologian of the Penitentiary; and Domenico Ursaya, a lawyer practicing in the Curia. Sparieri was hesitant, but Ursaya argued with an advocate's zeal for the existence of the papal power to dissolve and the desirability of its exercise. One example was worth one thousand: Pius V had exercised such power in *Romani pontificis*. The same reason for dispensation was present here as with the Indians whom it was "very harsh to separate from the spouses with whom they were baptized." In each case, compulsion "to leave a most beloved spouse was equally harsh and bitter." Exercise of the power was totally within the Pope's discretion. To grant dissolution was "a pure grace dependent solely on the will of Our Most Holy Lord," Benedict XIII. Ursaya was confident of "the celebrated piety and the clemency, never sufficiently praised, of Our Most Holy Lord." If the Pope could do so, he mercifully would dispense.[31]

The division of the consultors left the S.C.C. to decide the case itself. It responded enigmatically, even mysteriously, certainly with no suggestion that an established papal power was being routinely employed. It entered no judgment whatsoever in its records. Lambertini, recording the case as Secretary and writing about it later as Pope, seems to have believed that the dispensation was denied. Other evidence suggests the contrary: the records of Santa Maria de' Monti, a Roman hospice for catechumens, show that Abramo Ricci and "his wife Bianca" were baptized on January 20, 1728.[32] Perhaps the Penitentiary, whose theologian had favored this result, had obtained the dispensation for the couple when the S.C.C. had faltered. Yet, in that event, Lambertini, who was the canonist of the Penitentiary, would ordinarily have known of what had been done. The caution of the Curia as to advertising the papal power was such that Lambertini, the most informed lawyer in the Curia of 1727 and the ablest canonist ever to become Pope, was unable or unwilling to say that the power had been used.*

Dispensed and Deserted

From the time of Isaac to that of Innocent III to that of Gregory XIII, attention had focussed on the case of the convert. What of the born Catholic who married a pagan and was later deserted by him? No scriptural text could be cited expressly in his behalf; no decretal spoke to his condition. Prior to the eighteenth century the case does not appear to have been ruled on in Rome; at least no general or public ruling dealt with the issue.

Prior to the seventeenth century the possibility of the case aris-ing was not common. Only in this era did Rome grant dispensations to marry pagans, a concession to the requests of missionaries and a response to a shortage of male converts in the Far East. Then the case must have become common. Nothing guaranteed the success of these unions, and if they failed it would be legal civilly and expectable socially for the pagan spouse to divorce his Christian wife and remarry. Was she still bound for life? In 1708 the Holy Office under Clement XI was asked to rule on the state of a "number of Christian women" who had faced this question. Unable to remain continent, often commanded to remarry by their parents,

* Conceivably Esther could have died or made a religious profession between March 29, 1727, and January 20, 1728, making the request for papal dispensation moot. Discussing the case later, however, Benedict XIV did not mention any such event. Benedict XIV, *De synodo diocesana* (Rome, 1767), 6.4.4. As Secretary of the S.C.C., he had seemed to believe that "the very grave cause" necessary for apostolic dispensing power to be used was lacking, but that the marriage, con-tracted under Mosaic Law, might be null for a condition against indissolubility. Nothing, however, suggests that the marriage was dissolved on this ground.

So uncertain a precedent was the case of Abramo and Esther that in the nineteenth century the Third Plenary Council of Baltimore cited as controlling law the S.C.C.'s decision of 1680 in the case of Israel Pinto, Third Council of Baltimore, *Acta et Decreta Concilii Plenarii Baltimoriensis Tertii* (Baltimore, 1886), Decree 128, p. 65.

they had remarried. Their new husbands, pagans, like their old, were disposed to receive baptism if the new marriages were good. Were they valid? With its customary terseness the Inquisition answered, "No." [33]

Another effort was made to get a favorable response from Rome — this time in the pontificate of Benedict XIV by Clemente Colaso Leitão, the Jesuit Bishop of Cochin in the East Indies. Counting, perhaps, on Benedict's keen personal interest in marriage legislation, the bishop was disappointed by the Pope's death. On August 1, 1759, the Holy Office declared, "As long as the unbelieving spouse is alive, the believer cannot pass to other vows." "Cannot" seemed to pose a comprehensive barrier to remarriage, to reflect an irreversible decision of the Curia.[34]

The first moral theologian in the United States, Francis P. Kenrick, later Archbishop of Baltimore, thought otherwise in 1840. The marriage of the dispensed Catholic, he believed, "can always be dissolved if the unbeliever refuses to live with the believer." [35] He quoted the letter to the Corinthians, "If the unbeliever will leave, let him leave." Kenrick, writing in Philadelphia, had only Saint Paul at his fingertips, not the Roman documents. His teaching may have reflected what he had learned as a pupil at the College of the Propaganda in the 1820's; perhaps missionaries in the field acted on this teaching without asking Rome again. But Kenrick's theological position was unique; he could cite no author after Paul in its support, and the position of the Curia was clear: not only was there a repugnance to letting a Catholic undo a marriage he had begun with the special permission of ecclesiastical authority, but doctrine itself appeared to preclude remarriage. Repeatedly, in the course of the nineteenth century, the Holy Office gave the same answer — to an inquiry from China in 1852, to the Vicar-General of Siam in 1855, to the Bishop of St. Albert, Canada, in 1883. In a formal instruction to the Vicar Apostolic of Natal in 1866 the Inquisition asserted: "Marriage, even when contracted in unbelief, is indissoluble by its nature; and it can only be dissolved as to the bond by virtue of the privilege of the faith granted by Christ the Lord and promulgated by the Apostle Paul." No suggestion appeared in any of these Roman answers that the privilege of the faith was wider than, or distinct from, the privilege conferred by Paul and construed by *Gaudemus*. In these terms the rule was unbending: "Never, as long as the pagan husband is alive, can the Christian woman enter a second marriage." [36]

The extent of the Curia's commitment to the impossibility of re-marriage in this kind of case may be measured by the Parkhurst-Reid case described in Chapter VI. In the course of a dozen years of litigation in the courts of the Curia, before both Propaganda and the Rota, it was always assumed that the only ground which would permit Marie Reid to remarry was the invalidity of her original union with Parkhurst. His lack of baptism was established; he had divorced his wife; he had finally remarried; but not once was it suggested that Marie Reid could claim the privilege of the aban-doned convert. Dispensed and deserted, she could never marry in the lifetime of her first spouse. Not even the most knowledgeable of her counsel from the curial bar seemed to suspect the existence of an alternative route. Yet if her case had been presented only a decade after its rebuff by the Rota such an avenue would have been perceivable; three decades later it would have been open. The case in 1910 is a point from which the rapid evolution of doctrine may be measured.

DISSOLUTION OF MARRIAGE FOR THE SALVATION OF THE SOULS

According to respectable authority, *Romani pontificis* and *Populis et nationibus* were merely adjustments of the terms on which the convert's privilege recognized by St. Paul might be exercised; according to equally conventional authority, they were interpretations of the Pauline privilege. Neither theory separated the documents from Paul, neither recognized any extraordinary papal power exercised in them. In 1891 when Gasparri writing *De matrimonio* set these documents under the caption "Full Divorce — That is as to the Bond," he reviewed these positions and returned to the thesis of Sanchez that this exception to indissolubility de-pended on lawmaking power lodged in the Pope. Interpretation which extended a rule to a case not previously comprehended by the rule was true lawmaking; it presupposed lawmaking power in those making the extension. If the sixteenth-century Popes had had the power to extend Saint Paul's teaching about dissoluble marriage by interpretation of it, they had a large power over marriage. "If we take the words of Pius V and Gregory XIII in the obvious sense, it is plain [*palam*, open, evident] that they mean a dispensation in a lawful marriage." Could the Popes actually dispense from the bond of a lawful marriage, effect a full divorce as to the bond? The question could only be resolved, Gasparri said, *ex facto*, from what happened. If a Roman Pontiff acting in his capacity as Pope did something in a matter of morals, the inference was permissible that he was able to do it. The pontifical acts of dispensation from lawful marriage were proof of the pontifical power to dispense.[37]

In 1891 Gasparri's inferences were pure theory. Documents of the sixteenth century, so long obscured, debated, and limited, could not take on new force at once. They began, however, to be more generally known. Propaganda printed, for the use of missionaries, a collection of papal rulings, and, under the caption "Privileges in Favor of the Faith," the texts of *Romani pontificis* and *Populis et nationibus* appeared. No longer buried in rare sixteenth-century treatises, the documents were available for inspection by an interested, if still limited, audience. A committee of the Curia became their official sponsor.[38]

In 1894 "the Florentine case" recurred. Isaac and Rebecca, both Jews, were married as Jews and divorced as Jews. Rebecca became a Catholic. Isaac married civilly Antonia, a Catholic. He desired to become a Catholic if he could be religiously united to Antonia. The Prefect Apostolic for Morocco presented his case to the S.C.C. for instruction. The clear precedent of 1680 and the evasions of 1726 were not followed. On May 23, 1894, the S.C.C. recommended the dispensation be granted, and Leo XIII granted it.[39] As precedent in 1894, the case was worth nothing. The S.C.C. did not report it, nor did the *Acta Sanctae Sedis*. It was not commented on in the canon law journals nor in the next edition of Gasparri's treatise. It emerged into public light only forty years later, when Gasparri reported it in the final edition of *De matrimonio*. Unknown to a larger world in 1894, clothed in a secrecy which testified to curial ambivalence, the Morocco case told a small circle in the Curia that the power of which Gasparri had written was neither imaginary nor obsolete.

Codifying the law from 1904 to 1917, Gasparri found the opportunity to take another step. Canon 1125 of the new Code read:

Those matters which relate to marriage in the constitutions *Altitudo* of Paul III of June 1, 1537, *Romani pontificis* of Pius V of August 2, 1571, and *Populis et nationibus* of Gregory XIII of January 25, 1585, and which were written for particular places, are extended to other regions in the same circumstances.

On the surface, the significance of the new canon was escapable. It did nothing to resolve the dispute over what powers had actually been exercised in the decrees it extended. Avoiding language like "papal dissolution" or the milder "papal dispensation," it seemed to envelop everything in the bland phrase "those matters." Its practical effect seemed inconsequential: what regions in 1917 were populated by absent-minded Indian chiefs or by slaves torn from their spouses? If "the same circumstances" were meant literally, the documents might never apply again. But, if they were applied analogically, the possibilities opened up were large. Readers of *De matrimonio* knew that Gasparri viewed two of these documents as decrees of full divorce. Conservatism or the necessity of compromise prevented him from going beyond the invocation of their names. But to bring the decrees into the Code was to impart life to them. They emerged from their status of private exceptions to the law. They became part of the public universal law of the Church. Their actual texts, printed as appendixes to the Code, became accessible to all its readers. Fathered by the Curia of the sixteenth century, they were now fully acknowledged by the Curia of the twentieth century. That acknowledgment was the prerequisite of development.*

The Helena Case

Development did then occur, not in a straightforward unfolding of the sense of canon 1125, but obliquely, by a move which could scarcely have been made without Gasparri's bringing forward of the old decrees but which was, in fact, occasioned by another pro-

---

* Gasparri had proposed to cite these constitutions without quoting them. The Bishop of Panama objected that the texts were "generally unknown," and the same point was made by Cardinal Antonio Vico, by Patrick Delany, the Archbishop of Hobart, and by the ecclesiastical Provinces of Milan and of Salisbury. The Code responded to these observations by the texts in the appendixes, Puthota Rayanna, S.J., "De Constitutione S. Pii V Romani Pontificis (3 Augusti 1571)," *Periodica*, XXVII, 303.

vision of the new Code. According to a ruling of Benedict XIV issued in 1749, the marriage of a Protestant to an unbaptized person was null on the ground of undispensed disparity of cult.[40] The ruling — in itself an apparent exercise of papal authority over Protestants (all the baptized being taken as part of the Pope's flock) — had been a great boon in situations where such a marriage had later broken up, and one party to it wanted to enter a marriage with a Catholic; as Protestants and unbelievers never asked the Pope for permission to marry each other, all marriages between them were canonically invalid; no ecclesiastical barrier prevented the second union. Canon 1070 of the new Code eliminated the ruling and the benefit. In order to enlarge the number of canonically valid marriages, only persons baptized in the Catholic Church were to be bound by the law invalidating the marriage of Christians to unbelievers. "With this wise disposition," observed Joseph Creusen and Arthur Vermeersch, two leading Belgian Jesuits, "the Church has provided for the validity of more marriages." [41] The new provision also enhanced the difficulties of the divorced Protestant who sought to marry a Catholic. By canonical criteria the marital bonds of Protestants with unbaptized persons would now be binding in perpetuity.

Recognizing that the Code had created this kind of unprecedented difficulty, Creusen discussed a hypothetical solution in 1923, some six years after the Code's appearance. Invocation of Saint Paul was no help. The practice of the Church had determined the meaning of the Pauline privilege. That practice showed that the exception to indissolubility created by Paul had application only to a marriage contracted among unbelievers, of whom one became a convert, who, "called to peace" and radically transformed by baptism, was enabled to free himself of the servitude of marriage to his scoffing spouse. The privilege had never been available to those Christians who, as Christians, knowingly chose to enter marriage with the infidel. Canon 1120.2 now explicitly provided that the Pauline privilege in favor of the faith "does not obtain in a marriage between a baptized party and an unbaptized party which was begun with a dispensation for disparity of cult." By this specific provision of law Catholics, who could enter such marriages validly only by dispensation, were barred from invoking the Pauline privilege if the marriage failed. Should Protestants, who now could marry with canonical regularity without the dispensation, be better off than Catholics? Creusen thought not. But perhaps the Pope had the power to dissolve such marriages. The more common opinion of theologians was that, where one party to a marriage was unbaptized, the marriage was not sacramental. Only sacramental marriages were "fully indissoluble." If nonsacramental marriages were somehow dissoluble, it was the Pope, Creusen supposed, who could dissolve them, although, so far as he knew, the Pope had never dissolved the marriage of an unbeliever to a heretic. Should he reward "a lack of faith" by exercising his power? To push conjecture here, Creusen concluded abruptly, would be otiose.[42] Inferably, conjectures of this sort were in the process of being answered at a higher, more authoritative level.

In 1924 a series of decisions from the Holy Office gave the answer of the Curia. Elizabeth, a baptized Protestant, had married Charles Bukowicz, a Jew, in 1919. They were later divorced. Elizabeth became a Catholic and wanted to marry a Catholic. The Pauline privilege in the usual sense had no application: Elizabeth had been a Christian when she married Charles. Cardinal Adolf Bertram, Bishop of Breslau, sent her case to Rome. On April 4, 1924, the Holy Office, with Pius XI's approval, granted Elizabeth Bukowicz permission to remarry.[43] A second case, this time from mission territory, was determined on July 10, 1924. George, a baptized Protestant, married a pagan who soon abandoned him and remarried. George became a Catholic. A missionary permitted him to invoke the Pauline principle and marry a Catholic. Was his new marriage valid? Following the advice of the Holy Office, Pius XI dissolved the first marriage and permitted George to renew his marriage vows with the Catholic.[44] In the third case, Gerard G. Marsh, unbaptized, married Frances E. Groom, an Anglican, in September 1919. Less than a year later Marsh obtained a civil divorce, and Frances remarried. In 1922 Marsh sought to marry a Catholic, Lulu La Hood, and to become a Catholic; the Bishop of Helena, Montana, John P. Carroll, inquired if he had the authority to declare Marsh's first marriage null on the ground of disparity of cult. The Holy Office did not respond to this inquiry but converted it into an application by Marsh for "dispensation from the natural bond of the first marriage." The Congregation on November 5, 1924, voted to recommend such dissolution "in favor of the faith," and the next day Pius XI granted the grace.[45]

The Helena case was the best known of the series because it was the first publicized and because those most interested in this procedure were usually Americans. No case could better illustrate the creative role of the Curia and the way in which law was made in abstraction from the individuals affected. While the process went on in Rome, Gerard Marsh and Lulu La Hood married civilly, moved to Spokane, and on August 9, 1923, were married by a Maronite Catholic priest; they said nothing about Gerard's earlier marriage or the case pending in Rome and received a simple dispensation from the bishop of Spokane to permit Lulu to marry an unbaptized person. When the papal rescript reached Helena in 1924 the diocesan chancellor interpreted it as dissolving Marsh's marriage to Groom only if he became a Catholic: his desire for conversion had been put as a material fact in the petition to the Pope. As Marsh had married without conversion, the chancellor concluded that the marriage was invalid.[46] The extraordinary papal grace had no effect on either the couple or the local chancery. The rescript never reached the couple; they had moved and could not be found. The grace did not affect the chancery because it did not believe anything very significant had been done. Yet some canonists at once grasped the larger significance of the ruling: nothing in the rescript had made dissolution dependent on conversion; Marsh's lawful natural marriage had been dissolved by papal action.[47]

If the cases of Elizabeth Bukowicz, George, and Gerard Marsh were analytically dissected, they showed that the Pope would dissolve marriages which were valid, binding, and "naturally" indissoluble. They showed that the power to dissolve would be used in preference to the Pauline privilege; that it would be used to benefit either a former pagan or a heretic, a divorced spouse or a divorcing spouse; and that the phrase "in favor of the faith," until now restricted to mean "strengthening of the faith of a new Christian," would be the formula employed to explain dispensations permitting second marriages to Christians who had had valid marriages which were not sacraments. Above all, the case of Gerard Marsh showed that the Curia on its own initiative would undertake to extend the papal power to dissolve.

371

If the Code and these decisions had been lost for a thousand years and historians had then discovered them, a strong argument would have been made that they could not have been written within a few years of each other under the same curial administration. Surely, it would have been said, the Code and the decisions represent different epochs, or some part of the Code has not yet been found, or the decisions are forgeries, or a violent transfer of power occurred within the Curia. The Code's treatment of marriage and its dissolution was comprehensive and exhaustive. The Code knew nothing of a class of marriages dissoluble by papal action alone. No legal logic could account for this leap in legal development. Such a swift shift in law so thoughtfully planned as the Code would have been stamped as implausible, if not impossible, and the actuality of its occurrence challenged.*

The Curia was the same. No revolution had shaken its structure between 1917 and 1924. Cardinal Gasparri was in charge when the Code was enacted under Benedict XV in 1917 and when the new Pope, Pius XI, assented to the new policy in 1924. Achille Ratti,

* The relevant Code provisions ran:

Canon 1118. A valid, ratified, and consummated marriage cannot be dissolved by any human power or by any human cause except death.

Canon 1119. An unconsummated marriage between the baptized or between a baptized party and an unbaptized party is dissolved by the law itself through a solemn religious profession and by dispensation from the Apostolic See granted for a just cause at the request of both parties or of one although the other is unwilling.

Canon 1120.1. A lawful marriage between the unbaptized, although consummated, is dissolved in favor of the faith by the Pauline privilege.

Canon 1120.2. The privilege does not obtain in a marriage between a baptized party and an unbaptized which was begun with a dispensation for disparity of cult.

Canons 1121–1123. [On the interrogations to be used in discovering the will of the unbaptized party when the believer exercised the Pauline privilege to withdraw.]

Canon 1124. A believing spouse, although he has lived again matrimonially with the unbelieving party after the believer has been baptized, does not lose the right of celebrating a marriage with a Catholic person, and so he can use this right, if the unbelieving spouse changes his will and withdraws without just cause or does no longer cohabit peacefully without contempt of the Creator.

Canon 1125: *Supra* in text.

Canon 1126. The bond of the first marriage contracted in unbelief is only dissolved when the believing party in fact validly enters a new marriage.

Canon 1127. In a doubtful matter the privilege of the faith enjoys the favor of the law.

These canons were substantially identical with those which appeared in the draft code sent to the bishops of the world in 1912, *Schema codicis iuris canonici* (Rome, 1912), canons 395–404.

old librarian, new Pope, was not a person to have embarked on a personal adventure in remaking the law of marriage. No new demands of missionaries, no pressures from powerful archdioceses, no influence by secular authorities, no advocacy by lawyers had effected the creation of the new law. Nor had the vision or insight of theologians brought about the change. Creusen had mused about the possibility of papal action in his article in the *Nouvelle revue théologique*, but no prominent theologian had argued for it. When the *Helena* case was published in *Periodica*, the journal edited by Vermeersch, the leading moralist in Rome, it was carefully observed that the *stylus* of the Holy Office was not established by a single decision; perhaps it was a matter of "a very rare exception, the cause for which is hidden from us." [48] Nothing in this commentary suggested that the leading moral theologian was enthusiastic for this "truly noteworthy response." *

The change occurred — it could only have occurred — through a decision at the top of the Curia. The Holy Office which took this remarkable step on its own initiative was divided. Its Secretary was Rafaele Merry del Val; its next senior man was Gaetano De Lai. These were the intransigeants of Pius X's days. There was a Jesuit theologian, Louis Billot, and a Dominican diplomat, Andreas Frühwirth. The others belonged to Gasparri's administration — Gasparri himself, the Secretary of State; Basilio Pompili, Vicar of Rome; Wilhelm Van Rossum, Prefect of Propaganda; Donato Sbarretti, Prefect of the S.C.C.; Michele Lega, Prefect of the Sacraments; and Oreste Giorgi, Grand Penitentiary. Above all, Gasparri must have believed that now in the first years of the new pontificate a decisive break must be made. Precedent, practice, habit, and tradition called for maintenance of the old policy, for rejection of the

---

* Two studies of the literature have shown among theological writings no explicit support of papal power to dissolve such marriages before 1924. Kenrick's opinion in 1840 on the extension of the Pauline privilege appears to be the only theological support for dissolution prior to the papal action, see Damizia, "De dissolutione vinculi," pp. 164–170; Arthur Vermeersch, *Theologiae moralis principia–responsa–consilia* (Rome: Gregorian Univ., 3rd ed., n.d.), III, 689. (Damizia's reference to the Salamancans, *Cursus theologiae moralis* [Venice, 1750], II, "De matrimonio," 12:71–72, is to a passage which is merely an exposition of the ordinary Pauline privilege of converts.) Against dissolution in nonconvert cases stood a number of standard nineteenth- and twentieth-century theologians — Giovanni Perrone, S.J.; the team of Antonio Ballerini, S.J., and Domenico Palmieri, S.J.; Franz X. Wernz, S.J., see Damizia, "De dissolutione vinculi," pp. 160–162. Hence it was not in response to any impetus from the theologians that the Holy Office acted.

option to dissolve. In the same year in which the Folchi case was finally settled, Gasparri's Curia chose for innovation.

The Norms of 1934

Gasparri manifested the change in consciousness in the Curia in the version of *De matrimonio* which he published in 1932, at the great age of eighty, the first revision he had made of his fundamental textbook since he had put aside his individual work twenty-eight years ago to compose the Code. Now he asserted the new doctrine in a remarkable new section of the book bearing the caption, "The Dissolution of Legitimate Marriages by the Holy See When the Salvation of Souls Demands It and Scandal Is Absent." [49] He elaborated what he had held as early as 1892: Saint Paul's exception depended on legislation by the Pope; the apparent anomaly of the Pauline privilege was an instance pointing to a more fundamental power, a wider class. Paul had depended on Peter: "The Holy See approved the apostolic application and took care to preserve it." He was certain that the power extended to cases "far different from the Pauline privilege." He was convinced that the old decrees, *Altitudo, Romani pontificis, Populis et nationibus,* were all examples of the power. He was now sure of what was done at the Curia and not hesitant to go as far in revealing curial custom as the traditional secrecy of the Holy Office allowed: "Those who know well the practice of the Supreme Congregation of the Holy Office know that the Supreme Congregation, after a word with the Most Holy, has granted a dispensation of this sort not infrequently in times past, and also grants it in our day." The basis for the power to dispense from indissoluble nonsacramental marriages was a grant from God to God's Vicar on earth. It was a grant "in favor of the faith and for the salvation of souls." [50]

Were there any limits to a power with such high origins and such broad purposes? Gasparri held that the Pope could never act if his actions would give rise to scandal; the power was given for the welfare of souls and could not be validly used to the loss of souls. The limitation was a valiant attempt to put some boundary on papal discretion and to attach the severe sanction of invalidity to acts which overstepped the line. But the boundary suggested was a shifting and subjective one. Who in the Curia would think that any particular exercise of papal power would give occasion for true scandal — scandal which would arise from an onlooker's honest belief that something sinful was being done — rather than at most affording occasion for "pharisaical scandal," an onlooker's envy at a grace being given someone else? Who might not convince himself that the greater good being done for a soul outweighed the risk of even true scandal being caused by papal dissolution of a marriage?

Custom, however, as Gasparri did emphasize, put one limit. "Up till now," the practice of the Holy Office had been not to dissolve marriages where a Catholic had been dispensed to marry an unbeliever. In 1932 a marriage like Marie Reid's to Frederick Parkhurst would still have been indissoluble in fact. But nothing in Gasparri's theory prevented the dissolution of this kind of marriage. That it had begun with a dispensation was irrelevant. The Pope was not estopped to dissolve dispensed marriages. He could dispense from the impediment of consanguinity and then, if the marriage were unconsummated, dispense from the marriage; so here he could permit the Catholic to marry a pagan and later grant dissolution of the marriage. The custom of not dissolving in these cases "does not in the least prove that the Holy See lacks this power." To explain the repeated denials by the Inquisition that the Pope could do this, Gasparri looked at a single inquiry, that of the Bishop of Cochin, and said the Bishop had asked about the Pauline privilege, and so had been answered in terms of it in 1759.[51] The Bishop, he implied, should have asked about the Pope's power over the marriages of unbelievers. Gasparri did not acknowledge that, prior to 1924, "the privilege of the faith" had been used as coextensive with "the Pauline privilege," and that, if the Holy Office for two hundred years had taught that the marriage of a dispensed Catholic could not be dissolved, it was because the Church had known no power of dissolution except the power based on Paul.

What Gasparri, at the end of his long life, was able to teach to be the power of the Roman See was put in the form of administrative rules six months before his death.* The Holy Office, on May 1,

* Gasparri was no longer Secretary of State; enjoying honorable retirement he continued as a cardinal member of the Holy Office. Sbarretti was now its Secretary; Lega was still a member. Two other septuagenarians, Gaetano Bisleti, Prefect of the Congregation of Seminaries, and Lorenzo Lauri, who had succeeded

1934, issued these regulations under the title "Norms for the Dissolution of Marriage in Favor of the Faith by the Supreme Authority of the Sovereign Pontiff." Article I adopted the now-famous phrase of Gregory XIII in *Populis et nationibus*: marriages of unbelievers were marriages, but they were "not so confirmed that they cannot be dissolved if necessity urges." Added to this phrase was the significant qualification, "in favor of the faith, by the authority of the Supreme Pontiff." Dissolution by the Pope in these cases was "a privilege" or "a grace" which he did not have to confer. Only for cause, indeed only for "very grave cause," was the grace to be granted. Gasparri's limitation — no exercise if exercise would give scandal — was made explicit; and another limitation was added in a spirit of caution — no exercise if exercise would cause wonder (*admiratio*). These limitations were not, however, expressed as affecting the validity of any dispensation. The only *sine qua non* conditions were proof that at least one party to the marriage was not baptized when the marriage was begun and that no sexual intercourse had occurred between the parties after both were baptized. Although the petitioner for papal dispensation was asked if he had children and how he intended to provide for their religious education, emphasis was not placed on this part of the inquiry. In the spirit of the Parkhurst case, the focus was on the nonbaptism of one party to the marriage. The Norms told the bishops to interrogate the parents and other relatives "who know the whole course of life" of the person said to be unbaptized. The bishops were to investigate all the circumstances "from which it appears credible and probable that baptism had not been conferred." Inevitably, the cases were to become "baptism cases" rather than "marriage cases." The legal process was set up as inquiry into the fact of nonbaptism.[52]

Authority to dissolve resided only in the Pope. In theory his authority could have been delegated to the bishops of local dioceses throughout the world; and in practice, his authority was to be exercised by the Holy Office, to whom exclusive jurisdiction of the

---

Giorgi as Grand Penitentiary, were men of Gasparri's vintage. Two order men, Alexis Lépicier, a Servite, and Rafaele Rossi, a Carmelite, were more distinctly choices of Pius XI. New blood was represented by Gasparri's successor as Secretary of State, his old aide, Eugenio Pacelli; and Francesco Marchetti-Selvaggiani, who had performed the investigatory duties in the Washington phase of the Parkhurst case (see *Annuaire pontifical catholique* [1934], p. 848).

cases was assigned. The Assessor of the Holy Office in his weekly audience with the Pope would show him a set of dossiers, to which the Pope could nod approval. This ritual and the possibility of the Pope intervening in an individual case would give the form of personal papal action to the dissolutions. Effectively, the power was to be exercised by the Secretary of the Holy Office and the curial consultors to whom he sent the cases for review in Rome.

The reigning Pope when the Norms were issued was Pius XI, who had issued that small summa of Christian matrimony, *Casti connubii*, on December 31, 1930. In the encyclical Pius XI had quoted Luke 16, 18: "Whoever divorces his wife and marries another, commits adultery, and whoever marries a woman divorced by her husband commits adultery"; and the Pope had continued: "And these words of Christ refer to every marriage whatsoever, even those only natural and lawful; for indeed it is fitting that there be in every true marriage that indissolubility by which everything relative to the dissolution of the bond is removed from the good pleasure of the parties and from all secular authority." To the principle of indissolubility the Pope had then publicly acknowledged two exceptions: the unconsummated marriages of Christians, and "natural marriages contracted only betwen unbelievers." [53] Only those who noted the omission of "ecclesiastical authority" before "all secular authority" could have guessed at the existence of the power to be discovered in 1934.

In the recent light of *Casti connubii*, if the Curia was willing to systematize a new process of dissolution, it was not confident enough to inform the world at large of its dispositions. The Norms of 1934 were sent in secret to the bishops, "not to be made a matter of public law, but to be observed as the internal rule of the ecclesiastical tribunals." Laymen, and even priests outside of a bishop's chancery, had no means of knowing the content of the rules or even of their existence. When a bishop requested dissolution of a marriage pursuant to the Norms, he was directed to state expressly whether, "from the eventual granting of the grace some scandal, wonder or danger of calumnious interpretation is to be found among Catholics as if the Church by its practice favored too much the custom of divorce." [54]

Operationally, the Norms depended on the existence of civil divorce. In the typical situation, a marriage had been civilly terminated and one party now wanted to marry a Catholic. The divorce had effectively ended all relations of a marital kind; the old marriage existed only to bar union with a Catholic. In form, the petitioner sought the termination by the Pope of this tie. In fact, the Pope was being asked to rule that, if a new union were formed, the Catholic party to it would not be denied access to the sacraments because of the old bond. Functionally, the Pope was not "dissolving" a marriage which civil divorce had already ended; he was removing an impediment to an ecclesiastically valid union. His power, which looked so very large in theory, was in practice a modest regulation of the terms on which the sacraments of the Church would be made available.

The thrust of the changes was beneficent and merciful. They enabled more persons to marry and to remain eligible to receive the sacraments. The means of effecting this result bore comparison with the actions of Cardinal Giorgi on behalf of Filippo Folchi — to be merciful, to "help out" someone in difficulty, the easiest solution at the Curia was to put in motion the supreme power of the Pope. To do this was to avoid re-examination of the underlying problems, to eschew functional analysis, and to employ language which exalted the authority involved.

Ending an Exaggeration

The Norms were a phase in an evolutionary process which began to accelerate, first in theory, then in practice. The post-Gasparri curialists now spoke. Of these the most significant was Alfredo Ottaviani, a protégé of Gasparri, who in 1929 had promoted him, aged only thirty-nine, to be Substitute for Ordinary Affairs in the Secretariat of State. Ottaviani could not match Gasparri's older protégé, Eugenio Pacelli, in intellectual range and brilliance; his strength lay in his fidelity to basic concepts of Gasparri and the Curia; and his work was significant not because it was original but because it was so true to the spirit with which he was imbued.[55]

Unbelievers, Ottaviani taught, "belong by law to the Church." The reason for their legal status was that "Christ ordered the Church to do what was necessary to save them." In fulfillment of this mission, the Church could "bind and loose," as chapter sixteen of the Gospel of Matthew taught. Binding and loosening, the Church could legislate for unbelievers. True, Ottaviani added in a footnote, the power to bind and loose did not give the Church power over "temporal or merely civil matters." [56] But marriage was not a mere temporal or civil matter. It was in the domain of the sacred. As such, it fell within the Church's sphere; and within this sphere the Church could regulate the unbeliever. In addition, beyond the power conferred in Matthew upon the head of the Church, the Pope enjoyed additional power from Christ in his capacity as "Christ's Vicegerent over Christ's subjects." This vicarial power was extremely broad. Every human being was Christ's subject and so in some fashion under the authority of His Vicar. As far as the marriages of unbelievers were concerned, "what cannot be reached by virtue of the naked primacy received for the Church and in the Church can be done by virtue of the vicarial power of the Roman Pontiff." [57]

Not for Ottaviani to look functionally at the Pope's actions under the new Norms. In his view each papal dissolution "directly touches the rights and duties of the unbaptized party, as well as the rights and duties of the baptized": whatever the ecclesiastical allegiance of the party, by the papal action he was released from marital duties and deprived of marital rights. Analyzed in this fashion, the new papal power over marriage became itself a clear proof of the extensive competence of the Pope over unbelievers. Following Gasparri, and proving what the Pope could do from what the Pope in fact did, Ottaviani did not specifically cite the still secret Norms of 1934 to confirm his point. He did call upon historical precedent. Instances could be adduced, he said, to show that Popes had permitted unconverted Jews living in the papal territory to remarry after divorce. Some writers explained the practice as papal tolerance of the Mosaic law, or as a regulation made by the Popes in their capacity of civil rulers; others saw it as a true exercise of papal power over the unbaptized.* Ottaviani did not reject the latter opinion.

* Ottaviani, *Institutiones*, p. 229, citing Rudolf von Scherer, *Handbuch des Kirchenrechts* (Graz, 1898), II, 560, n. 61. Much later in the same line of argument, Joseph Greco, S.J., collected a series of papal rulings on purely Jewish marriages in Greco, *Le pouvoir*, pp. 115–127. These are as follows: (1) Martin V in 1418 orders that no one harass Misoli Angeli, a Jew of Ferrara, for divorcing his first wife and marrying again in accordance with Mosaic law; (2) The Grand Penitentiary, Cardinal Antonio Pucci, on June 15, 1534, grants a Jew of Bologna

These sweeping views on the power of the Church and Pope were not the excogitations of a hermit, the theses of a thirteenth-century controversialist, or the ranting of a religious visionary. They were the thoughts of a sober man from Trastevere who had spent thirty years of his life in the Roman Curia. They were ideas which, if not commonplace, were familiar and habitual in Rome and very far from being regarded by his peers as rash or dangerously novel. They embodied his teaching to students in canon law at the Lateran University. When they were published in 1936 as Institutes of Public Ecclesiastical Law he had become Assessor, or chief executive assistant, in the Supreme Congregation of the Holy Office. In a foreword to his book by the Secretary of State, Eugenio Pacelli, he was congratulated on making "complex and knotty questions clear in the full light of doctrine." [58]

His doctrine indeed was not made out of whole cloth. Even Ottaviani's boldest claims of papal power over the world could be matched in the giant curial canonists of the thirteenth century, Innocent III, Innocent IV and Cardinal Hostiensis. In the power asserted to move bishops from their sees a divine power over spiritual marriage had been said to be exercised in a fashion which could afford a precise parallel to the exercise of papal power over carnal marriage. Transferring the canonist Bernardo to the bishopric of Pavia from the bishopric of Faenza, Innocent III had spelled out the similarities:

Sacred Scripture has taught Us that "those whom God has joined together, no man may put asunder." But conjugal joining is of two kinds: one according to the flesh, which is called carnal, the other

permission "by apostolic authority" to marry a second time if the caononical judges determine that his assertion is true that his first wife is sterile; (3) The Camerlengo, Cardinal Giulio Ascanio, on June 26, 1555, grants Rafaele Angelo Levidici of Nepi "an indult to marry another wife." The petitioner had lived more than ten years with a sterile wife as established by witnesses. The permission is given to marry "freely, licitly, and with impunity," "as Holy Mother Church and our predecessors as Camerlengo and we have been accustomed to tolerate with God and without sin"; (4) Cardinal Ascanio, on June 23, 1561, gives a "license to marry another wife" to Rafaele Hacman, a Jew of Rimini; (5) Cardinal Ascanio on March 18, 1561, informs Salomone Abramo, a Jew of Fano, that he may marry a second wife in the lifetime of his first wife according to Jewish custom; (6) the Camerlengo, Cardinal Enrico Gaetani, on December 7, 1590, grants "a license to marry another wife in the lifetime of the first" to Moses Merlino, a Jew of Ferrara; (7) Pope Gregory XV on May 12, 1624, grants Giuseppe Toscano, a Jew of Rome, who has lived twenty years with his wife Giammilla without having children, "a license to be able to take a second wife," on the condition that the second wife lives outside of Rome during Giammilla's lifetime.

according to the spirit, which is not unfittingly called spiritual. The Apostle refers to both kinds — so that it is not lawful for man to divide those canonically joined in spiritual marriage as are a bishop and his church. It could seem from this that the Supreme Pontiff could not divide a spiritual marriage, that of a bishop and his church; but according to custom, which is the best interpreter of the laws, and according to the sacred canons, it may be held that by resignation, deposition, and translation, which are reserved to the Apostolic See alone, the Supreme Pontiff has plenary power over these affairs. That will cause no scruple of doubt in those who understand it properly; it happens not by human but by divine authority, which in this matter is carried out by the Supreme Pontiff, who is called not the vicar of mere man but the Vicar truly of the true God. Although We are successors of the Prince of the Apostles, We are not the vicar of any apostle or man, but We are the Vicar of Jesus Christ himself. Wherefore, whom God had bound by a spiritual union, not man — because not the vicar of man — but God — because the Vicar of God — separates, when We on occasion remove bishops from their sees by their resignation, deposition, or translation.[59]

The same teaching became decretal law in Innocent III's *Inter corporalia,* X.1.7.2. In turn this decretal was cited as controlling by Hostiensis when, explaining how the Pope can dispense from any vow made to God, he declared that the Pope acted "not by the authority of a mere man but by the authority of God: for he rules on earth in His place." In the same spirit Innocent IV opened his commentary on the *Decretals* by relating the Pope's divine role to his lawmaking authority: "To the Maker of the canons and the Vicar of the Creator is subject every creature." [60] The vicarial power over carnal marriage set out by Sanchez, Gasparri, and Ottaviani was rooted in these precedents.

Was there any limit to the papal power identified with Christ's? With unusual asperity Thomas Aquinas had remarked on the Pope's asserted ability to dissolve solemn religious vows: "The Pope cannot make one who has professed religion to be not a professed religious, although some jurists ignorantly say the contrary." [61] For Thomas some acts involved contradictions, and the nature of things set limitations. Joannes Andreas, the great lay canonist of Bologna, made a related comment on Hostiensis' view of papal power: "Hostiensis, however, acknowledges that as long as the Pope lives, he is called Lord, and he can change squares into circles and dispose of all things as Lord, saving violation of the Faith. Yet, truly speaking, neither he nor any other prelate is Lord." If, "truly speaking," the Pope was not Lord, there were limits to his power. Joannes Andreas nonetheless wrote these words while commenting on a canon permitting the Pope to be judge in his own case, a paradox or contradiction no greater than turning squares into circles, and he defended the canon: "It should not be presumed that He, the Vicar of God, will judge otherwise than God Himself would judge." [62] As long as the legal system insisted upon this kind of identification, no legal limit on papal power existed.

On March 2, 1939, Gasparri's old first assistant, Eugenio Maria Giuseppe Pacelli was elected Pope: Marcantonio Pacelli's grandson; Advocate Filippo Pacelli's son; Gasparri's right hand in 1904 when the composition of the Code began, Gasparri's successor as Secretary of State in 1930; the purest product of the Curia, armed with a strong grasp of the law, a very high view of papal authority, and an intellectual liking for large ideas. Not since Lotario de' Segni had a lawyer with such strong theological interests occupied the throne of Peter. In the twenty years of his pontificate, Pius XII made the marriages of the unbaptized a domain of papal authority, almost as, four centuries before, Alexander VI had treated the lands of the unbaptized as territory for the Pope to divide between Portugal and Spain — only here, as the domain was spiritual, a functional analysis of what Pius XII was claiming might have shown that the grand vision of papal imperium led in practice to a beneficent regulation of the reception of the Catholic sacraments. In theory, however, Pius XII proclaimed in the person of the Pope the view of the Pope's official power which Ottaviani had adumbrated in his lectures.

The grand vision was enunciated in a papal address to the Rota on the inauguration of the judicial year 1941–42. Preoccupied with World War II from the beginning of his administration, the Pope waited two years to give voice to his ideas, but now in the fall of the year in which the war had spread to Russia and to Africa, he turned his mind to marriage. By divine law, confirmed and consummated marriages were indissoluble. These marriages the Pope could only protect. The rest formed the domain. These other marriages could not be dissolved by the parties at will; in technical terms, they had "intrinsic indissolubility." They could be dissolved by higher extrinsic authority — God's, or the Pope's as God's delegate. "What God has joined together, let not man put asunder," he quoted, "that is to say, not man but God can put couples asunder; and hence, the putting asunder is null where God does not dissolve their bond." All marriages were indissoluble, but some marriages were more indissoluble than others. When, in the "indeed relatively rare" cases, he, the Pope, dissolved a marriage, he acted not as a man, but as the Vicar of God.[63]

The thesis of Sanchez and of Ottaviani on the vicarial power of the Pope to dissolve marriage had now been publicly accepted by the Pope himself. The power ascribed by Gasparri to the Pope had been formally claimed by the Pope whom he had trained. The decretal law of Innocent III was expanded in the Pope's claim of jurisdiction over marriage. In the most fundamental ecclesiological statement of the Pian regime, the encyclical letter *Mystici corporis*, the Pope identified himself with Benedetto Gaetani, Boniface VIII, the canonist whose reign from 1294 to 1303 is often taken as a turning-point in the history of the papacy. As Pius XII now put it: "Our predecessor of immortal memory, Boniface VIII, solemnly taught in the Apostolic Letter *Unam Sanctam* that in the world Christ and His Vicar constitute only one Head." *Unam Sanctam* had begun with the teaching of St. Paul that the Church was a mystical power whose head was Christ. But the Pope was also head of the Church. Did that mean the Church had two heads, "like a monster"? No, Boniface VIII had reasoned, it argued for a unity of the Pope with Christ; the logic of this unity meant that the Church held both the spiritual and temporal swords and that every human creature must be subject to the Pope. Pius XII did not claim the two swords. Later in his reign in a celebrated discourse on the relation of history to the Church he recognized the fundamental relativity of Boniface VIII's political pretensions for the papacy.* But he accepted the conclusion that the Pope bore Christ's "person on earth." [64] With this unity asserted, with Boniface VIII solemnly invoked, with *Unam Sanctam* itself — that flamboyant crest of the medieval papacy — actually quoted, Pius XII was prepared to rule

---

* "As the moon receives no light save from the sun, so no earthly power has anything save what it receives from the ecclesiastical power." Quoting these words of Boniface VIII to the envoys of Albert of Habsburg, Pius XII added, "That medieval conception was conditioned by the epoch," Pius XII "Vous avez voulu," Allocution to the Tenth International Congress of the Historical Sciences, September 7, 1955, AAS, XLVII (1955), 678.

the marriages of the world. His power had but one limit. "The supreme norm in every case," said Pius XII, must be "the salvation of souls." [65] With this open-ended restraint the single restriction on the supreme authority, Pius XII had proclaimed a new charter for the dissolution of marriage in the Curia.

In 1946, in the seventh year of the pontificate of Pius XII, in the first year after the American victory in Europe, Aloysius Willinger, Bishop of the diocese of Monterey-Fresno, California, forwarded to the Pope a petition to dissolve the marriage of a convert who, before her baptism, had been married before a Catholic priest to a Catholic who had been dispensed to marry her. The petitioner had been civilly divorced and was civilly married to another Catholic. The Bishop asked that the first marriage be dissolved by the Pope on the ground that it had not been consummated, a request for a papal action which had been run-of-the-mill since the seventeenth century. But the Holy Office found that the rigorous standards set for proof of nonintercourse had not been satisfied. The Holy Office — Marchetti-Selvaggiani now the Secretary, Ottaviani the Assessor — recommended dissolution, "in favor of the faith"; and on July 17, 1947, Pius XII dissolved the marriage. The Curia had at last decided to exercise the full power of the Pope over a marriage between a believer and an unbeliever and, by exercising it, to establish that the authority existed.[66]

Did it make a difference that dissolution was sought not by the dispensed Catholic, but by the originally unbaptized party? In 1950 Pius XII dissolved another marriage in favor of the faith of another convert-petitioner from Fresno. When Bishop Willinger asked if the dissolution meant that the Catholic party to the dissolved marriage was free to marry too, the Holy Office replied, on May 4, 1950, that it did.[67] One step more had to be taken: dissolution on the petition of a Catholic. In 1953 Bishop Willinger presented the case of Alfred Cinelli of Bakersfield, California, married in 1941 to Elinor Robbins. He was a Catholic, she was unbaptized. They had first married civilly, then united three weeks later in a Catholic church with a proper dispensation from disparity of cult. Cinelli was in the army. When he returned from overseas, he found his wife's attitude toward him had changed; in April 1946, she divorced him and remarried. Cinelli now wanted to marry again; his bride-to-be was not a Catholic but was taking instruction in the religion. Bishop Willinger asked the Pope to dissolve the first marriage in favor of the faith of Cinelli, in favor of the faith of the woman he wanted to marry, and in favor of the faith of any children born of this contemplated union, that they might be baptized and educated as Catholics; and he asked the favor further "because of the excellence of the merits of the petitioner and to preserve the name Cinelli and his offspring in the membership of the faith of his forefathers." The dissolution, the Bishop added, would not cause wonder among the people of the diocese; rather, it would be "the occasion of creating more good will toward the Church from those of the race and blood of the petitioner." The Holy Office approved, and Pius XII dissolved on January 23, 1955.[68]

If, by some extraordinary longevity, Marie Reid, Frederick Parkhurst, and Prince Rospigliosi had lived until 1955, would Marie Reid have obtained dissolution of her marriage by papal fiat? Surely in 1901, when she married Rospigliosi, or in 1910, when the Rota had decided against her, a papal dissolution would have caused *admiratio* if not scandal. The strict letter of the Norms could not have been met. But, after 1912, when Parkhurst remarried, it might have been hard to say that true scandal would have been given by permitting Marie Reid to remarry; and the risk of *admiratio* might have been more than counterbalanced by the excellence of the merits of the Rospigliosi family, the desirability of preserving the Rospigliosi offspring in the faith of their forefathers, the benefit to the faith of both the Prince and the Princess, the creation of good will among all those who believed that the Church should not, if it could help it, make a couple choose between obedience to the Church and marital embodiment of their love. In 1955 Franz Hürth, the leading Jesuit moralist in Rome, was an open champion of the power. In his view, if its exercise occasioned scandal or wonder, such reactions might be attributable to "an erroneous judgment as to an exaggerated indissolubility of marriages." [69] The unthinkable in 1912 would have appeared as the correction of an exaggeration in 1955.

The new power had its own name — "the Petrine privilege," to discriminate it exactly from the Pauline case. By the late 1950's sufficient information had been disseminated about its existence and exercise for other chanceries to follow the lead of Fresno. The power was worldwide in scope; its application was most frequent in America. The United States presented the combination of a large Catholic body — the largest and most prosperous Catholic body in the world — with a population many of whom were unbaptized and many of whom were divorced.[70] As civil divorce occurred on a massive scale in America, divorced Catholics and divorced non-Catholics who wanted to marry Catholics became petitioners for use of the Petrine power. In no country in the world did the number of requests amount to more than a tiny percentage of the potential applicants — both motivation and information were generally lacking. In terms of a system where divorce had been unknown, the numbers, running into the thousands in the United States, were significant.

The old American Catholic attitude toward divorce was not dead: the spirit personified by Cardinal Gibbons still stirred the hearts of many American bishops, who refused to permit Petrine cases to be processed within their chanceries. By 1960 the worry of these men had become so intense that the annual meeting of the hierarchy took upon itself the responsibility of alerting the Holy Office to the danger of giving scandal by the dissolutions. But the Roman practice was established; the American voice, more powerful than in 1910, was milder in its warning than Gibbons' uncompromising words to the Rota; and the Holy Office, acting through the Apostlic Delegate, Egidio Vagnozzi, replied with suavity that bishops should not process cases except to "regularize" existing marriages or "when exceptionally grave circumstances warrant the concession of the favor." [71] As anyone familiar with ecclesiastical usage might have guessed, the exception offered by "exceptionally grave circumstances" was a large enough loophole to accommodate any sympathetic case. By the late 1960's the practice of papal dissolution was so established that the Holy Office used printed forms in which the name of the particular petitioner could be inserted.* A fee first set at $75.00, then raised to $120.00,

---

* Standard forms have been provided me by several American chanceries. Some particulars are worth noting. The printed form is entitled "Dissolution of Marriage in Favor of the Faith," but provides as a condition of the petition that the petitioner will be baptized or converted. This phraseology is of course appropriate only to the Pauline privilege, which the form subsumes under the Petrine privilege. In the Petrine case the printed reference to baptism or conversion is crossed out by typewriter. The fee is typed in on the reverse side of the form granting the petition.

was charged by the Congregation for processing the papers. In 1969, 3,277 cases were forwarded to Rome by American dioceses and another 3,996 were pending in the United States.[72]

Louis Billot, a Jesuit cardinal created by Pius X and member of the Holy Office which had taken the first step in 1924, wrote in his treatise on the sacraments that there was a limit to papal power over marriage. "The most ample power of the keys given to the Church" could not dissolve a carnal, consummated marriage between two Christians. Only God Himself "by that way of dispensation which is like the operation of miracles" could dissolve such a union.[73] But if only a miracle could dissolve some marriages, were there not other marriages still outside the papal ambit which might be drawn within it?

Binding and Loosening Unbelievers

The evolution which reached a peak with Alfred Cinelli's case in 1955 did not stop. The rate of evolution had increased. It had taken over a thousand years for "the Pauline privilege" to be established beyond argument; it had taken 370 years for the Pauline privilege to be expanded to support special papal dissolutions of Indian and slave marraiges; it had taken another 340 years for these examples to be explicitly accepted by the Curia and made part of the general law in 1917; it had taken 30 years to move from the Code to the first Fresno dissolution; 8 years to come to the Cinelli case; and it took 3 years to reach what, in this series at least, had to be the ultimate term.

In 1892 Gasparri had written: "All admit that the Roman Pontiff can in no way dispense if both spouses remain in unbelief, for their marriage is not in the least subject to the Church." This statement disappeared from the 1932 edition of De matrimonio.[74] At the same time, in a catechism intended as a summation of the doctrine he had defended for over sixty years as a priest, Gasparri described the marriage of two unbelievers as "naturally indissoluble." If he meant that the Pope by supernatural power could dissolve such a union, few readers would have guessed his meaning. As of 1932 it seemed established that, if neither party to a marriage was a Christian, the marriage must always be beyond the jurisdiction of the Curia.[75]

Ottaviani in his book had put the marriages of unbelievers within the realm of the Church, but had not drawn the specific conclusion that the Pope could dissolve the union of two unconverted unbelievers. As Ottaviani in 1936 had gone beyond Gasparri, so in 1953 Ferdinando Lambruschini developed Ottaviani's doctrine by proposing its extended application. His essay, modestly entitled "A Disputation about the Vicarial Power of the Roman Pontiff over the Marriages of Unbelievers," had the marks of a trial balloon held up by a junior curialist (Lambruschini, a professor at the Lateran, was only forty-two), while a policy shift was being contemplated by his seniors in the Curia. Reasserting Ottaviani's theses on papal jurisdiction, he fortified them with further illustrations, among them the bull *Inter caetera* of May 4, 1493, of Alexander VI, in which the Pope, among other things, "by the authority of Almighty God granted to Us in Saint Peter and by the authority of the Vicariate of Christ Jesus which We enjoy on earth," gave to Ferdinand and Isabella authority over the lands of the New World they had discovered. The dedication of the entire world to the Sacred Heart of Jesus by Leo XIII in 1899 and the dedication of the world to the Immaculate Heart of Mary by Pius XII in 1942 rounded out the grosser exercises of authority culled from medieval history. Authority over unbelievers, proved to exist by these examples, had already been used over the marriages of unbelievers: Innocent III had determined in *Gaudemus* which of the canonical rules on incest bound converts before their conversion; whenever an unbeliever defended the validity of his marriage in a canonical court, the Church asserted competence to pass on the validity of a marriage made outside the fold; *Romani pontificis* and *Populis et nationibus* had turned the "naturally indissoluble" marriages of the Indians and slaves into dissoluble and dissolved unions. These well-known precedents were cited as prelude to a more explicit, more self-conscious assertion of the extent of papal power. As Vicar of Christ, the Pope was "at least in some way the head of humanity." In the modern world the very existence of "the sacred" was at stake; in a world which was physically and socially one it would be destroyed if it were not preserved by "a supreme spiritual authority." That supreme authority, protecting or judging the marriages of the world, could only be the Roman Pontiff.[76]

On March 12, 1957, in the eighteenth year of his pontificate and his fifty-fifth year as a member of the Roman Curia, Pius XII went beyond all his predecessors in explicit, self-conscious action affecting the marriage of two persons outside the Church. El Keir, aged sixteen, and his cousin, Sessya, aged fifteen, were married as Mohammedans, had three children, and were divorced by a Mohammedan cadi at El Keir's insistence. Sessya returned to her family with the one surviving child of the union. El Keir migrated to France and married civilly a young Catholic girl. He wanted to become a Catholic; canonically his civil marriage was concubinage; the local bishop would require him to separate from the girl for a year and a half to prepare for baptism. Instead of insisting on this painful separation, the priest advising him presented his case to Rome for a more immediate solution. In accordance with the Norms of 1934, El Keir's petition was submitted to the Holy Office, whose senior officer and public embodiment was its Secretary, Cardinal Ottaviani. On February 23, 1957, the Holy Office voted to advise the Pope to dissolve the marriage of El Keir and Sessya, both Mohammedans at the time of their marriage and at the time of its papal dissolution.[77]

El Keir's petition made it appropriate as a transitional case. He was seeking to be a catechumen; in time, after his baptism, he could have exercised the Pauline privilege. The papal dispensation merely accelerated the dissolution of a bond which, in any event, would not have survived; the unbeliever, whose faith was aided, had already placed himself at the door of the Church. But the transition once made, the papal power was exercised where neither party to the marriage had related himself in any way to the Church except as he had become involved with a Catholic he wanted to marry. Four more times, at least, in the remaining months of Pius XII's life, the Pope exercised his extraordinary jurisdiction over unbaptized spouses and dissolved marriages made in unbelief between unbelievers who remained outside the Church.[78]

Angelo Roncalli, John XXIII, with the Holy Office unchanged, continued his predecessor's policy. *Djarkata, August 19, 1959* exhibited its amplitude: Lo Ma, a Chinese pagan, was abandoned in

China by her husband, Phan, also a Chinese pagan. Phan migrated to Indonesia and married Dorothy, a baptized Catholic, who discovered the existence of her husband's first wife two years after her own marriage. She wanted to remain with Phan. Phan did not want to return to Lo Ma. Canonically, Phan and Dorothy were living in adultery. They were also raising five children, baptized and educated as Catholics, who were troubled by their mother's failure to receive the sacraments. Phan had no desire to convert, so the Pauline privilege was inapplicable. Lo Ma still being in Communist China, her disposition toward Phan or toward the Catholic Church was unproven and indeed unknown. John XXIII dissolved her marriage with Phan "in favor of the faith." In this usage the phrase encompassed, not conversion from unbelief as in the usage from 400 to 1934, but a wider range of spiritual benefits — the value to Dorothy of access to the sacraments and the value to her children of their mother sharing with them in the practice of the faith.[79]

Papal dissolution continued to be granted in the administration of Giovanni Batista Montini, Paul VI. Ralph and Estelle, a Jewish couple from Chicago, were married in 1954. Childless, they eventually separated. Ralph began to date Beatrice. In April 1964, Beatrice became a Catholic, and in the same month Estelle divorced Ralph. Ralph now sought to marry Beatrice, but he had no desire to become a Catholic himself, so that the Pauline privilege was inapplicable. The chancery of the archdiocese of Chicago prepared a petition for Ralph to sign asking the Pope to dissolve his union with Estelle. At the same time, the chancery prepared an endorsement of the petition for Cardinal Albert Meyer, Archbishop of Chicago, which summarized the facts making the papal grace appropriate: "the I.C.P." (Interested Catholic Party) was thirty years old, a girl of outstanding intelligence, unlikely to find another man so suited for her as Ralph. Processed by the chancery, endorsed by the Archbishop, reviewed in Rome by consultors of the Holy Office, the petition was acted upon in a papal audience to the Assessor. On February 7, 1964, Paul VI dissolved Ralph's marriage to Estelle.[80]

A Pause in the Process

Exercised by three Popes, papal authority over the unions of unbelievers was an established fact. Theoretically, the power knew
only one limit: exercise had to confer a spiritual benefit. This
limitation was so loose and so large as to be without practical significance. In the context of marriage cases someone's spiritual
status was always affected by the impediment of an existing marriage. Most of the marriages in the world were now in theory dissoluble by the Pope, for most of the world consisted of unbaptized
persons. Any spiritual advantage apparently could justify papal
dissolution of a union one party to which was not baptized. Practically, two limitations existed. Cases did not arise unless a Catholic
wanted to marry one of the unbelievers in the broken marriage:
there always had to be an I.C.P. Cases were not processed unless
the marriage to be papally dissolved was ruptured in fact. These
limitations supplied the contours of the power. The Pope was only
able to give Catholics access to the sacraments; papal dispensations
were available on a large scale only where civil divorce certified
that the prior union had in fact ended.

Civil divorce had a substantial relation to the new power. Where
it existed, the Church had ceased to be the primary agency for the
legal structure of sexual relations. No property rights, no custody
rights, no civil rights were determined by a papal dissolution of
marriage. The papal power, justified in the language of the medieval papacy, could expand without the check that Boniface VIII had
met, because it had no consequences — that is, no consequences
which were tangible, practical, social. All the palpable consequences of dissolution had already been determined by the civil
ruling which normally preceded the papal action. Practically speaking, papal dissolution effected results only in the intangible kingdom of the spirit and the spiritual-legal world of the sacraments.

Integration of civil divorce into a papal process, nonetheless, had
theoretical implications. The Popes proclaimed in word that marriage as a natural institution was indissoluble by any human agency.
Pius XII declared that the Church never recognized the validity
of the civil divorce of the unbaptized. The action of the Popes
conveyed a different message. When the Pope approved a rescript
processed by the Holy Office for the dissolution of "the natural

bond" of a marriage already civilly terminated, could anyone out-side the Church believe that it was the Pope's will which broke the tie? Could the unbelievers whose marriages were affected enter-tain the notion that, unknown to themselves, a marital bond had survived until the papal move was made? Within the Church, the papal acts inspired the kind of reflection visible in the description of absolute indissolubility as an exaggeration.[81]

Stress was laid in Rome on the gratuitous character of the new dissolutions; they were not one's right; they were in the free gift of the Pope. In the words of the Apostolic Delegate to the United States, "They entail an altogether extraordinary favor dependent on the vicarious power of the Holy Father." [82] The notion of a grace applied both to the few cases where the marriage of two unbelievers was dissolved and the more common cases where the Petrine privilege was used to end the union of a believer and an unbeliever. Difficult as this posture was to maintain when papal action was obtained by a routine licensing proceeding, the notion was not without consequences. What the Pope could freely give, he could freely stop.

Ottaviani had become emeritus in 1967. The old Holy Office, no longer styled "Supreme" and freshly baptized as the Sacred Con-gregation for the Doctrine of the Faith, was headed by a Yugo-slavian, Franjo Seper. Internationalized by the addition of two cardinals with major sees outside of Rome, and enlarged to eighteen members, the Congregation still was composed of the major policy-makers of the Curia. In the summer of 1970 the granting of Petrine dissolutions was suddenly suspended, catching the American dioc-eses with over 5,000 petitions in process. Cardinal Seper was ap-parently puzzled by the implications of the power and wanted it subjected to a new and profound examination; in December 1970 the cardinals of the Congregation voted to continue the suspen-sion.[83] Perhaps the seventeenth-century Curia's withdrawal after *Populis et nationibus* was to be paralleled in the 1970's. The im-plications for the theology of marriage were indeed profound: a new and deeper examination of the power to dissolve exercised by three Popes, over twenty years, in some tens of thousands of cases could only enlarge curial self-consciousness of the options available.

OPTIONS OF THE CURIA, OPTIONS
OF THE COMMUNITY

Superficially, after the development from 1924 to 1957, from the Helena case to El Keir's petition, the Pope possessed more power over the marriages of those outside the Church than of those within it. Functionally, his power was more extensive by far over the unions of the Catholic faithful. The marriages of non-Catholics could only be touched tangentially; to the extent that papal refusal to terminate a marriage meant that a Catholic believer would alter his relationship to some non-Catholic the Pope's acts had efficacy. What unbelievers' marriages were in themselves could not be affected for them by a power which they did not acknowledge and of which they might not have heard. It was otherwise with the marriages of members of the Church. At least since the twelfth century papal decisions had affected the substance of their marriages; and although social custom, inherited theology, and community beliefs were important components in the composition, the Curia was often the most important force in shaping the explicit structure, declared purposes, and recognized consequences of Catholic marriage.

For centuries the power of the Pope — or, more accurately, the power of the persons related to each other in the forms provided by the Curia — had been expressed in the policies governing the termination of marriage. These policies had been embodied in both substantive and procedural rules, and in the acts of officers of the Curia. Several kinds of marriage were officially terminable: the spiritual marriage of a bishop to his see, the unconsummated marriage of two believers, the consummated marriage of a believer to an unbeliever. Policy, that is, the preserving of other values, the meeting of other needs, the balancing of other virtues, was allowed to determine dissolution in these cases. But one kind of marriage was truly indissoluble in principle. Consummated marriage between two baptized Christians could, in the language of Cardinal Billot, be affected only by an operation of God in the manner of a miracle. The symbol of the union of Christ and the Church, that great mystery of the Epistle to the Ephesians was beyond formal subjection to policy. Entrustment of the symbol to a legal system made policy, nonetheless, inseparable from the vindication which the symbol was afforded.

Accommodation of values is necessarily the work — perhaps the chief work — of legal systems, whose most satisfactorily fulfilled function is to substitute peaceful compromise for resolution by combat. However high a priority is enjoyed by one value, it is certain to be, to a degree, sacrificed by a process which will take other values into account. Enthusiasts eager to make society revolve on their insights, dictators anxious for quick compliance with their will, theologians focused on a single transcendent truth are well advised to avoid the law. The canons concerning marriage were meant to teach a single lesson, to incorporate a single value — indissolubility was the *raison d'être* of the system; without it the whole enterprise would have lacked focus, connection, energy. But the tensions of the canonical process reflected the several values which the system in operation balanced. Because it responded to these multiple interests, because indissolubility as a symbol could not be single-mindedly served, the Curia was compelled to choose the marriages to be preserved, the marriages to be dissolved.

Options of Procedure

Prescriptions as to process — who could sue, when and where a case might be brought, when and where appealed, who could or must defend, who was free to judge — did not purport to exercise a power to bind or loose. Effectively, at only one remove from the decision of an individual case, rulings on these matters determined eligibility for dissolution and its likelihood of being granted. For example, the equity doctrine of clean hands, barring from the court a petitioner guilty of misconduct with respect to the subject matter of his suit, had been developed by the canonists themselves and applied by them in matrimonial litigation where the object of a suit was judicial separation. An adulterer could not, on the grounds of his spouse's adultery, obtain a separation; his own guilt kept him from judicial relief. Little legal imagination was necessary to have developed an analogous doctrine for annulment. Such a rule would have meant that the papal courts would have had very little marriage business to consider. Charles of Lorraine, Filippo

Folchi, Marie Reid, all involved in technically bigamous unions, would have been denied the opportunity to sue in the Rota. An absolute bar to litigation brought about by an adulterous union would have produced a lack of flexibility which the managers of the system sought to avoid; and clean hands were not made a requirement for matrimonial suits.

In the same spirit, the short statute of limitations apparently set by *Ad id* was overridden by the commentators and curial practice, although it stood on the books as good decretal law. The lack of any statute of limitations evidently produced the consequences such statutes are designed to prevent: ascertainment of what had happened at the time of consent became extremely difficult; perjury was easy. At the same time, absence of a cut-off on litigation meant that no one could ever be completely assured of his marital status. These evils, evident enough to the perspicacious lawyers who ran the system, were accepted because it was thought more essential to have flexibility. An escape-hatch, however small, could be glimpsed in any miserable marriage.

The welcoming of long-postponed litigation and the postponing of litigation which had begun were of a piece. From the date of Charles' marriage to Béatrice to the date of final judgment, nineteen years elapsed; from the date of Nicole's complaint to the Pope, fifteen; from the date of Charles' filing suit in the Rota, seven. The case was finally decided only after leading figures of the House of Lorraine had pleaded with the Pope to decide it, and after the Pope had obtained Charles' specific agreement to abide by the Rota's judgment. The process was paradigmatic of the system's moderation, and in this respect there was no distinction between the curial courts in their heyday and in their modern restoration. Perez de Guzman's case began thirty years after his marriage and took four years to be decided; Barberini's began the year of the marriage and ran five years; Reid's began sixteen years after the marriage and continued for ten years; Castellane's came sixteen years after the wedding and ran fifteen years; Folchi's began sixteen years after the wedding and lasted eighteen years. This procedure was inconsistent with a desire to put first the indissolubility of marriage. In effect, the system substituted delay for formal compromise.

Compromise is the normal achievement of a judicial system, but marriage in these cases could not be deliberately compromised. On the narrow issue, Is A married to B? the answer had to be either Yes or No. Doctrine permitted no surrender of half of a spouse's claims. Unable to produce compromise directly, the system substituted a process in which each person had the psychological satisfaction of believing that his rights would eventually be vindicated. While there could be only one winner, two could have hope of winning. In delay no one was forced to an absolute and irretrievable rupture with the Church. In delay there was the possibility that one person might die, that passions might cool, that reconciliation could be accomplished. Accepting delay as a method, the managers of the system tacitly acknowledged that the indissolubility of marriage could be subordinated to other values. Papal practice itself impaired the symbol of indissolubility.

Where the system did not work at all — where lack of lawyers, failure to institute effective tribunals, and the unavailability of information left potential litigants without access to the law — indissolubility, uncompromised, was affirmed by the impossibility of challenging a marriage once it was formed in appearance. In such circumstances, the circumstances of much of the Catholic world in the twentieth century, whatever union was publicly entered was untouched by the canonical process. *De facto* denial of legal process assured that most marriages would be unaffected by the subordination of indissolubility provided in the system. Only the powerful, the knowledgeable, or the lucky — and in any case only the persistent — were likely to encounter the system in its most developed form at the Roman Curia. For them a variety of values besides indissolubility came into play and entered into the ultimate conclusion of their suits.

The system itself could not escape the tension which must arise from reaching a decision on the basis of past events while looking ahead, even slightly, to the consequences flowing from the decision. Looked at in its judicial form, the system seemed incurably historical. Whether or not consent had been given to marry appeared a matter for discovery like whether or not a tort had been committed, a loan made, or a piece of land mortgaged. Yet charged with authority to affect the future lives of two persons, the system could not escape some orientation to the future. The more it looked to the future, even if only by delaying judgment, the more administrative discretion and pastoral concern predominated over strictly historical interest in what had once happened.

If indissolubility existed, it was because marital consent had actually been exchanged by the parties. The courts were interested in the truth, in what had happened at the moment of consent. Mere recital of a legal fiction in the fashion of many American divorce proceedings would not suffice to obtain dissolution of a marriage. Clumsily and haltingly, but earnestly, the system investigated the facts at issue.

Yet at the same time the realities of a case were submerged by the focus and formulas of testimony and argument. The efforts of lawyers to fit facts to the governing law often gave the courts a choice between two contrived accounts of palpable unreality. The actual circumstances were submerged in old cases and established commentaries. An intricate patterning of fact and citation was executed — in the courts of the seventeenth and eighteenth centuries with artistry — by the advocates employed to persuade the judges. So much time, care, energy, and thought were devoted to the proper patterning that the lawyers spent proportionately little time exploring the unique, factual constellation of their case. The system's interest in "the truth" — Had consent to marriage been given? — became less prominent than its educational concern.

The pedagogic impact of the system was, like that of other legal systems, chiefly upon its active participants: the lawyers, judges, and professors. The briefs and opinions interlaced with citations created a universe of intelligible discourse. Coral-like, the cases gave the law a rational structure into which the precedents initiated the system's managers. The active participants were provided with training in the art of analysis, the use of abstractions, the savoring of distinctions. They were taught to probe human motivation, question human veracity, and doubt human love. They acquired practice in affirming principle while tempering principle. The system formed the men who were the managers of the Curia so that they would be discreet, determined, patient, unillusioned, as self-limited as accountants, as mutually approved as diplomats.

Those who participated passively as parties — the Perez de Guzmans, the Pauline Baillys — received a much more uneven education. They had entered the system by accident. The system did not adjust to their capacities for instruction. The legal arguments, in the main, escaped them. Nothing suggests that any of them, save perhaps Parkhurst, read the briefs which their lawyers addressed to one another and the court, or the opinion which the court addressed to the lawyers. What the parties learned to value was the end result, the authoritative judgment of the court which bound them or loosed them. The education imparted was a lesson not so much in the indissolubility of a marriage, which might or might not be dissolved, as in the power of the papacy to determine their status and enforce its decrees.

The authorities of the system — the judges and professors of canon law — identified teaching with the written opinion, as they identified law with the written rule. Only what was said officially was teaching. They would have protested that any other education imparted was accidental and unintended, not to be charged against the system as its responsibility. By restricting their definition of teaching to the formal documents they were able to avoid seeing that they themselves in their own persons, by their own acts, were teachers who taught values other than those literally proclaimed.

For most of the lives of all of the litigants the system did nothing to preserve their marriages as effective symbols of the union of Christ and the Church. Setting out to defend a symbol of love, the active participants in the system seemed to have made the commonest of human mistakes, to have forgotten the purpose of their endeavor. Absorbed in the necessary operations of a sophisticated legal enterprise, they did not stop to ask how the education implicit in the process related to the reasons for defending the symbol.

Hospitableness to litigation by the knowledgeable, and secretiveness screening the existence and methods of the courts from the uninitiated; significance to litigants which was prospective, and formal focus centered on the past; concern concentrated on individual cases and subordination of the individuals to the symbolic value of their acts; commitment to an absolute choice between two exclusive alternatives and hesitancy to reach the terminal choice; judicial form dominated by the paternal and political features of the organization in which the form was set; dependence on principle for *raison d'être* and responsiveness to policy which overrode the sweep of principle; an educational mission directed to upholding a symbol of love in the community and educational methods which instructed the participants in legal technique and the use of power; responsibility for the symbolism of love and a forgetfulness of purpose such that love was lost — these were the characteristics of the canonical curial system as it worked in its prime and in its modern reconstitution. They were the price — was a price of this sort even avoidable? — of defending the symbol by a legal process.

Options of Substance

That the choices made by the Curia affected the content of the unions judged to be indissoluble needs little elaboration. Matthew, Mark, and Luke taught not to disunite those whom God had joined; the prevailing interpretation of Paul said that the physical union of man and wife symbolized the unbreakable union of Christ and the Church; popular piety often added that marriages were made in heaven. None of these authorities told when a couple had been joined by God, when a marriage had been made. Taking consent as the constituent of marriage, the Curia had to answer the questions, consent to what? what conditions, expressions or intentions qualify or destroy consent? who is sufficiently free to give it? who is physically capable of consenting? who is mentally and morally qualified? The answers to none of these inquiries was given by Scripture; all were open to decision; and decision meant adjusting theological ideals, the demands of reason, and social exigencies. The pattern of marriage could not be drawn out of the air, nor could the Curia act in a vacuum. Aware of certain traditional responses, attentive to the reflections of the academic theorists, embued in European, especially Italian, culture, the men of the Curia also had a range of discretion for magical improvisation, for creativeness. The answers given were no more a transcription of secular behavior than they were deductions from the Bible. Fusing Scripture, tradition, theory, Roman law, and European customs, the Curia approved the answers which determined when the consent of believers was beyond undoing and when apparent bonds were nullities.

The selection of options has been observed in the cases of Charles and Nicole, Luis Quifel Barberini and Joanna Almeida y Carnide, José Perez de Guzman and Ana Ponce de León, Filippo Folchi and Pauline Bailly, Boni de Castellane and Anna Gould,

Frederick Parkhurst and Marie Reid. In these cases choice had to be made between an ideal of personal freedom and a custom of arranged marriage; between a theology of virginal unions and a view of marriage as procreative; between the availability of a lawful form of sexual intercourse for everyone and the special requirements necessary to undertake the education of children and to preserve a lifelong relation; between the primacy of internal intention and the public character of a social institution; between the mores of a people and the construct of natural marriage; between deference to the stability engendered by apparently valid ceremonies and obedience to the technicalities set up for the distribution of papal power. The necessity for making these difficult choices made manifest the amplitude of the power possessed. Option after option was elected by the Curia, which shaped the substance of indissoluble marriage.

That this exercise of choice, inescapable for the managers of a legal system, should continue into the last quarter of the twentieth century was not in question — at least if the legal system survived at all — but the outcome of the development, whose beginnings under Gasparri have been examined, was more problematic. As the Church ceased to be identified with the social order, it became better able to shape marriage and the process of marital dissolution in accordance with theological demands. The Curia fought the disengagement — Paul VI opposed the introduction of civil divorce in Italy in 1970 as his nineteenth-century predecessors had opposed the introduction of civil government in Rome. But it was no more possible to maintain marriage as an institution theocratically ruled than it was to maintain government in its ancient sacred form. Ultimately the canon law would be stronger, free of doing the work of Italian domestic law, to design the processes and shapes appropriate to a sacramental community of believers. Already the course of change could be perceived in the courts of the Curia.

Mid-twentieth-century cases tended to fill out the pattern pricked out in the period of transition and to overcome the hesitations which attended the shift which started with the restored Rota. *Rennes, May 9, 1959,* for example, set a high standard for mental capacity to marry. *Tokyo, December 21, 1963* showed extraordinary sensitivity to an interior state of mind of unwillingness to marry, so that a mute internal dissent was allowed to cancel the assent publicly uttered in response to the pressures of convention.*

Rome, January 26, 1954, decided by Francis Brennan, the first American auditor of the Rota, could be viewed as vindication of the legal theory underlying the second Castellane decision, the Holy Office answer to Seattle of 1877, and one portion of Gasparri: a spouse's structure of personal values, set in the context of her country's customs, was treated as decisive in determining dissolubility. The traditional presumption that all men would wish to enter an indissoluble union, as instituted by the Author of Nature, yielded to anthropological evidence. The court recognized that "the immoderate desire for happiness" might be "more powerful than the sacred bond of marriage" and lead to the intent to enter a union whose durability would depend on its contribution to the

---

* *Rennes, May 9, 1959,* Sacred Roman Rota, *Decisiones seu sententiae,* LI, 237–243, may be compared with Ana Ponce de León's case two hundred years before. The bridegroom suffered from "a psychopathic condition of an intermittent nature." He was well enough to serve in the French army shortly after the wedding, and at a later stage in the case he had remarried civilly and was living contentedly with his second wife. Nonetheless, he had several breakdowns requiring hospitalization, and a psychiatrist testified that, at the moment of consent, "his freedom was not total because of the state of light exaltation he was in, and because of his puerile, vain, and mythomanic character." The Rota, through its most learned legal historian, Auditor Charles Lefebvre, held the marriage null. For a discussion of the trend of Rota decisions to look now for capacity to be faithful for life, to educate children, to sustain an indissoluble contract, see John R. Keating, *The Bearing of Mental Impairment on the Validity of Marriage: An Analysis of Rotal Jurisprudence* (Rome: Gregorian University Press, 1964), p. 179.

Tokyo, December 21, 1963, unpublished decisions of the Sacred Roman Rota, Rota archives, showed how far the Rota could now go in rejection of the kind of arranged marriage which had been the center of Charles of Lorraine's case. The bride, a Japanese Catholic, had entered a marriage negotiated by her sister because she was embarrassed to continue living in the home of her brother-in-law. Neither brother-in-law nor sister ordered her to marry or threatened her with punishment or inconvenience if she failed to marry. The situation spoke for itself: "Unless she entered marriage, she would feel herself a small person." She accepted without affection the man proposed for her and went through the wedding ceremony weeping; a few weeks after the ceremony, she ran away, back to her sister's house. Rotal auditor Ewers analyzed the case in terms of simulated consent. The bride's unusual breach of Japanese decorum, her tears at the wedding, showed that she could not have consented in her heart. Her public "Yes" was a pretense of internal consent, and the marriage was invalid. As in the *Rennes* case, the Rota still spoke in terms of the instant of the wedding, but it looked at the short entire life of the marriage. The criteria it applied were such that by them half the marriages of Europe might once have been invalidated: coercion, imposed by circumstance, and lack of love for the spouse accepted were equated with simulated consent. Justice to the interior region of the person brushed aside the words of consent uttered in the ceremony of outward appearance.

satisfaction of the spouses. The Rota would not treat such a union as indissoluble Christian marriage.*

Cases such as these continued an evolution whose foreseeable term suggested a substantive law very different from that established by the *Decretals* of Gregory IX and enforced by the curial courts up to the beginning of the twentieth century. The roots could be found in theory of the past, but everything was in the course of change. From a public exchange of promises interpreted by the ordinary rules of contract law, marital consent was becoming an interior acceptance to be interpreted by psychologists of the heart. Marital affection, to which lip service had for so long been given, was being more effectively acknowledged as a necessary quality of consent. Once a contract open to anyone, like any commercial bargain, canonical marriage was becoming an undertaking accessible only to persons who could be expected to be able to sustain lifelong commitments. Formerly an institution responsive to the social interests of a small governing class, in which the abstract honor given freedom to marry was combined with concrete arrangements for supporting parental choice, marriage was becoming the mutual choice of two persons in love. A type of social life which it was assumed that anyone wanting lawful sexual intercourse wanted to enter, indissoluble marriage was now becoming a form of spiritual life requiring personal perception of the values and personal dedication to their embodiment.[84]

The new character of marriage was not expressly acknowledged by the recent decisions of the Rota. Movement in this direction was evident. Reshaping the legal structure of marriage for believers coming before the Rota, the Roman Curia exercised the power to confirm or to dissolve. While theory and rhetoric dramatized the use of papal grace for participants in nonsacramental unions, a paral-

---

* *Rome, January 26, 1954,* Sacred Roman Rota, *Decisiones seu sententiae* (Vatican Press, n.d.), XLVI, 63–64. The language attributed to the petitioner, Aurelia, was virtually identical with that attributed to Anna Gould. A German living in Italy, Aurelia was said to have told relatives and friends before her marriage that she could always escape from matrimony if she were unhappy and that she would escape if unhappy. She was reported "to have said openly that if the marriage did not bring happiness she would have to free herself." She thought "it was immoral that two should be tied together when love between them was missing." The customs of her native land, Germany, bolstered her views: "If the marriage did not turn out well, she would get a divorce. For us in Germany that would be common. . . . She was a foreigner, and divorce was possible in Germany, and so she would follow the laws of her country."

lel use of power was occurring with regard to sacramental unions. When the two processes were viewed in conjunction, the forms of Catholic marriage were seen to be substantially enlarged.

By the second part of the twentieth century these classes of carnal marriage had been canonically established:

Class I. Sexual and indissoluble in intent; contracted by two baptized persons; consummated by sexual intercourse; indissoluble by any authority.

Class II. Virginal by vow, agreement, or intent; contracted by two baptized persons; dissoluble by religious profession or papal dispensation.

Class III. Sexual in intent; contracted by two baptized persons; unconsummated by sexual intercourse; dissoluble by religious profession or papal dispensation.

Class IV. Sexual, but limited or negative in procreative intent; contracted by two baptized persons; consummated by sexual intercourse; indissoluble or invalid at the option of the courts.

Class V. Impermanent by intention, custom, or assumption; contracted by two baptized persons; consummated by sexual intercourse; indissoluble or invalid at the option of the courts.

Class VI. Sexual in intent; contracted by at least one unbaptized person; consummated by sexual intercourse; dissoluble by the conversion and remarriage of the unbaptized in certain cases or by papal dispensation in all cases.

These classes varied in popularity and durability. Unconsummated marriages were uncommon. Virginal marriages, if not wholly hypothetical, were even more uncommon. Marriages which could be treated as valid or invalid at the option of the courts were transitional, and already decisions such as *Rome, January 26, 1954* exemplified a tendency to put outside the Catholic system unions where interior intention was counter to the required content. The marriages of most of the world were Class VI marriages, which could be terminated at the point they had an effect on marriages within the Catholic sphere. The ideal or normal type of Catholic marriage, Class I, was being purified by the new requirements made of it. Purification might make it rarer. No longer a necessity of social existence as it once had been in Western Europe, it could be expected not to disappear, to be more highly prized as it was more consciously chosen. Indissolubility was so tied to "the great mystery" of the Church, so developed as an ideal by the experience of the Christian community, so responsive to the profoundest thrust of human love that it would not vanish whatever other shapes were found for marriage.

That other shapes could be found even within the canonical system seemed implicit in the existing six divisions. No single characteristic of marriage entailed indissolubility — not procreative purpose, not completed sexual intercourse, not participation of the baptized. Precedent had been a barrier to the creation of new forms neither in the fifteenth century when papally dissoluble marriages were invented, nor in the twentieth when the naturally indissoluble marriages of unbelievers became certifiable as terminated by a process beginning with civil divorce and ending in an audience to the Assessor of the Holy Office. Marriage as a uniform institutional form did not exist within the system. In all but name plurality was recognized.

"What God has joined together, let no man put asunder." This great cornerstone of the Christian theology of marriage had not prevented the canonists from recognizing that, although Jesus had spoken to Jews, the marriages of unbaptized were, in more than one way, open to dissolution. The union of the baptized was the symbol of the union of Christ and his Church, as, in another way, the marriage of a bishop to his see was its symbol. The Curia had dissolved both sorts of union by means of a power put above the human and had stopped short only of formally dissolving the carnal unions of the baptized. For eight centuries of legal process, however, even the symbolic value of these unions had been balanced against other values in the system. Neither the theoretical construct of what nature demanded in marriage nor the express texts of Scripture, neither the absence of precedent nor the desire for uniformity, had barred innovation by the creative lawyers of the past. Variety in the unions already recognized — in their purposes, their stability, their manner of termination, their symbolism — was the ground which justified the belief that the last class of marriage had not been created.

APPENDIX A. *Citations by Type of Authority in Toul, January 15, 1653*

	Bible	Council of Trent	Corpus juris canonici	Justinian Codex or Digest	Cong. of Council	Rota Decisions	Rota Number of citations	Treatises Books	Treatises Number of citations
For Charles									
Ricci									
(Fact Brief)	0	0	0	0	0	8	17	6	6
Bottini									
(Law Brief)	1	0	7	1	0	17	29	53	102
Piccolomini									
(Law Brief)	0	0	9	6	0	26	52	62	155
Ronconi									
(Law Brief)	0	1	5	1	1	8	27	47	86
Vermiglioli									
(Law Brief)	2	0	2	0	1	10	10	2	2
Vizzani									
(Law Brief)	0	0	2	2	1	40	72	53	128
Joint Brief									
(Law Brief)	0	0	4	2	1	26	58	53	135
Total	3	1	29	12	4	135	265	276	614
For Nicole									
Saracinelli									
(Fact Brief)	0	2	1	1	3	10	25	5	28
Balbani									
(Law Brief)	1	2	5	6	0	88	104	56	115
Boncompagni									
(Law Brief)	0	1	5	3	0	44	77	41	85
Caprara									
(Law Brief)	0	0	3	1	0	24	33	60	120
Eugenii									
(Law Brief)	0	1	3	0	0	25	30	30	45
Eusebii									
(Law Brief)	0	0	3	2	0	43	56	54	106
Sarceni									
(Law Brief)	0	3	8	4	3	13	18	41	53
Total	1	9	28	17	6	247	343	287	552
The Rota	0	1	15	12	14	83	104	71	119

Authors cited by nationality

Italian	Spanish	French	Belgian	German	Portuguese	Polish	English	Greek	Uncertain
118	31	11	7	6	5	1	1	1	7

Authors cited by principal discipline

Canon Law	Civil Law	Moral Theology	Ethics	History	Uncertain
90	60	30	1	1	7

Authors cited by century

	pre-13th	13th	14th	15th	16th	17th	Uncertain	Total
Authors	3	5	14	22	89	49	7	189
Times cited	9	22	57	103	650	312	30	1183

APPENDIX B. Balloting in the Papal Election of 1921, according to Cardinal Piffl, "Notes on the Conclave of 1922," *The Tablet*, October 5, 1963, CCVI, 1060.

Ballot No.	1	2	3	4	5	6	7	8	9	10	11	12	13	14
Merry del Val	12	11	14	17	13	7	1	0	0	0	0	0	0	0
Maffi	10	10	10	9	1	0	0	0	0	0	0	0	0	0
Gasparri	8	10	11	13	21	24	24	24	19	16	2	1	0	0
La Fontaine	4	9	2	1	7	13	22	21	18	8	23	22	18	9
Ratti	5	5	6	5	5	4	4	5	11	14	24	27	30	42
Van Rossum	4	0	0	0	0	0	0	0	0	0	0	0	0	0
Bisleti	3	1	4	4	2	2	1	1	0	0	0	0	0	0
De Lai	2	2	1	0	1	1	0	0	0	0	0	0	0	1
Pompili	2	1	1	1	1	0	0	1	1	0	0	0	0	0
Mercier	1	0	0	0	0	0	0	0	0	0	0	0	0	0
Laurenti	2	4	3	2	2	2	1	1	3	5	4	3	4	2
Lega	0	0	1	1	0	0	0	0	0	0	0	0	0	0
Giorgi	0	0	0	0	0	0	0	0	1	1	0	0	0	0
Belmonte	0	0	0	0	0	0	0	0	0	8	0	0	0	0
Sbaretti	0	0	0	0	0	0	0	0	0	1	0	0	0	0

Abbreviations

AAS.	*Acta apostolicae sedis* (Rome: Vatican Press, 1908–).
Annuario pontificio.	*Annuario pontificio per l'anno* (Rome: Vatican Press, 1908–).
Bullarium.	*Bullarium Diplomatum et Privilegiorum Sanctorum Romanorum Pontificum* (Turin, 1858–1868).
Cerchiari.	Emmanuele Cerchiari, *Capellanes Papae et Apostolicae Sedis Auditores Causarum Sacri Palatii Apostolici seu Sacra Romana Rota ab Origine ad Diem usque 20 Septembris 1870: Relatio Historica—Juridica* (Rome: Vatican Press, 1920–1921).
Clementines.	Clement V, *Constitutiones, Corpus iuris canonici*, ed. E. Friedberg (Leipzig, 1881), volume II.
Codex Justiniani.	Justinian, *Codex, Corpus iuris civilis*, ed. Paulus Krueger (Berlin, 1895).
Council of Trent.	*Concilium Tridentinum: Diariorum, Actorum, Epistularum, Tractatuum Nova Collectio*, ed. Gorrës Society (Freiburg in Breisgau: Herder, 1964), volume IX.
Digesta.	Justinian, *Digesta, Corpus iuris civilis*, ed. T. Mommsen (Berlin, 1895).
Gratian.	Gratian, *Decretum, Corpus iuris canonici*, ed. E. Friedberg (Leipzig, 1881).
Hierarchia catholica.	*Hierarchia Catholica Medii et Recentioris Aevi sive Summarum Pontificum—S.R.E. Cardinalium Ecclesiarum Antistitum Series E Documentis Tabularii Praesertim Vaticani Co¹lecta—Digesta—Edita*, volume IV, Patrice Gauchat, O.F.M. Conv., ed. (Munster: Regensburg Press, 1935), and vols. V–VI, Remigius Ritzler, O.F.M. Conv., and Permin Sefrin, O.F.M. Conv., eds. (Padua: Il Messagero di S. Antonio, 1952, 1958).
Pastor.	Ludwig von Pastor, *History of the Popes From the Close of the Middle Ages*, volumes XXV–XXXIV, trans. by Ernest Graf (London: Kegan Paul, Trench, Trubner, 1935–1941), and XXXV–XXXVII, trans. E. F. Peeler (St. Louis: B. Herder Bond, 1949).
Pl.	*Patrologia latina*, ed. J. P. Migne (Paris, 1844–1855).
Schulte.	Johann Friedrich von Schulte, *Die Geschicte der Quellen und Literatur des Canonischen Rechts* (Stuttgart, 1880).
Sext.	Boniface VIII, *Liber Sextus Decretalium, Corpus iuris canonici*, ed. E. Friedberg (Leipzig, 1881), volume II.
Thesaurus S.C.C.	*Thesaurus resolutionum Sacrae Congregationis Concilii*, ed. Prospero Lambertini and various others, I–IV (Urbino, 1739–1740), V–CLXXVII (Rome, 1741–1968).
X.	Gregory IX, *Decretales, Corpus iuris canonici*, ed. E. Friedberg, (Leipzig, 1881), volume II.

Notes

CHAPTER I. THE STEADY MAN

1. On the life of Charles, see Fourier Bonnard, "Les relations de la famille ducale de Lorraine et du Saint-Siège dans les trois derniers siècles de l'indépendance," *Mémoires de la Société d'archéologie lorraine et du Musée historique lorrain* (1932, 1933), vols. LXX, LXXI; Augustin Calmet, *Histoire ecclésiastique et civile de Lorraine* (Nancy, 1728), vol. I, clxxxiii, with fuller details in vol. III, cols. 170–739; and F. des Robert, *Campagnes de Charles IV, Duc de Lorraine et de Bar, en Allemagne, en Lorraine, et en Franche-Comté* (Paris, Nancy, 1883), I, pp. v–xii, 4–7. Hereafter these works are cited respectively as Bonnard, Calmet, and Robert. On Pont-à-Mousson, *Les établissements des Jésuites en France depuis quatre siècles*, ed. Pierre Delattre, S.J. (Engheim: Institut superieur de théologie, 1956), IV, cols. 81–89, 95, 107.

2. On Nicole's age, see Bonnard, LXX, 166–168; Calmet, I, col. clxxxii; III, col. 543. At the trial two priests and a friar from Lorraine deposed that Nicole had been baptized in 1604, so that she would have been seventeen years old in 1621, *Summarium pro D. Carolo*, Sacred Roman Rota, Positio Number 189, Secret Archives of the Vatican. (All folio references to *Summaria* and Briefs are to the folio numbers stamped on by the staff of the Archives.) This testimony appears to be merely an error of recollection of a matter forty years old. The priests, called by Charles, had no motive for making Nicole older than she was. But her father and mother were not married until 1606, and modern historians agree in placing her birth in October 1608. On her disposition, see Calmet, III, col. 543. On her feelings toward Louis de Guise, see the testimony collected in *Summarium pro D. Carolo*, fol. 296v–298r.

3. A standard form of prayer for a dispensation stated that "grave enmities" between the petitioners' relatives would be composed by the petitioners' marriage. *Summa bullarii earumve Summorum Pontificum constitutionum*, ed. Stefano Quaranta (Venice, 1607).

4. Bonnard, LXX, 168–169. On the effect of Father Dominic's prophecies, see Nicole to Charles, undated letter circa 1637, *ibid.*, LXXI, 241.

5. *Summarium pro D. Nicole*, fol. 200r–200v. On the university celebration see Delattre, *Les établissements des Jésuites*, IV, col. 135.

6. Nicole to Charles, undated, Bonnard, LXXI, 239–242.

7. Robert, I, v–vii.

8. Henrietta's escape with Louis de Guise, now her husband, was an adventure of audacity and courage, see René Taveneaux, "Les mariages de la Maison de Lorraine-Vaudémont," *Le pays lorrain*, XXXII, 136; Calmet, III, col. 266.

9. Ch. Pfister, "Les mémoires du Comte de Brassac, gouverneur de Nancy (1633–1635)," *Mémoires de la Société d'archéologie lorraine* (1898), 48, 387. On her pension see Calmet, III, col. 543.

10. Charles to Nicole, *Summarium pro D. Nicole*, fol. 205; Charles to Nicole, April 6, 1634, *ibid.*, fol. 206r; Charles to Nicole, June 16, 1634, *ibid.*, fol. 206r.

11. Robert, I, 3.

12. Charles to Nicole, *Summarium pro D. Nicole*, fol. 207r–207v; and Charles to Nicole, *ibid.*, fol. 207v.

13. Robert, I, 277; Calmet, III, col. 325.

14. Phillipe Maréchal, *Une cause célèbre au XVII siècle* (Paris, 1919); Calmet, III, col. 325.

15. Robert, II, 376 (the 3000 masses); Bonnard, LXXXI, 326 (Charles' acknowledgment of paternity); Robert, I, 531 (the contract).

16. Delattre, *Les établissements des Jésuites*, IV, cols. 130–131 (Cheminot's expulsion); Robert, I, 378–380 (Cheminot's role as confessor). Henri Fouqueray, S.J., *Histoire de la compagne de Jésus en France* (Paris: A. Picard, 1925), V, 20–24, argues that it "is not certain" that Cheminot was Charles' adviser on the marriage and cites Charles' later denial that he took advice from him. But Charles' statement, made in the course of an official inquiry into Cheminot's conduct, is not credible. Why did Charles name him his confessor in March 1637? Fouqueray also does not know of Robert's account of the formal opinion or Guyot's testimony as to the date of the wedding.

17. Robert, I, 378.

18. So Cheminot explained the case in a memorial signed by Charles for presentation to the Pope, Bonnard, LXXI, 248, and the same arguments were doubtless made at the time of the wedding.

19. Robert, I, 377, 418–419. Fourier, a graduate of Pont-à-Mousson, was canonized in 1897, Jacques Choux, "Pietro Fourier," *Biblioteca Sanctorum* (Rome: Istitutó Giovanni XXIII: 1968) X, 829–837.

20. Fouqueray, *Histoire*, V, 22.

21. On Béatrice's portrait at Doubs, see Maréchal, *Une cause célèbre;* Charles' letter to his daughter Anne, March 2, 1656, *ibid.*, p. 250.

22. Testimony by Guyot in an inquiry held by the Archbishop of Besançon in 1639, Bonnard, LXXI, 232–234 (partial transcript of the inquest).

23. Testimony of Jean Dumény, the Duke's surgeon, in the same inquiry, *ibid.*, p. 235.

24. 2 Samuel 12:18–24. The paternity of the child born to Béatrice in September was the subject of a celebrated legal process, whose length af-

fords a comparison of civil procedures with canonical procedures, and whose twists and turns recall such other celebrated identity trials as that of James Annesley in eighteenth-century England, the Tichborne claimant in nineteenth-century England, or Anastasia, last of the Romanovs, in twentieth-century Germany. This case is described in Maréchal, *Une cause célèbre,* from whom the foluwing account is taken:

At stake was a large trust property (technically property in a *fideicommissio*). This estate went to the Count of St. Amour if Eugene, Prince of Cantecroix, died without issue. Cantecroix, however, believing Béatrice was pregnant by him, left the property to his child by her, appointing his mother Caroline as guardian. St. Amour got a judgment from the Parlement of Dôle as early as May 22, 1637, that Cantecroix had died without issue. However, Caroline refused to accept this result as definitive and sought the appointment of a guardian for the child in the womb of Béatrice (*ibid.,* pp. 27–28). The report of the child's death in November appeared suspicious to Caroline, a granddaughter of the Emperor Rudolph II and a woman of great determination. Her theory was that the true heir had been taken off to Flanders in disguise and another baby buried in his place. She believed that St. Amour, Charles, and Béatrice had conspired to this end — St. Amour to keep his property and Charles and Béatrice because they could not hope to overcome the legal presumption that a child born to a wife was taken to be her husband's, whatever she might say (pp. 58–61). In 1640 Caroline persuaded Urban VIII to issue a bull authorizing ecclesiastical inquiry into the disappearance of the child, and she had the Dôle judgment in favor of St. Amour appealed to the Grand Council of Malines (pp. 41, 65). In 1643 her efforts were rewarded by her lawyer, Pierre Maréchal, who located a six-year-old boy at Antwerp, and Caroline in an emotional scene recognized him as her grandchild (p. 89). She began legal proceedings to take him from the prostitute who had purported to be his mother and to establish her own guardianship. The Count of St. Amour intervened to defend his interests. The case began in 1643 and ended in 1662. During its course, the child himself came of age and intervened as a party (1653), the Count of St. Amour died and was replaced by his son (1658), and Béatrice herself was made a party (1659) (pp. 131–141). In 1660 the Council of Malines decided that the boy who died at Belle-Herbe in 1637 was not Béatrice's child, and Caroline had taken the first step toward winning. In 1662, however, she herself died, and died without a will. Her case collapsed, and the final decision of Malines in 1662 dismissed her claim.

A number of suspicious circumstances are developed in a partisan way in the book by Maréchal, who was a descendant of the family of Caroline's lawyer. Still, it is hard to believe that Caroline was right, and that Béatrice was unscrupulous enough to make a changeling of her child, whoever his father.

25. Calmet, I, col. clxxxii; III, col. 183.

26. Gabriel Hanotaux and the Duke de la Force, *Histoire du Cardinal de Richelieu* (Paris: Flammarion, 1943), V, 66–69; Robert, I, 13; Calmet, III, cols. 295–296.

27. Delattre, *Les établissements des Jésuites,* IV, cols. 112–116 (schooling of Nicolas-François); Bonnard, LXXI, 184 (brief of Urban VIII).

28. Taveneaux, *"Les mariages de la Maison de Lorraine-Vaudémont,"* XXXII, 131.

29. Bonnard, LXXI, 201–202; Calmet, III, cols. 258–259; *Biblioteca Sanctorum*, X, 836.

30. Hanotaux, *Histoire du Cardinal de Richelieu*, V, 34; Pflster, *Les mémoires du Comte de Brassac*, p. 379. On the whole affair see also Calmet, I, col. clxxxii III, cols. 257–259.

31. Nicolas-François to Nicole, April 1637, in Robert, I, 385–387; on Nicole's appeal to the Pope see Robert, II, 112.

32. Council of Trent, chapter 8, 34th session, November 11, 1563, *Acta*, IX, 970.

33. Congregation of the Council, *Liber decretorum* (Rome, Archives of the Congregation of the Council), book 47, 416–417 (bigamist to be given to Inquisition); Carena, *De officio Sanctissimi Inquisitionis*, part 2, title 5, *De polygamis*, 4.29 (regular penalty); *ibid.*, 11.58 (Cremona case). Carena took the position that if nullity of a first marriage was not clear and a spouse remarried, he would have to prove the nullity to the Inquisition. If he failed, he was punished as a polygamist; if he succeeded he would still be punished by the bishop for remarrying without a church court's judgment, *ibid.*, 5.30.

34. Urban VIII, *Magnum in Christo, Bullarium*, XIV, 595.

35. Bonnard, LXXI, 249.

36. *Ibid.*, pp. 250–251.

37. Fouqueray, *Histoire*, V, 28–29.

38. Judgment of Louis d'Amboise and Fernand de Ceuta in the name of Alexander VI, December 17, 1498, reproduced in Michel Lhospice *Divorce et dynastie* (Paris: R. Pichon and R. Durand-Auzins, 1960), p. 121. Judgment of Cardinals Joyeuse, Gaspardo Silingardi, and Orzaio del Monte, in the name of Clement VIII, December 17, 1599, summarized in *ibid.*, pp. 184–185. As Henri IV's chief negotiator in Rome advised the King's Secretary of State, Villeroy, there was "less rigor" when a marriage was entrusted to papal commissioners (D'Ossat to Villeroy, July 14, 1599, in Cardinal D'Ossat, *Lettres*, ed. Amelot de la Houssaie [Amsterdam, 1732], III, letter 189).

39. Calmet, III, col. 385 (Charles' request). Information on the bishops *Hierarchia catholica*, IV, 340 (Metz), 349 (Toul), 370 (Verdun). Henri de Bourbon was recognized as the temporal administrator of the bishopric of Metz. Verdun had been assigned to another "Charles of Lorraine," who in 1622 had resigned to enter the Jesuits, leaving the bishopric without a regular administrator until 1668, although François de Lorraine — Chalingy, a mercurial cousin of Duke Charles, occupied the see, Bonnard, LXX, 163.

40. Nicole to Charles, undated, Bonnard, LXXI, 239–242.

41. For a detailed study of the personnel of the office of the Secretary of State, Andreas Kraus, *Das Papstliche Staatsskretariat unter Urban VIII, 1623–1644* (Rome: Herder, 1964), pp. 12–20. "Cardinal-boss" (*cardinale-padrone*) appears in many interoffice memos designating Barberini; after 1640 the appelation "direction of affairs" is used.

42. Barberini may also have been advised by Giovanni Giacomo Panziroli, a rotal auditor who often assisted him on legal problems. See Kraus, *Das Papstliche Staatsskretariat*, pp. 30–31; Bonnard, LXXI, 252.

43. Fouqueray, *Histoire*, V, 26.

44. Bonnard, LXXI, 253.

45. *Ibid.*, pp. 232–238.

46. *Ibid.*, p. 254; Urban VIII, Bull of Excommunication, February 13, 1642, Calmet, IV, col. dxxvi (the Pope reviews what he had promised Charles at Cheminot's request).

47. Robert, II, 202.

48. The man assigned responsibility for Charles was no one to trifle with. A graduate of Louvain and a secular lawyer, Boonen had become a priest at the age of thirty-eight; he had been a bishop twenty-two years and had been made Archbishop of Malines in 1621, the same year Charles had married Nicole. Now sixty-six, enjoying the reputation of a reformer, Boonen could not have guessed that at the age of eighty-three he would become so involved in the Jansenist controversy as to find himself in contempt of a papal order and suspended as a priest by Innocent X (Pierre Claessens, *Histoire des Archêveques de Malines* [Louvain, 1881], pp. 254–260).

49. Barberini to Stravius, March 31, 1646, excerpted by Bonnard, LXXI, 256.

50. Fouqueray, *Histoire*, V, 28–36.

51. For an excellent description of the process see Giorgio De Santillana, *The Crime of Galileo* (Chicago: University of Chicago Press, 1955), pp. 187–306. Of Galileo, Urban VIII had once written: "We embrace with parental love this great man" (ibid., p. 171), but in directing the process to its tragic end he played a major role. True, there was more reason for him to feel personal pique toward Galileo than toward Charles. True, Galileo had a "record" of sorts with the Inquisition. But the basic feeling of frustration at being defied must have been dangerously alike in both cases. Possibly the more courteous handling of Charles owed something to Francesco Barberini being more completely in charge. In the Galileo business, he had prepared the summons that brought Galileo from Florence to Rome, and organized this in detail — such arrangements were his forte (*ibid.*, p. 268) — but when it came time to vote the actual condemnation of Galileo in the Congregation of the Inquisition he showed his mildness and intelligence by abstaining (*ibid.*, p. 310).

52. Urban VIII to Charles, October 5, 1640, excerpted in Bonnard, LXXI, 257–258; see also Urban VIII, Bull of Excommunication, February 3, 1642, in Calmet, IV, col. dxxvi.

53. Fouqueray, *Histoire*, I, 33; Calmet, II, col. 543.

54. Nicolas-François, *Protest*, Calmet, IV, cols. dxx–dxxii.

55. Calmet, IV, col. dxxvi; Fouqueray, *Histoire*, V, 34; Delattre, IV, col. 132 (on the reopening of the University). Cf. Urban VIII, Bull of Excommunication, February 13, 1642.

56. Fouqueray, *Histoire*, V, 36; Bonnard, LXXI, 258.

57. Urban VIII, Bull of Excommunication, February 13, 1642, Calmet, IV, col. dxxvi.

58. *Ibid.*, cols. dxxvi–dxxviii.

59. Bonnard, LXXI, 260–261.

60. Fouqueray, *Histoire*, V, 36.

61. "[E]ight whole years," etc., Béatrice to Pelletier, September 29, 1657, in Maréchal, *Une cause célèbre*, p. 259; on the actual separation, Calmet, III, col. 418.

62. *Toul, Of Marriage, June 26, 1648, Sacrae Rotae Romanae decisionum recentiorum*, ed. Prospero Farinacci et al. (Venice, 1616–1683), X, 380, Decision 233 (reference to removal of appeal). The papal rescript sending the case to the Rota is referred to in the final judgment, Calmet, IV, cols. dxxv–cxli.

63. Record of negotiations attested to by Nicholas de Guise, Calmet, IV, cols. dxxxi, clxxxii.

64. *Toul, Of Marriage, June 26, 1648*. An auditor often found it hard to satisfy the litigants in choosing a local judge to execute the remissorial letter, and had to be sure if he made his own choice that in a foreign land he picked someone both competent and reasonably impartial, Antonio Augustino y Albanella, *Praxis Rotae*, ed. Charles Lefebvre (Tournai: Desclée, 1961), p. 16. Augustino's treatise is a sixteen-page handbook for new auditors written by a Spanish auditor who took office in 1545. A century later its observations on points of practice such as this were presumably still valid.

65. Bonnard, LXXI, 264.

66. Calmet, III, col. 475 (the twenty-eight-month separation); cols. 475–476 (Béatrice's flirtations); Maréchal, p. 200 (Charles' reactions).

67. Calmet, III, col. clxxxiii.

68. *Ibid.*, III, col. 477.

69. Definitive recognition of Gratian as law is contained in Gregory XIII, *Cum pro munere pastorali*, July 1, 1580, printed in *Corpus iuris canonici*, ed. E. Friedberg (Leipzig, 1881), I, lxxix.

70. See Chapter II, section 3, "Before the S.C.C."

71. Pius IV, *In throno iustitiae*, December 27, 1561, *Bullarium*, VII, 156; Paul V, *Universi agri Dominici*, March 1, 1612, *Bullarium*, XII, 68.

72. On the justification for conflicts in rotal decisions: Jacques Emerix, *Tractatus seu Notitia S. Rotae Romanae*, ed. Charles Lefebvre (Tournai: Desclée, 1961), p. 100. Emerix, born in Belgium in 1626 and a nephew of the rotal auditor Jean Emerix, became an auditor himself in 1668 and Dean in 1686; on the importance of rotal practice; see Augustino y Albanella, *Praxis Rotae*, ed. Lefebvre, p. 18.

73. Pius IV, *In throno iustitiae*, December 27, 1561, *Bullarium*, VII, 156; Paul V, *Universi agri Dominici*, March 1, 1612, Bullarium, XII, 68.

74. Gratian, dictum *post* c. 4, C. 31, q. 2.

75. X.4.1.15.

76. *Digesta*, 23.2.22.

77. *Codex*, 2.4.13, *Interpositas*.

78. *Codex*, 2.20.7, *Si donationis;* Codex, 2.20.9.

79. Codex, 2.20.11, *Si per impressionem* (fear of intermediate authority); Codex, 2.20.6, *Ad invidiam* (fear of senator); Codex, 2.20.8, *Quum te domus* (fear of office); Codex, 2.20.2, *Quum te non solum* (payment without protest); Codex, 2.4.35, *Transactionem* (presence of friends).

80. Schulte, III, 737.

81. Sanchez, *De sancto matrimonii sacramento*, 4.6.7.

82. *Ibid.*, 4.6.11–16 (on the father's character and relationship to his offspring); 4.7.7–8 (on the coercive effect of importunities combined with reverential fear: the "more probable," although not the sole, opinion).

83. *Ibid.*, 4.13.3 (definition of just fear); 4.13.6 (examples of just fear); 4.13.1, 4.13.9 (answers to objections).

84. *Ibid.*, 4.23.3.

85. *Ibid.*, 4.23.4.

86. *Ibid.*, 4.13.6.

87. *Ibid.*, 2.34.3, 2.36.3, 4.18.5.

88. *Ibid.*, 2.32.7, 2.32.12.

89. Gratian, 29.1, *dictum.*

90. Sanchez, *De sancto matrimonii sacramento*, 2.36.3.

91. *Ibid.*, 4.18.1, 4.18.3, 4.18.11.

92. *Ibid.*, 4.18.1, 4.18.11.

93. For an extended discussion, see John T. Noonan, Jr., "Marital Affection in the Canonists," J. Forchielli and A. M. Stickler, eds., *Studia Gratiana* (Bologna: Institutum Gratianum, 1967), XII, 479–509.

94. For an understanding of marital affection at the court of Louis XIV, see Marie Madeleine de Lafayette, *La Princesse de Clèves*, ed. Albert Cazes (Paris: Société des belles lettres, 1934), part I, pp. 21–23, where the necessity of love for marital consent is pondered.

95. Sanchez, *De sancto matrimonii sacramento*, 4.18.6.

96. *Ibid.*, 2.37.3.

97. *Ibid.*, 2.37.11, 4.18.12.

98. Decision 326, *Sacrae Romanae Rotae Decisiones coram Alessandro Ludovico nunc. S.S. mo. D.N. Gregori XV* (Rome, 1622), p. 387. These opinions, advertised as given by the now-reigning Pope, had been edited and annotated by Oliverio Beltramino of the Rota bar. They were printed at the press of the Apostolic Chamber, had the imprimatur of the Master of the Sacred Palace, carried the papal arms, and were dedicated to the Pope's nephew, the Archbishop of Bologna. They were still only the decisions of a particularly astute auditor; the elevation of their author did not elevate them to papal law.

99. *Ibid.*, Decision 351, p. 414.

100. *Ibid.*, Decision 374.

101. *Ibid.*, Decision 392.

102. *Ibid.*, Decision 395, p. 435.

103. Giovanni, his son — by lawful marriage as the introduction to Buratto's work was at pains to make clear — gave Giovanni Francesco Ferentilli,

another member of the Rota bar, permission to publish his fifteen hundred decisions ten years after his death. Urban VIII granted Ferentilli the copyright, good for twenty years and backed by an excommunication, reserved to the Pope, of any infringer. The book was dedicated to the Barberini Pope, appeared with his arms as frontispiece, and opened with a special tribute to Cardinal Francesco Barberini. For further data on Buratto, see Cerchiari, II, 138.

104. Matteo Buratto, *Decisiones coram Matteo Buratto,* ed. G. F. Ferentilli (Rome, 1637), Decision 628.

105. *Ibid.,* Decision 86.

106. Three other decisions should be compared with this one: *Tortona, January 11, 1616,* before Ubaldo (*Decisionum recentiorum,* 41, Decision 204), holding that fear of death or imprisonment inflicted on the son by the girl's relatives invalidated his consent; and two cases holding that coercion by the girl's relatives had not been satisfactorily established: *Lisbon, May 2, 1616, January 26, 1617, and January 15, 1618,* before Pirovano (*Decisionum recentiorum* 4¹, Decisions 259, 600, and 605), where the facts alleged were not greatly different from the case of Emanuele and Bianca; and *Lisbon, November 16, 1622,* before Manzanedo, *January 27, 1624, July 1, 1625 and November 19, 1625,* before Pirovano (*Decisionum recentiorum,* 4², Decision 431, 4³, Decisions 526, 617, 625).

107. Congregation of the Council, *Liber decretorum,* I, fol. 94v–96r (1573).

108. The course of this case well illustrates the piecemeal decision-making of the Rota. The marriage was held null for fear on December 19, 1614 (Decision 86 in *Decisiones coram Matteo Buratto*). On December 14, 1615, the Rota decided that Bianca and Emanuele had been betrothed, but reserved judgment as to whether this conclusion affected the first decision (Decision 143). On July 20, 1616, it confirmed the betrothal (Decision 192). On December 2, 1616, it held that the establishment of the betrothal did not change its decision of 1614 on the nullity of the marriage (Decision 213). On April 10, 1617, it granted Bianca's counsel the right to argue that Emanuele should be made to carry out the betrothal (this action is referred to in Decision 273). On July 3, 1617, it heard Emanuele's request for remissorial letters to examine more witnesses in Portugal (described in Decision 273). On November 6, 1617, it denied the request for remissorial letters, finding this a dilatory tactic of Emanuele (Decision 273). On March 5, 1618, it decided that Emanuele should not be compelled to carry out the betrothal. Thus, with at least eight decisions over three years, final resolution of the case was delayed at the level of the Rota. How many years it had taken to reach this level of decision does not appear. I would say, certainly two and probably four to six.

109. *Decisiones coram Matteo Buratto,* Decision 205.

110. Council of Trent, Chapter 2, 25th session, November 20, 1563, *De reformatione monialium, Acta,* IX, 510. (Anyone coercing a woman to make a religious profession is *ipso facto* excommunicated. Bishops of dioceses are to ascertain the girl's freedom before profession is made.)

111. Pius IV, *In throno iustitiae, Bullarium,* VII, 155.

112. Cerchiari, II, 164–165.

113. *Ibid.*, II, 167; Pastor, XIV, 28–30.

114. If the stories of Henri and Charles were told a thousand years from now, some sharp-eyed critic would pronounce the tales to be doublets of the same basic legend and reasonably contend that there could only have been one impulsive gallant hero of Lorraine who performed the nucleus of deeds now magnified and improbably attributed to two. Like Charles, Henri had been destined for the Church and was a teenage bishop. At twelve, he had possessed nine abbeys; at fifteen he was Archbishop of Reims, one of the most famous sees in France. His eldest brother died in 1640 when he was twenty-six, and without resigning his see he became Duke of Guise. He courted Anne of Gonzague, daughter of Charles' cousin the Duke of Mantua, and, still Archbishop of Reims, married her. Disregarding this marriage, which suffered at least from failure to comply with Trent's requirement of a parish priest and two other witnesses, in November 1641 he publicly married Honorée de Glimes, daughter of the Count of Bossut. Urban VIII declared vacant the archbishopric of Reims. Henri spent Honorée's fortune and fell in love with Mademoiselle de Pons, a maid-of-honor to the French Queen. He brought suit in the Rota to annul his marriage with Honorée, and in 1646, just as Charles' case was getting launched, went to Rome to speed up the process in his own case. He attempted to ingratiate himself with Innocent X and Olimpia, but the case dragged on. Without waiting for the Rota's verdict, he married De Pons by proxy. Then some Neapolitans asked him to revive an old claim of the House of Lorraine to Naples and to become their king. He went to Naples, tried to start a revolution, was arrested by that city's Spanish government, and from April 1648 to July 1652 was a prisoner in Spain, being released some months before Charles turned up in Toledo as a Spanish prisoner. Henri passed the last years of his life at the court of Louis XIV, a hero without a cause, and, a court poet sang, "a husband without a wife and sick of being so." Henri de Guise, *Mémoires*, printed in Michaud, *Nouvelle collection des mémoires pour servir à l'histoire de France* (3rd ser., Paris, 1831), VII, 3–22. For his removal from Reims, *Hierarchia catholica*, IV, 245. For his later life see Louis Lacour, "Guise, Henri II," in *Nouvelle biographie générale* (Paris, 1887), XXII.

115. Pius IV, *In throno iustitiae*, *Bullarium*, VII, 155; repeated in Paul V, *Universi agri Dominici*, *ibid.*, XII, 67.

116. Of 1552 decisions of the rotal auditor Matteo Buratto in the period 1614–1627, only five cases and fourteen opinions involved the validity of marriage—less than 1 percent. See *Decisiones coram Matteo Buratto*. Of the five cases *Coimbra* and *Venice* are analyzed in this chapter and *Camerino* in Chapter III. The other two cases concerned whether particular phrases used in an exchange of promises amounted to present consent. (*Rome or Ascoli, June 2, 1623*, II, Decision 793, and *Besançon, December 19, 1625*, III, Decision 893.) Of 715 cases selected by Prospero Farinacci as leading Rota decisions for the years 1558–1616, 20 decisions out of 700, less than 3 percent, involved marriage. See *Sacra Romana Rota, Decisiones recentiores*. Of the decisions of Alessandro Ludovisi, only the decisions in the *Seville* case involved the validity of an existing marriage. *Parma, Of Status, April 10, 1606*, was an inheritance case turning on the validity of a marriage celebrated a century before, in 1502 (Ludovisi, *Decisiones*, Decision 247).

117. Emerix, *Tractatus*, p. 96, discussed in Charles Lefebvre, "La procédure du Tribunal de la Rota Romaine au 17 ième siècle d'après un manuscript inedit," *L'année canonique*, V, 143 (1957). As Lefebvre indicates, the cumbersomeness of this procedure and the disqualification of the best-informed person from voting were much criticized in the seventeenth century. The custom went back to a time when the judge-reporter was merely asking the advice of his confreres and their vote did not constitute the actual decision. For the law on procedural rulings see Pius IV, *In throno iustitiae*, *Bullarium*, VII, 155; repeated by Paul V, *Universi agri Dominici*, *ibid.*, XII, 67.

118. On the auditors of the studio see Emerix, *Tractatus*, p. 127; on the notaries, Gianbattista de Luca, *Tractatus de officiis venalibus vacabilibus Romanae Curiae* (Venice, 1735), c. 2.2, 2.8, 19.5.

119. See *ibid.*, especially c. 2 and 4.11, although the entire treatise of this curial cardinal of the late seventeenth century is devoted to "the salable offices" of the Curia.

120. Cerchiari, I, 61–65.

121. Cerchiari, I, 78.

122. Ansaldo de Ansaldi, *Decisiones coram Ansaldo*, "Preface" excerpted in Cerchiari, I, 95–98. Ansaldi, auditor in 1695, dean in 1717, describes the eighteenth-century Rota, which appears to be substantially the same as the seventeenth-century Rota.

123. Emerix, *Tractatus*, pp. 160–165. Emerix's figures for the last quarter of the seventeenth century must be about right for 1650. Cerchiari, I, 83, gives a slightly lower salary of 550 scudi from the Apostolic Treasury in 1541, so that over a century the compensation stayed fairly constant.

124. Emerix, *Tractatus*, pp. 141–149, 153–155, 166.

125. Cerchiari, II, 327–329. Of the eighteen auditors named from Rome itself in this period, eleven became cardinals.

126. De Luca, *Tractatus*, 4.11.

127. Cerchiari, II, 145–168.

128. Cerchiari, II, 146, citing the Diary of Auditor Pietro Ottoboni. Ghislieri came from the same family whose other branch had produced Michele Ghislieri, Saint Pius V, Pope 1555–1560. A recent distinguished relative had been the canonist Girolamo Ghislieri, deceased in 1625 ("Ghislieri," *Enciclopedia italiana* [Milan: Treves-Treccani-Tumminelli, 1932], XVI, 930). Innocent X had already shown confidence in Ghislieri by appointing him one of a three man commission to judge an internal dispute at the Vatican, Domenico Bernini, *Il Tribunale della S. Rota Romana* (Rome, 1717), p. 144.

129. Emerix, *Tractatus*, pp. 71–73.

130. A record of the confrontation with Ghislieri was made at the Pope's command by Angelo Celso and subscribed to by eight auditors. Celso's account is printed in Cerchiari, II, 147–150.

131. *Bullarium*, VII, 157, and XII, 69 (the reform bulls); Emerix, *Tractatus*, p. 108 (pooling of the *sportulae*).

132. Cerchiari, II, 151, citing the Diary of Auditor Pietro Ottoboni; *Hierarchia catholica*, IV, 311.

133. As it turned out, Ghislieri was to be the only auditor in history ever to have been even mildly censured for bribe-taking, Cerchiari, II, 330.

134. Cerchiari, II, 169.

135. Another relation was Niccolo Albergati-Ludovisi, made Archbishop of Bologna by Innocent X in 1645, *Hierarchia catholica*, IV, 118.

136. Cerchiari, II, 169.

137. The above description of the bar and what follows is taken from Emerix, *Tractatus,* pp. 129–133.

138. Ludovico Gomes, *Commentarii in iudiciales regulas Cancellariae* (Venice, 1575), "Proemium," Q. 1, fol. 3v. According to Gomes, a rotal auditor from 1529 to 1545, the old practice was to have only written argument, "following the counsel of Clement IV of which the Speculator speaks"; but this practice was abandoned during the pontificate of Alexander VI as a result of "the cupidity of some advocates." Gomes gives no good reason for the bar unanimously going back to the old practice under Paul III, and it seems unlikely that it returned voluntarily to a less lucrative practice. The counsel of Guy de Fulcodi, Clement IV, to which Gomes refers, consisted in his objection to advocates orally arguing cases before the advisers of a judge, after the judge had heard the case, Guilelmus Durandus, *Speculum juris* (Venice, 1566), 2.2, *De requisitione consilii.*

139. See the Rota's ruling of November 18, 1707, abolishing the consistorial advocates' privilege (Cerchiari, III, 466).

140. Emerix, *Praxis,* 91.

141. X.1.37.1–3 for the law.

142. Benedict XIV, *De Synodo diocesana,* 12.10.12 (on eighteenth-century practice, but in all probability true of the situation in 1650).

143. Pius IV, *In throno iustitiae, Bullarium,* VII, 156, repeated by Paul V, *Universi agri Dominici,* XII, 68.

144. Renazzi, *Storia dell'Università,* III, 202; Pastor, XXXI, 273 (on Vizzani); Schulte, III, 469 (on Vermiglioli).

145. *Hierarchia catholica,* IV, 126; V, 353.

146. See note preceding *imprimatur* to Silvestro Zacchia, *Lucubrationes ad Gallesuim de obligatione camerali* (Rome, 1647). Ronconi may well have been related to Cristoforo Ronconi, a sixty-seven-year-old lawyer from Faenza, who was a consultor of the Sacred Penitentiary and a referee in the Signature of Justice under Innocent X, see Bruno Katterbach, O.F.M., *Referendarii utriusque Signaturae a Martino V ad Clementem IX et Praelati Signaturae Supplicationum a Martino V ad Leonem XIII* (Vatican City, 1931, Vol. II of *Sussidi per la consultazione dell'Archivio Vaticano*), p. 315.

147. *Ibid.,* p. 325; Renazzi, *Storia dell'Università,* III, 203; *Hierarchia catholica,* V, 278. The later lawsuit in which Bottini appeared so prominently arose from the Pope's suppression of the College of Apostolic Secretaries. Those members who had paid money to their predecessors for their resignations contended that the Pope had a duty of restitution to them of these sums. In a series of decisions by Albergati, *Rome: The Price of Offices, June 16, 1679, June 19, 1680, and March 17, 1681,* Bottini successfully argued the Treasury position that no restitution was due for money it had never received, *Collectio jurium seu documentorum ac etiam informationum respon-*

sorum et decisionum super supressione Collegii secretariorum apostolicorum et restititione pretii (printed as an appendix in De Luca, *Tractatus de officiis venalibus*). On his service as Promotor of the Faith, see the account given by the man who became his assistant in 1708, Prospero Lambertini, in Benedict XIV, *De servorum Dei beatificatione et beatorum canonizatione* (Prato, 1839) I, 18.10.

148. Vittorio Spreti, *Enciclopedia storico-nobiliare italiana* (Milan, 1932), V, 683; Gaetano Moroni, *Dizonario di erudizione storico-ecclesiastica* (Venice, 1846), XXXIX, 251; XL, 312–314.

149. The related Popes were Ugo Buoncompagni, Gregory XIII (1572–1585), Alessandro Ludovisi, Gregory XV (1621–1663), and Pietro Ottoboni, then an auditor of the Rota, later Alexander VIII (1689–1691). Another collateral, Girolamo Buoncompagni, became Archbishop of Bologna in 1651.

150. Cerchiari, III, 383.

151. *Ibid.*, II, 198–199.

152. Moroni, *Dizonario*, XXXIX, 251.

153. *Summarium pro D. Carlo* (the above-quoted testimony and what follows is on fols. 291–301).

154. X.4.13.5: a spouse could testify to uphold his marriage as in *Venice, May 25, 1622.*

155. *Summarium pro D. Carlo*, fol. 303v; full text in Calmet, IV, cols. ccclv-ccclx.

156. *Summarium pro D. Carlo*, fol. 303v–305r.

157. *Ibid.*, fol. 305r–305v.

158. The letters are quoted above, part I.

159. The list of names was indispensable in giving personality to the witnesses, for in the body of the *summarium* they were identified only as "First witness, second witness," etc.

160. *Summarium pro D. Nicole*, fol. 197r–197v.

161. Cautious, ample, and drafted by a first-class draftsman, the bull of dispensation was proof against attack—no Roman lawyer thought it sensible to pursue Father Cheminot's charge of 1637 that the marriage was null for consanguinity.

162. *Summarium pro D. Nicole* fol. 197v–198v.

163. *Ibid.*, fol. 202v–203r.

164. *Ibid.*, fol. 203r–207v.

165. *Ibid.*, fol. 208r–211r.

166. *Ibid.*, fol. 211r–212r. Master Elepheus Bouillot, Nicole's proctor in Lorraine, had protested these gross irregularities, and his protest now found a place in the record.

167. *Ibid.*, fol. 212v–216v.

168. The briefs are available in the Sacred Roman Rota, Positio 189, Secret Archives of the Vatican; photostats are available in the Law Library, University of California, Berkeley.

169. No rotal decisions were cited before 1530, due largely to the accident that there was no good published collection of cases before that date.

Roughly 50 citations were made to decisions before 1600; another 50 came from the period 1600–1610. The decades 1610–1620, 1620–1630, and 1630–1640 each provided roughly 140 citations apiece. After 1640, citations again fell off, for lack of a published collection. To cite decisions after 1640 a lawyer had to find the opinion on his own. This was not always easy to do. There was no official Rota file of original opinions or even copies of opinions. Emerix, *Tractatus*, p. 110. Members of the bar must have borrowed from each other and made copies for their own use if the case seemed significant enough. Only the lawyer on the scene in Rome had much chance of being completely current with the case law. A second best was discovering a summary of a case in a treatise. Antonio Diana's *Resolutiones morales*, for example, provided some 14 of the citations to an important nullity of profession case decided by Arguelles on January 29 and December 10, 1646. Despite the handicap, there were roughly 70 decisions cited for the period 1640–1650. Finally, to the very recent opinions of the years 1651 and 1652, there were 10 references.

170. See Appendix A for a fuller analysis of authorities.

171. On Chifflet, see J. J. De Smet, "Chifflet, Jean-Jacques," *Biographie nationale* (Brussels, 1872), III, cols. 74–75.

172. Emerix, *Tractatus*, p. 98.

173. Sacra Rota Romana, *Decisiones recentiores*, XI, Decision 301.

174. Emerix, *Tractatus*, p. 98.

175. Cerchiari, III, 380–381. Publication of the vote was forbidden by Urban VIII, *Exponi vobis*, November 19, 1643, *Bullarium*, XV, pp. 286–289. The reason for the rule was to free auditors "from importunate and uncivil" pressures on reargument, Emerix, *Tractatus* 127.

176. *Decisiones recentiores*, XI, Decision 329; doubtless the need to determine marriage cases quickly was a cliché. The same observation is made by Ludovisi in *Seville, December 19, 1605*, Ludovisi, *Decisiones*, Decision 229.

177. Cerchiari, III, 384. The Pope's "fourteen years" apparently referred to the time when Charles first asked for a hearing in Rome.

178. *Decisiones recentiores*, XI, Decision 334.

179. Calmet, IV, cols. 485–498.

180. *Ibid.*, III, col. 491.

181. Charles to Nicole, February 28, 1655, in Robert Parisot, "Documents inédits sur la captivité de Charles IV à Tolède (1654–1659)," *Mémoires de la Société d'archéologie lorraine*, LX (1910), 338.

182. Charles to Nicole, January 14, 1657, *ibid.*, pp. 391–392.

183. *Ibid.*, p. 351.

184. Charles to Anne, undated, Maréchal, *Une cause célèbre*, p. 243.

185. Béatrice to Pelletier, August 13, 1657, *ibid.*, p. 257.

186. Béatrice to Pelletier, November 17, 1657, *ibid.*, p. 262.

187. Béatrice to Pelletier, September 29, 1657, *ibid.*, p. 258.

188. Calmet, III, cols. 545–546.

189. Béatrice to Pelletier, September 29, 1657, November 17, 1657, and November 30, 1657, respectively, in Maréchal, *Une cause célèbre*, pp. 258–261.

190. Bonnard, LXXI, 270.
191. *Ibid.*
192. *Ibid.*, p. 265.
193. Calmet, III, col. 609.
194. Béatrice, Testament, in Maréchal, *Une cause célèbre*, p. 420.

CHAPTER II "IF CONDITIONS ARE ATTACHED . . ."

1. *Commissum,* X.4.1.16.
2. Gratian, c. 1, C. XXVII, q. 2; *Licet praeter*, X.4.4.3.
3. Gratian, c. 40–45 inclusive, C. XXVII, q. 2.
4. Gratian, c. 19–26, C. XXVII, q. 2.
5. *Verum post,* X.3.32.2, and *Ex publico,* X.3.32.7.
6. St. Bede, "Commendation of the Author," *In S. Joannis Evangelium Expositio, PL* 92, cols. 633–635. Alexander III's adaptation of this approach: *Sane super eo, Compilatio I*, III, 28.9, *Quinque compilationes antiquae*, ed. E. Friedberg (Graz, 1956). On the whole development, see James A. Coriden, *The Indissolubility Added to Christian Marriage by Consummation: A Historical Study from the End of the Patristic Period to the Death of Pope Innocent III* (Rome: Catholic Book Agency, 1961), pp. 7–23.
7. *Ex parte,* X.3.32.14.
8. *Tua nos,* X.4.1.26.
9. Augustine, *De bono coniugali*, 29.32, *Corpus scriptorum ecclesiasticorum latinorum* (Vienna, 1886–) (hereafter cited as CSEL), 41.227. For a fuller treatment of Augustine's thought on procreation, see John T. Noonan, Jr., *Contraception: A History of Its Treatment by the Catholic Theologians and Canonists* (Cambridge, Mass.: The Belknap Press of Harvard University Press, 1965), pp. 119–137.
10. Gregory IX to the Prior of Tarvisino, *Bullarium Ordinis Praedicatorum* (Rome, 1729), I, 76. For the decretal's relation to the Cathars, Noonan *Contraception*, pp. 179–199. The development of conditional marriages in canon law began with an inquiry in Gratian; the contractual possibilities were most firmly asserted in the early thirteenth century by the Hungarian glossator Damasus, and the Spanish glossator Laurentius; by 1220 the teaching was common that conditional marriage was possible (Rudolf Weigand, *Die bedingte Eheschleissung im kanonischen Recht* (Munich: Max Hueber Verlag, 1963), pp. 414–421.
11. Headnote, *Tua nos,* X.4.1.26.
12. Sanchez, *De sancto matrimonii sacramento*, 2.29.11–12.
13. *Summarium pro Senatore L. Q. Barberini*, n. 9 (hereafter referred to as *Summarium*). A copy of the *Summarium* is filed under *West Lisbon, Nullity of Marriage, July 8, 1724*, Archives of the Sacred Congregation of the Council in the Secret Archives of the Vatican, *Positio* for July 8, 1724.

The *summarium* is an Italian translation of the material selected by Barberini's lawyer.

14. On Joanna's father, see her "Protest and Reclamation," May 5, 1718, an appendix to "Memorial for the Most Illustrious Lady Isabella de Favia Carnide, Mother of Joanna de Almeida y Carnide," filed with the Secretary of the Sacred Congregation of the Council, June 1724, by unidentified representatives of the Lady Isabella (hereafter to be referred to as Isabella, "Memorial"). On the low social standing of Joanna's parents and stepfather, Barberini, "Memorial to the Sacred Congregation of the Council," filed November 1719, *Summarium*, n. 20. Isabella stresses the high origins of her family, Barberini the low profession of her two husbands, and while the perspective is different there is no contradiction.

15. On Barberini's genealogy as stated by him, Nuncio Bichi to the Sacred Congregation of the Council, February 3, 1719, *Summarium*, n. 21. On the provenance of the Portuguese Barberini and their relation to the Counts of Anadia, see also *Armorial Lusitano* (Lisbon: Editorial Enciclopédia, 1961), I, 81; III, 195. The Portuguese Barberini are not mentioned among the descendants of Urban VIII's family, Pio Pecchiai, *I Barberini* (Rome: Biblioteca d'arte edifice, 1959).

16. Bichi to the Sacred Congregation of the Council, February 3, 1719, *Summarium* n. 21 (his position). Barberini, Deposition *Summarium*, n. 33 (his age). On the Senate of West Lisbon, Eduardo Freira de Oliveira, *Elementos para a História de Municipio de Lisboa* (Lisbon, 1899), part 1, XI, 172.

17. Barberini's testimony to the Inquisition as related by a notary of the Inquisition, *Summarium*, n. 35.

18. Joanna to Barberini, 1718 (five letters produced by Barberini before the court of the Patriarch in Lisbon and summarized in the *Summarium*, n. 1); on Joanna's dowry, Isabella, "Memorial"; on Barberini's sick brother, Barberini, "Memorial," *Summarium*, n. 20.

19. Testimony of De Goes, *Summarium*, n. 4.

20. Barberini's oath to the Virgin Mary is asserted as a fact in the Judgment of the Vicar General of the Patriarchate, *Summarium*, n. 15.

21. Barberini, Testament, October 10, 1722, *Summarium*, n. 32. In the explanatory notations of counsel in the margin, the impediment is stated as "the first degree of affinity." That consanguinity itself was being admitted seems unlikely supposing that Barberini intended to return to Portugal where incest between father and daughter was a crime punishable by death by burning; *Ordenacoes̃ e Leys do Regno de Portugal, confirmadas e establecidas pelo Senhor Rey D. João IV e agora impresso por mandado do Muyto Alto e Podoroso Rey D. João V* (East Lisbon, 1727), 5.10.

22. Testimony of Rodriguez, *Summarium*, n. 5.

23. Francisco Rodrigues, S.J., *História de Compania de Jesus na Assistência de Portugal* (Porto: Apostolado da imprensa, 1950), IV, 294–295.

24. Freira da Oliveira, *Elementos para a História*, XI, 93.

25. Testimony of Mother Maria Anna Giosefa, prioress of Santa Rosa, *Summarium*, n. 2.

26. Testimony of De Basta, *Summarium*, n. 6.

27. Testimony of João Ferreira Pinto, ecclesiastical auditor of the Patriarchate, *Summarium*, n. 7. On Cardoso see *Hierarchia catholica*, V, 234.

28. Testimony of Nicolo Fernandez Collares, *Summarium*, n. 10 Joanna claimed that her signature was procured to a blank piece of paper; "Protest and Reclamation" appendix to Isabella, "Memorial." This claim was not pressed or taken seriously even by the judges favorable to Joanna.

29. *Ibid.*, 11G-I.; testimony of Francesco Gomez Valenti, *Summarium*, 12B.

30. Testimony of Collares, *Summarium*, 11C.

31. Joanna Agnete de Almeida, *Libel*, May 14, 1718, *Summarium*, n. 14A; Ferreira Pinto, Notice of Service of Citation, *ibid.*, n. 14B.

32. Joanna Agnete de Almeida, Power of Attorney to Lourenço Alamez and Francesco de Aravio, *Summarium*, 14E; examination of the witness, *Summarium*, 10A, 12A.

33. Opinion of the Vicar-General of the Patriarchate, *Summarium*, n. 15. Counsel for Barberini could not refrain from putting in the margin of the *Summarium* the printed comment, "In favor of the adversary woman, against the express law."

34. On Almeida see *Hierarchia catholica*, V, 397; Lorenzo Cardella, *Memorie storiche de' cardinali della Santa Romana Chiesa* (Rome, 1794), VIII, 277; Cristovão Alão de Morais, *Pedatura Lusitana*, II², 411; Eduardo Brazao, *Subsídios para a História do Patriarcado do Lisboa* (Porto: Livraria Fernando Machado, 1943–1948), pp. 107–109. On the patriarchate, Eduardo Brazao, *Relacôes externos de Portugal: Reinado de D. João V* (Porto, 1938), II, 173.

35. Bichi to the Sacred Congregation of the Council, February 3, 1719, *Summarium*, n. 21.

36. *Hierarchia catholica*, V, 235 (Vincenzo), and 17 (Carlo); also Cardella, *Memorie storiche*, VIII, 251.

37. Judgment of Bernabo, *Summarium*, n. 17.

38. Data on João V, Henrique Schaefer, *História de Portugal* (Porto, 1898), IV, 676–688; H. V. Livermore, *A History of Portugal* (Cambridge: Cambridge University Press, 1945), p. 350; "João V," *Grande Enciclopédia Portuguese e Brasileira*, XIV, 262.

39. Bichi to the Sacred Congregation of the Council, February 3, 1719, *Summarium*, n. 21; Barberini to the Sacred Congregation of the Council, *ibid.*, n. 20.

40. Barberini to the Sacred Congregation of the Council, *Summarium*, n. 20.

41. Bichi to the Sacred Congregation of the Council, February 3, 1719, *Summarium*, n. 21.

42. Joannes Andreas, *Glossa ordinaria* on X.4.1.26.

43. Judgments of De Silva and Vilas, *Summarium*, n. 18.

44. Judgment of the criminal praetor, September 16, 1719, *Summarium*, n. 22.

45. Certificate of a notary of the Inquisition, *Summarium*, n. 35. The Inquisition was headed by a cardinal nominated by the king and was at this

time more active than it ever had been in the history of Portugal, Fortunato de Almeida, *História do Igreja em Portugal* (Coimbra: Imprensa académica, 1915), III³, 302.

46. *West Lisbon, March 16, 1720, Thesaurus resolutionum Sacrae Congregationis Concilii* (1739), I, 292.

47. *Ibid.*, p. 293.

48. On the whole affair, Almeida, *História de Igreja*, III, 92–103, Pastor, XXXIV, 37, 157, 181–183, 186–187, 189, 311, 403.

49. Order, July 9, 1720, *Summarium*, n. 23; Order, September 5, 1720, *Summarium*, n. 24.

50. On the Pope's moves see Pastor, XXXIV, 37; on Conti's title as Protector see *Notizie per l'anno 1720* (Rome, 1720), p. 116.

51. Pastor, XXXIV, 37.

52. Order, January 28, 1722, *Summarium*, n. 27.

53. Isabella, "Memorial." A certificate, dated January 3, 1720, and sworn to by Diego Nuñez Ribiero, a doctor of Lisbon, stated that Joanna had an abortion in December 1719; the certificate, too, was given to the Secretary of the Congregation. If the child were Barberini's, he would have been conceived just before Barberini's imprisonment in the Tower.

54. Order, July 27, 1722, *Summarium*, n. 29; on Barberini's imprisonment and release, certificates of the Sergeant Major of the Tower, *Summarium*, n. 28.

55. Certificate of two Madrid physicians, January 28, 1723, *Summarium*, n. 31, and certificates of three physicians of Lisbon, dated respectively March 15, 1722, March 17, 1722, and March 21, 1722, *Summarium*, n. 25.

56. Fiorenzo Romita, "Le Origine delle S.C.C.," in *La Sacra Congregazione del Concilio* (Vatican City, 1964), pp. 47–49. This memorial volume, put out by a curial group to celebrate the four hundredth birthday of the S.C.C., has the best collection of essays on its history. In the following description of its activities, I draw principally on it; R. Parayre, *La S. Congrégation du Concile* (Paris, 1897); A. Molien, "Concile, Congrégation du," *Dictionnaire de droit canonique*, III, cols. 1306–1311; and my own examination of *Libri decretorum* at the offices of the Congregation.

57. William I. Varsányi, "De competentia et procedura Sacrae Congregationis Concilii ab origine ad haec usque nostra tempora," *La Sacra Congregazione*, p. 120, citing an intervention in a rotal case in 1629.

58. In *Benedictus Dominum, Bullarium*, VII, 244, Pius IV ruled that only the Pope should interpret Trent. In *Alias nos nonnullos, ibid.*, p. 300, issued a year later in 1564, he set up a group of curial cardinals headed by Carlo Borromeo to execute the Tridentine decrees: this group became the S.C.C. In the curial reorganization of 1587 Sixtus V formally gave it the power to interpret Trent, *Immensa, Bullarium*, VIII, 991.

59. Based on inspection of its records, I estimate that, at its height in the seventeenth century, the S.C.C. had to decide over fifteen hundred items a year.

60. Pastor, XXXIV, 14, 22, 193, 316–318; Nicolo del Re, "I Cardinali Prefetti della Sacra Congregazione del Concilio delle Origine ad Oggi (1564–1964)," *La Sacra Congregazione*, p. 283; *Hierarchia catholica*, V, 28, 103.

61. Biographical data from Pastor, XXXV, 23–43; *Hierarchia catholica*, V, 375; Filippo Maria Renazzi, *Storia dell'Università degli studi di Roma dette communemente La Sapienza* (Rome, 1806), IV, 64. Lambertini's own role as an assistant in the Rota is set out in his letter of June 6, 1754, addressed to the auditors when he was Pope, printed in Cerchiari, III, 546–547.

62. Data on cardinals of the S.C.C. in 1720, *Notizie per l'anno 1720* (Rome, 1720); data on Barberini, see *Hierarchia catholica*, V, 17.

63. Data on cardinals of the S.C.C. in 1724 is from *Notizie per l'anno 1724* (Rome, 1724); on Origo's reputation see Pastor, XXXIV, 14, 22.

64. The special rescript is noted in Report of the Secretary, *West Lisbon, July 8, 1724, Thesaurus S.C.C.*, III, 41. The Memorial to the Pope is in the S.C.C. files for the case, as is the opinion of the anonymous theologians, dated June 1, 1723.

65. Barberini, Protest, November 6, 1723, *Summarium*, n. 34.

66. *In Coena Domini* had most recently been revised by Urban VIII, *Pastoralis*, April 23, 1637, *Bullarium* V, 125; as to its effect where unpromulgated because of governmental resistance, see Ferdinand Claeys-Bouüaert, "Bulle—In Coena," *Dictionnaire de droit canonique*, II, col. 1135.

67. Archbishop Firrao to the Cardinals of the S.C.C., March 24, 1724, in the file for *West Lisbon, July 8, 1724.*

68. Isabella, "Memorial."

69. Benedict XIV, *De synodo diocesana* (Rome, 1767), 3.22. A junior lawyer, Antonio Gerardo, also wrote a substantial fact brief, but his contribution was secondary and unremembered.

70. Schulte, III, 510; *Hierarchia catholica*, V, 22.

71. Francesco Maria Pitoni, *Disceptationum ecclesiasticarum in quibus frequentiora ecclesiastici fori litigia una cum decretis tam Datariae Apostolicae quam Sacrarum Congregationum particularium et generalium necnon decisionibus Sacrae Rotae Romanae continentur* (Venice, 1733), part 2, disputation 52, pp. 39, 51–53.

72. *Ibid.*, part 3, disputation 58, p. 52. Disputation 58 is a reprint of Pitoni's brief in the case, with some names omitted. At the end he added the account of what he had said when first consulted.

73. Francesco Maria Pitoni, *Restrictus iuris pro D. Senatore L. Q. Barberini*, in the files of the Sacred Congregation of the Council, Secret Archives of the Vatican, Position for July 8, 1724.

74. Gerardo de Petrasancto, *Sigularia iuris* (Paris, 1512). Instructively this old academic example was available to Pitoni, while the much more telling applications of the Inquisition for Bosnia in 1680 and for the Capuchin Missionaries in 1698 were not available because of the secrecy of this organ of the Curia.

75. Basilio Ponce de León, O.S.A., *De sacramento matrimonii* (2nd ed., Brussels, 1632), book IV, "Consent Due To Coercion or Error," 21.13. A description of the relation of Ponce's work to Sanchez' is in the preface: he is picking up, he says, "the gleanings."

76. Giacomo Pignatelli, *Consultationes canonicarum* (Venice, 1694), IX, consultation 136, p. 353. The names, of course, were fictitious, but Pignatelli reported the case as true.

77. Although the case was before a body whose jurisdiction was to interpret the Tridentine decrees, the Council of Trent was invoked only once and the S.C.C. cited only in reference to the Asti decision: the absence of published S.C.C. reports accounts for this striking lacuna. In contrast, fourteen Rota cases were cited, among them a decision of Albergati, *Tenancy of Diamonte, June 14, 1678, Decisiones recentiores S. R. Rotae,* XIX[1], n. 213, a pure commercial contract case used five times by Pitoni to show that contractual conditions must be complied with. Roman law and the *Corpus juris canonica* were treated equally—a dozen or so texts from each were used. The main reliance was on the commentators; over sixty authorities were cited more than two hundred times. To an extraordinary degree earlier legal authority was invoked: there were no eighteenth-century writers; two-thirds of the authors employed had also been used by counsel in 1650 in the case of Charles and Nicole; the most cited authority was still Sanchez.

78. The Report now appears as *West Lisbon, July 8, 1724, Thesaurus resolutionum S.C.C.,* III, 39–44.

79. Northcote Parkinson *The Law of Delay* (Boston: Houghton Mifflin, 1970).

80. Memorandum in the file for *West Lisbon, July 8, 1724.*

CHAPTER III. CAPTIVE IN MIND

1. On Benedict XIV's election, character, and reputation see Pastor, XXXV, 1–22; for the tribute from England, Horace Walpole, *Correspondence,* ed. Wilmarth S. Lewis (New Haven: Yale University Press, 1937), II, illustration reproducing the bust and inscription facing p. 79.

2. Benedict XIV, *Matrimonii perpetuum,* April 11, 1741, to the Bishops of Poland, Benedict XIV, *Bullarium* (Malines, 1826), I, 89.

3. *Notizie per l'anno 1720* (Rome, 1720), brought out under the direction of Luca Antonio Chracas and printed at the press of Giovanni Francesco Chracas near San Marco in the Corso. The series continued as *La Gerarchia Hierarchia* and continues today as *Il Annuario Pontificio.*

4. Benedict XIV, *Nimiam licentiam,* May 18, 1743, *Bullarium,* II, 123–134.

5. Benedict XIV, *Bullarium,* I, 166–177.

6. Henry of Ghent, *Quaestiones quodlibetales* (Venice, 1613), Quodlibet 5, q. 28; Thomas Aquinas, *In libros sententiarum Petri Lombardi,* 4.27.1. 3, Solutio 2: "before carnal coupling there is between the spouses only a spiritual bond," and this bond is broken "by the kind of spiritual death by which someone dying to the world lives to God." This view was nuanced when Boniface VIII ruled that only "a solemn religious profession" dissolved the marriage, Sext, 3.15.1; and "civil death" became the preferred metaphor, Antonino, *Summa theologiae moralis* (Venice, 1582), 3.1.21.

7. Hostiensis, *In libros decretalium commentaria* (Venice, 1581), III, 'De conversione conjugatorum,' 'Ex publico,' 9–16, followed by Joannes An-

dreas, *In quinque libros decretalium novella commentaria* (Venice, 1581), III, *De conversione coniugatorum*, 7, 'Ex publico.'

8. Antonino, *Summa theologiae moralis*, 3.1.21. Dispensations of Martin V from the Repertorium Germanicum IV, Archives of the Vatican, reproduced in Karl August Fink, "Frühe urkundliche Belege für die Auflosung des matrimonium ratum non consummatum durch päpstliche Dispensation," *Zeitschrift der Savigny—Stiftung für Rechtsgeschichte, Kanonistiche Abt.* XLVI (1960), pp. 434–442.

9. For the power, Tommaso de Vio, Cardinal Cajetan, *De matrimonio*, q. 1, in Cajetan, *Opuscula, quaestiones et quodlibeta omnia* (Venice, 1531), fol. 62B; Navarrus, *Enchiridion sive Manuale confessariorum et poenitentium* (Venice, 1579), 21.21. Against the power, Domingo de Soto, *In libros sententiarum Petri Lombardi* (Venice, 1570), 4.27.1.4. The provisions of Trent on dissolution by religious profession, "Canons Concerning the Sacrament of Matrimony," 24th session, November 11, 1563, Council of Trent, *Acta*, IX, 967.

10. The strongest negative evidence is furnished by Juan de Torquemada (the uncle of the famous Inquisitor). He was a Dominican, a cardinal, and part of Eugene IV's administration as Master of the Sacred Palace; he was keenly interested in marriage cases. But he knew of the practice only through Antoninus and favored the opinion that denied that the Pope had power to dissolve, Torquemada, *Commentarii in Decretum Gratiani* (Venice, 1578), at C.27, Q.3. When, later, Cajetan first referred to dispensations "in our day," he could have had in mind such cases as the dissolution of the marriage of Louis XII and Jeanne de France by judges-delegate of Alexander VI on August 31, 1498, on the basis of "the grounds declared in the process," in which consanguinity, spiritual relationship, and coercion had all been alleged along with nonconsummation, see the texts excerpted in Michel Lhospice, *Divorce et dynastie* (Paris: R. Pichon and R. Durand-Auzias, 1960), pp. 48–49, 121. Later, however, Cajetan reported advising Clement VII to solve a difficult marriage case by dispensation of the marriage as unconsummated and the Pope followed his advice, Cajetan, *Opuscula*, tract 28. Soto doubted that any cases actually existed, Soto, *In sententias*, 4.27.1.4. Navarrus does not say what happened to his advisees mentioned in *Manuale*, 21.21; although George Hayward Joyce, *Christian Marriage: An Historical and Doctrinal Study* (2nd ed., New York: Longmans, Green, 1948), p. 478, implies that he was successful. In 1950, when Jeanne de France was canonized, she was enrolled among the saints who were neither virgins nor martyrs, Pius XII, Act of Solemn Canonization, *AAS* XXXXII, 465 (1950). Hence, in hindsight at least, her case cannot be classified as a nonconsummation case, and no other case received publicity before the case of the Prince of Transylvania.

11. Pius V, *Romani pontificis* August 2, 1751, printed as Document VII in an appendix to *Codex canonici iuris* (Rome: Vatican Polygot Press, 1920); Gregory XIII, *Populis et nationibus*, June 25, 1583, Document VIII in *Codex canonici iuris*. Gregory XIII, an experienced canonist, seems to have grasped most clearly the potentiality of the power; he is said to have dispensed thirteen unconsummated marriages in a day, Enrique Henriquez, *Summa theologica moralis* (Venice, 1600), 11.8.2, cited in Tomás Sanchez, *De sancto sacramento matrimonii* (Venice, 1737), 2.14.

12. D'Ossat to Villeroy, July 14, 1599, letter 189 in *Lettres de Cardinal D'Ossat*, ed. Amelot de la Houssaie (Amsterdam, 1732), vol. III. D'Ossat observed drily, "The marriage will be dissolved in three months." In Henri IV's case, six months later, on December 17, 1599, his marriage to Marguerite de Valois was annulled by judges-delegate of Clement VIII on grounds of spiritual relationship, coercion, and failure of the papal dispensation to be seen by the Ordinary or read by the King (Lhospice, *Divorce et dynastie*, pp. 179–184).

13. Sanchez, *De sancto matrimonii sacramento*, 2.14.2.

14. Report of the Secretary, Genoa, *Of A Dispensation, May 20, 1719*, reprinted in Benedict XIV, *Quaestiones canonicae*, q. 168, *Opera*, (Prato, 1844), XII, 118. For practice earlier, at the turn of the century, see the report of two of his own cases by the advocate Domenico Ursaya, *Discreptationes ecclesiasticae* (Rome, 1717), II, 22. Ursaya cites precedents from the S.C.C. going back to 1608.

15. Benedict XIV, *Dei miseratione*, Benedict XIV, *Bullarium*, I, 175.

16. Alberto y Arturo Garcia Carraffa, *Enciclopedia heráldica y genealógica hispano-americana* (Madrid, 1954), LXXIII, 64. Luis' governorship of Jaén is mentioned by witnesses cited by the Secretary of the S.C.C. in *Córdoba, Of Nullity of Marriage, February 12, 1763, Thesaurus resolutionum Sacrae Congregationis Concilii* (Rome, 1763), XXXII, 36 (hereafter cited as *Thesaurus S.C.C.*). Ana's age is given on a baptismal certificate appended to *Restrictus facti et juris pro Josepho Perez de Guzman*, filed with the S.C.C. in *Córdoba, Of Nullity of Marriage, February 12, 1763* (hereafter referred to as *Restrictus facti*).

17. *Restrictus facti*, paras. 26–27 (testimony of Leonardo Carbanell, Bartolomé Hidalgo, and Francisco Delgado).

18. "Perez de Guzman, Gaspar Alonso," *Enciclopedia universal illustrada* (Madrid, 1921), XXXXIII, 685; "Perez de Guzman 'el Bueno,' Alonso," at p. 685. On the Guzman, see Miguel Cervantes, *Don Quixote*, chapter 13.

19. *Restrictus facti*, para. 2 (summary of testimony of several witnesses). On the Aguilera family generally, Garcia Carraffa, *Enciclopedia heráldica*, II, 76.

20. *Restrictus facti*, para. 3 (quotation from a later letter, in 1737, to Doña Juana from Herrera).

21. *Ibid.*, para. 4 (testimony of Juana).

22. *Ibid.*, para. 5 (dispensation quoted in Italian translation); and paras. 52–53 (Vicar-General's decree on the ratification of the marriage).

23. *Ibid.*, para. 10 (testimony of Sebastiano de Espexo, José's steward, who testified to being present both when Doña Ana declared her position to Don José and when Don José decided nonetheless to return to Córdoba with her).

24. *Restrictus responsionis facti et juris cum summario in calce*, filed in *Córdoba, Of Nullity of Marriage, February 28, 1763* (hereafter cited as *Restrictus responsionis*), para. 39.

25. *Ibid.*, para. 47, referring to a synopsis of the judicial record in the *Summarium* for Doña Ana.

26. The claim of relationship to the Duke of Medina Sidonia is made in the *Restrictus facti*, paras. 1, 77. Don José would not have succeeded to the dukedom, and it may be that his lawyers exaggerated his feelings for the family line, strong though such feelings would be in the heart of any gentleman of Spain.

27. Secretary's report in *Córdoba, Of Dispensation, September 20, 1760, Thesaurus S.C.C.*, XXIX, 178.

28. *Restrictus facti*, paras. 67, 71, summarizing the midwives' report. In the case of the Princess of Transylvania she had not been pressed to undergo this examination.

29. *Córdoba, September 20, 1760, Thesaurus S.C.C.*, XXIX, 178. On the ecclesiastics see *Notizie per l'anno 1760* (Rome, 1760), p. 157 (Barcia), and *Hierarchia catholica*, VI, 183 (Barcia); *ibid.*, p. 238 (Folch de Cardona).

30. On the cardinal members, *Notizie per l'anno 1760*; Pastor, XXXV, 355; XXXVII, 395.

31. Carlo Rezzonico, *Decisiones Sacrae Romanae Rotae* (Rome, 1759–1762). The accounting case began in the Rota as *Jaén or Baeza, January 30, 1733*, I, 362–364, and presented points for decision on December 4, 1733, and June 20, 1734; the tithes case was *Jaén, July 2, 1734*, II, 168–170. The benefice case began as *Córdoba, June 9, 1732*, I, 263–266, and ran until February 11, 1738. On Rezzonico's life, see Cerchiari, II, 226–227; Pastor, XXXVI, 158–159.

32. On Rossi, *Hierarchia catholica*, VI, 21, 100, 344; on Simonetti, *ibid.*, VI, 335; Pastor, XXXVII, 399.

33. Secretary's Report, *Córdoba, Of Dispensation, September 20, 1760, Thesaurus S.C.C.*, XXIX, 178.

34. Secretary's Report, *Córdoba, Of Dispensation, November 22, 1760, Thesaurus S.C.C.*, XXIX, 182. The witness is identified by name only in the *Restrictus facti*, para. 66.

35. Secretary's Report, p. 183. Reconsideration could still be granted after a wait of three months, rare though such a rehearing was, R. Parayre, *La Congrégation du Concile* (Paris, 1897), p. 236.

36. *Córdoba, Of Dispensation, September 20, 1763, Thesaurus S.C.C.*, XXIX, 178; *Restrictus responsionis*, paras. 6, 16.

37. Secretary's Report, *Córdoba, February 26 1763, Thesaurus S.C.C.*, XXXII, 36. On the Count's exclusion, *Restrictus responsionis*, paras. 8–11; and *Restrictus facti*, para. 29, on the pressure on the witnesses.

38. *Hierarchia catholica*, VI, 181–182. In the printed brief for Perez de Guzman in Rome, he is given the additional name "Fernandez de Córdoba."

39. Secretary's Report, *Córdoba, Of Marriage, February 26, 1763, Thesaurus S.C.C.*, XXXII, 39. On Durani see *Notizie per l'anno 1763*. He was not mentioned in the *Notizie* for 1762, and his co-counsel Niccolo Sala and Giovanni Ardvino, described as advocates in the brief, were not important enough to make the *Notizie* at all. Giovanni Pietro Brasca, presumably a writer not yet an advocate, was with them on the brief. Among other reforms of Benedict XIV had been one of the College of Advocates who were henceforth to nominate their own members for approval by the Pope,

Renazzi, *Storia dell' università*, IV, 201. Thus the advocates here employed had at least satisfied the senior bar of their qualifications.

40. *Restrictus facti*, paras. 16–18 (quotations from the medical conclusions; the deposition of the parish priest, Lorenzo de Cardenas; and the judgment of the Vicar-General). Also *ibid.*, paras. 58–59 (summary of the testimony of several witnesses for the petitioner), para. 110 (a sexton of San Andreas).

41. *Ibid.*, para 7. (Espexo), and para. 35 (Juana); *Restrictus responsionis*, para. 25 (Santos), para. 30 (the inference from refusal of intercourse).

42. *Restrictus facti*, para. 26 (Delgado quoted), para. 27 (Hidalgo quoted), para. 32 (quotations from the letters of Los Cobos and Morente to Juana); *Restrictus responsionis*, para. 33 (Santos quoted). *Restrictus facti*, para. 25 (Espexo) (the rock-throwing episode).

43. *Restrictus responsionis*, paras. 32–35 (the nun's deposition excerpted); para. 33 (Santos quoted); para. 37 (the uncle quoted); para. 43 (parish records); *Restrictus facti*, para. 66, and Secretary's Report in *Córdoba, November 26, 1763, Thesaurus S.C.C.*, XXXII, 36 (consummation).

44. Gratian, c. 26, C. 32, q. 7, ascribing the words to "Pope Fabius"; they are actually the Roman jurisconsult Ulpian's.

45. The tributes to his book appear at the front of the edition brought out by his nephew Lanfranco Zacchia, *Quaestionum medico-legalium opus* (Lyon, 1661). For his title from Innocent X and other biographical data, Gustavo Maria Apolloni, "Zacchia, Paolo," *Enciclopedia cattolica* (Vatican City, 1954), XII, 1762.

46. Zacchia, *Quaestionum*, at 2.1, "Dementia and Lesions of the Reason and all the Diseases Which Affect the Reason"; in particular 2.1.1 and 2.1.3.

47. In Roman law: *Codex Justinanus*, 6.36.5, "Nec codicillos." In the canons, Gratian, c. 14, C. 7, q. 11, *'Quamvis triste'* (resignation by a bishop). In the commentators, Raimundo of Peñaforte, *Summa casuum conscientiae* (Verona, 1740), 4.2.3: in "lucid intervals," a madman can "do all other things which others can do." In Zacchia, *Quaestionum*, 2.1.21.30: how the sanity of an act appeared from its quality.

48. Tomás Sanchez, *De sancto sacramento matrimonii*, 1.18.17. On the comatose and cataleptic see Zacchia, *Quaestionum*, 2.1.13.4, and 2.1.21.20.

49. "Captive in mind" was taken from Roman testamentary law, *Digesta*, 28.1.17. Zacchia describes the state at 2.1.9.2. For the pictorial tradition of the pathological melancholic, see Erwin Panofsky, *The Life and Art of Albert Dürer* (4th ed., 1953), pp. 158–159. The decretal *Quum dilectus*, X.3.27.3, a decision of Innocent III in a will case, taught generally that insanity was a fact to be proved. On the long debate over whether lucid intervals must be proved, Andreas Cuschieri, O.F.M., *De evolutione historica doctrinae et iurisprudentiae circa praesumptiones lucida intervalla respicientis* (Naples: M. D'Auria Editore Pontificio, 1970), pp. 12–34.

50. Avicenna, *Canon medicinae* (Venice, 1668), book 2, fen 1, tract. 3, c. 2; cf. *ibid.*, tract. 4, c. 7; Galen, *De affectorum locorum notitia* (*Opera*, Venice, 1560), 4.2; Zacchia, *Quaestionum*, 2.1.9.17–20.

51. Sanchez, *De sancto sacramento matrimonii*, 1.8.23.

52. Zacchia, *Quaestionum*, 2.1.9.20 (the old joke); 2.10.33–48 (on love).

53. Sanchez, *De sancto sacramento matrimonii*, 1.8.15; Zacchia, *Quaestionum*, 2.1.7.11.

54. Theodosius, *Code*, 16.1.2.

55. Sanchez, *De sancto sacramento matrimonii*, 1.18.17.

56. *Glossa ordinaria* at c. 26, C. 32, q. 7, "*Neque furiosus.*"

57. Zacchia, *Quaestionum*, 2.1.16.28. On the educating of offspring as part of the purpose of marriage see Thomas Aquinas, *In libros sententiarum Petri Lombardi*, (Paris: Vives, 1871–1880), 4.32.2.2, reply to obj. 1; Thomas Aquinas *Lectura in epistolas S. Pauli ad Corinthios*, (Turin: Marietti, 1953) 7.1. See the discussion of these texts in John T. Noonan, Jr., *Contraception: A History of Its Treatment by the Catholic Theologians and Canonists* (Cambridge, Mass.: The Belknap Press of Harvard University Press, 1965), p. 280.

58. Zacchia, *Quaestionum*, 2.1.7.11, 20–24; Sanchez, *De sancto sacramento matrimonii*, 1.8.15-17.

59. Zacchia, *Quaestionum*, 2.1.9.23.

60. Sanchez, *De sancto sacramento matrimonii*, 1.8.15-17.

61. Zacchia, *Quaestionum*, II, 447, Decision 54; also in Matteo Buratto, *Decisiones* (ed. J. F. Ferentilli, Lyon, 1660), III, Decision 763. Another indication of the rarity of insanity cases is that in Ferentilli's annotations to this case he gives a single earlier reference — to *Toledo, Of Marriage, December 10, 1625*. This case deals only with the intent necessary to establish domicile. Clemente Merlino, *Decisiones Sacrae Romanae Rotae coram Reverendissimo Patre Clemente Merlino* ed. Marcello Merlino (Venice, 1652), I, Decision 194. As to the sanity cases in Zacchia's appendix, they were six testamentary capacity cases: *Rome, Of Inheritance, November 13, 1592; Malta, Of a Will, February 17, 1612; Rome, Of Inheritance, November 13, 1624; Bologna, Of Inheritance, March 14, 1651; Tivoli, Of Inheritance, June 22, 1637; Rome, Of Succession, Jan. 29, 1629*. Four involving capacity to make a gift: *Rome, Gift of a Ring, May 10, 1589; Rome, Of a Gift, November 13, 1615 and December 12, 1622; Liège, Of the Castle of Mombech, December 15, 1634; Perugia, Of a Pension, December 9, 1650*. One appointment of a curator: *Rome, Of Property, June 26, 1609*.

62. *Lisbon, June 22, 1579* in Zacchia, *Quaestionum*, II, 364, and *Lisbon, November 16, 1588*, in *ibid.*, II, 371. Coincidentally, more than one Portuguese noblewoman had gone to Odivelas to annul an unconsummated marriage by religious profession, see Cristovão Alão de Morais, *Pedatura Lusitana*, II,[2] 399, 403, 413.

63. Secretary's Report, *Córdoba, Of Marriage, February 26, 1763*, *Thesaurus S.C.C.*, XXXII, 36–40.

64. *Gubbio, Of the Erection of Canonries, March 26, 1763; Ascoli, Of Jurisdiction, March 26, 1763; Bagnoregio, Of Martial Services, March 26, 1763*, *Thesaurus S.C.C.*, XXXII, 53–54.

65. Secretary's Report, *Córdoba. Of Nullity of Marriage, March 26, 1763*, *Thesaurus S.C.C.*, XXXII, 54.

CHAPTER IV. THE GOOD OF CHILDREN

1. Ferruccio Loreti, "Pietro Gasparri, Cardinale Ussitano" in *Il Cardinale Pietro Gasparri* (Rome: Lateran University, 1960), p. 151; Wilhelm Sandfuchs, *Die Aussenminister der Päpste* (Munich: G. Olzog, 1965), p. 94.

2. Pietro Pirri, S.J., "Per una storia del Card. Pietro Gasparri," in *Il Cardinale Pietro Gasparri*, pp. 31–33.

3. G. Oesterle, "Gasparri," *Dictionnaire de droit canonique*, V, col. 939; Pietro Palazzini, "Gasparri," *Enciclopedia cattolica*, V, cols. 1953–1955.

4. Appointments to the Institute at Paris where Gasparri went were controlled by the Roman Curia. The candidate the French had wanted received a bigger job as Nuncio to Vienna; the Curia judged an untried young man could fill the spot (Pirri, "Per una storia," p. 33). For an illustration of curial control from a somewhat later date, see the story of the appointment of Jacques Maritain as professor of philosophy at the behest of the Cardinal Prefect of Propaganda, over the strong objection of the Rector and part of the faculty, Raissa Maritain, *Adventures in Grace*, trans. Julie Kernan (New York: Sheed and Ward, 1945), p. 210.

5. Jacques Denis, "Le cardinal Gasparri, initiateur de l'enseignement du droit canonique à l'Université catholique de Paris, de 1880 à 1898," *Actes du congrès de droit canonique de Paris pour le cinquanténaire de la Faculté* (Paris: Letouzey et Ané, 1947), pp. 240–241.

6. *Ibid.*, p. 244. Such was Gasparri's devotion to the editor of the *Decretals* that it may not be wrong to see his hand in the anonymous proposal to raise the feast of Saint Raimundo to a "double of the first class"; Note, "Saint Raymond de Pennafort," *Le canoniste contemporain* (Paris, 1896), XIX, 353.

7. The forerunner of the printed volumes was Gasparri's notes lithographed in 1884 as *Commentarium in I, IV, V libros Decretalium*, see Charles Lefebvre, "De bonorum matrimonii exclusione secundum Card. Gasparri opera," *Apollinaris: Miscellanea in memoriam Petri Card. Gasparri* (Rome, 1960), XXXIII, 140.

8. Cardinal Francesco Roberti, recalling in 1959 what Giuseppe Palica, his professor of moral theology at the Apollinaris, said to him, Roberti, "Il Cardinal Pietro Gasparri" (speech given at the Lateran University, December 10, 1959, on the thirtieth anniversary of the Lateran Pact and on the installation of a bust of Gasparri), *Apollinaris*, XXXIII, 6. On the influence of Gasparri on the Rota see Kurt Schmidt, *Kardinal Pietro Gasparris Einfluss auf die Spruchpraxis der Sacra Romana Rota in Ehesachen* (Freiburg: Herder, 1963), p. 13.

9. Pietro Gasparri, *Tractatus canonicus de matrimonio* (Paris: Delhomme et Briguet, 1892), p. x (hereafter referred to as *De matrimonio*). Gasparri's own view, vigorously expressed at the end of his academic career in 1898, was that it was shameful, dirty (*turpe*) for a priest not to know the law, Denis, "Le cardinal Gasparri," p. 243.

10. *De matrimonio*, p. xii.

11. Pirri, "Per una storia," pp. 41–42.

12. Pietro Gasparri, "Storia della codificazione del diritto canonico per la Chiesa latina," *Acta Congressus Iuridici Internationalis* (Rome, 1937), IV, 4.

13. *Ibid.,* p. 4.

14. *Ibid.,* pp. 3–4.

15. Vittorio Spreti, *Enciclopedia storico-nobilare italiana* (Milan, 1930), III, 208; testimony of Filippo Folchi-Vici in *Summarium pro nobile viro domino Philippo Folchi-Vici* in *Rome, November 23, 1923,* Archives of the Sacred Roman Rota (hereafter *Summarium*), pp. 43–44. (Note that all further references to "Archives" will be to the file now kept under *Rome, November 23, 1923.*)

16. Folchi, Testimony, *Summarium,* pp. 42, 77.

17. The date of intercourse was the date eventually registered as the date of their marriage; Folchi, Testimony, *ibid.,* p. 78. The birthdate of Mario is given in an extract from the Register for Marriage for the City of Rome, 1893, *Summarium,* p. 57.

18. Giuseppe Folchi, Testimony, *Summarium,* p. 70.

19. Stanislao Folchi, Testimony, *ibid.,* p. 49.

20. Pauline Bailly to Filippo Folchi, December 27, 1887, *ibid.,* p. 60.

21. Filippo to Pauline, January 12, 1888, *ibid.,* pp. 57–58.

22. Filippo to Stanislao, January 27, 1888, *ibid.,* p. 59.

23. Filippo to the parish priest of San Vitale, April 4, 1888, *ibid.,* pp. 61–62.

24. Extract from the Register for Marriage for the City of Rome, 1893, *ibid.,* p. 57.

25. Stanislao Folchi, Testimony, *ibid.,* p. 49; Giuseppe Folchi, Testimony, *ibid.,* p. 70.

26. Pietro Della Porta, Testimony, *ibid.,* p. 135.

27. Giovanni Del Drago, Testimony, *ibid.,* p. 76; Pauline Bailly, Testimony, *ibid.,* p. 66.

28. *La Gerarchia cattolica* (Rome, 1875), p. 589; (Rome, 1891), p. 559.

29. Augusto Sili, Testimony, *Summarium,* p. 64.

30. *Ibid.,* p. 65.

31. Filippo Folchi, Testimony, *Summarium,* p. 77.

32. *Ibid.,* p. 78.

33. Tommaso Monti, Testimony, *Summarium,* p. 114.

34. *Ibid.,* pp. 114–115; Pauline Bailly, Testimony, *Summarium,* p. 53; Filippo Folchi, Testimony, *Summarium,* p. 43. The date of December 18, 1891, given in Filippo's libel as the actual wedding date (*Summarium,* p. 41) clearly seems a mistake, although the later Rota judgment adopts it.

35. Pauline Bailly, Testimony, *Summarium,* pp. 68–69.

36. Filippo Folchi, Testimony, *Summarium,* p. 79.

37. Pauline Bailly, Testimony, *Summarium,* pp. 53–54, 67.

38. Stanislao Folchi, Testimony, *Summarium,* p. 48; Pauline Bailly, Testimony, *Summarium,* p. 67.

39. Pauline Bailly, Testimony, *Summarium*, p. 69. The story of the communion is denied by Filippo, Testimony, *Summarium*, p. 80.

40. Extract from the Register for Marriage for the City of Rome, 1893, *Summarium*, pp. 56–57.

41. Princess Francesca Massimo, Testimony, *Summarium*, p. 74.

42. *Annuario della Nobilità Italiana* (1905), pp. 17, 47.

43. Filippo Folchi, Testimony, *Summarium*, p. 78.

44. *La Tribuna* (Rome), November 28, 1896.

45. *Il Popolo Romano*, December 24, 1896.

46. Filippo Folchi, Testimony, *Summarium*, p. 69; Pauline Bailly, Testimony, *Summarium*, p. 54.

47. Filippo Folchi, Testimony, *Summarium*, p. 79; Giovanni De Montel, Testimony, *Summarium*, p. 63. Biographical data on De Montel, *Annuaire pontifical catholique*, ed. Albert Battandier (Paris, 1903), p. 517; on Sinibaldi, *ibid.*, p. 525.

48. Louis Hardouin, Testimony, *Summarium*, pp. 45–48.

49. Pauline Bailly, Testimony, *Summarium*, p. 55.

50. Filippo Folchi, Testimony, *Summarium*, p. 43.

51. Filippo Folchi, Libel, *Summarium*, pp. 41–42.

52. *La Gerarchia cattolica* (Rome, 1895), p. 556.

53. *Annuaire pontifical catholique* (1899), p. 356; (1907), p. 450. For an example of an American, Francis MacNutt, using ecclesiastical influence to secure appointment to this sinecure, see the letter of William O'Connell to James Cardinal Gibbons, June 15, 1904, Baltimore Chancery Archives, Gibbons file.

54. *Annuaire pontifical catholique* (1899), p. 398; (1906), p. 516; *La Gerarchia cattolica* (1907), pp. 421, 468. On the functions of the Consistorial Congregation, see Michele Lega, *Praelectiones in textum iuris canonici, De iudiciis ecclesiasticis, in scholis Pontificis Seminarii Romani habitae* (Rome, 1898), II, secs. 209–215 (hereafter referred to as Lega, *De iudiciis*).

55. Filippo Folchi, Testimony, *Summarium*, p. 43.

56. A. Carabini, *Restrictus facti et iuris pro Filippo Folchi-Vici*, filed February 4, 1923 (statement that Giorgio was Folchi's counsel in the Vicariate). Biographical data on Giorgi, a native of Valmontone, a hill village southwest of Rome, Note, *Il monitore ecclesiastico*, XXIX, 40 (1917); *La Gerarchia cattolica* (1895), p. 659; (1908), pp. 352, 475, 504; *Annuaire pontifical catholique* (1899), p. 493; (1912), p. 297; (1917), p. 117; (1922), p. 55.

57. *Of Nullity of Marriage, December 6, 1909, Decisiones seu Sententiae Sacrae Romanae Rotae*, (Rome: Vatican Polygot Press, 1912), I, 160.

58. Filippo Folchi, Libel, *Summarium*, p. 42.

59. Filippo Folchi, Testimony, *Summarium*, p. 44.

60. Pauline Bailly, Testimony, *Summarium*, p. 52.

61. To the indignation of Bacchi's old assistant, the notary Tommaso Monti; Monti, Testimony, *Summarium*, p. 113.

62. Judgment summarized and dated in *Of Nullity of Marriage, January 17, 1912, Decisiones seu Sententiae Sacrae Romanae Rotae*, IV, 33–34.

63. Giovanni De Montel, Testimony, *Summarium*, pp. 63–64.

64. Note, *Il monitore ecclesiastico*, XXXII, 34 (1920); Pirri, "Per una storia," p. 45; *La Gerarchia cattolica* (1907), p. 245; *Annuaire pontifical catholique* (1917), p. 356; (1926), p. 126. As a canonist Sili, then in Calcara di Visso, was consulted by the S.C.C. in *Munster, Of Marriage, May 19, 1900, Analecta ecclesiastica* (Rome, 1900), VIII, 251–259.

65. See R. Parayre, *La S. Congrégation du Concile* (Paris, 1897), p. 241.

66. Genuario Bucceroni, S.J., "Casus Conscientiae Propositus et Solutus Romae, ad S. Apollinarem, in Cultu S. Pauli Apostoli," *Analecta ecclesiastica seu Romana Collectanea de disciplinis speculativa et practica* (Rome, 1901), IX, 318–321.

67. *Thesaurus S.C.C.*, CLXVI, 801–806.

68. Note, *Analecta ecclesiastica*, XII, 294–298. Note, *Le canoniste contemporain* (1904), XXVII, 676. A case from Bordeaux in 1890 had raised the same issue, but decision had been postponed. That case, too, was noted as "most rare" in a very brief annotation in *Le canoniste contemporain* (1890), XIII, 361. In 1907 the S.C.C. faced another case involving *Si conditiones* with enough of a flavor of incest to recall the original Barberini decision. In the Portuguese village of Montena, Isabella Laboreiro, thirteen years old, was raped by her stepmother's brother, Antonio Alfare, aged twenty-one. Alfare was sentenced to jail, but was promised his release if he married Isabella. Isabella's father would consent to her marrying only if the couple promised not to have marital intercourse. This agreement was made, Alfare was released from prison, and the couple were married. The S.C.C. avoided judgment on the validity of the marriage, but recommended that the Pope dissolve it as unconsummated. *Evora, July 27, 1907, Thesaurus S.C.C.*, CLVI, 390–416.

69. Folchi, Libel, *Summarium*, p. 42.

70. Folchi, Testimony, *Summarium*, pp. 43–44.

71. *Ibid.*, pp. 79–80.

72. Pauline Bailly, Testimony, *Summarium*, p. 53.

73. *Libro D'Oro* (Rome, 1965), XV, 505. For the dissolution of the cousin's marriage, *Thesaurus S.C.C.*, CLXI, 1021–1045. For the cardinal, *La Gerarchia cattolica* (1910), p. 104.

74. Giovanni Del Drago, Testimony, *Summarium*, pp. 75–76.

75. Filippo Folchi, Declaration, *ibid.*, pp. 82–83.

76. Niccolo Del Re, "I Cardinale Prefetti della Sacra Congregazione del Concilio dalle Origine ad Oggi (1564–1964)," *La Sacra Congregazione del Concilio* (Rome, 1964), p. 300.

77. *La Gerarchia cattolica* (1910), p. 433. On Pompili, see *Annuaire pontifical catholique* (1906), p. 541, and *Annuario pontificio* (Rome, 1924), p. 37.

78. Pius X, Rescript, October 30, 1908, Archives.

79. *Thesaurus resolutionum S.C.C.*, CLXVII, p. 644 (report of judgment without a report of the argument.)

80. William Cardinal O'Connell, *Recollections of Seventy Years* (Boston: Houghton Mifflin Company, 1934), p. 179.

81. Lega, *De iudiciis*, I, sec. 658.

82. Pius X, *Sapienti consilio, Acta*, IV, 150.

83. Cerchiari, II, 274.

84. *Ibid.*, II, 274, 289.

85. Charles Lefebvre, "Rote Romaine," *Dictionnaire de droit canonique* (Paris: Letouzey et Ané, 1965), VII, 739.

86. Pius X, *Sapienti consilio, Acta*, IV, 156.

87. Juan de Lugo, *De iustitia et iure* (Venice, 1751), disp. 34, sec. 1, n. 3.

88. Lega, *De iudiciis*, I, secs. 80–84, commenting on *De regulis iuris, Liber sextus decretalium*, 5.12.

89. E.g., Rafaele Merry del Val, *Memories of Pope Pius X* (London: Burns, Oates, and Washbourne, 1939), pp. 23–24.

90. Charles Ledré, *Pie X* (Paris: Spes, 1952), pp. 133–134.

91. Arturo Carlo Jemolo, *Chiesa e Stato in Italia negli ultimi cento anni* (Milan: Einaudi, 1957), p. 492.

92. Leo XIII, Allocution to the Cardinals, December 16, 1901, *Fontes iuris canonici*, ed. Pietro Gasparri (Rome: Vatican Polygot Press, 1925), III, 577–578. Scarcely had Leo XIII's pontificate begun before he issued the first encyclical letter on the indissolubility of marriage, *Arcanum divinae sapientiae*, February 10, 1880, *Acta sanctae sedis* (Rome: Vatican Press, 1889), XII, 385. This was followed by specific warning to the President of France on the social evils of divorce, *Les événements*, May 12, 1883, reproduced in *Les enseignements pontificaux, Le Mariage*, ed. by the Monks of Solesmes (Solesmes, 1954), p. 133. In addition, Leo XIII insisted on the divine institution of indissoluble marriage and the social evils which would attend the introduction of divorce in letters to the bishops of Hungary (*Quod multum*, August 12, 1886, *Acta*, VI, 153); to the bishops of Poland (*Caritatis*, March 19, 1894, *Acta*, XIV, 70); to the bishops of the United States (*Longinqua oceani*, January 6, 1895, *Acta*, XV, 15); to the bishops of Ecuador (*Dum multa*, December 24, 1902, *Acta*, XXII, p. 260). Although Pius X found far fewer occasions to pronounce on divorce—his denunciation of Bolivian divorce legislation in *Afflictum proprioris*, November 25, 1906 (*Acta sanctae sedis*, XXX, 65) stands out as an exception—it cannot be doubted that he shared Leo's outlook.

93. Thomas Aquinas, *Summa theologica*, I-II, q. 94.4 ad 4; and q. 97.4 ad 2.

94. Oreste Giorgi, Testimony, *Summarium*, pp. 121–125.

95. Del Drago to Giorgi, January 9, 1909, *ibid.*, pp. 96–97.

96. By the terms of *Sapienti consilio*, the S.C.C. was to be the competent tribunal in all cases relating to affairs committed to it "which it judges are to be treated as a matter of discipline." The Congregation of the Sacraments was given charge of "all relating to matrimonial discipline, such as dispensations" and the power to decide "questions of the validity of marriage," which could be decided summarily. Matters which were "major," "either by reason of the object or of the person," were excluded from the

Rota's ambit. Despite these limitations, matters which were not disciplinary — i.e., matters which were not appropriate for administrative rule-making — were to be referred by the S.C.C. to the Rota. The Sacraments was told to send the Rota all cases "where the judicial order should be kept." However vague the reservation of major questions, the Rota was to be the normal tribunal.

97. Pius X, Rescript, January 12, 1909, in Sacred Roman Rota, Archives.

98. Report of the Secretary of the S.C.C., in Sacred Roman Rota, Archives; Pius X, Rescript, May 24, 1909, in Sacred Roman Rota, Archives.

99. Biographical data on Many, *Dictionnaire de droit canonique*, VI, col. 725; on Heiner, *ibid.*, V, col. 1092; on Prior in J. J. Curtin, "Beda College," *New Catholic Encyclopedia* (1967), II, 215, and *Annuaire pontifical catholique* (1917), p. 646. Held over from the old Rota were Gustavo Persiani of Rome, aged sixty-seven, and Guglielmo Sebastianelli, aged fifty-three, a native of Castro dei Volsci, a former civil and criminal legal officer of the Vicariate, and a professor of canon law at the Apollinaris (see *Annuaire pontifical catholique* [1917], p. 656). New Italian appointments besides Lega were Giuseppe Mori, aged fifty-one, a native of Lorena-Piceno and a canon of the Lateran (*ibid.*, p. 632), and Federico Cattani Amadori, aged fifty-three, born in Moradi and formerly vicar-general of Modigliana (*ibid.*, p. 583). Many, born in Gespunsart, France, was sixty-two. Heiner, a native of Atteln in Westphalia, was sixty. Prior, born in Darlington, England, was forty-eight. The youngest member was the Austrian, Antonius Perathoner, aged forty-five, a native of Wollostein in the Tyrol and a former chaplain of the imperial court in Vienna.

100. R. Naz, "Michele Lega," *Dictionnaire de droit canonique*, VI, col. 371; Benedetto Lega, "Lega," *Enciclopedia cattolica*, VII, col. 1019; *Annuaire pontifical catholique* (1917), p. 120.

101. Lega, *De iudiciis*, I, Foreword.

102. Lega, Introduction, *Decisiones seu Sententiae Sacrae Romanae Rotae*, I (The first volume of published decisions of the new Rota) (Rome, 1912), pp. LIII–LIV.

103. Testimony of Pacieri, *Summarium*, pp. 88–90; of Frattini, pp. 90–91; of Fabi, pp. 91–92; of Antaldi, pp. 85–88.

104. Testimony of Stanislao, *ibid.*, pp. 93–94; of Saverio, p. 95; of Giulio, p. 96.

105. Del Drago, Testimony, *ibid.*, pp. 97–98.

106. Pauline Bailly, Testimony, *ibid.*, pp. 99–100.

107. On Sincero (born 1870 in Trino, diocese of Vercelli), see *Annuaire pontifical catholique* (1916), p. 741; on Parrillo (born in 1873, in Fontegreca, diocese of Isernia), *ibid.* (1922), p. 430; on Sacconi, *ibid.*, (1906), p. 671, and on his now being Folchi's counsel, testimony of Giorgi, *Summarium*, p. 120.

108. *Of Nullity of Marriage, December 6, 1909, Decisiones seu sententiae Sacrae Romanae Rotae* (Rome, 1912), I, 155–163 (opinion and judgment).

109. Composition of the Signature in 1910: Vincenzo Vannutelli, born in Genazzano in 1836, *La Gerarchia cattolica* (1910), p. 78; Antonio Agliardi, born in Cologna di Serio, diocese of Bergamo, in 1832 (*ibid.*, p. 78);

Francesco Satolli, born in Marsciano, diocese of Perugia, in 1839 (*ibid.*, p. 79); Sebastiano Martinelli, born in Santa Anna, diocese of Lucca, in 1848 (*ibid.*, p. 88); Francesco Segna, born in Poggio Ginolfo, diocese of Marsi, in 1836 (*ibid.*, p. 94); and Pietro Gasparri. For character sketches of the aristocratic Vannutelli and the nervous and inept Satolli, see O'Connell, *Recollections of Seventy Years*, pp. 148, 123–129. On Satolli's death, he was succeeded in June 1910 by Francesco di Paolo Cassetta, born in Rome in 1841, made a referee of the old Signature, in 1878, created cardinal by Leo XIII in 1899 (*Annuario pontificio* [1912], p. 78). On the use of consultors by the Signature, see Victor Martin, *Les cardinaux et la Curie* (Strasbourg, 1930), pp. 98–99. On Marini, *Annuaire pontifical catholique* (1917), p. 170.

110. Pius X, *The Proper Law*, Pius X, *Acta*, IV, 174–175.

111. Lega, *De iudiciis*, I, secs. 268–281.

112. Pius X, *Schema Codicis Iuris Canonici*, with notes by Cardinal Pietro Gasparri (Rome: Vatican Polygot Press, 1912), canon 1965.

113. Lega's feelings about the point were evident five years later when, now the Prefect of the Signature himself, he raised the point in a letter to the Pope and received explicit authorization for the Signature to hear marriage cases, Benedict XV, Note, *Attentis expositis*, June 28, 1915, *Acta apostolicae sedis* (1915), VII, 325; see also the discussion in G. Oesterle, "De restitutione in integrum," *Ephemerides Romanae ad canonicas disciplinas spectantes* (Rome, 1939), XIX, 177.

114. The judgment of the Signature is described by the Rota in its subsequent opinion, *Of Nullity of Marriage, January 17, 1912, Decisiones*, IV, 35–56.

115. Marini to Sacconi, quoted in *Restrictus facti et iuris pro Philippo Folchi-Vici*, filed February 4, 1923, Sacred Roman Rota, Archives.

116. Lega, *De iudiciis*, II, secs. 263–269.

117. Pietro Gasparri, *De matrimonio* (Paris, 1892), II, sec. 797.

118. "News of the Roman Curia," *Analecta ecclesiastica*, (1908), XVI, 85.

119. Giorgi, quoted in *Restrictus facti et iuris pro Philippo Folchi-Vici*, filed February 4, 1923, Archives.

120. Del Drago, Testimony, *Summarium*, pp. 100–106.

121. Giorgi, Testimony, *ibid.*, pp. 122–126.

122. *Ibid.*, pp. 120–121.

123. *Ibid.*, p. 121.

124. *Ibid.*, pp. 123–124.

125. Testimony of Giulio, *Summarium*, p. 106; of Pio, p. 111; of Pacieri, pp. 107–108; of Frattini, p. 108; of Antaldi, p. 107; of Serra, pp. 109–111; of Costantini, p. 119.

126. Pauline Bailly, Testimony, *ibid.*, p. 118.

127. Pius X, Rescript, Archives.

128. *Of Nullity of Marriage, January 17, 1912, Decisiones*, IV, 33–56.

129. Lega did not mention another curious circumstance, apparent from the record: Del Drago was a witness at the civil marriage of Filippo and Pauline in 1893 (Extract from the Register for Marriages for the City of

Rome, 1893, *Summarium*, p. 56). But the witnesses of the religious marriage in 1891 were Tommaso Monti and another whose name Folchi could not recall (Folchi, Testimony, *ibid.*, p. 43). It was at least surprising that Del Drago should have such precise knowledge of what was said just before the religious wedding at which he was inferably not present.

130. Pius X, *Arduum sane munus, Acta*, I, 219.

131. Pietro Gasparri, "Storia della codificazione del diritto canonico per la Chiesa latina," *Acta Congressus Iuridici Internationalis*, IV, 1, 9. The method by which the Code was composed is here lucidly set out by Gasparri, pp. 5–9. His close collaborators are described by Pirri in *Il Cardinale Pietro Gasparri*, p. 45.

132. See Lefebvre, "De bonorum matrimonii exclusione," pp. 139–156.

133. *Mutina, Of Marriage, August 19, 1724, and July 9, 1725, Thesaurus S.C.C.*, III, pp. 6, 161 (marriage null when feigned with a musical instrument repairman by a celebrated singer, Anna de Ambreville, as a means of escaping from a prison where she had been kept for four months to prevent her marrying a noble who was in love with her); *Asculana, Of Marriage, December 14, 1889, Thesaurus S.C.C.*, CXLVII, 866 (marriage of Angelo Bordoni and Anna Campatelli entered as a joke before their village priest held null).

134. See Lefebvre, "De bonorum matrimonii exclusione," pp. 144–145.

135. *Codex iuris canonici* (Rome: Vatican Polygot Press, 1918), canon 1086.

136. *Schema codicis iuris canonici*, canon 367.

137. See discussion of these decretals in Chapter I.

138. *Codex iuris canonici*, canon 1081.

139. John T. Noonan, Jr., *Contraception: A History of Its Treatment by the Catholic Theologians and Canonists* (Cambridge, Mass.: The Belknap Press of Harvard University Press, 1965), pp. 387–391.

140. See Chapter II, at note 12.

141. Gasparri, *De matrimonio* (1891 ed.), sec. 803.

142. *Ibid.*, sec. 855.

143. *Ibid.*, sec. 856.

144. *Ibid.*, sec. 856.

145. *Ibid.*, sec. 856.

146. Schmidt, *Kardinal Pietro Gasparris Einfluss*, pp. 113–119, 77.

147. *De matrimonio* (1932 ed.), sec. 842; italics in original.

148. See Noonan, *Contraception*, pp. 223–226.

149. Herbert Doms, *Vom Sinn und Zweck der Ehe* (Breslau: Ostdeutsche verlag, 1935), pp. 155–156.

150. *De matrimonio* (1891 ed.), sec. 510; (1932 ed.), sec. 528.

151. *De matrimonio* (1891 ed.), sec. 855.

152. *Ibid.* (1904 ed.), sec. 1004.

153. *Ibid.*

154. See the discussion by Lefebvre, "De bonorum matrimonii exclusione," p. 155.

155. See Noonan, *Contraception*, pp. 243–244, 497–498.

156. Thomas Aquinas, *Lectura super primam epistolam S. Pauli ad Corinthios*, 7.1 (Turin: Marietta, 1947), I, 280–281.

157. *De matrimonio* (1891 ed.), sec. 209.

158. *Ibid.*, sec. 859.

159. *Ibid.*, sec. 770; Sanchez, *De sancto matrimonii sacramento*, 2.26.1–6.

160. The Concordat provided, "The Italian State, willing to restore to the institution of marriage, foundation of the family, a dignity consonant with the Catholic traditions of its people, recognizes civil effects in the sacrament of marriage ruled by the canon law" (Concordat Between the Holy See and Italy, February 11, 1929, *Acta apostolicae sedis*, XXI, 290, article 34). Cases concerning "nullity and dispensations from a ratified, unconsummated marriage" were reserved to the ecclesiastical tribunals; their definitive judgments had civil effects when certified by the Signature and made executive by the appropriate civil Court of Appeals; *ibid.*, p. 290. The Curia moved to wipe out the sixty years of civil marriage: those entering civil marriages, "even with the intention of immediately celebrating religious marriage," would be treated as public sinners. (Sacred Congregation for the Discipline of the Sacraments, "Instruction to the Ordinaries of Italy," July 1, 1929, *Acta apostolicae sedis*, XXI, 352.)

161. *Of Nullity of Marriage, January 17, 1912, Decisiones*, IV, 33–56.

162. Ludwig von Pastor, *Tägebucher–Briefe–Erinnerungen*, ed. W. Wühr (Heidelberg: F. H. Kerle, 1950), pp. 719–720; Walter H. Peters, *The Life of Benedict XV* (Milwaukee: Bruce, 1959), pp. 260–272.

163. Folchi, Petition dated January 20, 1921, Archives.

164. *Annuario Pontificio* (1921), p. 661; Della Porta, Testimony, *Summarium*, p. 134.

165. *Annuario Pontificio*, (1923), p. 656; *Libro D'Oro* (1923), pp. 517–518; Orsini, Testimony, *Summarium*, p. 129.

166. Della Porta, Deposition of December 12, 1921, *ibid.*, pp. 126–127, and Testimony, *ibid.*, p. 134.

167. Orsini, Testimony, *ibid.*, p. 130.

168. Orsini, Deposition of December 10, 1921, *ibid.*, p. 126.

169. The Pope had contracted bronchitis on November 27, 1921; Carlo Falconi, *I Papi del ventisimo secolo* (Milan: Feltrinelli, 1967), p. 166.

170. *Annuario Pontificio* (1924), p. 444; *Annuaire pontifical catholique* (1917), p. 659. The order setting up the new turn, "with all to see," is in the Archives.

171. *Rome, November 23, 1923, Decisiones seu Sententiae S. R. Rotae*, XV, 273; Filippo Folchi, Petition to Pius XI, July 26, 1924, Archives.

172. Decision of April 19, 1922, referred to in Pius XI, Rescript, May 8, 1922, Archives.

173. Falconi, *I Papi*, pp. 174–191; see also *Annuario pontificio* for the years 1914–1918.

174. Falconi, *I Papi*, p. 391, citing the deposition of Monsignor Principi in the *Acta* for the beatification of Merry del Val, pp. 140–146.

175. Friedrich Piffl, "Notes on the Conclave of 1922," translated into English in *The Tablet*, October 5, 1963, CCVI, 1060. Piffl, Archbishop of Vienna, was a participant in the conclave. Not only had Sili become a cardinal after Gasparri had become Secretary of State, but Enrico Gasparri, a nephew, had been made a cardinal in 1923, so that the village of Ussita had three natives in the Sacred College, see Ferruccio Loreti, "Pietro Gasparri, Cardinale Ussitano," in *Il Cardinale Pietro Gasparri*, pp. 154–162, with accompanying pictures of "the three Ussitan cardinals."

For another illustration of Gasparri's sensitivity to the needs of his relatives — the reproach leveled at him in the Conclave of 1922 — consider this correspondence on behalf of his nephew Filippo Bernardini when Gasparri was the cardinal-president of the Code Commission. Bernardini had applied to the Catholic University of America for a job teaching canon law. In his own hand Gasparri wrote James Cardinal Gibbons, chairman of the board of trustees of the University. He recited "my nephew's" credentials, noted that Bernardini had assisted him in the work of codification, and asserted that when the Code was promulgated — God willing, in 1915 — Bernardini would be "better than anyone" at interpreting the canons, not only because of his familiarity with the work of codification but "because my support would certainly never fail him" (Gasparri to Gibbons, January 30, 1914, Archives of the Archdiocese of Baltimore, Gibbons file for 1914). When Bernardini was offered the job, but at a salary of $1,000 a year with the title of assistant professor and a teaching schedule of eight hours a week, he went to his uncle again, and his uncle again wrote Gibbons. "My secretary," said Gasparri, would like to be an associate professor at $1,200 a year but would waive the $200 to get the title; eight hours of law teaching a week is "beyond human powers," four hours would be appropriate. Such close negotiation and such effective intervention measured Gasparri's loyalty to his family.

176. On the conclave see also Falconi, *I Papi*, pp. 173–174; Luigi Salvatorelli, *Pio XI e la sua eredità pontificale* (1939), pp. 38–40; Francesco Maria Taliani, *Vita del Cardinal Gasparri, Segretario di Stato e povero prete* (Milan: A. Mondadori, 1938), pp. 164–165 (discussion of Giorgi's vote); Pastor, *Tägebucher*, pp. 725, 730. For the balloting, see Appendix B.

177. Pastor, *Tägebucher*, pp. 737–738.

178. Achille Ratti "Del monaco cistercense Don Ermete Bonomi milanese e delle sue opere," *Archivio Storico Lombardo* (Milan, 1895), pp. 355–356. Philip Hughes in his biography of the Pope notes that the passage was "an unconscious piece of self-portraiture," *Pope Pius XI* (London: Sheed and Ward, 1937), p. 24.

179. Tommaso Gallarati-Scotti, *La Vita di Antonio Fogazzaro* (Milan: Baldini & Castoldi, 1920), p. 45.

180. Achille Ratti, "La Vita della 'Signora di Monza' abbozzata per sommi copi dal Cardinale Federico Borromeo ed una lettera inedita della 'Signora' al Cardinale," *Rendiconti* (Milan: Reale Istituto Lombardo di Scienze e Lettere, 1912), XLV, 860.

181. Pius XI, *Ubi arcano*, December 23, 1922, *Acta apostolicae sedis* (1922), XIV, 684–685. Pius XI, *Casti connubii*, *Acta apostolicae sedis* (1930), XXII, 552.

182. Pius XI, Rescript, May 8, 1922, Archives.

183. Archives for Rome, November 23, 1923.

184. *Acta apostolicae sedis* (1922), XVI, 404.

185. Orsini, Testimony, *Summarium,* pp. 129-131.

186. Della Porta, Testimony, *ibid.,* pp. 134-136.

187. Smiderle, Testimony, *ibid.,* pp. 137-140.

188. The new *summarium,* now in the Archives, shows Prior as *ponens.*

189. *Of Nullity of Marriage, November 23, 1923, Decisiones seu Sententiae S. R. Rotae,* XV, 274.

190. Archives for Rome, November 23, 1923.

191. *La Gerarchia cattolica* (1908), p. 529; *Annuario pontificio* (1921), p. 420.

192. *Annuario pontificio* (1922), p. 8.

193. *Ibid.* (1912), p. 329; (1926), p. 501.

194. Opinion and judgment, *Of Nullity of Marriage, November 23, 1923, Decisiones seu Sententiae S. R. Rotae,* XV, 273-292.

195. See Chapter III, *supra* for earlier views of love as madness.

196. Biographical data, *Annuaire pontifical catholique* (1924): Joseph Florczak, born in Luciejow, Poland, in 1885, ordained 1910, entered as an advocate of the Rota bar in 1917, and appointed to the Rota in 1920 (p. 633); Ubaldo Mannucci, born in Montagnano, diocese of Boiano, in 1883, made archivist of the S.C.C. in 1914, appointed to the Rota, March 2, 1922 (p. 665); André Jullien, born in Pelusin, Loise, France, in 1882, a Sulpician, former professor of canon law at the Grand Seminaire of Lyon, 1912-1922, the assistant of the French auditor Many, appointed to the Rota, November 9, 1922 (p. 650); Rudolph Hindringer, born in Fraunstein, diocese of Munich, in 1880, appointed to the Rota, February 6, 1923 (p. 646); and Francesco Guglielmi, born in Andria, Italy, in 1875, assistant to Giorgi in the Congregation for Bishops and Regulars in 1907, appointed to the Rota, March 16, 1923 (p. 643).

197. The special papal commission to the Signature is reported by Lega in an edition of his own rotal opinions, including his opinion in 1912 in this case, which he published in 1926, *Coram Legam Habitae S. R. Rotae Decisiones sive Sententiae* (Rome: Vatican Press, 1926), p. 267.

198. *Annuario pontificio* (1924), p. 442.

199. Appendix to Rome, November 23, 1923, *Decisiones,* XV, 292. Folchi subsequently petitioned to be dispensed from paying costs, Folchi, Petition, July 26, 1924, Archives.
The Defender, Quattrocolo, became an auditor of the Rota on May 23, 1924, a month before the decision of the Signature; he served as auditor until 1945. Chimenti retired prematurely and became an auditor emeritus in 1925 (*Annuario pontificio* [1925], p. 486) instead of becoming Prior's successor as dean in 1926; Giorgi died on December 30, 1924 (*ibid.,* p. 64). Giovanni Del Drago died in 1956 at the age of ninety-six. *Libro D'Oro* (1965), p. 505.

CHAPTER V. DOES INTENT TO ENTER A MARRIAGE ONE BELIEVES TO BE DISSOLUBLE MAKE THE MARRIAGE DISSOLUBLE?

1. Jay Gould, Last Will and Testament, reprinted in Murat Halstead and T. Frank Beale, Jr., *The Life of Jay Gould* (New York, 1892), pp. 227–249; probate estimate given in *ibid.*, p. 219.

2. Boni de Castellane, *Comment j'ai découvert l'Amérique* (Paris: G. Cies et al., 1924), pp. 2–3; hereafter cited as Castellane.

3. *Ibid.*, p. 3.

4. *Ibid.*, pp. 38–50. The character of the schools Castellane attended may be inferred from the experience of Jacques Maritain as a zealous young Catholic convert in 1912. Given a teaching post at the Collège Stanislas, he found that he startled his pupils by opening class with a prayer and surprised the faculty by proposing to teach the philosophy of Saint Thomas, Raissa Maritain, *Adventures in Grace*, trans. Julie Kernan (New York: Sheed and Ward, 1945), pp. 100–101.

5. See Castellane, pp. 76–81; his self-description is at p. 173.

6. *Ibid.*, p. 4. On George Gould, see Edwin P. Hoyt, *The Goulds: A Social History* (New York: Weybright and Talley, 1969), pp. 99–101. A band of enterprising European investors who had attempted to oust the Goulds from control of the Union Pacific Railroad by ordinary financial tactics had been routed in 1892 by George Gould's cunning and decisiveness. Julius Grodinsky, *Jay Gould: His Business Career, 1867–1892* (Philadelphia: University of Pennsylvania Press, 1957), p. 590.

7. Castellane, p. 27; cf. Halstead and Beale, *Life of Jay Gould*, p. 67.

8. Castellane, pp. 5–31.

9. Henry James, *The Portrait of A Lady* (New York: Modern Library, 1951), vol. II, ch. 42, p. 191; ch. 54, p. 415.

10. *New York Times*, March 5, 1895, p. 2.

11. *Ibid.* The lead story, signed by the reporter Maurice M. Minton, beginning on the front page, taking up most of page 2 and ending with the exclamation "Long life and happiness to Count Paul and the Countess de Castellane!"

12. The conversations with Archbishop Corrigan are reported in New York, March 1, 1913, *Decisiones seu sententiae S. R. Rotae* (Rome, 1919) (hereafter cited as Cattani opinion), V, 188. The dispensation is reported in *New York, December 9, 1911, Decisiones* (hereafter cited as Lega opinion), III, 510. The witnesses to the ceremony are listed in Castellane, p. 34, and corrected by reference to the *New York Times*, March 5, 1895, p. 2.

13. *Ibid.*, March 5, 1895, p. 2.

14. Castellane, pp. 249–250.

15. *Ibid.*, pp. 158–166. The expenditures are described with even greater gusto in Lucius Beebe, *The Big Spenders* (Garden City: Doubleday, 1966), pp. 21–29.

16. Castellane, pp. 147, 173–174, 247–248, 251, 327.

17. *Ibid.*, pp. 330–337.

18. For a sad view of Anna in 1918, René Gimpel, *Diary of An Art Dealer*, trans. John Rosenberg (New York: Farrar, Straus and Giroux, 1966), p. 4; on her new husband, *Annuaire de la noblesse de France* (Paris, 1914), pp. 136–137.

19. Castellane, pp. 331–337.

20. Nazareno Padellaro, *Portrait of Pius XII*, trans. Michael Derrick (New York: Dutton, 1957), pp. 5–7.

21. *La Gerarchia cattolica* (1907), p. 503.

22. Lega opinion, p. 511.

23. *Ibid.*, p. 502. The case is still labeled a "New York" case in the title given to it in the Rota.

24. Cattani opinion, p. 174.

25. Lega opinion, p. 514.

26. Cattani opinion, p. 175.

27. *Ibid.*, p. 178. Catherine ("Kitty") Cameron was the daughter of Sir Roderick Cameron, a Canadian shipping man. Of her in his autobiography, Castellane says only that "she became one of my best friends"; Castellane, p. 290.

28. Cattani opinion, pp. 177–178.

29. *Ibid.*, pp. 179–180.

30. *Ibid.*, p. 186 (Luynes); p. 182 (Marquise de Talleyrand); p. 181 (Count de Montebello); p. 182 (Countess de Montebello).

31. *Ibid.*, p. 190.

32. *Ibid.*, p. 182 (Countess de Montebello); p. 178 (Del Drago).

33. *Ibid.*, pp. 183–184; Lega opinion, p. 509.

34. Lega opinion, p. 509 (Edward); p. 510 (Helen); Cattani opinion, p. 188 (the old friends).

35. Lega opinion, pp. 507–519.

36. *Ibid.*, p. 518.

37. Marquise de Castellane, Testimony, set out in Filippo Pacelli, *Summarium novum pro D. Comite Boni de Castellane* (Rome, 1912), pp. 20–21; Jean de Castellane, Testimony, in *ibid.*, pp. 24–25; Duke de Luynes, Testimony, in *ibid.*, pp. 22–23.

38. *Summarium novum*, pp. 25–29.

39. Filippo Pacelli, *Restrictus facti et iuris cum summario novo* (hereafter *Restrictus facti*) (Rome, 1912), pp. 19, 11 (on the first panel and Parrillo); pp. 8, 11–18 (on Anna); Filippo Pacelli, *Restrictus responsionis animadversionibus defensoris vinculi cum summario novissimo* (Rome, 1913), p. 3 (on Parrilo's reply).

40. *Restrictus facti*, pp. 3, 6, 14.

41. *Ibid.*, p. 4.

42 Francesco Parrillo, *Animadversiones alterae defensoris vinculi ex officio* (Rome, n.d.), pp. 6–9.

43. Cattani opinion, pp. 173–195; data on Cattani, *Annuario pontificio* (1921), p. 420; (1937), p. 53.

44. Robert Pullen, *Sententiae*, 7.29, *Patrologia latina*, 186, col. 947.

45. Gratian, c. 17, C. 28, q. 1.

46. E.g., Panormitanus, *In quinque libros decretalium commentarium* (Venice, 1571), 4.19.8.

47. See Joseph Greco, *Le pouvoir du Souverain Pontife à l'égard des infidèles* (Rome: Gregorian University Press, 1967), p. 72, for examples of the barrier to conversion created by existing marriages. Because of the rule upholding the pagan's first marriage, "the conversion of this people suffers incredible prejudice," wrote Manuel Diaz, Jesuit Visitor for China, writing in 1602, *ibid.*, p. 82. See also the similar report in 1614 of Luis Cerquira, Bishop of Japan, *ibid.*, p. 55.

48. Gabriel Vasquez, *ibid.*, p. 65; opinion of the Roman College Jesuits, Jean Chamerot, Niccolo Godringo, and Giovanni Lorini, *ibid.*, pp. 84–85.

49. See Chapter II, n. 12.

50. Tomás Sanchez, *De sancto matrimonii sacramento* (Venice, 1737), 2.29.11.

51. *Ibid.*, 5.12.3.

52. Greco, *Le pouvoir*, p. 55 (text of July 17, 1669 decree), pp. 96–97.

53. Juan de Lugo, *De sacramentis in genere* in *Opera omnia* (Venice, 1751), vol. V, disputation 8, sec. 8, nn. 125–136.

54. Oliver Wendell Holmes, Jr., "The Path of the Law," *Harvard Law Review* (1898) X, 466.

55. Lugo, *De sacramentis*, n. 71, at 8.8.136.

56. *Ibid.*, 8.2.52.

57. It is *de fide* that marriage is a sacrament (Council of Trent, Session 7, March 3, 1547, "The Sacraments in General," canon 1, *Acta*, V, 995; see also Sanchez, 2.10.2); that the spouses are its ministers (*ibid.*, 2.6.2); that the sacrament is conferred in the spouses' exchange of consent (*ibid.*, 2.5.6). Trent acted with the view before it of Martin Luther, expressed in the preface to The Babylonian Captivity, that there are only three sacraments— baptism, the Eucharist, and penance (Council of Trent, "General Congregation, January 17, 1547, *Acta*, V, 835).

58. Council of Trent, *De sacramentis in genere*, canon 11, *Acta*, V, 995. The definition of the Council responded to the declaration of Martin Luther, in his chapter on extreme unction in *De captivitate Babyloniana*: "Whatever we believe we shall receive, indeed we have received, whether the minister acts or does not act, whether he simulates or jokes." See the statement of the Council's theologians, *Errores haereticorum circa sacramenta in genere*, *Acta*, V, 836.

59. Lugo, *De sacramentis*, 8.3.30–36.

60. E.g., Thomas Aquinas, *Summa theologica*, 3.67.5.

61. Lugo, *De sacramentis*, 8.3.36.

62. Pietro Gasparri, "De la valeur des ordinations anglicanes" in *Revue anglo-romaine*, (Paris, 1895), I, 537.

63. On the campaign against validity as seen by the Anglican proponents: T. L. Lacy, *A Roman Diary and Other Documents Relating to the Papal Inquiry into English Ordinations* (London: Longmans, Green, 1910), p. 6;

Viscount Halifax, *Leo XIII and Anglican Orders* (New York: Longmans, Green, 1912), pp. 31, 217, 387. On Gasparri's responsibility for the issue of intention, see Gasparri to Abbé F. Portal, March 23, 1896, in Halifax, *Leo XIII*, p. 279. Gasparri was regarded by Halifax's party as friendly to the Anglicans, but not yet convinced of their claims; *ibid.*, p. 240. The decision itself: Leo XIII, *Apostolicae curae, Acta sanctae sedis* (1896), XXIX, 193–203.

64. Sanchez, *De sancto matrimonii sacramento*, 2.10.6.

65. Gasparri, "De la valeur des ordinations anglicanes," p. 539.

66. The relation of the marriage cases to the case of Anglican orders is explored at length in Francis Clark, S.J., *Anglican Orders and Defect of Intention* (London, New York: Longmans, Green, 1956), pp. 132–147.

67. Benedict XIV, *De synodo diocesana, Opera* (Prato, 1854), II, 13.22.7–9. The *West Lisbon* case is, of course, the subject matter of Chapter II.

68. Pius VI to the Archbishop of Prague, "Gravissimam," July 11, 1789, printed in *Iuris pontificii propaganda fidei*, ed. Rafaele de Martinis (Rome, 1891), IV, 340.

69. Holy Office to the Vicar Apostolic of the Sandwich Islands, December 11, 1850, *Collectanea S. C. Propaganda Fidei seu Decreta Instructiones Rescripta pro Apostolicis Missionibus* (Rome, 1907), I, 570, n. 1054; Holy Office, Instruction for Japan, March 11, 1868, *ibid.*, II, 11.

70. Holy Office to the Bishop of St. Albert, December 9, 1877, *ibid.*, XXII, 81–86, n. 1427.

71. Holy Office to Bishop of Nesqually [Seattle], January 24, 1877, II, 97–103.

72. Holy Office to Vicar Apostolic of Southern Japan, February 4, 1891, *ibid.*, II, 256–257, n. 1746.

73. Thomas Aquinas, *Summa theologica*, I–II, Q. 12, art. 4.

74. On the relation of intellect to will, *ibid.*, Q. 9, art. 1; on intention as an act of the will, *ibid.*, Q. 12, art. 4; on consent, *ibid.*, Q. 15, art. 1–3.

75. Gasparri, *De matrimonio*, sec. 863.

76. *Ibid.*, secs. 771, 776, 782.

77. Edith Wharton, *The Age of Innocence* (New York: D. Appleton, 1920), p. 109, 143–144. In 1890 there were 33,000 divorces in the United States, Paul H. Jacobson, *American Marriage and Divorce* (New York: Rhinehart, 1959), p. 90.

78. Lega opinion, p. 514.

79. Pacelli, *Restrictus facti et iuris*, p. 7; Lega opinion, p. 521.

80. Cattani opinion, p. 193.

81. *Ibid.*, p. 194.

82. Henry Woods, S.J., "Some Points Arising Out of the *Gould-Castellane* Case," *America* (October 20, 1913), X, 54–55; *New York Times*, January 26, 1914, p. 1 (a dispatch from Berlin).

83. *Ibid.*, June 1, 1913, sec. III, p. 3.

84. *Ibid.*, June 29, 1913, sec. III, p. 3.

85. On Patrizi, *Annuario Pontificio* (1914), p. 663. For his practice see the cases reported in *Acta apostolicae sedis* (1915). On his family, see

Francis MacNutt, *A Papal Chamberlain*, ed. John T. Donovan (New York: Longmans, Green and Co., 1936), p. 217.

86. *New York Times*, January 11, 1914, sec. II, p. 1. On Vannutelli, see *ibid.*, June 1, 1913, sec. 3, p. 3. The paper also observed that "the presence of Martinelli formerly Apostolic Delegate to the United States is especially valuable" (*ibid.*, June 29, 1914, sec. III, p. 3). But when the time came to vote Martinelli was sick (*ibid.*, January 10, 1914, p. 1). The Signature's actual decision on January 10 was a front-page news story in the edition of Sunday, January 11, 1914.

87. *Ibid.*, January 4, 1914, sec. III, p. 3 (a story purporting to quote Patrizi, but seriously garbled: the second decision was said to have been given by "Cardinal Lorenzelli" and Anna was said to have been prevented from testifying because "no woman is allowed to give evidence in person before the Vatican courts." In an earlier story Anna was quoted as believing that the Cattani case had turned on a forged letter in which she allegedly had declared her intention to remain a Protestant in order to be free to divorce, *ibid.*, March 16, 1913, p. 1. The letter was taken as genuine and as the basis for decision in a later pro-Castellane story which pointed out the social advantage to the Duchess de Talleyrand if she could be married to the Duke by the Church, *ibid.*, March 23, sec. IV, p. 5.

88. Apostolic Signature, Decision of January 10, 1914, in Sacred Roman Rota, Archives for *New York, February 8, 1915*. The decision was accurately reported on the front page of the Sunday *New York Times*, January 11, 1914.

89. Filippo Pacelli, *Restrictus facti et iuris cum summario novissimo pro Illustrissimo Domino Comite Boni de Castellane* (hereafter referred to as *1914 Restrictus*), p. 9.

90. Duchess de Talleyrand to Patrizi, March 28, 1914, Archives; *London Morning Post*, May 11, 1914, in Archives; *New York Times*, May 11, 1914, p. 5. The story added that the Duchess had received "an intimation from higher circles that in no case would she be allowed to win." Boni was reported to have been made "a semi-official agent for the Vatican" in dealing with the French government in problems caused by the Concordat. The story interpreted Anna's withdrawal as the end of the case.

91. Francesco Parrillo, *Animadversiones tertiae defensoris vinculi ex officio*, (Rome, n.d.), p. 2.

92. *Ibid.*, pp. 3–16.

93. *Ibid.*, pp. 17–23.

94. Pacelli, *1914 Restrictus*, p. 3.

95. In the Esztergom case it was argued that a marriage by a Catholic girl to a Calvinist in a Calvinist rite before a Calvinist minister was null because of an intent against indissolubility, and the advocate for the girl urged that the 1877 decision of the Holy Office for Seattle be followed. The Calvinists, he pointed out, believed marriage could be dissolved for adultery, and the couple must have married with this belief affecting their intentions. Seraphin Many, the rotal auditor, treated Calvinist belief as a mere error which had not been proved to infect the intention of either the Catholic or Calvinist party. *Esztergom, January 22, 1914*, Sacred Roman Rota, *Decisiones seu Sententiae* (Rome, 1922), VI, 7–25.

96. Dinah Smith to the Tribunal of Portland, Oregon, Sacred Roman Rota, Archives for *Portland, July 6, 1914.*

97. *Portland, July 6, 1914,* Sacred Roman Rota, *Decisiones,* VI, 244–252.

98. The provisions of canon 1086 ran: "1. Internal consent is presumed to be in agreement with the words or signs used in the marriage ceremony. 2. But if either party or both parties by a positive act of the will exclude marriage itself or all right to the conjugal act or some other essential property of marriage, the parties contract invalidly."

99. *New York, February 8, 1915,* Sacred Roman Rota, *Decisiones seu Sententiae,* VII, 23.

100. *Ibid.,* p. 27.

101. *Ibid.,* pp. 25, 34, 37.

102. *Ibid.,* p. 21.

103. *Ibid.,* p. 24.

104. *Ibid.,* pp. 30–37, 41.

105. Joseph Selinger, "Are Non-Catholic Marriages Valid?" *American Ecclesiastical Review* (November 1915), LII, 578–579.

106. The change in law was effected by Benedict XV in a note to Lega, *Attentis expositis,* June 28, 1915, *Acta apostolicae sedis* (1915), VII, 325.

107. Pietro Cardinal Gasparri, Secretary of State of His Holiness, to Guglielmo Sebastianelli, Dean of the Rota, Archives for *New York, February 8, 1915.*

108. *Annuario pontificio* (1915), p. 64; *Annuaire pontifical catholique* (1915), p. 126.

109. *Acta apostolicae sedis* (1915), VII, 292.

110. *New York Times,* October 17, 1915, sec. II, p. 9.

111. *Ibid.,* May 5, 1916, p. 18; May 6, 1916, p. 9; July 24, 1916, p. 16.

112. See note 98. Discussing *Castellane-Gould* in relation to Anglican orders, Francis Clark writes that the 1915 opinion of Prior "showed some hesitation about the admissibility *in foro externo* of the De Lugo-Gasparri principle"; and that this hesitation was "settled" by the Code (Clark, *Anglican Orders,* pp. 142–143). Clark's observation is a polite way of calling attention to the conflict of the opinion and the Code.

113. *New York Times,* July 12, 1924, p. 9.

114. *Ibid.,* September 18, 1924, p. 4; April 2, 1925, p. 21.

115. See Chapter IV, section 6, at note 129.

116. *New York Times,* April 2, 1925, p. 21; August 15, 1925, p. 11.

117. Gasparri, *De matrimonio* (1934 ed.), sec. 913.

118. *Ibid.,* sec. 807, n. 1.

CHAPTER VI. THE AMERICAN UNBELIEVER

1. *Libro D'Oro* (Rome, 1905), pp. 968–969.

2. William O'Connell, *Recollections of Seventy Years* (Boston: Houghton, Mifflin Company, 1934), pp. 211–212, 236, 266–269, 310–314. O'Connell's autobiography, formal and artful as it is, is a specimen of a rare genre, autobiographies of cardinals; indirectly, it affords much illumination.

3. *Nullitatis Matrimonii, June 30, 1910, Decisiones seu sententiae Sacrae Romanae Rotae* (hereafter referred to as Rota judgment), XI, 234–235.

4. Gregory XV, *Inscrutabili, Magnum Bullarium Romanum*, XII, 690–693. On the derivation of "propaganda" see *Oxford English Dictionary*.

5. John T. Noonan, Jr., *The Scholastic Analysis of Usury* (Cambridge, Mass.: Harvard University Press, 1957), p. 289.

6. John Tracy Ellis, "United States: of America," *New Catholic Encyclopedia* (New York: McGraw-Hill, 1967), XIV, 425, 434.

7. *Annuaire pontifical catholique* (1903), p. 568; O'Connell, *Recollections*, pp. 170–172.

8. John Tracy Ellis, *The Life of James Cardinal Gibbons* (Milwaukee: Bruce, 1952), I, 647–648; II, 487, 644.

9. *Annuaire pontifical catholique* (1902), p. 322; (1915), p. 315. Falconio had been first a missionary in the United States and Newfoundland, then in 1889 procurator-general of his order. In 1892 he had been made Bishop of Lacedonia in southern Italy, in 1895 Archbishop of Acerenza and Matera, in 1899 Apostolic Delegate to Canada.

10. Ellis, *Life of James Cardinal Gibbons*, I, 3–23, 163; II, 131.

11. *Ibid.*, I, 275; II 47–48, 453–455.

12. *Ibid.*, I, 326 (the trip with Gibbons).

13. Obituary of Frederick H. Parkhurst, *Bangor Daily News*, February 1, 1921, p. 3; this is also the source of the following biographical details except his love for Marie; on that, see Rota judgment, sec. 13, p. 231.

14. *Holyoke v. Holyoke, Maine Reports* (1886), LXXVIII, 411.

15. *Revised Statutes of the State of Maine* (Portland, 1884), c. 60, sec. 2.

16. Letter to the author from the Clerk of Penobscot County (Maine) Superior Court, June 25, 1970.

17. *Revised Statutes of the State of Maine*, c. 60, sec. 12.

18. *Bangor Daily News*, February 1, 1921, p. 3.

19. Rota judgment, sec. 7, subpara. 6, p. 226.

20. *Il Codice Civile*, art. 102.

21. *Libro D'Oro* (1905), p. 969.

22. *New York Times*, September 28, 1913, sec. 4, p. 2.

23. Sacred Congregation for the Propagation of the Faith, "Instruction," *Collectanea S. Congregationis de Propaganda Fide seu Decreta Instructiones Rescripta pro apostolicis missionibus* (hereafter referred to as *Collectanea*) (Rome, Polygot Press 1907), II, 172, no. 1587; a similar decision by the S.C.C. in *Acta Sanctae Sedis* (1870), II, 137–147.

24. Third Plenary Council of Baltimore, Decrees, n. 131, *Acta et Decreta Concilii Plenarii Baltimoriensis Tertii* (Baltimore, 1886), p. 64.

25. O'Connell, *Recollections*, pp. 211–212.

26. Marie Rospigliosi's petition for annulment accused O'Connell of being influenced in a hostile way by Archbishop Chapelle. In fact, O'Connell and Chapelle had been friends since at least 1888, when O'Connell went to baptize a convert at St. Matthew's whom he had instructed in Medford, Massachusetts, and Chapelle was "most kind and courteous in everything." William O'Connell, *The Letters of His Eminence William Cardinal O'Connell* (Cambridge, Mass.: Riverside Press, 1915), p. 137. This book, in the form of letters to correspondents, seems to have been O'Connell's idealized account of what he might have written on a number of occasions. It was withdrawn from sale when the authenticity of the letters was challenged. While the genre is fictional autobiography, there is little reason to doubt that real incidents are described and that the writer's true feelings toward most of the people mentioned are revealed. I am indebted to John Tracy Ellis for drawing my attention to this book, providing the history of its circulation, and making available one of the few existing copies.

27. Lombardi was a professor of canon law at the Roman Seminary, auditor of the Cardinal Vicar of Rome, substitute notary of the Holy Office, *Annuaire pontifical catholique* (1902), p. 588.

28. Marie Rospigliosi, "Petition for A Declaration of Nullity of Marriage," a document now filed under *Baltimore, June 30, 1910* in the Archives of the Sacred Roman Rota (hereafter in this chapter referred to as Archives).

29. Propaganda to O'Connell, January 10, 1902, Archives.

30. "Instruction," cited in note 23.

31. O'Connell to the Vicar-General of Portland, March 26, 1902, Archives.

32. Interrogation of Marie Rospigliosi, May 28, 1902, Archives.

33. Interrogation of Placide Chapelle, June 1, 1902, Archives.

34. Interrogation of Mrs. Reid, July 5, 1902, Archives.

35. Interrogation of Frederick Parkhurst, August 14, 1902, Archives.

36. Archives; O'Connell's failure to answer the Prince had also been criticized in Marie Rospigliosi's Petition.

37. Evaristo Lucidi, *Votum*, Archives.

38. Sacred Congregaton for the Propagation of the Faith, General Congregation, May 16, 1904, Archives.

39. Gotti to O'Connell, June 13, 1904; Gotti to Falconio, June 16, 1904, Archives.

40. O'Connell to Propaganda, July 1904, Archives.

41. Chancellor of the Archdiocese of Philadelphia to Marchetti-Selvaggiani, August 2, 1904, Archives.

42. Marchetti-Selvaggiani, Declaration, August 9, 1904, Archives.

43. Interrogation of Chapelle, September 19, 1904, Archives.

44. Interrogation of Stonor, September 20, 1904, Archives.

45. O'Connell, *Recollections*, pp. 193, 212; *Annuaire pontifical catholique* (1902), p. 301.

46. Lucidi, *Votum,* and Steyaert, *Votum,* Archives.

47. *New York Times,* March 22, 1905, p. 5, and May 4, 1905, p. 12.

48. Marie Rospigliosi, "Request for the Judicial Examination of Prince Rospigliosi," May 1905, Archives.

49. Sacred Congregation for the Propagation of the Faith, General Congregation, May 22, 1905, Archives.

50. Gotti to O'Connell, June 23, 1905, Archives.

51. O'Connell to Gotti, July 15, 1905, Archives.

52. Vittorio Spreti, *Enciclopedia storico-nobiliare italiana* (Milan, 1932), V, 800.

53. Pius X, *Sapienti consilio, Acta.* (Rome, 1914), IV, 153.

54. Marie Reid, *Petition,* March 18, 1909, Archives.

55. Parkhurst to the Sacred Roman Rota, June 26, 1909, Archives.

56. Parkhurst to Princess Rospigliosi, January 10, 1910, Archives.

57. Parkhurst, *Argumentum in casu,* Archives.

58. Parkhurst to Francesco Parrillo, January 30, 1910, Archives.

59. Gibbons to Michele Lega, January 26, 1910, printed in *Animadversiones Defensoris Vinculi,* Archives.

60. *Mémoires et correspondance du Roi Jérome et de la Reine Catherine* (Paris, 1862), I, 172; III, 365.

61. Leo XIII, *Longuinqua oceani spatia,* January 6, 1895, *Acta,* XV, 15.

62. Gibbons to Merry del Val, May 25, 1910, Archives of the Archdiocese of Baltimore, Gibbons File (1910), item M5.

63. Santucci to Serralunga, January 10, 1930, published in *Chiesa e Stato nella Storia D'Italia,* ed. Pietro Scoppola (Bari: Editori Laterza, 1967), p. 560.

64. Santucci, *Restrictus iuris.*

65. Archives.

66. Gratian, *Decretum,* dictum post c. 14, C. 28, q. 1.

67. Peter Lombard, *Sententiae* (Quarrachi ed., 1916), 4.39.1.

68. Tomás Sanchez, *De sancto matrimonii sacramento* (Venice, 1747), 7.71.5–8.

69. Thomas Aquinas, *Scriptum super sententiis Magistri Petri Lombardi,* ed. M. F. Moos (Paris, 1947), bk. 4, D. 4, Q. 2, art. 2, 5.

70. E.g., Benedict XIV, *Magnae nobis admirationis,* To the Primate and Bishops of Poland, June 29, 1748, in Benedict XIV, *Bullarium,* VI, 67–76.

71. Henry first attacked the dispensation as null because of obreption: it had been asked for on the ground of making peace between England and Spain, and this ground was false, see "Articles of the English," a summary of Henry's points made to the Curia, printed in Stephen Ehses, *Romische Dokumente zur Geschicte der Ehescheidung Heinrichs VIII von England* (Paderborn, 1884), pp. 216–219.

72. Sanchez, *De sancto matrimonii sacramento,* 8.17.4.

73. Council of Trent, *Canones de reformatione,* sess. 25, ch. 18, *Acta,* IX, 1093. Sanchez, *De sancto matrimonii sacramento,* 8.17.10. Technically, the

Council provided that if the reason was not known to the dispenser, the dispensation "is to be judged subreptive." Decretal law treated a dispensation gained by subreption (concealment of a relevant and significant fact) as void; X.3.4.11, and the Sext 1.11.2.

74. Pius IX gave his approval on July 26, 1863; see George Eagleton, *The Diocesan Quinquennial Faculties, Formula IV* (Catholic University of America Studies in Canon Law, no. 248, Washington, 1948), p. 19.

75. Formula D is printed in Antoninus Konings, *Commentarium in facultates apostolicas quae episcopis et vicariis apostoliciis per modum formularum concedi solent, ad usum venerabilis cleri Americani concinnatum*, rev. by Joseph Putzer, C.S.S.R. (New York, Chicago, and Cincinnati, 1893), art. 3, p. 335 (basic delegation), and final para., p. 361 (restriction to serious reasons). After July 1, 1946, the bishops were empowered to dispense for Jewish-Catholic marriage; Eagleton, *Diocesan Quinquennial Faculties*, p. 58.

76. Secretary of State, *Instruction*, November 15, 1858, in *Collectanea*, I, 637, no. 1169.

77. Sacred Congregation for the Propagation of the Faith, *Encyclical Letter*, March 11, 1868, *Collectanea*, II, 10–11.

78. Third Plenary Council of Baltimore, *Decrees*, n. 131, *Acta et Decreta Concilii Plenarii Baltimoriensis Tertii* (Baltimore, 1886), pp. 66–67.

79. Holy Office to the Vicar of Bosnia, August 14, 1822, repeated in Sacred Congregation for the Propagation of the Faith, *Instruction*, May 9, 1877, *Collectanea*, II, 10–11.

80. *Instruction*, cited in note 76.

81. Third Council of Baltimore, *Decrees*, n. 131. *Acta et Decreta*, pp. 66–67.

82. Formula D, art. 8, in Konings, *Commentarium*, p. 359.

83. On the whole development, Francis J. Schenk, *The Matrimonial Impediments of Mixed Religion and Disparity of Cult* (Catholic University of America Studies in Canon Law, no. 51, Washington, 1929), pp. 50–56.

84. *Encyclical Letter* of March 11, 1868, cited in note 77.

85. *Of Nullity of Marriage, June 30, 1910, Decisiones seu sententiae*, pp. 219–237.

86. Sanchez, *De sancto matrimonii sacramento*, 8.26.4–5.

87. Ledóchowski to Gibbons, August 2, 1901, *Analecta ecclesiastica* (1902), X, 61.

88. Second Plenary Council of Baltimore, Decree 339 (*Concilii Plenarii Baltimoriensis II Decreta* [Baltimore, 1868], p. 176).

89. *Relatio collationum*, Archives of the Archdiocese of Baltimore, Gibbons File, November 1883, item L.20.

90. S.C.C., *Ne temere*, August 2, 1907, Article XI, published in Pius X, *Acta* (Rome, 1914), IV, 40–46.

91. Lega to Gibbons July 1, 1910; Lega to O'Connell, July 1, 1910, Archives.

92. Obituary, *Bangor Daily News*, February 1, 1921. The second marriage took place in Bangor, June 1, 1911, before the Reverend Alva Roy Scott.

Communication to the author, September 15, 1970, from the City Clerk, Bangor, Maine.

93. *Acta apostolicae sedis* (1911), IV, 157.

94. Holy Office, Decree, June 21, 1912, *Analecta ecclesiastica* (1912), XXIV, 198–199.

95. Louis Walsh to Gibbons, December 12, 1912, Archives of the Archdiocese of Baltimore, Gibbons File.

96. *Ibid.*

97. *New York Times*, June 8, 1913, Part III, p. 2.

98. *Ibid.*, September 24, 1913, p. 4.

99. *Analecta ecclesiastica* (1910), XVIII, 342–348; *Acta apostolicae sedis* (1910), II, 584–600.

CHAPTER VII. THE SEVENTH CLASS

1. Only recently the suggestion has been made that Paul regarded the marriage made in unbelief severed by conversion; the convert was a new creation, all his old relations were ended; but if he chose he could reinstate his old marriage by intercourse. David Daube, "Pauline Contributions to a Pluralistic Culture: Re-Creation and Beyond," *Jesus and Man's Hope*, ed. Donald G. Miller and Dikran Y. Hadidian (Pittsburgh: University of Pittsburgh Press, 1971), pp. 232–239. That such a striking analysis of the foundation of Paul's thought could only now be put forward suggests how obscured Paul's text became.

2. Augustine, *De sermone Domini in monte*, ed. Almut Mutzenbecher, *Corpus Christianorum*, Latin series, vol. XXXV (Turnholt: Benedictine monks of the Abbey of St. Pierre de Steenbrugge, 1967), 1.16.48.

3. See Heinrich J. Vogels, *Ambrosiastri qui dicitur commentarius in epistulas paulinas*, CSEL (Vienna: Hoeller–Pichler–Tempsky, 1966), 81, XII–XVII; Alexander Souter, *The Earliest Latin Commentaries on the Epistles of St. Paul* (Oxford: Clarendon, 1927), pp. 45–68. Arguments against Isaac as the author are summarized by Prosper Schepens, "L'Ambrosiastre et Saint Eusèbe de Verceil," *Recherches de science religeuse* (1950), XXXVII, 235 ff. They are unpersuasive. Isaac's name was blotted out because in bloody battle for the see of Rome he was not only on the losing side, but accused the successful candidate, Damasus—later Saint Damasus—of the capital crime of adultery. (See A. Van Roey, "Damase," *Dictionnaire d'histoire et de géographie ecclesiastique*, XIV, 48–53.)

4. *Commentarium in Primam Epistolam B. Pauli ad Corinthios*, 7.13, printed in *PL* as an appendix to the works of Saint Ambrose; *PL* 17, col. 219.

5. Hugo of St. Victoire, *De sacramentis Christianae fidei*, 2.11.13, *PL* 186, col. 510.

6. Gratian, *Decretum*, dictum post c .2, C. 28, q. 2.

7. Robert Pullen, *Sententiae*, 7.29, *PL* 186, col. 947.

8. William of Auxerre, *Summa* (Paris, 1500), fol. 291n.

9. Hostiensis, *Commentaria in quinque libros decretalium* (Venice, 1481), 4.19.7.

10. Thomas Aquinas, *Scriptum super sententiis Magistri Petri Lombardi*, 4.39.1.5, corpus and reply to obj. 1.

11. Hugo of St. Victoire, *De sacramentis christianae fidei*, 2.11.13, *PL* 186, col. 507. For an extensive review of the canonical development, see Othmar F. Rink, "Die Lehre von der Interpellation beim Paulinischen Privileg in der Kirchenrechtsschule von Bologna, 1140 bis 1234," *Traditio* (1952), VIII, 305-365.

12. Celestine III, *Laudabilem*, printed in full in the Friedberg edition of the *Decretals*, 3.33.1. For a modern appreciation of Celestine III's action, see R. Weigand, "Unauflöslichkeit der Ehe und Eheauflösungen durch Päpste im 12. Jahrhundert," *Revue de droit canonique* (1970), XX, 63-64.

13. Pullen, *Sententiae*, 7.29; *PL* 186, col. 947; Gratian, *Decretum*, dictum post c. 17, C. 28, q. 1. The theologians: William of Auxerre, *Summa aurea in quartos libros sententiarum* (Paris, 1500), bk. 4, *De libello repudii*, fol. 289n; Thomas Aquinas, *Liber de veritate catholicae fidei contra errores infidelium seu Summa contra gentiles*, ed. Celsa Pera, Peter Marc, and Pietro Caravello (Turin: Marietti, 1961), 3.123.

14. Innocent I to Rufus and Eusebius, Bishops of Macedonia, Epistle 17, *PL* 20, col. 526; Gratian, dictum ante c. 1, C. 28, q. 2.

15. Tommaso de Vio, O.P., Cardinal Cajetan, "Ad septemdecim quaesita responsiones," ed. V. M. Pollet, *Angelicum* (1937), XIV, 551.

16. *Altitudo* is now printed as Document VI in an appendix to the *Codex iuris canonici*. On the letter to Toledo, see Ludwig von Pastor, *Geschichte der Päpste seit dem Ausgang des Mittelalters* (Freiburg im Br.: Herder, 1925), V, 720.

17. Alfonso de la Veracruz, Preface, *Speculum coniugiorum*, p. 8.

18. *Ibid.*, 2.2 (on marriage customs of the New World); *ibid.*, 2.4.13 and 21 (on the validity of these marriages); *ibid.*, 2.28 (on the gentleness of the spouses and the converts' position).

19. *Ibid.*, 3.18.

20. *Romani pontificis* is now Document VII of the appendix to the *Codex iuris canonici*.

21. Veracruz, *Speculum coniugiorum*, ed. Giovanni Batista Piccaia (Milan, 1599), 3.18. (The Milan edition follows the third edition, produced at Alcalá in 1572, which in turn follows the second edition published in Salamanca in late 1571.) For the reference to Cajetan, *ibid.*, 2.6. For the *motu proprio* on privileges of the religious which Veracruz helped obtain from Pius V in 1567, see *ibid.*, appendix, where it is reproduced. On Veracruz's role in obtaining this document, Ennis, *Fray Alfonso de la Vera Cruz*, p. 167.

22. Navarrus, *Consilia* (Rome, 1590), "De conversione coniugiorum," Counsel 2. *Romani pontificis* is not mentioned by name.

23. *Ibid.*, Counsel 3. The case of the Indian was dropped from the second edition of the *Consilia*, arguably because Navarrus himself felt the incon-

sistency with his own opinion on Lazarus, Puthota Rayanna, S.J., "De constitutione S. Pii Papae V. *Romani Pontificis* (3 Augusti 1571) (Canonis 1125)," *Periodica de re morali* (1938), XXVII, 320.

24. *Populis et nationibus* is now Document VIII in the appendix to the *Codex iuris canonici*. On the circumstances of its issue, Joseph Greco, *Le pouvoir du Souverain Pontife à l'égard des infidèles* (Rome: Gregorian University Press, 1967), pp. 41–42. (The request of Cristovoam Gonada, S.J., was presented by Aquaviva on July 24, 1583.) A draft decree, done by an anonymous aide to the Pope, said, "not to be judged entirely consummated and indissoluble," instead of "not to be judged so confirmed." The memorandum is reproduced in Greco, *Le pouvoir*, p. 44.

25. Sanchez, *De sancto matrimonii sacramento*, 7.74.10.

26. Sacred Congregation for the Propagation of the Faith, General Congregation, December 5, 1631, *Collectanea*, I, 17–18, n. 71. Urban VIII had issued pontifical decrees on October 20, 1626, and September 20, 1627, dissolving the marriages of converts contracted in unbelief. Alfonso de' Ligouri, *Theologia moralis* (Turin, 1827), Bk. VI n. 897.

27. Greco, *Le pouvoir*, pp. 96–97.

28. The reference to *Romani pontificis* in Sanchez is *De sancto matrimonii sacramento*, 2.42. Basilio Ponce set out *Populis et nationibus* in his *De matrimonio*, 7.48.22. In this way it was quoted to the S.C.C. in 1726, see Domenico Ursaya, *Disceptationes ecclesiasticae* (Venice, 1728), VI, 389. Ligouri refers to the decrees in his *Theologia moralis*, bk. VI, no. 897, citing Benedict XIV.

29. S.C.C., *Liber decretorum*, July 1, 1679 (Archives of the S.C.C.), XXX, fol. 352–353r, and April 13, 1680, XXXI fol. 89v. Also noted in Prospero Lambertini, *Thesaurus S.C.C.*, III, 346, 350. Printed in *Analecta ecclesiastica* (1906), XIV, 306.

30. *Florence, July 27, 1726*, *Thesaurus S.C.C.*, III, 346, 350, and *Florence, March 29, 1727*, *Thesaurus S.C.C.*, IV, 38. The same material appears in Benedict XIV, *Quaestiones canonicae et morales*, q. 546. The opinions of Ponsi and Zavaroni are reproduced in Ursaya, *Disceptationes*, VI, 387–398, part II, dispute 44. Opinion of Sparieri in *ibid.*, pp. 398–399. He upheld the Pope's power to dissolve, but wondered if the cause was sufficient and the danger of creating precedent too great.

31. Ursaya, *Discreptationes*, VI, I, dispute 32, pp. 136, 141, 142. Ursaya was quoting from *Praxis dispensationum* by Cardinal Corradini, former Prefect of the S.C.C. and Lambertini's old mentor.

32. Greco, *Le Pouvoir*, p. 101.

33. Holy Office, Response of June 14, 1708, set out in Holy Office to the Bishop of St. Albert, December 9, 1874, *Collectanea*, II, 87.

34. *Codicis iuris canonici fontes*, ed. Pietro Gasparri (Rome: Vatican Polygot Press, 1951), pp. 90–91. On the seventeenth-century dispensations to marry pagans, Francis J. Schenk, *Matrimonial Impediments of Mixed Religion and Disparity of Cult* (Washington: Catholic University of America Press, 1929), p. 45.

35. Francs P. Kenrick, *Theologia moralis* (Philadelphia, 1843), III, 320.

36. Holy Office to Nanking, March 5, 1852, Sacred Congregation for the

Propagation of the Faith, *Collectanea* (Rome, 1907), I, 576, n. 1070; Holy Office to Siam, July 4, 1855, *ibid.*, I, 593–594, n. 1114; Holy Office to St. Albert, December 9, 1874, *ibid.*, II, 81–88, n. 1427; Holy Office to Natal, *Fontes codicis iuris canonici* IV, 300.

37. Pietro Gasparri, *De matrimonio* (1892 ed.), secs. 1084, 1109.

38. S.C.P.F., *Collectanea* (Rome, 1893), nos. 1305–1307. The documents are also in *Appendix ad Bullarium Pontificum*, printed about 1859 at Propaganda.

39. S.C.C., *Vicariate of Morocco, May 23, 1894*, reported in Gasparri, *De matrimonio* (1932 ed.), sec. 1163.

40. Benedict XIV, *Singulari Nobis*, February 9, 1749, to Henry Cardinal and Duke of York, Benedict XIV, *Bullarium* (Malines, 1827), VII, 10–33. (The marriage of a Jewish man to a Protestant woman held null on the ground that the Protestant was bound by ecclesiastical law.)

41. Joseph Creusen, S.J., and Arthur Vermeersch, S.J., *Summa nova juris canonici* (Malines: H. Dessain, 1918), sec. 433.

42. Joseph Creusen, S.J., "Privilège paulinien et mariages mixtes," *Nouvelle revue théologique* (1923), LVI, 88–89.

43. "De privilegio Fidei. Solutio ex S.C.S. Officio, April 2, 1924," *Periodica de re morali canonica liturgica* (1931), XXI, 170; translated in T. Lincoln Bouscaren, *The Canon Law Digest* (Milwaukee: Bruce, 1934), pp. 551–552.

44. Holy Office, Rescript, July 10, 1924, translated in Bouscaren, *Canon Law Digest* (1934), pp. 551–553, first reported, *L'Ami du Clergé* (1925), p. 409.

45. Supreme Congregation of the Holy Office, Decree, November 5, 1924, printed in Note, "Dispensation from Natural Marriage 'In Favorem Fidei' —An Important Decision," *The Ecclesiastical Review* (February 1925), LXXII, 188; reprinted in *Nederlandsche Katholieke Stemmen* (1925), p. 65, and in *Periodica de re canonica et morali* (1926), XIV, 19–20; translated in Bouscaren, *Canon Law Digest*, pp. 553–554. In the published accounts M and G are substituted for Marsh and Groom.

46. J. C. Willging, chancellor of Helena, to W. J. Metz, Vicar-General of Spokane, December 13, 1924, Archives of the Diocese of Helena; Metz to Willging, December 16, 1924, containing a copy of the dispensation to Lulu to marry a non-Catholic and a reference to both their civil and Catholic marriages; Willging to Metz, February 27, 1925, closing the file with the Marshes still not informed of the papal rescript.

47. H. A. Ayrinhac, S.S., "Indissolubleness of Non-Catholic Marriage," *The Ecclesiastical Review* (April 1925), LXXII, 409; Joseph P. Donovan, C.M., "Doubtful Baptisms Again," *The Ecclesiastical Review* (May 1925), LXXII, 624. Donovan noted that a case similar to the Helena case had been submitted to the Holy Office by the Bishop of Indianapolis in 1922 but decided on other grounds.

48. "Notes" following the decree of the Holy Office printed in *Periodica* (1926), XIV, 20–21.

49. Pietro Gasparri, *De matrimonio* (rev. ed., Rome, 1932), p. 231. There is no hint of this doctrine in a book he prepared for the laity at about the same time, Pietro Gasparri, *Catechismus catholicus* (13th ed., Rome: Vatican

Press, 1932). In the catechism, marriage "can never be dissolved except by death"; and the Pauline privilege is the only other exception noted, pp. 234–235.

50. Gasparri, *De matrimonio* (1932 ed.) secs. 1164–1165. Following Gasparri's lead, efforts have been made to give a venerable pedigree to the papal power by focusing on the sixteenth-century papal documents such as *Romani Pontificis* and interpreting them as clear, positive exercises of the power, e.g., Puthota Rayanna, S.J., "De constitutione S.Pii V *Romani Pontificis* (3 Augusti 1571) (Canonis 1125), *Periodica* (1938), XXVII, 295; Joseph Greco, S.J., *Le pouvoir du Souverain Pontife à l'égard des infidèles* (Rome: Gregorian University Press, 1967). These efforts at historical foundation have produced interesting evidence. But clearly *Romani Pontificis* in its own time was an ambiguous compromise.

51. Gasparri, *De matrimonio*, p. 238, secs. 1164–1165. The same lame explanation was later given by the leading Jesuit moralist in Rome, Franz Hürth, S.J., "Notae quaedam ad Privilegium Petrinum," *Periodica* (1956), XLV, 1–21.

52. These regulations, still unpublished and officially still secret, are kept at diocesan chancery offices. I cite from a copy provided me by Peter Shannon of the archdiocese of Chicago.

53. Pius XI, *Casti connubii, Acta apostolicae sedis,* XXII, 574; the general indissolubility of marriage is stated at p. 552.

54. The first public reference to the Norms appears to be a Latin article by the American Sulpician, P. J. Lydon, professor of canon law at St. Patrick's Seminary, Menlo Park, California: "De juridica conditione in Statibus Fed. Americae Septentrionalis," *Ius pontificium* (1938), XVII, 168, where Lydon notes that the Norms are not "public law." In the same issue Vitomiro Jelicić, a Franciscan professor at the Antonianum, said that the papal power here could be used if the good of the faith "demands it or urges it," De privilegio fidei ejusque fundamento juridico," *ibid.,* p. 160. Professor Stephan Kuttner informs me that the Norms would have been known at Schools of Canon Law.

55. *Annuario pontificio* (1936), p. 659. Born in 1890 and ordained in 1916, Ottaviani began his curial career as a *minutante* in Propaganda, but by 1921 had moved to the Secretariat of State. By the end of Gasparri's regime, in 1929, he had become Substitute for Ordinary Affairs (*Annuaire pontifical catholique* [1928], p. 720, and [1934], p. 886), a highly responsible position to be held by one not yet forty. Pacelli, succeeding Gasparri as Secretary of State in 1930, left Ottaviani in this high post until his transfer in 1936 to the Holy Office, where he must have appeared as Pacelli's man.

56. Alfredo Ottaviani, *Institutiones iuris publici ecclesiastici* (3rd. ed., Rome, 1947), II, 227–228, sec. 346 and n. 77.

57. *Ibid.,* p. 724.

58. Eugenio Pacelli to Alfredo Ottaviani, March 12, 1936, *Institutiones iuris publici ecclesiastici,* I, vii.

59. Innocent III to Bernard, August 8, 1198, Othmar Hageneder and Anton Haidacher, eds., *Die Register Innocenz' III* (Graz-Cologne: Hermann Böhlaus Nachf., 1964), I, 472–473.

60. Hostiensis, *Summa aurea* (Venice, 1583), on X.3.34, '*De votis*,' at n. 4. Innocent IV, *Apparatus super libros decretalium* (Venice, 1571), '*De constitutionibus*,' c. 1

61. Thomas Aquinas, *Summa theologica* (Leonine ed., Rome, 1882), II–II, q. 88, art. 11.

62. Joannes Andreas, *In libros decretalium commentaria novella* (Venice, 1581), on X.2.1.12, *Cum venissent.*

63. Pius XII, "Allocution to the Auditors and other Officials and Ministers of the Tribunal of the Sacred Roman Rota and to the Advocates and Proctors of the Tribunal," October 31, 1941, *Acta apostolicas sedis* (Rome, 1941), XXXIII, 424–425.

64. Pius XII, *Mystici corporis, Acta apostolicae sedis* (1943), XXV, 211; Boniface VIII's *Unam Sanctam* appears in the *Corpus juris canonici* in the *Extravagantes communes*, 1.8.1.

65. Pius XII, "Allocution to the Auditors," October 31, 1941, *Acta apostolicae sedis*, XXXIII, 424–425.

66. Holy Office, Rescript, July 18, 1947, text in Giuseppe Damizia, "De dissolutione vinculi initi cum dispensatione ab impedimento disparitatis cultus," *Apollinaris* (1960), XXXIII, 181; first published in English translation by *The Canon Law Digest* (Milwaukee, 1953), III, 485; published in Spain in I. Prieto, "Una nueva aplicación del Privilegio de la Fe," *Revista Española de derecho canónico* (1955), pp. 233–236. As long as the Holy Office does not make its records public, it cannot be proved wtih certainty that the Fresno case was the first of its kind. However, there is the reasonably informed testimony of Gasparri in 1932 that such cases were not known. The Italian church historian, Arturo Jemolo, writing in the early forties, knew of no such cases, *Il matrimonio nel diritto canonico* (Milan, 1941), pp. 74–76; nor did the Spanish canonist E. J. Regatillo, "Disolución de matrimonio," *Sal Terrae* (1940), V, 371–372.

67. Holy Office, Rescript, May 4, 1950, translated in Bouscaren, *The Canon Law Digest* III, 488.

68. Holy Office, Rescript, January 23, 1955, translated in Bouscaren, *The Canon Law Digest* (Milwaukee Bruce, 1958), IV, 349–350.

69. Hürth, "Notae quaedam ad Privilegium Petrinum," p. 379. The term Petrine Privilege was coined by Hürth in 1946 to designate the papal prerogative to dissolve a marriage in which one party was baptized and the other was not, Urban Navarrete, S.J., "De termino 'Privilegium Petrinum' non adhibendo," *Periodica* (1964), LIII, 323. "Privilege of the faith" is the curial expression used when establishing the competence of a Roman Congregation to treat of cases in this area, see Paul VI, "Integrae servandae," December 7, 1965, *AAS* (1965), LVII, 954; Paul VI, "Regimini Ecclesiae Universae," August 15, 1967, LIX, 898. The literature is reviewed in Heinrich Molitor, "Die Auflösung von Naturehen durch papstlichen Gnadenakt," in Karl Siepen, Joseph Weitzel, and Paul Wirth, eds., *Ecclesia et Ius* (Paderborn: Ferdinand Schöningh, 1968), pp. 513–535.

70. In the single year 1950, there were 381,000 divorces in the United States (Paul H. Jacobson, *American Marriage and Divorce* [1959], p. 90).

71. Egidio Vagnozzi, Apostolic Delegate to the United States, Circular letter to the heads of American dioceses, July 31, 1966.

72. Michael O'Callaghan, "Case-Load for 1969 in American Tribunals in Formal Trials, Privilege of the Faith (PF) and Ratum (RNC) Cases," Canon Law Society of America, *Proceedings of the Thirty-Second Annual Convention, October 6–8, 1970.*

73. Louis Billot, S.J., *De ecclesiae sacramentis: Commentarium in tertiam partem S. Thomae* (7th ed., Rome, 1929), II, 441.

74. Compare Gasparri, *De matrimonio* (1892 ed.), sec. 1108; and *De matrimonio* (1932 ed.).

75. Gasparri, *Catechismus catholicus* (3rd ed., Rome: Vatican Press, 1932), p. 235.

76. Ferdinando Lambruschini, "Disputatio de potestate vicaria Romani pontificis in matrimonium infidelium," *Apollinaris* (1953), XXVI, 175–197. Lambruschini cited among other documents Nicholas V to Alfonso of Portugal, June 18, 1452, in *Ecclesia et status: Fontes selecti historiae iuris publici ecclesiastici*, ed. Giovanni Batista LoGrosso (2nd ed., Gregorian University Press, Rome: 1952), pp. 237–238; Alexander VI, *Inter caetera*, May 4, 1493, in *ibid.*, p. 241; Leo XIII, *Annum Sacrum, Acta sanctae sedis* (1899), XXXI, 646–649; Pius XII, Radio broadcast to the Christians of Portugal, October 21, 1942, *Acta apostolicae sedis* (Rome, 1924), XXXIV, 319 (a broadcast in honor of Our Lady of Fatima).

77. First reported in André Bride, "L'actuelle extension du Privilège de la Foi," *L'année canonique* (1958), VI, 77–79; also reported in René Leguerrier, O.F.M. Cap., "Recent Practice of the Holy See in Regard to the Dissolution of Marriages Between Non-Baptized Persons Without Conversion," *The Jurist* (1965), XXV, 456.

78. *Ibid.*, pp. 454–460.

79. *Ibid.*, pp. 460–461. Two other dissolutions by John XXIII are reported in J. M. Kautz, "The Petrine Privilege: A Study of Some Recent Cases," *The Jurist* (1968), XXVIII, 486.

80. Holy Office, *Rescript*, February 7, 1969, protocol number 2645/1962M, reported by Peter Shannon of the Chicago chancery and translated in T. Lincoln Bouscaren, *The Canon Law Digest: Annual Supplement through 1966* (Milwaukee: Bruce, 1967), at canon 1127.

81. For a short history of natural indissolubility see John T. Noonan, Jr., "Indissolubility of Marriage and Natural Law," *American Journal of Jurisprudence* (1969), XIV, 79–94. For Pius XII's statement, see his "Allocution to the Auditors, Advocates, and Other Officials of the Sacred Roman Rota," October 6, 1946, *Discorsi e Radiomessagi*, VIII, 255.

82. Egidio Vagnozzi, Circular letter to the heads of American dioceses, December 21, 1965. One other practical consequence of conceiving the papal power as part of the extraordinary competence of the Vicar of Christ is the conclusion that it cannot be delegated. In 1954, Leopold Brellinger, S.J., the Bishop of Tientsin in Communist China, petitioned that, "given the circumstances of the Church in China," the power to dissolve in favor of the faith be delegated to him for his diocese. The Holy Office replied that "the Holy See cannot delegate the power to dissolve marriage 'in favor of the faith' since that belongs to the Supreme Pontiff through the vicarial power" (Holy Office to Propaganda, May 28, 1955, quoted in Antonino Abate, "Delegabilitá del Potere Vicario Sul Vincolo Coniugale,"

Pontifical Commission for the Revision of the Code of Canon law, eds., *Acta conventus internationalis canonistarum* [Rome: Vatican Polygot Press, 1970], p. 537). Abate, on the other hand, argues that the vicarial power may be delegated; he points to the action of Gregory XIII in *Populis et nationibus*.

83. As to the power's suspension, Franjo Seper, as reported by Luigi Raimondi, Apostolic Delegate to the United States, to Joseph Bernardin, General Secretary of the United States Catholic Conference, August 28, 1970. As to continuation of the suspension, Canon Law Society of America, *Newsletter*, April 1971. The statistics as to the cases in process appear in "Case-Load for 1969," cited in note 72. According to chancery officials I have spoken to, dissolutions were granted up to June 1970; by July petitions were being returned with the notation individually marked on each one "it is not expedient." Only with the Delegate's letter in late August were the bishops informed that the suspension was in effect. Papal dissolutions of marriage would still be granted if the petitioner was a non-Catholic who would become a convert in cases distinct from those covered by the Pauline Privilege. To this extent, the Petrine Privilege remained in effect; but the usual case of dissolutions without conversions had, for the time being, been eliminated.

84. A modest step was taken by the revisers of the Code in 1971, who proposed that incapacity to consent be recognized as arising from "a serious psycho-sexual anomaly," Commission for the Revision of the Code of Canon Law, *Communicationes* III (Rome, June 1971), p. 77. In general, however, the proposals of the revisers did not go as far as I have gone in the text in suggesting the likely outcome of present developments. Nor did the Commission reflect the breadth of such recent Rota decisions as *Niterói, Of Nullity of Marriage, April 21, 1970,* where the Spanish auditor, Salvador Canals, ruled in a case from Brazil that a serious mistake as to the moral quality of a spouse would amount to a mistake as to person, rendering the consent to marriage invalid, *Il diritto ecclesiastico* (1970) LXXXI, part 2, pp. 1–22.

Index   Papal Legislation   Cases and Rulings

Index

Abate, Antonino, 461n82
Abortion: and intention against off-spring, 215–216; of Ana Ponce de León, 144; of Joanna Almeida y Carnide, 106
Abramo, of Florence, 362–364
Absolution: refusal of to parent coercing, 42
Acceptance of persons: defined, 184; in dispensation, 326; in Parkhurst case, 320, 322–323; in procedural rulings, 187
Acts fit for generation of offspring, 211–215
Adams, Addie Woodward, 254
Ad id, 28–29, 39, 256, 288, 395
Admiratio, 376, 385; defined, 318
Adultery: legislation against, 13–14
Advocacy, oral: in Rota, 55–56
Advocates: in Rota, 55–57; for poor, 290; in Maine, 312; standards of illustrated, 255, 257–259, 259–260, 288, 300. *See also* Balbani; Beltramino; Bottini; Buoncampagni; Caprara; Durani; Eusebii; Ferentilli; Giorgi; Grazioli; Lambertini; Lombardi; Pacelli; Parrillo; Patrizi; Piccolomini; Pitoni; Ricci; Ronconi; Sacconi; Santucci; Saraceni; Saracinelli; Sincero; Ursaya; Vermiglioli; Vizzani
Age of marriage: for children, 3–4, 153; for aged, 212–213
Agliardi, Antonio, Cardinal, 438n109
Aguirre, Felipe, 216
Albergati, Antonio, 54, 71–75, 419n147
Albergati-Ludovisi, Niccolo, Cardinal, 419n135
Albert of Hapsburg, 383
Alberti, Giuseppe, 260
Albizzi, Francesco, Cardinal, 331

Alessandro de Nevo, 118
Alexander III, Pope: on coercion, 28, 34; on estoppel of bigamist, 206; on marital affection, 38; permits marriage dissolution by religious profession, 80–82
Alexander VI, Pope, 16, 349, 382, 388, 428n10
Alexander VII, Pope, 54, 58, 59, 78
Alexander VIII, Pope, 420n149
Alfare, Antonio, 436n68
Alimony: during annulment suit, 22
Almeida, Tomas de, Patriarch, 95, 96, 98
Almeida y Carnide, Joanna Agnete de Almeida: genealogy, 89; courted by Senator Barberini, 90; writes him, 91; relation to him, 93; agreement with him, 89, 95; marries him, 96; lawsuits against him, 96–98, 102; miscarries, 106; foils Portuguese process, 111; in S.C.C., 112; marriage annulled, 120
Ambreville, Anna de, 440n133
Ambrose, St., 70
Ambrosiaster, 454n
America, 284
American Ecclesiastical Review, 295, 457n45, n47
Ami du Clergé L', 457n44
Anglican orders, validity of, 271–273, 449n112
Anne, daughter of Charles and Béatrice, 23
Annulment of marriage: delays in, 24, 75, 395, 421n176; by private authority, 7–8; instances of, 15–16, 28, 120, 42, 44, 148, 155, 176–177, 234, 237, 262, 401–402, 436n68, 440n133, 448n95, 457n40, 461n84; parallel treatment of religious profession, 45–47, 155–156; rules for, 125–128; time limit on, 28–29, 39, 262, 395

Index

Index

Index

Index

Index

Index

Index